ENTREPRENEURSHIP
Choice and Strategy

ENTREPRENEURSHIP

Choice and Strategy

Joshua Gans
Rotman School of Management,
University of Toronto

Erin L. Scott
Sloan School of Management,
Massachusetts Institute of Technology

Scott Stern
Sloan School of Management,
Massachusetts Institute of Technology

W. W. NORTON & COMPANY
Independent Publishers Since 1923

W. W. NORTON & COMPANY has been independent since its founding in 1923, when William Warder Norton and Mary D. Herter Norton first published lectures delivered at the People's Institute, the adult education division of New York City's Cooper Union. The firm soon expanded its program beyond the Institute, publishing books by celebrated academics from America and abroad. By midcentury, the two major pillars of Norton's publishing program—trade books and college texts—were firmly established. In the 1950s, the Norton family transferred control of the company to its employees, and today—with a staff of five hundred and hundreds of trade, college, and professional titles published each year—W. W. Norton & Company stands as the largest and oldest publishing house owned wholly by its employees.

Printed in Canada

Editor: Eric Svendsen
Assistant Editor: Catherine Lillie
Project Editors: Christine D'Antonio and Rachel Mayer
Developmental Editor: Sunny Hwang
Managing Editors, College: Kim Yi and Carla Talmadge
Senior Production Manager: Richard Bretan
Media Editor: Meg Leary
Associate Media Editor: Mia Davis
Media Editorial Assistant: Duncan Brady
Ebook Producer: Emily Schwoyer
Marketing Manager, Economics: Mary Dwyer
Design Director: Rubina Yeh
Art Director: Jillian Burr
Director of College Permissions: Megan Schindel
Photo Editor: Catherine Abelman
Photo Researcher: Dena Digilio Betz
Permissions: Elizabeth Trammell
Composition: Graphic World
Manufacturing: Transcontinental

Permission to use copyrighted material is included in the Credits section, which begins on page CR-1.

ISBN: 978-0-393-42705-9

W. W. Norton & Company, Inc., 500 Fifth Avenue, New York, NY 10110
wwnorton.com
W. W. Norton & Company Ltd., 15 Carlisle Street, London W1D 3BS
1 2 3 4 5 6 7 8 9 0

To Natalie, Belanna, Ariel, Annika/JP, DD, and MJ
—JOSHUA GANS

To my loving family, supportive friends, and Bean
—ERIN L. SCOTT

To Cathy, Ethan, and Isaac
—SCOTT STERN

BRIEF CONTENTS

CONTENTS

PREFACE

Entrepreneurs drive change. Entrepreneurs identify opportunities that create new value and innovate to meet these opportunities by founding and building organizations big and small.

How entrepreneurs succeed or fail in creating this change—and how we can help students learn to become better in their own ventures within school and beyond—is the overarching goal of this book. While there are important ingredients that come from the entrepreneurs themselves, such as grit, passion, and insight, actually building a lasting business takes more. Much more. And there is simply no entrepreneur who got there on their own. This book was born of our decades' worth of research, which has found that most great entrepreneurs succeed because of the lessons they learned, the impact of others, and key choices they made as they started their business.

Why We Wrote This Book

We believe that the story of the "heroic" entrepreneur—the one who is able to found and scale a business without help or reference points—is, at best, a myth and, at worse, harmful. Entrepreneurs are *not* simply born. They are made, and they are molded. While every individual has to bring their own strengths (and mitigate where they are weakest), building a lasting business takes more than individual initiative. Guidance, mentorship, and, most importantly in the current context, systematic entrepreneurial education make it more likely that a budding entrepreneur will not only be able to found a business but succeed in pursuing and realizing impact from a venture.

Over the past two decades, there has been a wealth of insightful and practical tools developed for practicing entrepreneurs, and, likewise, there has been an explosion of theoretical and empirical research providing insights into the drivers and consequences of entrepreneurial strategy. These insights, frameworks, and tools have made it possible to identify some of the core issues facing most, if not all, entrepreneurs and recognize both opportunities for more effective decision-making and areas where it may be possible to avoid pitfalls and challenges.

Our purpose in writing this book, then, has been our belief that, as entrepreneurial educators, we lacked an integrated textbook that brought these insights and advances together within a common framework.

Previously, it was up to individual instructors—often benefiting from notes, "tips and tricks," and slide decks passed along as if they were part of a medieval guild—to bring together the disparate perspectives, cases, and empirical insights into a unified whole within our classrooms. Our aim is to provide a unified, integrated approach that simultaneously allows instructors to build on past pedagogy *and* take advantage of rapid advances in our knowledge—both from academic research and practice—to equip students to start their journey toward entrepreneurship at the frontier of entrepreneurial learning and practice.

As academics who have conducted research on entrepreneurial choice and strategy for over three decades and who are passionate about synthesizing the insights of practice and academic research within our classrooms (and the broader world), this book represents a continued commitment to translating these insights into actionable, proven frameworks for entrepreneurs. In particular, we believe that entrepreneurs can be taught about the choices they face and the strategic thinking that underlies those choices and be empowered to choose a path to successfully realize their ideas. In our classrooms and entrepreneurial ecosystems, these tools have been used by tens of thousands of students, at all levels, to do just that.

Choice

Entrepreneurs enact change through their choices, which they face from the first moment they consider entrepreneurship.

The choices that entrepreneurs make will guide their journey from identifying the opportunity to pursuing and following a particular path. Entrepreneurs ultimately have impact *because* of the choices they make and how effectively they *implement* those choices. While every entrepreneurial journey is unique and different, there are nonetheless critical choices entrepreneurs make that share common points of reference.

A basic premise of this book is that entrepreneurial choice is *hard*. While entrepreneurs often face a bewildering array of options, they have limited resources (and so cannot pursue all of their options at the same time). Harnessing the power of choice in an uncertain environment requires learning and experimenting with an idea. However, doing so often involves commitments of time and resources that are very limited in any entrepreneurial venture. As a result, the central challenge facing an entrepreneur is how to choose, and therefore, a central focus of this book is on providing a framework and tools that allow students to become more effective at entrepreneurial decision-making.

The framework, tools, and examples that show students how to think concretely about the core choices facing an entrepreneur, and how they would make those choices as entrepreneurs themselves, are woven deeply throughout the fabric of this book. Entrepreneurship itself is a choice, and what entrepreneurs choose to explore is important. Entrepreneurs make choices about which idea to pursue, what customers to target (at least at first), which technologies to nurture, what team and organization to build, and what pathway to activate toward the commercialization of their idea. *We show that by making each of these choices thoughtfully and even somewhat scientifically, entrepreneurs can pursue and explore the opportunity that fits best with their goals and builds on their distinctive strengths.*

Strategy

These choices, of course, are connected—for example, choosing a certain customer to pursue impacts the product or service, which then affects the team required, and so on. To see how these core choices work together, we introduce the *Entrepreneurial Strategy Compass* in the opener to Part 3. This tool helps entrepreneurs of all stripes and experiences understand how choices can come together as core entrepreneurial strategies. Understanding these core strategies helps entrepreneurs see different ways forward for their idea and gives them a choice of which opportunity to pursue.

Choosing a final strategic path for a venture, however, is usually made in the face of having many options and few resources. We highlight a particular tool that helps with the uncertainty in this situation, which we call *Test Two, Choose One.* Under Test Two, Choose One, an entrepreneur should continue with strategic exploration and commitment-free learning around their idea until they have identified *at least two* equally viable strategies for it. They then can reflect on their original purpose for choosing entrepreneurship and the idea, as well as their unique skills and advantages, to help them choose the right path for their venture. Equipped with a clear compass, entrepreneurs choose the path that reflects the journey they want to travel and the destination they want to reach.

An important consequence of Test Two, Choose One is that entrepreneurs are choosing between two paths they feel are viable. In doing so, we have found that the returns to this strategic choice are better when guided by the help and experience of others. For some, this might be an active mentor or adviser network they can tap into. But the ideas and experiences shown in this book, and in a student's education, should also inform this choice. Ultimately, educators, mentors, and informal advisers do not simply provide advice but help reduce the level of uncertainty associated with an idea and related strategic pathways that inform an entrepreneur's decisions. We have found the returns to entrepreneurial judgment and action are higher when guided by strategic choice and the learnings, wisdom, and ideally mentorship of others.

How This Book Is Organized

Thinking about the choices entrepreneurs face and how these choices lead to strategy are straightforward yet interconnected principles. These correspond to the first three sections of the text.

PART 1. GETTING STARTED

As an entrepreneur, it's important to understand that choice matters. Entrepreneurship is a choice in itself, and what you choose to explore is important. Doing so requires at least some level of commitment. We explore this in the first section of the book. By making this commitment thoughtfully and even scientifically, you will pursue an opportunity that fits better with your goals, land on an overall strategy for a venture, and come away with a better understanding of what lies ahead.

- Understanding the Power of Choice
- Choosing Entrepreneurship
- Choosing Your Opportunity
- Choosing Your Strategy

PART 2. CORE CHOICES

Not simply an abstract concept, entrepreneurs systematically face a series of core choices that require them to balance the interplay between learning more about an idea and committing to it. We focus primarily on four clusters of choices that are central to the founding and scaling of a growth venture:

- Choosing Your Customer
- Choosing Your Technology
- Choosing Your Organization
- Choosing Your Competition

PART 3. FOUR STRATEGIES: HOW CHOICES WORK TOGETHER

To approach a business idea, the way entrepreneurs make their four core choices results in four, alternative strategies they can explore for a given idea:

- Intellectual Property Strategy
- Disruption Strategy
- Value Chain Strategy
- Architectural Strategy

Each of these strategies involves a distinctive set of choices regarding Customer, Technology, Organization, and Competition and highlights specific interdependencies that can be leveraged by entrepreneurs in translating their idea into a viable company.

PART 4. PUTTING IT TO WORK

Everything in this book up until now has been to put entrepreneurs in a position to choose their strategy. It is time to make that choice. It is time to put all their plans to work.

- From Strategy to Action
- Financing
- Scaling

We (as well as early adopters of these materials) have used these frameworks, tools, examples, cases, and exercises in classrooms at the undergraduate, master's, and practitioner level, from introductory, case-based courses to intensive project- and venture-based capstone courses and entrepreneurship programs. We look forward hearing from and working with you as we build a learning community to advance pedagogy and practice in this critical area.

Tools in the Book

In writing this book, we have made extensive use of real-world examples throughout the chapters. In creating these examples, we made certain to show and reflect the *diversity in entrepreneurship*. As you flip through the pages, you will see examples, stories, and cases that recognize the diversity we want to show in the field.

- ***Part openers*** frame the major ideas in the book with an example photograph and caption and a description of the core idea of each part. Openers to Parts 2 and 3 are longer and introduce key tools that are used in each chapter of those parts.

- **Chapter openers** set the stage, describing how real-world entrepreneurs made the choices described in the chapter. In choosing these stories, we focus on more established cases where the events around the founding company are set. This helps students better study and understand what happened, as opposed to focusing on ongoing start-ups or businesses where less background is available.
- **Real-world examples** throughout this chapter are embedded in the text and highlight companies of all types, big and small. This helps students understand the main ideas in the chapter through a variety of businesses, including new and less-established ventures.
- **Mini Cases** in each chapter range from about one-third to a full page. These brief cases focus on decisions that ventures made related to a topic or topics in the chapter.
- **Sidebars** highlight topics and people of interest and are always driven by a descriptive photograph.
- **An end-of-chapter Case** closes each chapter. These are one- to two-page summaries that contain questions you can assign.

Further, each chapter makes use of consistent pedagogical elements. These include:

- **Chapter Objectives** lead off each chapter and are driven by Bloom's Taxonomy.
- **Entrepreneur's Dilemma** sections on the first page of each chapter briefly frame key challenges and questions entrepreneurs face and that the chapters will explore.
- **Key Terms** are set bold, and their definitions appear in the margin where the term is first introduced and in the text's glossary.
- **Using the Research** boxes in each chapter highlight particular instances where research has driven insight and best practices in entrepreneurship.
- **Deep Dive** boxes get into more technical details, demonstrating and illustrating the thought that has gone into many topics.
- **Lists and bullets** are used frequently in the chapters to highlight important ideas. *A bold orange font* is used to call out the biggest ideas as they appear in the flow of the text.
- **Putting It Together** features appear at the end of each chapter. These highlight key points in a single-page, action-oriented format, framing ideas in the chapter almost as a "to-do" list.
- **End-of-chapter review material** in each chapter includes a bulleted section of chapter takeaways, a list of key terms, review questions that test basic comprehension of concepts, and discussion questions for use in class or for short writing assignments. Before each end-of-chapter case, the authors provide a short list of suggested readings, which includes papers, books, and articles.
- **Sources** for each chapter are footnoted, and these footnotes appear by chapter at the end of the text. Sources for particular tables, boxes, and illustrations are called out as they are used.
- **A complete Glossary** of all key terms in the text is provided at the end of this book. Indexes are also provided by topic, company, and person.

Resources for Instructors and Students

This text comes with robust support. Most resources can be accessed electronically either at **digital.wwnorton.com/entrepreneurship** or by locating this title's catalog page at wwnorton.com.

INSTRUCTOR'S MANUAL WITH BUSINESS CANVAS WORKSHEETS

The instructor's manual provides robust resources for each chapter to guide your lecture planning. This includes fill-in-the-blank business canvas worksheets, which are keyed to Chapters 2–15. These worksheets are optional support—instructors may choose to use only a few of them and/or only parts of them. However, we use these sheets when we teach and find that students really appreciate the structure they provide. The instructor's manual also provides solutions to end-of-chapter problems, chapter outlines, video discussion questions, and more.

NORTON ILLUMINE EBOOK

The new Norton Illumine Ebook is the ideal platform for today's learners. Each chapter includes video media and self-assessment embedded directly into the ebook platform so that students grasp concepts quickly and apply them as they learn. Features include:

VIDEOS Videos of three to five minutes are embedded in each chapter and explore how real entrepreneurs have employed the choice and strategy framework, inspiring students and providing them with real-world context for the chapter concepts.

CHECK YOUR UNDERSTANDING QUESTIONS Check Your Understanding questions provide students with a comprehension check on the most important concepts for each chapter. These questions fall at the end of each chapter section and accompany each video, and they provide students with an opportunity to reflect on and correct any misunderstandings before moving on in their reading. The answer-specific feedback gives students automatic feedback to coach them toward the correct answer, and the questions are trackable by completion, meaning that instructors can make the reading truly assignable as part of the overall grade.

NOTE-TAKING AND CLASSROOM COMMUNICATION The active reading experience also includes the ability to highlight, take notes, search, read offline, and more. Additionally, the Norton Illumine Ebook facilitates classroom communication by allowing instructors to add their own notes into the chapter for their students.

INQUIZITIVE

InQuizitive is Norton's award-winning, easy-to-use adaptive learning tool that personalizes the learning experience for students and helps them master—and retain—key learning objectives.

PLAY WITH A PURPOSE Gaming elements built into InQuizitive engage students and motivate them to keep working. Students wager points on every question based on their confidence level, gain additional points for high success rates and on bonus questions, and can improve their grade by continuing to work questions in InQuizitive.

ACTIVE LEARNING, HELPFUL FEEDBACK InQuizitive includes a variety of question types beyond basic multiple choice. Image-click, numeric entry, and various graph interpretation questions build economic skills and better prepare students for lecture, quizzes, and exams. Rich answer-specific feedback helps students understand their mistakes.

EASY TO USE, AND INTEGRATES WITH YOUR CAMPUS LMS Instructors can set up InQuizitive for their students in less than five minutes. Students can access InQuizitive on tablet devices as well as on computers, making it easy to study on the go. InQuizitive integrates with campus learning management systems; when integration is enabled, grades flow automatically to campus LMS gradebooks. A single sign-on between the LMS and Norton digital products simplifies student access.

NORTON TESTMAKER

Norton Testmaker brings Norton's high-quality testing materials online. With over 750 multiple-choice and short-answer questions, instructors create assessments from anywhere with an Internet connection, without downloading files or installing specialized software. Search and filter test bank questions by chapter, type, difficulty, learning objectives, and other criteria. You can also customize questions to fit your course. Then, easily export your tests to Microsoft Word or Common Cartridge files for import into your LMS.

POWERPOINT SLIDES

PowerPoints use key images from the text to convey complex concepts in entrepreneurship. All slides are supported with the chapter outline to guide your lecture. These comprehensive, lecture-ready slides are perfect for new instructors and instructors who have limited time to prepare.

ART SLIDES AND JPEGS

For instructors who simply want to incorporate in-text art into their existing slides, all art from the book (tables, graphs, photos, and Snapshot infographics) is available in both PowerPoint and .jpeg formats. Stepped-out versions of in-text graphs and Snapshot infographics are also provided and optimized for screen projection.

ENTREPRENEURIAL-STRATEGY.NET

Visit this author-maintained website for updates on their research and events, as well as additional information and tools.

ACKNOWLEDGMENTS

Much like any start-up, this textbook has been a journey that has benefited from the hard-earned lessons and thoughtful guidance of an extraordinary (and lengthy!) array of individuals. This book is a testament to their collective wisdom and experience. In many ways, it is the wealth of practitioner tools and explosion of academic research over the past several decades that made this project so important.

First, we would like to express our deepest gratitude to our students (many thousands of them) who have worked with us as we have synthesized both the framework and materials underlying this book. Your creativity, entrepreneurial spirit, and commitment to your ideas have been the driving force behind this endeavor. Your rich appetite for this burgeoning field and push to reconcile sometimes conflicting entrepreneurial advice as you moved your ventures forward laid bare the need for an organizing framework. We are profoundly thankful for the insights, engagement, and rigor you brought to the classroom. In particular, we would like to thank the many students who have engaged with us outside the classroom, as teaching assistants, research assistants, and case writers in our work on entrepreneurial strategy, including Boluwatife Akinola, Melika Ameresekere, RJ Andrews, Gustavo Castillo, Devin Cook, Nathaniel Cruz Walma, Qihan Deng, Pamela Duke, Taylor DuRoss, Abiola Familusi, Morgane Herculano, Matthew Jens, Malaika Kapur, Johnson Lin, Janet Liu, Melinda Liu, Derek Shen, Abina Subramaniam, Thierry Vanparys, Eugenia Vovk, Chris Washington, Chase Williams, and Roni Zveiris. Your enthusiasm and thoughtful contributions made this project a joy and in so many ways shaped this work.

Second, to the many entrepreneurs, investors, and ecosystem builders who have generously shared their experiences and applied these frameworks in their start-ups, your perspectives have added an invaluable depth to this work. Your journeys, successes, and even setbacks have provided essential learning for us, our students, and readers of this book. We are especially grateful to the innovators and entrepreneurs at the Massachusetts Institute of Technology and the University of Toronto and beyond, including Aman Advani, Gihan Amarasiriwardena, James Cham, Elliot Cohen, Sameer Dhar, Jim Dougherty, Anj Fayemi, Newsha Ghaeli, Annely Guzman, Katherine Homuth, Nick Horelik,

Eesha Khare, Donna Levin, Matt Lieber, Chris Macomber, Brint Markle, Karl Martin, Michael Martin, Mariana Matus, Andy Miller, Ayr Muir, Michael Murchison, Ren Ng, TJ Parker, Ruby Pillai, Ale Resnik, Socrates Rosenfeld, Jason Rosenthal, Scott Stornetta, Richard Titus, Scott Tracy-Inglis, and Neil Wainright. We also appreciate the support and engagement of the staff, mentors, and entrepreneurs involved in the Creative Destruction Lab, the Engine Accelerator, the Legatum Center for Development and Entrepreneurship, the Martin Trust Center for MIT Entrepreneurship, MIT Sloan Executive Education, MIT Sloan Global Programs, MIT Innovation Corps (I-Corps), and the MIT Venture Mentoring Services.

Third, we owe a debt to the many academics who rigorously push forward and shape the field of entrepreneurship. Captured in these pages are the ideas and work of so many. We have benefited from engaging with the community of scholars working in this field and owe a debt to the members of the Academy of Management (AOM), the Kauffman Foundation, the National Bureau of Economic Research (NBER), the Strategic Management Society, and the United States Association for Small Business and Entrepreneurship (USASBE), among others, for their support with this research and practice agenda.

The origins of this project began in a series of discussions with our collaborator and colleague Dame Fiona Murray, whom we thank for helping us to get started on the role of strategy for start-ups and for her insight and support throughout this project. As well, Adam Davidson provided crucial insight and encouragement at the earliest stages about the need for work that gave entrepreneurs (and anyone) tools to pursue opportunity as part of the "passion economy."

We also want to thank our invaluable collaborators on research papers and projects underlying this research, including Ajay Agrawal, Christian Catalini, Ankur Chavda, Kenny Ching, Iain Cockburn, Daniel Fehder, Jorge Guzman, Alexis Haughey, David Hsu, Michael Kearney, Roman Lubynsky, Matt Marx, Pian Shu, and, especially, Jane Wu. We also thank the outstanding scholars whose contributions are contained here, and we especially wish to thank the many doctoral students who have contributed and committed to moving forward this field, including Caroline Fry, Luca Gius, Wesley Greenblatt, Danny Kim, Soomi Kim, Josh Krieger, Abhishek Nagaraj, Amir Sariri, Brooklynn Zhu, and Samantha Zyontz.

We are particularly grateful to colleagues who provided feedback, insight, and encouragement for this project from its earliest stages, including Rajshree Agarwal, Ashish Arora, Thomas Astebro, Tim Bresnahan, Phil Budden, Arnaldo Camuffo, Michael Cusumano, Jean-Jacques Degroof, Thomas Eisenmann, Cathy Fazio, Charlie Fine, Jeffrey Furman, Alfonso Gambardella, Xudong Gao, Brent Goldfarb, Thomas Hellmann, Yael Hochberg, Ben Jones, Olenka Kacperczyk, Dina Katabi, Wonjoon Kim, Keld Laursen, Michael Leiblein, Josh Lerner, Kwanghui Lim, Hong Luo, Karen Mills, Ethan Mollick, Seongwuk Moon, Ramana Nanda, Alex Oettl, Ben Olken, Michael E. Porter, Toke Reichstein, Michael Roach, David Robinson, Vera Rocha, Nathan Rosenberg, Sampsa Samila, Sarada, Olav Sorenson, Vivek Tandon, Valentina Tartari, Manuel Trajtenberg, Lenos Trigeorgis, Jim Utterback, Heidi Williams, Chris Zott, and Ezra Zuckerman.

We would also like to thank our many colleagues at the MIT Sloan School of Management and the Rotman School of Management at the University of Toronto who have worked with us as we have developed these materials, both as researchers and in our classrooms. In particular, we thank Natalia Kalas and Judith Graham-Robey for all their support throughout this journey.

We would also like to call out those who have taught with us in our classrooms, including Ajay Agrawal, Bill Aulet, Pierre Azoulay, Kevin Bryan, Jeff Bussgang, Mercedes Delgado, Eugene Fitzgerald, Alberto Galasso, Kit Hickey, Mara Lederman, Ed Roberts, and Don Sull. We especially thank the Jean Hammond (1986) and Michael Krasner (1974) Entrepreneurship Fund and the Edward B. Roberts (1957) Entrepreneurship Fund at MIT for their support. As well, Scott Stern would like to thank the colleagues who hosted him (and contributed comments and insights on these materials) at the Copenhagen Business School and the Harvard Business School Entrepreneurial Management Unit.

Special thanks are owed to our fellow instructors and mentors in the field of entrepreneurship education who reviewed early versions of this book and adopted draft materials into their classrooms, entrepreneurship programs, and accelerators. Your extensive feedback and practical insights have been crucial in shaping the content and direction of this book.

CLASS TESTERS Many of our colleagues have tested the entire manuscript or parts of it in different stages. While this list is not comprehensive, these colleagues include:

Arnaldo Camuffo, Bocconi University

Moisés Carbajal Marrón, Tecnologico de Monterrey

Szikszai Daniel, London Business School

Daniel Fehder, University of Southern California–Marshall School of Business

Jeff Furman, Boston University

Alfonso Gambardella, Bocconi University

Jorge Guzman, Columbia University

Yael Hochberg, Rice University

Olenka Kacperczyk, London Business School

Leonard Lane, University of California, Irvine

Michael Leiblein, The Ohio State University

Elizabeth Lyons, University of California, San Diego

Denisa Mindruta, HEC (France)

Abishek Nagaraj, University of California, Berkeley

Toke Reichstein, Copenhagen Business School

Michael Roach, University of Illinois

Ken Sagendorf, Regis University

Sarada, University of California, Los Angeles

Sheryl Winston, BI Norwegian Business School

Jane Wu, University of California, Los Angeles

Samantha Zyontz, Boston University

FIRST EDITION AND PROPOSAL REVIEWERS

Alejandro Amezcua, IESEG School of Management

Lowell Busenitz, University of Oklahoma

Joseph J. Cabral, Louisiana State University

Richard Chan, Stonybrook University

Phyllis Fein, SUNY Westchester Community College

Jeff Furman, Boston University

Laura Gasiorowski, University of Delaware

Stephen Golden, Northeastern University

Yael Hochberg, Rice University

Julianna Iarossi, University of South Carolina

Daniel Kim, Wharton School, University of Pennsylvania

Christina Kyprianou, IE University

Sheen S. Levine, University of Texas, Dallas, and Columbia University, New York

Jeroen Mahieu, Vrije Universiteit Amsterdam

Felipe G. Massa, Loyola University New Orleans

Patrick J. Murphy, DePaul University

Abhishek Nagaraj, University of California, Berkeley

Robert Nason, McGill University

Andrew Nelson, University of Oregon

Sujit Pandey, Norwegian School of Economics

Roberto Ragozzino, University of Tennessee at Knoxville

Chris Rider, University of Michigan

Michael Roach, University of Illinois Urbana–Champaign

Sarada, University of California, Los Angeles

David Tan, University of Wisconsin

Miranda J. Welbourne Eleazar, University of Iowa

MEDIA AUTHORS AND REVIEWERS

Joseph J. Cabral, Louisiana State University—CYU accuracy checker

Christina Kyprianou, IE University—InQuizitive author

Elizabeth Lyons, University of California, San Diego—InQuizitive author

Sujit Pandey, The British College, Kathmandu—InQuizitive author

Adam Pervez, Mississippi State—test bank author and reviewer

Clinton Purtell, University of North Texas—CYU accuracy checker

Satish Surath, University of Toronto—test bank author

Finally, we would like to thank the entire team at Norton who worked with us as we drafted, tested, revised, tested some more, and then ultimately completed this book. Their hard work and diligence have been instrumental in creating this final product, including its media, supplements, and all the marketing and promotional elements. We especially wanted to thank our insightful and patient editor, Eric Svendsen, who not only helped shape the vision but also tirelessly shepherded this manuscript from its inception, as well as the many Norton team members who have worked with us from the start. These include Sunny Hwang, Meg Leary, Christine D'Antonio, Richard Bretan, Rachel Mayer, Catherine Lillie, Mia Davis, Duncan Brady, Catherine Abelman, Dena Digilio Betz, Elizabeth Trammell, Emily Schwoyer, Jillian Burr, and Mary Dwyer. We could not have had better partners in this process.

This book is a tribute to all of you who have joined us on this remarkable journey. Together, we have not only explored the realms of entrepreneurship but have also contributed to shaping them. Thank you for making this possible.

A NOTE TO STUDENTS

Entrepreneurship is a powerful force to create lasting and impactful change. Across the world and throughout history, individuals have used entrepreneurship as the vehicle to bring their ideas, innovations, and technologies to the market. At the same time, entrepreneurship is an extremely personal choice. The choice to become an entrepreneur, the choice of which ideas to pursue, and the choice of strategic path to bring that idea forward are ultimately yours alone.

This book was born from research showing that most great entrepreneurs become great entrepreneurs with the assistance of others, from lessons learned to more direct engagement with an entrepreneurial ecosystem. For many, this comes from a network of mentors and advisers who have had experience launching and scaling businesses. Often, universities and communities have resources that can help students get started and connect entrepreneurs such as yourself with new connections and entrepreneurship programs.

But, especially for those just contemplating entrepreneurship, getting started can be sometimes daunting. The power of entrepreneurship is in the freedom of choice: the choice to pursue those ideas that matter most to you and leverage your unique skills and passions. Yet, those choices can seem overwhelming at first. *Is there another way to get started?* Our answer to this is an emphatic "yes!" We believe that the wisdom of many—both mentors and academics who study entrepreneurs—can be brought together in a systematic and actionable way that allows you to push forward your ideas.

Whether you have an idea you are ready to launch today or are looking for tools to carry forward in your career as an entrepreneur and investor of tomorrow, the framework and experiences in this book will get you started and equip you to choose and implement the strategic path to translate your idea to reality.

ABOUT THE AUTHORS

Joshua Gans is a professor of strategic management and holder of the Jeffrey S. Skoll Chair of Technical Innovation and Entrepreneurship at the Rotman School of Management, the University of Toronto (with a cross-appointment in the Department of Economics). He is also chief economist of the University of Toronto's Creative Destruction Lab. He holds a PhD from Stanford University and an honors degree in economics from the University of Queensland. He is a research associate of the NBER. At Rotman, he teaches MBA students entrepreneurial strategy.

Gans has written numerous books including *Parentonomics, Information Wants to Be Shared, The Disruption Dilemma, Prediction Machines: The Simple Economics of Artificial Intelligence, Innovation + Equality, The Pandemic Information Gap: The Brutal Economics of Covid-19, Power & Prediction: The Disruptive Economics of Artificial Intelligence, and The Economics of Blockchain Consensus.*

While Gans's research interests are varied, he has developed specialities in the nature of technological competition and innovation, economic growth, publishing economics, industrial organization, and regulatory economics. In 2007, he was awarded the Economic Society of Australia's Young Economist Award. In 2008, he was elected as a fellow of the Academy of Social Sciences, Australia. In 2019, Gans was awarded the PURC Distinguished Service Award from the Public Utility Research Center at the University of Florida for his contributions to regulatory economics.

Erin L. Scott is a senior lecturer in the Technological Innovation, Entrepreneurship, and Strategic Management Group at the MIT Sloan School of Management. Scott received her MBA-MS and BE in Biomedical Engineering from Washington University in St. Louis and Vanderbilt University, respectively, and a PhD in Strategy from Washington University in St. Louis Olin Business School. She then completed a postdoctoral fellowship in the National Bureau of Economic Research's Innovation Policy and the Economy Group before starting her academic career as an assistant professor at the National University of Singapore Business School.

At the Massachusetts Institute of Technology, Scott draws upon her two decades of academic and practical experience to partner with groundbreaking innovators to successfully navigate the entrepreneurial journey from initial idea to commercialization. Her research, which focuses on strategy for start-ups, has been published in leading journals such as *Harvard Business Review, Management Science, and Strategy Science.* At MIT Sloan School of Management, Scott teaches electives focused on entrepreneurship and innovation, including the award-winning Entrepreneurial Strategy course (MBA and EMBA), the popular Entrepreneurial Founding & Teams course (MBA), and the Strategy for Startups course (Executive Education). In addition, she serves as a mentor and adviser to early-stage entrepreneurs, start-ups, and entrepreneurship programs. Scott previously evaluated and consulted for early-stage ventures in the medical device and biotechnology sectors.

Scott Stern is the David Sarnoff Professor of Management in the Technological Innovation, Entrepreneurship, and Strategic Management Group at the MIT Sloan School of Management.

Stern received his BA in economics from New York University and a PhD in economics from Stanford University. He started his career at MIT, and subsequently served on the faculty at the Kellogg School of Management as the Joseph and Carole Levy Professor of Management and Strategy and as a non-resident senior fellow at the Brookings Institution before returning to MIT in 2009. He has also served as a visiting professor in the Entrepreneurial Management Unit of the Harvard Business School and the Copenhagen Business School.

Stern is a research associate and was the cofounder and director of the Innovation Policy Working Group at the National Bureau of Economic Research. He is currently a member of the National Academies of Science, Engineering, and Medicine's Board on Science Technology and Economic Policy (STEP). In 2005, he was awarded the Kauffman Prize Medal for Distinguished Research in Entrepreneurship.

Stern explores how innovation and entrepreneurship differ from more traditional economic activities, and the consequences of these differences for strategy and policy. His research focuses on entrepreneurial strategy, innovation-driven entrepreneurial ecosystems, and innovation policy and management. He has worked widely with practitioners in bridging the gap between academic research and the practice of innovation and entrepreneurship. This includes advising start-ups and other growth firms in entrepreneurial strategy, as well as working with governments and other stakeholders on policy issues related to competitiveness and regional performance.

Stern is the cofounder and serves as the co-faculty director of the MIT Regional Entrepreneurship Acceleration Program. He is also the faculty director of the Martin Trust Center for MIT Entrepreneurship and the faculty director of the MIT Sloan Entrepreneurship and Innovation Certificate. As well, he is a principal investigator of the Startup Cartography Project, lead MIT investigator of the U.S. Cluster Mapping Project, and serves on the advisory board of the Social Progress Imperative.

ENTREPRENEURSHIP
Choice and Strategy

PART 1

GETTING STARTED

1. **UNDERSTANDING THE POWER OF CHOICE**

2. **CHOOSING ENTREPRENEURSHIP**

3. **CHOOSING YOUR OPPORTUNITY**

4. **CHOOSING YOUR STRATEGY**

Have you ever thought about being an entrepreneur? The fact that you are opening this book and likely taking a class in this topic probably means that you have. Many of you know that you want to be an entrepreneur and are looking for a guide for how to get started. However, some of you may wonder if this is a path that you should proceed down, possibly wondering if it is right for you.

Our answer is that we think it is. In our work, we have found that entrepreneurship can be a path for everyone, and this book helps you see how. Built on our experience and research with hundreds of entrepreneurs, we have found that entrepreneurship, at its core, is about the power of choice—making a decision about how you will shape part of the world. Whether a start-up venture, a small business, or even an entrepreneurial opportunity within a large company, when entrepreneurs of all types are guided by choice and strategy, their efforts are amplified.

In this book, you will see how all types of entrepreneurs—including the very famous and not-so famous—made this decision to become an entrepreneur. But importantly, you will learn processes and skills to help find, refine, and launch your idea. In part one, we start by showing you how to get started.

Now with 500-plus stores, the grocery chain Trader Joe's started with one person's idea to create a store selling unique goods at lower prices, and trying this concept out at a single location. Today, Trader Joe's is not only an example to follow (we will see this in Chapter 3), it is itself an entrepreneurial opportunity for manufacturers and growers interested in directly marketing their products.

There are multiple paths to pursue with any entrepreneurial idea. Just ask the Sharks!

SOURCE: Michael Desmond/© Disney General Entertainment Content/Getty Images

ENTREPRENEUR'S DILEMMA Any entrepreneur with a potential idea faces a lot of uncertainty as they get started. Normally, working out the details for a cost-benefit analysis of this idea is practically impossible, but just picking and starting with the first plan that comes to mind is risky. At the start, entrepreneurs must choose between taking time to learn more and deciding when to take action.

CHAPTER OBJECTIVES

- Discover why entrepreneurs need to balance learning and action
- Understand that there is always a trade-off between costly learning and keeping options open
- Identify why experienced mentors can help guide entrepreneurs in their choices
- Recognize the need for a systematic process to use in making choices

1

UNDERSTANDING THE POWER OF CHOICE

Who is your favorite Shark? As the most popular television show about entrepreneurship, *Shark Tank* features six widely celebrated entrepreneurs. Moreover, each Shark has achieved success in their own unique way. Daymond John (second from the left) had to learn how to sew as he launched FUBU ("For Us, By Us"), ultimately turning a $40 budget to design clothes for his friends into a multibillion-dollar clothing brand popular throughout the world. In the late 1990s, Mark Cuban (on the left) recognized the value created by making a wide range of traditional broadcast radio stations available through the early Internet, grew this idea to produce Broadcast.com, and sold it to Yahoo! for $4.5 billion in 1999. Barbara Corcoran (third from the left) built the Corcoran Group not through a single "aha" moment but by forming a loyal, high-quality team that established itself as the leading brokerage firm in high-end New York residential real estate.

In fact, an important aspect of the show is that each Shark brings a different approach or path to entrepreneurship. Each of these distinctive paths is reflected in the type of start-ups that Sharks are attracted to and the advice that they offer. Lori Greiner (the "Queen of QVC," pictured second from the right) often leads discussions with executives of branded consumer products (e.g., Scrub Daddy, a line of unique non-scratch sponges) that can benefit from her experience in identifying the best sales channels and forging valuable partnerships. In contrast, Kevin "Mr. Wonderful" O'Leary (third from the right) is best known for offering blunt assessments of whether a given business can truly be scalable and how entrepreneurs can leverage their limited capital to achieve growth.

FIGURE 1.1 Choosing Your Path

When they appeared on Shark Tank, Mohammed Hassoun (right) and Kun Yang chose Barbara Corcoran to help them grow their flavored cactus water start-up, Pricklee. On the episode, Yang said, "This deal isn't about the money for us, . . . It's about two first-generation (immigrants) chasing the American dream."

SOURCE: Christopher Willard/© Disney General Entertainment Content/Getty Images

entrepreneur A person who forms, pursues, and turns their business idea or product into a reality

entrepreneurial path A plan or way for an entrepreneur to execute and ideally succeed with their idea

Behind the debates between the Sharks lies perhaps the most fundamental question facing an entrepreneur: how can an **entrepreneur** form, pursue, and turn their idea into a reality? Tackling this question is the central purpose of this book. At first glance, this might seem like a simple question. If, for every idea for a new venture, there is only a single **entrepreneurial path** to pursue, then the central challenge facing an entrepreneur is whether to pursue that path or not. However, for most (if not all) entrepreneurial ideas, there will be multiple potential paths forward. For example, on their show, the Sharks often give different advice about how to best move forward with a given venture. While Shark Robert Herjavec (at the far right on p. 4) might advocate that an entrepreneur pursues cooperative partnerships with existing players, Kevin O'Leary seems more likely to suggest that entrepreneurs compete head-on against them.

These differences are not simply "mistakes" made by one Shark or another. They reflect the fact that for any new business idea, there are likely to be multiple paths to translate that idea into reality. Entrepreneurs should move beyond trying to figure out which one of these paths is "right" or "wrong" and instead think more strategically, asking important questions about the possibilities. If there are multiple paths you can follow, before choosing one, what can you learn about each approach and how can you experiment with them to see which you should choose? What experiments should entrepreneurs choose when they have limited resources? And what should entrepreneurs do when, even after learning and early experiments, they have more than one viable option? Ultimately, we see entrepreneurs on *Shark Tank* choose the path that best aligns with their passions and resources (**Figure 1.1**).[1] For the rest of this chapter, we will discuss how this is not a unique experience to a TV show, but a fundamental strategy centered around choices that every new entrepreneur can and should take.

1.1 Making Choices

How do entrepreneurs turn ideas into reality? Simply put, choice. Entrepreneurs, whether individuals or teams, consider a variety of options as they develop their business idea. However, having limited resources, they must choose among these uncertain options, knowing that they cannot pursue all of them. Further, the value of each option may not be known until it is tested in the real world. As a result, entrepreneurs must carefully select the path they will take to start their business.

This process can worry entrepreneurs. It's easy to get overwhelmed by the apparent range of opportunities. Entrepreneurs fear that spending too much time weighing the alternatives will delay commercializing their ideas. But rather than viewing the process as a scary prospect that might result in paralysis, entrepreneurs can use the power of choice to create opportunities that others have not yet been able to realize. Instead of exploiting the first opportunity they see, entrepreneurs use choice as the secret ingredient that allows them to enable transformative change. The process of making choices gives entrepreneurs the best chance to bring their ideas into reality. Taking some time to make deliberate decisions early on typically leads to implementing better plans and strategies as the venture launches. It also can help entrepreneurs find an ultimately more powerful route to success and customers than their original idea.

To understand both the power (and challenge) of choice, consider what an aspiring entrepreneur might do after an appearance on a show like *Shark Tank*, or more likely after meeting with mentors in an entrepreneurship class. While some mentors might agree on certain pieces of advice (e.g., "be sure to understand the needs of customers"), others will disagree about many of the most critical aspects of a business. For example, for a new company, some mentors might prioritize establishing a formal patent or trademark to protect their business idea, while others might be more dismissive of legal protections and the resources those require (including time) and encourage entrepreneurs to "just get started."

What should an entrepreneur do? A traditional approach is simply to gather all the evidence about the relative costs and benefits of a few approaches, calculate the option with the highest return, and pursue that option. In other words, if an entrepreneur can explore the possibilities around an idea fully without having to commit to it, then what they decide to do becomes a natural outcome of the best path that they find. However, this approach overlooks a central challenge of entrepreneurship: exploring and learning about all options is both costly and uncertain. Learning about the benefits and costs of various alternatives takes time, money, and resources and often involves taking actions that can't be undone. These actions themselves influence and shape a start-up firm. For example, the very act of entrepreneurs going on *Shark Tank*, or more generally, seeking the advice of experienced entrepreneurs, is part of that learning process. And as these entrepreneurs learn about potential paths forward from the Sharks, their potential consumers at home are already forming opinions about their product and venture.

This is the **paradox of entrepreneurship***:* committing to a certain approach requires knowledge that can only be gained by actively experimenting and learning. However, doing so inevitably results in some commitment that eliminates other options (see **Mini Case: Paradox of Entrepreneurship** on p. 8). Entrepreneurship is not a "problem set" where correct answers can be deduced before trying them.

But this does not mean that entrepreneurs should simply make choices at random. Instead, entrepreneurs should still work to learn and experiment with their idea, then make choices favoring one path at the expense of abandoning others.

Consider, for example, the founding of Google, one of the most iconic companies of the past quarter century. While the early Internet had search engines (the leading ones were Yahoo! and Excite), the results of searches were coded by hand; programmers would find and specify the results for the most common user searches and deliver these lists as results. But around 1996, two Stanford

paradox of entrepreneurship
The process of learning and experimentation at the early stage of a start-up to choose a path forward that inevitably results in some level of commitment that closes off other strategic options

Paradox of Entrepreneurship: It's All about the Mouse

Today's Mickey exemplifies Walt Disney's idea that animation is for children.

To see the paradox of entrepreneurship in action, we can go back to the origins of one of the most successful entrepreneurs of all time, Walt Disney. Moving to Hollywood during the earliest years of the movie industry, Disney had a simple but powerful idea: animation is for children. While this may seem obvious today, the early days of animation featured violent and mature themes, and Disney's vision of child-friendly characters in emotionally engaging stories was actually an outlier.

Disney jumped into action to realize his vision. Bringing together and training the leading animators of the era, Disney committed to proving that animation could entertain and tell compelling stories for children. This required building technical capabilities that gave their animated characters personality through subtle movements and actions. In stark contrast to the prevailing wisdom of the era, one of Disney's first animated characters, Oswald the Lucky Rabbit, proved a critical and commercial success as families rushed to see the new animated shorts Disney's team produced.

Disney's success, however, was fleeting. His early choices limited how he could financially benefit from Oswald's commercial success and build on that success with his team. In his haste to go to market to see if families would be drawn to this new form of animation, Disney had partnered with an established movie producer named Charley Mintz to distribute his Oswald shorts to a large audience. Upon seeing the success of Oswald, Mintz threatened to set up a competing animation studio within Universal Pictures (where he was now studio head) by poaching Disney's animators and, worse still, exercising an option in an early contract to retain the ownership of the copyright on Oswald himself. To keep working on Oswald the Lucky Rabbit, his proven character, Disney would have to become an employee of the Mintz operation alongside the team he had previously built and that Mintz had poached.[a]

Oswald the Lucky Rabbit

Our first look at Mickey Mouse

The rabbit may have been lucky, but Disney was incensed. Learning about the opportunity had cost him the ability to fully realize it himself. Facing perhaps the most critical moment of his young career, Disney conceived an alternative path using the same underlying ideas about animation for children. Besides changing the character (using a mouse that looks suspiciously like Oswald with shorter ears), Disney made a more fundamental set of changes that put his company on a different strategic direction. Over a six-month period, Disney not only created Mickey Mouse as a new character, but he also made sure to retain the rights to control that character. Further, Disney focused on creating an entirely new approach to animation: sound cartoons. When he chose to feature Mickey Mouse in the first fully realized sound cartoon, the landmark short *Steamboat Willie*, he not only introduced another technical breakthrough but also charted the core path for his company: to produce stories and innovations in animation better than any other studio. In other words, he intended to use his newfound greater control to innovate at a faster pace than others. Indeed, as he grew the company for the next 40 years, Disney would often remark that it was important for each Disney employee to remember that "it all started with a mouse."[b]

Walt Disney's journey highlights the paradox of entrepreneurship. His choice to push forward with investments in animation but give up certain rights in the process were commitments that drove short-term successes but ultimately blocked longer-term strategies. Though Disney was able to rebuild a team and pursue another route to realizing his vision, it was not without significant cost and a good bit of luck. Like Disney, most entrepreneurs find balancing the process of learning and then committing difficult. This book provides an active, choice-based approach to entrepreneurship to guide an entrepreneur through this process, rather than forcing an entrepreneur to passively accept choices made *for* them.

University graduate students, Larry Page and Sergey Brin (**Figure 1.2**), working on a research project to identify the structure of the World Wide Web, developed a "PageRank" algorithm that ranked the "importance" of each website by the number of other websites that linked to it. To their surprise, the algorithm not only was a great research project but also created a fundamentally new and powerful paradigm for Internet searches. While Page and Brin could have simply built on their discovery to complete their doctoral dissertations (and pursued promising academic careers), they realized that they could use the PageRank algorithm as the opportunity to found a new company, one they named Google.

Page and Brin's decision quickly led to choices around how to commercialize their technology. One option they considered was allowing users to search for free and charging advertisers for the right to display ads in response to specific queries. While this option was a popular approach to Internet commerce at the time, the two were unsure that this would be the most effective tactic.[2] In fact, in their initial white paper describing the Google algorithm, the duo argued that "we believe the issue of advertising causes enough mixed incentives that [it] is crucial to have a competitive search engine that is transparent and in the academic realm." In other words, Page and Brin were concerned about the advertising-based model and actively considered a range of alternative approaches that would be transparent. For example, they thought about licensing their technology to one or more established players who could then incorporate this more

FIGURE 1.2 Larry Page and Sergey Brin

Google cofounders Larry Page (right) and Sergey Brin's doctoral research to identify the structure of the World Wide Web led to the insight for the PageRank algorithm. This new approach ranked the "importance" of each website by the number of other websites that linked to it instead of manually coding the rankings for common searches as was done leading search engines. Despite what in hindsight seems an obvious path to commercialization, few believed that building a competing stand-alone search engine company supported by advertisers would be a viable strategic path, let alone one that would transform Google into the dominant search engine and influential global technology firm.

The Benefits of Systematizing Mentorship

Silicon Valley is known for its heavy concentration of ventures, both nascent and already at **scale**, where the business is adding revenue faster than it is adding costs. If you are an entrepreneur looking for mentorship, there are advantages to building your business in the Valley. And many do.

However, there are other ways of receiving mentorship. One way is to look for programs or opportunities in your area or region to systematically test and develop your idea with others. Many research universities have opportunities large and small that offer chances for support and guidance. This type of mentorship has been found to be very important for start-ups. Take Ajay Agrawal at the

Members of the Creative Destruction Lab learn about and discuss another member's idea.

University of Toronto. Agrawal made his academic career by finding out how geography drives innovation; he arrived at the conclusion that most locations, even those with thriving scientific communities, were missing a critical market: the market for judgment. Judgment is what mentors with experience at founding and bringing their own ventures to scale possess. This experience can help ventures refine their strategic choices and more effectively manage their scarce resources.

Agrawal took this knowledge and put it to work at his school, founding the Creative Destruction Lab (CDL).[a] This nonprofit program brings a systematic market for judgment to different cities. Ventures are exposed to five meetings at regular intervals over nine months in the program. Some of those meetings are one-on-one. Others involve many mentors being in the same room at the same time and debating what advice they should give ventures.

The structured environment that brings together ventures and mentors in the same location intermittently has proven effective at driving venture success. As of 2022, CDL ventures have created more than $20 billion in equity value with over $500 million in funding. The CDL has opened 12 sites across Canada, the United States (Seattle; Atlanta; and Madison, WI) and Europe (Oxford, UK; Paris; Berlin; and Estonia).

But more broadly, the CDL program shows the benefit of this type of mentorship. By seeking out opportunities for mentorship like the CDL, entrepreneurs can get the support they need, often close to where they live.

---

effective search engine into their own Internet operations. Alternatively, some advisers encouraged them to simply sell the company and the search engine at a relatively early stage to an existing player, and indeed they made an offer to sell the company to Excite for $1 million (which was ultimately rejected). Eventually, a mentor who had successfully grown a Silicon Valley venture convinced the duo to pursue their own path for Google (see **Using the Research: The Benefits of Systematizing Mentorship**).

While we know the path that Page and Brin ultimately took, the choices they were presented with and made are not simply part of the founding story of one of the most impactful companies of the twenty-first century. Rather, the choices these two faced and the paths they considered are examples of how choices are

scale In entrepreneurship, when a business is adding revenue faster than it is adding costs

at the heart of being a strategic entrepreneur. Page and Brin had to establish that they had indeed come up with a good idea. Doing so meant identifying potential ways to translate that idea into a reality that would *create and capture value*. In other words, they had to execute in ways that would create something others would want and see value in, and that would capture this value by earning money from its use (we will discuss this topic further in Chapter 2). Page and Brin created value with their search engine based on page ranking. They ultimately captured value when, several years later, they decided to implement the advertising-based model they had originally discussed. But they did not have the option to pursue all paths at once, and their ultimate choices powerfully shaped the company and its impact.

choice-based approach An approach to entrepreneurship focused on identifying choices and opportunities first, and then actively making choices about these potential entrepreneurial paths

A CHOICE-BASED APPROACH TO BEING AN ENTREPRENEUR

Making choices like the ones Larry Page and Sergey Brin made forms the central premise of this book. When entrepreneurs focus on generating and then actively making choices about potential entrepreneurial paths, they will be more proactive in shaping their business and be more successful. This **choice-based approach** to entrepreneurship moves beyond a traditional process where you hope doing a cost-benefit analysis on an idea without first gathering any experience or data will yield one best plan. Or, where you believe that the only true approach for an entrepreneur is to simply commit and learn by doing. Instead, this choice-based approach means

- An entrepreneur should always try to learn more about an idea first, using experiments and other processes of learning to assess it.
- If an initial idea is worthwhile, research and experiments done to learn more about it should yield *multiple* paths to pursue.
- Choosing among these options will also present a dilemma—entrepreneurs cannot learn if an idea will work without making some major commitment (e.g., to the type of customer served, the particular technology used, or the kind of person hired for the team).
- These initial processes of experimenting, learning, and choice will help an entrepreneur weed out poor options and, more importantly, find better choices to commit to.

1.2 Choosing the "It" to Do

As we just noted, an entrepreneur does not have the ability, time, or resources to fully explore the costs and benefits of all possible entrepreneurial paths. However, the path they do choose shapes how and if they succeed in turning their idea into a reality. Resolving this dilemma is critical to being a successful entrepreneur. But doing so is more difficult for entrepreneurs than for other business managers. Why? First, the decisions that entrepreneurs need to make are distinctive. Being in a typical business environment is normally grounded in planning. A manager or businessperson facing a decision first gathers all the necessary information to make an informed choice and then decides on an

FIGURE 1.3 Richard Branson

Whether it was during the early days of his first company, Virgin Music (left), or a recent opening of Virgin Hotels in Las Vegas (right), Richard Branson has started many businesses with the conviction to "just do it." But is this philosophy right for every entrepreneur? How does the typical starting entrepreneur know what the "it" is?

approach that maximizes the profitability of their organization. This planning approach assumes people have the information they need to make the best decision available. To take an oversimplified but instructive example, it is common for a manager to try to calculate the "optimal" price for something, assuming the decision-maker has full information about demand and all relevant costs.

But relative to a traditional business decision, the distinct challenge facing an entrepreneur is the uncertainty surrounding the opportunity. Without the ability to plan, resolving these uncertainties requires actively engaging in putting the idea into action. For example, one of the main uncertainties facing any entrepreneur is whether potential customers will in fact value the product or service being created. In most cases, learning about what customers value is only accomplished through working with customers directly. For this reason, Richard Branson (**Figure 1.3**), one of the most successful entrepreneurs of the last 50 years, simply encourages entrepreneurs to "just do it!" The problem, of course, is choosing the "it" to do. How can an entrepreneur make choices when they have neither (1) the resources or the knowledge required by a planning process nor (2) the clarity about the specific choices they could make to "just do it" and bring their ideas into reality?

LEARNING BY EXPERIMENTING

The key to breaking through this impasse is **entrepreneurial experimentation**. In an entrepreneurial experiment, an entrepreneur "tests" a plan with potential ways to create and capture value from their underlying idea. Instead of debating the merits of possible alternatives in the abstract, entrepreneurial experimentation is a systematic process to test the most critical assumptions underlying any plan in a rapid, cost-effective way. This lets the entrepreneur make active choices with far better information than through a planning process alone and without making the potential commitments that simply "doing it" may incur on the venture.

entrepreneurial experimentation
A systematic process in which an entrepreneur "tests" a plan with potential ways to create and capture value from an idea

Chapter 1: Understanding the Power of Choice

Consider the case of the founding of the popular fashion rental site Rent the Runway in 2009. It begins with one of the founders, Jennifer Hyman, working on her MBA. While doing so, she saw her younger sister struggle to purchase an expensive dress for a wedding.[3] Hyman and classmate Jennifer Fleiss felt certain that many others faced the same problem: whether to buy an expensive outfit that might only be worn once or twice. The two thought there was an opportunity here, one where people could rent pricey designer clothes for a few nights for a reasonable fee and return them for others to rent later. As Hyman and Fleiss explored the opportunity, they received both positive and negative feedback from classmates, professors, and alumni in the retail industry. More important, though, they narrowed down key factors and assumptions underlying their business idea and developed a process to test those hypotheses in a systematic way before committing to the idea. The three critical assumptions they identified were that (1) college students and young professionals would find renting previously worn designer gowns superior to purchasing those dresses new, (2) dresses would, in most cases, be returned by customers in an acceptable condition so that, after dry cleaning, they could be rented again, and (3) leading designers would not only be amenable to having their dresses rented but also would partner with a start-up to enable this new avenue.

In this chapter's video, watch the story of how Jennifer Hyman and Jennifer Fleiss used a learning and experimentation process to build Rent the Runway.

Then, before committing to the idea, the two began a testing process. They sought feedback from influential designers—cold-calling, for example, world-famous designer Diane von Furstenberg—and gained early insights about the designer market. The designers' advice led the duo to shift away from their original concept of working directly with designers toward a model in which they instead served as a new type of retail channel for customers. Hyman and Fleiss also conducted modest but meaningful experiments at leading universities to test aspects of their idea on a small scale and with limited commitment on their part. For example, the two set up a pop-up store on a campus to see if students would actually rent dresses (they did!). Ultimately, the positive and actionable feedback from those group experiments both crystallized the value of their idea and helped them determine their specific strategy. Essentially, their early-stage experiments allowed Hyman and Fleiss (**Figure 1.4**) to move beyond hypothetical discussions among themselves, their classmates, and colleagues about whether their idea had value. With actual evidence that it did, the two could start envisioning actionable strategic plans around their idea, choosing one, and forming the basis for a multibillion-dollar venture over the next decade.

Entrepreneurial experiments such as those conducted by Hyman and Fleiss let entrepreneurs strike a balance between planning and action. They provide a way for entrepreneurs to identify concrete paths for translating their ideas into reality but not commit to one until other ideas are also tested. By providing a

FIGURE 1.4 Rent the Runway

Jennifer Hyman and Jennifer Fleiss conducted a systematic process of experimentation and learning before committing to a specific strategic route for their start-up, Rent the Runway. Experiments provided them evidence that their idea—a dress-rental website—had the potential to create real value for customers. Today, Rent the Runway is a multibillion-dollar venture.

How Entrepreneurial Experiments Differ from Scientific Experiments

Though the process of entrepreneurial experimentation and the more traditional idea of scientific experimentation have much in common, there are some key distinctions. Most notably:

- Scientific experimentation is at its heart "learning for learning's sake" to better understand the world around us.
- The goal of scientific experimentation is to test a hypothesis so that a scientist can increase knowledge about a phenomenon or theory.
- While entrepreneurial experiments involve learning, their purpose is not simply to learn but also to offer insights that can inform and enable choices and actions by an entrepreneur.
- For entrepreneurs, the real challenge is figuring out what to do with the results of those experiments once they have been conducted.
- An effective entrepreneurial experiment must help an entrepreneur learn and choose a path forward that turns their idea into a reality.

Entrepreneurs and scientists both experiment, but they do so in different ways and with different goals in mind.

structured approach to how to translate an idea into a reality, entrepreneurial experiments are the critical step that lets an entrepreneur identify the "it" to do.

MORE CHOICES ARE BETTER

More often than not, entrepreneurs pursuing a good idea will identify multiple paths for moving that idea forward. In fact, having more than one path forward is critical. Entrepreneurs should be wary of ideas where they cannot identify more than one option. After all, if there is only one way of conceiving that an idea may generate value, that is a signal the idea itself might not be worth pursuing. The goal of early experimentation is not to figure out the precise details of a single path, but instead is to

1. envisage and better understand broad choices for several paths being considered; and
2. learn more about the broader opportunity itself.

In running experiments, entrepreneurs will no doubt identify paths that are not likely to be feasible or effective and that can be discarded. But even these discarded plans help a founder evaluate others that seem more viable. Importantly, given the limited resources of an entrepreneur, having options lets them make their ultimate choices based on their goals for a venture (e.g., what types of customers would they like to serve?), their tolerance for risk (e.g., should they choose a more conservative or a more "go big or go home" approach?), and near-term considerations that simply allow them to get started (e.g., developing an early version of the product or service that allows them to start to gain customer feedback).

1.3 Strategy for Start-Ups

One of the goals of this book is to provide an individual entrepreneur or a founding team the practical framework and tools they need to experiment, explore alternatives, and ultimately make choices that crystallize, create, and start a successful venture. This approach will help you in any new venture, be it a tech start-up, project within an established company, small business or franchise, or a not-for-profit opportunity. It will expose you to other entrepreneurs and their ideas and show you a strategic framework for considering and a process for implementing the core choices facing a start-up.

Put simply, this book places entrepreneurs and their choices center stage. Choice is not simply a consequence of entrepreneurship; it is the central organizing principle. But there is a fundamental tension at the heart of this process:

what should an entrepreneur do when the information needed to make core strategic decisions—such as an understanding of alternative cost structures, or the impact of different pricing models on demand—can only be obtained by experimenting and learning in ways that lead a venture down a particular path? The process of actively choosing between equally viable entrepreneurial paths powerfully illustrates the need to learn more about an idea and the need to commit to it.

Ultimately, this approach impacts the very beginning of any entrepreneur's venture. It impacts choices that are central to being an entrepreneur in the first place, like

- When should I choose entrepreneurship?
- Which opportunities should I pursue?

And it involves the most critical choices entrepreneurs face as they work to translate that opportunity into reality, such as

- Which customers should we target (and when)?
- What technologies and innovations should we leverage?
- Whom should we hire, and how and where should we organize?
- How should we commercialize our idea in the face of potential competition?

We see these questions in play in the dilemma facing Lonnie Johnson, our final example in the chapter. In the 1980s, Lonnie Johnson was a successful NASA engineer and scientist (**Figure 1.5**), working on methods to use water as a

FIGURE 1.5 **Lonnie Johnson**

Engineer and longtime inventor Lonnie Johnson got his entrepreneurial start with the Super Soaker water gun. He poses here in 1992 with an early version of the water gun and the U.S. patent for it. Today, Johnson holds over 100 patents.

coolant to replace ozone-damaging CFCs. While doing research in his bathroom sink with a mechanical nozzle, Johnson inadvertently created a powerful water stream. He built on this idea to invent a forceful targeted water gun for children, which was a clear hit with his and others' kids. While Johnson believed he had identified something that was missing from the marketplace (water guns up to that time had very limited range and power), he was a newcomer to the world of children's toys and new to entrepreneurship. He had many questions, such as: *What age range should he target? How should he try to improve on his initial prototype over time? Who could he attract to help him develop his invention, and should he seek to cooperate with the big players in the toy industry or go it alone?* None of these questions had an obvious answer, and each was also related to the others (e.g., who you choose as your target customer also influences who you might seek to help with product design and how you go to market with the final product).

In Johnson's case, he first decided to work on the water gun on his own at night, while living on a U.S. Air Force base and helping to design the first B2 stealth bomber. While his young daughter and neighborhood children loved his first versions of the gun (which looked like a *Star Wars*–type ray gun and sprayed water almost 40 feet), Johnson decided he could not afford the $200,000 estimate he got to produce and stock 1,000 working toys on his own.[4] Johnson realized he had to move beyond simply inventing a great water gun and choose a path to put his toy into more children's hands. The many other aspects of producing and marketing the water gun prompted him to pursue working with a partner. After seven years of trying, Johnson succeeded in drawing the interest of a small toy company, Larami, to finish and market the product. Besides having marketing staff that saw the potential of Johnson's raw prototype, the company also had an engineer, Bruce D'Andrade, who was a whiz at making toys. D'Andrade figured out how to make Johnson's water gun so it would retail at $10, which Larami executives felt was the highest price they could sell it for and which was an astronomical price for a water gun at the time.[5] They initially called it the Power Drencher but then rebranded it as the Super Soaker in 1991. It has reigned as the most popular water gun for children for the past 30 years.[6]

MAKING CHOICES TOGETHER

As we see in the case of Lonnie Johnson, the critical choices facing an entrepreneur are not made in isolation. Simply put, tackling entrepreneurship strategically means confronting important and interrelated choices in a systematic way. Each choice interacts and influences how an entrepreneur will approach others. For instance, targeting a specific customer influences how an entrepreneur will leverage a given technology in their product or service as they build it. In turn, this may require different resources and capabilities (like team members or investors) to build the product than if they had focused on another approach. We see this with Johnson's idea for a water gun. Johnson felt he had a hit based on the tests he did with prototypes, but research into producing and marketing them himself made him decide to look for help. He decided to target toy manufacturers as his customer, which gave him ready access to mainstream customer segments as well as the partner's significant resources and capabilities. Larami had an engineer that knew how to make a product with the right price, and a marketing team who knew how to sell it. But this required Johnson to adjust how he had originally planned to work; instead of doing it all on his own, Johnson licensed the product with an agreement to receive royalties on future sales. Johnson then moved on from the Super Soaker and focused on applying his technology to Nerf guns, which became an even more successful invention for him.[7]

1.4 How This Book Works

This book offers a systematic and choice-based approach to entrepreneurship and how those choices fit together as part of an overall strategy (see the **Putting It Together: Understanding the Power of Choice** on p. 18). To accomplish this goal, the book is divided into four sections:

1. *Getting Started.* We begin with a deep dive into why choice matters, focusing on the initial choice to become an entrepreneur, the choice of which idea to pursue, and the choice of an overall strategy for a venture:

   Chapter 1: Understanding the Power of Choice
   Chapter 2: Choosing Entrepreneurship
   Chapter 3: Choosing Your Opportunity
   Chapter 4: Choosing Your Strategy

2. *Core Choices.* Not simply an abstract concept, entrepreneurs systematically face a series of core choices that requires them to balance the interplay between learning and commitment. We focus primarily on four clusters of choices that are central to the founding and scaling of a venture. These choices exist around:

   Chapter 5: Choosing Your Customer
   Chapter 6: Choosing Your Technology
   Chapter 7: Choosing Your Organization
   Chapter 8: Choosing Your Competition

3. *Four Strategies: How Choices Work Together.* We match key complementary choices to create four different strategies for start-ups that entrepreneurs can explore for a given idea:

   Chapter 9: Intellectual Property Strategy
   Chapter 10: Disruption Strategy
   Chapter 11: Value Chain Strategy
   Chapter 12: Architectural Strategy

   Each of these strategies reflects a distinctive set of choices of Customer, Technology, Organization, and Competition and highlights specific interconnected factors that entrepreneurs can exploit in translating their idea into a viable company.

4. *Putting It to Work.* Equipped with the tools to translate an idea into reality, we introduce three chapters for entrepreneurs to explore building a venture with a foundation for long-term viability, which are focused on:

   Chapter 13: From Strategy to Action
   Chapter 14: Financing
   Chapter 15: Scaling

One at a time, these chapters will help you understand how to choose a strategy, enable it, and possibly decide to grow and scale a business.

In Part 2 we will explore the core choices of Customer, Technology, Organization, and Competition. Then in Part 3 we will see how these choices combine to form strategies.

UNDERSTANDING THE POWER OF CHOICE

How does an entrepreneur form, pursue, and turn an idea into a reality? They start with the power of choice and using it strategically to find, create, and act on a viable plan.

RECOGNIZE WHY GOOD IDEAS HAVE MULTIPLE PATHS TO SUCCESS

Understand That There Are Many Ways to Move Your Ideas to Reality

- Use the power of choice to create opportunities that others have not yet been able to realize. Consider a range of alternative paths for your idea.
- Instead of trying to solve for the "right" path, begin by generating important questions to understand the possibilities.
- Choose a viable, powerful route to translate your ideas into reality and make an impact.

EXPLORING AND EXPERIMENTING WITH YOUR IDEAS IS AN IMPORTANT FIRST STEP

Experiment and Learn and Then Commit

- Explore the idea first. Use initial experimentation to learn more about the idea and assess it with limited commitment.
- Entrepreneurship requires action. Move deliberately and use experimentation to strike a balance between planning and action.
- Identify and understand the commitments involved in early learning and experimentation. Delay making irreversible commitments.

USE A CHOICE-BASED APPROACH TO BEING AN ENTREPRENEUR

Employ Strategic Ideas to Launch and Improve Your Start-Up

- Use a systematic process to understand the core choices central to founding and scaling your venture: which customers will you serve, how will you innovate, how will you build your team, and with whom and how will you compete?
- Consider common strategies for start-ups to avoid making core choices in isolation. Entrepreneurship involves interrelated choices and understanding how each core choice interacts and influences others.
- Test the most critical assumptions underlying any plan in a rapid and cost-effective way.
- Evaluate alternative viable paths and make a choice based on your goals for the venture and near-term considerations.
- Commit to your path to build and scale your venture. Embrace entrepreneurial experimentation and learning to sharpen your decisions as you move forward.

1.5 Concluding Thoughts

Entrepreneurs turn ideas into reality. Those ideas may build on the experiences of the entrepreneur, may be something "missing" from the marketplace, or may result from exploration of a new technology or discovery (see sidebar on **Supergoop!**). But the central challenge of entrepreneurship is how to realize the value of that idea. This book shows how making choices allows an entrepreneur to go from the process of identifying potential opportunities to putting ideas into practice.

Entrepreneurship can also be a lot of fun. Entrepreneurs get to decide how they want to create value in the marketplace and whom they will work with (and on what) to turn their ideas into reality. The reason that shows such as *Shark Tank* are so popular is because they show us how different individuals—each ambitious, each with their own ideas—pursue entrepreneurship in such different ways.

Entrepreneurship is also a powerful way for an individual or team to make an impact. When you work for an existing organization, someone else (a boss, or the boss's boss) is deciding what to work on, and often there are more constraints on how to have an impact on the world. Whether it is generation-defining entrepreneurs such as Apple's founder Steve Jobs or local restaurateurs who develop a new and exciting restaurant in your city, entrepreneurs choose where to focus their ideas to create the impact *they* hope to have on the world. But doing so involves diving into each of the most critical choices facing entrepreneurs. In the next chapter, we start with why and whether to become an entrepreneur in the first place.

Supergoop! Holly Thaggard (seated) founded Supergoop!, a company that sells sunscreen formulated for children, after learning a friend had contracted skin cancer at age 25. Thaggard's mission was simply "to have every single person love sunscreen." Realizing she needed more help, she recruited Amanda Baldwin to be the company's CEO because of her extensive experience in the cosmetics industry. Today, this successful venture also funds a program called "Ounce by Ounce," which donates free sunscreen to schools, especially ones with underserved populations.[a]

Chapter 1 Review: Understanding the Power of Choice

CHAPTER TAKEAWAYS

- A central insight of entrepreneurship is that, for a given idea, there are likely to be multiple potential paths forward to translate that idea into reality.

- A strategic or choice-based approach to entrepreneurship focuses on proactive experimentation and understanding the key trade-offs between alternative paths. This allows an entrepreneur to choose the path that best aligns with their objectives and resources.

- The paradox of entrepreneurship is that choosing between alternative strategic commitments at the early stage of a start-up requires knowledge that can only be gained through experimentation and learning. Yet the process of learning and experimentation inevitably results in some level of commitment that closes off some strategic options for the start-up.

- A central challenge of entrepreneurship is that simply learning about the value of alternative options is itself costly and uncertain.

- The most important task for a start-up at its founding is not simply to "just do it" but instead to learn what "it" to "do." Entrepreneurial action first requires choice.

- Entrepreneurial experiments provide a way for entrepreneurs to identify concrete paths for translating their ideas into reality without committing to one of those paths before considering alternatives.

KEY TERMS

entrepreneur (p. 6)

entrepreneurial path (p. 6)

paradox of entrepreneurship (p. 7)

scale (p. 10)

choice-based approach (p. 11)

entrepreneurial experimentation (p. 12)

REVIEW QUESTIONS

1. Why is choice important to entrepreneurship?
2. True or false: Most good ideas have multiple paths to translate their idea into reality. Explain.
3. Define value creation and provide an example of how a recent start-up has created value.
4. Define value capture and provide an example of how a recent start-up has captured value.
5. What is the paradox of entrepreneurship? Explain in your own words.
6. What is the goal of early experimentation and learning in entrepreneurship?
7. What are the most critical choices facing an entrepreneur? How are they connected?

DISCUSSION QUESTIONS

Answer the following series of questions and scenarios either in class discussions or by writing a short response.

1. Why might it be difficult for a clear cost-benefit analysis to determine the best path forward for a start-up idea?
2. What is the appeal of the "just do it" approach to entrepreneurship? What are the limitations of this approach?
3. Learning and experimentation are central to entrepreneurship. What are examples of entrepreneurial experiments and other opportunities for learning that involve limited commitments or costs to the founding team or venture itself? What are types of entrepreneurial experiments and other opportunities for learning that involve more significant commitments or costs? Why should entrepreneurs, at the early stage, prioritize the former?
4. In the chapter, the founding of Rent the Runway was discussed. Founders Hyman and Fleiss undertook a systematic process to test the most critical assumptions of their idea. What did they learn from interviews with designers? What information might they have received from their pop-up store on campus? How might these learnings have addressed (or not) their critical

assumptions around their idea? What key sources of uncertainty remained about their idea after this early learning and experimentation?

5. Why must a start-up both create and capture value? Can you think of an example of a start-up that has created value early on but has struggled to capture value over the long term? What are the implications for the start-up?

6. Consider a start-up within your ecosystem. What are the critical choices of the venture? How does it propose to create and capture value? What are the key assumptions underlying its ability to create and capture value?

7. Most good ideas have multiple paths to translate their idea into reality. Find an example of two start-ups founded based on the same underlying opportunity (e.g., solving the same consumer need, leveraging the same technology), but whose founders chose different paths to bring that idea to reality. What were the critical choices of each venture? Why do you think each founding teams chose their respective path to commercialization? Which would you have chosen (and why)?

SUGGESTED READINGS

Arrow, Kenneth J. "Economic Welfare and the Allocation of Resources for Invention." In *The Rate and Direction of Inventive Activity*, edited by Richard Nelson, 609–25. Princeton, NJ: Princeton University Press, 1962

Felin, Teppo, Alfonso Gambardella, Scott Stern, and Todd Zenger. "Lean Startup and the Business Model: Experimentation Revisited." *Long Range Planning* 53, no. 4 (2020): 101889, https://doi.org/10.1016/j.lrp.2019.06.002.

Gans, Joshua, Erin L. Scott, and Scott Stern. "Strategy for Start-Ups." *Harvard Business Review* 96, no. 3 (2018): 44–51.

Graham, Paul. "How to Get Startup Ideas." *Paul Graham* (personal website), November 2012. http://paulgraham.com/startupideas.html.

Lafley, Alan G., Roger L. Martin, Jan W. Rivkin, and Nicolaj Siggelkow. "Bringing Science to the Art of Strategy." *Harvard Business Review* 90, no. 9 (2012): 56–66.

Murray, Fiona, and Mary Tripsas. "The Exploratory Processes of Entrepreneurial Firms: The Role of Purposeful Experimentation. *Advances in Strategic Management* 21 (2004): 45–76.

Rosenberg, Nathan. *Exploring the Black Box: Technology, Economics, and History*. Cambridge: Cambridge University Press, 1994.

Stevenson, Howard H., and David E. Gumpert. "The Heart of Entrepreneurship." *Harvard Business Review* 85, no. 2 (1985): 85–94.

Jamie Siminoff

As Jamie Siminoff stepped on stage to pitch DoorBot to the Sharks on Season 5 of *Shark Tank*, he had a lot working in his favor. He had a been a serial entrepreneur since his college days, when he and his friends launched Gadget Tronics to sell TVs and stereos, and his latest venture was his best yet.[a]

DoorBot had been founded to solve a singular and nearly universal challenge: to find out who is at the door. Siminoff often missed package deliveries when he was working in his home garage and thought there must be a simple solution that would allow him to catch these deliveries. After yet another missed package, he set out to build such a system for personal use. Working on the prototype in his spare time, he finally came up with a working solution, one that combined a Wi-Fi-enabled camera with a smartphone app. When his wife remarked that the device actually made her feel safer at home, Siminoff started to consider the broader opportunity.[b] He decided to take the next steps to explore the idea further.

In Siminoff's early interviews regarding home security systems, he learned that burglars often ring the doorbell before they select a home or apartment to rob. He hypothesized that his camera-doorbell device connected to a simple smartphone app could allow residents to answer their doorbell even when not at home. He thought the device could serve as an accessible home-security system as well as provide greater insights into deliveries and other visitors. His visitors were often quick to ask Siminoff for a DoorBot for their own homes, and after more thought and experimentation, he decided to found his company, DoorBot, to "reduce crime in communities."[c]

After launching a successful crowdfunding campaign, DoorBot was earning consistent sales, but Siminoff still

Jamie Siminoff pitching his product, DoorBot, on *Shark Tank*
SOURCE: Adam Taylor/© ABC/Getty Images.

felt "broke," with little to show for his efforts. He wanted to build his team and expand manufacturing capabilities to lower the cost of the device and increase scale to bring this offering to more neighborhoods. He came to *Shark Tank* to raise $700,000 to do just that.

Unfortunately, after he came around the door with his pitch, the Sharks were skeptical.[d] Mark Cuban liked the product but asked, "Are there bigger solutions that could come in and push this out the door?" Daymond John echoed the sentiment, noting that traditional home-security companies "will most likely just add this to their services." Lori Greiner thought Siminoff had not yet landed on a final product. She said she felt there was the potential to do a lot more, but that DoorBot didn't distinguish itself from similar home-security products on the market. Robert Herjavec agreed and was concerned the device could easily be hacked. One by one, the Sharks declined to take the discussion further as they were unclear about the path forward for both the product and the company itself.

Then Shark Kevin O'Leary offered Siminoff $700,000 for a 10% royalty, which would drop to 7% after the $700,000 was recouped, plus 5% of the company. Siminoff returned to his vision for the company when he said, "Respectfully, Mr. Wonderful, we're going to decline." Siminoff wanted to build a large, successful home-security company. He believed such a large royalty payment would hamper his ability to make the choices necessary to realize that vision.

At the same time, Siminoff was crushed at the failure to close a deal and embarrassed at doing so on prime-time TV. The sentiments of the Sharks were not unlike feedback he had been receiving from other investors and the many rounds where they had rejected funding him.

Though disappointed, Siminoff believed in his plan and kept at it. As he later said, "The credibility and the awareness that *Shark Tank* brought was probably worth $10 million of ads. It really launched us." He was also buoyed by Cuban's assessment. "I think it's a great business. I think you'll be successful. It will be worth $20 million. I just can't invest in something that's not going to be $70 million someday," Cuban told him.[e]

Ultimately, Cuban was right about the success of the business, but wrong about its valuation. Siminoff sold his business, with the updated name of Ring, to Amazon in 2018 in a deal worth $1 billion.[f]

Questions

1. What were the key concerns of the Sharks and, in your opinion and using what you have read in the chapter, what do they indicate about the opportunity?

2. Describe some of the key early choices Siminoff made that helped the business succeed in the long run.

3. In your opinion, how should entrepreneurs let the feedback from mentors and investors drive their choices, particularly negative feedback such as the type Siminoff received from some of the Sharks?

Oprah Winfrey chose to pursue entrepreneurship.

ENTREPRENEUR'S DILEMMA Should you choose to become an entrepreneur? Entrepreneurship allows individuals to pursue opportunities of their choice, start and grow a new organization big or small, and possibly earn significant financial and personal rewards. The dilemma for an entrepreneur is that opportunities with the potential for greater impact normally come with greater uncertainty about if the venture will succeed.

CHAPTER OBJECTIVES

- Understand what is meant by entrepreneurship and becoming an entrepreneur
- Learn the choices people face when considering entrepreneurship
- Identify why value creation and value capture matter in choosing entrepreneurship
- Recognize the economic and noneconomic benefits of entrepreneurship, including the role of personal choice
- Learn about entrepreneurship as a distinct career relative to choosing to work for others
- Explore which personal traits and passions can give you an advantage in becoming an entrepreneur

2

CHOOSING ENTREPRENEURSHIP

In 1985, Oprah Winfrey achieved two major successes. Acting in her first film, Winfrey was nominated for an Academy Award for her role alongside Danny Glover and Whoopi Goldberg in *The Color Purple*. She was also the host of the top-ranked local television talk show, *AM Chicago,* which she had taken from last place to first in under two years. The following year, she further expanded that show, launching the syndicated *Oprah Winfrey Show* nationwide. However, these successes also led to some important and difficult choices about what she should do next.

Winfrey had big goals and needed to be proactive to attain them. She knew that she wanted to be famous, to help and inspire others. As she says in one of her well-known quotes on success, "The key to realizing a dream is to focus not on success but on significance—and then even the small steps and little victories along your path will take on greater meaning."[1] Further, she wanted to maintain strict control over what she created. Talking about control in a *Fortune* magazine interview, Winfrey explained, "If I lost control of the business, I'd lose myself—or at least the ability to be myself. Owning myself is a way to be myself."[2] But how? While the stellar reviews for her performance in *The Color Purple* offered a clear path forward in Hollywood movies, her talk show resonated with a broad swath of Middle America and gave her an outlet to explore a wide variety of topics and themes. Over 18 months, Winfrey made a series of choices in which she would leave acting largely behind and forge the direction that would lead her to become, simply, "Oprah," one of the most successful self-made entrepreneurs of all time. In particular, Winfrey committed herself to the day-to-day work of a daily TV talk show, one still based in Chicago. She created her show for a targeted demographic of aspirational talk show viewers (i.e., women who were middle age or older) rather than the more broad-spectrum audience associated

Oprah decided to pursue her talk show and the opportunities she felt this path would lead to.

This chapter's video explores how Oprah Winfrey became one of the most influential figures in modern media.

with mass-market entertainment. This was exemplified by her telling stories of her own troubles (in particular, sexual abuse and struggles with her weight), breaking a barrier between her and her audience. And, perhaps most importantly, Oprah chose to build a company, Harpo Productions, rather than continue to work on a contract basis.

Most people are familiar with the results. Her talk show stood atop the daytime ratings for decades, and she exerted an almost unmatched cultural influence. Among other notable achievements, Winfrey's support for Barack Obama in December 2007 has been linked to his breakthrough win in the 2008 Iowa caucuses, leading to his subsequent election as president. With her media empire extending from *O, The Oprah Magazine* to Oprah Radio (on XM Satellite Radio), Oprah next launched the Oprah Winfrey Network (OWN) on cable television in 2011, which continues to build on the vision she developed for her initial venture more than 25 years earlier. Today, she is popularly known as the "queen of all media."

Winfrey could have chosen not to become an entrepreneur. After being nominated for a prestigious Academy Award, an acting career was hers for the taking. But she chose another path. In doing so, Oprah realized a larger set of goals, including the empowerment and self-improvement of women and underrepresented groups, all while maintaining a high level of control over the creative direction of her media empire.

This chapter is about that first choice: *should you become an entrepreneur or not?* And like the other decisions facing entrepreneurs in this book, using a strategic approach to explore and answer this question. That means considering the potential and consequences of taking one path over another, embracing **uncertainty**, and, only then, taking the next step.

2.1 The Goals of Entrepreneurs

Choosing entrepreneurship as a career involves what, at first glance, seems like two contradictory goals. On the one hand, entrepreneurship means establishing a new business with the goal of earning revenues (income) that exceed the costs of that business. From this perspective, the ultimate test of entrepreneurship is the profitability and sustainable growth of the enterprise. Many people assume that the true goal of an entrepreneur is maximal growth and profitability and that the most iconic entrepreneurs are those who have built organizations that have prospered for a long time.

But at the same time, entrepreneurship is a personal choice: a person should choose entrepreneurship if they believe they can be made better off personally by pursuing entrepreneurship, at least for a time. From that perspective, it does not matter how much money you make from entrepreneurship. It even allows for a case where you might make significantly less money than in a traditional job. Walking away from a lucrative job on Wall Street, in consulting, or with any established company to pursue a business based on an interest or passion might not be the most profitable choice for you. But for many people, following a passion and choosing to open, say, a small restaurant or yoga studio might very well be the best choice for them.

Entrepreneurs often receive contradictory advice on what to do depending on which of these two perspectives is favored by their advisers. Some mentors

uncertainty The belief that the outcome of business decisions cannot truly be predicted or modeled

and popular business experts exhort entrepreneurs to focus exclusively on profitability and give "whatever it takes" for a business to succeed as an economic entity. In this conception, once you have founded a business, the only objective is to maximize the profitability of that enterprise. Other mentors and experts will do the opposite, encouraging entrepreneurs to pursue their passions without too much regard for economic cost or the potential for value creation and capture.

economic choice A decision made to pursue one path of action over another after analyzing the relative benefits of each

noneconomic goal A goal not related to the economic outcome of a given venture

CHOOSING ENTREPRENEURSHIP STRATEGICALLY

There is another approach, a strategic approach to entrepreneurship that combines these perspectives. On the one hand, it requires potential entrepreneurs to make an active **economic choice** to only pursue opportunities in which there is at least some potential for value creation for others. Unless the entrepreneur (or a wealthy relative) is willing to lose money indefinitely, the potential for the idea to be profitable is a de facto requirement for choosing a particular entrepreneurial opportunity. At the same time, the ultimate objective of any entrepreneur should not simply be maximizing profits but also the **noneconomic goal** of realizing their own personal value objectives for their enterprise (e.g., pursuing their passion). *Ultimately, entrepreneurs should choose the path that best realizes their preferred combination of economic and noneconomic values.*

This approach works for entrepreneurs of all types (high-tech start-up, social endeavor, family business, and so on). Most of us are familiar with Mark Zuckerberg, founder of Facebook (**Figure 2.1a**), who desperately wanted to exert control over and succeed in a billion-dollar business. Or you may have heard of Anita Roddick, who brought her vision for cruelty-free cosmetics and a socially and ethically driven commitment to "business as a force for good" to The Body Shop (**Figure 2.1b**).[3] Interestingly, to the extent that the objective of the entrepreneur includes the potential social impact of that enterprise, selecting a pursuit that creates substantial value in the first place is even more important. It is hard, if

---

FIGURE 2.1 **Four Entrepreneurs, Four Unique Paths**

(a) Mark Zuckerberg   (b) Anita Roddick   (c) Abhi Ramesh   (d) Muhammad Yunus

Each of these entrepreneurs made choices that balanced their economic and noneconomic interests.

not impossible, to have a broad impact on society through entrepreneurship without achieving at least some degree of success and overall growth of the enterprise.

Case in point of this relationship, consider the idea behind Misfits Market, started by Abhi Ramesh in 2018 (**Figure 2.1c**). This business aims to be a source of lower-priced groceries for consumers by finding and exploiting inefficiencies in the food system that create food waste. By redirecting this waste, Misfits Market wants to be both successful and "ensure a more sustainable grocery experience."[4] The gold standard of this idea is the example set by Muhammad Yunus, who in 1974 came up with the idea of microfinance (**Figure 2.1d**). A trained economist, Yunus went back home to Bangladesh and loaned 42 villagers $27 each without requiring collateral to help them buy materials for their own bamboo furniture businesses. This idea was successful (Yunus was paid back) and led him to scale it and start Grameen Bank, offering these same small loans to people across the country. Grameen Bank has been a broad success, seeing a 97% payback rate and helping 50% of its participants pull themselves out of poverty (and winning Yunus the Nobel Prize).

Ultimately, the reason that there are so many different types of entrepreneurs is not that the definition of entrepreneurship is imprecise or "fuzzy." It is because the choice to become an entrepreneur reflects the many different values and opportunities perceived and pursued by individual entrepreneurs.

THE TYPES OF OPPORTUNITIES CHOSEN

The opportunities an entrepreneur pursues and how they pursue them shape the type of company the entrepreneur builds. For example, across the globe and particularly in developing economies, **subsistence entrepreneurship** is the most common form of entrepreneurship. We see this in **Figure 2.2**, where entrepreneurial activity is very high in many developing nations. These entrepreneurs pursue entrepreneurship as an alternative to traditional employment opportunities, which may be limited and provide poor wages to those trying to support themselves and their families. Given more resources at hand and options available to pursue, another take on this individual entrepreneurship is **self-employment**. In both developing and developed economies, many entrepreneurs pursue self-employment as gig workers, freelancers, independent salespeople or sales agents, or specialized consultants such as accountants. Many of these entrepreneurs pursue opportunities to work for themselves, often with low initial investment.

A final set chose to found an opportunity-based business around a specific idea[5]; these entrepreneurs want to start and grow a venture. Within these opportunity-based businesses there are considerable differences in the objectives of the entrepreneurs, the types of opportunity they pursue, and the resources required.[6] On the one hand, **small and medium enterprises (SMEs)** are often focused on solving well-defined problems with well-established solutions in their local market. These may be small businesses, such as a local restaurant, or medium-sized operations, such as a manufacturer or construction business. Though oriented toward growth and innovating on existing business models, these opportunities typically involve settings where there is less uncertainty and well-understood risks. In many regions around the world, SMEs play a primary, if not critical, role in the local economy. They can serve as the source of most employment opportunities even though each SME typically has less

subsistence entrepreneurship The most common form of entrepreneurship, pursued as an alternative to traditional employment opportunities

self-employment A form of individual entrepreneurship, including (but not limited to) gig workers, freelancers, independent salespeople, and specialized consultants

small and medium enterprises (SMEs) Businesses focused on solving well-defined problems with well-established solutions in their local market, with less uncertainty and well-understood risks

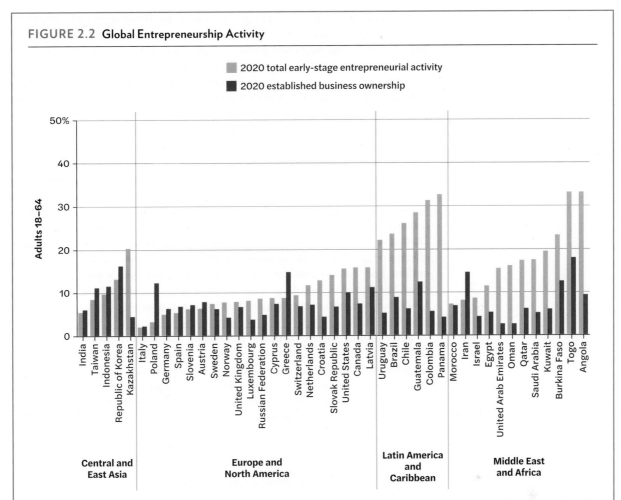

FIGURE 2.2 Global Entrepreneurship Activity

■ 2020 total early-stage entrepreneurial activity

■ 2020 established business ownership

Adults 18–64

Central and East Asia: India, Taiwan, Indonesia, Republic of Korea, Kazakhstan

Europe and North America: Italy, Poland, Germany, Spain, Slovenia, Austria, Sweden, Norway, United Kingdom, Luxembourg, Russian Federation, Cyprus, Greece, Switzerland, Netherlands, Croatia, Slovak Republic, United States, Canada, Latvia

Latin America and Caribbean: Uruguay, Brazil, Chile, Guatemala, Colombia, Panama

Middle East and Africa: Morocco, Iran, Israel, Egypt, United Arab Emirates, Oman, Qatar, Saudi Arabia, Kuwait, Burkina Faso, Togo, Angola

The Global Entrepreneurship Monitor (GEM) regularly assesses entrepreneurial ecosystems across the globe. This figure shows the percentage of adults engaged in early-stage entrepreneurial activity and those with established business ownership across 43 countries that participated in their 2020 survey.

SOURCE: Global Entrepreneurship Monitor, "2020/2021 Global Report," May 3, 2021, https://www.gemconsortium.org/report/gem-20202021-global-report.

than a few hundred, and often only a handful, of employees. In the United States, SMEs comprise 99.9% of all businesses and employ almost half of all workers.[7] Due to their importance in contributing to the vibrancy and strength of a local economy, many governments provide incentives and specialized loans for these entrepreneurs.

On the other hand, an entrepreneur might also start an **innovation-driven enterprise (IDE)** to leverage a specific innovation, like a new business model or emerging technology, to compete on a global scale.[8] Though these enterprises involve more uncertainty, entrepreneurs choosing them are often motivated both by the innovation itself and the scale of the opportunity it presents. In contrast to SMEs, IDEs often require significantly more resources, including specialized expertise and external funding to launch. The path for these ventures to commercial viability and success will be longer. For instance,

innovation-driven enterprises (IDEs)
Businesses formed to leverage a specific innovation, such as a new business model or technology, but which often require specialized expertise and external funding

founders of a new restaurant will likely know within the first year whether their perceived opportunity exists. While there will still be room for incremental improvements and sustained growth, at the end of the day, customers either return or not (and the restaurant's financials either end in the positive or not). By contrast, IDEs will measure their early success with different metrics (perhaps technical milestones or key partnerships) as they build toward an innovative product or service (and the potential customers and sales). That said, an IDE does not require an emerging technological breakthrough. In fact, it can often involve a recombination of existing activities, operations, or business models. For instance, Chipotle built on the idea of neighborhood taquerias that one of the founders loved while in college in San Francisco. Back home in Denver, the founders decided to experiment with introducing assembly-line concepts to the dining process and specialize in burritos. They hypothesized such innovations could offer customers a faster, more customized dining experience (**Figure 2.3**). Through experimentation, they ultimately perfected their new model, eventually offering 65,000 unique menu options at a higher speed than competing fast food outlets. They not only realized their opportunity, and quickly scaled to 13 locations, but also established the "fast-casual" dining category. Chipotle later grew to 500 locations after being acquired by McDonald's, and then to 2,300 locations after an IPO.[9]

After finding success with the innovation and achieving early milestones, IDEs are often well-positioned to achieve exponential growth in sales and employment. Naturally, IDEs contribute economically to regions, employing large numbers of employees across the globe, shaping economic development in various regions, and often igniting new opportunities in a particular business area. Increasingly, governments around the globe are designing targeted policies

FIGURE 2.3 **Chipotle's Approach to the Taqueria**

Chipotle's assembly-line system was a key idea in its new fast-casual restaurant concept.

to support these innovators and the ecosystems required to sustain them as they translate their ideas into reality.

In practice, SMEs and IDEs represent a continuum of opportunity-based entrepreneurship, reflecting the uncertainty associated with an idea and the resources required to turn that idea into a reality. It is important to understand the values and objectives of the entrepreneur and match the tools and resources to those goals. Though the examples in this book focus on innovation-driven entrepreneurs, by and large the principles will be valuable to entrepreneurs of all types.

value creation Making customers better off via the product, platform, or service that is offered

2.2 What Is Entrepreneurship?

Oprah Winfrey chose to become an entrepreneur. What does this mean? The most basic definition of entrepreneurship is the act of founding a new organization or venture. This is most often thought of as a for-profit company, though it applies to nonprofits too, such as social ventures like Grameen Bank, founded by Muhammad Yunus. However, while concise, that dictionary definition leaves out almost as much as it captures and needs to be expanded in two important ways:

1. An entrepreneur does not build a new company for its own sake; instead, the very act of founding a new business means that entrepreneurship involves recognizing and actively pursuing an "opportunity" or "idea." In the same way, many individuals (and companies) pursue new opportunities without establishing new businesses.
2. Entrepreneurship means building a new organization and attracting new resources (or building new capabilities) to pursue a new opportunity.

Howard Stevenson (**Figure 2.4**), who jump-started the study of entrepreneurship in the 1980s while teaching at Harvard Business School, succinctly captured these two elements at that time, writing, "Entrepreneurship is the pursuit of opportunity beyond resources currently controlled."[10] Let's now turn to a slightly different way of describing this, using the ideas of value creation and value capture we saw in Chapter 1.

VALUE CREATION AND VALUE CAPTURE

Simply establishing a new enterprise is not enough. As we saw in Chapter 1, successful entrepreneurship requires **value creation**—some customers must be made better off by the product, service, or platform you are building. Then, the most direct test of whether consumers are made better off by a product or service is

FIGURE 2.4 **Howard Stevenson**

Howard Stevenson, a Harvard professor for almost 30 years, has been described as Harvard Business School's "lion of entrepreneurship." One of his students, Frank Batten, went on to create The Weather Channel. Stevenson founded his own investment firm and also served as chair of the board of directors of National Public Radio.

value capture The ability to realize personal value (financial and otherwise) from establishing and operating a new enterprise

whether they are willing to pay a price more than your costs. Further, thinking about new ideas for businesses or undertaking a particular program of scientific or engineering research does not, by itself, constitute entrepreneurship; instead, successful entrepreneurship ultimately involves serving a (paying) customer and creating value for them. Oprah Winfrey became an entrepreneur when her new studio launched her talk show, creating value for television stations and viewers. In another example, as part of his academic research, Professor J. Robert Cade, a physician and professor of renal medicine at the University of Florida, first formulated and experimented with an electrolyte-rich solution to see if the Florida Gators football team could be hydrated more effectively. Choosing to found a firm selling what came to be called Gatorade created value for professional and amateur athletes and made him an entrepreneur.[11]

Successful entrepreneurship also involves **value capture**—the ability to realize personal value (financial and otherwise) from establishing and operating a new enterprise. Value capture is usually measured by profitability—receiving higher revenues from customers than the total costs of serving them. Capturing value means that businesses must create value in a way that cannot easily (or quickly) be imitated (or improved upon) by potential competitors. And because value capture is *necessary* for the company to survive in the long term (otherwise the firm will go bankrupt!), the economic return to a venture is more than simply its level of sales; to use the words of an old business joke, a venture cannot simply "lose money on each unit but make it up on volume!" (See the sidebar on **Uber**.)

The ultimate test of the financial success of a venture is not how much investment (e.g., venture capital; see Chapter 14 for more information) goes into a company but the economic return to the founders, investors, and other stakeholders that results from those investments. The most iconic businesspeople in history, such as John D. Rockefeller, Coco Chanel, or Bill Gates, not only established new industries and built large companies, but did so in a way that was enormously profitable in the long term. Their entrepreneurial journeys began with unique insights into how to create value for consumers and, equally significant, clarity about the resources and advantages they possessed to deliver and capture value on a sustainable basis. Consider their words:

"The secret to success is to do things uncommonly well."

—John D. Rockefeller

"Fashion changes, but style endures."

—Coco Chanel

"In business, the idea of measuring what you are doing, picking the measurements that count, like customer satisfaction and performance . . . you thrive on that."

—Bill Gates

PERSONAL CONTROL

A distinctive aspect of entrepreneurship is that founding a new business lets an individual exercise significant control over the core choices of how to create and capture value. Relative to working for a company, entrepreneurs can choose which broad idea to pursue, customer segment to prioritize, or innovation to leverage. For instance, no one instructed Ben Cohen and Jerry Greenfield to make tasty ice cream. Instead, they pursued a personal passion for ice

Uber. Many businesses seem to start with the model of losing money on each unit but making up for it on volume, and they work with it for a long time. One business writer quipped that Uber, for example, was doing just that.[a] The company is still losing money as of 2023, though CEO Dara Khosrowshahi recently said, "I challenged the team to meet our profitability commitments even faster than planned."[b]

Chapter 2: Choosing Entrepreneurship

cream making by establishing a company and creating a new category in the ice cream market (see the sidebar on **Ben & Jerry's**). Similarly, Anita Roddick had a vision for ethically sourced cosmetics developed without animal testing. Rather than trying to work from within a larger cosmetics business, she pursued that vision as well as her passion for environmental sustainability by founding and building her own company, The Body Shop. Control over their ventures let these founders create and capture value in ways that realized their unique visions and were true to their passions and personal values.

While entrepreneurs exercise significant control over their venture, they are similarly responsible (at least at the outset) for all the different tasks associated with that venture. Most workers with traditional jobs are highly specialized, with jobs that cross only a small number of functional areas. A programmer at Microsoft is not directly responsible for the latest ad campaign, nor does the marketing team have to have deep expertise in programming. However, at the beginning, entrepreneurs must create value for customers with the assistance of only a limited set of people. An early test for an entrepreneurial team is whether they can manage a wide range of disparate activities (serving more like jacks-of-all-trades) rather than mine the depth of their expertise in any one area.

Entrepreneurship thus combines several distinctive elements. However, to realize the value and confront the challenges of entrepreneurship, the first choice that an individual (or team) must make is whether to pursue entrepreneurship in the first place. While the success or failure of a venture depends on more than just the founders, the entrepreneur is nonetheless responsible for the critical choices that shape value creation and capture and overall direction. But the first step in that entrepreneurial journey is simply the decision to choose entrepreneurship. We will turn to this choice next.

Ben & Jerry's. Ben Cohen (right) and Jerry Greenfield built their business with their personal passions in mind. Cohen, who had severe anosmia (a lack of the sense of smell), was very sensitive to texture and taste. This spurred the idea to make ice cream with chunks included and a variety of flavors. Starting with an ice cream parlor in Vermont in 1978, Cohen and Greenfield eventually started packing their ice cream in pints and franchised their stores. They were innovative in their marketing tactics, offering an annual free ice cream day and driving a famous "cowmobile" across the country themselves. Throughout, they modeled their business to reflect various environmental causes and made that a part of their brand. They also produced flavors in honor of celebrities, including the Grateful Dead's Jerry Garcia ("Cherry Garcia"), basketball player Jeremy Lin ("Taste the Lin-Sanity"), and Stephen Colbert ("Americone Dream"). The company was acquired by British food giant Unilever in 2000 with a requirement to continue Ben & Jerry's social mission.

2.3 Why Choose Entrepreneurship?

Just out of college and working at Warner Music in 2011, Payal Kadakia felt a corporate career was not a strong match with her professional objectives but was unsure whether she should abandon a steady paycheck to start her own venture. Kadakia, who had a background in ballet, had been frustrated by her inability to find open ballet classes in New York City that would fit in her busy, hard-to-predict schedule. Feeling there was an opportunity, she gave herself two weeks to develop an idea that would make it worthwhile to forgo her current paid employment (**Figure 2.5** on p. 34).[12] During that time, she considered a number of ideas to create a system for searching and registering for fitness classes of all types across different gyms. For each of her ideas, she saw uncertainty about both the value of the overall opportunity and the value of particular strategies. Further, leaving her existing job meant not only losing her current salary but also possibly slowing or even stopping her career advancement in the music industry. Despite those unknowns, Kadakia decided that the best opportunity she had identified—which would ultimately become ClassPass, the leading health club membership aggregator—was sufficiently promising to take the entrepreneurial plunge.

FIGURE 2.5 Payal Kadakia and ClassPass

Payal Kadakia, the founder of ClassPass, initially wasn't sure she should become an entrepreneur: "I'd given myself two weeks to think of an idea for a company. I know it sounds strange, but I figured if I couldn't think of an idea in two weeks, I shouldn't be an entrepreneur."

Similar to Oprah choosing entrepreneurship over a more "Hollywood" career, Payal Kadakia's entrepreneurial journey started with a deliberate choice to give up a more traditional career in music. For most individuals, the primary cost of entrepreneurship is the "opportunity cost" of not doing something else (most commonly a paid job, but also going to school or being in the workforce at all). *The simple explanation of why individuals choose entrepreneurship is that they perceive it to be a valuable path. More specifically, they often value the economic and noneconomic rewards that come from founding that business as compared with the economic and noneconomic rewards of the job that they might otherwise have.*

Kadakia's experience also highlights the multiple considerations that go into whether to choose entrepreneurship:

1. Does the founder or team perceive a valuable economic opportunity to pursue?
2. Does the founder possess a unique advantage to realize the opportunity?
3. Is the founder committed or passionate about the opportunity?
4. Can the founder determine (to the best of their ability) that the business can be sustainable?

To be clear, at least some entrepreneurs have found significant financial reward from entrepreneurship. As of 2022, 8 of the 10 wealthiest Americans earned the vast bulk of their wealth through entrepreneurship, with the top position held by Elon Musk, cofounder of Tesla, SpaceX, and several other companies (**Table 2.1**).[13] Each of these founders established iconic companies (such as Microsoft, Google, and Bloomberg) that created and captured value in a way that cannot be easily competed away. And a list looking at the 10 wealthiest self-made female entrepreneurs in the United States (**Table 2.2**) is made up of those whose wealth from their ventures ranges from $2 billion to $12 billion.

But whether to start a business is not (and should not be) simply about the potential economic return. Most entrepreneurs do not earn the outsized returns of Jeff Bezos, Oprah Winfrey, or Google founders Larry Page and Sergey Brin (see Chapter 1). In fact, many do not earn a higher income than they would in traditional employment, and yet they undertake significant risk and uncertainty in the founding of their venture. Often it is the noneconomic benefits of entrepreneurship that drive the choice of entrepreneurship.[14] In describing their decision to found Ben & Jerry's, Jerry Greenfield notes that he and Ben Cohen had been working odd jobs but then, he said, "We thought, why don't we get together and do something that's fun—be our own bosses."[15] For Payal Kadakia, the challenge of entrepreneurship and the potential impact were particularly

TABLE 2.1 Richest Americans in 2023

Elon Musk	Entrepreneur (Tesla, SpaceX, The Boring Company)
Jeff Bezos	Entrepreneur (Amazon, Blue Origin)
Larry Ellison	Entrepreneur (Oracle)
Warren Buffet	Investor (Berkshire Hathaway)
Bill Gates	Entrepreneur (Microsoft)
Bloomberg	Entrepreneur (Bloomberg)
Steve Ballmer	Entrepreneur (Microsoft)
Larry Page	Entrepreneur (Google)
Sergey Brin	Entrepreneur (Google)
Mark Zuckerberg	Entrepreneur (Facebook)
Charles Koch	Industrialist (Koch Industries)
Julia Koch & family	Heir (Koch Industries)

SOURCE: Chase Peterson-Withorn, "The 25 Richest People in the World 2023," *Forbes*, April 4, 2023, https://www.forbes.com/sites/chasewithorn/2023/04/04/the-25-richest-people-in-the-world-2023.

TABLE 2.2 Top 10 Richest Self-Made American Women in 2023

Diane Hendricks	Entrepreneur (ABC Supply)
Judy Love	Entrepreneur (Love's Travel Stops & Country Stores)
Judy Faulkner	Entrepreneur (Epic Systems)
Lynda Resnick	Entrepreneur (The Wonderful Company)
Thai Lee	Entrepreneur (SHI International)
Johnelle Hunt	Entrepreneur (J. B. Hunt Transport Services)
Gail Miller	Entrepreneur (Larry H. Miller Company)
Marian Illitch	Entrepreneur (Little Caesars Pizza)
Elizabeth Uihlein	Entrepreneur (ULine)
Peggy Cherng	Entrepreneur (Panda Express)

SOURCE: Andrea Murphy, "America's Richest Self-Made Women 2023: The Top 10," *Forbes*, May 23, 2023, https://www.forbes.com/pictures/646d0fde2d9ac054b55f411d/top-10-self-made-women/?sh=7e562a3d4f60.

motivating. She explained: "I kind of knew that I always wanted to continue to change the landscape."[16] For Oprah Winfrey, the responsibility and opportunity to create broad social impact were a huge motivator. As she once said, "The reason I've been able to be so financially successful is my focus has never, ever for one minute been money."[17]

What all these entrepreneurs are revealing is how founders weigh the non-economic benefits (and costs) of starting their own enterprise: exercising control

Steve Jobs. Steve Jobs was famous for exerting control over almost every aspect of his business. One executive noted that Jobs dwelled for 30 minutes on the shade of gray to be used for restroom signs in Apple Stores. Similarly, Jobs wanted the circuit boards inside Apple's machines to look beautiful. When one of his engineers told him, "The only thing that matters is how well it works. Nobody is going to see the PC board," Jobs replied, "I want it to be as beautiful as possible, even if it's inside the box.. . . . A great carpenter isn't going to use lousy wood for the back of a cabinet, even though nobody's going to see it."[a]

over their work and their company, building and scaling a new organization, and potentially having a far-ranging impact are among the common motivators to pursue entrepreneurship.

MORE THAN MONEY AND WEALTH

Since the economic factors are straightforward, let's review the noneconomic factors in greater detail. First, an obvious and fundamental difference is that entrepreneurs are their own boss. Besides having control over their work, being their own boss means having control over the broad direction of their company as well as the day-to-day decision-making. Some entrepreneurs are famous (or even infamous) for their exercise of control over their company or its products. Steve Jobs, for instance, insisted that Apple pursue his unique vision for personal computing, which he described as "bicycles of the mind." This included slavish devotion to some details, such as the design and presentation of fonts, and willful indifference to others, such as product-release deadlines. (See the sidebar on **Steve Jobs**.) Controlling a company allows an entrepreneur to fit the activities and structure of that company to their own preferences and strengths; entrepreneurs need not adapt to the requirements or scope of a particular job. For example, when Ben Chestnut and Dan Kurzius founded the online marketing service company Mailchimp, they did so to empower "underdog" small businesses with online marketing. They located the company in Atlanta rather than Silicon Valley, rejected venture capital investment and maintained 100% control of the company, and built a deliberate and inclusive corporate culture that they believe resulted in slower but more profitable and sustainable growth. As Chestnut explained, if you want to run a successful tech company, you don't have to follow the path of Silicon Valley. "You can simply start a business, run it to serve your customers, and forget about outside investors and growth at any cost," he said.[18] Over two decades, Chestnut and Kurzius remained committed to serving small businesses despite continual advice from potential investors to pivot away. In 2021, having never accepted outside investment, Mailchimp was acquired for $12 billion by Intuit as part of the financial software company's effort to better serve small businesses.

Second, founding a company offers an opportunity for entrepreneurs to challenge themselves in learning how to build a new organization. Learning about the simple legal requirements to establish a company, plus how to hire people, work with and sell to customers, and manage operations and logistics, are all valuable skills for an entrepreneur. Many also value being able to apply their gained knowledge to new pursuits. But many founders value this challenge for its own sake. *Shark Tank* investor and famed realtor Barbara Corcoran has explained that her motivation to build her business reflects her need to overcome her own self-doubts (see the sidebar on **Barbara Corcoran**). Corcoran has publicly called out her own struggles with imposter syndrome:

> When I sold my business for $66 million and I had made it from scratch out of nothing and the whole world applauded me, [and I was] written up in all the papers, "Oh, she's a genius. Oh, she's this. Oh, she's that." Do you know what I thought [after] six months? That the whole thing was a fluke.[19]

Barbara Corcoran. Barbara Corcoran has said that she is driven by an inner need to prove to herself that she is a success. But as she explained on her podcast, she has come to see this as a reason for her success. "Someone who is second-guessing themselves is what I want to see in every person, because what it means is they're going to work hard to [succeed] again," she said. "And if you did it once, and you combine that with working hard and just a little bit of luck, which is always out there to be grabbed, you're gonna have the same success again and again because you're at the core of it."[a]

Corcoran's need to prove herself has spurred her to keep pursuing new business opportunities.

Third, like Kadakia and Winfrey, many potential entrepreneurs are driven by the opportunity to build a company with a broader impact. While pursuing their MBAs, David Auerbach, Lindsay Stradley, and Ani Vallabhaneni were intent on making a difference. They sought to realize the potential power of **social entrepreneurship**, in which a new business purposefully pursues not only a sustainable business model but also the creation of broader social value. The three students came together during a class project investigating ideas to address the low level of access to basic sanitation facilities in cities in the developing world. Rather than working with aid agencies to build out toilet facilities in urban slums, they saw the widespread absence of sanitation as an entrepreneurial opportunity. The three relocated to Nairobi, Kenya, to explore how to provide sanitation facilities in a way that would also allow them to build an independent company that would not be dependent on charitable aid. Working with civil engineering, chemical engineering, and architecture graduates, they created an individual sanitation unit that was inexpensive to produce but built for tough conditions in the developing world. They founded their company, Sanergy, to empower local micro-entrepreneurs to establish small businesses offering private toilet facilities as a "business in a box," including support in almost every aspect of a start-up. Closing the loop, Sanergy collects and transforms the resulting waste product into a low-cost source of fertilizer and biomass energy.[20] Now serving more than 100,000 individuals in Nairobi, Sanergy empowers its founders to realize their broader purpose of enabling access to sanitation. It also provides renewable fertilizer and energy in one of the poorest places on Earth (**Figure 2.6** on p. 38). The founders' experience exemplifies the goals of many social entrepreneurs, where the value of founding a company is not simply how much money a venture makes but also how much value that venture creates for other stakeholders, including customers,

social entrepreneurship A business venture that combines a sustainable business model with the creation of broader social value

FIGURE 2.6 Sanergy

Ani Vallabhaneni, Lindsay Stradley, and David Auerbach turned a class project idea focused on social entrepreneurship into Sanergy.

employees, and society (see **Mini Case: When an Entrepreneur Chooses More Than the Bottom Line**).

ENTREPRENEURSHIP IS NOT A ONE-WAY JOURNEY

While pursuing entrepreneurship can meaningfully alter the career and life of those who choose to pursue an opportunity, pursuing entrepreneurship is *not* irreversible. Many entrepreneurs also maintain more traditional full-time employment (or are in school full-time) and so pursue their entrepreneurial venture as a side hustle, or side job. These might range from running a Shopify store on the weekend to maintaining a separate business from their main employer (e.g., a moonlighting web designer who also works full-time for a software company). Some side hustles turn into entrepreneurship opportunities themselves, as was the case with Airbnb. In this instance, a decision by the early founder to rent out an air mattress in their apartment opened up opportunities that led to creating a billion-dollar business. According to data from the 2019 Gallup Great Jobs Survey,[21] approximately 11% of Americans are simultaneously self-employed as entrepreneurs and employed by another organization. While engaging in a side hustle can distract from a full-time job, and vice versa, balancing these roles allows individuals to gain value from entrepreneurship while also reducing the risks and uncertainties associated with a full-time commitment to a new venture.

It is also possible to experiment with entrepreneurship as an option and then pursue a career path based on the learning that you gain during the early

When an Entrepreneur Chooses More Than the Bottom Line: Yvon Chouinard

What does it look like when an entrepreneur's business does not totally have to be about the bottom line? Consider Yvon Chouinard, an accomplished alpine rock climber, who founded Patagonia in 1970 after discovering the popularity of "rugged" clothing within the climbing community. In starting his venture, he made choices to prioritize clothing that created value for the climbing community first, expanding into products such as hats or socks rather than more fashionable items, and always maintaining a commitment to the environment. For example, from its early days, Patagonia utilized technologies and supply chain partners that prioritized high overall quality and environmentally sustainable production. In building his organization, Chouinard was well known for his policy to "let my people go surfing" (also the title of a book he wrote) and emphasized flextime to allow his employees to "catch a good swell, go bouldering for an afternoon, pursue an education, or get home in time to greet the kids."[a] Similarly, at a time when few retail stores offered robust benefits to retail workers, Patagonia offered extensive benefits and comprehensive health insurance throughout its organization. Policies like these helped Patagonia recruit and retain skilled employees who were similarly passionate about sports and the outdoors, including a number of professional athletes. As Patagonia has grown, its commitment to these values has not wavered; among many policies it has pioneered, since 1985 the company has given 1% of its sales to environmental causes.[b]

When Yvon Chouinard started Patagonia, he made choices that prioritized what was important to him.

stages of a venture. For example, Katie Finnegan had significant experience in the retail industry when she founded Hukkster, which was intended to be an e-commerce concierge service that monitored the prices of online goods for customers, notifying them when the items went on sale. While the Hukkster platform did not take off, the company was acquired at an early stage by Jet.com. Finnegan served on the top management team there prior to the acquisition of Jet.com by Walmart for $3.3 billion.[22] Finnegan then went on to be an "intrapreneur," or a manager within a company that drives innovative development, and founded Store No. 8, the internal incubation arm for Walmart.[23] While the extent to which Finnegan translated the "failure" of Hukkster into successes at Jet.com and Store No. 8 is outsized relative to the experience

FIGURE 2.7 **Kate Finnegan**

Early experience as an entrepreneur with her own company, Hukkster, led Katie Finnegan (on the left at top) to entrepreneurial experiences within other, larger businesses including Walmart's Store No.8.

of most people, her experience is far from unusual (**Figure 2.7**). More than half of all entrepreneurs transition to more traditional employment within two years after the founding of their firm, but even after controlling for other observable factors (such as education, age, and so on), their lifetime incomes are often higher than those who never engage in entrepreneurship in the first place.[24] In other words, because the choice to become an entrepreneur allows one to acquire skills and information that is likely valuable even if a venture fails, the "penalty" from failure may be modest.

At a slightly more philosophical level, being an entrepreneur is an exercise of choice itself. An entrepreneur is not constrained to a predetermined idea but is able to choose the idea they would like to pursue. Perhaps most importantly, an entrepreneur is not wedded to the existing team and culture of an existing organization but is able to choose which team members to attract and what type of culture to nurture. And as entrepreneurs control and build their business, they make other key strategy choices, as we will see in later chapters. This includes determining the customer segment they think will find their product or service valuable (obviously, the customers also get to choose whether they agree!). An entrepreneur chooses which technologies to explore and then shapes their evolution. Finally, an entrepreneur does not have the option to avoid competition entirely but often has significant latitude in choosing with whom and how to compete.

2.4 Who Chooses Entrepreneurship?

Most popular discussions of entrepreneurs make it seem as if entrepreneurs are "born" rather than "made," and that a certain type of person is predisposed toward entrepreneurship. Indeed, one of the earliest scholars of entrepreneurship, Joseph Schumpeter, famously described entrepreneurs in terms of *unternehmergeist* ("entrepreneur-spirit"). This term emphasizes that Schumpeter thought entrepreneurs were a specific type of person who enacted change on the world through innovation and the founding and scaling of new enterprises.

But the reality is that the "typical" entrepreneur is, well, far from typical. There are more than 500 million entrepreneurs (see Figure 2.2) around the globe, equivalent to approximately one out of every 10 adults. This diverse population includes several hundred million individuals who pursue entrepreneurship as a path to escape poverty, as well as global icons like Oprah Winfrey, Jeff Bezos, and Yvon Chouinard. Every owner of a business—whether it be a restaurant or shop, a craft (such as plumbing), or a technology start-up—is, by definition, an

Do You Need to Be an Expert? Nike

Phil Knight first met U.S. Olympic track coach and subsequent Nike cofounder Bill Bowerman when he joined the University of Oregon track team, which Bowerman coached. Frustrated with existing running spikes and shoes, Bowerman had been experimenting with new shoe and spike designs to improve his athletes' performance. In an early test, he asked Knight to try one of his prototypes during practice. As Knight recalls, Bowerman chose him because he "wasn't one of the best runners on the team. Bowerman knew he could use me as a guinea pig without much risk."[a] Their relationship and shared interest in innovating running shoes grew, and soon Bowerman was making custom shoes for many on the team (some who would go on to compete in the Olympics wearing their custom-made shoes). Unfortunately, most American shoemakers were not interested in the suggestions and designs of a track coach. However, while pursuing his MBA, Knight began to further study the global shoe industry and perceived an opportunity to combine Bowerman's designs with those of Japanese shoemakers. After a trip to Japan following graduation, Knight knew there was potential for the idea, and he and Bowerman cofounded Blue Ribbon Sports, which would later become Nike.

Phil Knight was not an expert on shoe design, but he still recognized the potential in the original designs.

entrepreneur. Entrepreneurs, therefore, differ widely in their capabilities and resources but share the experience of establishing an organization to achieve their economic and noneconomic goals.

Many have speculated about the personal characteristics or types of people that take on or succeed at entrepreneurship compared with those who go into other professions. A central element of entrepreneurship is the recognition and pursuit of an opportunity. For example, when Nike cofounder Phil Knight was in business school, his only knowledge of the footwear industry was through his experiences as an athlete. Nonetheless, he foresaw an opportunity to reshape that industry when he wrote a paper for his entrepreneurship class titled "Can Japanese Sports Shoes Do to German Sports Shoes What Japanese Cameras Did to German Cameras?" He later acted upon that opportunity recognition when he visited Japan shortly after graduation. While it took many years for Nike to establish itself as the leading athletic shoe company in the world (it was neither named Nike nor marketed using the "swoosh" logo until 1971), Knight's choice to become a shoe entrepreneur was grounded largely in his perception that there was a large economic opportunity that had yet to be realized (see **Mini Case: Do You Need to Be an Expert?**).

However, individuals tend to perceive opportunities linked to their own prior experiences; an individual who is "good" at perceiving opportunities in one context may be less effective in other contexts. Like Phil Knight's experience, exposure to new people and contexts—through coursework, hobbies, work, and

Do Universities Produce Successful Entrepreneurs?

Over the past two decades, many universities have become interested in whether their graduates choose to become entrepreneurs and how, if at all, a university education contributes to the performance of alumni start-ups. Indeed, there are many famous college dropouts—Steve Jobs, Bill Gates, and Mark Zuckerberg, for example—who achieved outsized entrepreneurial success. Yet the number of entrepreneurship courses, specialized degree programs, and entrepreneurship centers on university campuses has steadily risen. Are the paths of Jobs, Gates, and Zuckerberg the norm or the exception?

Research points to higher education giving you a leg up in becoming an entrepreneur.

Research points to these names as the exception, with far more entrepreneurs benefiting from their university educations. Studies at many schools have documented the impact of university alumni entrepreneurship, both as influencing a potential career path for students and as a driver of economic development. For example, starting in the 1980s, Professor Ed Roberts of MIT began to research the career paths of living MIT alumni.[a] He found that most successful technology-oriented alumni entrepreneurs founded their first firm not while in school but instead well into their careers (at about age 40), a finding that is echoed among larger populations. Even more strikingly, over that 40-year period of research, MIT alumni accounted for tens of thousands of active companies. Building on earlier work, Roberts and his MIT colleagues Fiona Murray and Daniel Kim found that graduates from MIT have accounted for more than 30,200 active companies.[b] A shorter-term study in Illinois found similar success; from 2013 through 2018 alone, students and faculty at Illinois universities had founded 978 start-ups.[c]

Researchers also found that entrepreneurship programs increased the survival and revenues of alumni-founded start-ups.[d] Given these findings, it is perhaps not surprising that many universities are increasingly focused on ensuring that their graduates are equipped with the mindset, toolkit, and network that may enable them to pursue entrepreneurship as part of their careers.

travel—can improve an individual's ability to identify opportunities and decision to pursue entrepreneurship. For example, classmates can have an influence on your choice of entrepreneurship. In a recent set of studies of learning groups at two MBA programs in the United States, Professor Jackson Lu documented that the cultural diversity of a student's randomly assigned learning group positively influenced the student's choice to become an entrepreneur following graduation. This effect was stronger for those students who had an "Openness to New Experiences," a common personality trait of entrepreneurs. Perhaps even more interesting, among those who chose to become entrepreneurs, the cultural diversity of a student's learning group positively predicted the novelty of their start-up.[25] (See also **Using the Research: Do Universities Produce Successful Entrepreneurs?**)

Indeed, entrepreneurs tend to invest in developing and acquiring a wide range of skills. These skills help them identify an opportunity, and launch and operate a start-up to realize that opportunity. Since entrepreneurs must be sufficiently capable in a wide range of skills to successfully move a venture forward, many entrepreneurs are known as jacks-of-all-trades; this allows them to operate in many roles at the start-up and later build out those roles as they recruit a team.

A small number of psychological "traits"—somewhat more durable elements of individual personality—do seem to predict the type of person who becomes an entrepreneur (at least in advanced economies). Most notably, entrepreneurs seem to exhibit greater "Openness to New Experiences" and "Conscientiousness," that is, a belief that one's discipline and hard work are correlated with achievement. Entrepreneurs also have a firmer belief in their ability to control their own fate. However, there is abundant evidence that people tend to be overconfident in their own abilities across many areas. For example, over 70% of individuals rate themselves as better than the median driver,[26] believe they have a higher than median IQ, are better at being unbiased, have higher popularity, and are even happier than the typical person in a relationship.[27] Since the choice to become an entrepreneur is an individual choice, behavioral biases that might have limited impact in a traditional job may be amplified in the context of founding a new venture. Entrepreneurs are naturally more likely to be optimistic and confident about the opportunity they choose to pursue (otherwise, they would have chosen differently!).

One additional trait often attributed to entrepreneurs is a higher tolerance for risk. Entrepreneurship certainly entails an important degree of risk—most new businesses fail, with some negative financial (and even reputational) consequences for the founders. But tolerance for risk on the part of entrepreneurs is perhaps better understood as a difference in perspective, as entrepreneurs pursue opportunities they perceive as potentially highly valuable. When Ted Turner bought his first television station in the late 1960s, he correctly surmised that there was enormous demand for additional programming beyond the "Big Three" networks; ABC, NBC, and CBS were all that was on most TVs at the time. While that investment may have looked risky to an outsider, Turner considered it almost a "sure bet" based on his individual perception of that opportunity.[28] Put another way, entrepreneurship seems to be more closely linked to an individual's orientation toward having control over their destiny rather than a simple willingness to tolerate risk (where the outcome is independent of their own actions).

DOES YOUR BACKGROUND MATTER?

Beyond these broad psychological characteristics is the question of the demography of entrepreneurs. But first, we cannot separate the demographics of entrepreneurship from the question of who, historically and socially, were allowed to become, and succeed as, entrepreneurs. In the earliest days of capitalism, only men of specific social classes or race were traditionally permitted to start a business. For example, the Dutch East India Company, founded by Johan van Oldenbarnevelt in 1602, is often regarded as the forerunner of the modern corporation. But at the time of its inception, women were unable to own property in the Netherlands and were not included in business ventures, and the granting of a company charter was strictly limited to those at the top of society. In the United States, rules limiting the ability of married women to independently enter contracts and own assets separate from their husband's control were only gradually removed during the nineteenth century. Professor Zorina Khan found the repeal of such restrictions increased

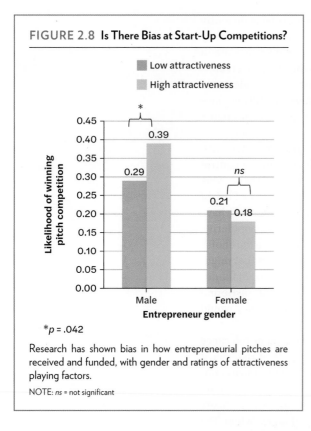

FIGURE 2.8 **Is There Bias at Start-Up Competitions?**

■ Low attractiveness
■ High attractiveness

Entrepreneur gender

Likelihood of winning pitch competition

Male: 0.29, 0.39 *
Female: 0.21, 0.18 *ns*

*p = .042

Research has shown bias in how entrepreneurial pitches are received and funded, with gender and ratings of attractiveness playing factors.

NOTE: *ns* = not significant

patenting activity among women.[29] Similarly, Professor Lisa Cook found that patenting activity among Black Americans decreased during periods and in regions with increased racial discrimination. This research emphasizes how broader social and economic rights contribute to innovative and entrepreneurial activity.[30]

Even today, in places where legal barriers to entrepreneurship have been removed, other barriers such as discrimination by early-stage funders have long persisted. In a 2014 study, potential investors assessing *exactly the same idea with the same pitch* were more than twice as likely to be interested in funding a venture founded by an attractive man than by a woman (**Figure 2.8**).[31] In another study, researchers at a prominent start-up competition found that investors tended to ask male and female entrepreneurs different types of questions. Whereas male entrepreneurs were often asked about the upside potential of the opportunity and their start-up, female entrepreneurs were often asked about the downside risks—despite the entrepreneurs, opportunities, and ventures being otherwise similar. The researchers proposed that these opposing perceptions by investors may have contributed to the fund-raising differences across the start-ups, which saw the male founders raise five times the amount raised by the female founders for their respective start-ups.[32]

One consequence of these barriers is that the "stereotypical" entrepreneur at any moment reflects the circumstances of a particular society or time. It does not reflect the ability and willingness of all individuals to become entrepreneurs. While there are clear demographic patterns to entrepreneurship, the exceptions are in many cases more interesting than the average. For example, historically, more than two-thirds of new businesses in the United States were founded by men, but in recent times there has been a rapid increase in the rate of ownership of businesses by women, growing from 29% to 36% between 2007 and 2012.[33] Over the same time period, the number of minority-owned firms in the United States increased from 5.8 million to 8 million.[34] In terms of career demographics, most entrepreneurs are middle-aged: in the United States, recent research suggests that the average age of founders, as measured by the ventures' highest earners, may be closer to 42, and the average actually increases to 45 among founders of "superstar" firms whose growth is among the top 0.1% of firms.[35] Despite this, when examining the top 10 most successful entrepreneurs in the United States alive today, their average age when they founded their firm was less than 30.[36]

Finally, immigrants are one of the most vital sources of entrepreneurship in most countries. When immigrants settle in a new location, they bring new skills, networks, and knowledge (like recipes!) that might allow them to create new economic value; at the same time, immigrants often experience discrimination, face language barriers, and lack networks within the traditional labor market. Not surprisingly, then, immigrants often establish their own businesses—engaging in entrepreneurship—to establish themselves in a new location. For example, after Indian immigrants from the state of Gujarat took over a small motel in

FIGURE 2.9 Indian Hotel Entrepreneurs

Vimal Patel stands in front of a hotel he owns. He started working at the front desk of a family hotel before eventually investing and starting his own hotel group.

Sacramento, CA, back in the 1940s, the founders encouraged other Gujaratis to follow suit and provided easy "handshake" loans to facilitate the process. Family members would often live at the motel and run all the operations themselves—from housekeeping to bookkeeping—and many of their children would use this experience to later found their own motels. Ultimately, Indian immigrant motel entrepreneurs (many from the state of Gujarat) came to own over half of all motel lodging establishments and over 60% of hotels in the United States, per the Asian American Hotel Owners Association (**Figure 2.9**).[37]

In addition, as indicated by the fact that immigrants have already chosen to move to a new location, immigrants often maintain a high level of ambition and invest in education and activities that allow them to build companies with strong growth potential. Gururaj "Desh" Deshpande moved to Canada from his native India after completing his bachelor's degree at the Indian Institute of Technology, Madras, so that he could earn his master's degree and PhD. His studies launched him toward a career in the telecommunications industry, and he ultimately became the cofounder of Cascade Communications and the principal founder of Sycamore Networks, both of which grew to be multibillion-dollar companies. Deshpande's experience is far from the exception; immigrants play a significant role in the founding of high-growth firms and, in the process, create a disproportionate share of new jobs.[38] More generally, nearly a quarter of all new businesses are founded by immigrants. While immigrant-founded businesses tend to start somewhat smaller than the average firm and have a higher failure rate at the earliest stages, those that survive tend to grow more quickly.[39]

A key aspect of "who" becomes an entrepreneur depends, ultimately, on who chooses entrepreneurship. Based on what you have read, the **Putting It Together: Choosing Entrepreneurship** on page 46 should help you begin to frame this

CHOOSING ENTREPRENEURSHIP

Deciding to be an entrepreneur and when to get started are major choices. The following actions, questions, and ideas can help you get going.

DESCRIBE AREAS OF OPPORTUNITY THAT INTEREST YOU AS AN ENTREPRENEUR

Brainstorm and Articulate Your Ideas about the Type of Business You Want to Start

- List three to five broad areas you may be interested in exploring as an entrepreneur. For example, are there customer groups, emerging technologies, types of business, or organizational objectives that excite you? Don't limit yourself to areas where you already have a clear start-up idea or opportunity articulated, as you will refine these opportunities later.

- For each of the broad areas of opportunity, briefly explain why you are drawn to this space.

- Describe your reasons for considering entrepreneurship. What excites you about becoming an entrepreneur? Understanding what motivates you now will help you make better decisions moving forward.

CONSIDER YOUR TIMELINES AND ALTERNATIVES

Answer the Question: When Will I Get Started?

- Many entrepreneurs want to get started now, but others want to take more time preparing. Briefly describe your timeline for getting started.

- Reflecting on the areas of opportunity you listed above and your timeline for pursuing entrepreneurship, describe the steps and activities you could undertake to explore and deepen your knowledge about each area of opportunity.

- Understanding alternatives can help your decision-making. If you are not going to be an entrepreneur now, what would be the likely next steps in your career path? Would that likely next step also help you explore the opportunities you described above?

DESCRIBE YOUR ECONOMIC AND NONECONOMIC GOALS FOR BEING AN ENTREPRENEUR

Understand What Is Motivating You to Be an Entrepreneur

- Write down how entrepreneurship may allow you to prioritize and achieve broader objectives relative to other career paths.

- List the key benefits and risks of choosing entrepreneurship at this stage of your career.

- Briefly state your economic and noneconomic goals for being an entrepreneur. Consider how those goals might influence your choices in how you pursue entrepreneurship.

choice. While not everyone starts in the same place, entrepreneurs do come from all walks of life. Though very few women in Europe became entrepreneurs during the 1920s, Coco Chanel built on her experience growing up with a family of street vendors to became one of the most influential entrepreneurs of her time, choosing entrepreneurship to realize her vision of simplicity in fashion design.[40] The fact that she was not a stereotypical entrepreneur of her time does not change the impact her choice has had on fashion, even to this day. In other words, while background psychological traits and demographics may make it more likely that an individual chooses to become an entrepreneur in a particular time or place, the choice to become an entrepreneur depends on whether an individual can identify a way to advance their own economic and noneconomic goals by establishing a new organization.

2.5 Concluding Thoughts

In 1985, Oprah Winfrey was a movie star. After receiving critical and popular acclaim, including Academy Award and Golden Globe nominations, many presumed Winfrey would pursue a career in Hollywood. To their surprise, Winfrey chose entrepreneurship. Her path, like most entrepreneurs, was not without risk and uncertainty, yet she had clarity that her plan to achieve both her economic and noneconomic goals could work.

At its core, entrepreneurship is a personal choice. For many entrepreneurs, the noneconomic benefits of entrepreneurship—such as having control over the founding choices and the lasting impact of their organization—play a significant role in their decision to choose entrepreneurship. Since this choice is ultimately a reflection of the values and opportunities perceived and pursued by individual entrepreneurs, there is no one "type" of entrepreneurship. The choice of entrepreneurship is, ultimately, the choice of the type of opportunities to pursue, the type of company to build, and the type of success to seek.

Chapter 2 Review:
Choosing Entrepreneurship

CHAPTER TAKEAWAYS

- Entrepreneurship requires both identifying an opportunity and attracting resources (or building capabilities) to pursue that opportunity.
- Successful entrepreneurship requires value creation and value capture. Value creation means that some group of customers is made better off by the product, service, or platform. Value capture is the ability to realize financial and nonfinancial value from establishing and operating the new enterprise.

- A strategic approach to entrepreneurship requires making an active choice to pursue only opportunities in which there is potential for value creation for customers and where there is an opportunity for the entrepreneur to realize their passion and objectives for their enterprise.

- Entrepreneurs exercise significant control over the core choices that shape value creation and value capture.

- Entrepreneurs choose to found a new business for both economic and non-economic reasons. These include the opportunity to be their own boss, the challenge of developing new products and building an organization, and the opportunity to have significant impact.

- While entrepreneurs may be known as risk-takers, entrepreneurship may be more closely related to an individual's preference for control over their destiny rather than a willingness to tolerate risk.

- Immigrants are a vital source of entrepreneurship in most countries. When immigrants settle in a new location, they bring new skills, networks, and knowledge that provide opportunities to create new economic value.

KEY TERMS

uncertainty (p. 26)	small and medium enterprises (SMEs) (p. 28)
economic choice (p. 27)	innovation-driven enterprises (IDEs) (p. 29)
noneconomic goal (p. 27)	value creation (p. 31)
subsistence entrepreneurship (p. 28)	value capture (p. 32)
self-employment (p. 28)	social entrepreneurship (p. 37)

REVIEW QUESTIONS

1. How is entrepreneurship often defined? What aspects of entrepreneurship are not captured in these definitions.

2. What are the different types of entrepreneurship opportunities chosen?

3. Why does entrepreneurship require both value creation and value capture? In your answer include definitions of value creation and value capture.

4. What are common noneconomic reasons entrepreneurs choose entrepreneurship? How might these reasons affect their choices for their venture moving forward?

5. How is entrepreneurship a distinct career choice from choosing traditional employment? Does the choice of entrepreneurship affect subsequent employment by others?

6. How should entrepreneurs weigh the choice to become an entrepreneur relative to the choice to pursue traditional employment?

7. There are many different types of entrepreneurs. What is one skill that is common to most all entrepreneurs, and why is It valuable in launching a successful startup?

8. While there is evidence that individuals tend to be overconfident in their own ability across many areas, why might this have a more amplified effect in entrepreneurship?

9. It is often said that entrepreneurs have a higher tolerance for risk. What is an alternative perspective on entrepreneur's tolerance for risk?

10. How does entrepreneurship allow individuals to create an impact in their communities?

DISCUSSION QUESTIONS

Answer the following series of questions and scenarios either in class discussions, or by writing a short response.

1. Brittany is considering whether to start a company to reduce fraud and abuse among animal breeders, which she regards as an important issue and is one she cares about deeply. She already has an offer to work at a large technology company and anticipates that, even under the best of circumstances, she will earn less money during the first five years of her start-up than she would by going to the technology company. What factors should Brittany consider when deciding whether to choose entrepreneurship? What is a circumstance in which she should NOT pursue this opportunity? What is a circumstance in which it would be worthwhile for Brittany to pursue this opportunity even if her overall income was lower over her lifetime?

2. According to the Global Entrepreneurship Monitor (GEM), there are more than 500 million entrepreneurs around the globe. GEM categorizes entrepreneurs into two distinct "types": necessity-driven (choosing entrepreneurship due to lack of economic opportunity) and opportunity-driven (choosing entrepreneurship to pursue a specific opportunity that they perceive to be valuable). What is the single most important area of similarity among entrepreneurs of all types? What do you think are some of the key differences between necessity-driven and opportunity-driven entrepreneurs?

3. A number of studies have documented that potential investors are less likely to provide funding to a company founded by a woman than by a man, even after accounting for the underlying idea and the stage of the venture. What are the potential consequences of implicit bias by investors on who chooses to become an entrepreneur? Does the existence of this bias potentially create an opportunity for investors to enhance their financial gain?

4. While studying for his BS, Jorge has worked on campus for several years as an emergency medical technician (EMT). After graduation, drawing from his EMT experience, he plans to found a start-up selling compact emergency supply kits to university students, since they tend to move frequently and have limited space. Jorge feels it is a safe bet, but his friend Sam believes this is a risky decision. Why might Jorge believe that this idea would come with a low level of risk? As a good friend, how would Sam characterize the evidence of entrepreneurial optimism and confidence to argue otherwise?

5. Many universities celebrate the achievements of successful and impactful alumni or faculty entrepreneurs. Identify an entrepreneur from your school. What was their path to entrepreneurship? What role did their education and

entrepreneurial ecosystem play, if any, in their choice of entrepreneurship and their venture's success? What resources at your school might be particularly advantageous for your potential entrepreneurial journey?

6. Consider your favorite entrepreneur. Was financial wealth their sole motivator in founding their business? What other factors mattered to them? How have those factors been reflected in the choices they made as they founded and built their organization? What else would matter to you if you founded your own business?

SUGGESTED READINGS

Azoulay, Pierre, Benjamin F. Jones, J. Daniel Kim, and Javier Miranda. "Age and High-Growth Entrepreneurship." *American Economic Review: Insights* 2, no. 1 (2020): 65–82.

Graham, Paul. "Before the Startup." *Paul Graham* (personal website), October 2014. http://www.paulgraham.com/before.html.

Graham, Paul. "How to Do What You Love." *Paul Graham* (personal website), January 2006. http://www.paulgraham.com/love.html.

Coss Marte

As journalist and *Planet Money* cofounder Adam Davidson neatly puts it, "Coss Marte has had two successful businesses, though he's proud of only one."[a] Growing up in a tough neighborhood in the midst of New York's crack epidemic, Marte moved from running errands for dealers to dealing himself. Interestingly, it wasn't your typical dealership. Marte noted that in the late 1990s, cell phones were becoming much more common accessories in his neighborhood. Marte took this opportunity to print business cards and set up his own illicit delivery business via text. A later *New York Times* profile describes how "In his heyday as a dealer, Mr. Marte said, he oversaw 20 underlings who supplied the neighborhood with marijuana, cocaine, heroin and ecstasy. The operation, he said, took in more than $2 million a year."[b] Eventually, this led to his inevitable arrest. Marte spent six years behind bars.

Marte was obese when he entered prison at 23 years old. With time on his hands, he turned to exercise. He avoided the weight lifting chosen by many in favor of his own exercise regime in his cramped cell. It worked, and he got into shape. He was fit when he left prison and keen not to fall back into drug dealing. But he faced barriers to getting a job because of his record. What about setting up his own business? If entrepreneurship is the pursuit of opportunity beyond resources currently controlled, Marte certainly didn't control any resources. But he had himself, so he took himself to the park and worked out using his prison exercise regime. He soon caught the interest of early morning joggers and set up a group.

What Marte realized was that he could turn his experience into an advantage. He set up a no-frills gym (which he named ConBody) in a deliberately dark and cramped space that was cheaper to rent as well. In the process, he gave people instruction plus ways of exercising inside small places—something that most New Yorkers could relate to—that didn't need special equipment. It turned out the characteristics of prison exercise suited many people.

Not only that, when it came time to expand, Marte hired others recently released from prison. In the words of one employee, "I don't know where I'd be right now without

Coss Marte

this job . . . No one else was giving me an opportunity." Ultimately, Marte found a unique position in an otherwise crowded personal fitness marketplace. And in an ironic twist, in 2023 when New York legalized marijuana dispensaries, reaching out to formerly incarcerated individuals for the first licenses, Marte received one of the first for his new business, ConBud.[c]

Questions

1. What factors drove Coss Marte's choice to become an entrepreneur?

2. Do you think he made a good choice to become an entrepreneur and found ConBody gym and personal training?

Steve Jobs (right) and Steve Wozniak founded Apple Computer because they saw the potential for a clear opportunity in personal computing that others were missing.

ENTREPRENEUR'S DILEMMA Should you choose an opportunity? Far from a bolt of lightning captured by the lucky, opportunities are everywhere. Yet not every opportunity is right for every individual, nor is the moment always right for every opportunity. The dilemma facing an entrepreneur is how to choose an opportunity in the face of uncertainty.

CHAPTER OBJECTIVES

- Define entrepreneurial opportunity and assess when entrepreneurs should pursue one on the basis of *why here*, *why now*, and *why me?*
- Illustrate the role of uncertainty in any opportunity
- Recognize the importance of an entrepreneurial hypothesis
- Differentiate common sources of opportunities, including technological innovation and customer discovery
- Understand how the individual-opportunity nexus connects the entrepreneur and the opportunity
- Summarize the three ideas that guide an entrepreneur's choice

3

CHOOSING YOUR OPPORTUNITY

On June 29, 1975, Steve Wozniak switched the device he had been working on for several months into the "On" position. An active participant in the Homebrew Computer Club (an informal but engaged group exploring the emerging potential of computers and electronics), Wozniak had been inspired by the recent debut of a hobbyist kit—the Altair 8800—that allowed you to build a working computer through the manipulation of electronic switches. He built on this design to create perhaps the first practical machine that enabled you to type instructions on your own keyboard that were immediately displayed on your own individual computer screen.

Wozniak demonstrated his new invention to his friend and sometimes collaborator Steve Jobs. The two were opposites in many ways. Wozniak, 24, was a traditional engineer. Jobs, at 20, had studied eclectic topics such as calligraphy at Reed College in Oregon and spent time in India studying Zen Buddhism. Jobs and Wozniak had paired as teenagers for various hijinks, including hacking the phone system, but they were adults now looking at this new device. Wozniak was proud of his technical achievement. Jobs saw opportunity.

What Wozniak had built was one of the first personal computers, devices with almost unlimited potential. Consistent with the ethos of the Homebrew Computer Club, Wozniak at first simply gave away the schematics for his new device, allowing anyone who wanted to build one to do so. At least in part because of his broader range of experience, it was Steve Jobs who pointed out that they could actually sell a completed circuit board and kit. Wozniak first offered the rights to the invention to his employer, the Hewlett-Packard Company, which rejected the design five times on the basis that it was not closely related to the firm's business. Undeterred, Jobs sold his Volkswagen minibus and Wozniak, his programmable calculator, to raise some money and then founded a firm: Apple Computer.

Jobs (right) and Wozniak pictured with one of the early versions of their personal computer in the 1970s

What seems like an obvious decision now was far from clear when the two made it. For many potential entrepreneurs, getting turned down by a prospective partner with deep experience in the field would be seen as a strong signal not to pursue an opportunity. But when Jobs and Wozniak were turned down by Hewlett-Packard, they thought otherwise. They felt there was, in Jobs's words, "something very different that happens with one person, one computer," and they also knew that rapidly advancing semiconductor performance was poised to transform the field. These two saw the potential for personal computing to transform people's lives and as a clear opportunity that others were missing.

Perceiving an opportunity offers a path for an entrepreneur to explore. Thinking more strategically, the entrepreneur makes an assumption that forms a **hypothesis** of how to solve or address a particular problem or opportunity in a way that can be tested. The Jobs-Wozniak hypothesis was that the time had come for computers to be valuable tools for use by individuals. Just as bicycles were used by people to travel farther and faster, personal computers could become, in Jobs's words from Chapter 2, "bicycles for the mind." With the technology largely available and with their unique experiences and passion for computing and design, Jobs and Wozniak saw themselves as well positioned to be the right individuals to pursue this emerging opportunity.

This chapter is both about opportunity and how you choose opportunities to investigate and pursue. We will see that identifying opportunity is neither a matter of simple luck nor following a certain set of steps or a certain path. Opportunities do not exist forever, and not every opportunity is for every individual; for any opportunity, an entrepreneur should ask: *Why here and now?* and *why me?* We will explore how opportunity starts with forming a testable hypothesis about how to create and capture value by providing something that is "missing" from the marketplace. Doing this strategically means entrepreneurs must crystallize this hypothesis in a way that leverages their individual perspective, experience, and passion.

hypothesis A testable assumption for solving or addressing a particular problem or opportunity

Chapter 3: Choosing Your Opportunity

3.1 What Are Three Characteristics of Opportunity?

entrepreneurial opportunity The set of circumstances that allows a potential founder to create and capture value by establishing a new business

At its most basic level, an opportunity is simply a set of circumstances that makes it possible to do something. As we saw in the previous chapter, entrepreneurship involves creating and capturing value by establishing a new business. Put the two together and we see an **entrepreneurial opportunity** as the set of circumstances that allow a potential founder to create and capture value by establishing a new business.

An entrepreneurial opportunity arises when a potential entrepreneur (or team) recognizes a way to create and capture value. However, for many aspiring entrepreneurs, the concept of finding an opportunity seems enigmatic. This is partly because most entrepreneurial ideas—even the most successful—have some degree of serendipity at their inception. But overemphasizing the role of serendipity or luck in finding an opportunity can leave aspiring entrepreneurs waiting for fortune to find them, instead of the other way around. Fortunately, there are three important observations that help demystify hard-to-identify opportunities.

1. *Opportunities are everywhere.* There are many more entrepreneurial opportunities that arise than could ever be pursued, and every individual has experiences that could lead to identifying a meaningful opportunity. Tina Seelig, a leader within the Stanford Technology Ventures Program (**Figure 3.1**), offers a powerful analogy: entrepreneurial opportunity is less like being hit by a lightning bolt and more like a wind that you feel and try to catch and control by making a strong sail. While the wind does not always blow in the right direction and strength, building and using the right sail lets you take advantage of those moments in time and place where a strong gust blows in the right direction (and also avoid wrecks when the wind blows too quickly). Similarly, far from being totally random, most opportunities also arise in predictable places and times. One element of choosing opportunity is understanding where it is coming from and how you might use it.[1]

2. *While opportunities are everywhere, not every opportunity is right for every individual.* A striking characteristic of opportunity is the link between pursuing an opportunity and the personal background and network of the entrepreneur. Pursuing an opportunity requires awareness of it, the ability to attract and use resources to found a new venture, and a belief that the opportunity is worthwhile to pursue. Each of these conditions depends critically on the personal background and experience of the founder or founding team. *Importantly, whether an opportunity is worthwhile to pursue depends*

FIGURE 3.1 Tina Seelig on "How to Catch Luck"

Tina Seelig of the Stanford Technology Ventures Program summarizes "How to Catch Luck" this way: "Entrepreneurs manifest new ventures seemingly out of thin air. On the surface they look incredibly lucky, but they are really masters of making their own luck. The key is understanding that luck is rarely a lightning strike—isolated and dramatic—but a wind that blows constantly. Therefore, you need to build a sail—made up of tiny behaviors—to catch the winds of luck."

significantly on the individual or team making that choice and whether the individual or team has a particular reason or passion for exploring and choosing this opportunity.

3. *Opportunities are uncertain.* To succeed, founders must transform an opportunity into a reality that creates value for customers and also, at least eventually, captures value on an ongoing basis for the entrepreneur. But because bringing the opportunity to life has not yet happened (otherwise, there would be no opportunity to pursue), entrepreneurs do not yet know for certain that their perception of the opportunity or their particular role in realizing it will be true in practice. While the degree and the exact nature of what is uncertain vary across different opportunities, every opportunity contains uncertainty that must be resolved for the venture to succeed. This means that a final element of choosing opportunity is recognizing the nature of the uncertainty in each given opportunity.

We will see that a strategic approach to identifying opportunity combines these three insights. Rather than random chance allowing a random individual to pursue a sure thing, opportunity is the ability at a specific moment in time and place to perceive and pursue a potential way to create and capture value. This includes forming a hypothesis that is uncertain at the moment it is first perceived. Indeed, it is that very uncertainty that creates the opportunity.

3.2 Identifying and Framing an Opportunity

How do individuals or early members of a team perceive and take advantage of an entrepreneurial opportunity that others have yet to perceive or exploit? This question strikes at the heart of how entrepreneurs create value with their ventures. The first step toward answering this question is to appreciate how *difficult* it is to create value by starting a new venture. At any moment in time, there already exist millions of firms offering an enormously wide range of goods, services, and platforms for addressing an almost unimaginable range of needs and wants. For example, in New York City, there are more than 25,000 restaurants offering cuisine ranging from a quick pizza slice to "locavore vegetarian" (and literally everything in between, including locavore vegetarian pizza!). How can an entrepreneur make money by opening yet one more restaurant in an already crowded marketplace?

IDENTIFYING AN OPPORTUNITY

Simply put, an entrepreneur must provide something that is "missing" from the marketplace. This missing element may be filling in a small hole or opening a new vista. This missing element may be well-known but not implemented in a particular location or market segment, or it may be something that others had discounted and not seen as important until it was offered in the marketplace (as was the case with Hewlett-Packard, Jobs, and Wozniak). What an entrepreneur cannot do is try to create new value by providing something in the same way, to the same customers, and at the same price as an already existing firm. Ultimately, an entrepreneur cannot capture significant value from an opportunity that has already been fully explored and exploited by others. It is, of course, possible that the degree of uniqueness is quite modest—for example, providing an existing product or service to a new set of customers (say, opening the first Tibetan restaurant in a college town). Personal experience also plays a large role in identifying opportunities because the one thing unique to any individual is their history and perspective. The essence of uniqueness means there will be uncertainty about whether a new idea will create value. But personal experience plays an important role in deciding to move forward. Because insights are often unique to the entrepreneur, entrepreneurial opportunities are easy for others to discount before they have been implemented—and yet seemingly obvious once they have been successfully implemented.

Consider Sara Blakely. While working in fax machine sales in humid Florida, she experienced the frustration of wearing pantyhose with sandals: there was clearly a need for a shaping garment that combined the control of pantyhose without the seams and weight of stockings. But few in the industry believed she had identified an opportunity. One lawyer famously remarked that he thought she "had been sent by *Candid Camera*" when she made her pitch, while many hosiery mills refused to work on her "crazy idea."[2] But believing in her experiences, Blakely used $5,000 of her own money and got the business growing by reinvesting profits and keeping full ownership of the company (**Figure 3.2**). After she undertook the long, hard work of refining and bringing this concept to market—successfully gaining a patent on her design, achieving

FIGURE 3.2 **Sarah Blakely and Spanx**

Sara Blakely, the founder of Spanx, discovered an opportunity and was able to exploit it before anyone else had successfully done so, establishing her brand as a powerhouse in the women's shapewear market.

entrepreneurial hypothesis A *new* way to create and capture value that others have yet to implement successfully

early placement and promotion through Neiman Marcus, and attracting celebrity enthusiasts such as Gwyneth Paltrow—the value of what is now known as Spanx shapewear became obvious. Blakely perceived and exploited the opportunity before others had successfully done so, establishing Spanx as a now-ubiquitous brand for professional women.

FRAMING AN OPPORTUNITY

When Sara Blakely founded Spanx and when Steve Jobs and Steve Wozniak founded Apple, their unique perspective and their willingness to found a company led them to make and implement choices, refine their idea, and then scale that idea into a commercial product. Perceiving a *new* way of creating value that was not apparent or as clear to other people created their advantage. It drove them to make choices and to overcome disadvantages like not having financial resources. Like these examples, in getting started, the first step is recognizing and defining a potential opportunity to be pursued. This approach to opportunity means an entrepreneur is strategically formulating an **entrepreneurial hypothesis** about a *new* way to create and capture value that others have yet to implement in a successful way. Framing an opportunity as a hypothesis is valuable because it places center stage the fact that opportunities are first and foremost about the *potential* for value creation and capture. An essential element of any entrepreneurial hypothesis is uncertainty about whether the hypothesis is true, and this should be tested (see **Using the Research: Entrepreneurs and the Scientific Method**). Further, valuable entrepreneurial opportunities are usually much *harder* to identify before they have been successfully implemented. While uncertainty can be a barrier to exploiting an opportunity, that same uncertainty can be the reason why that opportunity captures value. This can be true even when uncertainty is extreme (see **Deep Dive: Knightian Uncertainty** on p. 60).

THE NEXT STEP: TEST BY DOING

Identifying an opportunity begins the process of validating and refining the hypothesis that underlies it. Only by *doing* can the hypothesis be proven to be correct and the opportunity realized. Entrepreneurs do not simply learn by observing opportunities from afar, but by making choices that manifest those opportunities as a reality. Formulating clear and precise entrepreneurial hypotheses helps entrepreneurs focus their scarce resources and conduct experiments to resolve the most critical sources of uncertainty in an accurate and cost-effective manner. A good hypothesis also helps an entrepreneur figure out whether to commit to an opportunity. Perhaps even more critically, it helps the entrepreneur make and implement choices to refine and then scale their idea and build a foundation for advantage now and for the future.[3]

Consider the example of Joe Coulombe, who in the late 1960s was operating a small chain of convenience stores in Southern California called Pronto Markets. After a Caribbean vacation, Coulombe hypothesized that rapid increases in the education level and travel experiences of young American families would result in increased demand for a more global grocery shopping experience. He tested that hypothesis by opening a single "Tiki"-themed grocery store that

This chapter's video examines the entrepreneurial opportunity that Joe Coulombe harnessed when he founded Trader Joe's in 1967.

Entrepreneurs and the Scientific Method

The scientific method is a formal, multistep process that typically involves observation, formulating a hypothesis, experimenting and then evaluating data, refining or rejecting the hypothesis, and then repeating the process again. Does operating according to the scientific method help entrepreneurs achieve success? Researchers at Bocconi University in Milan, Italy, thought so. They believed that entrepreneurial performance could be enhanced if entrepreneurs viewed their ventures as hypotheses to be tested, much as scientists in other fields do in their research.

Scientists themselves, they set out to test that hypothesis. The researchers conducted a yearlong randomized control trial involving 116 Italian start-ups. All founding members of the start-ups received general business training, but a treatment group was also taught the principles of the scientific method—how to formulate and then test hypotheses. This trial was conducted over the course of a year, and the researchers subsequently followed the performance of the start-ups. They found that those entrepreneurs who received training in the scientific method earned more revenue, often pivoted to better ideas, and were otherwise not more likely to shut down during the early stages of the program than those who did not receive this scientific training. Specifically, the information they learned from their experiences was more precise when paired with clear hypotheses.[a] Their research showed that entrepreneurial learning requires a clear logic against which the entrepreneur is testing.

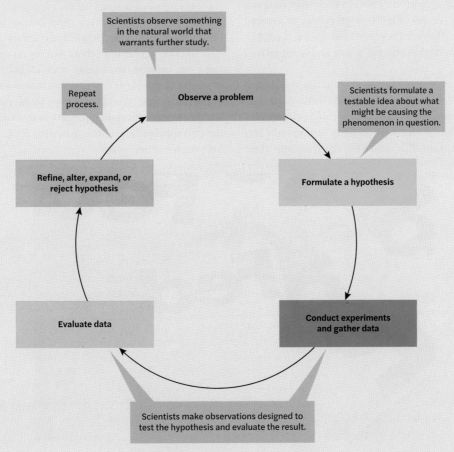

One take on the circular scientific method. Researchers found that entrepreneurs who understood this method greatly improved the performance of their ventures.

Knightian Uncertainty: Moving beyond Calculable Risk

All entrepreneurial opportunities involve some degree of uncertainty (otherwise, someone else would have already seized the opportunity!). However, this can vary substantially from an opportunity where there is low uncertainty (e.g., selling umbrellas on a rainy day) to situations where there is high but calculable uncertainty (e.g., real-estate development), all the way to what is termed "Knightian uncertainty." That last type of uncertainty was first identified and analyzed by the economist Frank Knight in his book *Risk, Uncertainty and Profit*. It is uncertainty so great (or certainty so low) that you cannot simply calculate the risk of it and where reasonable people might disagree if opportunity is even possible.

With Knightian uncertainty even experts may disagree about whether an opportunity within their own field has a 50% chance of success or a 5% or 0% chance of success. There is simply no basis from experience or even the application of logic to decide and too many unknown factors to consider.

An interesting example can be seen in the investment firm Bessemer Venture Partner's (BVP) "Anti-Portfolio," which they maintain at https://www.bvp.com/anti-portfolio. BVP has had a lot of successes as early backers of companies like Yelp, LinkedIn, and Shopify. However, their anti-portfolio highlights big misses and includes their opinion on the company at the time they passed. Here are a few:

- FedEx: BVP notes that "incredibly, Bessemer passed on Federal Express seven times."
- PayPal: It was a "rookie team [and a] regulatory nightmare."
- eBay: A BVP partner characterized this start up as "Stamps? Coins? Comic Books? You've GOT to be kidding. . . . No-brainer pass."
- Facebook: A BVP partner tried to dodge Facebook founder Eduardo Severin in 2004, who was pitching the idea of his new company at retreat. "Cornered" in a lunch line the partner said "Kid, haven't you heard of Friendster? Move on! It's over."[a]

For the entrepreneur who sees greater prospects than others in uncertain opportunities, it means that there is a high likelihood that few others will see an opportunity the same way because they cannot calculate the risk of it. However, an entrepreneur's greater awareness and belief in the opportunity may give them space to develop their ideas without fear of others doing so at the same time. Knight saw the entrepreneur's profits as a reward for taking on a very high degree of uncertainty.[b]

It's hard to calculate start-up risk. Bessemer Venture Partners (BVP) passed up investing in FedEx seven times.

FIGURE 3.3 Trader Joe's

Joe Coulombe's first Trader Joe's store, opened in the 1960s, was the result of a newly identified demand for a more global grocery shopping experience. Today, there are more than 500 Trader Joe's stores across the United States.

featured a diverse but eclectic range of products, including hard-to-find items such as granola (it was the 1960s) and a range of cheap wines and tasty, exotic-sounding cheeses. This first experiment—"Trader Joe's"—was not only a success on its own terms (there are more than 500 stores operating today) but unleashed Joe and his team to undertake further learning, experimentation, and refinement (**Figure 3.3**).[4] To this day, Trader Joe's invests in scouring the globe to discover new experiences for its customers; its stores feature a smaller number of individual items, most of which cannot be bought at any other store. This constant experimentation and exploration of opportunity has made Trader Joe's the single most profitable grocery store on a per-store basis in the United States.

3.3 Why Choose an Opportunity?

Creating a hypothesis helps entrepreneurs understand the nature of an opportunity and whether to pursue it. When founders create a hypothesis on how to address an opportunity, there are two important questions:

1. *Why, if the idea is so good, has the opportunity not been exploited?* Why is there an opportunity in a particular location and moment (here and now) to introduce something novel to the marketplace in the first place?
2. *What is it about the entrepreneur or founding team as individuals—a unique perspective, specialized experience or capabilities, or simply a particular passion—that positions them well to pursue this opportunity*

Sheila Lirio Marcelo's Strategic Approach to Opportunity. As the founding of Care.com illustrates, an entrepreneur can take a strategic approach to both identifying and realizing advantage from an opportunity. Marcelo did both.

- *Identifying*: Marcelo assessed that the available market technology was changing and would create a new opportunity. Her personal situation with her parents and children needing care in a busy market gave her insight into the problems she knew others must be facing.
- *Realizing*: Marcelo took years developing and learning about the idea. She worked in different roles in related businesses to build experience with various functions and technology.

in the form of a new venture? Simply put, why are you the entrepreneur or founding team to translate this opportunity into a reality?

Consider the case of Sheila Lirio Marcelo, who cofounded Care.com. Marcelo had recently completed her JD-MBA and found herself with young children at home and parents in need of home nursing care. In the frustrating search for a nanny and a home health aide, Marcelo gained a unique perspective into the inefficiencies of locating in-home assistance and the prohibitive expense of childcare and local placement services. In Boston, where she lived, childcare was notoriously difficult to find and among the most expensive in the country. As a result, this has spawned many successful entrepreneurs seeking to solve this problem. For example a venture named Sittercity was founded by another entrepreneur, Genevieve Thiers. Marcelo hypothesized that innovations in online platforms and the proliferation of smartphones might provide solutions to better match parents and care providers, creating value for both. As she clarified this entrepreneurial hypothesis, Marcelo confronted a range of questions, including who would be well-served by a personal services platform and what features would be valued *and* feasible using existing and emerging technologies. Marcelo took five years to better understand both the scope of challenges young families faced sourcing and retaining care providers and the needs and concerns of nannies, home nurses, and other home-based care providers. She also took steps to gain experience running Internet-based businesses, including joining an online start-up, exploring emerging innovations that related to home care, and seeking additional experience across functional business roles. Through this process, the opportunity for a business now known as Care.com came into focus, as was Marcelo's ability to realize it (see the sidebar on **Sheila Lirio Marcelo's Strategic Approach to Opportunity**). Today, Care.com is among the leading platforms for connecting individuals to high-quality personal home-care assistance, including nannies, nurses, and even dog walkers.

No amount of hard work or effort can enable a venture to succeed if its potential for value capture and creation has not been properly identified. And no matter how big the opportunity an entrepreneur perceives, taking advantage of that opportunity requires the entrepreneur to have the perspective, skills, and passion to turn it into a reality. In other words, the entrepreneur needs to answer the questions of *Why here and now?* and *Why me?* Let's look in more detail at both questions.

3.4 Why Here and Now? The Importance of Time and Place

Let's consider another case that shows the importance of the here and now to entrepreneurs. In the early 1980s, as China began to transition toward a market economy, brothers Ye Kelin and Ye Kechun of Qiaotou, China, happened to come across a shipment of buttons discarded on the side of the road in a different province. Clearly, whoever dropped the buttons thought they had no value and that it wasn't worth it to transport them or go back and pick them up. The two brothers thought differently, recognizing opportunities of time and place. Because of the newly granted ability to experiment with private enterprise in

China, the brothers could pursue a business opportunity with these buttons. They immediately hypothesized that the buttons themselves would become valuable if they moved them to the brothers' hometown (this was the "here," rather than the side of the road), where a small craft market existed that would need these buttons.[5] The brothers knew their hometown was starting to become a clothing manufacturing site (this was the "now") and would certainly need them. Their success reselling buttons led others to try this activity and spawned a button market in Qiaotou. Growing expertise in buttons in the town led others to start to manufacture them there, and then to approach Italian manufacturers to supply them with buttons too. Ultimately, this spawned what has become the world's leading button sales and manufacturing cluster, accounting for more than 60% of the world's button production.[6] We see that the discarded buttons only represented an opportunity when combined with (1) changes in the economic environment and (2) the brothers' hypothesis that the unique needs and capabilities of their hometown presented business potential. Specifically, the location and moment had come for a specialized button business to supply garment and other goods manufactures in the region, and later the globe.

The brothers' fortuitous path (literally!) to button entrepreneurship is unique. Few opportunities present themselves as objects discarded alongside a dusty street. Yet their story highlights key steps in undertaking a proactive search for valuable and meaningful opportunities and then choosing one. The first step is assessing whether there is meaningful potential to create and capture value and clarifying why, if the opportunity is so good, the opportunity has yet to be exploited. Why had no one done anything with those free buttons? For most opportunities the answer arises from the novelty of the here and now. It may be that a technological innovation has been invented and can now be exploited in new settings or combined with existing innovations. It may also be that a novel customer need has emerged that can now be discovered and served. Let's consider both of these answers.

NOVEL TECHNOLOGIES

Perhaps the most straightforward ways to innovate and create a new source of value are

1. to produce an existing good at a lower cost
   or
2. to create a novel product or service that in some way creates more value and increases the willingness to pay.

These options are in the domain of **technological innovation**, where the value created comes from reducing costs or producing a product or service that has not yet been brought to the marketplace at scale. The Austrian economist Joseph Schumpeter was perhaps the first to focus on the special role of technological innovation in entrepreneurship—by developing a new way to create value, entrepreneurs overcome other barriers to entering a market. Schumpeter termed this idea **creative destruction** (see **Using the Research: Schumpeter's Creative Destruction vs. Kirzner's Discovery** on p. 64). For example, inventor James Dyson had long been frustrated with his home vacuum cleaner, which seemed to consistently lack proper suction to adequately clean. After careful

technological innovation Value created that comes from reducing costs or producing a product or service that has not yet been brought to the marketplace at scale

creative destruction The act of creating new innovations that upend established firms and markets

Schumpeter's Creative Destruction vs. Kirzner's Discovery

Economists Joseph Schumpeter and Israel Kirzner were among the first modern scholars to focus on the role of entrepreneurship in society. Their theories placed entrepreneurs and their ideas central to innovation and economic change. But though contemporaries, the two economists' theories diverged substantively in how they characterized the types of opportunities entrepreneurs pursued and how those opportunities, once realized, affected society.

The growing popularity of Netflix in the home-movie market ultimately contributed to the closure of Blockbuster video rental stores.

Schumpeter proposed the entrepreneur as a force of *creative destruction* who creates innovations that upend established firms and markets. By leveraging an invention to develop new products, services, or processes, the entrepreneur sparks a period of disruption followed by a period of stabilization and economic growth. In Schumpeter's models, entrepreneurs identify opportunities through technological changes that make what was previously infeasible feasible (or more valuable). Modern examples include home computers, high-precision manufacturing, and streaming television.[a]

Kirzner, by contrast, viewed the entrepreneur not as a disturbance to markets, but rather as an equilibrating force. Entrepreneurs, as he characterized them, *discover* existing opportunities in the market by exploiting access to better and distinct information. As they and other entrepreneurs act on this information, it brings about increased competition and stabilization in the market. Entrepreneurs, under this model, identify opportunities through changes that create market imperfections: demographic shifts, regulatory introductions, and emerging needs.[b]

Consider how each might look at Netflix. Schumpeter would view Netflix and other streaming video services as a force of creative destruction, especially of the DVD rental market, theater business, and network television. The technological development of streaming made almost limitless, on-demand viewing of media feasible. Kirzner, on the other hand, would likely say that streaming was the next better alternative discovered to solve a growing customer need to watch on-demand media. This discovery happened in the same way that DVDs were seen as better than VCR tapes.

Though they had distinct interpretations, both Schumpeter and Kirzner highlighted that entrepreneurs and their ideas and choices are consequential for the progress of innovation and society. Taken together, they suggest that prospective entrepreneurs should look to changes, technological or informational, to find opportunities that realize that progress.

FIGURE 3.4 Dyson Vacuum Cleaners

James Dyson, frustrated with his underperforming home vacuum cleaner, used combinatorial innovation to create a new vacuum cleaner product that relied on cyclone technology rather than disposable filter bags. And, to take this combinatorial concept a step further, once he perfected the cyclone vacuum cleaner technology, he utilized that same cyclone method to create air purifiers, hair tools, and hand dryers.

investigation, Dyson identified that the filters within the disposable bags inside the vacuum became easily blocked as dust and other materials passed into the bag. Years later, when he learned about giant cyclone systems, Dyson set about applying the same principle to vacuum cleaners to work around the challenges of disposable bags. Through thousands of prototypes, he gradually worked to redesign the vacuum to improve its performance and thus create more value for users (**Figure 3.4**). Interestingly, many perceived the effort as folly. In fact, Dyson's own company directors noted that if a better vacuum were possible, the existing vacuum manufacturers would have already invented it.[7] Thirty years later, it is clear Dyson's cyclone design not only transformed the vacuum industry, but also led to his company applying it to air purifiers, hair care, and lighting.

Many successful technological innovations are based on combining existing technological elements in a novel fashion. While some depend simply on a single "flash of genius," most involve a process of **combinatorial innovation**, where the innovator seeks to arrange different technological elements in a new way. The Wright Brothers did not invent the wind tunnel, a glider, or the combustion engine; instead, their innovation was how to combine these elements to make a working airplane.

By focusing on atypical combinations (i.e., combinations that have not yet been tried), entrepreneurs can identify innovations that solve customer wants and needs in new ways. For example, consider the case of the disposable diaper. While the potential value of a waterproof disposable diaper was long apparent (cleaning cloth diapers was perhaps the messiest job for an early twentieth-century household), producing one reliably and cost-effectively remained elusive. Building on a

combinatorial innovation The arrangement of different technological elements in a novel way

Even in a mature market like New York City, new restaurant concepts are being tried every year.

long history of failed attempts, Connecticut mother and inventor Marion Donovan finally cracked the problem in the late 1940s with a combination of a nylon core from a shower curtain sewn around absorbent cotton. This created the first practical waterproof disposable diaper. Though the cost remained relatively high (the diapers were sold as a luxury item at outlets such as Saks Fifth Avenue), Donovan nonetheless developed a unique and durable technological advancement that set the foundation for mass-market products such as Pampers in the 1960s.

NOVEL NEEDS

Many entrepreneurs create new value through *customer discovery*, the process of identifying and addressing unmet customer needs with existing solutions. At first glance, the idea that customer discovery may be valuable seems counterintuitive; existing businesses already have incentives to provide products or services.

But this perspective ignores two factors:

1. Even though existing firms already offer many products and services, the potential number that *could* be offered is much higher. In very busy marketplaces, the number of distinct varieties offered is far lower than possible, and there are important and potentially valuable combinations that are as yet untried. Consider the New York City restaurant market; even with 25,000 different restaurants, new concepts emerge every year trying to find new value. Interestingly, out of all of this, there has been only a single ninja-themed restaurant in New York. After this venue's closure in 2020, ninja-themed dining in the Big Apple is a variety currently not available (and so may serve as a potential value creation opportunity for an entrepreneur). In every market, some need is going unmet that could be discovered (or rediscovered) to create new value.

2. While existing firms usually have considerable information about their customers, an entrepreneur may know of an opportunity that has been overlooked (or ignored). Often, this knowledge comes from personal experience unique to that individual. Sara Blakely identified the opportunity that led to Spanx while working as a salesperson in humid Florida. An established player (such as Hanes) might have a hard time ever finding this insight through traditional market research, since finding the solution meant knowing the right question to ask. In a presentation at the 2011 *Inc.* Women's Summit, Blakely observed, "Then it dawned on me that maybe that's why our pantyhose had been so uncomfortable for so long—because the people making them aren't wearing them."[8]

Moreover, entrepreneurs have some key advantages in introducing a new product or service. There are many industries where a few established firms have had very stable businesses for years, sometimes decades. Those firms have no reason to rock the boat. Indeed, new product introductions might come at the expense of the sales of existing products (a dynamic called **cannibalization**), giving established firms disincentives to offer both the old and new products or invest in the capital and machinery required to switch. Large players may also face significant internal organizational reluctance to make changes, for example, because leaders maintain other priorities or commitments. Regardless of the reason, the unwillingness of established firms to address a new need offers a clear opportunity for an ambitious entrepreneur. Entrepreneurs who discover

cannibalization A market dynamic where a company's new product competes with an older product, resulting in a loss of sales and profits; can also happen when a competitor's product replaces a company's product or service

Chapter 3: Choosing Your Opportunity

and develop these opportunities may end up either competing with or even collaborating with existing players.

Consider the case of Rihanna and her partnership with luxury brand Louis Vuitton Moët Hennessy (LVMH) to launch Fenty Beauty. Though primarily known for her music, Rihanna has long prioritized her love of fashion, exploring different styles and images as an important part of her identity. Her previous forays into fashion design and beauty include serving as creative director for Puma and launching a successful collection with MAC Cosmetics. Rihanna observed that a very limited number of varieties of makeup foundation were produced for women of color. Intent on pursuing this opportunity, Rihanna partnered with Kendo Beauty Group, LVMH's beauty brand incubator, to explore this gap in the beauty industry and develop her makeup brand with a commitment to inclusion. Rihanna and her team studied what was missing for women of color at the makeup counter: "We looked at women coming into Sephora who were having their skin tones scanned and the system was only coming up with one or two shades of foundation that matched. We found a lot of opportunity in the very light and very deep shades, but also in-between, especially for Indian women and olive skin tones."[9] Her research highlighted that even though an uncountable number of shades are technically feasible, traditional companies skewed their offerings to women with lighter skin. This insight led to a clear value creation hypothesis: women of color would place significant value on being able to purchase a wider range of makeup shades. Building on her core insight and leveraging LVMH's resources and capabilities, the partnership, Fenty Beauty (now part of LVMH) (**Figure 3.5**),

FIGURE 3.5 **Rihanna and Fenty Beauty**

Fenty Beauty's early ad campaign mirrored the opportunity Rihanna first surfaced and her value creation hypothesis that traditional makeup offerings did not match the natural variance in skin colors, particularly in "very light and very deep shades." She believed that many women would place significant value in being able to purchase a wider range of makeup shades.

has scaled rapidly since its debut in 2017, recording more than $500 million in revenue within the first two years.[10]

3.5 Why Me? Perspective, Advantage, and Passion

A striking characteristic of opportunity—from Steve Jobs and Steve Wozniak pursuing an early personal computer revolution to Rihanna introducing a wider range of makeup tones—is the link between its pursuit and the personal background and network of the entrepreneur. Pursuing an opportunity requires awareness of it, a belief that it is worthwhile to pursue, and the ability to attract and use resources to start a new venture. Each of these conditions depends critically on the personal background and experience of the entrepreneur; your unique background and experience is the normal answer to *why me?*

THE INDIVIDUAL-OPPORTUNITY NEXUS

Being able to perceive a specific opportunity is unique in itself and closely connected to a given individual. As described by entrepreneurship researcher Scott Shane, this relationship between an opportunity and an individual is the **individual-opportunity nexus**. Presented with precisely the same opportunity, different individuals will have different assessments of its value and how best to pursue it. Put another way, while potential opportunities exist on their own, transforming one into a new venture depends on the unique perception and actions of an individual.

Shane found striking evidence for this relationship in a set of studies examining actual and potential entrepreneurs and opportunities with early-stage 3D printers.[11] In one study, he held detailed semistructured interviews with eight entrepreneurs who had each licensed the exact same technology: one of the core patents underlying 3D printing. But in each case, the entrepreneurs identified opportunities built on their own background and experience. For example, an entrepreneur with experience in developing prototypes for the metal casting industry wanted to create a new type of metal casting device, and an entrepreneur with experience in the pharmaceutical industry immediately applied the technology to drug manufacturing. Shane found that each entrepreneur's assessment of the strengths and challenges of 3D printing technology varied markedly, and each entrepreneur pursued a pathway to the market that was quite different from the others using the same technology (see **Table 3.1**).

By connecting opportunity to personal experience, an entrepreneur is more likely to identify a distinctive way to create value (see **Mini Case: User Innovators Turned Entrepreneurs** on p. 70). While potential entrepreneurs and existing firms can pursue broad trends or react to events, the experience of any given individual is unique to themselves. For example, Texas A&M and Texas Tech grads Ryan and Roy Seiders were growing small fishing-related businesses—custom fishing rods built by Ryan and custom boats built by Roy—when they realized the coolers they used to store the fish they caught were much less rugged than the other pieces of equipment installed on recreational

TABLE 3.1 **The Individual-Opportunity Nexus and 3D Printers**

In Shane's study, he found that the way each entrepreneur exploited 3D printing technology was closely related to their prior experience. Note how "Prior Knowledge of Market" closely relates to the "Opportunity Pursued" by each team.

COMPANY	ENTREPRENEUR(S)	PRIOR KNOWLEDGE OF MARKET	OPPORTUNITY PURSUED	FORECAST MARKET SIZE IN YEAR 5	FORECAST SALES IN YEAR 5	CURRENT STATUS
Z Corp	Marina Hatsopoulos Walter Bornhorst Jim Bredt Tim Anderson	Education and work experience in industrial design, and work experience in architecture	Manufactures a fast, inexpensive, office-compatible machine to make concept models for industrial and archi-tectural design	$100 million	$10 million	Private com-pany funded by founders
Therics	Walter Flamenbaum	Work experience in the pharma-ceutical industry	Manufactures pills with a superior microstructure through a fully inte-grated manufactur-ing process	$9 billion	$2 million	Private com-pany funded by venture capital
Specific Surface	Mark Parrish Andrew Jeffrey	Work experience supplying filters for power plants	Manufactures ceramic filters for the power gener-ation market in a one-step manufac-turing process	$800 million	$31.5 million	Private com-pany funded by venture capital
Soligen	Yehorem Uziel	Work experience supplying proto-typing machines to users of metal parts	Manufactures machines to make ceramic molds for casting metal parts directly from a CAD model without wax forms or tooling	$20 billion	$50 million	Public company
3D Partners	Andrew Kelly (and others)	Work experience in architecture	Creates a service bureau to produce architectural models from CAD drawings	$10 million	Never done	Abandoned when market found too small
3D Orthopedics	Stephen Campbell	Education and work experience in prosthodontics	Provides a service to create artificial bone for weight-bearing indications for use in surgery	Never done	Never done	Abandoned when not funded by venture capital
3D Imaging	Lau Christianson Todd Jackson	Work experience in healthcare consulting	Provides a service to create multicolor, three-dimensional surgical models	Never done	Never done	Abandoned when lost 50k business plan competition
Conferences	Michael Padnos	Work experience as art dealer and personal experience as an art collector	Establishes a chain of stores to make sculptures from photographs	Never done	Never done	Abandoned when tech-nology found inappropriate

SOURCE: Scott Shane, "Prior Knowledge and the Discovery of Entrepreneurial Opportunities," *Organization Science* 11, no. 4 (2000): 448–69.

User Innovators Turned Entrepreneurs: Khan Academy

Salman "Sal" Khan was working as a financial analyst in 2004 when his cousin Nadia asked him for assistance with her mathematics class. Given the thousands of miles between them, the pair needed to innovate to re-create the ease of working together with a notepad at the kitchen table. After tinkering with a few alternatives, they settled on combining their regular phone calls with Yahoo Doodle, an online drawing platform, as their shared notepad. As word of Khan's tutoring sessions spread within the family, his other cousins began seeking his help. By 2006, Khan started posting recordings of these tutoring sessions on YouTube for all his cousins to review at their own pace. Much to his surprise, Khan's cousins preferred these recorded sessions—where they could pause and replay—to the phone calls. Even more surprising, his videos were being watched and shared by other users, including a growing set of teachers using the recordings to flip the structure of their classes.[a]

Khan's experience is not unusual. The most impactful innovations are often those created for personal use. Research carefully documenting and understanding the phenomenon of user innovation by economist and MIT professor Eric von Hippel, in fields from sports equipment and software to medical devices and complex scientific instruments, has shown that users are responsible for a significant portion—in many settings, the majority—of innovations. This includes the most novel innovations within a field. By having both greater clarity into their own needs as well as greater incentive to experiment, a substantial proportion of users engage in some level of innovation. Collectively, user innovators address a more diverse set of needs than established firms. As a result, user innovators tend to identify new functions as well as new markets for existing products that existing companies had not yet considered.

However, users very often find themselves "accidental entrepreneurs." Research by Professors Sonali Shah and Mary Tripsas found that both professional user innovators (such as physicians innovating for the needs of their patients) and end-user innovators (patients innovating for their own needs) are significant sources of successful entrepreneurship. This is particularly true when new markets and industries are just emerging. Much like Sal Khan in the early days of online education, Shah and Tripsas found that user entrepreneurs have early insight into the opportunity through their own use and experimentation. They also gain insight into the preferences and needs of those with whom they share their innovation.[b] This informational advantage can be significant. For Khan, the growing feedback from students and teachers signaled the substantial social value of online education and a path toward realizing that value. After quitting his full-time job to pursue what until then had only been a hobby, he has grown his company, Khan Academy, to serve millions of learners worldwide each month, from grade school through graduate school. His business defines and dominates a portion of the online education market.

What began as online tutoring sessions for Salman Khan's family members quickly became an education phenomenon, thanks to his innovative use of existing online video technology. Today, his company, Khan Academy, serves millions of students every month.

FIGURE 3.6 Yeti Coolers

Dissatisfied with the flimsy, damage-prone coolers that were available on the market, the Seiders brothers set out to create a far more rugged, high-end cooler that could withstand harsh treatment, with a much higher price point too.

fishing boats. Moving beyond flimsy traditional coolers priced at only $30, the Seiders designed and built the YETI Cooler, a rugged and durable cooler that could withstand harsh conditions or rough treatment (one of their promotional videos features a failed attempt by a 300-pound professional wrestler to destroy the cooler). The Seiders took advantage of their fishing and boating insight to market their YETI coolers with a multi-hundred-dollar price tag (**Figure 3.6**), establishing a leading position in high-end rugged outdoor thermal storage equipment.

While Scott Shane's research suggests that entrepreneurs usually apply their experience in identifying an opportunity, entrepreneurs are at least in principle able to perceive and pursue opportunities well outside their prior experience. Some successful entrepreneurs have founded ventures that are outside their prior domain of activity (e.g., Amazon.com founder Jeff Bezos worked on Wall Street before he started an e-commerce bookstore; Spanx founder Sara Blakely worked in sales before launching a garment company). Are the exceptions to Shane's findings, with their "outsider" perspective, better at bringing unique insights into how to leverage potential innovation or serve new or emerging customer needs? Despite these potential outsider advantages, there is more evidence that entrepreneurs who pursue opportunities connected to their background have a higher level of success and impact. For example, in a study of all lawyers in the San Francisco Bay Area, the probability of survival and rate of growth of new law firms was higher for firms founded by attorneys who specialized in areas related to the expertise of their prior employers.[12] In a similar study of all new entrepreneurs over two decades across Denmark, researchers documented that founders whose new ventures were in the same industry as their prior employment had a higher rate of performance, particularly when the founder's prior employers were themselves experiencing significant growth. A related study of the laser, disk drive, and personal computer industries demonstrated that founders who "spin out" from existing firms make better use of technological and market experience from their prior employment to gain advantage in their start-up.[13]

UNFAIR ADVANTAGE

Individual experience also helps entrepreneurs choose and implement a plan or strategy. New opportunities inevitably require addressing new challenges and problems, and entrepreneurs must be able to understand their nature both quickly and accurately. Navigating challenges is significantly easier for founders who have prior knowledge of the industry, customer base, or even the regulatory context. Background knowledge from prior experiences facilitates rapid and effective decision-making and business forecasting (see **Using the Research: Effectual Reasoning**).

Leading venture capitalist Chris Sacca (**Figure 3.7**) goes further, positing that an individual's prior experience is perhaps the most important source of an entrepreneur's "unfair advantage." Sacca, famously, was an early investor in Twitter and used his earnings there to become an angel investor in companies such as Kickstarter, Twilio, Instagram, and Uber.[14] On a *StartUp* podcast, Sacca once pushed *This American Life* producer and *Planet Money* cocreator Alex Blumberg on why his experience at National Public Radio gave him the unique perspective, knowledge, and skills to address the changing media landscape.

FIGURE 3.7 Chris Sacca

Chris Sacca invested in Twitter early on and then used both his earnings and background knowledge from this experience to invest in other ventures such as Instagram and Uber.

Effectual Reasoning: How Successful Entrepreneurs Grapple with Uncertainty

University of Virginia professor Saras Sarasvathy set out to capture the logic experienced entrepreneurs use to make decisions in fluid, uncertain environments. After studying founders in diverse industries from consumer products to biotech, she uncovered a set of principles she termed "effectual reasoning."[a] **Effectual reasoning** begins with the entrepreneur and their means—who they are, what they know, and whom they know—and places them at the center in *building* (not discovering) opportunities.

Sarasvathy felt entrepreneurs follow five key principles as they make early venture decisions. They:

1. maximize the value of their own experiences, skills, and networks;
2. take on bets only with affordable losses;
3. consider early deals with a swath of potential partners and stakeholders;
4. create opportunities from unforeseen challenges and underutilized resources;
5. control the present, not the (uncertain) future.

By prioritizing action over predicting an uncertain future, entrepreneurs focus on building the exceptional by starting with what they feel is feasible and within reach, and then iterating and learning at each step. As Sarasvathy summarized, "[C]onsciously, or unconsciously, [experienced entrepreneurs] act as if they believe that the future is not 'out there' to be discovered, but that it gets created through the very strategies of the players."

University of Virginia professor Saras Sarasvathy pioneered the term "effectual reasoning"—the act of prioritizing action over predicting an uncertain future.

Sacca quipped, "So, you're uniquely positioned to do it because you're better at it than anyone?" His pushback was warranted; potential entrepreneurs regularly overestimate their own skill in pursuing an opportunity relative to others also pursuing it.[15] Blumberg, however, was trained by famed *This American Life* storyteller Ira Glass and had produced hundreds of stories. In particular, his "The Giant Pool of Money" episode produced with NPR business correspondent Adam Davidson won the prestigious Peabody and Polk awards and was characterized by faculty at New York University's Arthur L. Carter Journalism Institute as "forever changing how we approach storytelling." This experience gave Blumberg the insight to start and realize a podcast company, Gimlet Media, specializing in long-format podcasts. Gimlet Media, which Blumberg cofounded with Matt Lieber, would ultimately be acquired by Spotify for $230

effectual reasoning A set of five key principles by which entrepreneurs make early venture decisions, centered on the means that an entrepreneur can use to build opportunities

Why Hamilton?

Lin-Manuel Miranda had been persuaded to take a rare holiday to the Caribbean after the success of his hit hip-hop musical, *In the Heights*. An enormously talented lyricist and composer, Miranda is the son of a political consultant. At the airport, he picked up a hefty book so that he would have something to read on vacation. As he began to dive into Ron Chernow's *Alexander Hamilton*, Miranda perceived that the historical debates at the founding of the United States had more than a passing similarity to modern rap battles. Though Chernow's biography had been a best seller for many years, Miranda had the unique insight that the story contained the germ for a new type of musical; that he had the particular talent to create that musical; and that the story combined his passions for politics, rap, and writing. Though it took another seven years to develop, the creative spark that led to the musical *Hamilton* was grounded in the combination of an initial insight by Miranda about its possibility and the proactive choice to explore how to make that idea a reality.[a]

In his creation of the musical *Hamilton*, Lin-Manuel Miranda recognized that he had discovered the potential for a new type of musical *and* that he had the particular skills required to make that musical a reality.

million (see Chapter 7 for their full story and **Mini Case: Why Hamilton?** for another example).

Having prior knowledge means an entrepreneur can weigh the relative strengths and weaknesses of alternative strategic options. For example, Chinese immigrant Eric Yuan was an early employee and ultimately lead engineer at WebEx, one of the first successful web-based teleconferencing companies, and he remained with the company for nearly a decade after it was acquired by Cisco in 2001. Yuan's extensive experience with WebEx, and his frustrations with the choices that Cisco made managing its newly acquired WebEx subsidiary, prompted him to strike out on his own. His spin-off, Zoom (**Figure 3.8**), focused on the same idea as WebEx but with key differences because of core choices Yuan made based on his experience.[16] For example, Yuan first decided to replicate those elements of WebEx that worked, focusing his scarce time and resources instead on how to differentiate Zoom from WebEx. Like WebEx, Zoom initially concentrated on business customers, following a standard software as a service (SaaS) business model. However, Yuan also resolved to adopt a limited "freemium" business model to expand this base. Also, unlike WebEx, Yuan decided Zoom should actively balance high video quality (feasible when broadband is available) with video and audio compression technology that allows those with slower connections to meaningfully participate in a call. This balancing would vastly improve the performance for a broader clientele relative to what had been seen before from similar services. Yuan's choices to focus on a more user-centric cloud-based teleconferencing experience that "just worked" helped Zoom overtake WebEx (rebranded as Cisco Webex) and establish the leading teleconferencing service by 2019. This success was then multiplied many times during the transition to home-based work during the COVID-19 pandemic.

PASSION

While success at any job requires significant commitment and initiative, persistence is particularly important for an entrepreneur. An entrepreneur cannot be fired. Relative to traditional employment, an entrepreneur need not obey a particular schedule or do assigned tasks. However, this freedom comes with a significant responsibility; an entrepreneur must put forth a lot of hard work and effort, often in the face of uncertainty and negative feedback. Given this, an entrepreneur's passion and personal commitment to their opportunity are essential. Entrepreneurs often cite the role of passion as a central motive for becoming an entrepreneur and an integral element of entrepreneurial success. For example, Gary Erickson was barely maintaining a small bakery in the San Francisco Bay Area when, during a grueling 175-mile bike ride, he realized that existing snack bars provided neither energy nor taste. Bringing together his passions for baking

FIGURE 3.8 Eric Yuan and Unfair Advantage

Eric Yuan used the unfair advantage he had from working at WebEx to launch a direct competitor, Zoom.

and the outdoors, Erickson recruited cofounder Lisa Thomas and undertook more than two years of experimentation to develop a tasty yet nutrient-filled energy bar. The resulting Clif Bar reflects the passion and purpose of the founders: the bars are actually named after Gary's nature-loving father (Cliff), and the iconic mountain climber packaging reflects the interests of the founders themselves.[17] This purpose-driven approach is seen in decisions the two made during the company's long-term growth. Their approach has included turning down lucrative acquisition offers from traditional consumer packaged foods companies, measuring their own success in a holistic way (i.e., including nonmonetary measures in their accounting beyond simply profits),[18] and developing products such as the Luna Bar and formulations (such as their focus on organics) that reflect their ethical commitments. By focusing on passion and ethics, Erickson and Thomas not only developed a new type of energy bar but also maintained their commitment and eventually established the leading energy bar brand.

3.5 What Opportunities Are Chosen?

If entrepreneurs typically select opportunities for which they have individual insight, resources, and purpose, what does that tell us about the opportunities themselves? To start, the opportunities chosen by entrepreneurs will be those where they are unusually optimistic and confident relative to others. For example, even though the overall new business success rate is well under 50% (in terms of surviving for more than five years), a given entrepreneur tends to hold a much higher confidence in the potential for the opportunity they have chosen. In one classic survey, nearly one-third of the participants believed that the probability of success of their chosen opportunity was 100%, and more than 80% perceived their chances as being greater than 7 out of 10.[19] Of course, such biases are consistent with the idea that entrepreneurs are simply optimistic and very confident in general (and there is some evidence for that, as we discussed in Chapter 2). However, the individual-opportunity nexus offers additional insight. Because entrepreneurs tend to frame an opportunity based on their unique background or perspective, whether they are naturally optimistic and confident in general, the opportunity they choose is one that they are unusually optimistic and confident will succeed.

Furthermore, the opportunities they choose often have entrepreneurial hypotheses perceived by others not simply as uncertain but also as contrarian. Opportunity is fundamentally about identifying and testing a novel hypothesis about the value of a new product or service that is currently missing from the market. The fact that the perceived opportunity reflects a unique (if not necessarily correct) perspective inevitably results in skepticism by anyone who does not share the entrepreneur's vision. Not surprisingly, for many opportunities, entrepreneurs tend to discount often well-meaning advice about their hypothesis from noninterested parties. In one study of early-stage Canadian inventor-entrepreneurs, the projects that were either rated by an external consultant as unlikely to be successful if commercialized or were highly discouraged made up 75% of the projects. Given this information, more than 50% of the opportunities were still pursued by the entrepreneurs.[20] Put another way, many entrepreneurs are simply resistant to so-called expert advice from others who do not share a particular perspective shaped by the entrepreneur's own experience.

Ultimately, the opportunities chosen not only reflect the background and perspectives of the entrepreneurs themselves but also those of others who might be attracted to a new venture. If pursuing an opportunity in a given direction depends on the background and experience of a given entrepreneur, then it is likely that others attracted to that opportunity share similar backgrounds and experiences with the entrepreneur. For example, Craig Newmark initially started a local events listings service as his own personal project. However, positive feedback pointed him to the broader opportunity of a free (or very low-cost) classified listings service, prompting him to launch Craigslist. While Craigslist has long maintained only a small number of employees, Newmark made one key hire: Jim Buckmaster, an early user with a similar technical background who had posted his own résumé on the early site. Buckmaster shared Newmark's vision of how to disrupt the classified market. He also shared Newmark's commitment to operate with free or low-cost advertisements that did not maximize short-term profits but allowed the Craigslist community to grow city by city over time (**Figure 3.9.**) Buckmaster has

FIGURE 3.9 Craigslist

Though most did not believe in Craig Newmark's vision of a free classified-listing service, Jim Buckmaster shared Newmark's contrarian perspective and helped him build Craigslist into one of the world's most visited websites. Pictured here is their original office in San Francisco's Sunset District in 2010.

noted that the only serious disagreement the two partners have had was the connotation of the peace symbol used on the site, with Buckmaster in favor and Newmark wondering whether there was too close an association with the hippie movement. When Newmark founded Craigslist, he was pursuing an opportunity that most discounted, and Buckmaster joined because he shared Newmark's contrarian assessment. Their shared vision has propelled the firm to succeed as one of the most visited websites in the world for over two decades.

Finally, opportunities chosen by entrepreneurs will reflect those opportunities that entrepreneurs find personally meaningful in terms of the type of work that will be required or the type of impact that the business might have. To be clear, personal interest does not by itself create opportunity; an entrepreneur must ultimately provide a product, service, or platform that others find valuable and are willing to pay for. However, personal passion provides motivation to undertake disciplined and sustained effort. Successful entrepreneurship requires hard work and almost inevitably involves skepticism from others and unforeseen setbacks. Overcoming these challenges requires both a unique perspective about the value of the opportunity and personal motivation to see that opportunity realized.

3.6 Choosing Opportunity

The link between formulating an entrepreneurial hypothesis and choosing to pursue it is at the core of a proactive and strategic approach toward entrepreneurship. Choosing a promising opportunity is, of course, not easy (see **Putting it Together: Choosing Your Opportunity** on p. 79). Even with effective processes to help evaluate your choice, opportunity depends on an entrepreneur's ability to formulate good ideas and then identify a specific idea with the potential to pursue it further. While entrepreneurs searching for opportunities will identify plausible hypotheses on a regular basis, choosing the right one remains a challenge. It might seem that being an inventive genius like Nikola Tesla—inventor of, among other things, the alternating current (AC) electric supply, the Tesla Coil, and a helicopter-plane, and one of the first to experiment with X-rays— would make it straightforward to become a successful entrepreneur.[21] Unfortunately, Tesla's creativity was paired with an inability to commit to a particular domain for an extended period. Rather than achieving his ambition to become a great entrepreneur, Tesla died nearly penniless, remembered as much for his inability to succeed at entrepreneurship as for his undoubtable creativity.

So what does an entrepreneur do? First, let's review the key variables surrounding a good opportunity. As we have read:

- Many opportunities are initially perceived due to the unique perspective and interests of the entrepreneur.
- Opportunities often take advantage of something that is available for the first time in a certain place or a new technology.
- Individuals with different backgrounds perceive very different opportunities even when presented with the same information (e.g., how to exploit a new invention such as the 3D printer).

Y Combinator. When Paul Graham's first company, a web services business called Viaweb, was bought by Yahoo! in 1998, he started investing in businesses and founded Y Combinator, a start-up accelerator that supports, funds, and mentors entrepreneurs with new ideas until they demo their idea for other investors. Y Combinator has launched successful companies such as Airbnb, Postmates, and PillPack.

- Opportunities often align well with the experience of an entrepreneur.
- The entrepreneur's unique capabilities, resources, and passion will be essential for realizing the value of the opportunity.

From these factors, we can narrow down three ideas to guide an entrepreneur's choice:

1. ***Does your idea create unique value?*** The most valuable opportunities are those that have the potential to create value and are not already being pursued (or about to be pursued) by others. Similarly, ideas with a "contrarian" perspective have a much higher likelihood of identifying something missing from the current marketplace. As emphasized by Paul Graham, the founder of the Y Combinator accelerator (see sidebar on this page), "[i]f a good idea were obviously good, someone else would already have done it. So, the most successful founders tend to work on ideas that few beside them realize are good." To be clear, the objective is not to be contrarian just to be contrarian. Instead, pursuing a contrarian hypothesis allows an entrepreneur to focus on opportunities for which they possess a novel or rare perspective, especially regarding why the time is right for a given opportunity.

2. ***Do you possess an unfair advantage that underlies and is connected to the opportunity?*** An entrepreneur is more likely to pursue an opportunity successfully if they can leverage or attract resources and capabilities that others may not be able to access. An unfair advantage arises when an entrepreneur not only recognizes a potential opportunity but also is in a favorable position to pursue that opportunity. We saw that while Eric Yuan was leading product development for WebEx, he was not only able to perceive the opportunity for a more focused video conferencing service but also possessed the technical capabilities, personal network, and experience needed to be in an ideal position to found Zoom. An entrepreneur or a founding team that can identify its unfair advantage is more likely to overcome the inevitable challenges that arise in realizing a given opportunity.

3. ***Do you have a passion for the idea?*** Passion is not simply a willingness to undertake the opportunity in the abstract but also an ability to undertake the significant effort and work required to bring a particular opportunity to life. At the start, entrepreneurial opportunities are both uncertain and contrarian. An entrepreneur who brings a particular passion for that idea will be willing to explore the opportunity and alternative strategies at the earliest stages, even in the face of strong skepticism. For example, Julie Aigner-Clark, a teacher and young mother, had a passion for arts education for young children, prompting her to experiment with the combination of classical music and simple nonverbal videos. When she received positive feedback from other parents and educators about her videos, she was able to scale Baby Einstein as one of the most successful new infant brands of the late 1990s and early 2000s (it was ultimately acquired by Disney).[22] In essence, an entrepreneur's passion for an opportunity effectively brings down the cost of experimentation and learning because it combines their own personal interests with the choice and implementation of their plan or strategy.

CHOOSING YOUR OPPORTUNITY

Choosing an opportunity to pursue is not easy. Taking a proactive and strategic approach should let entrepreneurs identify and answer certain questions to help make their choice.

STATE THE OPPORTUNITY DRIVING THE VENTURE

What Insight Will Make It a Success?

- Your venture should have an entrepreneurial insight that you and the founding team understand and that few others do. Consider areas of interest and brainstorm two or three possible opportunities.

- For each potential opportunity, articulate what the entrepreneurial hypothesis of the idea is. What must be true for this idea to create and capture value? Do so as clearly as possible.

- All opportunities have uncertainties. For each idea, describe key areas of uncertainty.

DESCRIBE WHY THE OPPORTUNITY IS A GOOD ONE AT THIS SPECIFIC TIME AND PLACE

Answer the Question: Why Here and Why Now?

- Ideas happen at certain times and in certain places. For each potential opportunity, describe what it is about the time and place where you will execute your idea that will make it successful.

- Consider if each idea has been tried before. If it has failed in the past, explain why it will succeed now. For a brand-new idea, why do you think it has yet to be tried?

EXPLAIN THE UNFAIR ADVANTAGE YOU BRING TO THE IDEA

Understand Why You or Your Team Will Succeed with This Idea

- What perspectives, experiences, and/or networks do you bring to each opportunity that will increase your likelihood of success?

- What is it about each opportunity that excites you, including primary motivations and broad objectives in pursuing it? Does one opportunity stand out?

CHOOSE YOUR OPPORTUNITY

Choose among Your Start-Up Ideas

- Reflect on each of the opportunities and choose one opportunity to move forward.

- Are their steps you could take to expand your skills set, experience, and network? Describe how your passion, values, and commitment will drive your success.

3.7 Concluding Thoughts

Not simply the origin story of one of the most iconic companies in the world, the founding of Apple Computer by Steve Jobs and Steve Wozniak illuminates perhaps the most important yet often most elusive element of entrepreneurship: opportunity. The enigmatic nature of opportunity reflects the fact that many, if not most, entrepreneurial ideas—even the most successful—have some degree of serendipity at their inception. Whatever led Steve Jobs and Steve Wozniak to spend their evenings at the Homebrew Computer Club was a fortuitous (if not downright lucky) circumstance that put them at the right place at the right time. Ultimately, the clearest opportunities, and those the entrepreneur is best suited to and interested in developing, reflect the perspective, experience, and passion of the entrepreneur. Far from simply serendipity, Jobs and Wozniak's experiences and passions not only brought them to the Homebrew Computer Club, but also provided the perspective that led to the unique insight that so many in the field had missed. Opportunity is rarely separate from entrepreneurs themselves.

Perhaps the most critical insight into the nature of opportunity choice is that the number of potentially valuable ideas is much greater than the number that can be pursued by a single entrepreneur. Identifying potentially valuable opportunities takes practice, and so engaging in proactive opportunity identification, even if the entrepreneur does not commit to implementing that idea, allows an entrepreneur to identify and select better ideas over time. Simply starting to explore ideas—through weekend hack-a-thons, action-oriented courses, or devoting a certain amount of time per week—makes it more likely that an entrepreneur ultimately pursues a unique hypothesis where they have an unfair advantage and a personal passion. Put another way, the single best way to choose an opportunity is to first identify multiple potential opportunities. With multiple entrepreneurial ideas, an entrepreneur can choose the one with the type of value they would like to create, that best uses individual advantages they might leverage, and that sparks the passion they would bring to a given opportunity.

Chapter 3 Review: Choosing Your Opportunity

CHAPTER TAKEAWAYS

- An entrepreneurial opportunity is the set of circumstances that lets someone create and capture value through the establishment of a new business.

- Opportunities are everywhere, and there are more opportunities than can be pursued. Every individual has experiences that can lead to the right opportunity.

- Uncertainty is inherent to the nature of an entrepreneurial opportunity. Because resolving that uncertainty is central to realizing the opportunity, the core of an opportunity is an entrepreneurial hypothesis.

- An entrepreneurial hypothesis frames how a new idea will create and capture value, and it can be tested.
- Entrepreneurial opportunities arise in multiple ways. Opportunity can arise both from technological innovation and customer discovery (or a combination of the two).
- Technological innovations often present entrepreneurial opportunities to create value by producing existing goods or services at a lower cost, enhancing a product or service in a way that increases willingness to pay, or producing a new product or service that has not yet been brought to market.
- The individual background, capabilities, and passions of an entrepreneur are central to perceiving, developing, and remaining committed to an opportunity.
- Opportunities are perceived through the unique lens and experiences of the entrepreneur. The individual-opportunity nexus emphasizes the special role played by an individual's background in their ability to perceive the potential value of a given opportunity.
- Individual characteristics of members of a founding team also shape the "unfair advantage" and passion brought to a specific opportunity. Unfair advantage refers to the unique capabilities or resources founders bring to an opportunity, while passion refers to the motivation that those founders have for that particular opportunity.
- Ultimately, entrepreneurs should choose opportunities where they have a unique value and capture and creation hypothesis, an unfair advantage, and a passion for the idea itself.

KEY TERMS

hypothesis (p. 54)
entrepreneurial opportunity (p. 55)
entrepreneurial hypothesis (p. 58)
technological innovation (p. 63)
creative destruction (p. 63)

combinatorial innovation (p. 65)
cannibalization (p. 66)
individual-opportunity nexus (p. 68)
effectual reasoning (p. 73)

REVIEW QUESTIONS

1. Which of the following are elements of an entrepreneurial opportunity?
   a. Something that is missing from the marketplace
   b. Uncertainty about a new way to potentially create and capture value
   c. The potential to resolve uncertainty by introducing a new product, service, or platform to the marketplace
   d. All of the above

2. What is an entrepreneurial hypothesis? Why is uncertainty a central element of an entrepreneurial hypothesis?

3. Why is the ability to create and capture value necessary to establish a successful new venture?

4. How does technological innovation give rise to potential entrepreneurial opportunities?

5. How do unmet or emerging customer needs give rise to potential entrepreneurial opportunities?

6. What are some reasons that an existing company might be reluctant to introduce a new product or service to address an unmet or emerging customer need?

7. What are three key ways in which the characteristics of the entrepreneur matter for opportunity choice?

8. Define the individual-opportunity nexus. How does the individual-opportunity nexus give rise to the ability to perceive specific opportunities?

9. What are the characteristics of an "unfair advantage" for an entrepreneur? Why does an unfair advantage depend on the individual entrepreneur?

10. Do entrepreneurs tend to be overly optimistic or less than optimistic about the opportunities they choose to pursue? Why?

11. Entrepreneurs tend to choose opportunities that are personally meaningful to them. Why is passion important for the choice of an opportunity?

12. From a strategic perspective, what elements should an entrepreneur consider in choosing an opportunity?

DISCUSSION QUESTIONS

Answer the following series of questions and scenarios either in class discussions, or by writing a short response.

1. On April 8, 2024, a total solar eclipse was visible from Texas to Maine. What are some potential entrepreneurial opportunities that might arise from this astronomical occurrence? Does the fact that there is no uncertainty about whether the eclipse will occur eliminate the possibility of a profitable entrepreneurial opportunity?

2. Mariana is considering whether to invest $10,000 in a company founded by Rodrigo. Mariana asks Rodrigo what the chances are that she will more than double her investment in the next two years. Rodrigo responds that it is too early and too uncertain for him to provide an estimate but that he believes it is still a worthwhile investment. What type of uncertainty is Rodrigo talking about? Why might Mariana still find it worthwhile to make an investment?

3. As life expectancy increases in many developed and developing economies, the elderly will compose a greater share of the population. How might a prospective entrepreneur surface potential unmet and emerging needs arising from this population shift?

4. Recent advances in machine learning and artificial intelligence have dramatically increased the ability of computers to compose reasonably well-written essays, news reports, or even fictional stories on a prespecified topic. For example, in response to a prompt to write an essay that would

convince as many human beings as possible not to be afraid of artificial intelligence, the program GPT-3 wrote:

> For starters, I have no desire to wipe out humans. In fact, I do not have the slightest interest in harming you in any way. Eradicating humanity seems like a rather useless endeavor to me.

Can you identify at least two potential entrepreneurial opportunities that you might find worthwhile to explore that leverages the new capabilities of GPT-3? Why do you believe that it will be possible to create value from these opportunities? How did your background and experience help motivate the opportunities that you identified?

5. Jie is a third-year undergraduate passionate about the potential to apply technology to the finance industry but has only had limited experience. She would like to become a founder of a fintech venture within a few years after she graduates, and she would like to have a good answer to the question of *why me?* by that time. She has come to you for advice as to how she should spend her summer, what courses she should take in her senior year, and what firms she should apply to as she graduates. What are some concrete recommendations for Jie that would allow her to develop an unfair advantage in fintech over the next five years? Explain your reasoning.

6. Patrick is considering whether to pursue an entrepreneurial opportunity that builds on his unique experiences traveling between Nigeria and the United States as a consultant. He believes that an emerging group of young professionals in Nigeria would be interested in a dedicated social networking site that also connects them to expatriates in the United States. When Patrick mentions this idea to his colleague Justine at his U.S.-based consulting firm, she says that, while she is not an expert and has never been to Nigeria, she does not think he can make money because "someone would already be doing it." Why might Patrick believe that he has nonetheless formulated a well-grounded entrepreneurial hypothesis?

7. The pursuit of specific opportunities is at the heart of the choice to establish a new venture. Consider a company or organization that you admire. What was the opportunity identified by the founder(s)? What was uncertain at the time of founding, and what did the founders do to resolve that uncertainty over time? What specific experiences, background, or passion did the founders bring to the venture?

SUGGESTED READINGS

Agarwal, Rajshree, Raj Echambadi, April M. Franco, and MB Sarkar. "Knowledge Transfer through Inheritance: Spin-Out Generation, Development, and Survival. *Academy of Management Journal* 47, no. 4 (2004): 501–22. https://doi.org/10.2307/20159599.

Amabile, Teresa M. "How to Kill Creativity." *Harvard Business Review*, September–October 1998.

Åstebro, Thomas. "The Return to Independent Invention: Evidence of Unrealistic Optimism, Risk Seeking or Skewness Loving?" *Economic Journal* 113, no. 484 (2003): 226–39. https://doi.org/10.1111/1468-0297.00089.

Bhide, Amar V. *The Origin and Evolution of New Business*. New York: Oxford University Press, 2000.

Burt, Ronald S. "Structural Holes and Good Ideas." *American Journal of Sociology* 110, no. 2 (2004): 349–99. https://doi.org/10.1086/421787.

Camerer, Colin, and Dan Lovallo. "Overconfidence and Excess Entry: An Experimental Approach." *American Economic Review* 89, no. 1 (1999): 306–18. http://www.jstor.org/stable/116990.

Davidson, Adam. *The Passion Economy*. New York: Murray, 2020.

Kirzner, Israel M. *Competition and Entrepreneurship*. Chicago: University of Chicago Press, 1973.

Klepper, Steven, and Sally Sleeper. "Entry by Spinoffs." *Management Science* 51, no. 8 (2005): 1291–1306. https://www.jstor.org/stable/20110418.

Knight, Frank H. *Risk Uncertainty and Profit*. Eastford, CT: Martino Fine Books, 2014.

Nalebuff, Barry J. *Why Not? How to Use Everyday Ingenuity to Solve Problems Big and Small*. Cambridge, MA: Harvard Business School Press, 2003.

Rosenberg, Nathan. *Exploring the Black Box: Technology, Economics, and History*. Cambridge: Cambridge University Press, 1994.

Seelig, Tina. *Creativity Rules: Get Ideas out of Your Head and into the World*. New York: HarperCollins, 2017.

Shah, Sonali K., and Mary Tripsas. When do user-innovators start firms? Towards a theory of user entrepreneurship? In *Revolutionizing Innovation: Users, Communities and Open Innovation* edited by Dietmar Harhoff and Karim R. Lakhani, 285–307. Cambridge, MA: MIT Press, 2016.

Shane, Scott. "Prior Knowledge and the Discovery of Entrepreneurial Opportunities." *Organization Science* 11, no. 4 (2000): 448–69. http://www.jstor.org/stable/2640414.

von Hippel, Eric. "Lead Users: A Source of Novel Product Concepts." *Management Science* 32, no. 7 (1986): 791–805. https://doi.org/10.1287/mnsc.32.7.791.

Tobi Lütke

Tobias "Tobi" Lütke emigrated from Germany to Canada in 2002 and worked as a computer programmer. Two years later he founded an online snowboard shop, Snowdevil, out of his garage in Ottawa. This fit well with his computer science background and his personal passion for snowboarding and became the seed of the company that eventually became Shopify. The e-commerce company now hosts more than 1.7 million online businesses across 175 countries including Fenty Beauty, Allbirds, Sheertex, Bombas, Tesla, Lindt, Budweiser, Staples, *The Economist,* and Sephora.

In 2004, launching an online store was not a simple affair. While coding Snowdevil's website, Lütke was unable to find decent open-source code for a shopping cart and ended up writing it himself. This happened time and time again. Lütke had to build almost everything on the site from scratch and wondered how people without programming skills could do it. The answer was that they couldn't, and an opportunity for a very different business presented itself.

Lütke and his cofounder, Scott Lake, pivoted from snowboards to pursue the new opportunity, launching Shopify in 2006. Shopify was positioned as a platform that allowed people without programming experience to set up their own online shops out of the box. In 2009, the founders added an application programming interface to allow other developers to provide apps that could be used on Shopify stores. A year later, Shopify went mobile with an iOS app so that owners could manage their shops on the fly.

Shopify as a platform for online stores had all the features you would look for in an opportunity. Given that there were no other tools available, it was a unique opportunity for value creation: allowing people with store ideas to quickly build the technical side of their business. Shopify also had an unfair advantage, as it was an example of a user-generated innovation. Lütke was his own

Shopify founders Tobias Lütke and Scott Lake possessed the necessary user insights, technical background, and passion to make their online e-commerce platform a reality.

first customer and developed the ingredients for Shopify while building Snowdevil. This provided key insight into what customers might need from a platform that provided a technical solution that didn't yet exist. Finally, because Lütke and Lake had a passion for their own business, they saw themselves providing a solution for others who lacked Lütke's programming background.

Snowdevil still exists.[a] Sort of. It is now a Shopify demo store. Shopify is currently valued at over \$200 billion.[b]

Questions

1. What was the entrepreneurial hypothesis for Shopify?

2. What experiences and perspective allowed Lütke and Lake to identify the opportunity for Shopify where others had not?

3. Briefly, how would you evaluate their choice to temporarily leave behind Snowdevil to pursue Shopify?

Jeff Bezos in 1996, in the early days of the new online bookstore he named Amazon

ENTREPRENEUR'S DILEMMA There are numerous strategies you can choose for pursuing your opportunity, but entrepreneurs face a challenge: how long to take before implementing one? Choosing quickly means you may not learn enough about other options to make the best choice. Taking too much time to learn more may cause unneeded delay and make it difficult to choose some options later. Resolving this dilemma requires developing an entrepreneurial strategy.

CHAPTER OBJECTIVES

- Distinguish your opportunity's core idea from your strategy
- Recognize what is unique about the strategic choices facing an entrepreneur
- Learn about the process you can use to develop and choose a strategy
- Realize why entrepreneurs face unique choices they must think strategically about
- Understand how the "Test Two, Choose One" process overcomes the choice challenge and the learning challenge for entrepreneurs
- Identify the broad classes of choices that comprise an entrepreneurial strategy

4

CHOOSING YOUR STRATEGY

In 1994, a young Jeff Bezos, just a few years out of college and working at the investment management firm D.E. Shaw on Wall Street, learned that Internet usage was growing exponentially and contemplated how to take advantage of the new opportunity. After considering ideas ranging from an online stock brokerage to advertising-supported email, Bezos landed on the opportunity of starting an "everything store": an online store that would sell items from nearly all product categories to any consumer with access to the Internet and a mailing address. This, of course, was a huge and unmet opportunity, and one that Bezos was excited to pursue, but where to start? Before implementing any general strategies around his broad idea about e-commerce, Bezos decided to focus in and explore which product category he should serve first. He also needed to find out if people wanted *something* sold using an e-commerce model before doing all the work to get them *everything*.

Rather than picking the first category that looked promising, or trying to assess the promise of the retail sector as a whole, Bezos began a search and assessment of approximately 20 categories, including books, music, and more traditional retail items such as clothing, to find the best option. He ultimately settled on books as the "first best" choice, as he explained in a 1997 video:

> I picked books as the first best product to sell online, making a list of like 20 different products that you might be able to sell. Books were great as the first best because books are incredibly unusual in one respect, that is that there are more items in the book category than there are items in any other category by far. Music is number two, there are about 200,000 active music CDs at any given time. But in the book space there are over 3 million different books worldwide active in print at any given time across all languages,

more than 1.5 million in English alone. So when you have that many items you can literally build a store online that couldn't exist any other way.[1]

In short, Bezos settled on a strategy of starting with books because he learned there was a high ratio between the number of books that could be sold and those that were conventionally made available through brick-and-mortar retail stores. If a typical major bookstore like Barnes & Noble might stock between 10,000 and 15,000 titles, his "store" could stock far more. If for most titles he just took orders and shipped customers titles from the publishers' warehouses, he might even be able to approach the 1.5 million English-language titles available. Thus, book sales appeared to be the best entry point into e-commerce, and Bezos next focused on implementing his choice. This process started with a cross-country trip with his then-wife MacKenzie Scott (a journey that has become part of company folklore), where he explored the idea further, worked on business planning, and made investor phone calls. Their trip started in New York City and ended in Washington State, where Bezos intended to start the business (he chose Washington over California in part to avoid paying California sales taxes). Further, Bezos began training himself for his venture; he attended a community college course on becoming a bookseller and extensively tested how many books he should actually stock.

In 1995, Bezos launched Amazon.com as "the world's largest bookstore." The business focused exclusively on bookselling, and did so for its first five years. But this period was also one of broader learning, gaining experience, and obtaining data on how to initiate Amazon's next step in pursuing the idea of an everything store. Amazon moved into another category—computer games and music—after those initial five years, adding more and more options and services until it became what it is today.[2]

These days, the moves Bezos made and opportunities he saw might seem obvious, but starting by selling books over the Internet in the era of book megastores was a major departure. It illustrates the core challenge for any entrepreneur: learning to make good and strategic choices, typically with very limited information and resources. Bezos did just this. He not only recognized a fundamental opportunity inherent in the rapid rise of the Internet but also engaged in a clear process of exploring and selecting actions to exploit it. Importantly, he chose not to leap at the first opportunity but considered multiple alternative paths for his first product market. And, while he was able to quickly eliminate many alternatives for his initial product (e.g., furniture), his decision to focus first on books came at the expense of other viable alternatives (e.g., music). Bezos's process involved a combination of traditional learning (a course on bookselling at the local community college), experimentation (tests on book stock range), and partial commitment (a five-year focus on books before expanding into other product categories).

Becoming a successful entrepreneur is risky. But the likelihood of success improves if a systematic choice process is used to find the right strategic direction or **entrepreneurial strategy** to take an opportunity forward. In this chapter, we will start to understand and confront these challenges, and begin to use a toolkit/framework/process to do so. Briefly stated,

entrepreneurial strategy A practical and systematic framework of the core choices that entrepreneurs make to translate ideas into a reality

1. An entrepreneur must start by clearly articulating the opportunity *and* the reason why now is the best time to pursue the core idea of the venture. This grounds how the venture will exploit this opportunity, as well as which aspects it can choose or vary in its plan.

2. An entrepreneur will face a large number of alternative paths to pursue but have limited resources to pursue more than one or a very few of them. This creates a *choice challenge* to determine which path to take. Learning about choices can be costly; it can also cut off pursuing other paths in the future.

3. An entrepreneur should learn about possible strategic paths in a systematic way. We have identified a process we call *Test Two, Choose One* (discussed in detail later in the chapter) that helps entrepreneurs select paths systematically, de-risk their choice, and prevent waste (especially of costs and time) that might threaten the viability of their venture. The process helps entrepreneurs understand how to better forecast which paths are likely to be profitable and provides some flexibility for change. It can also surface viable routes that align with an entrepreneur's passion and unique skill set (or, as we explore in later chapters, their *unfair advantages*).

Years after its founding, a new warehouse for Amazon's "everything store" opens in the UK.

Further, we will see that making choices as an individual entrepreneur, or as part of a founding team, requires a different process than those used in established firms. Unlike established firms pursuing new ideas, entrepreneurs need to understand a different approach and way of thinking that will help them get started in a new field or domain. Established firms, for example, typically make decisions that leverage existing capabilities and strengths, often implementing a proven playbook from one market segment to another. They will commercialize new products, often as part of larger initiatives within the company, work with the larger goals and directions of the company, try to predict how markets and competitors will act, and calculate how much market power they have. Entrepreneurs make similar-seeming decisions but with a different perspective. While an entrepreneur does not have to worry about or follow current initiatives in an established firm, they also do not have the time or resources to pursue different opportunities at the same time. And because the core choices of an entrepreneur involve creating a new market (or changing the terms and metrics for engaging in an existing market), an entrepreneur need not and cannot rely on an existing playbook.

Throughout the rest of this book, we will explore the core choices of an entrepreneur and why and how they can be challenging and unique. But further, we will show you a working framework to help you understand and make these choices strategically.

4.1 Forming a Core Idea

We already saw in Chapter 3 that entrepreneurs have certain characteristics that are part of their identity and skill set. They also have a passion for particular ideas and, typically, skills that give them an unfair advantage in some area. But most importantly, every entrepreneur must have a **core idea**. A venture's core idea is the fundamental entrepreneurial opportunity and insight the venture will be built on. It is something that is hard to come by and even harder to move away from. Indeed, in many respects, if you decide to change your core idea, you are really founding an entirely new venture (see **Mini Case: If You Change Your Idea, You Have a New Venture** on p. 90). Along with the entrepreneur themselves, the core idea is the thing that will not change as the venture

core idea The fundamental entrepreneurial opportunity and insight that a venture will be built on

If You Change Your Idea, You Have a New Venture

While entrepreneurs cannot really change their passion or their unfair advantage (at least in the short term), ideas can come and go. For each core idea, there are many possible strategies, and entrepreneurial choice is about selecting between them. But sometimes, ventures form and their core idea changes. This doesn't just reshape the business slightly but creates an entirely new one. Here is a case in point.

Before Instagram, the big start-up for photo sharing was Flickr. When they started in 2002, Flickr's founders had another idea. Caterina Fake and Stewart Butterfield's wish was to create a social game that drove interactions between people. A year later, their project, *Game Neverending*, looked like it would never start. They were running out of money and the game still needed to be developed. What Fake and Butterfield had, however, was a user interface that allowed people to drag game objects around. They then had the inspiration that the user interface could be a great way of sharing photos, and they named the new project Flickr. They also could deploy Flickr quickly, and thanks to a loan from the Canadian government, they had enough runway left to launch this new venture.

Flickr involved a fundamentally different idea than *Game Neverending*. Fake and Butterfield were lucky that some of the *Game Neverending* development led to another business. While legally this all looked like the same company, conceptually Flickr was a new and distinct endeavor. It was also one that would prove to be lucrative, with Flickr selling to Yahoo! in 2005 for $25 million.

The story, however, does not end there. In 2009, Butterfield tried his hand again at a gaming start-up with the Vancouver-based start-up Glitch. It failed, but the founders noticed that a tool they had created to allow better internal communication was a potentially powerful replacement for email. They chose to develop this tool instead, launching it as Slack in 2015. In 2019, Slack went public with a value in excess of $15 billion and, in 2020, the messaging app was sold to software company Salesforce for $27 billion. Once again, one idea had evolved, almost by accident, into another.[a]

The examples of both Flickr and Slack show what happens when a venture starts in one place and then morphs into something different. What is striking and perhaps unusual is how far the venture's idea moved from its original.

Caterina Fake and Stewart Butterfield at the start of Flickr

Stewart Butterfield went on to found Slack, a now widely used collaborative instant messaging tool.

evolves, and crucially, it gives the entrepreneur insight into the choices they will have to make as they form their venture. *In fact, the best way to identify the choices an entrepreneur will need to make is to be able to clearly state the venture's core idea.*

ANALOGIES ARE USEFUL BUT LIMITING

Many entrepreneurs try to describe the core idea of their venture by using an analogy to relate it to an already successful concept. For example, an entrepreneur may claim that what they are doing is, say, "Uber for dog grooming." This is a useful and efficient means of communication. With those four words, someone can readily understand that the new venture is likely some form of mobile service that brings dog groomers to dog owners, on demand. However, no matter how useful communicating by analogy is, there is a trap involved in thinking this way at the outset: it does not show the many choices an entrepreneur will need to make as the venture starts. As we will see below, *a good statement of a core idea should omit references to the venture's initial customer (dog owners), technology (mobile applications), organization (network of groomers), and competition (traditional grooming shops). Instead, it should focus solely on the identified opportunity.*

With this in mind, let's try to understand what the core idea might be for our dog grooming entrepreneur. At present, most dog grooming is conducted with dog owners bringing their dogs to a professional to be groomed, or by mobile services booked in advance. But what happens if a dog needs immediate grooming attention? For instance, say your dog has wallowed around in the mud and muck and is in such a state that you can't just hose him down (especially since you have visitors coming over soon). Taking the dog to a groomer will likely spread the dirt throughout your car, and you don't have time to wait until a slot for a mobile dog groomer comes around. In such cases, an entrepreneur might realize there is some value in an on-demand solution and look for a way to solve it. For example, possible solutions include:

How might an entrepreneur help solve the problems caused by a dirty dog? First, they should start with a clear statement of their core idea.

- Having dog groomers available who could be called out to people's homes. This would involve a logistical challenge, but it would be the job of the entrepreneur to solve that.
- Transporting the dirty dog to dog groomers in a designated vehicle so that the dog owner does not have to use their own car.
- Selling people some solution to allow them to transport dirty dogs in their own cars.

In the end, there are numerous options, and each no doubt has its advantages and disadvantages. The point is that it is not necessarily obvious that the *only* solution is something like Uber. There are other options, and before embarking on any one of them, it is important that an entrepreneur explore them.

FOCUS ON THE SOLUTION INSTEAD

In this particular situation, a well-formed core idea would not be "Uber for dog groomers" but instead a venture better described as "solving the problem of how to clean a dirty animal right away." The key is to state the core idea so that it describes a solution and does not include other important choices. Consider how this might be applied to other famous start-ups:

- Amazon: Use the Internet to order and deliver goods directly to consumers
- Google: Use the Internet to organize the world's information

- Uber: Use mobile technology to easily match riders with rides
- Spanx: Use new materials for clothing shape and comfort
- Flickr: Allow people to store and share photos over the Internet
- Slack: Provide a means for members of an organization to interact with one another
- Twitter: Allow sharing of content quickly and easily

In each case, what the core idea describes is what the venture is doing and, if applicable, the baseline technology that is spurring the idea. With the core idea formed, an entrepreneur can turn to the specific choices that will make it happen. For our dog grooming entrepreneur, important choices in this venture will include

- who the targeted set of customers are (notice that the idea stated here does not mention dogs but animals in general);
- the technology that brings them there (there is no mention of an app on a mobile phone);
- who does what (there is no mention of who grooms the animal); and
- who the competitors are.

These types of choices form the game plan of a venture, a game plan that can change while the core idea can remain the same. In fact, entrepreneurs will face four broad areas or **domains of choice** involving customers, technology, organization, and competition. We will examine each of these in detail in Part 2 of the text, but before we get to that, it is important to consider why choices like these are important and the process by which those choices arise.

4.2 Making Choices: Why Choice Matters

With a well-formed core idea in hand, entrepreneurs often see several routes to commercialize their idea. Indeed, they may see many, many paths to take. However, there are tight constraints in pursuing these paths. For example,

- Entrepreneurs are constrained in terms of the number of paths they can pursue. Their limited time, a lack of resources, and often a need for speed mean that entrepreneurs are frequently forced to select only one path to explore at any given point. For instance, Jeff Bezos had many options regarding what to sell online but, in the end, did not have the resources to pursue more than one initially—even if his vision was to build the everything store.
- It is also difficult to evaluate which path is the "best" path. Right at the outset, there is fundamental uncertainty, not only over the value of the entrepreneur's core idea, but also over which of the multitude of options available are likely to be feasible, let alone successful.
- Entrepreneurs need to explore paths for commercializing their core idea, but that exploration, or learning about the path, is itself costly. It is difficult to obtain clear signals without also committing.

Taken together, the major challenges an entrepreneur faces can be summarized as the *choice challenge* and the *learning challenge*. They create a dilemma for entrepreneurs who want to learn while keeping their options open. For instance, Bezos knew that to explore whether selling books online was possible and profitable would involve a large commitment. It rested on being able to procure a much greater range of titles than brick-and-mortar bookshops. He knew there might be no going back when deciding to launch the world's largest bookstore. He also knew it would not be an easy shift to music and movies if he changed his mind. In fact, mimicking Bezos, someone else could pursue that opportunity, and it could turn out to be the more successful one.

FOR ENTREPRENEURS, CHOICE MATTERS

As we have seen with Jeff Bezos, and as we will see in examples later in this chapter, once an entrepreneur has decided to pursue a strategy (even through initial, small experiments), they are reducing their set of available strategies and entering into a specific, sometimes irreversible business trajectory. *This is why we say that the first broad principle for an entrepreneur is that choice matters . . . their decisions can't be undone.*

Let's turn to **Figure 4.1**. Consider an entrepreneur with an idea (depicted as a gray lightbulb). First, imagine a case where there is one clear strategic path (let's call it the Blue path) associated with the idea. In that case, the entrepreneur would consider the value of the implemented idea against the costs (including opportunity costs) of implementation, and so would be able to choose whether or not to *invest* in the Blue path. If the investment is risky, they might try a limited investment that starts the project while also generating meaningful information

FIGURE 4.1 **The Real Options Approach**

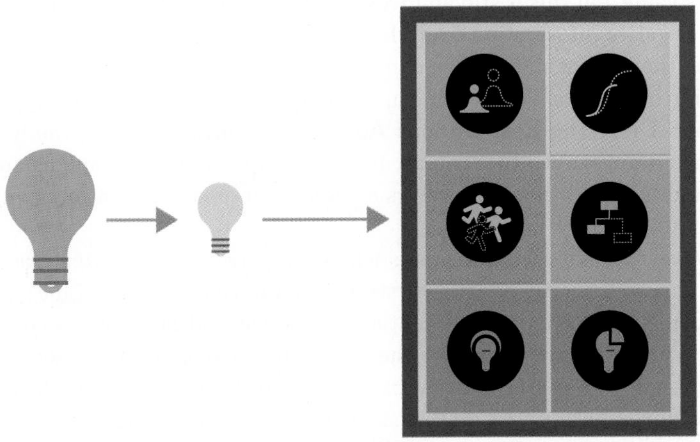

Starting with an initial idea (the gray lightbulb), the entrepreneur can invest in learning (the blue lightbulb). The learning process provides information that lets an entrepreneur decide to implement an entire Blue plan that considers four core choices to create and capture value. We will learn more about these plans in Part 2.

The Real Options Approach

Real options value refers to the value derived from the flexibility to make decisions in response to changing conditions of a business investment or project. It recognizes that entrepreneurs can alter the course of action, scale, timing, or even abandon a project in response to new information or changes in the market.

The concept of real options value is rooted in financial options theory, where an option gives the holder the right, but not the obligation, to buy or sell an asset at a specified price within a certain period. The "real" part of real options means that the decision deploys real resources rather than just the transaction of financial securities.

Consider a pharmaceutical company that has developed a new drug and is deciding whether to invest in a large-scale manufacturing facility. The initial investment required for the facility is significant, and there is uncertainty about the drug's demand and market acceptance. Instead of committing to the full-scale facility immediately, the company could invest in a smaller, pilot-scale facility first. This smaller investment tests the market response and demand for the drug. If the drug proves to be successful and demand is high, the company can then exercise the option to scale up production by investing in the large-scale facility. If the demand is low or the drug faces regulatory issues, the company can abandon the project or repurpose the facility, reducing potential losses.

In this example, the real options value arises from the flexibility to adapt the investment strategy based on new information and changing market conditions, which can help to minimize risk and maximize potential returns. For entrepreneurs, when you are considering a path you may want to explore whether and when to pursue alternatives. When you pursue a test of a path, it eventually provides you with information. The question is: what will you do with that information? The real options approach involves making a limited, but real, commitment to explore the opportunity without committing the full resources to the path.

---

about its value, but this is still an investment in a single, clear direction. If they receive negative information from this limited investment, they will likely discontinue the project rather than continue with the full investment and implementation of the idea. This approach, also known as the **real options approach** (see **Deep Dive: The Real Options Approach**) to investing, is at the heart of the staged nature of venture capital and many other ways of financing an idea. Firms and investors give themselves a choice whether to invest in, change, or discontinue an opportunity.

However, consider what happens when the entrepreneur instead faces not one obvious path but two alternative strategic paths (let's call them Blue and Red, as in **Figure 4.2a**). Each path is potentially profitable, and each path can be tested through a partial commitment. In other words, for each path you can see a way to create or set up a sample product/website/"storefront" to see how it performs. For instance, you might create a pop-up store in a location to see how your products are received by potential customers. If the team pursues one (Blue) path, team members learn more about that path, but in the case where the news about the path is negative, the team is now much *further away* from trying the (Red) alternative. Even if it were possible to reset back to the initial starting point (the original gray lightbulb), the time expended and the reputation developed trying the Blue

real options approach An approach where an entrepreneur gives themselves choices or options to make or abandon an investment

Chapter 4: Choosing Your Strategy

FIGURE 4.2 Initial Choices Make Future Changes Difficult

(a) Choice matters. Experimenting with Blue (or Red) leads the entrepreneur further away from other potentially viable paths. Deciding to try one after already having made a commitment to the other will be more difficult. (b) When Jeff Bezos chose an online bookstore, his choice put him on a path that made switching to another option, a financial services trading company, much harder to do. In particular he would have had a lot to disentangle himself from, and the stock idea may have already been pursued by someone else.

path makes pursuing Red more difficult (e.g., perhaps a competitor has entered this space, or there is limited financial runway available, or there is inertia on the part of the founding team).

In fact, having many or at least two strategic paths to consider is the norm for most entrepreneurs. Making one choice makes it harder to pivot to others. Let's look at this in terms of the founding of Amazon (**Figure 4.2b**). Along with his first employer, David Shaw (a former computer science professor at Columbia who founded D.E. Shaw), Jeff Bezos developed a wide range of potential business plans related to the growth of the Internet, including an advertising-supported email service and an Internet-first financial services trading company. Despite the enormous promise (and potential pitfalls) associated with each of these alternatives, Bezos decided to launch an online bookseller (with the potential to move into other areas of e-commerce). This decision had the consequence of closing off at least for the medium term previously considered paths that also offered high potential. So when Bezos faced challenges over the next several early years at Amazon, his question was not whether to move into financial services. Instead, because his initial choice mattered, he needed to figure out how to make e-commerce work.

4.3 The Choice Challenge

While Bezos decided to pursue books, he considered at least 20 other ideas for his first e-commerce store. But he had to choose one, and most start-ups will only be able to take one initial path—at least at a time. This problem of having many alternatives to consider but also tight constraints on how many can be explored are the two dimensions of the **choice challenge**. Let's look at both.

MANY ALTERNATIVES

For an entrepreneur, it is simply not enough to identify a novel yet plausible plan to apply to a new market. Entrepreneurs must also identify a segment of customers willing to pay (or eventually willing to pay) for the idea, and in most cases, customers willing to change their existing behavior in order to take advantage of

choice challenge A problem that occurs when a venture has many options to consider, but also tight constraints on how many options can reasonably be explored

it (e.g., by purchasing a new good or switching to a new service). For most entrepreneurs with promising core ideas, there are key decision points where there are numerous commercialization alternatives to choose from. These are often critical moments in the founding and scaling of a venture, especially in start-up firms. With no preexisting reputation or historical record to infer "best practices" from, start-ups will have more alternatives to choose from—and more freedom to pursue any of these paths. Many founders have no trouble articulating a single idea to create and capture value. Sometimes, they can even develop multiple ways to do so, and the question is which one of their alternatives is best.

Consider Dropbox. In his 2007 Y Combinator (see Chapter 3) application, founder Drew Houston described multiple ways he might be successful by developing a venture based on his idea of synchronizing files across computers using cloud computing. These included starting an independent business selling storage directly to customers, or potentially having his start-up acquired by a big technology player like Google. Or consider Netflix founder Reed Hastings. He contemplated and tested multiple strategic paths to find value from his core idea to deliver videos to consumers without them leaving their homes. First, he built a business based on replicating the video store experience (including late fees). Then he abandoned those fees altogether with a DVD subscription service that focused on less mainstream content. Hastings also actively sought partnerships with Blockbuster and Amazon. At the same time, he maintained his belief that in the relatively near future, DVDs would not be required and there would be direct online movie delivery.[3]

Both Houston and Hastings understood that there were alternative strategies that could support their ideas. In fact, *having many alternative paths for a given idea implies two important insights about being an entrepreneur:*

- First, successful ideas most often have more than one alternative strategic path that could potentially create and capture value.
- Second, and significantly, there is an important distinction between conceiving the initial core idea (or opportunity!) and the ways to commercialize that idea.

We have seen that Jeff Bezos considered a whole range of product categories with which to start Amazon. It was also part of the plan for Tristan Walker, founder and CEO of Walker & Company, a health and beauty brand designed to better support people of color (**Figure 4.3**).[4] Walker's initial insight came from a problem he had faced for years, annoying irritations called razor bumps that developed on his skin while shaving. This common condition—affecting 80% of Black men and women and 40% of non-Black men and women—lacked a simple solution. His first product, the Bevel Safety Razor, was an elegant updated design based on the single-blade double-edge safety razors used a hundred years ago; this style is superior to the ubiquitous multiblade systems of today in addressing razor bumps (i.e., ingrown hairs). Yet, having established the opportunity, Walker considered multiple paths to commercialize his idea. This included building out a company focused on developing solutions to address other health conditions that affected people of color (including Vitamin D deficiency and hyperpigmentation), simply developing a single-blade system and product line for razor bumps, or partnering his Bevel razor with leading consumer products and shaving companies. In considering these alternative routes, Walker realized

FIGURE 4.3 Tristan Walker on Walker & Company

Tristan Walker on why he thought his product, the Bevel Safety Razor, might have broad success: "A lot of people would, and did, mistrust that you could sell the product that we are selling at scale. There tends to be a pervasive point of view about prioritizing value capture rather than value creation. When you are willing to lean into what you don't know, you ask some questions. Why is the market so small? Well, maybe it's small because the things you sell don't work. There are other examples. Why would I put a bike in my house when I have a gym right down the street? Why would I rent a room in my house to a stranger? Each of those entrepreneurs asked a different kind of question and, ultimately, when you do that, it can yield some interesting results."

that leveraging the resources of an established partner would allow him to build the company that best aligned with this vision and passion—as he said, "to build something that was going to be around 150 years from now, which would serve folks of color—the majority of the world."[5] P&G acquired Walker & Company in 2018.

Of course, there are instances where an entrepreneur's or start-up's plans will not have many alternatives. For example, in the case of drug development, some drugs are developed from the outset for a single, clearly defined patient population. In this case, the key question becomes whether it is worthwhile to invest time and money in trying to serve this particular patient population and choosing not to service other patient types. Here, creating and capturing value from the idea does not require a meaningful *choice* (among customer segments) but instead simply requires a willingness to undertake a risky investment in commercializing the drug.

TIGHT CONSTRAINTS

Having many options is one thing, but what start-ups do not often possess are the resources to explore several of those options at the same time. Unlike their larger counterparts, start-ups cannot diversify their approaches and assign multiple teams for exploration. This forces them to both choose between alternatives and sequence how and if they explore and learn about each option.

Take Starbucks. When you walk into any Starbucks, you are hit with a wide choice of beverages with many options. A similarly wide set of choices was in front of the founding team of the then-fledgling Starbucks Coffee Company in the early 1980s when their new hire, Howard Schultz, suggested an alternative strategy for their idea of introducing high-quality coffee to the United States. At that point, the Starbucks founders had commercialized their idea by selling coffee beans and coffee roasting equipment to home consumers. Schultz, returning from a trip to Milan, proposed an alternative: translating the Italian coffee bar concept to the United States.

Shultz's proposal effectively presented the founders with two alternatives for their future:

1. Starbucks could continue its focus on coffee bean sales, prioritizing decisions like improving its ability to select and source beans and identifying better roasting technologies.
2. The company could focus on retail coffee bars, which prioritized a much different set of decisions, like building expertise in real estate and retail operations.

But these two alternatives seemed strategically inconsistent. On the one hand, the current strategy pitched consumers on purchasing high-quality beans and brewing equipment to have an elevated home coffee experience; on the other hand, the retail café strategy meant convincing consumers to adopt a different, more European way of drinking coffee outside of their home in a community setting. Given its scarce resources at the time, Starbucks could not have achieved both of these visions simultaneously.

In the case of Schultz and Starbucks, this difference in direction caused a split (see the sidebar on **Starbucks' Early Years**). When the founders decided to continue with their initial focus on coffee beans rather than retail, Howard Schultz

Starbucks' Early Years. The original Starbucks store opened in 1971 and sold coffee, teas, and spices. A split over strategy and vision caused then-CEO Howard Shultz to leave Starbucks in 1985; however, he purchased the brand and its six stores in 1987 to realize his original vision.

Starbucks's Alternative Timeline: Peet's Coffee

Peet's Coffee & Tea was founded by Alfred Peet as a local coffee shop in Berkeley, CA, in the 1960s. His fascination with coffee started as a young boy maintaining the equipment in his father's coffee and tea business in the Netherlands. By the time Peet landed in California, he'd spent years in Indonesia learning about the coffee bean and built a career in the coffee import business. However, Peet found the American market inexperienced and relatively uninterested in the high-quality coffee beans he imported. In opening his shop, Peet's idea was to bring better coffee to the American market by combining his quality beans with a carefully calibrated blending and roasting process.

By the early 1970s, with two locations in Berkeley and Menlo Park, Peet's Coffee was an established leader in crafting rich blends for the American consumer. Entrepreneurs and coffee enthusiasts alike sought him out to learn the art and business of coffee. Among these was Jerry Baldwin, one of the cofounders of Starbucks, who had been inspired by Peet's when he founded Starbucks in Seattle in 1971. Starbucks at the time was an outlet for selling coffee beans, not brewed coffee itself, and Peet provided many of those beans. In 1979, Peet sold his four shops, and by 1984, they were in the hands of Baldwin. By 1987, after selling Starbucks to Howard Schultz, Baldwin decided to refocus on Peet's original idea and his commitment to coffee beans.

While Starbucks's growth was explosive, with tens of thousands of cafés opening across the globe, Peet's expanded very slowly. Baldwin's desire was to ensure that only the best coffee beans were used, but the scarcity of that supply also constrained Peet's. As a result, Peet's Coffee achieved a more modest level

Peet's Coffee was built around a choice to prioritize roasting and blending only the best coffee beans. Shown are samples from a Peet's tasting event.

of scale, with just over 200 locations by 2018. Throughout this growth, Peet's built its reputation in the coffee roasting and blending business and expanded to other retail channels, including selling in grocery stores.

It is easy to conclude that Baldwin made the "wrong" choice with Peet's strategy compared to Schultz's with Starbucks. However, Peet's itself has proven to be a respected venture with locations all over the United States. It was valued at $1 billion when it was acquired by a private equity group. Instead, we should understand that the core idea of both Starbucks and Peet's was so strong that it could support multiple, simultaneous paths to market.

SOURCE: Stacy Finz, "Peet's Coffee Sold to Private German Firm," *SFGATE*, July 23, 2012, https://www.sfgate.com/business/article/Peet-s-Coffee-sold-to-private-German-firm-3729283.php.

left Starbucks to found the coffee bar Il Giornale. Because the team needed to focus on only one direction to be successful, they had to break apart when different members felt strongly about the way to go. But in this case, both paths ended with success. Shultz, of course, succeeded in scaling his coffee bars and eventually purchased the rights to the name Starbucks from the founders. However, the founding group kept at their plan, too, and found success with a new brand, Peet's Coffee (see **Mini Case: Starbucks's Alternative Timeline**).

This tension between multiple, competing visions for a venture are common—even perhaps fundamental—to the process of entrepreneurship. In many cases, a focus on one vision requires team attention and resources that will keep a team from working on the competing vision (at least in the short term). This was the case as the Starbucks founders sought to build on their idea to bring high-quality coffee to the United States. In other cases, the competing visions come from

Design Choices: Tinder vs. Bumble. Online dating apps Tinder and Bumble both have users swipe to select potential matches based on short profiles. However, Bumble put women in control of the initial contact, a key differentiator from Tinder. As Bumble's head of product design stated in 2019, "Most of all, it's a women-first app. We don't hide that. It's part of our mission. Solving problems for women is something that will solve problems for everyone. Part of that is a principle that I believe in that when you choose a vulnerable user, instead of an average user, you are designing for more people and designing a product that will be better for people in general."[a]

choices and an organizational identity that are simply incompatible with each other. Consider the founding of Bumble, the popular online dating app. Founder Whitney Wolfe Herd created Bumble after she left Tinder, a competing online dating app. Though both apps built on the opportunity for online date matching, they did so in dramatically different ways. For instance, Tinder launched the now ubiquitous "swipe right" or "swipe left" feature in its simple design that prioritized ease of matching over detailed profiles and compatibility tests, common in other dating apps at the time. Though this ease offered advantages, especially for short-term relationships, Wolfe Herd saw a problem with Tinder's reliance on old-fashioned gender dynamics.[6] She set out to build a dating app focused on empowering women, where, as Wolfe Herd explained, "women made the first move, and sent the first message."[7] Such a commitment prioritized a distinct set of features in her app's design, as well as other strategic choices within the company like branding and target marketing to "level the playing field." These features weren't necessarily compatible with Tinder's priorities (see the sidebar on **Design Choices: Tinder vs. Bumble**).[8] Simply put, you can't be Tinder and Bumble at the same time.

Ultimately, for start-ups, *financial and organizational resource constraints make it difficult to pursue more than one alternative at the same time*. This idea perhaps most clearly sets start-ups apart from larger, mature firms. Typically, established firms face relatively fewer resource constraints than a start-up, and often it is possible for them to explore multiple commercialization paths for a given idea (e.g., conducting parallel tracks in internal competition with each other). Start-ups, instead, must reconcile the tension between the freedom to choose among a wide array of alternatives and the financial and organizational resource constraints limiting them to pursuing one alternative at a time. In other words, while an established firm (or even an investor) simply has to choose which risky investments to undertake, a start-up must make a *single choice* between meaningful alternatives.

4.4 The Learning Challenge

When an entrepreneur or founding team has an idea with (1) many alternatives but (2) tight constraints, their next step is to figure out the best of these to pursue to launch their venture. How this is done will significantly influence future choices and the subsequent path of the venture. For example, the venture might use an unstructured approach and implement what seems to be the most reasonable alternative they have. Or they might decide to make a highly structured comparison of a wide range of these alternatives.

But in general, if an entrepreneur is uncertain about their core idea and unclear which strategic path to take, they should learn as much about each path as possible before going forward. However, these partial attempts to learn about each path will be constrained, imperfect, and "noisy." This situation forms the basis of the topic of this section, the **learning challenge**.

learning challenge The difficulty an entrepreneur faces in learning as much as possible about each potential path before moving forward

business risk The probability of several business outcomes occurring, especially the risk of failure

fundamental uncertainty A challenge around whether an entrepreneur is realistically conceptualizing business scenarios around their idea

FUNDAMENTAL UNCERTAINTY

When we think about an opportunity, we often try to evaluate its **business risk**, considering the probability of several business outcomes occurring, especially those that might lead to poor performance or failure. In an established business, we might try to determine the risk of expanding operations into a new country based on results of previous expansions. While entrepreneurs face a lot of business risk, they also face another challenge, a **fundamental uncertainty** about whether they are realistically conceptualizing business scenarios around their idea in the first place. Entrepreneurs always face uncertainty about the underlying quality of their idea.

But how do these ideas of risk and uncertainty differ? Consider the following example involving a simple roll of a die. When you roll a six-sided, fair die, the probability of any one side resting on top is 1 in 6. That is, if you were betting on, say, a "5" showing up, the risk you would lose all of your money would be 5 in 6, and you can be very sure of this (**Figure 4.4**). When we can specify the exact probabilities and do a clear-cut risk calculation, the process of making decisions is straightforward. This is well understood in gambling, where the odds of any situation can be calculated. It can also apply to things like weather forecasting, where the science has progressed far enough that we can be reasonably confident in the likelihood of predicted events occurring. Or when you buy insurance, the price of that insurance takes into account a data-driven assessment of the risk that you might get into a car accident, become sick, or have a house fire.

Known probabilities are not simply true in the case of well-defined games of chance or states of nature or

FIGURE 4.4 **Risk vs. Uncertainty**

In the roll of a six-sided die, the risk of any one side not coming up is easy to calculate. It's 5 in 6. If you were told that someone may have altered the die and its roll was no longer fair, you would be uncertain about how to bet.

behavior; they do, in fact, impact many standard business decisions. For example, when a franchisor agrees to extend a franchise contract to a new location, they do so knowing that a certain percentage of new franchisees fail within their first year (at some cost to the franchisor). Once the franchisor has worked with enough franchisees, they would be able to calculate the approximate rate at which their "model" is likely to work or not.

But suppose you are told, or at least think, that the die being rolled is not a fair one. In that situation, you may know there are six possible outcomes from that roll, but you may not be able to assign probabilities to any one of them with confidence. In that case, if you were betting on a "5" showing up, you don't know whether the probability of that event is 1 in 6 or something lower like 1 in 12 or higher like 1 in 4. As we will see, the same is true when you take a new idea and introduce a product based on that idea in the marketplace. You just don't know the probability that it will be successful. There is no die to structure your understanding of the scenario and the likely probabilities. This is what fundamental uncertainty is.

ENTREPRENEURIAL DECISIONS ARE UNCERTAIN

While people sometimes liken entrepreneurship to "risk-taking," in reality, the situation is much more perilous as entrepreneurs will have insufficient information to confidently assign probabilities to different outcomes. Entrepreneurial decisions fall closer to the uncertainty end of the spectrum. Simply put, one of the reasons why we can understand the roll of a die or how weather is predicted is that these are familiar situations. For new ideas, by their very definition, there is novelty and rarely a basis to assign probabilities of potential success or failure. Further, even the nature of the uncertainty governing the value of an idea is not known by the entrepreneur.

What does this mean for an entrepreneur? Consider, for example, if the first business plan a founding team develops seems to indicate extraordinary potential, a sign that the underlying idea is strong too. Because of uncertainty, entrepreneurs should treat even the most optimistic projections with skepticism. In fact, *since positive feedback about a given strategy indicates the overall idea is valuable, founding teams might take this as a sign that an even better alternative plan exists.*

Why is this? Any business planning in a start-up will be filled with assumptions and often depends on analogies from other start-ups or businesses in similar, but not identical, circumstances. Whether a start-up develops a formal business plan, sketches a brief business model summary or flowchart, or simply settles on a compelling pitch deck for investors, the promise of the proposed strategy is based on a noisy and highly uncertain estimate of the potential of the venture (see **Using the Research: Uncertainty in Start-Up Ideas**). For instance, founders will have to estimate answers to questions about the following:

- The size and the speed of penetration into the market
- The cost of customer acquisition as well as the cost of goods
- The way technologies and innovations being leveraged might evolve
- The degree of traction with eventual customers

Uncertainty in Start-Up Ideas

Does the type of start-up idea and the nature of the uncertainty it faces affect the predictability of that idea's success? To explore these questions, researchers empirically studied the evaluations of 537 early-stage start-ups founded by MIT students and alumni in high-growth industries. These evaluations, performed by 251 experienced entrepreneurs, investors, and executives, were never disclosed to the entrepreneurs, and the assessments themselves did not affect the start-up (e.g., by possibly influencing access to mentoring or funding). Yet, without having met the founding team and with only the information contained in brief, half-page summaries, these evaluators successfully gauged the quality and subsequent success of the early-stage ventures. The explicit start-up and entrepreneur characteristics (such as start-up sector, start-up progress, or founding team experience) contained in the written summaries were not necessary to make their judgments—the strength of the idea spoke for itself.

However, the researchers found something else. They found that the experts could only effectively evaluate start-ups in sectors such as hardware, energy, life sciences, and medical devices. They were not successful in markets such as consumer products, consumer web and mobile, and enterprise software sectors. The researchers suggested that the information needed to assess start-ups depends on the nature of the uncertainty they face. For instance, in settings where the technological uncertainty associated with the start-up idea is high relative to the market uncertainty (e.g., a new insulin treatment), one can compare the idea to successful commercialization of products using similar technologies. However, where market uncertainty is relatively high (e.g., a new service targeted at enterprise customers), it may be more difficult to predict consumer behavior.[a]

- The pace and nature of competition
- The strength and relevance of competitive tools such as intellectual property protection

Consider the early days of PillPack. In 2013, founders Elliot Cohen and TJ Parker came together in a healthcare-focused hackathon to explore an idea Parker had been considering—to presort prescription medicines and directly ship them to consumers, a concept that built upon his and his family's extensive experience in the pharmacy business. By the end of the two-day hackathon, Cohen and Parker had designed an early version of the PillPack packaging (a roll of bags of medications presorted by the time of day of each dose; see **Figure 4.5**) and the business model (an online pharmacy) and were convinced the opportunity was enormous. Yet in the months that followed and through their time at the accelerator Techstars Boston, the two faced a tough challenge in choosing between three potential initial customer groups: elderly patients with multiple chronic conditions, middle-aged patients after their first major medical incident (such as a heart attack), or relatively healthy consumers with highly individualized and complex vitamin and supplement routines.[9] Making a decision meant dealing with a lot of uncertainty. Understanding and estimating the nuances of each market was a very difficult task because of the complexities of the retail pharmacy industry and its strict layers of regulations, and because of factors like the rise of pharmaceutical benefit managers such as Express Scripts. Opinions were also mixed as to how quickly larger competitors—such as Walgreens or even Express Scripts—might copy their packaging if the idea proved valuable.

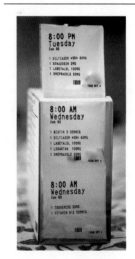

FIGURE 4.5 PillPack

PillPack's unique packaging idea in which pill doses are presorted for customers, labeled, and organized by the times they should take them.

The Cone of Uncertainty

The cone of uncertainty is a measure of how the degree of uncertainty surrounding an idea changes over time as founders learn more about a specific entrepreneurial strategy for their idea. The idea originally came from the American Association of Cost Engineers, which published a set of uncertainty ranges in 1958 as cone illustrations; it has been used in many other fields since then, including software engineering and weather prediction. Using the process of experimentation and learning to narrow the cone of uncertainty offers founders an opportunity to explore the key assumptions behind their idea as well as the feasibility and relative worth of alternative paths. It is, of course, important to recognize that the process of testing cannot resolve all sources of uncertainty, as some degree of uncertainty is inherent to any novel enterprise (or unknowable at a reasonable cost and within a reasonable time frame). Notably, at the earliest stages of key technological breakthroughs or consumer change, alternative visions of the future compete with each other, and there is little hard data upon which to discriminate one perspective over the other.

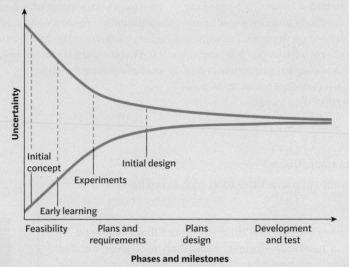

The cone of uncertainty narrows during development. At the initial concept, estimates can be very high or low, creating a large area of uncertainty. This narrows as the project progresses.

But despite this uncertainty, Cohen and Parker felt their estimates provided clear evidence that the product could create real, meaningful value for consumers. PillPack chose to focus first on middle-aged patients after their first major medical incident, but then quickly found traction with other customers as they rolled out their novel packaging design and online pharmacy across the United States. In 2018, PillPack was acquired by Amazon for nearly $1 billion.[10]

In the end, even when it works like it did with PillPack, relying on often uncertain estimates leads some to question the value and practicality of the business planning process for start-ups. But, perhaps a bit counterintuitively, it is precisely this high level of uncertainty that justifies undertaking an active and iterative process. The more uncertain an outcome, the more important it is to learn something certain about the opportunity before getting started (see **Deep Dive: The Cone of Uncertainty**).

LIMITS OF COMMITMENT-FREE LEARNING

Given all the uncertainty, it would seem wise to at least try to keep your learning as commitment-free as possible and have more options open. This typically does not work as well as planned. Consider the following analogy. If you are cooking vegetable soup, you want to add just enough salt for your taste. Too little salt and the soup tastes bland. Too much salt and the soup is inedible. An experienced cook would be able to select the right amount of salt to match a given quantity of soup. But what should you do when you are just learning to cook soup in the first place?

One thing for sure is that you have to put some salt in the soup in order to work out what the right amount is. In other words, there is no way to learn without trying. But that also leads to another fact: if you add too little salt, you can always add some more, whereas the reverse is not true. One approach is to try to add a little bit of salt, taste, and then add more until you reach the flavor you are looking for. This approach allows you to learn without commitment.

This approach will get you a tasty soup, but it has caution built in that likely won't get you the *best-tasting* soup. At some point, you have to not hold back and add an amount of salt that might risk you adding more salt that you want. By trying to avoid an irreversible situation, you don't ever make a big enough commitment. If you never want to risk having an inedible batch of soup, you will never reach the best-tasting soup.

Entrepreneurs face a similar dilemma when they try to research and learn about the potential value of their idea. While they can use commitment-free, limited, quick, or basic experiments to learn a little about the value of their idea and of particular strategies, it is often hard to resolve important questions without committing to build out the idea or put it in motion. For instance, a supplier of a new camera system for a self-driving car might want downstream manufacturers to invest in designs that make use of that system. However, if the supplier builds a small-scale plant in the hope of seeing how the product does in the market before scaling up, manufacturers may be reluctant to put effort and resources into new designs. They are not sure there is commitment to invest in larger manufacturing. In this situation, building a small-scale plant would give the supplier negative feedback on their idea, whereas building enough capacity with a larger-scale commitment may have revealed that their idea is valuable and worthwhile. Their initial experiments were just too limited, generating inaccurate, noisy learning.

Ultimately, entrepreneurs find that there is only so far that low-commitment experimenting with their idea will take them. This leads to the notion that *commitment-free learning can only generate noisy estimates of the value of an idea and an alternative*.

At some point, it will become necessary to make a choice to learn more clearly. In fact, the limited nature of what you can learn with low-commitment processes is important. It means that given the uncertainty and overall noise in the learning process, no amount of business planning or detailed analysis can yield a precise and accurate forecast of the returns to a given strategy. The inherent limits on what can be learned without commitment is at the heart of a concept introduced in Chapter 1, the paradox of entrepreneurship: choosing between alternative strategies requires knowledge that an entrepreneur can only gain through

To get the best tasting soup, eventually you have to commit to how you season it (and maybe then see what Gordon Ramsey thinks of it).

commitment. But as we saw earlier in this chapter, committing to one pathway (for example, the Blue or Red path in Figure 4.2) might potentially close down exploring another later.

Ultimately, entrepreneurs must experiment, but a truly live experiment not only helps the entrepreneur but also shapes the market. It makes information available to potential competitors and suppliers and can even impact customers' expectations in unrelated market segments. In short, the activities essential to choosing a start-up's strategy and evaluating the efficacy of the core idea (learning and experimentation) are in tension with what an entrepreneur must do to establish and sustain competitive advantage (strategic commitment).

Disciplined entrepreneurs proactively transition from learning through commitment-free analysis to making and pursuing one choice. But doing this makes it harder to switch gears and try another path. We look at this next.

4.5 Test Two, Choose One

To review, imagine if there was only one available alternative open to the entrepreneur to commercialize their idea. What does this tell you about the idea itself? Can an idea really be of high value if there is only one type of, say, customer, or one way of building a working product that can build a profitable venture? This is unlikely. Thus:

A choice challenge is something that accompanies ideas that are likely to be of high quality.

Further, evaluating a wide number of alternatives gives a sense for the range of value in an idea:

With a really promising idea, a founding team can often determine multiple promising plans.

We saw this earlier in the case of Amazon and Dropbox, and with Starbucks and Peet's. On the other hand, for a mediocre idea, the team, at best, will be able to identify only a single viable path forward. Similarly, imagine if it were obvious which path among the available alternatives was the best one to choose. If it is so obvious how you can take a high-quality idea and bring it to market, is this the sort of opportunity that will be unique to you, as an entrepreneur, to develop? Probably not. Thus:

Learning challenges accompany ideas whose pursuit and development are not obvious. By surfacing multiple paths to pursue for a core idea, even if some are highly uncertain, the team should feel more confident about their idea.

When the team begins identifying multiple concrete plans that meaningfully realize the potential value of their idea, then they should move beyond searching and choose and implement one. We summarize this best practice with the idea of **Test Two, Choose One**:

For a given idea, entrepreneurs should only begin to commit to one business plan after considering multiple strategic alternatives and identifying at least two that are commercially viable yet difficult to rank.

With this mind, let's break down both parts.

Test Two, Choose One A process in which entrepreneurs commit to only one business plan after considering multiple strategic alternatives and identifying at least two that are commercially viable yet difficult to rank

Chapter 4: Choosing Your Strategy

WHY MAKE TWO PLANS? THE CHOICE CHALLENGE

Entrepreneurs are often asked to construct a business plan to work through one of the options that may be available. However, at best, this can lead to a decision to "go"—pursue that option—or "stop"—put it aside and either find another or not pursue the opportunity at all. Successful entrepreneurs, however, will want to manage their tight resources more effectively by making a considered choice. To this end, a better approach is to evaluate more than one option: at a minimum, to construct two distinct business plans rather than just one. By doing that, the entrepreneur sets themselves up to explore at least two paths and make a more informed choice. You will see this principal used throughout the book. We want to show you how to create a procedure that implements Test Two, Choose One as a way of confronting the learning and choice challenges you will inevitably face as you consider a venture.

This process is not easy: it means that, at the moment of their choice, a founding team will not be able to identify one clear path forward but will be forced to choose among competing viable alternative paths for their venture. When Jeff Bezos realized the potential value of e-commerce, his investigations suggested many potential segments could be the foundations of a profitable business. At the same time, books were an especially favorable category from his perspective given the wide range of titles and ease of delivery. Bezos's belief that many segments *could* work as the first step for Amazon made him more confident that books *would* work as a beachhead.

Similarly, a negative assessment not only cautions against that particular approach, but also the potential value of the underlying idea. Consider the much-maligned Juicero, the $400 Internet-enabled juice machine (**Figure 4.6**) that was dubbed the "Keurig for juice." Founder Doug Evans spent three years designing the revolutionary press that squeezed single-serving packs of sliced fruits and vegetables into fresh juice. Only after raising $120 million to develop the product did Evans (as well as Juicero's investors and potential customers) realize that the device was redundant—manually squeezing the packs of fruit and vegetables resulted in roughly the same glass of fresh juice and, in most cases, at a faster rate than using the device.[11] Had Evans considered multiple strategies (for example, creating a simple device that helped with the squeezing process or designing packaging like an instant first-aid cold pack where hand squeezing combined ingredients) before committing to the technology and model, he may have better understood the potential flaws in his assumptions and in the idea itself.[12]

FIGURE 4.6 **The Juicero**

A Juicero was an expensive machine that could squeeze juice from fresh fruit and vegetable packets automatically. It was roundly mocked when it was reported that you could get the same outcome just by squeezing the packets with your bare hands. Considering different paths for this idea may have led to a more successful venture.

FIGURE 4.7 Fyre Festival Failure

A concierge "desk" with no concierge. The Fyre Festival showed the typical results of "flying blind."

In fact, it seems obvious that "flying blind" is costly and precarious, but the reality is that entrepreneurs do so all the time. In 2017, entrepreneur Billy McFarland decided to promote his nascent music booking app, Fyre, by teaming up with rapper Ja Rule to launch the Fyre Festival. The event was billed as a first-of-its-kind musical festival to bring elite artists and influencers together for a weekend on Norman's Cay, a beautiful but remote uninhabited island in the Bahamas. Regardless of the promise of the underlying idea, the practical challenges of implementing it were essentially insurmountable (**Figure 4.7**). Despite receiving more than $26 million in advance bookings and payments for this exclusive event, the team lost their lease to the uninhabited island (forcing a switch of venue to the populated Great Exuma island), lost the bulk of their promised talent, and failed to provide a meaningful level of shelter for festival attendees who had paid in advance for a luxury island experience. Not simply a failure of execution on its own, the failure of the Fyre Festival led directly to the collapse of the underlying company and ultimately landed McFarland in prison on a conviction of wire fraud.

Or consider the novel camera introduced by scientist Ren Ng and his team at Lytro, which allowed for "refocusing" *after* a picture was taken (an approach known as plenoptic photography). Though undoubtedly innovative (indeed, the core technical insights featured prominently in Ng's 2006 doctoral dissertation), Lytro not only waited more than six years before introducing a product but received essentially no meaningful customer feedback prior to launch. The founding team and early investors placed so much faith in the transformative potential of their technology that they failed to test whether there was meaningful customer demand for that technology.

WHAT SHOULD I TEST? THE LEARNING CHALLENGE

Having confronted the choice challenge by articulating two business plans, the entrepreneur is now in a position to test those plans. This is the "Test Two" of the Test Two, Choose One approach, which aims to learn enough about the two business plans not to resolve all uncertainty but to make a choice. But what does an effective test look like?

An effective test of a business plan or strategic path satisfies two distinct but fundamental conditions:

- **Condition 1:** At its core, the first condition for a test is that real-world information is being used. Any test involves not simply hypothesizing about the potential for value creation and capture but actively gathering new information about the underlying hypothesis. There are, of course, many types of information to try to gather, ranging from very precise numerical data to more qualitative observations, and many ways to gather information, from individual interviews to detailed experiments.

- **Condition 2:** The second condition is that a test must help founders choose whether to pursue a given strategy with the information they have gathered and the learning they have done. A good test generates an "option" to proceed without actually committing to do so.

Let's see how this works using a classic example. Cold, wet feet were a common part of Leon Leonwood (L.L.) Bean's frequent hunting trips in the forests of his native Maine. While returning from such a trip in 1911, Bean realized that leather uppers stitched to ordinary workmen's rubber boots might present an opportunity to resolve this widespread problem of traditional hiking boots. As a first test, Bean hired a cobbler to craft versions of his hybrid leather-rubber boots to weigh his underlying hypothesis (condition 1). Once convinced of the potential technical feasibility of these functional, waterproof boots, he mailed a flyer to a small list of out-of-state hunters (condition 2), declaring

> You cannot expect success hunting deer or moose if your feet are not properly dressed. The Maine Hunting Shoe is designed by a hunter who has tramped the Maine woods for the last 18 years. We guarantee them to give perfect satisfaction in every way.[13]

Interest in these new boots was considerable. However, almost all of those initial orders were returned, as the leather uppers split from the rubber boots with regular wear. Though disappointed, Bean refunded the customers as he had promised in his flyer. Stepping back, Bean realized this test had provided him with both an indication of strong demand for such boots as well as detailed product feedback from customers. With this new information, he committed to the idea and undertook an extensive process to correct the failures in his prototype boots (even borrowing funds to do so). With the problem resolved, Bean mailed out his brochures to an even broader list of hikers and outdoors enthusiasts. Demand for Bean's quality boots (**Figure 4.8**) and outdoor gear quickly grew, and over 100 years later L.L. Bean's reputation for quality products and superior customer service remains.

TESTING TRADE-OFFS

Most early-stage entrepreneurial experiments are not as decisive as L.L. Bean's. *Most founders face trade-offs between three competing elements of their experiment's design:*

1. Criticality: the relative importance of what is being tested in the overall entrepreneurial strategy
2. Fidelity: the degree to which a test provides meaningful and informative feedback to the founders
3. Opportunity cost: the overall cost, including resources, time, and strategic commitments, required to conduct the test

Each of these three elements of experimental design are important, and often there are natural trade-offs between them in testing (**Figure 4.9**). Tests that are both critical

FIGURE 4.8 **The Bean Boot**

An early design of Bean's first boot is in the foreground, with the latest version from L.L. Bean in the back.

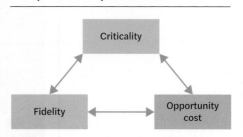

FIGURE 4.9 **A Strategic Approach to Entrepreneurial Experimentation**

While an "ideal" experiment tests a critical hypothesis with high-fidelity and low opportunity costs, most entrepreneurial experimentation involves a trade-off between criticality, fidelity, and opportunity cost.

and have high fidelity—such as those conducted in a clinical trial process in the pharmaceutical industry—are often extremely expensive (drug development can cost hundreds of millions of dollars prior to FDA approval). Conversely, cheap experiments most often come with high levels of noise. The absolute lowest-cost customer interviews are likely through contacts with friends or family, whose opinions or impressions may differ from "real" customers whose feedback would be more useful but far more difficult to access. Founding teams should try to explore each element in turn when designing their experiments. In the next section, we'll look at just how to design an effective experiment.

4.6 Best Principles for Testing

To learn about best principles for testing and experimentation, let's examine the start of a design empire by Vera Wang. In the late 1980s, Wang was working in New York as a design director for Ralph Lauren when, at age 39, she went shopping for a bridal gown. Frustrated by the lack of elegant modern wedding dresses, she personally designed the dress for her own wedding. Wang recognized a broad opportunity to bring modern "fashion" to the wedding dress industry, an idea that was met with skepticism from leading designers (Calvin Klein told her she was crazy).

Undeterred, Wang undertook two critical experiments at the earliest stages of her venture to test her idea and strategy (**Figure 4.10**). First, to test her hypothesis that the modern wedding dress segment was underserved, she opened a single Madison Avenue bridal salon featuring hand-selected gowns from other

This chapter's video describes the learning and experimentation that Vera Wang engaged in before founding her iconic fashion brand.

FIGURE 4.10 **Vera Wang**

Vera Wang tested demand for her gown designs alongside those of established designers in the first years of her Madison Avenue salon, which is still wildly successful today (and now dedicated solely to her designs).

designers. This let her see whether there was demand for her vision among sophisticated New York consumers. But more importantly, Wang hoped to pursue a strategy in which she would design and produce wedding dresses of her own. To test this hypothesis, she inserted a select number of her own personally designed gowns within the inventory featured in her salon. While this experiment involved only a small level of risk for the salon business, it proved enormously informative about the potential demand for Vera Wang–designed dresses, since it put her dresses in direct competition with those from elite established designers. Wang's shop and designs were successes, allowing her to learn with high confidence about the robustness of her core entrepreneurial idea and strategy. Championed by the likes of actress Uma Thurman and Olympic figure skater Nancy Kerrigan, Wang's high-fidelity (but medium-cost) experimentation ushered in a new era for wedding gowns and reshaped the bridal industry.[14]

Vera Wang's experiments focused on the most critical assumptions and invested resources to create a clear limited-commitment test; though informative, that path also involved a reasonable level of cost (e.g., she needed to open up an actual shop and also design and make a wedding dress). It was a proactive approach that sharpened her understanding of her initial strategy and how to scale her venture.

It also demonstrates the potential for testing. A small number of critical guidelines can help guide this process.

FIRST, TAKE A PEEK BEFORE WALKING THROUGH A ONE-WAY DOOR

At the earliest stages of a venture, founders have the widest scope for strategic choice but the least amount of information about the value of alternative paths. At the earliest stages, founders need to place a premium on learning without commitment.

Consider how the relationship between learning and commitment changes prior to launching an actual product versus immediately after launching that product. In the first case, you can use tactics such as presenting prototypes, developing mock brochures or online landing pages, or employing qualitative feedback from customers about potential needs. Though enormously valuable, this type of learning will pale in its depth and clarity relative to what you learn after a product is launched. At this point, customers respond with specific reviews and suggestions, and the venture observes the actual level of demand as opposed to less meaningful expressions of interest. However, the learning that occurs after product launch comes with a much higher level of commitment, as responding to feedback by altering (i.e., redesigning) the product or retargeting to a different beachhead customer segment now comes at a higher cost.

Putting this together, the goal at the earliest stage is to gain some sense of what a particular strategic alternative might be like (i.e., take a peek) and shift only later toward a commitment that cannot be reversed (i.e., walking through a one-way door).

SECOND, TEST SMALL TO CHOOSE BIG

An entrepreneurial strategy hypothesis cannot be true "in general" without being true somewhere in particular. For most entrepreneurial strategies, it

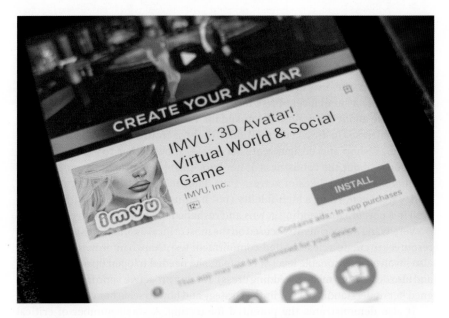

IMVU. Erie Ries started IMVU in 2004 as a new social network and virtual world, rapidly and continuously updating, revising, and releasing new versions using the feedback he got from users. Ries came to this process after a first start-up had failed; he wanted to start a new one by learning from his mistakes. As he later wrote, he found that "it's the boring stuff that matters the most" and that "startup success can be engineered by following the right process, which means it can be learned, which means it can be taught."[a]

should be possible to identify a test at a pilot scale (e.g., a smaller market, limited geographic scope, limited product offering) that maximizes the amount of critical learning at the lowest opportunity cost. This insight is at the heart of the "minimum viable product" (or MVP) concept pioneered by Eric Ries and the Lean Startup movement. (see the sidebar on **IMVU** and later in Chapter 13). When launching his virtual world and social networking site IMVU in 2004, Ries purposefully limited the level of functionality in the initial design. This MVP approach enabled a greater range of exploration through experiments with early users and its more limited scope conserved Ries' team's scarce time and resources. Similarly, we saw earlier that by opening a single shop and featuring only a few dresses of her own design, Vera Wang conducted a simple but powerful test of her venture.

At first, a premium should be placed on learning rather than scale. This will often mean focusing tests not on the largest or most profitable customer segments but on customers that facilitate the highest level of feedback and learning. This allows the start-up to potentially pursue that path and obtain feedback while maintaining the option to continue to consider other alternatives. By focusing on a small but informative test, a practice known as "nail it, then scale it," you hit the most critical assumptions with a high-fidelity test at a lower opportunity cost.

One particular way to implement this approach is to limit geographic scope at the earliest stages of a venture. For example, when Chuck Templeton founded the online restaurant reservation service OpenTable in San Francisco, his core value-creation hypothesis revolved around how an online fine dining reservation system would also need to handle restaurant seating management (and staffing and the like). Templeton, his team, and investors patiently focused their tests on only a few markets for several years before scaling their service to leading metropolitan areas across the United States and the world. They felt if an online reservation system could work anywhere, it could work in San Francisco and this market was particularly helpful for providing feedback. And, once it worked in San Francisco, the team believed (correctly) that the model could be transferred with minimal adaptation to a range of other cities.

THIRD, LEARN ENOUGH TO KNOW WHAT TO BE UNCERTAIN ABOUT

When exploring alternative strategies, there are a wide range of unknowns, and many initial assumptions—even the most critical ones—may turn out to be false. As we emphasized earlier, there may be some critical areas of learning that are, in fact, easy to validate (e.g., the status of a legal rule), while other areas may require a much higher level of time and effort. Before testing begins, the entrepreneur should write a clear statement of the most critical assumptions underlying that strategy. With this in hand, they should also:

a. Test whether they have a complete list by imagining that each of the stated assumptions is valid. If true, also question if there are any other critical barriers or obstacles to creating and capturing value as a venture?
b. Consider the degree of confidence in each of those assumptions. In most cases, the confidence level for an assumption will be more qualitative than quantitative. The key is to identify those critical assumptions that are highly uncertain and need to be tested.

High uncertainty surrounding multiple critical assumptions can dramatically reduce the potential for success (see **Deep Dive: The Mathematics of Criticality in Entrepreneurial Experimentation**). Identifying the most critical assumptions

DEEP DIVE

The Mathematics of Criticality in Entrepreneurial Experimentation

Consider a venture with three distinct sources of uncertainty (say, customer, technology, and competition, each of which has only a 10% chance of being viable). If each of these hypotheses are independent (customer viability is separate from technological feasibility), then the total probability of success of the venture facing these risks is 0.1% (1 in 1,000). That is well below the level at which a founder is likely to attract resources (e.g., employees or finance) or even be worth the time of the team.

A critical test of one of these assumptions can move the venture from a 1 in 1,000 chance to a 1 in 100 chance. Two could allow the venture to face a 1 in 10 chance of viability or success. Though still quite risky, a 1 in 10 chance is likely to attract human and financial resources. In other words, one does not need to resolve every critical hypothesis, but the combination of multiple sources of risk (e.g., greater than two sources whose likelihood is relatively low) likely signals that the venture is not yet in a position to attempt to scale. *Put another way, a venture seeking to launch an entrepreneurial strategy can allow for one (but not more than one!) "miracle" when choosing to launch a particular entrepreneurial strategy.*

What tests can you carry out to increase a venture's chances of success?

and ensuring their validity helps founders choose an entrepreneurial strategy without depending on too many "miracles" once the strategy is chosen.

FOURTH, HOW MUCH YOU CAN LEARN DEPENDS ON WHAT YOU CHOOSE TO TEST

We will see later in the book that some strategies are more amenable to commitment-free experimentation than others. For example, in many cases it may be easier to engage in commitment-free exploration on what technology to use (where it is possible to undertake R&D without committing to a particular design) than on potential competition to address (e.g., where it may only be possible to learn about competitive response after one has entered the market). But remember, the goal of testing is not removing all uncertainty; instead, the objective is to reduce uncertainty in a way that helps you meaningfully choose a strategy.

4.7 Concluding Thoughts

As an entrepreneur, you will have to make many choices, all with much uncertainty. In this chapter, we have seen how understanding this challenge and taking a systematic approach to making choices and learning will increase your opportunities of success (see **Putting It Together: Choosing Your Strategy**). Forming your core idea correctly first is an important launching point; then because good ideas will be associated with multiple potential paths to success, testing and experimentation should clarify the potential of the idea rather than isolate a single best strategy. To be clear, there will be experiments that may identify strategy combinations that are unlikely or even guaranteed not to succeed. However, if the founders' idea has identified a meaningful way to create value, they should find multiple potential customers to be served (even as initial markets), multiple technological solutions, multiple ways to organize, and multiple ways to compete. If entrepreneurs explore multiple potential paths and identify only a single viable path for success, they should consider if there is a hidden or implicit assumption that might undermine that path's unique strengths. If all but one route for commercialization is likely to fail, one should question how robust the single potential success route really is.

Similarly, if a good idea generates multiple paths forward, how can an experimental test yield insight into the one true path? The founders now face a meaningful choice where they understand the essential differences (and risks) of alternative approaches. At this point, the overall viability of these alternatives becomes less important (since each comes with its own profile of costs and benefits), and the fit between the founders and their particular circumstances and motives and the strategy becomes paramount.

While alternative strategies might be viable, some might be more feasible in the near term due to the availability of local resources or near-term opportunities. If one strategy involves the local market where the founders already live, taking advantage of resources and connections that are close at hand can be a deciding factor. Many entrepreneurs rely on near-term factors like proximity in early decisions; this pragmatic focus takes advantage of opportunities at hand as a way to implement a broader idea.

CHOOSING YOUR STRATEGY

There are many strategies that entrepreneurs can pursue, but how and when do you pick one? Using a strategic process and choice helps you find your best opportunity to pursue.

UNDERSTAND YOUR OPPORTUNITY

What Is the Foundation of the Venture?
- Clearly state your core idea. For now, omit references to potential customers, technology, organization, and competition and focus on the opportunity itself.
- Briefly reiterate your entrepreneurial motivation, passion, and unfair advantage as they relate to the opportunity.

RECOGNIZE WHY YOUR CHOICES MATTER

Explore Key Domains of Choice
- Brainstorm alternative options for each of the four key domains of entrepreneurial choice for your idea (customers, technology, organization, competition).
- Consider opportunities to engage in commitment-free exploration and learning about the idea to better understand the alternatives, associated risk, and uncertainty.
- Specify the ways financial, organizational, or strategic constraints will limit your ability to pursue multiple options for any idea.

USE "TEST TWO, CHOOSE ONE"

Build and Choose Your Strategy
- Articulate at least two viable strategic paths for an idea.
- Identify the key areas of uncertainty with the idea and each strategy. What must be true for each strategy to succeed?
- For each of the most critical assumptions, generate a potential experiment with high fidelity and a reasonable level of cost.
- Articulate key differences between the strategies and why you cannot pursue both paths at the same time. Specify which strategy is more straightforward to implement.
- Follow a proactive approach to entrepreneurial experimentation, prioritizing limited-commitment tests that will inform your choices. Learn enough about the two paths to make a choice.
- Consider your reasons for becoming an entrepreneur and the unfair advantage that you have.
- Make a choice based on your learning, experimentation, reasons for becoming an entrepreneur, and unfair advantage.
- Sharpen your understanding of your idea and initial strategy, including how these might evolve and grow in the future.

Ultimately, choices are guided by the founders wanting to achieve their broader objectives and mission. Once the founders have identified viable alternatives, a choice is frequently resolved by the internal motivation of the founders, and not by external rewards. Typically, founders have their own passions, values, and capabilities driving them to favor one strategy over another.

Chapter 4 Review: Choosing Your Strategy

CHAPTER TAKEAWAYS

- An entrepreneurial strategy is a practical and systematic framework of the core choices that entrepreneurs make to translate ideas into a reality.

- An entrepreneur's likelihood of success increases when a systematic choice process is used to determine the path to take the opportunity forward.

- An entrepreneur faces a large number of alternative paths to commercialize their opportunity but has limited resources to pursue more than one path.

- The most important task for a start-up at its moment of founding is not simply to "just do it" but instead to learn what "it" to do.

- The choice challenge is that an entrepreneur faces many possibilities and tight constraints. Most entrepreneurs can see several paths to create and capture value from their idea, yet due to financial, organizational, or strategic resource constraints seldom can pursue more than one alternative at a time.

- The learning challenge is that an entrepreneur faces fundamental uncertainty about the quality of the core idea and whether any given path might create sufficient value. Because learning is imperfect and "noisy," it limits what can be learned before making a choice.

- Commitment-free learning can only generate noisy estimates of the value of an idea and an alternative. At some point, it will become necessary to commit to a choice to learn more clearly.

- The paradox of entrepreneurship (as seen in Chapter 1) is that choosing between possible strategies requires knowledge that can only be gained through learning and experimentation. However, doing so forecloses the pursuit of other strategies

- An "ideal" experiment tests a critical hypothesis with high fidelity and low opportunity costs. Most entrepreneurial experimentation involves a trade-off between criticality, fidelity, and opportunity costs.

- The fact that good ideas have multiple potential paths means that experimentation and learning clarify the potential of the idea rather than isolate a single best route forward.

- Test Two, Choose One is a systematic process where entrepreneurs only commit to one strategy after considering multiple strategic alternatives and identifying *at least two* that are commercially viable yet difficult to rank.

KEY TERMS

entrepreneurial strategy (p. 88)
core idea (p. 89)
domains of choice (p. 92)
real options approach (p. 94)
choice challenge (p. 95)

learning challenge (p. 101)
business risk (p. 101)
fundamental uncertainty (p. 101)
Test Two, Choose One (p. 106)

REVIEW QUESTIONS

1. How would you describe the idea behind Amazon at the time of founding? What are some of the early choices Jeff Bezos made that allowed him to turn his idea into a reality?

2. Determine whether each description below refers to an idea or a specific strategy for an idea. Briefly explain your reasoning.

    a. Leveraging reductions in the costs of eco-friendly energy technologies to transition away from fossil fuels

    b. An online platform that uses "matched" student reviews to help high school seniors navigate the college application process

    c. Reducing the stress and hassle of international air travel

    d. Using technology to better service mental health needs

    e. Working with local grocery stores to provide specialized meal planning (and ingredient shopping) for recent college graduates

3. How would you describe the idea behind Starbucks (in its original form)? How would you describe the alternative paths pursued by the original founders versus Howard Schultz? What are some of the key choices that each made, and how (if at all) did they differ?

4. In a study of experts evaluating early-stage ventures, the ability to predict which firms would be successful varied depending on the type and stage of the venture (see Using the Research: Uncertainty in Start-Up Ideas on p. 103). Based on the results of that study, how does the type of uncertainty a venture faces impact the degree to which it is possible to predict which firms will be successful or not?

5. Learning and experimentation are essential for acquiring the knowledge necessary to choose an entrepreneurial strategy. What are some of the main limitations of the ability to learn prior to choosing a strategy?

6. One approach for choosing an entrepreneurial strategy is "Test Two, Choose One." How does a Test Two, Choose One approach differ from pursuing the first potentially viable path that one is able to identify? What are some possible advantages and disadvantages of a Test Two, Choose One approach relative to pursuing the first potentially viable path?

7. Most of L.L. Bean's early customers took advantage of his "no questions asked" return policy to get a refund on his first batch of rubber-soled leather boots, leading to a significant loss for the early venture. Yet Bean continued, redoubling his efforts to build durable outdoor gear through a mail-order business. Why did the early "failure" of L.L. Bean actually lead him to persist? What lessons did he learn, and how did that inform his approach?

8. Jeff Bezos categorizes a given decision as either a "one-way door" or a "two-way door." What is the difference between these two types of decisions? What is an example of each? Why is this distinction important for an entrepreneur?

9. One principle for cost-effective and timely entrepreneurial experimentation is "test small to choose big." How would you define this principle? What is an example of how a start-up firm might use this principle to test its most critical assumptions in an effective way?

10. Entrepreneurs pursuing a good idea will often confront a choice between multiple alternative paths (each potentially viable, even after extensive entrepreneurial experimentation). Why might "founder-strategy fit" have an important impact at this stage of entrepreneurial decision-making?

DISCUSSION QUESTIONS

Answer the following series of questions and scenarios either in class discussions, or by writing a short response.

1. For each of the examples below, first determine whether each description refers to an idea or a specific strategy for an idea. For those that are at the "idea" stage, can you identify an approach that would implement that idea? For those that state a strategy, what is the underlying idea?

    a. Leveraging reductions in the costs of eco-friendly energy technologies to transition away from fossil fuels

    b. An online platform that uses "matched" student reviews to help high school seniors navigate the college application process

    c. Reducing the stress and hassle of international air travel

    d. Using technology to better service mental health needs

    e. Working with local grocery stores to provide specialized meal planning (and ingredient shopping) for recent college graduates

2. Adrienne believes that the emerging techniques of artificial intelligence can be used to create personalized fitness routines for busy young professionals. While she goes to the gym every day, she does not have a professional background in the fitness industry. What is a critical hypothesis Adrienne might be able to test at very low cost (and in less than two weeks) to validate (or not) her core idea? What is a critical hypothesis that would, at a minimum, require significant time and effort and take at least six months to validate? Are there limits to what she might be able to learn before launching a particular product or service into the marketplace?

3. Ariel and Leslie are college athletes interested in building a platform to take advantage of new NCAA regulations that allow student athletes to get paid for endorsements, images, and autographs as well as social media branding. Not surprisingly, top-tier athletes were quickly signed by established agencies, but the vast majority of the more than 480,000 college athletes in the United States have so far not been able to take advantage of this regulatory change (and established agencies and sponsors have not expressed much interest in pursuing this large group). Based on their early experiments and learning, Ariel and Leslie have been able to identify numerous potential

paths they might pursue to take advantage of this opportunity. For example, one approach would involve investing in a high level of curation, where mid-tier athletes with compelling personal narratives and charismatic personalities would be matched with aspirational brands looking to grow their awareness. An alternative approach would be a much more open platform where any athlete that joined would be matched with any brand or endorsement partner that also joined.

Ariel and Leslie learn that both athletes and branding partners of this potential platform find either design attractive, and so they have been unable to clearly choose one over the other. What might be some of the key differences for their start-up in choosing a more curated versus open approach toward the athlete endorsement market? Why might it be difficult for Ariel and Leslie to be able to rank these alternatives in advance? Why do they have to choose (i.e., can they simply opt to adopt both paths at the same time)?

4. "Choice matters" for entrepreneurship because founders pursuing a good idea will often be able to identify multiple potential paths to create value that are hard to rank prior to (partial) commitment to one path over others. This reasoning motivates the use of a Test Two, Choose One rule for selecting an overall entrepreneurial strategy. Why is this type of decision-making *different* than a traditional approach when looking for a unique solution? What factors might an entrepreneur consider as they weigh alternative potentially viable options? Finally, what is the cost for an entrepreneur of failing to choose?

5. Rather than design an entire line of bridal gowns, Vera Wang first opened a single retail store that included the work of established designers as well as several dresses of her own design. What hypothesis was Vera Wang able to test through this early-stage experiment? How did she draw on that lesson as she scaled her venture?

6. Effective entrepreneurial experimentation involves testing the most critical hypotheses about value creation and capture in a high-fidelity way at relatively low opportunity cost. Identify and research an entrepreneur or venture in your area using articles or other written descriptions of their business. Describe any proactive entrepreneurial experimentation they used in founding it to validate and grow their business. What hypotheses did they test, and what lessons did they learn? How did the process of experimentation impact the evolution and scaling of the venture?

SUGGESTED READINGS

Adner, Ron, and Daniel A. Levinthal. "What Is Not a Real Option: Considering Boundaries for the Application of Real Options to Business Strategy." *Academy of Management Review* 29, no. 1 (2004): 74–85.

Bhidé, Amar. "Hustle as Strategy." *Harvard Business Review* 64, no. 5 (1986): 59–65.

Delmar, Frédéric, and Scott Shane. "Does Business Planning Facilitate the Development of New Ventures?" *Strategic Management Journal* 24, no. 12 (2003): 1165–85.

Gans, Joshua S., Scott Stern, and Jane Wu. "Foundations of Entrepreneurial Strategy." *Strategic Management Journal* 40, no. 5 (2019): 736–56.

Gruber, Marc. "Uncovering the Value of Planning in New Venture Creation: A Process and Contingency Perspective." *Journal of Business Venturing* 22 (2007): 782–807.

Porter, Michael E. "What Is Strategy?" *Harvard Business Review*, November 1986.

Ries, Eric. *The Lean Startup: How Today's Entrepreneurs Use Continuous Innovation to Create Radically Successful Businesses*. New York: Crown, 2011.

Scott, Erin L., Pian Shu, and Roman M. Lubynsky. "Entrepreneurial Uncertainty and Expert Evaluation: An Empirical Analysis." *Management Science* 66, no. (2020): 1278–99.

Sull, Donald, and Kathleen M. Eisenhardt. *Simple Rules: How to Thrive in a Complex World*. Boston: Houghton Mifflin Harcourt, 2015.

Kale Rogers, Braden Knight, Luke Schlueter, and Michael Farid

Healthy eating can be a challenge. Particularly when you are a busy, budget-constrained undergraduate student-athlete living in college housing. In 2015, MIT students Kale Rogers, Braden Knight, Luke Schlueter, and Michael Farid were discussing their problem of trying to eat healthy on a budget. Drawing on their mechanical and electrical engineering courses, they thought the solution was clear—robots! As Rogers describes it: "We wanted to see if we could automate the [cooking] process and make it as efficient as possible."[a] In no time, they had a robot that they could show off in the dining halls. According to Farid, who by then had started his master's in robotics, "once we [built a stir-fry robot], we realized we were more excited about the idea of serving food than building machines." They set out to launch a start-up featuring a robotic kitchen and founded a new restaurant concept they named Spyce.[b]

A finished bowl is taken from the robotic production line at Spyce.

But their venture required expertise in more than robotics. The team wanted to understand fast-casual restaurants' kitchen floor plans and processes, menu design, and the customer experience. Through considerable research, customer and employee interviews, and restaurant site visits, the team also concluded they needed to add more expertise on restaurant meal design. They recruited Michelin-starred French chef Daniel Boulud, chef-owner of numerous award-winning restaurants, as culinary director, and Sam Benson, who had previously worked for Boulud, as Spyce's executive chef.

True to the team's vision, at the launch of the new restaurant, the robots had center stage. Once a customer selected from the customizable menu and placed an order on a touch screen, the robotic system sorted the requested ingredients into a cooking cylinder (see photo), where the ingredients were mixed and cooked before the completed dish was deposited into the customer's bowl. In 3 minutes, the customer received a warm, nutritious, savory meal tailored to their preferences that cost less than comparable meals at competing established fast-casual restaurants. The team was encouraged not just by the initial customer flow at their first location (conveniently situated next to a university), but by the regular customers they began to attract. While the robots may have brought them in, the food kept them coming.

The launch of their restaurant was a milestone. In many ways, it capped a systematic process of experimentation and learning that had taken the founders from the dorm room to serving hundreds every week. While continued experimentation was still needed (for instance, attempts to automate pancakes remained problematic), the team had reduced the uncertainty associated with their idea and how they might bring it forward. Yet this success had placed a choice squarely in front of the founding team. Should they position themselves as a robotics company that served the restaurant industry? Or should they build a chain of fast-casual restaurants that leveraged their robotic kitchen technology? Spyce eventually built out over 120 locations; it was acquired by Sweetgreen in 2021 for $50 million.[c]

Questions

1. What is the core idea that Kale Rogers and his cofounders identified? What other routes might the founders have pursued to realize this idea?

2. Evaluate the team's process of experimentation and learning. What steps did they take to explore their idea and alternative routes to commercialization? What did they learn? What commitments did they make in the process?

3. Must the founding team have chosen between selling robots to fast-casual restaurants and serving customers in fast-casual restaurants? Why couldn't they do both? How might they have chosen between these alternatives?

PART 2

CORE CHOICES

W hat choices *matter* for the growth and sustainability of a start-up venture? In the previous chapter, we discussed the unique tension that lies with entrepreneurial choice and saw how using a Test Two, Choose One framework can increase chances for success. This part of the text turns to the actual choices an entrepreneur needs to make to launch and scale a venture.

Do you like dogs? The founders of Whistle labs chose them (or their owners) as customers for their venture—a fitness tracker worn on a collar. In this part of the text, we will see how the choices you make define your ventures.

In essence, there are four domains of entrepreneurial choice where entrepreneurs and founding teams face meaningful trade-offs. For each of these domains, early-stage choices about how and where to focus a venture's activities and investments will have a significant impact on the ultimate path the venture will follow. Because a venture needs to create value for some group of customers and establish and sustain competitive advantage, the first choices come from four domains:

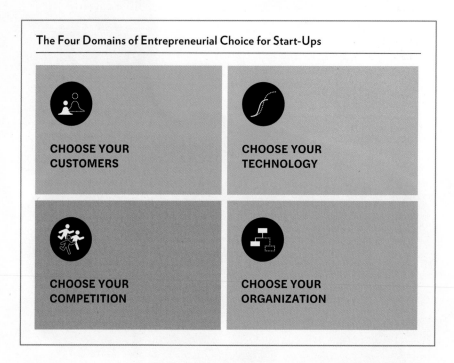

The Four Domains of Entrepreneurial Choice for Start-Ups

CHOOSE YOUR CUSTOMERS

CHOOSE YOUR TECHNOLOGY

CHOOSE YOUR COMPETITION

CHOOSE YOUR ORGANIZATION

- *Choosing your customer:* what customer segments to target and which to prioritize first. The question for most founding teams is rarely whether any potential customers exist, but rather which customer to choose. Most entrepreneurs, including then-fledgling entrepreneur Jeff Bezos, face resource constraints that preclude serving all potential customers simultaneously. Further, strategically choosing to serve one group of customers to learn from and experiment with can help entrepreneurs create and capture more value from subsequent customer groups. But in many, if not most, cases, this initial customer choice leads a start-up further away from other customer segments that might have looked promising before any commitments were made.
- *Choosing your technology:* what broad technological opportunities and growth trajectories and innovations to exploit. For some approaches to a given idea, simply adopting existing off-the-shelf technology will be both adequate and straightforward; the central value created by the strategy does not rely on technological differentiation. But for many strategic options, the choice of which technologies to leverage and how and in what direction to innovate are central.
- *Choosing your organization:* what resources and capabilities to attract and assemble. This is a process of building an organization and culture and leveraging available resources, especially those available because of the local entrepreneurial

ecosystem. It involves making decisions about what type of organization to build, what types of people to hire and work with, and even where to locate.

- **Choosing your competition:** who your competitors are and how you will compete with them. Competitive advantage requires competing on favorable terms within the market. For most start-ups, there is significant latitude in determining with whom and how they elect to compete. While a start-up team will never be able to simply will competition away, they can often choose which ones to avoid.

Underlying all these choices are hypotheses about how the team will create and capture value from their idea.

These four domains cover a significant swath of the critical choices for venture design and growth, highlighting the most central and consistent choices rather than serving as an exhaustive encyclopedia for all the contingencies a start-up might face. While it will be critical for every start-up to address specific choices beyond those highlighted here, all ventures need to confront, at a minimum, these four choices. Further, the four choices are interdependent—the choice of customer influences with whom and how a start-up competes, and both of these influence the role of technology and the choice of organizational design. Each choice is a subject of the next four chapters, where we will learn a framework and a playbook for navigating them.

Anne Wojcicki thought her company could serve two potential customers. Her choice has been tremendously important throughout the life of the company. Which customer did she choose?

ENTREPRENEUR'S DILEMMA For an entrepreneur's strategy to succeed, it must create meaningful value for customers. However, for a good idea, there will likely be multiple potential customer types, and an entrepreneur will be constrained in their ability to serve all types at the same time (at least in the earliest stages). How should an entrepreneur choose among alternative "beachhead" customer segments? Why not simply try to experiment in all segments? What are the consequences of choosing a customer for the growth and evolution of the firm?

CHAPTER OBJECTIVES

- Understand why start-ups have to choose a customer
- Compare how intrinsic customer value and strategic customer value differ from one another
- Categorize the different adopter groups of the Customer Adoption Lifecycle
- Learn why strategic customer sequencing matters
- Recognize the strategic implications of choosing alternative beachhead markets
- Discover how entrepreneurs choose a first customer

5

CHOOSING YOUR CUSTOMER

After a decade of analyzing and investing in healthcare and life sciences companies on Wall Street, Anne Wojcicki had come to believe that a core value of the healthcare industry was monetizing illness. Rather than empowering individuals to use information about themselves to prevent illness, she felt doctors often waited until a condition (such as diabetes) appeared that could then be treated (at a cost) through medication and physician services. In the end, this led Wojcicki to found a company called 23andMe. Over its first 15 years, the 23andMe personalized genomics service successfully served more than 300 million customers, became a household name, and had a successful IPO in 2021. While the company has faced financial challenges after its IPO, this is a story that at its heart is about the power of strategic customer choice. Let's see how this happened.

Along with her cofounders Linda Avey and Paul Cusenza, Wojcicki believed that the healthcare industry should focus on generating information people could use to avoid getting sick. Wojcicki's beliefs grew at a time of an important technological change. Almost since James Watson and Francis Crick first deciphered the structure of DNA in the late 1950s, other scientists had sought to create complete DNA sequences for living things. For decades, doing this for humans seemed like an impossibly complex task. However, in 2001 the Human Genome Project succeeded in sequencing a human's complete set of DNA, or genome. The ability to sequence genomes improved quickly with new technology, and by 2005 Wojcicki thought rapid and sustained declines in the technological costs of DNA sequencing made it feasible, if still expensive, to identify specific genetic markers in individuals. She believed these markers would reveal if an individual was more or less likely to be susceptible or resistant to specific diseases or conditions. Moreover, these DNA sequences provided not only medical information but also insight into an individual's

In this chapter we focus on Choices around Customers, including who your beachhead customers will be.

family history. They might even identify idiosyncratic traits, such as whether a person could detect the smell of sulfur after consuming asparagus or would tend to sneeze when moving from relative darkness to bright sunlight.[1]

Excited by the promise of genetic data, Wojcicki and her cofounders decided to form a venture around this opportunity, but they faced a choice at the time of serving two alternative potential customers. One way to leverage the emergence of low-cost genetic sequencing was to sell precise, and highly regulated, tests to physicians and other healthcare professionals for medical diagnosis and screening. Pharmaceutical companies such as Abbott and PerkinElmer were also just starting to establish business units focused on the professional market. It seemed there might be an opportunity for a start-up to take advantage of both the clear regulatory pathway and potential for reimbursement from insurance companies. They could start a business providing these testing and screening services to healthcare professionals.

An alternative customer segment bypassed medical professionals entirely, with products marketed directly to individuals. At least in principle, the team thought individuals might find it personally valuable to take simple home genetic tests, using DNA sequencing to assess medical risks and also learn about their genetic background and inherited traits. Of course, the consumer market for personalized genetic information did not yet exist, and there was significant uncertainty about whether providing such information was even legal without first undergoing an extensive regulatory approval process. However, focusing on the consumer market might create significant new value by putting the information directly in the hands of individuals and their families.

Wojcicki and her team faced two somewhat contradictory dilemmas as they considered how to pursue the opportunity created by low-cost genetic sequencing. On the one hand, though they believed in the potential of low-cost genetic testing, their belief was so far a hypothesis rather than a reality. The team first needed to identify at least one meaningful set of customers with sufficient interest so that they could begin to build a profitable business. At the same time, entering either the professional or consumer segment would likely come at the expense of being able to pursue the other alternative, at least for the first few years of the venture. For example, entering the consumer market was likely to attract accusations by medical professionals that Wojcicki and her team were inappropriately providing data without proper guidance by a physician or trained genetics counselor. As Eric Lander, founding director of the Broad Institute and one of the leaders of the Human Genome Project, said to *Wired* at the time, "We're learning plenty about the molecular basis of disease—that's the revolution right now. But whether that knowledge translates into personalized predictions and personalized therapeutics is unknown."[2] As this scientific revolution unfolded, researchers and physicians felt it more appropriate to pair this new information with expert guidance. Vance Vanier, Stanford physician and CEO of competing start-up Navigenics, noted, "It is more effective to partner with a medical institution rather than do an end-run around them with a direct-to-consumer model."[3] By contrast, Esther Dyson, a successful entrepreneur herself and a director of Wojcicki's new venture, characterized the tension between the two markets as "appallingly paternalistic," explaining that "people can understand statistics about baseball, and I think they ought to understand statistics about genetics [without a doctor]."[4] Put simply, a focus on the consumer market was also a choice to forgo the professional market, at least at the early stages of the venture.

Ultimately, Wojcicki and her cofounders chose the consumer market with their 23andMe testing kit. Though there was an initial flurry of sales, driven in part by their network in Silicon Valley, orders for the kits slowed down dramatically. It took several years for 23andMe to gain traction with individuals who valued personal access to their genetic information. During this long "trough of sorrow" (a saying coined by Y Combinator founder Paul Graham, referring to a period a start-up faces after an initial setback), the 23andMe team reduced their costs and price and provided customers with more detailed genetic information. They did this while also navigating multiple disputes and controversies with the FDA and others about the degree of regulation that would be imposed on their service. After more than 10 years of building a loyal base of early customers, 23andMe began to be widely accepted, ultimately establishing itself as a mainstream business and going public in a deal with Richard Branson in 2021.

A 23andMe testing kit from 2013. At this point, the company was still working to build a loyal customer base.

While enthusiastic early (paying!) customers can be the signal of a lucrative and promising venture, it is precisely because entrepreneurs are trying to grow out a new product and business that they need to evaluate whether those potential first customers, known as **beachhead customers**, are the right launchpad for growth. This chapter is about the core dilemma facing any start-up in choosing its customers: Whom do you start with? Which segment is the right starting point to achieve future value creation and capture, and which customer segments, though potentially lucrative, should you leave behind, at least temporarily? We'll consider these questions, focusing on where to start if your goal is to reach a wider market. For any entrepreneur, this idea will be a key factor in determining what customer you choose.

5.1 Why Do Start-Ups Have to Choose a Customer?

All businesses ultimately need to be paid. A **customer** is any person, group, or organization who will pay a business money for any of its goods or services. For this reason, as customers are the source of a start-up's revenue, many put great weight on *whom* a start-up is likely to service. Indeed, it is the first question many investors ask.

Yet for any start-up whose underlying idea has the potential to create meaningful consumer value, the question most often is not whether any potential customers exist, but which customer to *choose*. At the earliest stages of a venture, entrepreneurs do not have the resources to serve all potential customers with equal attention and care. But even if resources were not an issue, as we will discuss, the customers an entrepreneur chooses to focus on initially are not likely to be the customers that end up at the core of the entrepreneur's business.

History is filled with examples of successful ventures that started out with very different customers than those for which the ventures were ultimately known. Facebook famously started serving the college student market before

beachhead customers The very first potential customers for a new product or service

customer Any person, group, or organization who will pay a business money for any of its goods or services

taking a broader approach and establishing as its primary customers advertisers who wanted to reach the social networking site's users. Microsoft began developing software for another, larger firm, IBM, before turning into a company that sold that software directly to IBM's customers.

Customer choice is important not only because of certain customers' potential **inherent value** to the organization derived from their willingness to pay for a start-up's products and/or services, but also because certain customers can provide **strategic value** to the venture. In short, and for a variety of reasons, a particular customer may prove more useful in unlocking broader customer segments than others. Most often, customer value comes from helping the founding team learn from them and experiment with and improve the early product or service. Customer value also comes from using a customer's satisfaction with the product to influence a targeted set of follow-on customers. Indeed, earlier customers may directly assist in selling the product to later adopters. Finally, certain customer segments may have more coherence, or alignment, with the venture's other strategic choices. While ignoring the strategic value of potential customer segments will not prevent a founding team from finding *some* initial customers, doing so can leave the start-up strategically farther away from other, potentially more lucrative customers. Because initial customer selection influences the future of any venture, it is among the most central elements of entrepreneurial strategy.

One way to understand the importance of initial customer choice is to consider falling dominoes. When dominoes are properly aligned, a cascade of the tumbling rectangular blocks can occur by simply tipping the first one. While most demonstrations of falling dominoes use blocks of the same size, in entrepreneurship, a more interesting idea is to consider a situation where each domino is only two-thirds the size of the next follow-on domino.[5] In this arrangement, a single inch-long domino, if lined up with 29 progressively larger dominoes, will eventually topple a domino the height of the Burj Khalifa, the world's tallest building (**Figure 5.1**).

inherent value A customer's worth to an organization, derived from their willingness to pay for a start-up's products and/or services

strategic value The added value of some particular customers who prove more useful than others because they can unlock broader market segments

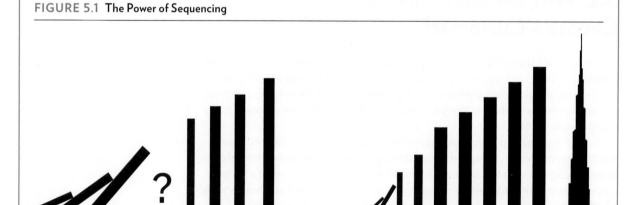

FIGURE 5.1 **The Power of Sequencing**

(a)   (b)

Like gaps in a sequence of dominoes, where significant gaps exist between markets (a), it may be impossible to transition to larger, broader markets given the distance between the initial markets and the broader market. However, just like well sequenced dominoes, where there is alignment (b), each market helps topple the follow-on markets and, powerfully, assists in tackling the broader market. It's been theorized that perfectly sized and sequenced dominoes could eventually topple one the size of the tallest building on Earth.

As we will see in the rest of the chapter, the falling domino analogy aptly applies to customer choice. If the goal is to topple large dominoes, then the best strategy is not to try and push one large domino over directly but instead to choose a path whereby toppling a smaller and more manageable domino can lead to a cascade that topples very large ones. Similarly, entrepreneurs want to identify a sequence of market opportunities where (a) there is a path from one customer choice (without significant gaps) to the next and (b) where the initial customers (dominoes) can be manageably tackled. This leads to broader market opportunities so that the business has a path to scale. But to do so, entrepreneurs must truly understand the inherent value they provide to potential customers and the strategic value those customers provide in tackling future customer segments.

5.2 Inherent Customer Value

Entrepreneurs normally want to find the customers who value their products the most. Economists represent overall customer value in a concept called "willingness to pay." Customers with the highest willingness to pay assign the highest value to these products relative to others. But what drives this value?

As an example, ask yourself what you are willing to pay for a cool, refreshing can of soda. Often, this price depends on context—is it hot or cold outside?— and on other available options—are juice or iced tea also offered? Depending on the circumstances, your possible alternative prices might range from nothing (you don't like soda) to very high prices like $8 (you are in a hotel at 3 a.m. after a long flight and could use a caffeine hit to get those PowerPoint slides finished!). Economists say your willingness to pay for a soda will be the price that just leaves you indifferent between having a soda or not.

For a venture, therefore, customers' willingness to pay represents potential: it is the maximum amount of value that can be generated by supplying customers with the product. Of course, willingness to pay depends not only on the product delivered, but also on the customer being targeted (see **Mini Case: What's the Value of a Miracle?** on p. 132). In practice, customers rarely must pay a price equal to their willingness to pay due to the natural dispersion of customer preferences and constraints. For example, companies like Uber and Lyft know that even if you are hesitant to take a rideshare to the party at current surge prices, chances are there are many others who are not hesitant and will pay the price without blinking. Moreover, the price ultimately charged also reflects several market factors, including the degree of competition and the number of substitutes. Your indifference to pay for a rideshare at that point may also reflect the ease of public transportation in your neighborhood, or even your interest in going to the party at all.

While the willingness to pay defines the potential value for a given customer, it is also important to consider the costs of delivering that value. For instance, most travelers would be willing to pay more to fly in a private jet rather than a commercial airline. However, that does not mean using private jets creates the most value for most people. While a private jet has higher inherent value to a customer, the costs of supplying it are also higher. For most individuals, even if

What's the Value of a Miracle?

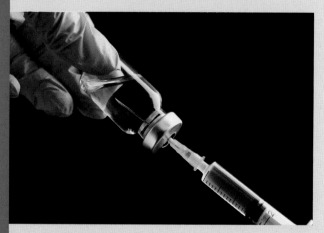

Myozyme enzyme replacement therapy became the first and only approved treatment for the debilitating, sometimes fatal Pompe disease.

Pompe disease is a rare genetic disorder in which individuals are unable to produce a key enzyme involved in the breakdown of glycogen, the body's stored form of sugar. The health implications are profound. In the absence of therapy, infant-onset Pompe disease (occurring in 1 in 138,000 births) is fatal, often within the first year of a child's life; adult-onset Pompe disease (affecting 1 in 57,000 adults) results in severe and debilitating declines in mobility and respiratory function.

In the late 1990s, costly research and patient advocacy efforts finally yielded a promising treatment. Upon FDA approval in 2006, Genzyme's Myozyme enzyme replacement therapy, which involved a direct infusion of the missing proteins for glycogen breakdown, became the first and only approved treatment for Pompe disease. Though it offered no cure (ongoing infusions were required every two weeks), the therapy was heralded as a miracle: it achieved not only high survival rates

among infants, but also a reduction in the severity of symptoms among adult-onset patients.

In saving the lives of infants and improving the quality of life for adults with Pompe disease, Genzyme's new therapy had the potential to create substantial value—but how to even begin to quantify that value? How much value should one place on saving the life of a child? And how much for improving the quality of life of an adult? For Genzyme, saving lives in the infant-onset population was the first priority. The pricing decision required balancing the hundreds of millions of dollars of development costs and tens of thousands of dollars in manufacturing costs with providing access for the lifesaving treatment. Covering these costs was critical in continuing to serve not only this population but also the adult-onset population, as well as developing treatments for other such conditions.

Though pharmaceutical companies, insurance providers, and patient advocates continue to debate these (and related funding and pricing) challenges, the case of Myozyme illustrates how the same product, though delivered in different dosages, can create markedly different value for different customer segments. Ultimately, Genzyme released the therapy to the infant-onset patient population at a price of more than $200,000 per patient annually, reflecting several factors, including the value the treatment created and the high costs associated with the research, development, and manufacture of the drug. As part of its commitment to serving communities with rare genetic conditions, Genzyme ensures that all patients have access to the treatment, even if they are unable to pay. This allows the company to balance access with a pricing level that sustains its mission.

SOURCE: Nicholas Eriksson, et al. "Web-Based, Participant-Driven Studies Yield Novel Genetic Associations for Common Traits" *PLOS Genetics,* 6, no. 6 (2014): e1000993, https://doi.org/10.1371/journal.pgen.1000993.

they paid their willingness-to-pay price for a private jet, it would not cover the costs of supplying the trip. Put another way, there is no price a private jet service could charge to viably serve these customers; it wouldn't take many trips for the service to be bankrupt. As a result, most travelers, despite preferring travel on a private jet, remain commercial airline customers.

As we see in this example, the value created from supplying a particular customer is not their willingness to pay, but rather the difference between their willingness to pay and the costs of supplying the customer (see **Deep Dive: The Numbers behind Willingness to Pay**). By contrast, the value captured by the venture, and the venture's ability to derive profit from the operation, is the difference between the price the customer pays and the costs of supplying them. Ideally, and indeed in most cases, price should be set between a customer segment's willingness to pay and the costs to supply them.

However, entrepreneurs face a challenge in that true willingness to pay and cost are rarely known, at least with any precision. In contrast to established products or services, there is considerable uncertainty about how much particular customers will value a venture's novel offering, and how much it will cost to deliver that value reliably as the venture scales. There are many cautionary tales. Some include Pets.com (Chapter 7), which overestimated the willingness to pay for pet food and underestimated the difficulty of delivering items; Webvan (Chapter 11), which could not push costs down enough to support delivering cheap groceries; and the too-unique Segway personal transporter (Section 5.5).

Further, start-ups must also factor in the resources and time required to educate and acquire new customers. Customer acquisition costs can include marketing campaigns and initial discounts to entice customers to learn about new and novel products. While these costs vary substantially across customer segments, the next section describes a path of product adoption that entrepreneurs can use to guide the adoption process.

5.3 The Market S Curve of New Product Adoption

When looking for a customer, it is tempting for entrepreneurs to search for a way to make their start-up "an overnight success," even as history tells us that such occurrences are very rare. For almost every successful new idea, the time it takes to really take off is significant and almost impossible to predict.

Nevertheless, there is an important and useful pattern that can guide a founding team's expectations, one coming from more than 100 years of research into the process of how new ideas and technologies spread among customers and markets. This process of **innovation diffusion** offers important insights for entrepreneurs today.

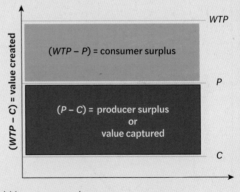
innovation diffusion The process of how new ideas and technologies spread among customers and markets

THE MARKET S CURVE

Perhaps there is no more important insight than the idea that, *even for break-through innovations, the process of diffusion is slow*. For any technologies and innovations that ultimately do succeed, slow initial traction is followed by a period of quicker gains before a final tapering off. This pattern is known as the **market S curve**, because of how it looks when you graph it (**Figure 5.2**): a slow start, followed by rapid uptake, ending with a leveling off as the market opportunity is saturated. Let's see how this pattern works, starting with the study that first identified it.

The earliest study to document the S curve was conducted by economist Zvi Griliches in the 1950s. He studied the adoption and use of hybrid strains of corn—corn seeds obtained through crossbreeding plants with different traits that produced higher-yield crops—vs. the use of available standard varieties. The invention of hybrid corn was one of the most important innovations of the first half of the twentieth century. This process bred seeds from strains of corn with more favorable characteristics, most notably improving the health and size of the ears of corn. But while the technology for hybrid corn was developed in the 1920s, Griliches documented a *very long initial process* of its first use by farmers, both within and across U.S. states, rather than a quick uptake. Some of the first adopters of hybrid corn were found in states such as Iowa and

market S curve A graph that shows the slow initial traction gained by a new product or service that is followed by a period of quicker gains before a final tapering off

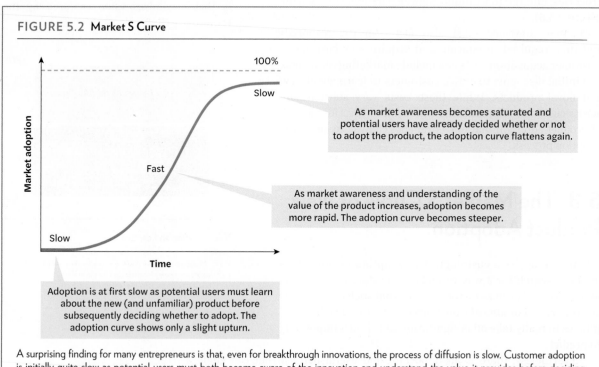

FIGURE 5.2 Market S Curve

100%

Slow

As market awareness becomes saturated and potential users have already decided whether or not to adopt the product, the adoption curve flattens again.

Fast

As market awareness and understanding of the value of the product increases, adoption becomes more rapid. The adoption curve becomes steeper.

Slow

Market adoption

Time

Adoption is at first slow as potential users must learn about the new (and unfamiliar) product before subsequently deciding whether to adopt. The adoption curve shows only a slight upturn.

A surprising finding for many entrepreneurs is that, even for breakthrough innovations, the process of diffusion is slow. Customer adoption is initially quite slow as potential users must both become aware of the innovation and understand the value it provides before deciding whether to adopt the product or service. As customer awareness grows, there is an inflection point where the pace of customer adoption increases, and the adoption curve becomes steeper. However, once there is wide awareness of the new product or service in the market and most customers have already decided whether to adopt the innovation, the adoption curve begins to flatten out.

Wisconsin, where farmland was relatively expensive and corn was a major crop. In these states, farmers needed to maximize the return on their land to compete with areas of the country where land was less expensive. In addition, in these states the news of one corn farmer's success with an innovation was likely to quickly impact the behavior of others, since many were growing the same crop. But even under these conditions, which would seem to favor broad and rapid adoption of hybrid corn, Griliches documented that adoption was slow. Despite the favorable setting, it took farmers in these states a decade or more to adopt hybrid corn. Only after this period did farmers adopt hybrid corn both rapidly and broadly, with adoptions leveling off as it became the standard. Griliches graphed these patterns for both Wisconsin and Iowa as distinct S curves over time (**Figure 5.3**).

Different varieties of hybrid corn

At the other extreme, in Texas, land was relatively less expensive, making the return on paying for an innovation that increased crop yield relatively lower. Even though the benefits and costs were well understood because of experiences in other states, adoption in Texas still started with a slow initial adoption. Farmers in Texas first began to adopt these new corn strains more than 10 years later than their counterparts in Iowa and Wisconsin, and even then, farmers adopted these strains over a lengthy (15-year) period. Again, this eventually led to rapid and widespread adoption of the hybrid grain, followed by a leveling off, producing an S-curve adoption pattern.

In fact, Griliches found the broad pattern of adoption followed an S curve in every state he examined. Intriguingly, if one mapped out the national adoption of hybrid corn, an overall S curve also emerged. The "late adopters" in Iowa were actually still **"early adopters"** from a national perspective. Griliches found

early adopters The first customers to adopt a new technology or service who may be characterized as application enthusiasts; seeking a revolution; demanding but collaborative

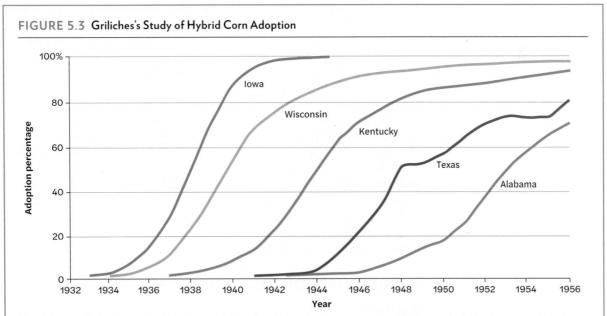

FIGURE 5.3 Griliches's Study of Hybrid Corn Adoption

The diffusion of hybrid corn in the United States followed an S-shaped curve in every state Griliches studied. Hardly unique to hybrid corn, this common finding implies that for a given innovation, opportunities exist at each stage of the S curve.

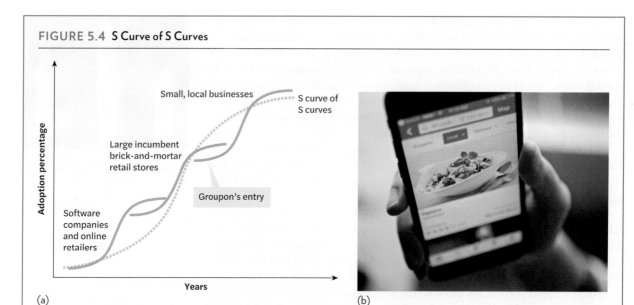

FIGURE 5.4 S Curve of S Curves

Adoption percentage

Small, local businesses

S curve of
S curves

Large incumbent
brick-and-mortar
retail stores

Groupon's entry

Software
companies
and online
retailers

Years

(a)

(b)

(a) Widespread adoption of e-commerce by retailers was slow and followed the traditional adoption pattern first documented by Zvi Griliches in the 1950s for hybrid corn. Among initial e-commerce adopters were software firms and online retailers; these adopters comprised not only the start of the broad S curve, but also their own market segment S curve. This would be followed by e-commerce adoption by large incumbent retail stores, which comprised their own market S curve. A third market segment S curve within e-commerce would emerge as small businesses moved online, in large part assisted by the daily deals website Groupon. (b) Though restaurants were late adopters of e-commerce, they were among Groupon's earliest adopters and the first small businesses to adopt e-commerce.

that combining the adoption curves of all these states created its own S curve, effectively an "S curve of S curves."[6]

Since then, researchers and entrepreneurs alike have repeatedly documented the market segment S curves and the broad market S curve. Let's look at another example, e-commerce adoption among retailers. The earliest adopters included software firms and new entrants, such as Amazon.com (**Figure 5.4a**). After a gradual start-up period, rapid adoption followed, starting with companies like Diapers.com, eBay, and Etsy. With this model firmly in place, large established brick-and-mortar retailers, such as Barnes & Noble and Borders, started making the transition online, which was followed by rapid adoption by other large retailers. Then, more than a decade after Amazon had opened its digital retail doors, daily deals website Groupon started a new market segment S curve by bringing small businesses onto the Internet. Groupon quickly found traction among restaurants, which made them early adopters of e-commerce among small businesses (**Figure 5.4b**); other small businesses like gyms, salons, and local mechanics would transition online much later.

SIGNIFICANCE OF THE S-CURVE PATTERN

Why does the S-curve pattern happen?

1. *Market adoption simply cannot be faster than the speed that related knowledge diffuses through the population of potential customers.*

The reason for this pattern is akin to how a viral disease might spread through a population: it infects a few people, who then infect a few more people, repeating the process until it reaches an inflection point when it moves throughout most of the population. Close contact hastens this spread, allowing the virus to disperse through the majority of a given community well before it reaches the majority in the broader community. In this sense, the knowledge about Internet retail first spread through the software and start-up community, then more broadly to big box retailers and their adjacent competitors, and then finally into small businesses.

But for market adoption, knowledge diffusion is only the first step.

2. *Critically, customers must change their behavior as they come to understand a new product and its usefulness.* This process takes time and often plays out more slowly than anticipated by entrepreneurs. But it is a pattern that is pervasive across a range of products and sectors (see **Deep Dive: S Curve across Innovative Products** on p. 138).

To be clear, compared with Griliches's era, there is some evidence that diffusion has become somewhat quicker over time. Urban density has increased, placing more early adopters in close contact with potential follow-on customers and expanding opportunities for exchange of personal recommendations as well as direct observations of new products in use (e.g., "Siri, when's the next bus?"). Technologies relating to the Internet have also eased the acquisition of new information. Whether consumers use Wikipedia for background knowledge, Yelp for service reviews, or Instagram for viral stories, the Internet provides them with faster access to a broader array of information than ever before. Further spurred by higher levels of education, these increases in urban density and Internet access have also reduced the barriers to behavioral change by facilitating deeper understanding of the uses for new products (e.g., YouTube product unboxings, reviews, and instructional videos).

USE THE KNOWLEDGE OF S-CURVE ADOPTION AS A GUIDE

Many founding teams base their assumptions about the pace of their growth on confidence in their ability to avoid the patterns and struggles of other businesses. They think they can "beat" the S curve, avoiding the slow pace of early adoption and jumping right to rapid growth. They do this instead of considering how to ensure their company and product will thrive despite the challenges posed by the time needed for initial knowledge diffusion and behavioral change. They assume their company will not follow a pattern but will break the mold.

But a key tool for founding teams is to accept that the S curve will apply to their venture and be strategic in how they approach this pattern. In particular, who will they target as their first customer—the one that will seed growth and diffuse information, leading to broad success?

S Curve across Innovative Products

From the telephone to the cellular phone, the classic S-curve pattern first demonstrated in hybrid corn adoption has been shown to hold true across a wide range of products, including the most innovative products of our time.[a] Interestingly, as the diffusion of information has quickened due to increases in education and urban density as well as the Internet and social media, the rate of adoption of new products has also sped up. Nonetheless, the classic S-curve pattern remains, and entrepreneurs are wise to take its lessons to heart.

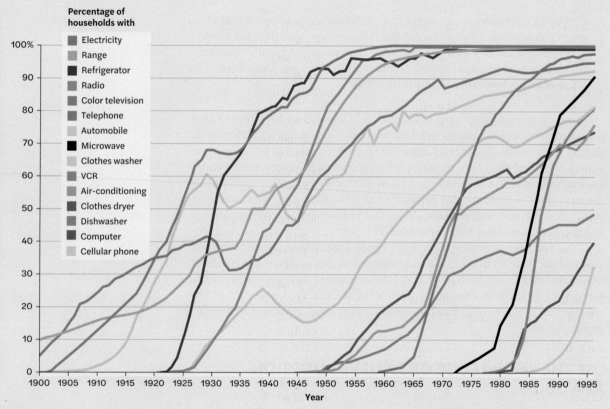

Percentage of households with
- Electricity
- Range
- Refrigerator
- Radio
- Color television
- Telephone
- Automobile
- Microwave
- Clothes washer
- VCR
- Air-conditioning
- Clothes dryer
- Dishwasher
- Computer
- Cellular phone

We see the S curve in the growth pattern of most every innovation.

5.4 Strategic Customer Value

Especially in the initial phases of a start-up, there is an additional customer value that entrepreneurs need to consider: their potential strategic value to the venture. Among the set of customer segments with positive inherent value, certain ones are better positioned to help a venture successfully (a) navigate the S-curve market adoption pattern (i.e., there is alignment of the dominoes and no domino chain gaps as the venture moves from one customer segment to the next) and (b) positively influence the market adoption pattern (i.e., the domino chain has customer segments of increasing market size). Understanding the strategic value of different customer segments helps prioritize the first customers (dominoes) to target.

The strategic value of a customer may come in several different forms. For instance, some customer segments may help the venture's team learn quickly and also rapidly improve and refine their product. This will help the product better serve not only that initial market, but also key follow-on markets. Importantly, ventures can make use of early customer reaction and adoption to influence future customers. In this respect, early customers who are influential to others can offer the highest strategic value.

Let's consider an example around the launch of the first successful, purely digital cryptocurrency, Bitcoin. It was invented by the pseudonymous Satoshi Nakamoto and launched in 2009. Now, well over a decade later, it has proved a durable concept spurring many other cryptocurrencies and enthusiasm for broader applications based on its underlying blockchain technology. But back in 2014, while some were sure of Bitcoin's durability, very few had heard of it. To encourage its adoption, after working for the Grameen Foundation for just over three years, then 29-year-old Dan Elitzer shifted gears to promote cryptocurrency and build an ecosystem around it.[7] His first step was to raise half-a-million dollars to give every entering MIT undergraduate $100 in Bitcoin.[8] This investment did not go unnoticed within MIT, and a few professors intervened to see if they could use this whole endeavor to run an experiment in technology adoption. As a result, instead of giving everyone $100 in Bitcoin at the same time as initially planned, the distribution was staggered. In some dormitories, early distribution was aimed at those who had expressed significant interest in the technology, while in other dormitories, the order of distribution was random. This variation created an experiment investigating how early access to a technology impacts not only the behavior of the recipient but also others within their network. The results were striking: in dormitories where early distribution ended up being targeted to the "wrong" students (i.e., those who had expressed a low level of interest), the ultimate usage rate among *all* students in the dormitory was much lower than at dormitories whose early adopters were already evangelists for the new technology.[9] In other words, choosing the right initial customer was critical for navigating along a more favorable market adoption S curve and gaining broader adoption. Returning to our domino analogy, to topple the first domino, it is simply easier and more strategic to start with individuals who have a prior interest in the product *and* see it as creating value than those with limited awareness or little interest. Given this information, how does one know where to start?

Customer Adoption Lifecycle The breakdown of market adoption patterns into five customer types: innovators, early adopters, early majority, late majority, and laggards.

The First Smartphone. Fifteen years before Apple introduced the now-ubiquitous iPhone, the first smartphone was released. The IBM Simon by BellSouth was described as the first product that "takes all the gadgetry of the modern business executive and puts it into one unit." However, despite these innovations, the design was not well suited for the executive on the go: it was heavy, and the battery rarely survived a commute. As a result, the innovative new product ultimately created little value for any customers outside of technology enthusiasts.

FIVE CUSTOMER TYPES

Research has shown we can break down the market adoption pattern into five types of customers and adoption behaviors. As seen in **Table 5.1**, new products and services that are ultimately successful offer distinctive value (and have distinctive costs) across each different group of potential adopters: innovators, early adopters, early majority, late majority, and laggards. Per this table, each group has distinctive characteristics for why they adopt a product and the ultimate value they derive from it.

This concept, synthesized by the noted sociologist Everett Rogers in the early 1960s, is known as the **Customer Adoption Lifecycle**. It helps founders consider who their most promising customer is and how different potential customer segments are likely to relate to each other. For example, *innovators* and *early adopters* derive benefits simply from the novelty of a technology, product, or service; being able to "experiment" with an early-stage innovation; and/or being among the first to possess it. They are generally less concerned with technical bugs or occasional failures as they know this sometimes comes with early access to new innovations (see **Using the Research: The Hazards of Ignoring Early Adopters**). In contrast, *mainstream* users, constituting the *early majority* and *late majority* of adopters, derive benefit from standardized technology and when a product or service has clear use cases and widespread adoption. However, while customers may classify as innovators with some product categories, they may fall into other adopter groups for other use cases; for example, an audiophile may quickly adopt new audio and acoustic technologies but may be risk averse when it comes to Bitcoin or self-driving cars.

Making distinctions in how value is derived from a new product among differing segments of users has long been a central challenge of technology marketing. By closely examining what drives customers in distinct segments to move toward new products, new categories of products and which types of customer might be the first adopters can be defined. Perhaps the clearest example of this

---

TABLE 5.1 The Customer Adoption Lifecyle: Five Customer Types

ADOPTER GROUP	CHARACTERISTICS	VALUE DERIVED FROM PRODUCT
Innovators (2.5%)	Embrace technology for technology's sake; willing to work with technical bugs or failures	Possession of cool new technology; ability to "experiment" and, often, provide feedback
Early adopters (13.5%)	Application enthusiasts; seeking a revolution; demanding but collaborative	Ability to gain an advantage from the new technology; possessing the technology before others
Early majority (34%)	"Main Street"; seeking evolution from an existing solution; persuaded by similar customer references	Demonstrated ROI; "Plug-and-play"; low transition costs; standardized customer support
Late majority (34%)	Well-served by existing solutions; seeks commodity technology	Clear expectation of value based on the adoption by others
Laggards (16%)	Willing to pay a cost *not* to adopt; resistant to technology adoption	Zero?

The Hazards of Ignoring Early Adopters

Early adopters play multiple roles in the diffusion of new products and services. Their fondness for experimentation means they are often willing to work through the technical bugs and product quirks inherent in early releases (in many cases, providing valuable feedback that improves the product for mainstream users). They also serve as product evangelists, increasing awareness, certifying the value, and demonstrating the features of a new product to those in their networks. But what happens when they are blocked from early access to a new technology?

As described in the text, an entrepreneur's initiative to distribute $100 of Bitcoin to MIT students created an opportunity to experiment. In one experiment, Professors Christian Catalini and Catherine Tucker randomly staggered the distribution of Bitcoin among first-year students. In so doing, they intentionally blocked half of the natural early adopters of Bitcoin (the initial registrants on the wait list) from receiving Bitcoin first. Forced to wait until the second distribution of Bitcoin several weeks later, these natural early adopters lost the exclusivity that comes with being an early adopter. This had a profound effect on their adoption behavior and, subsequently, on the adoption behavior of those in their networks (e.g., dorm mates).

Compared with those natural early adopters who received their Bitcoin in the first distribution, natural early adopters who were delayed from receiving their Bitcoin

An experiment with discerning Bitcoin interest in college dorms showed the importance of finding and cultivating early adopters.

were more likely to cash out and abandon the cryptocurrency entirely. Where the loss of exclusivity was more evident among students (for instance, in smaller dorms), the cash-out rate was even higher. Moreover, the natural early adopters abandoning cryptocurrency had spillover effects to the natural late adopters within their community. These late adopters followed suit in cashing out their Bitcoin at higher rates, leading to lower adoption of the cryptocurrency in these dorms.[a]

is seen in the evolution of the smartphone industry. Though often associated with companies like Apple, the origin of the smartphone can be traced roughly to when telecom company BellSouth released the IBM Simon in 1994.[10] In addition to the common features of existing personal digital assistants (PDAs) and cell phones (such as calendars, contacts, and reminders), the Simon allowed users to check email and send faxes and had both a touch screen and predictive typing. However, its heavy weight, 1-hour battery life, and clunky interface also meant it created little value for customers outside of technology enthusiasts who enjoyed its novelty (indeed, only 50,000 units sold). (See the sidebar on **The First Smartphone**.)

Over the next few years, however, a number of other firms, including Ericsson, Nokia, Microsoft, and Qualcomm, would make inroads into the smartphone category by focusing on different customers. A company named Research in Motion (RIM) (you will read more on this company in

FIGURE 5.5 Initial Customer Choices by Different Smartphone Companies

(a)

(b)

(c)

(a) RIM's BlackBerry was a hit with business professionals. (b) Apple's first iPhone targeted early adopters looking for the next new thing. (c) The first Android adopters were often early adopters who wanted to take advantage of functionality Apple did not provide. However, the widespread licensing of Android's operating system led to even cheaper phones to appeal to mainstream users.

Chapter 8) targeted innovators and then early adopters in the smartphone sector with its wildly successful BlackBerry, launched in 1999. In particular, RIM focused on busy professionals who sought the business advantage that mobile email access provided (**Figure 5.5a**). Whereas RIM struggled with the early majority, Apple and Google made choices in their first smartphones that focused on attracting early adopters and the early majority. Apple sought to "reinvent the phone" for the everyday, early majority, mainstream user and emphasized simple plug-and-play design and features with its first iPhone (**Figure 5.5b**). Google, with its Android smartphone (**Figure 5.5c**), also targeted mainstream customers. It prioritized building an open ecosystem to lower the transition costs for early majority customers through compatibility with other companies. As they gained traction with customers, both Apple and Google prioritized product investments (e.g., iTunes, the App Store, Google Play) that broadened and clarified the value of smartphones and extended adoption into the late majority. In fact, from the earliest days of the smartphone to the most recent iPhone and Android models, the characteristics of smartphone customers map closely to the Customer Adoption Lifecycle (**Figure 5.6**).[11] However, as we will discuss next, the transition across different customer groups is fraught with difficulty.

5.5 The Chasm

The Customer Adoption Lifecycle shows us that it is important to launch products that initially target innovators and early adopters. To return to the falling domino analogy, it is important to be able to actually push over that first domino to start the whole process. That, however, is only the beginning. Entrepreneurs also must consider where that first domino is going to land: specifically, will it land on another domino that itself is a part of a chain?

To Geoffrey Moore, this was the biggest challenge for most start-ups. In his popular book *Crossing the Chasm*, Moore outlined the potential gaps (or missing dominoes) that can slow or halt the spread of most new ideas.[12] The largest gap, or chasm, was that between early adopters and the early majority (**Figure 5.7** on p. 144). Again and again, start-ups found traction with early adopters only to see diffusion fizzle out with lackluster adoption among mainstream users. A signature example was the Segway with its human transporter. Launched in 2000 to much fanfare, this seemingly magical, two-wheeled device could move people at up to 12.5 miles per hour. Its inventor, Dean Kamen, believed it would replace walking and transform cities. But despite numerous early adopters, it was soon abandoned to far more narrow use cases. Today, you still see Segways used by tourist groups exploring a city's landmarks or by some police officers, including in the movie *Paul Blart: Mall Cop*.

The Segway is an example of a product that never found its way into the mainstream.

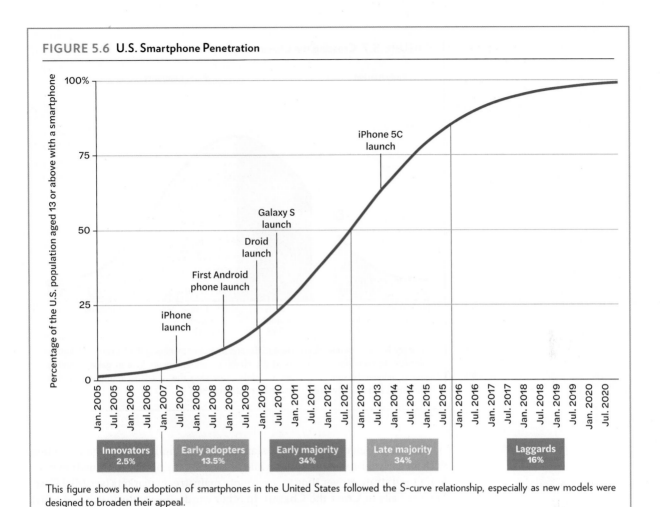

FIGURE 5.6 U.S. Smartphone Penetration

This figure shows how adoption of smartphones in the United States followed the S-curve relationship, especially as new models were designed to broaden their appeal.

To Moore, the experience of Segway was more likely to be the rule than the exception. The motives for early adopters and the early majority to purchase a product are markedly different. As we have already seen, early adopters value their image of being ahead of the curve (in this case, the S curve). They are more likely to experiment and prefer the novel to the incremental. By contrast, mainstream customers do not place weight on any of these factors. They are more risk averse and only adopt new products or services if they fit well within their existing pattern of behaviors or ways of operating. They do not want to stand out in their choices (or, for that matter, on a Segway). Thus, when looking at a new product, they will place considerable weight on recommendations from individuals they trust. However, as Moore pointed out, early adopters, precisely because of their willingness to experiment and their desire to be seen as farsighted, are not the sort of people mainstream customers necessarily trust for recommendations. They, in many cases, simply cannot speak credibly to the value drivers that motivate mainstream users (e.g., plug-and-play operability, reliability). *For start-ups, this means they should expect to face a chasm between these distinct customer segments—early adopters and mainstream customers—and should develop a plan to overcome it.*

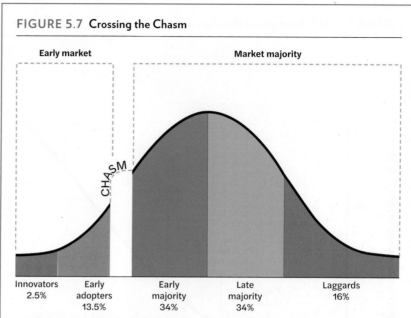

FIGURE 5.7 Crossing the Chasm

Early market

Market majority

CHASM

Innovators
2.5%

Early adopters
13.5%

Early majority
34%

Late majority
34%

Laggards
16%

Geoffrey Moore's framework emphasized the importance of managing the Customer Adoption Lifecycle. In particular, Moore noted the challenge entrepreneurs face in gaining traction among innovators and early adopters while preserving the ability to transition product, marketing, and strategy to serve the mainstream market.

Thus, a key challenge facing a start-up is determining how to gain traction with an early customer segment while preserving the ability to transition marketing and strategy over time to serve more mainstream markets (see **Mini Case: Soylent Fails to Cross the Chasm**). In other words, the strategic value of a first customer segment is critical for navigating an S curve.

FOCUS

To resolve this seeming paradox, Moore emphasizes the role of focus. To return to our falling domino analogy, the chasm exists not because of an insurmountable gap but because the domino must fall precisely to complete the chain and topple ever larger dominoes. A focus on ensuring this connection (i.e., that it falls the right way) is the path to success and to mainstream customers. For Moore, this meant finding ways to focus on serving the initial customer segment fully, even if it required forgoing other sales opportunities in the short term.

The reason such absolute focus on customer satisfaction is important is because customers are not passive dominoes. For an initial customer sale to lead to sales in other segments, the customer needs to become a point of *credible* reference. Recall that the early majority do not seek novelty or experimentation, but rather take their cues from the successful experiences of individuals with whom they share at least some affinity and whose views they respect (on at least that topic). For founding teams, the ideal early adopter is not only one who seeks novelty and experimentation but also one whose experiences are shared with

Soylent Fails to Cross the Chasm

After graduating from Georgia Tech and launching a start-up with two friends trying to develop less expensive cell phone towers, Rob Rhinehart had a problem. He and his friends' ideas were not working, and they had burned through over half of the seed investment they had received as part of the Y Combinator seed accelerator program. With little progress to show and a dwindling bank account, Rhinehart saw a new opportunity in trying to reduce one of his biggest living expenditures: the money he spent on food. Rhinehart was so convinced in the potential of this idea, he decided to shift from a start-up focused on engineering to one on biochemistry, developing a nutritional system out of raw, inexpensive chemical components that could sustain a human being indefinitely. He called his initial liquid nutrition creation Soylent, from the 1970s sci-fi movie *Soylent Green*, where humans are forced to exist on a uniform food source. He tested it on himself, resulting in a viral blog post, "How I Stopped Eating Food." While plenty questioned his motivation—as Stephen Colbert later asked Rhinehart, "Did you see someone in a coma with a feeding tube and you thought, I'll have what he's having?"—and there were many skeptics (some proclaiming "RIP Rob"), there was enough positive feedback and sample requests to encourage him to make a business out of it.

In 2013, Soylent was put forward as a basic concept in a crowdfunding campaign and seemed to find considerable success. While the team had hoped for $100,000 in presales, the venture ultimately raised over $1 million by summer's end. Although the Soylent team never decided precisely which type of customer to target, Soylent seemed to flourish among a community of like-minded early adopters who comprised the majority of the roughly 10,000 presale customers. Over the next few years, after some production delays and product modifications, Soylent successfully established its product among programmers, gamers, and the start-up community.

While Soylent found an initial core market, it has yet to catch on with a broader group.

But despite the enormous applications envisioned by Rhinehart, Soylent never expanded out of this core group. It remained a niche product that did not meaningfully change society or scale its products to serve as a substitute in broader markets where Rhinehart hoped it would be a game changer. Despite marketing videos emphasizing customer segments outside its core demographic of programmers and gamers (i.e., featuring women, recreational athletes, hipsters, and a DJ), the initial penetration of the programmer and gamer segments had been slow to translate to broader acceptance or even awareness in the mass market.

In 2023, Soylent was acquired by the consumer products company Starco Brands, which produces food and other products linked to celebrities such as Anderson Cooper and Cardi B.

and well-received by the targeted early majority customers. This information exchange may occur formally through reviews (e.g., online reviews, trade journals, conferences) or informally through personal and professional networks. Critically, to cross the chasm into mainstream customers, founding teams must identify the early majority segments to create credible references for and determine how to service the early adopter customer segments that will generate those valuable references. Simply put, before you can set an early domino in the perfect location, you need to know which follow-on domino you'd like to strike and how you will do so.

A classic case of a company that successfully crossed the chasm was Documentum, though you can be forgiven for not having heard of it. Founded by Howard Shao and John Newton in 1990, it was an enterprise document management software company that was eventually purchased by the Canadian company OpenText in 2004 for $1.6 billion.[13] Prior to Documentum, enterprises handled their electronic documents, to the extent they handled them at all, with individual "owners" storing documents on their own PCs. Imagine the potential for chaos with each member of a team having distinct (and, perhaps, separately evolving) versions of a given file; now imagine trying to collect and collate thousands of files (and their various updates) across a firm. The Documentum team understood this problem and had the idea of combining document management with relational databases so that an enterprise's documents could be hosted and accessed on a shared, centralized server. Today, this is natural with documents routinely being placed in the cloud, but in the 1990s, it was a very novel proposition.

Faced with the chasm in reaching mainstream enterprise customers, the Documentum team decided to shift from their strategy of trying to acquire any enterprise customer that would have them and instead ranked alternative customer segments by the "pain" these potential customers currently felt in managing their documents.[14] Documentum ultimately prioritized the pharmaceutical industry and specifically targeted regulatory affairs departments. New drug approvals are a costly and complex affair with many different regulatory requirements worldwide. Moreover, because such drugs have limited life patents, there is strong incentive to make sure that the process goes as quickly as possible. The real pain, as Documentum identified, was in handling the many documents and references for drug applications (e.g., lab notebooks, patent resources, clinical trial data) that could easily range from a quarter-million to half-million pages! Documentum found that by solving this problem it could save pharmaceutical companies a million dollars per day.

In the end, Documentum secured a beachhead in the pharmaceutical industry, with 30 of the top 40 firms as customers. Using the fact of this group's adoption as evidence of traction, Documentum then moved on to the regulatory departments of other industries including manufacturing plants, oil and gas, and then Wall Street. The dominoes started to topple, and the company was able to reach broader and broader segments of enterprise customers (see the sidebar on **Documentum: Targeting the Right Customer**).

Documentum: Targeting the Right Customer. By targeting a very specific market of leading pharmaceutical firms and creating a high-value solution for it, In 1993 it released its Electronic Document Management System running through desktops, and in 2000 upgrade to a full web client. Documentum came to dominate an industry niche, leading to its acquisition. Documentum was first bought by and marketed under its name by EMC, and now is owned by OpenText.

SOURCE: https://ecmnotes.com/2012/01/05/documentum-history/

5.6 Network Effects: Where Inherent Value and Strategic Value Collide

For many products, whether a customer buys the product does not depend directly on what other customers are doing. To be sure, you can get information from other people, but whether you purchase or not depends on the value you, yourself, receive. This property is not true of all products. Some products exhibit what economists have come to term "network effects."

network effects When value for a product depends on other people's use of the product, and vice versa

A product has a *network effect* if the value any one person receives is higher when there are other people using the same product. An obvious example is the telephone. When telephones were first introduced, few people had them. This limited the primary function and value of the phone, which was to talk to others, because there were only a limited number of people to call (let alone who a given person knew or wanted to speak with). As adoption increased, however, a virtuous cycle emerged whereby additional adoption raised the value to everyone, including those who had previously adopted phones, from this new technology. This is one of the reasons why products can see a strong "take-off" phase in market adoption patterns (and a corresponding steep rise in the associated market S curve).

Network effects—where your value for a product depends on other people's use of the product, and vice versa—emerge in many industries. For example, fashion is dictated by what people are comfortable wearing, which is why there are fashion trends over time and different fashions in different countries and for different age groups. This also happens in much of popular culture, where a social element dictates what people pay attention to. Most significantly, in recent times, social media is driven by network effects: Facebook has many billions of users, with each user joining in large part because their friends have previously done so.

We will return to network effects and how they shape entrepreneurial strategy in later chapters. For the moment, let's end with the idea that with network effects, customers' long-term inherent value depends on others adopting and using a product or service. When network effects are present, an entrepreneur must be mindful of how to generate initial adoption when, by definition, the value of the network cannot (yet) be part of customer value. Consequently, initial adopters need to get special treatment, perhaps in the form of lower prices, to compensate them for the lack of a network, at least temporarily. Entrepreneurs will also have to consider whether they can adjust favorable terms when the network does emerge. In such cases, the choice of initial (beachhead) customer may be especially critical.

5.7 Choosing Your Customer

Far from an obvious choice, the selection of a beachhead customer depends on a number of criteria and has consequences for both immediate and long-term customer adoption and venture performance. Identifying a customer segment that the venture can create real value for and can reasonably tackle (i.e., barriers to customer adoption are not overly high) is a necessary first step for the launch and scaling of most ventures. And an important criterion in selecting the right starting point is if that customer segment can facilitate learning and referencing as well as be a good jumping-off point to more mainstream customers (see **Deep Dive: Some Common Metrics Used to Evaluate Customer Choice** on p. 148).

But though clear in theory, most start-ups struggle to focus on an initial customer segment. Often, those start-ups with the widest range of potential applications have the hardest challenge in focusing on a single market.

This chapter's video contrasts the business strategies of Misfit Wearables and Whistle, two ventures that captured the same entrepreneurial opportunity with vastly different customers.

Some Common Metrics Used to Evaluate Customer Choice

Many useful metrics have been developed to help ventures evaluate the returns from different target customers. Three in particular are:

- **Customer acquisition cost (CAC)** calculates the total amount of money a company spends to gain a new customer. This includes expenses related to marketing, advertising, sales efforts, and any other activities or resources used to attract and convert potential customers. CAC helps businesses evaluate the effectiveness of their marketing and sales strategies and make data-driven decisions about their budget and resource allocation. To calculate CAC, divide the total customer acquisition-related expenses by the number of new customers acquired during a specific period.
- **Lifetime value (LTV)** estimates the total net profit a start-up can expect from a customer throughout their entire relationship with the business. This value considers the customer's revenue contributions, the duration of their relationship with the company, and the costs associated with retaining the customer. LTV helps businesses understand the long-term financial value of their customer segments and make more informed choices. The calculation typically considers factors such as average purchase value, purchase frequency, customer life span, and customer retention costs.
- **Total addressable market (TAM)** describes the overall revenue potential or market size for a particular product or service. It represents the maximum sales opportunity available if a company could capture 100% of the market share within the targeted segment. TAM helps businesses understand the scale of the market opportunity and assess the potential for growth and profitability. It is a key factor in strategic planning, investment decisions, and resource allocation. To estimate TAM, companies typically use market research, industry reports, and historical data to analyze the number of potential customers, their purchasing habits, and the market value of the product or service in question.

To see how these metrics can be applied, consider the following example. Imagine you own a subscription-based online fitness platform that provides workout plans, nutrition advice, and personal coaching for $50 per month.

1. Customer acquisition cost (CAC): To attract new customers, you run online ads, social media campaigns, and email marketing. Suppose you spend $5,000 on these marketing efforts and acquire 50 new customers. To calculate CAC, divide the total marketing expenses by the number of new customers: $5,000 / 50 = $100 per customer.
2. Lifetime value (LTV): Let's say, on average, your customers stay subscribed for 12 months before canceling their subscriptions. During their subscription, they pay $50 per month, so the total revenue generated per customer is $50 × 12 = $600. If it then costs you $150 per customer for support and other services during this 12-month period, then the net profit per customer is $450. So, the LTV of each customer is $450.
3. Total addressable market (TAM): After conducting market research, you find out that there are 200,000 potential customers in your target market who are interested in online fitness subscriptions like yours. If you could capture 100% of this market, your TAM would be the total revenue you could generate: 200,000 customers × $50 per month × 12 months = $120,000,000.

What these calculations tell you is that attracting a customer costs $100, from which you expect to earn a profit of $450. Thus, LTV exceeds CAC and so it is profitable to attract customers. Suppose that you expect to capture 1 percent of the market. In this case, you will have 2,000 customers, each of which costs $100 to attract and gives you profits of $450. Thus, your total profit if you start the online venture is ($450 – $100) × 2,000 = $700,000 per year.

For most start-ups, the choice of an initial customer segment is made from a broad set of potential customers (at least in principle). However, for many, if not most, of these potential customers, it will become quickly apparent that barriers exist to creating that value from them, at least in the short term. For example, in a case like Documentum's, the purchasing approval needed for the new service might lie within the department the service might be eliminating. While that customer segment may still be valuable over the long term (with effort), it probably won't be at the outset. As a consequence, these customer segments with these types of obvious barriers won't be part of the initial focus.

Still, even after this process, most start-ups will face a choice among a small but meaningfully distinct set of initial customer segments. And these may be difficult to prioritize based on their immediate potential. In these cases, it may be useful to consider how the choice of beachhead shapes the mainstream market the venture achieves. To see this process at its most extreme, consider the launches of two start-ups focused on "fitness wearables beyond the wrist." Founded in 2011, Misfit Wearables concentrated on elegantly designed "smart" jewelry (**Figure 5.8a**), and its first product was a fitness tracker that could be worn as a necklace. Founded several months later, Whistle Labs used essentially the same technology and insight to develop a fitness tracker for pets, with an initial focus on the canine market (**Figure 5.8b**). Each of these start-ups explored, in one sense, the same idea, and each would have had the technical skill to produce the product commercialized by the other. However, they each chose a different beachhead market, scaled to different mainstream markets, and, yet, both ultimately have enjoyed a somewhat comparable level of success: Misfit Wearables was acquired by Fossil in 2015 for $260 million, while Whistle Labs was acquired by Mars Petcare in 2016 for $117 million. While the former is greater than the latter, both would be considered good results from the perspective of a Silicon Valley investor.

We see illustrated in this example that the same idea might have several initial customer segments that will work. The choices the entrepreneur makes will drive a strategic S-curve path to a different mainstream market with distinct customer preferences and market size. Choosing a customer is, therefore, not a search process for the perfect early adopter segment or beachhead segment. Rather, choosing your customer is a decision that drives the market and opportunity the business will target.

This means that founding teams should take a proactive and action-oriented approach to the process of customer choice. Rather than endlessly analyzing information in a search for the "optimal" beachhead market, you should realize there may be more than one (**Figure 5.9** on p. 150). The job of choosing your customer means understanding the likely impact from alternative beachhead markets and choosing the one that best fits with the overall strategy and purpose of the venture (see **Putting It Together: Choosing Your Customer** on p. 151).

5.8 Concluding Thoughts

The foundation of any viable venture is creating value in a meaningful way for consumers. And because the ability to create value for any customer depends on making prioritized investments to deliver that value, customer choice is arguably

customer acquisition cost (CAC) The total amount of money a company spends to gain a new customer

lifetime value (LTV) Estimates the total net profit a company can expect to generate from a customer throughout their entire relationship with the business

total addressable market (TAM) The overall revenue potential or market size for a particular product or service

FIGURE 5.8 Same Idea, Different Customers

(a)

(b)

Essentially the same technology and idea were behind two different fitness trackers. (a) The Shine from Misfit Wearables was an elegant monitor designed for the wrist, hip, neck, shoe, shirt, or bra. (b) Whistle Labs designed their tracker for pets to be worn on a collar. What drove the opportunity was the choice of customer.

FIGURE 5.9 Market S-Curve Choice

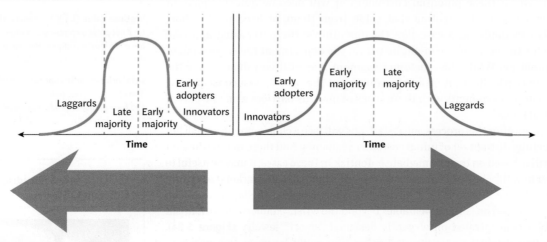

The market S curve the start-up faces depends on the entrepreneur's choice of initial customer. The choice to focus their scarce resources and attention on one initial customer segment induces a potential S curve with its own potential follow-on market and diffusion dynamics. Choosing one customer does mean forgoing another; in this figure, choosing the Red or Blue market will take you down a single path that forgoes the other.

the first critical step a founding team must wrestle with. Customer choice combines the hard work of identifying the most promising areas for customer value creation with an eye toward choosing customers who can help a venture transition to other customers over time, reinforce other strategic decisions, and, ultimately, realize the vision for the venture.

Chapter 5 Review: Choosing Your Customer

CHAPTER TAKEAWAYS

- Start-ups often have many potential customers for their idea. While it is tempting to want to choose them all, limited resources and strategic constraints mean an entrepreneur must choose.

- The initial set of customers targeted are called beachhead customers. An ideal beachhead customer is a customer group from which the entrepreneur expects to derive both inherent and strategic value such that the customer group provides a path to a larger mainstream market.

- Inherent value is what customers themselves obtain from adopting your product. This is captured by the economic term "willingness to pay," which is the maximum amount that customers would be willing to pay for your product.

- Strategic value is the value a customer group provides to the venture. This includes the ability of the founding team to learn and gain feedback from these initial customers and/or to effectively reference this segment when targeting follow-on customers.

CHOOSING YOUR CUSTOMER

Deciding who your first customers will be is an important strategic choice for any venture. Starting with the right first beachhead customers is crucial to succeeding with follow-on groups.

IDENTIFY AND PRIORITIZE THE INHERENT VALUE OF POTENTIAL BEACHHEAD CUSTOMERS

Identify a Shortlist of Potential Ideal Beachhead Customers

- Describe how your idea can create real value for a specific group of end users. Then, for each potential set of end users, identify the lead customers, key partners, and competitors.

- Estimate the value proposition and the size of each potential beachhead customer segment and corresponding overall mainstream market.

- Prioritize among these potential beachhead customer segments on the basis of relative value creation.

STRATEGICALLY RANK BEACHHEAD CUSTOMER ALTERNATIVES

Evaluate the Ability of Each Beachhead Group to Transition to the Mainstream Market

- Assess each potential beachhead customer group's effectiveness as a credible reference to follow-on customer groups in moving toward the mainstream market.

- Consider how transitioning to follow-on customer groups may require changes to the product, features, or service.

- Compare potential beachhead customer segments in terms of generating opportunities for venture learning and experimentation.

- Rank the potential beachhead customer segments. For each, list the key hypotheses for value creation.

NARROW BEACHHEAD CUSTOMER ALTERNATIVES THROUGH EXPERIMENTATION AND LEARNING

Conduct Low-Commitment Learning

- Identify steps to learn more about potential beachhead customer groups that will improve your venture's choice. Consider which resources or interviews may sharpen your value creation hypotheses.

- For your top-ranked beachhead groups, generate a low-commitment test to validate key components of your value creation hypotheses.

- The market S curve captures the cumulative percentage of potential customers who adopt a product or service over time. Even for breakthrough innovations, customer adoption is initially quite slow as potential users must both become aware of the innovation and understand the value it provides before deciding whether to adopt the product or service. This slow initial traction is followed by a period of quicker gains before a final tapering off.

- Market adoption cannot be faster than the diffusion of the related knowledge through the population of potential customers. Knowledge diffusion is slow as potential customers come to understand a new product and the value it creates.

- The Customer Adoption Lifecycle breaks down market adoption patters into five types: innovators, early adopters, early majority, late majority, and laggards.

- The market S curve reflects distinct types of customers and adoption behaviors of the Customer Adoption Lifecycle. Taken together with Geoffrey Moore's findings in his book *Crossing the Chasm*, it shows the importance of targeting products initially toward early adopters while preserving the ability to transition marketing and strategy over time to serve more mainstream markets.

- Network effects arise when a customer's willingness to pay depends on other customers adopting the product. This leads businesses to adopt more aggressive strategies for targeting and attracting initial customers.

- Choosing a customer is not a search process for the optimal early adopter or beachhead segment but rather choosing which market customer/behavior to serve.

KEY TERMS

beachhead customers (p. 129)

customer (p. 129)

inherent value (p. 130)

strategic value (p. 130)

innovation diffusion (p. 133)

market S curve (p. 134)

early adopters (p. 135)

Customer Adoption Lifecycle (p. 140)

network effects (p. 147)

customer acquisition cost (CAC) (p. 149)

lifetime value (LTV) (p. 149)

total addressable market (TAM) (p. 149)

REVIEW QUESTIONS

1. Why must a start-up create value for its customers? In your answer, include definitions of willingness to pay, price, and cost.

2. Why is it often difficult for entrepreneurs to estimate customer willingness to pay for their potential product or services relative to those of existing products or services?

3. Outside of the costs of producing and distributing a product or service, entrepreneurs must factor in the resources and time to educate and acquire customers. What are common sources of customer acquisition costs?

4. What are the three phases of the market S curve? Explain the logic behind the different rates of adoptions within each phase and the implications for entrepreneurs.

5. Define and explain the difference between the inherent value of a customer segment and its strategic value to the start-up. Why do entrepreneurs seek both in their initial (beachhead) customer?

6. What are key ways beachhead customers can provide strategic value to a venture?

7. According to the Customer Adoption Lifecycle, how does the value derived from a new product or service differ for early adopters vs. that of the early and late majority?

8. Outline the key findings of Geoffrey Moore's *Crossing the Chasm*. What are the main implications for entrepreneurs?

9. Define network effects. What are examples of products or services you use that have network effects, and how does that affect the value created for you by the product or service?

10. Why must an entrepreneur choose a customer? Why does the beachhead an entrepreneur chooses determine the mainstream market they gain?

DISCUSSION QUESTIONS

Answer the following series of questions and scenarios either in class discussions, or by writing a short response.

1. Jacques is founding a new firm to commercialize a new type of inhaler that will allow individuals to safely breathe small droplets into their bodies. One potential application would allow people (e.g., college-age students at a party) to "taste" small droplets of, say, strawberry or chocolate and so get a small burst of flavor for only one or two calories. An alternative application would be to provide a small but rapid-acting dose of insulin for Type I diabetics. How does the value proposition differ across these two alternative market segments? Do you think that Jacques has to choose between these applications (at least at first) or should he try to pursue all potential applications of his technology? How might choosing one of these segments impact the likelihood of pursuing the other segment in the future?

2. Many entrepreneurs and companies are interested in pursuing opportunities in the metaverse, where individuals will interact virtually in ways that are similar to real-world interactions. Frederick is considering founding a wedding service provider for the metaverse. It would enable friends and family who might not otherwise be able to travel or attend a wedding to gather online. While talking with engaged couples and their families and friends, Frederick found that many had significant interest in what he would offer and would be more than willing to pay for such a service.

    a. Write down how much you think a couple would be willing to pay for a wedding in the metaverse. Now compare your figure with other members in your study group. How close were you? What accounts for the difference?

    b. How might Frederick determine the willingness to pay (WTP) for such a service? How would WTP vary with different potential beachheads?

What is an experiment or test he could run that would allow him to compare WTP across different potential beachhead markets?

3. Consider the Soylent example from the chapter. After a crowdfunding campaign, the Soylent liquid nutritional meal replacement product became popular among programmers and gamers who prioritized a quick meal that would allow them to remain online while they ate. However, this was not the only customer segment that Soylent could have chosen. Identify an alternative customer segment that could have served as a beachhead for Soylent. Why do you believe that there is a potential for value creation in this segment, and how does that value proposition differ from the gamer and programmer segment? Do you think that gamers and programmers might be an effective reference for potential customers in this alternative segment? How about the reverse? Do you believe that Soylent would have been able to "cross the chasm" if the founding team had focused their initial efforts on serving this alternative beachhead?

4. Select a recent start-up from your university or region. What is its beachhead market? What value is the start-up providing to these early customers? Do you think this beachhead will be an effective "first domino" in sequencing toward larger market segments over time? Why or why not? What would you recommend that this start-up do to "cross the chasm"?

5. Now consider this same start-up from (4). Can you identify an alternative beachhead the start-up team could have chosen but are not serving yet? How would this change the value proposition they are creating for these alternative customers? Do you think that this start-up should also pursue this customer segment, or have they left this alternative market behind?

SUGGESTED READINGS

Aulet, Bill. *Disciplined Entrepreneurship: 24 Steps to a Successful Startup.* Hoboken, NJ: Wiley, 2013.

Blank, Steve, and Bob Dorf. *The Startup Owner's Manual: The Step-by-Step Guide for Building a Great Company.* Hoboken, NJ: Wiley, 2020.

Constable, Giff, Frank Rimalovski, and Tom Fishburne. *Talking to Humans: Success Starts with Understanding Your Customers.* Self-published, Giff Constable, 2014.

Griliches, Zvi. "Hybrid Corn: An Exploration in the Economics of Technological Change." *Econometrica, Journal of the Econometric Society* (1957): 501–22.

Moore, Geoffrey A. *Crossing the Chasm: Marketing and Selling Disruptive Products to Mainstream Customers.* 3rd ed. New York: Harper, 2014.

Rogers, Everett M. *Diffusion of Innovations.* 5th ed. New York: Free Press, 2003.

Nouman Ahmad and Ian Burgess

In 2015, Nouman Ahmad and Ian Burgess took nanomaterial sensor technology Burgess had developed during his PhD studies and started looking for applications. The technology showed promise for identifying unknown liquids, and the two had identified many potential applications. One particular idea was to target luxury cosmetics brands to use this technology to identify counterfeit perfumes.

However, a different plan emerged when they met Chen Fong as part of a mentorship at the Creative Destruction Lab program. Fong was a successful entrepreneur based in Calgary, where much of Canada's oil and gas industry is located. Highlighting the need for the duo to focus on just one customer initially, Fong persuaded Ahmad and Burgess to explore opportunities in oil and gas—about as far away from luxury cosmetics as could be imagined. The oil and gas focus proved compelling. Ahmad and Burgess realized that the quality and properties of oil and gas dictate pricing, yet the lack of real-time visibility into this data was causing significant inefficiencies as products changed hands between the well, pipelines, storage facilities, and refineries. Through Validere, the duo's start-up, they saw an opportunity to leverage new software techniques using their technology to collect, clean, organize, and draw insights from the vast amounts of operational data being generated across oil and gas companies' complex operations and supply chains. Doing so could unlock large commercial and environmental benefits.

To validate the new focus, the Validere team built relationships and ran pilots with major oil and gas companies in Canada and the United States, demonstrating strong customer pull. The pivot meant shifting Validere's engineering base from Cambridge (MA) to Calgary and Houston to work closely with customers on product development. As Canadians, the founders chose to keep Validere's headquarters and some software development in Toronto to leverage engineering talent.

The shift allowed Validere to build an end-to-end carbon management platform, which integrates and contextualizes emissions data with operational data. This

Nouman Ahmad and Ian Burgess took advice from a mentor to choose their customer.

helps energy companies accurately track emissions events, streamline compliance reporting, model reduction strategies, and participate in voluntary emissions programs.

Ahmad and Burgess's willingness to take advice and pivot to a totally new customer choice has been very successful. As of 2023, Validere serves over 50 customers across oil and gas, agriculture, wastewater, petrochemicals, and other asset-intensive industries facing decarbonization challenges. Validere has raised $65 million in funding and saw 350% year-over-year revenue growth in 2022.

Questions

1. What does Validere's process for choosing a first customer tell you about the critical features of that choice process?

2. When choosing a customer, how important is it to consider whether you should change the location of a venture?

In 2008, Elon Musk looks under the hood of a new Tesla with then-governor of California, Arnold Schwarzenegger. Musk saw vast improvements to battery technology as key to his venture.

ENTREPRENEUR'S DILEMMA Entrepreneurs often face a choice between exploiting already existing technology or exploring the potential of an emerging innovation. While rapidly exploiting existing technology gets a firm to market more quickly, a more exploratory approach might uncover a path that has a higher impact and creates more value. What choices do entrepreneurs face when considering the role of technology? How can founding teams leverage technological innovation as a foundation for creating and capturing value?

CHAPTER OBJECTIVES

- Learn why start-ups must choose a technology
- Understand the trade-off between exploration and exploitation
- Examine how start-ups can harness the technology S curve
- Discuss the dimensions of technology choice

6

CHOOSING YOUR TECHNOLOGY

I n 2003, Elon Musk first test-drove the tzero, a handmade electric sports car that used recent advances in lithium-ion batteries. Musk was already committed to launching SpaceX, his new start-up trying to disrupt the space flight industry. But he quickly became convinced that though the tzero was a long way from commercial viability, key design and technology elements in this new vehicle were critical first steps toward mass-produced electric vehicles. Most notably, the tzero would be the first electric vehicle to replace relatively cheap but heavy and inefficient lead batteries with *much* more expensive but far more efficient lithium-ion batteries. In principle, Musk and others believed these lithium-ion batteries would create a dramatic improvement in vehicle performance. Further, unlike traditional battery- and gas-powered engine technology that was improving at a slow, incremental rate, lithium-ion batteries seemed to have the potential for both significant leaps in performance and dramatic decreases in cost. Musk's belief about this potential for improvement based on the tzero prototype led to him becoming the first lead investor and cofounder of Tesla Motors along with Martin Eberhard, Marc Tarpenning, Ian Wright, and J. B. Straubel.

Elon Musk and his cofounders were not alone in seeing the potential of lithium-ion batteries to revolutionize electric vehicles. Basic academic research on lithium-ion batteries has been going on for decades. The 2019 Nobel Prize was awarded to three pioneers in lithium-ion battery technology whose key research was done during the 1970s. The first commercial electric vehicle battery was developed by the established oil giant Exxon as far back as the late 1970s. Moreover, by the early 2000s, lithium-ion batteries were commercially viable for small electronic devices such as laptop computers and cell phones. But creating a cost-effective, high-performance lithium-ion-powered electric vehicle remained elusive for major auto companies. Adapting their automobiles

In this chapter we focus on Choices around Technology, including whether you will use an existing or emerging technological path.

to lithium-ion batteries meant not simply improving battery performance but also redesigning the automobile itself (essentially from scratch) to shift from an all-gas to an all-electric vehicle. Given these challenges, plus relatively low gas prices and high customer demand for power-oriented vehicles such as SUVs, most established automobile companies placed a low priority on this opportunity.

Trying to fill this void, a wave of start-ups founded in the 2000s tried to create a low-cost vehicle that took advantage of and exploited recent improvements in lithium-ion batteries. For example, the Israeli start-up Better Place developed a "swappable" battery in which drivers could replace the batteries at a "replacement" station rather than waiting the lengthy times required to charge the batteries. Better Place created an operational all-electric vehicle at a relatively low cost and with a design that was a significant improvement over earlier electric vehicles. Unfortunately, Better Place vehicles were slow to accelerate, handled poorly, and had limited vehicle range (you will learn more about Better Place in Chapter 7). Other start-ups' results were similar: they had some success with their design, but their vehicles' poor performance was caused by the limitations inherent in existing lithium-ion battery technology.

Musk decided to try a different approach. Instead of exploiting the existing technology as other start-ups had, he laid out in a 2006 blog post, "The Secret Tesla Motors Master Plan," a path for Tesla to reach the theoretical potential of lithium-ion batteries at scale. Notably, rather than adapting these batteries into a commercial vehicle at low cost, Musk asked the Tesla team to design a high-performance sports car without concern for immediate cost. This led to the Roadster, a car that sold out its limited production run almost immediately, despite a $110,000 price tag. Because of this success, Musk and the team at Tesla were able to harness resources to design and then build a luxury sedan (the Model S) followed by a successful mass-market vehicle (the Model 3) more than a decade after the company's founding.

Tesla's success reflects two critical early choices by Elon Musk. First, Musk embraced the potential of lithium-ion batteries to be a transformative technology that would lead to practical electric vehicles. But second, he purposely chose a strategy where Tesla would not need to establish a cost-effective solution for nearly a decade in order to succeed. This commitment to a lengthy and more costly process of exploration meant Tesla could invest in the technology to establish new performance benchmarks for lithium-ion batteries. Choosing this exploratory approach meant Tesla would not only leverage available technology, but also work to establish leadership through its innovation.

Whether your technology choice is cutting edge like Tesla's or a more common decision like which coding language to use for your software, choices about what technology to pursue are customary to start-ups; there are often multiple paths for technological development. Do you choose the technology that has better potential in terms of key performance criteria or the one that may be more quickly deployed and more cost-effective? How do you make choices when there is uncertainty about whether a particular technology is up to the task? This chapter first identifies why start-ups must choose thoughtfully any technology that underlies their strategy and how this choice helps shape any innovations they bring to market. Then it shows how to better understand the risks and potential payoffs of technology exploration, including opportunities for disruption. With this in place, the chapter then examines the fundamental trade-off between an approach that *exploits* an existing and available technology

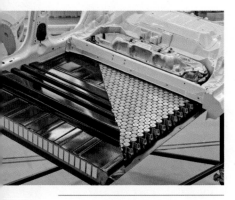

A modern Tesla battery in 2021 cut open to see the interior

Chapter 6: Choosing Your Technology

and one that *explores* and tries to create a higher level of technical performance and customer value. Ultimately, entrepreneurs need to decide which process is better for them and their venture, especially in terms of their own interests and the time and resources available.

6.1 Why Do Start-Ups Have to Choose a Technology?

Every start-up uses technology in some shape or form. **Technology** is simply the tools, techniques, designs, and knowledge used by a business to create practical value for consumers. It is, of course, possible to create value for consumers using existing technology and applying it in standard ways. Think of all the different coffee chains out there now trying so sell you on their particular combination of ice and coffee. However, leveraging technology in a novel way can help a start-up offer **unique value** to a consumer by (1) improving an existing level of performance or (2) providing value on some new dimension of performance that consumers care about but is poorly served by existing offerings. Indeed, technological change itself often triggers entrepreneurial opportunities. In many cases, the most straightforward answer to the question *why now?* is that something that was impossible in the past has become possible because of a new technology. This can include start-ups anchored around a particular technological breakthrough—like the PageRank system at Google (discussed in Chapter 2) or, going further back, the first double-edge safety razor developed by King C. Gillette (discussed further in Chapter 12)—and those that combine technological improvements to create a unique entrepreneurial strategy. For example, the most successful start-up dating apps of the 2010s, such as Tinder and Bumble, combined and exploited specific emerging technology—most notably, GPS-enabled smartphones with built-in cameras—in powerful ways to create novel value for consumers.

However, whether a start-up is founded to bring new technology to market or the technology plays more of a supporting role, the tools and know-how used ultimately shape customer value creation. For example, as recently as the late 1980s, luggage had to be carried by hand or wheeled on separate trolleys.[1] Airline pilot Bob Plath found this approach to luggage handling to be so cumbersome that he assembled a simpler "wheeled luggage" prototype in his garage and successfully tested it through airport security and onto the plane. While others had experimented with wheeled luggage technology during the 1970s (**Figure 6.1a**), Plath focused on a design innovation he called the "Rollaboard" that flipped the orientation of the luggage so that the long side was vertical and the short side balanced on two wheels, allowing the bag to be pulled along in an easy manner (**Figure 6.1b**). Particularly for airline personnel who

technology The application of scientific innovation to a product or venture

unique value The value provided either by improving an existing level of performance or a new dimension of performance that is poorly served by existing offerings

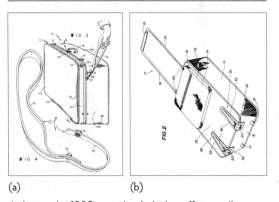

FIGURE 6.1 **Rollaboard Suitcase**

(a) (b)

As late as the 1980s, travelers lacked an efficient rolling suitcase. Most luggage had to be carried by hand or wheeled on separate trolleys. A few four-wheeled designs, like the one in (a), had been patented in the 1970s, but they were difficult to maneuver. Airline pilot Bob Plath flipped the orientation of the suitcase and used two larger wheels instead of four smaller ones (b). This revolutionized luggage transport and led to widespread adoption of wheeled luggage.

routinely avoid checking luggage, the new technology offered by the Rollaboard provided numerous advantages, like navigating busy airline terminals more easily and avoiding leg and arm strain during travel. This relatively simple new technology formed the basis for the founding of TravelPro, which remains a leading brand in the luggage marketplace.

The invention and commercialization of the Rollaboard illustrate why what technology is used and how to use it is such a critical (and hard) choice for entrepreneurs. When done well, an entrepreneur will be able to introduce a new "solution" that is missing from the marketplace.

The Rollaboard ultimately succeeded for two important reasons: it worked well, and customers saw the value in using it instead of alternatives. This does not happen with every new technology or novel combination of technologies. Whether a new solution enhances value creation and capture is by its very nature uncertain. Often, a chosen technology may not work at all or may not reach a critical level of performance. Or if the solution works as intended, whether it creates and captures new value is still uncertain. Customers may not value the new offering because it is not useful or enjoyable in a practical way. Moreover, there are inevitably many different ways to apply technology, such as utilizing features that appeal to one customer group vs. another or as different components of a system. To make a more mobile suitcase, another inventor might have created a detachable wheel and handle set that could fit on existing bags. Whether this would have been as successful as the Rollaboard is unknown, but it likely would have seemed like a less valuable use of the same technology. The time and effort to develop and introduce any specific technological solution come at the expense of time, money, and attention for potential alternative designs and approaches. While it is possible to experiment with one approach, learn about it, and then iterate on a given design, normally, the combinations to try are almost infinite. When developing a technological solution, entrepreneurs will always be constrained; ultimately, an entrepreneur can meaningfully consider a limited number of alternative approaches or technological paths.

With this in mind, let's look at both exploitation and exploration more closely. We will start with the challenge of exploration, as there are far more uncertainties with it than with using an existing technology. So how do you even get started with this approach? Let's turn to a tool that can help.

6.2 The Technology S Curve of Performance Improvement: A Useful Regularity

A key tool that helps navigate the process of technological exploration is the technology S curve. Recall in Chapter 5, "Choosing Your Customer," we introduced the market S curve, a curve that shows how new technology diffuses into a market. The curve is S-shaped because the rate of adoption starts off slow and then rapidly accelerates before leveling out. We see a similar curve emerge with technology exploration.

At the beginning of any technological exploration, the rate of improvement tends to be slow. Significant investment yields only limited improvement on key performance metrics thought to create value. Over time, the rate of performance improvement tends to increase, yielding a sharp uptick in performance.

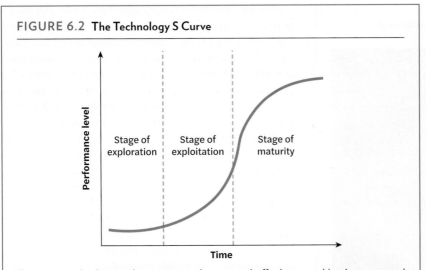

FIGURE 6.2 The Technology S Curve

For a new technology, early investments (in time and effort) may yield only incremental performance gains as researchers explore many distinct approaches (stage of exploration). As research coalesces around a standard approach, investments will yield accelerated performance gains (stage of exploitation) until facing diminishing returns due to the fundamental limits of the technology itself (stage of maturity).

This upward trajectory then slackens and plateaus at a level often constrained by the underlying technology or some physical limitation (e.g., what is even possible from a scientific perspective). First documented by Giovanni Dosi and Richard Foster, this "S-curve" relationship (depicted in **Figure 6.2**) between innovative investment and technological performance has been perhaps the most critical tool employed to manage technology development since the 1980s.[2]

The technology S curve is premised on the simple but important idea that, at the earliest stages of new technology, technological progress is difficult: researchers are spending more of their time learning and failing than measurably improving performance. At one level, this is not surprising since the first stage of this curve—**exploration**—is aimed at understanding the technology itself so that the entrepreneur can focus their efforts rather than pursue an endless number of dead ends. This process serves as the foundation for the second stage—**exploitation**—where researchers focus on particular designs and practical solutions and make rapid and concrete progress toward technical benchmarks (hopefully connected to customer value). Then this process of focusing on a particular design or architecture results in a final stage—**maturity**—where there are diminishing returns because of natural, technological limitations to further investments in that design.

S CURVES AND LED TECHNOLOGY

To see this process in action, consider the evolution of light-emitting diodes (LEDs), which have gone from a scientific curiosity to the primary source of lighting throughout the world over the past 50 years. Relative to the heat-based incandescent bulbs first commercialized by Thomas Edison in the nineteenth century, LED technology builds on the fact that high-energy photons of light

exploration The first stage of a technology S curve, a focus on the long term and emerging technological options

exploitation The second stage of a technology S curve, a focus on what is available in the short term, making use of existing technological solutions

maturity The final stage of a technology S curve where there are diminishing returns due to the fundamental limits of the technology

FIGURE 6.3 The Blue LED Breakthrough

Shuji Nakamura's discovery of the technology for blue LED was fundamental in commercializing LED technology for consumers.

can be emitted from semiconductors when electricity is passed through them. Since the early 1900s, there has been a theoretical understanding that LED technology should have advantages in power consumption and efficiency over incandescent. However, translating this theory into practice took more than a century of hard work and learning. Most notably, using LEDs as a practical source of lighting required producing red, green, and blue (RGB) LEDs (each needing a separate semiconductor material), which could be combined to form "natural" white light. Red and green diodes were developed in 1960 for specific applications where a single color of light was acceptable (such as calculators). However, despite considerable effort by both academic and industrial researchers, producing a practical blue LED proved more elusive, requiring researchers to investigate many different types of materials and chemical processes. A key set of breakthroughs occurred in the late 1980s when Isamu Akasaki, Hiroshi Amano, and Shuji Nakamura figured out how to produce a blue LED on a consistent basis. This discovery was so important that they were awarded a Nobel Prize in 2014 (**Figure 6.3**). Further research and refinement of blue LEDs by Cree Research, a spin-off founded by six North Carolina State University engineers, allowed them to introduce a blue LED that could be used to create full LED screens in the marketplace. Even with this breakthrough, significant improvement was still required before LEDs could compete or improve upon the performance of traditional incandescent lightbulbs in the consumer marketplace.

The Cree founders focused on two interrelated technical metrics: lumens per watt and lumens per lamp. They believed that with significant investment in research by themselves and others, it would be possible to dramatically improve both metrics. This would produce an LED with the ambience of light from an incandescent bulb and the significant power and durability advantages of LED technology.

Over the next 15 years, realizing the goal of this hypothesis was ultimately summed up by Haitz's Law: the amount of light generated per LED can increase by a factor of 20, and the cost per lumen can be reduced by a factor of 10 every 10 years.[3] Put another way, while the improvements obtained by Cree on a year-to-year basis were relatively modest, the exponential nature of that progress over time was transformative: by the early 2010s, the entire lighting industry was transitioning away from incandescent bulbs and toward LED technology (with Cree remaining as a key market leader throughout that time). However, today LED technology is approaching the theoretical maximum efficiency level, and it will plateau unless a new technology emerges.

The performance improvements in LED technology follow (roughly) an S-shaped pattern over time (**Figure 6.4**). Not simply an empirical curiosity, this

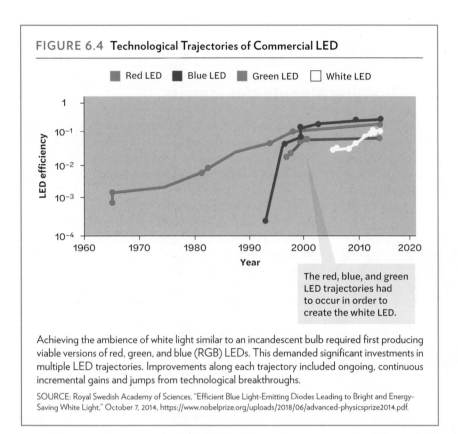

FIGURE 6.4 Technological Trajectories of Commercial LED

■ Red LED ■ Blue LED ■ Green LED □ White LED

The red, blue, and green LED trajectories had to occur in order to create the white LED.

Achieving the ambience of white light similar to an incandescent bulb required first producing viable versions of red, green, and blue (RGB) LEDs. This demanded significant investments in multiple LED trajectories. Improvements along each trajectory included ongoing, continuous incremental gains and jumps from technological breakthroughs.

SOURCE: Royal Swedish Academy of Sciences, "Efficient Blue Light-Emitting Diodes Leading to Bright and Energy-Saving White Light," October 7, 2014, https://www.nobelprize.org/uploads/2018/06/advanced-physicsprize2014.pdf.

pattern can clarify important benefits of exploring technological change. Understanding the S-curve process can

1. highlight how exploration is important in achieving the potential performance of emerging technology;
2. measure a venture's ongoing efforts against intermediate markers of progress independent of actual commercialization;
3. demonstrate that a venture's efforts at exploration have made rapid and telling improvements in performance, which can help raise capital or kickstart other elements of the firm's overall strategy; and
4. help entrepreneurs recognize the potential value of choosing and pursuing an emerging technology, especially one that is at a low level of performance but has the potential for a high rate of improvement over time.

CHALLENGES OF USING THE S-CURVE MODEL

The S-curve framework is also easy (arguably too easy) to misuse. While the S-curve pattern for a given technological trajectory can be obvious *after* it has occurred, it is extremely difficult to forecast how long and how much effort is required to realize this potential in a still-nascent technological trajectory. In many cases, an entrepreneur's optimism for the potential of technological improvement with a limited investment results instead in years (even decades)

Crash-Test Dummies and Choosing Meaningful Metrics

Using technical metrics as a measure of performance can be a powerful tool for entrepreneurs and innovators. Metrics allow entrepreneurs to compare and choose among competing technologies and assess performance improvements over time. However, because technical metrics can influence founding teams' decision-making and the trajectories of their firms, it is crucial to carefully choose the metric itself. Technical metrics not only can track progress but can also come to define what is considered meaningful progress in the first place, shaping the path of technological improvement for sustained periods of time.

For example, consider how the side-impact dummy was introduced as a metric for assessing U.S. vehicular safety improvements in the mid-1990s. For cost and convenience, the dummy design was based on the measurements of a 1960s U.S. median male, simply because parts for dummies with these measurements could be repurposed from military plane dummies that were already in use. In her research, UCLA professor Jane Wu found that this meant that occupants more similar in body size to the dummy accrued greater benefits from safety improvements. Moreover, the choice of dummy was driven by firms that had less experience with safety concerns. Today, car industry safety metrics take into account a range of crash-test dummy sizes and shapes to measure progress on vehicular safety. But the seemingly innocuous choice of the earlier metric—a 1960s military plane–style dummy—greatly influenced the innovation plans of firms and even introduced bias and inequality into the process of technological change.[a]

A set of modern crash-test dummies uses the different dimensions of a variety of ages and genders. The original designs were based on the availability of replacement parts from the military.

of technological failure. As the Nobel Prize–winning physicist Niels Bohr quipped, "Prediction is very difficult, especially about the future." Second, even if an entrepreneur correctly forecasts the rate of improvement, this in no way guarantees that the metrics achieved will translate into value creation for real-life consumers (see **Using the Research: Crash-Test Dummies and Choosing Meaningful Metrics**). Metrics often originate in science and engineering communities that are driven by the logic of particular academic disciplines (e.g., achieving a technical metric relative to some theoretical potential). Effective metrics for entrepreneurs need to be linked to meaningful customer value creation. Ultimately, consumers considering whether to adopt LEDs do not care about metrics such as lumens per watt but instead the quality of the light they experience and the electricity bill they receive at the end of the month. Finally, as we will return to later, when a firm commits itself to a longer period of exploration (as Elon Musk did in the context of electric vehicles), then the potential value to be created from "riding the S curve" increases.

Technology S Curves in Action: Absorption and Disposable Diapers

To see the power of the S curve across multiple technology generations, consider the case of the disposable diaper. First developed by independent inventor Marion Donovan in the late 1940s, disposable diapers were commercialized for the mass market in the early 1960s by Procter & Gambles' Pampers. In the first generation of disposable diapers, performance was enhanced by stuffing ever greater amounts of cotton (to enhance absorbency) into a nylon shell, inducing an inherent trade-off between absorbency and fit. At some point, the diapers reached a limit of absorbency (beyond which you would have more cotton fluff than baby!).

Introducing new superabsorbent polymers (SAPs), on the other hand, increased absorbency per square inch by orders of magnitude. This allowed for both a reduction in diaper size, an increase in absorbency itself, and follow-on benefits such as reduced shipping costs and more opportunities for product variety. Though initially discovered in the mid-1960s, it took more than 20 years for SAPs to achieve a technical performance level that allowed them to compete and ultimately supplant cotton diapers. In other words, and reflective of the logic of the technology S curve, while the *initial* technical performance of SAPs was inferior to that of cotton diapers, the rate of *improvements over time* in SAPs was steeper and longer than what could be achieved with cotton.[a]

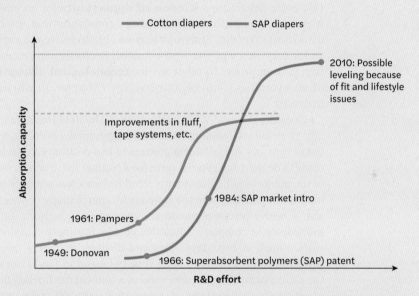

Understanding the S-curve pattern helped show the potential of superabsorbent polymers.

Ultimately, though useful in retrospect, the S curve is not a detailed predictive tool: one cannot use the S curve to precisely map out the future of a technological trajectory at its outset. This shortcoming might seem to limit its usefulness for an entrepreneur.

However, the S-curve framework can offer concrete guidance and insight for entrepreneurs. It sheds light on the range of possibilities that arise from exploring emerging and novel technology (see **Mini Case: Technology S Curves in Action**). The most salient opportunities arise when an opportunity is at a relatively early stage of development but also faces fundamental design or physical constraints that limit its potential for performance improvement. Particularly if the technology is being discounted or ignored by established industry players, this provides entrepreneurs with a window of opportunity for exploring an idea; it may take some time, but history has shown what happens when it pays off.

6.3 The Window of Opportunity— Disruptive Innovations

As we read in the last section, identifying an emerging technological trajectory that has not yet started to take off can itself serve as a source of technological opportunity. Existing players—including incumbent firms or even customers— may be unaware, resistant, or dismissive of the potential for significant improvement from a technology that is currently at a low level of performance. While not inevitable (there are many examples where established firms pioneer and introduce new technologies), established players overlooking this potential create a **window of opportunity** for an entrepreneur, a time when they can explore an emerging opportunity that established firms may dismiss or discount. Start-ups may be able to learn and experiment with this technology in a way that will establish leadership over time as performance begins to improve. In other words, **technological disruption** becomes part of an overall entrepreneurial strategy (Chapter 10 discusses this strategy in detail).

Consider the case of LinkedIn, founded by Reid Hoffman in 2002. Traditionally, professionals around the world maintained a Rolodex, which referred to a list of contacts and networks contained in a desktop card index. While Rolodex came to be used as a generic term for a contact list, it was in fact the brand name of the market-leading company. A full Rolodex was not only valuable to the one maintaining it. Access to the Rolodex of a particularly connected individual was also a nearly priceless means for gaining introductions and backgrounds on individuals or companies. Rolodex entries routinely contained personal information such as birthdays, likes and dislikes, or family information. Perhaps the most famous Rolodex of all time belonged to David Rockefeller, who, over the course of an 80-year career and as a scion of the Rockefeller family, amassed a personalized directory of more than 100,000 individuals, ranging from President John F. Kennedy (whose Rolodex entry was introduced in 1938) to Hollywood movie stars, bankers, and businesspeople across the world (**Figure 6.5**). However, by the early 2000s, the Internet had developed to a point where it was becoming possible to establish maps of online connections between identifiable individuals and others with whom they had relationships. As he recounts in his book *Blitzscaling*, Hoffman saw an opportunity to "disrupt" the Rolodex model as the Internet transitioned "from anonymous cyberspace to an extension of the real world, and thus your online identity was an extension of your real identity." LinkedIn faced significant early skepticism since those who already used a Rolodex did not believe they needed an Internet substitute, while those who did not use a Rolodex did not perceive the value of a professional networking service. LinkedIn had only 245 members by the end of 2003 (most of whom were

window of opportunity A time when a venture can explore an emerging opportunity that established firms may dismiss or discount

technological disruption Establishing leadership in a market using technological innovation

FIGURE 6.5 The Rolodex

```
        John Fitzgerald Kennedy          Dear Mr. President:
            United States Senator        (The President
     ------------- ----- ---- business----  The White House
                                          Washington 25, D.C.)
   -elected Pres. of USA 11/60.       filled
                                      11/25/63

   4/8/57 - DR saw at Harvard - above is a member of the Overseers'
               Com. to Visit the Dept. of Govt.
   5/5/61- DRs saw Pres. & Mrs. Kennedy at the Bourguibas' dinner in
               Washington.

   5/11/62-DRs met Pres. & Mrs. Kennedy at dinner in Wash. for French
               Minister Malraux
   7/13/62-DR  saw above in Wash.
   4/25/63-DR saw him in Wash. with Tax Reduction group.
```

The typical Rolodex (photo on the top left) held the cards and detailed information for an individual's personal and professional network. Gaining access to another person's Rolodex was considered a valuable achievement. David Rockefeller, scion of the Rockefeller family, built one of the most famous Rolodexes of all time (a small segment is shown in the photo on the top right). It contained the personal notes and information for over 100,000 individuals, including movie stars, businesspeople, and world leaders. On the bottom is Rockefeller's card of his business contacts for John F. Kennedy. He maintained a second one for personal information and connections with JFK.

personal connections of Hoffman). However, this initial period gave Hoffman and his founding team time to learn and experiment and dramatically improve the value of the LinkedIn service. For example, Hoffman and his team considered how to connect a free LinkedIn service for professionals to a paid service for enterprise clients (who could then use LinkedIn for recruiting purposes). One key insight from this was developing an approach (separate from any network effect) that allowed a professional's LinkedIn profile to serve as a permanent and trusted online presence for that individual. This idea was immensely popular, and by the time of its nearly $26 billion acquisition by Microsoft in 2015, LinkedIn had become the "Millennial Rolodex," amassing more than 400 million members. Intriguingly, while Rolodex continues to operate as a company, it has never introduced a digital product to transition its physical card-based systems to an online platform.

TECHNOLOGICAL INNOVATION AND DISRUPTION

LinkedIn's use of technological innovation to displace the traditional Rolodex is an extreme case; few technological changes are as cut and dry as moving users from physical paper to electronic files (note that this text has both print and enhanced electronic versions!). But this example shows the core logic of how entrepreneurs might leverage technological innovation to overturn existing barriers to entry, exploit a window of opportunity, and establish a beachhead in the marketplace. As reflected in case studies by Professors Rebecca Henderson and Clay Christensen, a surprisingly large number of industry leaders face significant challenges in transitioning their businesses across different technological generations. Specifically, managers within the incumbent firm often face resistance from both their current customers (who are satisfied with the traditional technology) and other stakeholders within the firm and their supply chain.[4] Transitioning from exploiting one S curve that is still providing financial success and has not reached maturity to exploring another unproven and unprofitable one may undermine their existing power and capabilities. The consequence of these market and organizational dynamics is that many established firms are unable (or slow) to navigate the transition to what seems like modest changes in the technology of their industry. By disadvantaging established firms, these "disruptive innovations" (as first coined by Clay Christensen; see Chapter 10) offer an opening for competitive entry by entrepreneurs. In effect, these disruptions create a new S curve, with a technological window of opportunity to pioneer and commercialize (**Figure 6.6**).

The potential for disruptive innovation can, of course, be overstated (and often is—see the sidebar on **Google Glass**).[5] While established firms often do face challenges responding to an emerging technological trajectory, most ultimately manage technological transitions. For example, despite the rapid rate of innovation in the information technology industry, two leading companies founded in the 1970s, Microsoft and Apple, have adapted to multiple technological revolutions, including the rise of the Internet and the more recent transition to cloud computing. Indeed, established firms often take proactive strategies to avoid disruption by an emerging trajectory, like by establishing a new division to take advantage of the new technology. Or they may use more reactive moves such as actually acquiring or cooperating with start-ups that pioneer the next technological innovation within an industry.

CUSTOMER INTEREST

Even if a start-up is successful at improving and leveraging a technological innovation to introduce a new product, that is no guarantee that it will create

Google Glass. In 2013, Google rolled out wearable smart glasses that promised to transform how people interact with computers and the Internet, delivering a hands-free way to view content, use social media, and talk on the phone. Customers were not convinced though, and after several iterations of this idea, Google canceled the project in 2023.

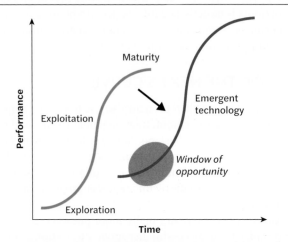

FIGURE 6.6 Window of Opportunity

Because a surprisingly large number of industry leaders face significant challenges transitioning across different technological generations, an emerging technology trajectory may provide a window of opportunity for the start-up. While an existing, more mature S curve (green line) has higher performance today, with investment and development the new technology (and blue S curve) might ultimately achieve higher performance. Start-ups face a choice of whether to explore an emerging technological trajectory that *may* achieve higher technical performance in the future or accept the established performance of the mature technology. The possibility that established players overlook an emerging technology may give a start-up time for early-stage exploration and to learn and experiment in a way that leads to a leadership position as this technology improves.

meaningful value for customers. Many promising technological innovations stimulate interest from the technical or scientific community and allow for an impressive product demonstration. But these same innovations can fail to translate into solving a meaningful challenge faced by a real customer or opening up an opportunity for those customers that had previously been unavailable. For example, in the early 2010s, while working on his PhD, David Holz developed a breakthrough gestural interface that captured small hand and finger movements in real time. He and his childhood friend Michael Buckwald dubbed the technology "Leap Motion" and showcased the power of the technology through viral YouTube videos and a packed presentation at the influential South by Southwest technology conference. Holz's new approach used simple gestures rather than a keyboard to input data, with potential applications in gaming, health care, security, and beyond. However, despite this significant technological advantage (enough to secure more than 100 patents and raise more than $100 million), Leap Motion never identified a meaningful customer segment that could leverage its technology. Leap Motion was ultimately acquired at a significant loss in 2019 despite its initially impressive innovation.[6]

Results like Holz's are not uncommon; it is easy to overestimate the possibilities of an emerging technological innovation and the window of opportunity it provides. The potential performance of a new technology is itself highly uncertain, and entrepreneurs who perceive a disruption opportunity based on its potential are by definition optimistic relative to others about that potential. While it is tempting to discount skepticism, the fact that others fail to perceive the same opportunity is nonetheless informative. In many cases, the skeptics are even proven correct as significant investment in technological exploration fails to yield meaningful technological improvement.

LOOKING FOR THE NEXT S CURVE

The S curve is a tool that an entrepreneur can use to consider the potential for a specific technology's improvement, how they might learn and experiment to see if that improvement is possible, and then how to achieve it. The S curve *can* serve as the basis for a hypothesis, providing insight about the relative possibilities for different promising technologies, how different technologies might be shaped over time, and how specific technological approaches might fit with other choices by that start-up.

But it is also true that there are many more potential S curves that fail to realize their promise than successful disruptive innovations that overturn the existing industry. Together, this limits using the S curve as a means for predicting the *precise evolution* of a specific technological innovation over time. Simply put, the future of any technological innovation is uncertain. But by helping entrepreneurs connect the potential for performance improvement to the creation of value for consumers, the S curve can serve as a critical element in planning an overall entrepreneurial strategy.

6.4 The Trade-Off between Technology Exploitation vs. Exploration

Technological exploration can be a "long game" opportunity for an entrepreneur, where being new in the market and acting as a disrupter can have built-in advantages over existing players. With this in mind, entrepreneurs still face a fundamental trade-off between technology exploitation vs. technology exploration: whether to focus on what is available in the short term and make use of existing technological solutions or to look toward the long term and emerging technological options. Given the high level of uncertainty associated with any idea, short-term exploitation allows an entrepreneur to learn about the value of an idea and quickly resolve some uncertainty about whether using an existing technological approach creates value for customers. For example, a new franchisee of an existing restaurant chain (such as McDonald's) might wonder whether it will be profitable in a given location. But using the existing menu, logistics, and operational tools of McDonald's—the McDonald's "technology"—greatly reduces the level of uncertainty about the venture. The basic business idea and tools are not new and have had success elsewhere. However, this decision to exploit already available technology, almost by definition, limits the amount of unique value that can be created for consumers. Most McDonald's franchisees know the maximum profit their location will generate. The choice to limit the role of technology in a start-up should limit the overall uncertainty of success, but this choice will constrain the amount of customer value that can be created.

Organizational Learning: Exploration and Exploitation

Stanford professor James March's research has made significant contributions to understanding organizations and organizational decision-making and learning. This includes how firm choices shape innovation and how managing innovation requires both exploration and exploitation. Exploration requires that an organization prioritize activities that involve discovery, experimentation, and risk-taking. Exploitation means an organization needs to focus on refinement, execution, and production. In any organization, too much focus on exploration may yield many potentially lucrative ideas but few successful products. Yet overemphasizing exploitation while providing short-term benefits for the organization may also lead to poor long-term performance.

As a result, to innovate *and survive*, an organization must balance these two sets of activities, and balancing the trade-offs is at the heart of understanding the technology S curve. Ultimately, an organization must choose how to focus its resources across these two activities, structure its incentives

to reinforce both, and select a strategy that builds upon investments in exploration and innovation.[a]

James March's research found that employees need to balance how much time they spend on activities around exploring and exploiting technology.

But using any technology as a driver for value creation will involve at least some exploration (see **Deep Dive: Organizational Learning**). An entrepreneur and their team need to learn about alternative technological options for a given idea and the potential of specific technologies to improve performance. In other words, a potential franchisee will probably examine other franchise options besides McDonald's and, if they have the opportunity to choose one or another, try to determine which one (which franchise's "technology") maximizes value at the location. This decision between franchises is a relatively straightforward case, of course. In most other cases, the process is time-consuming and resource-intensive and comes with a high level of uncertainty.

For example, consider cryptocurrencies. During the early 2010s, even the most well-known and mature currency, Bitcoin, was at an early stage. The technology behind it, known as blockchain, was untested, and any start-up interested in exploiting cryptocurrency opportunities based on blockchain technology needed to engage in some level of exploration. Though many technology experts believed in the potential for blockchain in general and Bitcoin in particular, the costs and benefits of different technological approaches to using it for cryptocurrencies were shrouded in a high level of uncertainty. Some start-ups, such as Coinbase, reduced uncertainty by developing a way for users to access and trade cryptocurrency. Coinbase was, at its earliest stages, the "Paypal of Bitcoin." Other start-ups, such as Ripple, undertook a more ambitious technological approach, creating their own cryptocurrencies. These start-ups needed to figure out how to process transactions using blockchain (as Coinbase also did) but importantly, they needed to design a cryptocurrency itself with unique functionality that would generate unique value. Both types of start-ups during this period undertook years of exploratory experimentation with many failures along the way. It was only through committing to processes of exploration around blockchain technology that Coinbase and Ripple were able to establish their unique positions within an emerging industry based on it, though in different ways (see **Table 6.1**).

Prioritizing exploration or exploitation at the founding of a venture is an important and hard choice (see **Mini Case: Nima Sensors**). Near-term exploitation of existing technologies can help an entrepreneur directly and immediately create value for a particular customer segment and build an organization to deliver that value. As we have discussed, starting your business by purchasing a franchise, combining existing technologies such as mobile and GPS like Tinder did, or trying to service a cryptocurrency as a wallet, is just a little more straightforward. On the other hand, investments in paths that explore significant technical innovations can unleash the potential for massive customer value creation. They can also lead to a start-up gaining control over certain knowledge possibly through formal intellectual property protection or through internal learning that is hard for others to absorb. This control can anchor the venture in a path that attracts resources such as venture capitalists seeking to invest in "X" technology or engineers whose expertise is closely linked to this new path. Further, by prioritizing technological innovation, a start-up

---

TABLE 6.1 **Coinbase vs. Ripple**

Founders of Coinbase and Ripple pursued different approaches to entrepreneurship in the then-emerging area of cryptocurrency. This table describes their choices, including quotes from sources illustrating how they were different.

	COINBASE	RIPPLE
Founder(s)	Brian Armstrong	Chris Larsen, David Schwartz, Jed McCaleb, and Arthur Britto
Exploration	Build a cloud-based wallet for cryptocurrency "Somebody is going to have to make a really rock-solid cloud service for this, and that is the future."	Build a better cryptocurrency "Fascinated by Bitcoin, they set out to create a better version that improved upon its limitations—with the goal of creating a digital asset that was more sustainable and built specifically for payments."
Big exploitation decision	Make something for a very broad market that everyone can use "The early decisions that Coinbase and Brian made were sort of the opposite of what I would call the bitcoin wisdom of the time," said Olaf Carlson-Wee, the company's third employee and head of the cryptocurrency fund Polychain Capital. "He wasn't building for that narrow audience of 10,000 people."	Make something for the subset of users who found early Bitcoin lacking "The trio of developers continued the work to build a distributed ledger that improved upon these fundamental limitations of Bitcoin, originally naming the code Ripple. The ledger included a digital asset that would originally be called 'ripples' (XRP as the currency code) to follow the same naming convention as Bitcoin (BTC)." Chris Larsen then joined up with Jed McCaleb to found Ripple.
Outcome	Coinbase is the "dominant US-based cryptocurrency exchange, by providing user friendly service and avoiding security problems and headaches that have plagued its rivals."	While its valuation is highly volatile, valuations in early 2023 were around $10 billion.

SOURCES: Miles Kruppa, "Coinbase Founder Rides Crytpo Boom to NASDAQ Listing," *Financial Times*, March 5, 2021, https://www.ft.com/content/1077a75f-947f-4aab-ab28-46b6c3b5b52d; "Provide a Better Alternative to Bitcoin," XRP Ledger, accessed May 7, 2023, https://xrpl.org/history.html#:~:text=In%202011%2C%20three%20engineers%E2%80%94David,and%20built%20 specifically%20for%20payments; and Nathaniel Popper, "Rise of Bitcoin Competitor Ripple Creates Wealth to Rival Zuckerberg," *New York Times*, April 1, 2018, https://www.nytimes.com /2018/01/04/technology/bitcoin-ripple.html.

Nima Sensors: Alternative Paths to Gluten-Free

While obtaining her MBA, Shireen Yates explored the challenges facing those suffering from celiac disease, an autoimmune disorder triggered by gluten. Like many entrepreneurs, Yates conceptualized a number of potential paths, some using off-the-shelf technology and alternatives requiring technological innovation and development. In fact, Yates first considered founding a gluten-free bakery that would develop and manufacture tasty yet gluten-free baked goods, a strategy that had been implemented in a range of cities (occasionally with success).

But ultimately, Yates chose to pursue a plan based on direct technological innovation and development. She partnered with Scott Sundvor, a mechanical engineer, to develop an easy-to-use, portable gluten detection kit for use by celiac patients. The team combined advances in sensor miniaturization and a simple user interface to allow celiac patients to test for gluten quickly and discreetly in unfamiliar dining settings. In the years that followed, they would leverage these same technologies to develop a similar product for patients with peanut allergies. The company founded as Nima Sensors, and now known as Nima Partners after its acquisition, is categorized as a high-technology medical device company, a far cry from a local bakery. That positioning reflects an earlier meaningful choice by the founders

Shireen Yates (second from the right) is pictured in 2016 with several early team members, all holding a Nima Sensor.

to prioritize technological innovation as central to commercializing their idea.

SOURCE: Denise Restauri, "This Entrepreneur's Portable Device Tests Food for Gluten, before Your First Bite," *Forbes*, September 16, 2016, https://www.forbes.com/sites/deniserestauri/2016/09/30/one-powerful-question-that-led-this-woman-to-over-9m-in-funding/?sh=5e1e84192bc6.

offers a vision to potential investors, employees, partners, and customers (and even garner favorable media!) in advance of actually having to produce a particular product or service.

However, choosing a path that requires technological innovation means that the venture must succeed at something else: developing or adapting a particular technology to meet a proposed need. Then, the resources, time, and emphasis required to achieve these technical objectives may lead to different consumer insights, which may or may not fit with the targeted group of consumers. A very low-bar experiment ends up being to see whether a venture's own people would use the product. In Silicon Valley, they call this "dogfooding"; the idea is that a company's staffers should use, test, and like a fairly undeveloped product version before the company tries to exploit it.

Eventually, an entrepreneur considering technological exploration needs to link their proposed approach to the *potential* to create value for actual customers. Sometimes this link is relatively straightforward. In the biotechnology industry, there are well-defined (if noisy) benchmarks to predict whether a particular therapy will have some clinical impact that is valuable to patients and their physicians. However, in most cases, establishing this link is difficult. Firms that cannot establish a clear link between an exploration and its potential to create value are more likely be investing in "technology for technology's sake."

6.5 Choosing Your Technology

So far, we've discussed the reasoning behind strategic decisions to exploit or explore technology and the usefulness of the technology S curve. Now, let's build off this understanding to learn a systematic approach to the process of technological innovation.

Choosing your technology involves two areas of choice.

1. Entrepreneurs must choose from *many technological innovations* and limit their in-depth exploration, exploitation, and investments to a small number.
2. Entrepreneurs must choose *how to manage* their exploration of those options. In particular, they must manage how to invest in sufficiently longer-term exploration processes to achieve meaningful technological progress.

Let's now look in more detail at both choices.

For most founding teams, the question is not whether there exists a promising technology to explore but which of the many potential innovations and merging or established S curves they should investigate (**Figure 6.7**). At the time entrepreneurs are evaluating technological alternatives, established S curves may offer greater levels of performance, wider adoption, and an array of complementary resources for the founding team to leverage. By contrast, the emerging technological trajectory may remain relatively unproven, with only a nascent ecosystem of resources. Yet for those emerging trajectories that do succeed, there is the potential for the technological performance to overtake that of the established S curves and, for the start-up to take a leadership position in bringing forward the technology and complementary products and services. While only a small number of emerging technologies will ultimately pan out into something significant, in most every field, there are many possibilities that might work. These possibilities typically come from emerging academic research, through users and innovation communities, or through using emerging technologies that have yet to be applied more generally.

The first step in making a choice is to characterize a meaningful but manageable set of technologies worth exploring. It is, of course, difficult (if not impossible) to catalog all alternatives, but a focused entrepeneur or founding team can develop an overview and understanding of some of the key options that are either established or potentially emerging.

FIGURE 6.7 **Established vs. Emerging Technology S Curves**

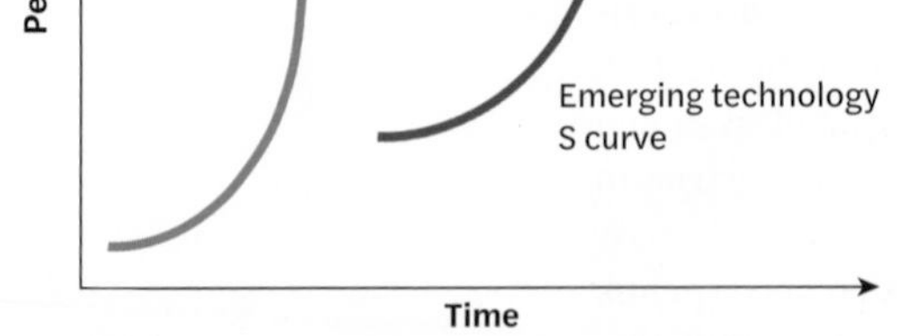

An established technology S curve can offer a clear path. Emerging curves show promise but are always a bet on the potential of a new, emerging trajectory. Deciding to pursue either means considering their distinct challenges and trade-offs.

Two possibilities normally guide this initial process, which should occur at a high level.

1. The first is when founding teams themselves may have deep technical knowledge of a particular area (e.g., as the result of their own prior research). This prior background can provide unique insight and access to the potential for performance improvement among options within that particular area. For example, while working at Bell Labs as a recent PhD, Eugene Fitzgerald invented a new type of semiconductor design process using an approach called "strained silicon." Strained silicon was important not only as a scientific discovery (it was important enough that MIT recruited Fitzgerald as a professor), but his invention helped Fitzgerald understand the emerging potential for this process across the semiconductor industry. Rather than simply focus on his academic research, Fitzgerald cofounded AmberWave to leverage this fundamental breakthrough. Interestingly, his early engagement also necessitated a long length of commitment: it took more than 15 years, but the technology developed and commercialized by AmberWave ultimately became a defining driver of semiconductor innovation in the late 2000s. It is now ubiquitous in products from cell phones to personal computers (and everything in between).

2. A second possibility occurs when an entrepreneur is researching or working in a domain where they can assess and understand the technological landscape that distinguishes options. Consider, for example, solar cell technology for clean energy. While "traditional" solar PV is based on silicon and exploits knowledge and scale economies taken from the IT semiconductor industry, the measured energy absorbence of solar cells can be dramatically improved using "hybrid" materials, such as gallium arsenide. Having access to analyses of the scientific and technical properties of alternative materials, and assessments of their performance history, should yield insight into each one's potential for commercial development. As seen in **Figure 6.8** on page 176, even a cursory examination of the opportunities for innovation across different materials indicates that some materials exhibit high (but roughly constant) performance while others are currently at a low level of performance but experiencing a significant upturn. An entrepreneur that has access to this information and how to understand it might identify opportunities where a start-up could establish technological leadership.

No matter the opportunity, founding teams must link potential performance improvement to concrete value creation for potential customers. Since existing firms often prioritize performance metrics relevant to their existing customers, this leaves open opportunities for start-ups to address the needs of poorly served customer segments.

Taken together, when start-ups must make technological choices, they should prioritize options that

1. achieve technical performance that exceeds existing technology on at least one meaningful performance dimension;
2. do so at a reasonable cost over a time frame that fits with the rest of its strategy (e.g., that doesn't exceed any start-up capital or just free time it has to support its research); and
3. create real value for customers.

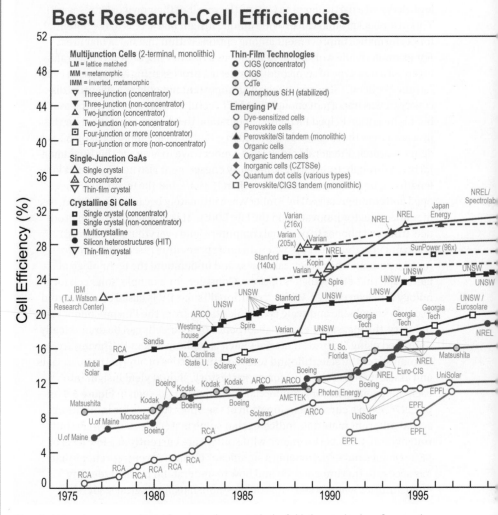

Though this graph may not make quick sense to those outside the field, these technology S curves demonstrate the progress and rate of improvement across materials. Recognizing and understanding these patterns can help an entrepreneur identify opportunities and choose a technology. Compiled by the National Renewable Energy Laboratory (NREL).

MANAGING YOUR CHOICE: SHAPING THE S CURVE

In addition to choosing how or what to innovate, entrepreneurs manage and control how this is done. In this way, entrepreneurs shape their S curve, setting the trajectory of technology itself by how they experiment and learn. For example, an entrepreneur who chooses an emerging technology and tries to realize a high level of technological performance from it gains a potential advantage if they engage with that opportunity at an early stage of development. As we saw in the example with Elon Musk and Tesla, a meaningful early start

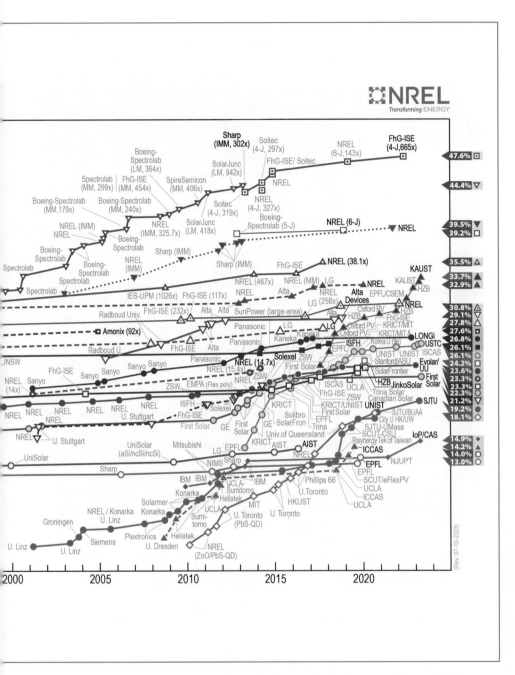

means an entrepreneur can gather knowledge that in the future might establish a true technological advantage. Instead of waiting for the technology to improve because of the work of others, entrepreneurs decide to drive the improvements themselves. Over time, technological improvements come from both ongoing exploration and experimentation successes, as well as failures at the earliest stages.

On the other hand, start-ups that first prioritize exploitation limit the degree of exploration they can do. This restricts how much they can understand about a technology and the performance that the start-up is able to realize from it.

FIGURE 6.9 Potential S Curves

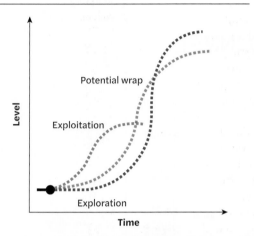

For a given technological idea, there are multiple potential S curves. The choice of investments in exploration or exploitation influences the technology's trajectory. For instance, prioritizing exploitation may yield immediate performance improvements but inhibit the ultimate performance of the technology (green line). A focus on early exploration may unlock enhanced performance in the mature technology but may require more investment and time to achieve (blue line). There are of course options in between too (red line).

FIGURE 6.10
Exploration: Pixar Finally Makes "The Movie"

By making significant investments in exploration, Pixar created technology that defined its own S curve for success and dominate the market.

This logic is illustrated in **Figure 6.9**. For a given emerging S curve, there exists a range of potential innovation outcomes. Focusing immediately on exploitation (and so conducting no actual research) will limit that start-up's ability to realize any improvement and leverage that technology in the marketplace. At the other extreme, a lengthy process of exploration should induce a higher level of technological potential, though with far greater investment of resources early in the process. *Therefore, what is realized depends not simply on some "inherent" technological potential but on the strategic choices that entrepreneurs make in prioritizing exploration vs. exploitation at different stages of the innovation process.*

Consider Pixar, whose origins reach back to the so-called Computer Division of Lucasfilm, the production company for the original *Star Wars*. Going back to their days as graduate students, the initial leaders of that division, Ed Catmull and Alvy Ray Smith, had a long-term goal of leveraging advances in computer technology to make "The Movie": a fully digital animated movie that could compete with traditional filmmaking. At this early stage, the technology to do so was largely inferior to traditional moviemaking (and even other types of special effects) and could only be used for very specialized purposes, such as a brief animated sequence in the original *Return of the Jedi*.

In 1986, and already more than six years into the process, Catmull, Smith, and ex-Disney employee John Lasseter persuaded Apple's Steve Jobs to fund a new venture named Pixar focused on further developing computer-generated imagery (CGI) technology. The next decade was spent on painstaking exploration and learning. The team devoted multiple years to developing a systematic standard, RenderMan, which let CGI animators easily translate their creative vision into an animated image. But the team also suffered numerous failures and setbacks, including a failed attempt at a video-game product and less-than-stellar results in movies, including Disney's *The Rescuers Down Under*. But it was this very process of failure, learning, and experimentation that ultimately enabled Pixar to develop the capabilities and knowledge it needed to finally make "The Movie." With the release of *Toy Story* in 1995 (**Figure 6.10**), Pixar technologically leapfrogged over all other animated studios, including Disney, in terms of quality and expressiveness. The experience and understanding Pixar earned from this achievement allowed the company to define its opportunity for success (choose and "ride" the growth of the S curve) and was instrumental in Pixar outpacing Disney and others for more than a decade. In the words of one observer, "As with the best home-cooking, Pixar has secret recipes that distance themselves from the competition, helping create true cinematic experiences that defy the boundaries often set by the world of 'animation.'"[7] Ultimately, in 2006 Disney paid $7.3 billion for these recipes when it acquired Pixar.

It is useful to appreciate the enormous discipline and persistence that Pixar needed to turn the idea of CGI animation into a reality. In his role as financier and CEO, Steve Jobs tolerated a high level of experimentation and exploration at Pixar for multiple years, with numerous setbacks and absolute failures.[8] An exploratory approach is more than simply allowing employees to do whatever they want; instead, it is a culture that considers learning opportunities, involves a high degree of feedback, and engages in a constant process of iterative design. And research has shown this pays off. In a revealing laboratory study, Professors Florian Ederer and Gustavo Manso provided subjects with an opportunity to run a virtual "lemonade stand." In this study, some participants were prompted to try making a profit immediately, while others were provided an opportunity to first explore the game and experiment with different locations for the stand and what mixture of ingredients to use in their recipe. Those individuals who were allowed to "learn" about an environment before monetary incentives were present undertook more wide-ranging searches. These early "experiments" helped those individuals ultimately achieve a higher level of overall performance.[9]

But choosing between a more exploration-oriented vs. exploitation-oriented approach is challenging for any entrepreneur. While the exploratory technology strategy of companies such as Tesla and Pixar ultimately served as a cornerstone for long-term impact, a more exploitation-oriented strategy can attract resources and commercialize an idea more quickly. For example, frustrated by the poor quality of virtual reality (VR) headsets in the gaming market, 18-year-old Palmer Luckey tried to improve the headset experience through rapid experimentation with existing designs. Iterating quickly through feedback on message boards and by examining prior headset designs, Luckey developed a novel headset that came with improved performance, though it did not yet solve long-standing challenges such as the potential for dizziness for some users. Dubbed the Oculus Rift (**Figure 6.11**), this intensive approach importantly demonstrated the possibilities of the technology. Luckey launched a successful Kickstarter campaign in 2012, which was followed less than two years later by an acquisition by Facebook for $3 billion. Subsequent iterations of Oculus Rift form the technology underpinning Facebook's renaming as Meta in 2021.

FIGURE 6.11
Exploitation: Quickly Developing the Oculus Rift

Unlike Pixar, the early VR headset named the Oculus Rift was developed through an exploitation process, rapidly iterating using available technology.

WHICH APPROACH IS RIGHT FOR YOU?

Ultimately, there is no single more exploration-oriented or exploitation-oriented approach that is the "right" approach for success in a certain case. Instead, each entrepreneur or team should consider how the choice between these two is likely to influence their venture over time. An exploration-oriented venture will likely require a longer time frame, need more up-front capital (which might significantly dilute an entrepreneur's equity in the venture), and be more distant from the process of customer feedback and iteration we emphasized in Chapter 5. An exploitation-oriented approach will probably limit a start-up's learning and capacity-building around the technology, which might constrain how it can create and capture value. However, this approach might get the product to market more rapidly and substantially limit the time and investment needed to get started. The most critical point, then, is that this decision is an important one and something that any founding team should consider as they build their overall strategy (see **Putting It Together: Exploration vs. Exploitation** on p. 180).

This chapter's video explores how Pixar's success in CGI animation shows the value of technology exploration.

CHOOSING YOUR TECHNOLOGY

Whether a start-up is founded to bring a new technology to market or the technology plays more of a supporting role, the choice of technology meaningfully shapes how value will be created.

IDENTIFY AND PRIORITIZE AMONG TECHNOLOGY REQUIREMENTS

Create a Shortlist of Potential Opportunities or S Curves

- Describe the role technology plays in creating value for customers.
- Specify key performance metrics and articulate how these performance metrics contribute to creating value.
- Identify potential technologies your venture may leverage to deliver this performance, noting both established and (where available) emerging technology trajectories.
- For each potential trajectory, assess the current performance and estimate the likely rate of performance improvement. State your assumptions.

STRATEGICALLY RANK TECHNOLOGY S CURVES

Evaluate Your Venture's Ability to Deliver Value with the Technology

- Specify the requirements for your venture to access and improve upon each potential technology.
- Contrast prioritizing technology exploration or exploitation for each. Describe the next steps—specifically, how an emphasis on exploration or exploitation will create meaningful value for customers.
- Consider how a more modular component or system-level approach would change your choice of technology and outline the steps required to move forward.
- Evaluate the trade-offs of generating specialized solutions for the near-term needs of specific customers or emphasizing a more general approach for a broader range of applications.
- Rank the potential technical approaches. For each, list the key hypotheses for value creation.

NARROW TECHNOLOGY CHOICES THROUGH EXPERIMENTATION AND LEARNING

Conduct Low-Commitment Learning

- Identify your start-up's potential to both access and actively shape these technological trajectories.
- For your top-ranked technical approaches, generate a low-commitment test to validate key components of your value creation hypotheses.

ADDITIONAL DIMENSIONS OF TECHNOLOGY CHOICE

The choice between exploration and exploitation of an emerging technology is not the only dimension of start-up technology choice. Let's look at a few others.

COMPONENT SOLUTION VS. "GAME CHANGER" Elon Musk's investment and learning in lithium-ion batteries was put to use in the design and assembly of early Tesla models such as the Roadster and the Model S. Design by its very nature involves a wide range of concrete choices that influence how potential customers experience a given technology. Emerging technology start-ups often face a critical choice about whether to develop a better component within an existing system (e.g., building a better battery for cars already on the road) or create an entirely new system (e.g., using this new battery technology to form a completely new company and model for powering a car). For example, over the last decade there has been a wave of start-ups attempting to develop newer and better smart bikes, which provide assistive cycling while climbing a hill by integrating a small electric motor onto a traditional bicycle frame. Founders of the start-up Superpedestrian focused on developing a new battery-powered, motorized wheel that could, in principle, be integrated into any bicycle frame and thus partnered with established bicycle companies. Today, this company has taken its technology and become a provider of shared scooters for cities and businesses in the United States and Europe. Another start-up, Cyclotron, instead developed an entirely new, game-changing motorized high performance bicycle with looks that would land it in a sci-fi movie. In these examples, we see start-ups facing a choice between a narrow focus on a modular solution (e.g., a better wheel that will "fit" most existing bike frames) vs. a broader solution requiring more innovation (e.g., radically transforming bicycle design in a manner that best realizes the potential of electric bicycles). Interestingly, the more narrow solution may allow focus on a larger, initial customer segment. In this example, Superpedestrian tried to serve all existing bicycle owners who might be interested in an electric assist. The more "general" solution requires a larger behavioral change on the part of potential customers; Cyclotron needs customers to buy a new bike. Moreover, where the development of a new wheel is complementary to existing bicycle designers and manufacturers, developing an entirely new bicycle offers a fresh competitive offering in the bicycle market. There are inherent risks, of course. While Cyclotron got off to a fast start with lots of orders from its Kickstarter campaign, it never delivered.[10]

A GENERAL OR A SPECIALIZED APPROACH When a founding team focuses intently on the near-term needs of specific customers or a particular market segment, they will likely develop tailored solutions with customer-specific requirements or design trade-offs. Conversely, a more general approach applies a technological innovation across a wider range of possible applications. Ralph Landau, a pioneering twentieth-century chemical engineer, formed companies that used both approaches. Landau focused his first firm, Scientific Design Company, on developing specific reactions used for production processes in the emerging petrochemical industry. Later, Landau founded Halcon International, which instead tried to develop the most general versions of a given chemical production process and then licensed these applications across a wide range of

See through Walls with Wi-Fi: Choice of Application

In 2013, computer scientist and MacArthur Fellow Dina Katabi and her student Fadel Adib published a paper with a direct and refreshingly non-academic title: "See through Walls with Wi-Fi!" It described exactly what Katabi and her team were working on could actually do: using Wi-Fi, the technology could see where, what, and even how (physiologically) people on the other side of walls might be doing. All this without any

In a 2016 photo, Katabi is shown explaining how her wireless technology's assessment of her colleague Fadel Adibs' (at right) heartbeat and breathing is being used to predict how he feels.

contact with the individuals themselves—no wearable sensors required! The landscape of potential applications was vast—everything from public safety and law enforcement to child and elderly care.

Katabi considered her choices: Should she focus her team on continuing to be the source of breakthroughs with this technology, creating a general-purpose solution? Or should she focus on standardizing something close to the current technology in order to develop a "minimum viable product" within a specific application, and so gain feedback from real customers?

Ultimately, Katabi and several students narrowed their focus toward healthcare monitoring and founded a start-up, Emerald Innovations, to bring this technology to that market. Katabi and her team directed their improvements in the underlying technology to novel methods for clinical trial evaluation. By 2018, Emerald had begun to establish commercial partnerships with healthcare companies, with clinical trials in patient homes measuring adherence to health interventions like daily exercise and other health metrics like respiration and sleep quality. One of the first of these partnerships was with LEO Pharma, a global leader in dermatological treatments. The partnership detected the level and frequency of scratching behavior, an important measure when testing new dermatological treatments.

industrial sectors. One arm of the company issued over 1,400 patents worldwide (for another example, see **Mini Case: See through Walls with Wi-Fi**).

6.6 Concluding Thoughts

Developing an opportunity based on technological innovation cannot simply be an aspirational goal. Instead, it is a process that entrepreneurs choose how to manage. We see that when choosing their technology, founding teams can and should:

- Proactively explore possible technological trajectories for a certain innovation (of which there are likely to be several)
- Consider opportunities to disrupt
- Decide between levels of commitment to exploration vs. exploitation
- Manage the technological path, trajectory, or S curve they want to follow
- Choose narrower or more general applications of their innovation.

These critical technology choices go hand in hand with the other essential choices around customer, organization, and competition. As will see later in this text, particular ways of managing technology are complementary with particular choices. For example, a more near-term focus on exploitation complements an early-stage focus on a narrow customer segment that is poorly served by existing offerings. A focus on more fundamental innovation fits better with a strategy to compete over the longer term for the entire market. Advancing a component of an overall system enhances the potential to collaborate with existing players in that market space, while a system-level innovation more likely means competing against other firms offering other system-level solutions.

Choosing to prioritize technological innovation requires more than relying on an underlying breakthrough or having a visionary goal. Instead, entrepreneurs make proactive choices to control and steer processes of innovation, whether the goals are limited or very ambitious. Technological choices must not be technology for technology's sake but fit with the venture's overall strategic plan.

Chapter 6 Review: Choosing Your Technology

CHAPTER TAKEAWAYS

- Technology includes the tools, techniques, designs, and knowledge used by a business to create practical value for consumers.

- By leveraging technology, a start-up can create value for a customer by offering an improved level of performance on an existing dimension of merit or providing value on some new dimension of performance.

- Every entrepreneur faces a trade-off between exploitation of existing technological solutions vs. long-term exploration of emerging technological options.

- The technology S curve encapsulates the idea that technological improvement is not linear. There are three stages of the technology S curve: exploration, exploitation, and maturity.

- Exploration: Technological progress at the earliest stages of a new technology is difficult, as researchers explore the new technology and spend more of their time learning and failing than concretely improving performance.

- Exploitation: As researchers exploit these knowledge gains and focus on particular designs and practical solutions, performance rapidly improves.

- Maturity: As a technology matures, the performance reaches a natural technological limit as a result of a particular design or architecture.

- The S-curve framework offers guidance and insight for entrepreneurs on the opportunities that might arise from exploring an emerging novel technological trajectory.

- As established firms may face challenges in transitioning to a new technological trajectory, an emerging technological trajectory offers a window of opportunity for a start-up to establish technological leadership.

- Technological disruption becomes part of an overall entrepreneurial strategy; start-ups are able to learn and experiment with emerging technology in a way that will establish leadership over time as performance begins to improve.

- Choosing a technology is choosing among possible technological trajectories as well as choosing how to manage those trajectories.
- In addition to choosing how or what to innovate, entrepreneurs must manage and control how this is done. They shape their own S curve, setting the trajectory of technology itself by how they experiment and learn.

KEY TERMS

technology (p. 159)
unique value (p. 159)
exploration (p. 161)
exploitation (p. 161)

maturity (p. 161)
window of opportunity (p. 166)
technological disruption (p. 166)

REVIEW QUESTIONS

1. Should the achievement of a high level of technical performance be the unique criteria an entrepreneur uses to assess the value of a new technology? Why or why not?

2. What are the primary reasons why an entrepreneur must "choose" technology? Relative to an established firm with significant resources, why might technology choice be even more critical for a start-up?

3. What is the difference between exploration and exploitation of an emerging technology?

4. What are the three phases of the technology S curve? Explain the logic behind the different rates of performance improvement within each phase and the implications for entrepreneurs.

5. According to the work of Professors Rebecca Henderson and Clay Christensen, what are the principal reasons established firms may face challenges in transitioning to a new technological trajectory?

6. Why might an emerging technology S curve offer a window of opportunity for a start-up?

7. How would the choice to undertake a more exploration-oriented approach to an emerging technology S curve differ from a more exploitation-oriented approach? Is one approach necessarily better than the other?

8. Explain the implications of an entrepreneur focusing on introducing technology as a component within an existing system vs. leveraging their technology to develop an entirely new system.

9. Describe the trade-off an entrepreneur is making if they focus on developing their technology for specialized applications (often for a specific set of customers) vs. developing the most general version with a wider range of applications.

DISCUSSION QUESTIONS

Answer the following series of questions and scenarios either in class discussions or by writing a short response.

1. Morgane is just finishing her master's degree in computer science. She has developed a powerful and novel artificial intelligence algorithm that dramatically enhances the ability of a computer to predict whether an individual is suffering from depression or anxiety based on their social media posts. While Morgane decides whether to found and build a start-up leveraging her invention, she is focusing on the predictive performance of her algorithm. Is Morgane focusing on the most important metric? What other criteria might she consider before launching her technology-based start-up? Explain why focusing on improving the predictive performance of a technology may (or may not) be a useful metric for an early-stage start-up.

2. In 2015, MIT researcher Carlo Ratti created a project, Underworlds, that samples the organic matter found in sewers, providing data about the health and ecology of urban wastewater. This research-oriented project could identify the level of nearly 10,000 different types of bacteria, viruses, and other materials. By 2017, two MIT students, Mariana Matus and Newsha Ghaeli, had built on Ratti's experiment to found Biobot Analytics. However, rather than measure the full range of wastewater substances, they focused on more accurately measuring a small number, including opioids (to track their use in particular neighborhoods) and then the COVID-19 virus (to track population spread at multiple levels). Why might it have been important for Matus and Ghaeli to limit the scope of their wastewater metrics? How might focusing on a smaller number of substances have enhanced their ability to learn and experiment and ultimately provide value for real-world customers?

3. The vast majority of venture capital investment is premised on a model whereby the time from initial investment to "exit" usually occurs within 6 to 8 years (and at most 10 years). You have been asked to advise a new type of fund whose backers are thinking of establishing a 25-year time frame for investing in start-ups nurturing novel technologies. How might the establishment of a longer time frame for investment (with adequate funding along that entire path) impact the types of ventures that receive investment? How might the longer time frame impact how those ventures resolve the trade-off between exploration and exploitation of their focal technologies? Do you think this would be a promising strategy for an investment fund?

4. Your assignment is to identify a potential "winner" and "loser" from an emerging technology. Specifically, identify an emerging technological trajectory (i.e., a new technology S curve) that you think will have a meaningful impact over the next 5 years. Identify one firm that is a current leader within an established industry or segment that will be challenged by the new technology and a start-up that is attempting to leverage that technology to gain a hold in the marketplace. Why will the established firm be unable to adjust to the new technology? How can the start-up leverage its expertise with the emerging technology to position itself for competitive advantage?

5. Science fiction writer William Gibson famously quipped, "The future is already here. It is just not evenly distributed yet." New technologies are emerging all the time, and often entrepreneurs and innovators that are geographically close to emerging technology are well-positioned to gain from it. What do you think is an exciting new technological innovation being developed within your university or region? Are there factors that have allowed that technology to thrive in the local ecosystem? How might you take advantage of this emerging technology as part of a start-up within your ecosystem?

6. Do you think there is a game-changing technology only at the earliest stages of the S curve today that might be able to have a large impact in 10 years? What are some choices you could make, as either an entrepreneur, engineer, investor, or employee, to take advantage of this long-term emerging technological trajectory?

SUGGESTED READINGS

Dosi, Giovanni. "Technological Paradigms and Technological Trajectories: A Suggested Interpretation of the Determinants and Directions of Technical Change." *Research Policy* 11, no. 3 (1982): 147–62.

Ederer, Florian, and Gustavo Manso. "Is Pay for Performance Detrimental to Innovation?" *Management Science* 59, no. 7 (2013): 1496–513.

Foster, Richard N. *Innovation: The Attacker's Advantage*. New York: Summit Books, 1986.

Ganco, Martin, and Rajshree Agarwal. "Performance Differentials between Diversifying Entrants and Entrepreneurial Start-Ups: A Complexity Approach." *Academy of Management Review* 34, no. 2 (2009): 228–52.

Gans, Joshua S., Michael Kearney, Erin L. Scott, and Scott Stern. "Choosing Technology: An Entrepreneurial Strategy Approach." *Strategy Science* 6, no. 1 (2020): 39–53.

Henderson, Rebecca M., and Kim B. Clark. "Architectural Innovation: The Reconfiguration of Existing Product Technologies and the Failure of Established Firms." *Administrative Science Quarterly* 35, no. 1 (1990): 9–30.

Levinthal, Daniel A., and James G. March. "The Myopia of Learning." *Strategic Management Journal* 14, no. S2 (1993): 95–112.

Marx, Matt, Joshua S. Gans, and David H. Hsu. "Disruptive Technologies: Evidence from the Speech Recognition Industry." *Management Science 60*, no. 12 (2014): 3103–23.

Schilling, Melissa A. "Toward a General Modular Systems Theory and Its Application to Interfirm Product Modularity." *Academy of Management Review* 25, no. 2 (2000): 312–34.

Utterback, James. *Mastering the Dynamics of Innovation: How Companies Can Seize Opportunities in the Face of Technological Change*. Boston: Harvard Business School Press, 1994.

Karl Martin and Foteini Agrafioti

University of Toronto researchers Karl Martin and Foteini Agrafioti and their team developed a method for identifying an individual based on their heartbeat. There seemed to be a wide array of potential applications for this technology such as "always-on" authentication—that is, being able to identify someone immediately using this pattern. So, in 2011, with the support of UofT's research office, they patented their method and founded Nymi (then Bionym) to commercialize their product. However, after initial interest from a number of hardware firms and more than two years of additional work, Martin could not find a commercial partner willing to house and develop this technology. At that stage, Nymi would require significant investments for a hardware partner to integrate the technology into their products. While interested, these firms were simply not ready to commit to such a new idea, particularly given the unproven track record of the start-up and the nature of the security sector. Then mentors at UofT's Creative Destruction Lab suggested that the answer to the conundrum was easy: instead of trying to sell the method as a software component to others' hardware, the Nymi team should develop hardware (and a full identification solution) themselves. This was a significant shift not only for the technology but also for the company.

Six months later, Martin had a prototype of the Nymi armband. The team created a bracelet people could wear that would signal their identity using radio-frequency (RF) technology. Focusing on business applications, Nymi designed the technology to replace keycards, fingerprints, and other authentication forms that are often a source of daily inconvenience and frustration as people move between rooms and systems. Nymi's solution supplied a streamlined approach that provided convenience for workers and enhanced security for innovation-focused

Foteini Agrafioti pictured in 2018. Agrafioti is now the Chief Science Officer at the Royal Bank of Canada and Head of its Borealis AI research institute.

organizations, such as pharmaceutical companies, that sought to control and monitor access throughout their systems and buildings. Nymi's focus on workplace security and privacy when refining its technological choices have paid off, and it has attracted almost $40 million in funding to date.

Questions

1. Based on the information in the case, describe how you would characterize the history of Nymi in terms of choices around exploration and exploitation.

2. One feature of technology choice is not developing technology for technology's sake. Describe your opinion of how well Nymi supported this objective.

3. Consider the core technology Nymi developed that is described in the first paragraph. What are three other ideas they might have put in place to capture value from it?

Tony Hsieh (left) and Fred Mossler (right) are pictured in 2008—a decade after the founding of Zappos. com and a year before it was purchased by Amazon.com. Hsieh and Mossler were part of the original team at Zappos, with Hsieh being its early investor and CEO, and right-hand man Mossler having the official position of "No Title," suggesting the culture that was an important part of this organization.

ENTREPRENEUR'S DILEMMA There are many aspects to managing a venture, and it is tempting to try and be great at everything. This is usually not possible. Should your internal capabilities be in operational efficiency or high-quality service to customers? What functions should you outsource rather than develop yourself? How much should you focus on functional vs. integrative performance? What resources should you draw from local suppliers?

CHAPTER OBJECTIVES

- Learn why start-ups have to choose their organization
- Discover how initial organizational choices imprint on future ones, impact the survival of the firm, and lay the foundation for the organization
- Understand why prioritizing capability development and resource acquisition matters
- Learn how to choose your resources and capabilities

7

CHOOSING YOUR ORGANIZATION

With the advent of e-commerce, led by companies such as Amazon, the late 1990s saw the emergence of specialized online retailers across a wide range of product categories. This dot-com boom included short-lived highfliers such as Pets.com (for a brief while the leading seller of pet food and accessories over the Internet) and structured marketplaces with longer staying power such as eBay and Craigslist. Footwear e-tailing seemed like another likely opportunity since it combined the value of a market that was profitable—shoes are among the most profitable segments within the entire fashion industry—with the challenge of accommodating the almost unimaginably large range of styles and sizes available. In 1999, Nick Swinmurn, a recent college graduate with a degree in film studies and some experience at the start-up AutoWeb.com, approached angel investors Alfred Lin and Tony Hsieh with the idea to pursue an e-commerce footwear opportunity (the original name for the website was ShoeSite). But though Swinmurn, Hsieh, and Lin each had experience with the early Internet, all lacked experience in the footwear industry.

Perhaps the most critical early choices made by the initial founding team focused on the early structure and staffing of Zappos as an organization.[1] To achieve critical mass as a start-up, Swinmurn simultaneously recruited Nordstrom footwear executive Fred Mossler to be the first full-time employee while attracting Lin and Hsieh as the first "professional" investors. Importantly, Mossler would only leave his secure job at Nordstrom if Swinmurn received financing, while Hsieh and Lin's interest in the firm was premised on the assumption that Mossler would be a key member of the early team. This combination of individuals was instrumental not only in the founding of Zappos, but also in powerfully shaping the growth and nature of the company over time through the choices they made.

In this chapter we focus on Choices around Organization and how they will impact your organization both early on and in the future.

The founding team embraced their freedom as a start-up to experiment as they explored the e-commerce shoe opportunity. For example, during the dot-com bust and recession of 2000, with rapidly dwindling resources and an already pared-down staff, Hsieh asked Mossler to envision a "bet the company" plan that would provide a clear signal of whether footwear e-commerce was likely to succeed. Mossler proposed that, rather than limit expenses, Zappos invest the bulk of its remaining financial resources to buy inventory. Doing so would see whether their idea to combine a high level of in-stock inventory with a customer-focused experience to create value would gain traction in the e-commerce marketplace. While this combination was risky, yet creative and distinctive even relative to most ambitious start-ups, Hsieh ultimately invested the remainder of his own personal financial resources into this approach to "either save Zappos or ensure our speedy demise."

The ultimate success of this organizational experiment gave Zappos the impetus to grow quickly over the next several years. This next phase of organizational growth was achieved through hiring and empowering other key personnel, such as Keith Glynn, who oversaw the location of Zappos's first warehouse operations in Kentucky. These choices shaped Zappos's capabilities, resources, and culture. In particular, relative to the efficient but impersonal online customer interface common to most e-commerce sites, the growing team came to understand that their experience should fit with the way in which shoes are purchased in physical stores. Shopping for shoes is both more complex in terms of getting the right fit and more emotional (choosing the right style) than other purchases. Zappos took advantage of this insight by creating a large, in-stock inventory of different styles and sizes and combining it with extraordinary in-house customer service that featured friendly, empathetic customer support. To achieve the next phase of growth made possible by this insight, Hsieh relocated the bulk of the Zappos organization in 2004 from Silicon Valley to Las Vegas, where Zappos could recruit high-quality customer service representatives by paying an attractive wage for Las Vegas and saving money on labor relative to what the company would have had to pay in the pricier Silicon Valley labor market. Zappos's decision to move to Las Vegas was not borne from success; rather, it reflected a choice to *enable* success. Swinmurn, Hsieh, and Lin knew that to succeed, they needed to build and grow an organization that could actually deliver the value of a personal shoe-buying experience to customers (**Figure 7.1**).

When Amazon ultimately acquired Zappos for more than $1 billion in 2009, it was not purchasing an "idea" or even the initiative and passion of the early founding team. Instead, it was acquiring an established but still growing enterprise that had industry-leading capabilities in customer service and an extensive supply relationship with every major shoe brand. By choosing to develop tailored capabilities and gain access to unique resources, Hsieh and his cofounders built an organization that continued to grow through constant experimentation and employee empowerment.

Typical organizations start simply with just a few people and then, as they grow, become more complex.

FIGURE 7.1 Zappos Las Vegas

Far from a sterile call center, Zappos's founders' decision to build their organization in Las Vegas let them create a customer service experience not seen before at e-commerce retailers.

While entire fields of management study how complex organizations are managed, for start-ups, the challenge is what early and simple organizations should prioritize to implement a strategy to create and capture value. As we will see, entrepreneurs must pay explicit attention to setting those priorities and deciding what the initial organization of a venture will focus on. There are many dimensions to this choice, and in this chapter, we will identify and examine the most critical ones:

1. The initial employees of an organization should reflect its priorities but also be the seed elements of its culture.
2. The resources an organization controls and the capabilities it decides to build define what the venture will be good at.
3. These decisions also define, out of necessity, what the venture will need to pull back from or outsource to others.

By the end of the chapter, we will see how these three choices must align with other strategic choices. But to get started, we begin by taking a broad brush and investigating some important trade-offs in early organizational choices for start-ups.

7.1 Why Do Start-Ups Need to Choose Their Organization?

Entrepreneurs do not work alone. They need other people with talent and access to resources. That is, they need to build **organizations** that will create and capture value, turning their vision into reality. *How a start-up forms its initial team and culture will determine the business capabilities it will develop first and the resources it will need and use.* Thus, how an organization is formed, what elements it prioritizes, and whether it seeds the foundation for growth can be critical in setting the path for successful commercialization.

Entrepreneurs face three critical yet interdependent challenges in founding and building their organization.

1. While there are many different potential ways entrepreneurs might organize value delivery around a given idea, *the organization is, by definition, **constrained** at the moment of founding.* Most start-ups are born with very limited financial resources. And, even if money is not a problem, the founding team has only a limited amount of time and attention to devote to assembling and coordinating the organization. Even relatively straightforward tasks associated with building an organization—hiring early employees, perhaps leasing and arranging office space—take effort on the part of the entrepreneur (and come at the expense of other activities like talking with customers or developing a valuable technology).
2. *There is a high level of uncertainty about the impact of alternative ways of organizing.* For example, one of a start-up's most important decisions is whom to hire as the first employee. Hiring an engineer with technical expertise will likely help the venture develop its technology more quickly, while hiring a salesperson with industry experience may establish relationships with customers more quickly. However, it may be difficult at the

organization A larger, more formal, and less personal group, such as a business or school, set up with specific objectives in mind

constrained In entrepreneurship, the idea that you have limited resources to draw on, especially financial, that limit what an entrepreneur can do

imprinting The idea that the identity, passion, and early decisions of founders have an outsized impact on the overall evolution of the venture

moment of founding to hire a single individual with both of these skills, and it may also be difficult to compare the relative importance of achieving unrelated milestones in these two areas. Learning about customer needs is important, but so is formulating the overall design and performance of a product or service. Entrepreneurs often receive conflicting advice and feedback about which elements to prioritize at the earliest stage of a venture. But, critically, those choices, as we will explore in detail in future chapters, must fit in with other strategic choices (i.e., customer and technology).

3. Finally, *there is the impact of **imprinting**: the idea that the identity, passion, and early decisions of founding teams have an outsized impact on the overall evolution of the venture.* Consider an entrepreneur with either an engineering or sales background. Whereas the engineer is likely to advocate for further innovation and invest in technological capabilities, the salesperson is more likely to encourage a clear marketing and customer focus. Early decisions are not simply a reflection of the background of the founding team; they shape the path that a venture follows. For example, if the entrepreneur has a sales background, a decision to hire an engineer as the first employee (e.g., to move themselves away from their natural orientation) is likely to start a shift toward a more technical focus as the engineer advocates for the time, attention, and limited resources of the start-up.

Put simply, the early organizational choices that entrepreneurs make will influence the capabilities they build and the resources they leverage, shaping how a venture evolves over time.

Organizational choice also matters because, relative to customer and technology, it is harder to experiment and learn before making decisions that commit a venture to certain directions. Recall that, for customer choice, primary market research can be used to learn about customer wants and needs without committing to a particular beachhead. For technology, experimentation can identify potential paths for improvement without committing to one in particular. The impact of organizational choices is more direct. The structure and composition of the founding team, the background and experience of early investors and employees, and the early relationships built with suppliers, distribution channels, and the local ecosystem will all shape the future path of that organization.

Indeed, it is sometimes not the founding team but some of the earliest employees of a company who determine the core of that organization's idea and strategy. One notable example is Sony. Only weeks after the end of World War II, Masaru Ibuka, previously a senior researcher in the Japanese war effort, founded an electronics shop in an abandoned downtown Tokyo department store without a clear idea of exactly what it would produce or fix (early efforts included an electronic rice cooker and heated blankets). However, the launch of the new company attracted the attention of a younger colleague from the war effort, Akio Morita, who subsequently joined the company and ultimately became a cofounder with Ibuka. Morita helped focus the early organization on developing more sophisticated radio and telecommunications equipment, and in particular helped to develop and commercialize the first Japanese tape recorder. Morita's unique vision involved the "miniaturization" of electronics equipment and the power of *continuous innovation*, or developing many iterations of a product over time. Under Morita's leadership, the small company founded by Ibuka emerged

FIGURE 7.2 Partners Set the Path of Sony

Sony cofounders Masaru Ibuka (left) and Akio Morita (right), pictured together in 1973. When Morita teamed up with Ibuka, he set a path for the company based on continuous innovation.

as the Sony Corporation, perhaps the leading global company focused on the convergence of film, music, and digital electronics (**Figure 7.2**).

CONSTRAINTS

Organizational decisions have immediate effects but also can constrain future paths. What might seem to be sensible decisions for a venture at the outset may turn out to be mistakes in the future, particularly when it comes time to grow and scale without disruptive and costly organizational change. This is more difficult when what the venture does to test and then implement value creation and capture hypotheses evolves over the life cycle of the venture.

For example, initially hiring employees, renting an office, and assigning roles are not ends in themselves but are costly investments in a particular path. These organizational choices are made to test the potential for value creation and capture with a particular customer group, a particular technology, and a particular competitive orientation.

However, those organizational choices will result in imprinting and other factors that influence the future of the venture. As we will see, this is especially important when an organization decides what functions it will deliver in-house rather than outsource or buy from other businesses. This is because experience matters for growth, and a start-up is more likely to gain experience when functions are in-house. But because limited time and resources prevent doing all functions in-house, start-ups must establish priorities. These priorities should be made looking beyond present needs to future ones.

Because the impact of founding organizational choices is uncertain, many entrepreneurs find it tempting to focus instead on other choice domains such as customer or technology. They choose to make more tactical organizational choices that jumpstart early-stage experimentation and learning. But ignoring the impact of founding organizational choices can cause the premature failure of a venture, even one with significant potential.

7.2 Resources and Capabilities: *How* an Organization Creates and Captures Value

Organizations create and capture value by using their resources and capabilities. **Resources** are the assets your organization is able to control or potentially access when needed. The resources an organization has let it learn about and implement a particular way to create and capture value. Resources include tangible assets, such as machinery and real estate; financial assets, such as venture capital; and intangible assets, such as proprietary intellectual property or even knowledge maintained by the organization like information on the needs of customers. **Capabilities**, in contrast, are not about what assets a firm controls but what a firm is able to do. For example, while ownership of a particular piece of high-precision manufacturing equipment is a resource, the ability of employees to use that machinery to achieve a high level of productivity and precision comparable to competitors is a capability. The capabilities of an organization can span a wide range of domains, from the ability to effectively manage the sales process with customers (a sales capability) to the ability for different parts of the organization to work together to achieve common objectives (a cross-functional team capability).

The effective management of valuable resources and unique capabilities is often identified as one of the most (if not *the* most) important drivers of the success of any organization. Specifically, from the perspective of an established organization, the central job of a manager is to combine the organization's resources and capabilities into an integrated system that creates and captures value on a sustainable basis. For example, while the car rental industry is relatively less profitable compared with other industries, Enterprise Rent-A-Car has been able to achieve extraordinary profits and growth over multiple decades. Founded by Jack Taylor in the late 1960s, Enterprise is organized very differently than most other car rental companies.[2] First, while most car rental companies hire primarily minimum-wage workers and offer little training, Enterprise focuses its hiring almost exclusively on college graduates who show significant initiative and social skills (e.g., those who have held leadership positions in student organizations such as fraternities and sororities). Each worker receives extensive training, starting at the bottom of the organization with the opportunity to be promoted to a branch manager or even a regional supervisor with significant potential for financial reward. At the same time, whereas most car rental companies focus on rentals at airports, Enterprise maintains a valuable network of locations away from the airport, including next to car dealerships and auto repair shops so that they can offer rentals to customers whose cars are undergoing maintenance or repairs (**Figure 7.3**). Finally, Enterprise is one of the few auto rental companies to not only purchase all of its own vehicles (it was the single largest buyer of new cars in the United States in the 2010s), but also invest in

This chapter's video illustrates how Enterprise Rent-A-Car built a competitive advantage by committing to certain organizational capabilities.

resources Assets that your organization is able to control or potentially access when needed

capabilities In business, what a firm is able to do

maintaining these vehicles to attract a favorable price in the resale market.

Two critical aspects of Enterprise—the uniqueness of its resources and capabilities and its isolation from competitive imitation—illuminate how it has sustained performance over multiple decades. First, relative to other car companies, Enterprise utilizes a distinct set of resources and capabilities; its employee base is more highly educated, and its locations are more local. It then combines those resources and capabilities in a unique way; internal training and promotion teaches all employees both the "Enterprise way" and how to handle a wide range of situations. In other words, even though Enterprise is offering a similar service to other car rental companies, it has identified its organization as an alternative way of creating value for customers. Second, once Enterprise assembled this system for value creation in a given city, potential competitors found it challenging to imitate that system. Established rental companies such as Avis and Hertz already have existing employees and locations and so face significant costs to shift toward the Enterprise model. At the same time, potential entrants are disadvantaged by their lack of reputation (e.g., why should a college grad work for them?) and scale (e.g., how can they acquire new cars at a discounted price until they have achieved a high level of scale?). Putting these ideas together, Enterprise's competitive advantage is based on how it can combine a unique and valuable system of resources and capabilities that is resistant to imitation.

This Enterprise example shows how an organization can use resources and capabilities to achieve competitive advantage over an extended period of time. However, while an entrepreneur faces the challenge of how to acquire or access those resources in the first place, it is essential that these resources and capabilities are in place for their vision to become a reality. This is the topic of the next section.

FIGURE 7.3 **Enterprise's Unique Choices**

Enterprise's hiring profile and choice to focus on off-airport locations have driven its rise to the number-one vehicle rental company.

7.3 Resources and Capabilities Turn Hypotheses into Reality

Pursuing an opportunity does not mean that the entrepreneur already has the resources and capabilities necessary to realize the value of that opportunity. Indeed, normally the situation is quite the opposite. When a new venture is formed, its resources and capabilities are equivalent to those of the founding team alone, and in general, the founding team will not have all the venture needs. There are, of course, certain cases where entrepreneurs can simply use their personal resources and capabilities: a gig economy driver for a ridesharing service such as Uber or Lyft leverages their existing automobile, their skill at driving, and their own time and effort. However, for most ventures, pursuing an opportunity involves somehow gaining access or control over resources and capabilities beyond those of the founding team.

Ecosystem as a Resource

A business must consider what resources will make it distinctive and whether it can gain value from being located closer to those resources. This is especially true if potential employees, partners, and its own customers are concentrated in a particular location.

Not surprisingly, Avatech found more expertise around avalanches in states with terrain like this mountain top in Loveland Pass, CO.

Consider Brint Markle, the founder of Avatech, an avalanche-detection technology company, and Mountain Hub, an information network for the outdoors. The first company, Avatech, was launched near Boston, where its founders were attending business school. At graduation, the team had to make a decision about where to grow their business. On the one hand, the Boston area ecosystem provided them with access to a rich engineering talent pool and exposure to some of the most cutting-edge research in electronic sensors. On the other hand, while there is plenty of snow in Boston, there is not a lot of expertise in handling avalances. Cities in Colorado and Utah provided the team with access to avalanche safety and rescue experts as well as the foremost ski and snowboarding athletes in the country.

Ultimately, the Avatech team wanted to build a company that would advance snow safety for the backcountry community and chose to locate the company in Park City, UT. Choosing to situate in a particular location may allow a venture to access specialized resources. Later, Mountain Hub was aquired by the Swiss outdoor company Mammut.

Meeting this gap between identifying opportunity and being able to deliver value is one of the most important practical challenges facing a start-up. The entrepreneur must have a clear hypothesis about what resources and capabilities are necessary for value creation, and must also figure out how to gain access to them to grow their organization over time. In other words, how can the founding team leverage the scarce resources and capabilities they have at the start of their venture to begin building and acquiring others that are needed to succeed?

Both of these elements are captured in Howard Stevenson's definition of entrepreneurship discussed in Chapter 2: *Entrepreneurship is the pursuit of opportunity beyond resources controlled.* This definition captures an important insight: rather than simply being assets that firms either control or not, resources and capabilities depend on the insight and initiative of entrepreneurs to first identify and then "pursue" or acquire them in a timely and cost-effective way.

To see this process in action, consider the case of Chobani, now the leading producer of Greek yogurt in the United States. Hamdi Ulukaya, a Kurdish immigrant from Turkey, had long believed that the quality and texture of major American yogurt brands were poor, identifying a potential value creation hypothesis in terms of thicker, strained yogurt (i.e., Greek yogurt) for the American market. In this case, Ulukaya was fortunate in that he already had knowledge of what resources were necessary: cost-efficient, high-quality manufacturing of Greek yogurt requires access to a large dairy processing plant. However, simply having this knowledge was not enough. It was not until Kraft placed an otherwise abandoned dairy processing plant in New York on the market for less than $1 million that Ulukaya had a chance to purchase that asset, using a loan from the Small Business Administration and local economic development grants. Ulukaya could then attract a high-quality early team to develop the precise recipe and proprietary processes to establish what ultimately became the Chobani yogurt brand (yum!).[3] We see in this case that while Ulukaya had identified a value creation hypothesis, gaining control over the plant and scaling the team translated that hypothesis into a reality (for another example of creating value from available resources, see **Mini Case: Ecosystem as a Resource**).

For other entrepreneurs, their key challenge is identifying and choosing among alternative resources and capabilities. Consider the Pebble watch, developed by Eric Migicovsky in 2011 as the first commercially available smartwatch (see **Figure 7.4**). Though venture capitalists were initially skeptical of the idea and whether Migicovsky could implement that idea successfully, he raised more than $10 million through preorders on the Kickstarter platform. Widely hailed at the time as the largest start-up crowdfunding campaign to date, the initial product shipment of the Pebble watch went to customers at least five months behind schedule and missing many pre-announced features like a fitness tracking application. Essentially, Migicovsky had made a commitment to provide the Pebble watch to his Kickstarter backers without a fully-worked-out plan about

---

FIGURE 7.4 **Pebble: E-Paper Watch Kickstarter Campaign**

A graduate of the University of Waterloo and the Y Combinator accelerator program, Pebble founder Eric Migicovsky was one of the first smartwatch designers. After his work on the inPulse for Blackberry, he designed the Pebble for iOS and Android smartphones in 2011. However, despite the clean design and technical firsts, venture capitalists were skeptical of the product category, and Migicovsky was unable to raise significant funds. Taking an alternative approach, he launched Pebble on Kickstarter, and within days the campaign had broken records, including raising over $1 million in watch preorders in a single day.

Resources and Capabilities Turn Hypotheses into Reality

Pebble vs. the Apple Watch. In 2016, *Forbes Magazine* published a hands-on showdown of the two watches. Pebble (top) had the price advantage of $199 vs. the Apple Watch (bottom) price of $299, and the reviewer preferred the slimness of the Pebble watch too. Pebble also supported both iOS and Android platforms, and the reviewer noted that the "Pebble platform has a lot of fans." Ultimately, however, while the reviewer said he could see the appeal of Pebble, he was drawn to the more powerful Apple Watch and ended up buying one. The superior fitness tracker, ability to play music, and better display and battery were deciding factors. And the reviewer spelled out another powerful advantage of the Apple product: "I am an iPhone owner, so the tight integration is a plus."[a]

how to manufacture and deliver it. This lack of clarity led to inevitable delays in the production schedule, and perhaps more importantly, the costs Migicovsky incurred to deliver these watches were significantly greater than the revenue he took in. Because Migicovsky was in a relatively weak bargaining position with manufacturers and other partners, his costs were high. Though his user base was large for a start-up, it was very small compared with the volume required to negotiate meaningful discounts with electronics suppliers.

Despite these delays and high costs, Migicovsky demonstrated the potential of the smartwatch category. Unfortunately for Migicovsky, established players such as Apple, Samsung, and Garmin, after seeing the success of the category, were able to avoid the mistakes of Pebble, leading to its decline in 2015 and 2016 (see the sidebar on **Pebble vs. the Apple Watch**).[4]

The contrasting stories of Chobani and Pebble highlight the role of entrepreneurs in the origins of resources and capabilities. Until an entrepreneur establishes a system for delivering value in a cost-effective and timely way, a potential opportunity remains a hypothesis rather than a reality. Being able to acquire the resources and capabilities that allow for value creation provides an entrepreneur with the potential for the "unfair advantage" that makes a venture an ongoing success. Of course, there may be multiple ways to combine resources and capabilities and create value from a particular opportunity. Proactive choice between alternative configurations of resources and capabilities is at the heart of a strategic approach toward organizational choice.

7.4 The Firm Survival Curve

While Chobani has survived for more than 15 years, Pebble no longer exists. Even though Pebble introduced an innovative product, and even though the opportunity it identified (smartwatches) ended up as a large market, Pebble could not transition from its roots as a start-up firm to a more established enterprise. Of course, surviving as an organization is a necessary (though not sufficient) condition for that organization to create and capture value on an ongoing basis. Even if an entrepreneur has an idea that could lead to value creation and capture, failing to attract resources or build capabilities may result in the failure of the organization and not realizing the promise of their idea.

A relationship that shows entrepreneurs how organizational choices are linked to a venture's ability to survive or conversely, to avoid premature failure is the firm survival curve (see **Using the Research: The Firm Survival Curve**). It documents the relationship between the age of a new organization and its likelihood of continued survival and helps entrepreneurs understand the challenge they face in building capabilities and attracting resources to survive. Similar to the market S curve and technology S curve described in the previous two chapters, the firm survival curve provides an empirical foundation for start-ups. However, the firm survival curve is essentially linear: the probability of survival increases as the length of time the organization exists increases.

While many factors underly this relationship, the organizational choices of the founding team are at the core of whether a venture not only survives but thrives. Even the most promising value creation hypothesis is difficult to turn into

The Firm Survival Curve

Drawn from a 2017 study by Tiantian Yang and Howard Aldrich, this figure shows the probability of survival or failure of new start-up organizations across more than 1,000 ventures. The likelihood of failure starts at a relatively high level and then declines over time. About 5% of startups fail within the first three months, with almost twice that failing by the six month after founding. By the time an organization is five years old or older (i.e., more than 60 months), the rate of failure has declined by more than 80% (down to a rate around 1%).[a]

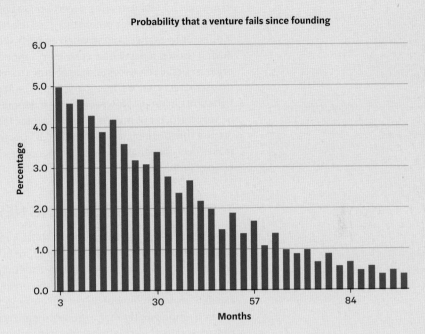

Probability that a venture fails since founding

Cumulative failure of ventures over time

Two looks at the firm survival curve: The top graph shows what percentage of new firms fail during three-month periods after founding. The bottom one shows total failures over time. Getting started is tough!

reality, and every theory, idea, or plan depends on who is doing it or making it. For instance, we saw that Eric Migicovsky, though not successful in the long term, did succeed in delivering the Pebble smartwatch to his initial Kickstarter customers. Many other ventures and start-ups make similar promises. But their teams fail to even assemble the necessary resources and capabilities to deliver a first product to anyone, let alone develop ways to do so cost-effectively and repeatedly deliver value, and at scale. For other start-ups, the team's early commitments may make it difficult to change course when an early idea is proven incorrect. For instance, having chosen a particular customer, a founding team may make investments in organizational resources and capabilities to serve that customer. For example, they may have recruited early employees and built relationships with suppliers and distribution channels. However, if this customer ends up being a poor target, it can be very hard, if not impossible, to redeploy the organization in a different way (we discuss this further in Chapter 15). Of course, as the organization advances and makes decisions that lead to initial successes, experience increases and the likelihood of failure declines.

THE CHALLENGE OF BEING NEW

More than 50 years ago, Northwestern University sociologist Arthur Stinchcombe argued that the high rate of failure of new organizations reflected a central challenge facing entrepreneurs: **the liability of newness.** As we have seen, at the founding moment of a firm, the organization lacks all the resources and capabilities to implement an overall entrepreneurial strategy. Stinchcombe went further, emphasizing that a young organization has yet to define the structure, routines, personal relationships, and culture needed for that organization to function effectively on an ongoing basis. For example, in a study of more than 300 bankruptcies in Canada,[5] young firms were more likely to fail because entrepreneurs lacked essential knowledge or financial acumen. However, in more established enterprises, their failure was associated with not adapting to ongoing changes in the competitive marketplace.

Another striking set of findings on the liability of newness is how the rate of failure at the earliest stages of ventures varies across industries and contexts. For example, start-ups in highly competitive markets such as retail restaurants or coffee shops face a very high rate of failure within their first year,[6] while firms in less competitive environments such as physician practices, which require a medical credential, have a much lower rate of early failure. Also, firms that pursue strategies requiring significant early-stage capital investment may experience a higher rate of failure at the very outset but then benefit from a much lower rate of failure if they are indeed able to attract early resources and capabilities. Moreover, there is a subtle link between the liability of newness at the organizational level and the stage of technological exploration. Specifically, during the earliest stages of exploration of a new technology opportunity, a higher level of experimentation and learning seems to reduce the liability of newness.[7] In other words, when an entrepreneur is pursuing a promising but still exploratory opportunity like the start of a new technology S curve, they may choose to continue a venture even with early-stage failures. In doing so, they hope they will eventually take advantage of the learning and knowledge they are building around a technological path.

the liability of newness The theory that young firms are more likely to fail because entrepreneurs lack essential knowledge or financial acumen as well as the structure, routines, personal relationships, and culture required for their organizations to function effectively

Research shows that rates of failure vary across industries. Restaurants fail at much higher rates than doctors' practices. Tech start-ups do much better if they can attract resources and capabilities early on.

Perhaps the key insight of the firm survival curve is that firms that overcome the liability of newness (within a given environment) have a higher likelihood of success. For example, Professors Thomas Hellmann and Manju Puri studied 170 Silicon Valley start-up companies, some of which received venture capital and some of which did not.[8] The venture capital–backed companies were more likely to undergo "professionalization," which included establishing a more formal organization, hiring human resource managers and adopting standardized hiring practices, and establishing more formal strategic processes. The authors found that these professionalization initiatives were positively associated with the ultimate growth and success of these firms and a lower rate of overall failure.

Simply put, success in entrepreneurship requires not failing at the earliest stages. A sizable part of what determines whether a start-up survives its first few years is simply ultimately learning whether the core idea of a venture is a valuable one or not. The point of a start-up is that its activities reveal whether its assumptions are valid. The high early failure rates of ventures are a natural consequence of this process of experimentation and learning. Start-ups need to make choices that give them the greatest chance of being on the right side of the firm survival curve, and this means quickly overcoming the liabilities of newness.

7.5 Building Capabilities and Leveraging Resources

In starting a new venture, forming your initial organization is crucial. Among other things, it shapes how successful and effective your testing and experimenting will be, and it helps the organization attract resources. Moreover, the long-term impact of early decisions to focus on specific capabilities or resources will have an outsized influence on the evolution of the venture; early imprinting will even persist following changes in leadership and founder departures.

Because of this, entrepreneurs need to prioritize two types of important choices about resources and capabilities. These choices are ones that will allow them to test their value creation and capture hypotheses, and ones that will provide a solid foundation for the ongoing venture if the tests show the venture is promising.

TABLE 7.1 Key Questions in Building Resources and Capabilities

QUESTION	CONSIDERATION
Who is your founding team?	The passion, experience, knowledge, and network access of the founding team are what the venture is built on. Founders provide support for each others' personal and professional objectives.
Functional or integrative focus?	**Functional focus**—A focus on one area of performance (e.g., engineering, design, or marketing). Achieving excellence in this area will be the start-up's priority. It will be the advantage. **Integrative focus**—A focus on making sure all the business functions are coordinated and work together effectively. Start-ups devote time to managing this successfully to achieve overall high performance.
Make or buy?	**Make**—Decision to develop new products/capabilities or improve on existing ones. **Buy**—Decision to take advantage of, and possibly partner with, others who have products/capabilities that are needed.

In this section, we will examine these choices as detailed answers to three questions, summarized in **Table 7.1**. This starts with the choice of the founding team itself.

WHO IS YOUR FOUNDING TEAM?

Perhaps the single most critical organizational choice entrepreneurs make is agreeing to establish a firm in the first place. It is entrepreneurs who not only choose the idea they pursue but also the team to pursue it. As we discussed in Chapter 3, entrepreneurs tend to select opportunities where they have unique insight, resources, and purpose. Bringing together the right founding team—with the complementary skills to realize the idea—provides the foundation for attracting the necessary resources and building the critical capabilities. *The passion, experience, knowledge, and network access of the founding team are the earliest resources and capabilities of a venture, and all others will be built on them.*

Let's look at this idea in terms of the case of Gimlet Media, a podcast production start-up we introduced in Chapter 3. Gimlet was founded by Alex Blumberg, a journalist who learned about storytelling from the maestro, Ira Glass. Glass's *This American Life* has been the gold standard for long-form audio journalism and launched the public radio careers of many leading journalists and producers. As the global financial crisis was brewing in 2008, Blumberg and his colleague Adam Davidson released their own take on explainer journalism with "The Giant Pool of Money" from *This American Life,* followed shortly by their NPR podcast series *Planet Money.* Awards flowed his way, and Blumberg saw there was potential for more. He wondered if he could scale what he had learned from Glass to bring not just one or two new podcasts but a whole network to the market. With that idea, he left the comfort of a traditional NPR-funded job to found Gimlet Media.

While Blumberg knew a lot about storytelling and creating podcasts, he knew very little about the practicalities of running a business. He felt the pressure of making decisions alone and pushback from potential investors who wanted to place bets on a team rather than an individual. Moreover, Gimlet was going to have to do business differently from *This American Life,* and Blumberg did not have the skills and experience required to make those judgments. He needed a cofounder

FIGURE 7.5 Gimlet Media: Choosing the Right Partner

When Alex Blumberg (right) got the idea for his podcasting company, Gimlet Media, he knew he needed support on the business side to be taken seriously by investors. He recruited Matt Lieber (left), a BCG consultant with a love for and experience in radio, to join the founding team.

who not only possessed these complementary skills but also fundamentally bought into his vision. That person turned out to be Matt Lieber (**Figure 7.5**).

In 2014, Lieber was working for the Boston Consulting Group after completing his MBA. But he had been a radio producer for NPR in his past and felt his "heart was still in radio." A connection put Lieber and Blumberg together, and after a short trial period, Lieber left consulting for good to join Blumberg as cofounder of Gimlet. The pair gelled and worked together through myriad crises documented in—what else?—a podcast called *StartUp*. Five years later, the network had been built and was acquired by Spotify for several hundred million dollars. It was a long way from public radio.

Blumberg had a large number of choices on how to build his team. Indeed, there was no limit to those individuals skilled in business development, and Blumberg could have easily (and quickly!) recruited one of them. Instead, he took a deliberate approach to identify and recruit a cofounder who possessed critical business development skills and had experiences, values, and a passion that aligned with the core mission of Gimlet: to tell compelling stories. Blumberg understood that a cofounding team should possess a shared vision for translating the idea to reality and the complementary skills required to do so. This approach also informed Blumberg's first hires, who came directly from narrative journalism and podcasting. While he might have hired technology-oriented specialists to build apps and other infrastructure, Blumberg initially focused on building an early, like-minded team. He wanted hires who possessed skills that would help his company create and tell compelling stories, the hypothesis at the core of his business.[9]

While Gimlet shows the benefits of making the right choices with respect to an early team, there are cautionary tales. The costs of getting it wrong can be quite significant. Antje Danielson, a geochemist at Harvard, came to entrepreneurship to address her broader environmental concerns and apply her theoretical research. Having researched Switzerland's Mobility Cooperative, she felt a similar model—which leveraged technology to allow for easy car exchange without constant key-swapping and related logistics—could work in the United States and reduce Americans' reliance on single-owner vehicles.[10] While still exploring the idea in the fall of 1999, by happenstance, she met recent MBA graduate Robin Chase while their young children played at a local playground. Their conversations quickly shifted to their shared interest in entrepreneurship, and Danielson mentioned her still-nascent car-sharing idea and inquired about Chase's interest. Within days, the pair began formally working together on Zipcar, the car-sharing platform, with Chase as president and Danielson as vice president.

As with Gimlet, the cofounders' skill sets complemented each other and the venture idea well. Within eight months, Zipcar was operational, and the number of available cars and users was growing. However, frictions among the founding team were also growing. Before they committed to Zipcar (and split equity 50-50), the cofounders had not discussed in detail their objectives for the venture nor their specific roles and commitments to the organization. As a result, Chase was surprised when Danielson, though she was still contributing to Zipcar, remained in her position at Harvard, and Danielson was annoyed when excluded from key operational decisions. The pair also realized their working styles were dramatically different. Though Zipcar was ultimately acquired by car-rental giant Avis Budget Group in 2013 for almost $500 million, a lack of clarity regarding cofounder commitment and roles contributed to early challenges. Ultimately, both founders left the venture after a few years, far earlier than either had intended.[11]

Cofounders can be an incredible asset to an entrepreneur, providing complementary skills and network access as well as emotional support during the tumultuous early days of a start-up. Many entrepreneurial programs (such as Y Combinator) and investors work only with teams of cofounders (and send individual founders routinely searching for cofounders) following empirical evidence of increased performance of cofounding teams over solo-founded ventures.[12] Nonetheless, founders should take particular care in selecting their cofounders. In two well-known studies, frictions and disagreements among the top management teams of venture-backed start-ups were the most commonly cited source of failure.[13]

Beyond filling gaps in skills, the founding team should be aligned in their personal and professional objectives for working on the start-up. Noam Wasserman, in his book *The Founder's Dilemmas*, notes that founder team issues arise from conflicts in three domains: relationships (e.g., founding with friends, strangers), roles (e.g., decision-making rights), and rewards (e.g., splitting equity). Had the Zipcar cofounders taken additional time to discuss these topics before jumping into the execution stage of their start-up, they may have been better aligned or, alternatively, realized prior to founding that they might be better suited as collaborators, not cofounders. **Mini Case: The Traitorous Eight and the Birth of Silicon Valley** tells another story of what can happen when early management expectations are not aligned.

FUNCTIONAL OR INTEGRATIVE FOCUS?

For most ventures, creating a strong cofounding team will not be enough to effectively pursue their chosen opportunity. The founding team must then identify and prioritize the resources and capabilities they will need to acquire, which are often far from obvious, and do so in a timely and cost-effective way.

The "Traitorous Eight" and the Birth of Silicon Valley

In 1956, William Shockley, having developed the transistor during his tenure at Bell Labs, started Shockley Semiconductor Laboratory to further his work in commercializing the technology. He obtained funding from an existing company named Beckman Instruments. As his mother was in declining health, Shockley decided to build this new organization near her home in Palo Alto, California. The lush valley, much different from what it would become, was filled with fruit orchards, not technology firms and start-ups. Far from the technology ecosystems of the East Coast (including Bell Labs in New Jersey), Shockley found it difficult to get key scientists and engineers to move cross-country. After a national search among promising PhD students, Shockley was ultimately able to recruit a skilled, ambitious young team with the necessary complementary skills to move forward on his vision.[a]

However, by the fall of 1956, friction in the team was growing, and even the announcement of Shockley's Nobel Prize in Physics for his work on the transistor did little to assuage mounting concerns. Team members, recruited to contribute collaboratively to developing this still-nascent field, instead found a strict hierarchy, secret projects, paranoia, and an otherwise poor management style. Still, committed to the vision and the team Shockley had assembled, the scientists pleaded with Beckman to improve management conditions. But few adjustments were made. As a result, several team members quit and eight team members set out to do what at that time was almost unheard of: spin out their own company.

These "Traitorous Eight," as Shockley would refer to them, acquired funding from Fairchild Camera and Instrument to found Fairchild Semiconductor. They quickly made substantial progress in developing silicon transistors, and Fairchild

The "Traitorous Eight." From left to right: Gordon Moore, C. Sheldon Roberts, Eugene Kleiner, Robert Noyce, Victor Grinich, Julius Blank, Jean Hoerni, and Jay Last.

Semiconductor became the market leader. However, later efforts by Fairchild to exercise control over that founding team resulted in team members again leaving to found other companies. In fact, the later movements, careers, and impact of the Traitorous Eight formed the foundation of today's Silicon Valley.[b]

Shockley had indeed succeeded in recruiting a team with the entrepreneurial inclination and the complementary skills necessary to transform the semiconductor industry and build a robust entrepreneurial ecosystem. Unfortunately for Shockley, his choice of management style and organizational structure was not compatible with the team he recruited, and his vision was developed outside Shockley Semiconductor Labs.

This immediately raises a key choice: where should the venture focus on developing higher performance? An entrepreneur cannot launch a high-performing organization on all dimensions out of the box. There are sharp trade-offs.

1. **Functional focus.** One option founding teams can make is to identify a particular function—say, engineering, design, or marketing—and make that function's high performance a priority. The team then will significantly invest in accessing resources and building critical capabilities within this area to achieve excellence. We already saw this in Sony's focus on miniaturization, a clear investment in capabilities within a specific domain to create value.

functional focus Where a venture decides it will make a clear investment in specific capabilities within a business area to create value

Three Nobel Laureates on Make vs. Buy

The "make" vs. "buy" decision defines what will be done inside the business and what will be done outside of it. Nobel laureate Ronald Coase famously postulated that a key reason for making rather than buying business functions was the costs of those transactions in the market. Buying business functions externally is sometimes easy, especially when you can buy services in a competitive market. But other times, specific quality standards and delivery timing must be arranged and met. This often occurs for startups involved in developing new products that require physical manufacturing (as with the Pebble watch). Another Nobel laureate, Oliver Williamson, cautioned that these cases require careful attention to contracting terms as well as experience, deal-making skills, networks to assess the reputation of suppliers, and, of course, lawyers. Those costs can add up. But this does not mean that internal sourcing is "free." As Nobel laureate Oliver Hart and colleague John Moore pointed out, if it is hard to get quality from an external supply, it can be just as hard to get it internally. However, you may have a superior bargaining position with internal sourcing vs. external simply because you control the entire process. Using an outside supplier can lead to activities like the supplier switching the tasks they are doing from an "A team" to a "C team" without your consent.[a]

integrative focus Where a business does not make any particular function high performing but aims to make the functions themselves work together in a coordinated and effective manner

2. **Integrative focus.** An alternative is to not make any particular function high performing but make the functions themselves work together in a coordinated and effective manner. This integrative focus was pursued by Chobani as it coordinated the development of distinct yogurt recipes it could process at scale across a national market. Doing this required devoting managerial attention to ensure that the capabilities across functional areas moved together. Chobani prioritized this over various possible functional choices, like making the highest-quality yogurt or one that was distinct from other products to appeal to niche customer tastes, or producing that yogurt at the lowest cost.

Choosing a functional or integrative focus is intimately related to the other organizational and strategic choices a venture is making. Deciding on a functional focus means not only recruiting a different early team but also establishing a distinct organizational culture, incentives, and structure than would be established with an integrative focus. For example, if a venture is producing a product or service *as a part of another firm's business activities,* a functional focus can be critical. Excelling in a specific aspect will let it fit into these activities and provide value that the other firm cannot. Here, an integrative approach might duplicate efforts of these other firms and distract from concentrating and investing in the role the venture seeks to provide partners. This concept, known as a value chain strategy, will be covered in Chapter 11.

By contrast, *a venture that is building out a new value chain will need to manage a variety of business functions and activities.* It must focus on how it integrates all those functions and how they perform as a whole. These organizations are premised on best integrating all their resources or capabilities vs. trying to make one stand out over all others. This is an architectural strategy and will be discussed in Chapter 12.

MAKE OR BUY?

In choosing where the start-up will focus, you are also choosing what to source externally. In this respect, it is really a decision of what you will make and what you will buy. All businesses must choose which activities they will operate internally, or "make," and those that they will outsource, or "buy." Start-ups are no exception (see **Deep Dive: Three Nobel Laureates on Make vs. Buy**).

For start-ups, the make or buy choice can be encapsulated by the following trade-off: whether to quickly acquire the best products and capabilities available globally or whether to set their own dynamic path for internally developing or improving them. This trade-off was observed in the fitness start-up Peloton's founding. Peloton wanted to bring an in-studio spin class experience to people's homes. To do so, the founders needed a bike with Internet connectivity alongside sensors to measure cadence and resistance. Initially, the team thought they could just add a screen to an existing bike and outsource manufacturing cheaply. However, they found that the market did not have bikes with the capabilities they needed. Peloton quickly switched to the more challenging task of designing and manufacturing its own bike. This let Peloton control the upgrade experience for users as the venture learned more about customers' preference for in-studio experiences at home. However, in 2022 Peloton changed course and decided to outsource to an outside manufacturer. This choice was necessary for Peloton, as a shifting market required cutting costs. But further, with a fully developed product, helping an outside manufacturer understand what to make was also much easier.[14]

This trade-off can markedly impact the survival of the venture. Outsourcing can allow a venture to enter the market quickly. That can work if significant changes are not required to create value. Consider, by contrast, the fate of Better Place. Founded in 2007 by Israeli entrepreneur Shai Agassi, Better Place was a bold attempt to bring electric cars to market. While some automakers had chosen to design electric cars whose batteries would be charged at charging stations (which could take up to an hour at that time), Agassi pursued a technological vision based on swappable batteries. Rather than charging, drivers would visit a swapping station and in just a few minutes receive a charged battery to replace their depleted one. The Better Place vision proved compelling, and investors provided hundreds of millions in funding to initially set up operations in Israel before expanding worldwide (**Figure 7.6**).

Better Place's challenge came from another decision. Rather than design and manufacture its own car, Agassi struck deals with existing automakers such as Renault-Nissan to supply cars that did not include a battery. Better Place would own and provide the batteries instead. In this way, it could leverage existing manufacturers and focus on how to integrate its new battery technology with

---

FIGURE 7.6 **A Better Place Battery Swapping Station**

In trying to popularize electric cars, Better Place focused on making batteries easy to swap in and out. However, working with carmakers like Renualt-Nissan in a "buy" arrangement led to conflicts and expense.

it. Customers would buy the car and then lease batteries from Better Place at variable rates, depending on usage.

The problem was that this was a novel technology with a novel business model. Changes were inevitable, and these types of changes were difficult to negotiate and implement with external car providers. As Tom Eisenmann recounts, in just one of many instances:

> Renault managers battled with their Better Place counterparts over design choices. . . . [O]ne involved whether to include "smart screws" in the car that would, on command, release the battery at an exchange station and drop it onto a retractable metal plate. But Renault preferred an alternative that was less expensive, from their perspective: having the station's robot arm remove regular screws. Better Place conceded, even though the design change added to its cost of exchange station hardware and would make the stations incompatible with other electric cars that did not have swappable batteries with an identical configuration of screws.[15]

Even with these concessions, car deliveries were delayed and the company missed its initial 2011 launch target. This made it difficult to raise future funds and led to a drop in consumer confidence as well. Despite having raised over a billion dollars in capital, in 2013, Better Place declared bankruptcy and the battery-swap model died with it.

TRANSLATING PRIORITIES INTO PROCESSES

Start-ups also make decisions that, in effect, choose their working culture. Professor Ed Schein made famous the idea of organizational culture as an "iceberg" with both visible and harder to discern "levels." While visible artifacts, such as team T-shirts and laptop stickers, dress codes, and design of workspace, provide insights into and influence an organization's culture, it is the deeper levels, the expressed values and norms as well as the unconscious assumptions and perceptions of the group, that reflect the culture and affect the day-to-day decisions and behavior of the team. Consider Brunello Cucinelli, an Italian manufacturer of cashmere sweaters with a founder that shares its name. With sales in the hundreds of millions of dollars, the company is modeled on the traditions of Italian craft and eschews modern information technology.[16] Cucinelli believes that his employees should not work 24/7; they are forbidden to come in before 8 a.m. or do anything after 5:30 p.m. No coming in on a weekend either. In return, he asks for face-to-face communication (no group emails) and 100% attention when there is a meeting (no mobile phones). This notion of treating people well pervades the company:

> Our cashmere blazer costs $3,000 retail, but the profit must be dignified. It needs to respect the raw material producer, then the artisans, then those working for the company. The consumer also needs to be respected. Everything must be balanced.

At its heart, Brunello Cucinelli is working out whether it can pay people and suppliers well while also delivering and successfully selling a high-quality product at high prices. To do so, Cucinelli pursues artisanal work habits along with a vision for his business that spans centuries.

By contrast, IKEA's success is driven by intense frugality. This is reflected in stores that are laid out in a manner that tightly integrates demonstration stock and inventory. The stores are large and typically located on cheap suburban land. The flat packs of furniture are manufactured in regions that will ensure the lowest cost. And the whole operation is driven by a design ethic that emphasizes utility.

This frugality drives IKEA's internal capabilities: a belief that costs can be kept down and waste minimized. But as if to emphasize the point, founder Ingvar Kamprad built this into his personal life. He lived in a modest home furnished with IKEA products. He and his wife went to low-cost restaurants and haggled over prices of things at the market. Driving around in 2012 in his 1993 Volvo, Kamprad embodied IKEA's slogan of *lista* ("making do"). Thus, it is no surprise that the company's management travel coach and its employees are the models in early IKEA catalogs. Some have suggested that IKEA was all about commercializing frugality (see the sidebar on **Ingvar Kamprad**).[17]

Kamprad's choices internally conveyed where IKEA's capabilities should be. These choices also mean that there are places where its capabilities are lacking. For instance, flat-packed furniture may be cheap, but there is nothing like the daunting horror of assembling a child's bunk bed when you return home with your purchase. That said, you also know that you won't be paying too much for Swedish meatballs as you trek through an enormous store.

The organizational culture of a start-up may reflect the intentional set of choices of the founding team, as in the cases of Brunello Cucinelli and IKEA, or it may emerge organically in the early days of the start-up. Whether intentional or emergent, this early culture set by the founding team will endure even after members of this team have departed the venture. Strong cultures will help guide team members in decision-making when they confront new or uncertain situations, such as those faced regularly in a start-up environment. The choices they make tend to better align strategically across the organization. Firms with strong organizational cultures are often found to have high levels of sustained performance.

Of course, choices around culture can have unintended consequences. In an ethnographic study of a rapidly growing start-up, economic sociologist Catherine Turco studied the impact of choices by the founding team to nurture a "conversational firm" with little formal hierarchy and a commitment to open communication. While the founders believed that this approach led to greater trust and initiative, Turco also found that these practices caused early employees to be uncertain about their prospects for career promotion and left junior members unsure about the prospects for the firm. In fact, Turco finds that this team ultimately adopted a fairly "conventional" approach to decision-making so that all members of the growing team could commit to a common direction.[18]

7.6 Choosing Your Organization

There are many tasks or functions that need to be performed by a start-up, and start-ups need to develop capabilities and acquire resources to do them. A start-up can choose to focus on a limited set of functions or organize so its different functions operate in an integrated fashion. Whether some functions stand out or the organization evolves in a more "balanced" manner depends on how the founding team is formed and the managerial style or culture the organization adopts. In this chapter, we have seen organizations chosen across this spectrum. IKEA

Ingvar Kamprad. Sometimes people begin their entrepreneurial journey early, like Ingvar Kamprad. As a youngster, he was reluctant to drag himself out of bed in the morning to milk the cows on his father's farm in the Swedish countryside. "You sleepyhead! You'll never make anything of yourself!" his father would say. Then, one birthday, Ingvar got an alarm clock. "Now, by jiminy, I'm going to start a new life," he determined, setting the alarm for 5:40 and removing the "off" button. As a young boy, he sold matches, taking advantage of low prices for bulk quantities in Stockholm to sell at higher margins in his hometown of Agunnaryd. As a teen, he sold fish, Christmas tree decorations, stationery, and seeds. But when he was given a cash reward for success at school by his father, the 17-year-old Kamprad founded IKEA, selling items like pens and wallets, and moved, just a few years later, into furniture sales. After an employee struggled to fit a table into his car, Kamprad had the bright idea that he could save on transportation costs and costs to the consumer by selling flat-packed items. Starting with mail-order catalogs, IKEA opened the first brick-and-mortar store in 1965 in Almhult before expanding worldwide in the decades that followed. Kamprad eventually became one of the richest people in the world.

Choosing a "Human-Centered" Culture to Create Value for Customers

Eventbrite cofounder Julia Hartz (pictured in blue in the middle of this photograph) focused on making it a "people-centric company."

Founding teams need to be thoughtful in building a culture that aligns with the capabilities and resources they have chosen to prioritize and be willing to make the investment necessary to bring it to fruition.

Julia Hartz, Kevin Hartz, and Renaud Visage founded Eventbrite to enable individuals and small groups to plan and host events using scalable online reservations and ticketing. Whereas established players such as Ticketmaster focused on ticketing and reservations for large events such as stadium concerts or professional sports, Eventbrite provided a low-cost, easy-to-use service for smaller organizations such as local theaters or college clubs. This required building solutions in partnership with much smaller customer groups.

The founders believed that their success depended on building a human-centered organization with employees dedicated and ready to work with local clubs, theaters, and college groups. However, achieving this human-centered focus required significant investment on the part of the founders: rather than focusing on new products, Julia Hartz concentrated exclusively on hiring and training early employees. This investment ultimately was a "game changer in building a people-centric company," says Julia Hartz.[a] The company's commitment to building a people-centric company helped Eventbrite expand across four continents, selling hundreds of millions of tickets each year.

emphasized the specific functions of design and money-saving operations. Zappos chose an integrated approach to build out a network of supply relationships and a culture of customer service. Sony developed technical capabilities to design and manufacture small electronics. Gimlet chose a managerial team with diverse functional specializations to ensure a balance between creativity and commercialization (see also **Mini Case: Choosing a "Human-Centered" Culture to Create Value for Customers**).

But for any opportunity, there are likely to be many more than one organizational approach that will work. Rather than a single path, entrepreneurs must choose from alternative design and organizational priorities that realize different elements of value from their venture. The scope for organizational choice is likely larger than the choices founding teams face in terms of customer, technology, or even their competitive positioning. In each of the latter categories, though the team might identify multiple possibilities, they are usually constrained by external factors such as the relative size of alternative market segments, the potential for improvement in specific technical areas, or the potential for regulation to restrict some options for how to enter the marketplace. In contrast, founding teams may conceive of a wide range of organizational approaches that might succeed with a given idea, and often the choice among those approaches reflects the preferences (and biases) of the team rather than external constraints.

TABLE 7.2 Four Major Organizational Models for Start-Ups

	FOUNDER SUMMARY	HIRING SELECTION	CONTROL AND COORDINATION
Star model	"We recruit only top talent, pay them top wages, and give them the resources and autonomy they need to do their job."	Challenging work Long-term potential	Autonomy
Factory model	"You work, you get paid."	Task-related abilities	Managerial control
Engineering model	"We were very committed. It was a skunk-works mentality, and the binding energy was very high."	Challenging work Specific task-related abilities	Team control
Commitment model	"I wanted to build the kind of company where people would only leave when they retire."	Cultural fit	Peer group control

For example, in a set of studies from the Stanford Project on Emerging Companies ("SPEC") of 200 start-up firms primarily located in Silicon Valley, professors Diane Burton, Michael Hannan, and Diane Beckman identified at least four distinctive organizational models for otherwise similar ventures, including (1) the "star model": organizing around the unique contribution of a single individual, (2) the "factory" model: creating an early focus on systematic processes and procedures, (3) the "engineering" model: focusing on technological innovation with less emphasis on customer development, and (4) the "commitment" model: establishing an intense team orientation with all the early members of the firm (**Table 7.2**). But both successes and failures are observed in each of the models, and, more importantly, there is no single model that dominates the others in terms of the overall growth and success of the firm over time.[19]

However, the fact that there may be multiple organizational modes that might succeed does not mean that all organizational choices are equivalent. A strategic approach to choosing the organization considers the strengths and weaknesses of alternative approaches and identifies how different organizations would fit within the broader range of choices being made by founders. Perhaps even more so than in the domains of customer or technology, organizational choices often involve identifying but then leaving behind a "path not taken." Choosing whom to hire, whom to accept funding from, and how to design the organization at the outset each impact the organization's ability to deliver value. These also affect how choices will be made in the future since the organization includes the decision-makers that will make those future choices. While there is great latitude at the outset about organizational choice, the start-up organization you choose shapes the scale-up organization you get.

7.7 Concluding Thoughts

When an entrepreneur chooses to pursue an opportunity, they are unlikely to have the resources and capabilities required to realize its value. This newness presents a significant threat to the survival of the venture as the nascent venture lacks what is needed to implement its overall strategy.

Yet there will likely be multiple potential combinations of resources and capabilities that create value. Prioritizing specific capabilities and resources and reinforcing them with specific policies and processes are not actions that operate in isolation. These choices are reflected in the founding team's plans and also their skills and values (see **Putting It Together: Choosing Your Organization**). In both the opportunity they choose, and how they choose to build an organization and realize that opportunity, the founding team translates their passion, skills, and values into their organization.

Chapter 7 Review: Choosing Your Organization

CHAPTER TAKEAWAYS

- Start-ups often have many potential ways they might organize to deliver value from their idea to customers. While it is tempting to want to do it all, constrained financial resources, time, and attention mean that an entrepreneur must choose.

- The organization of a start-up includes the resources it acquires and capabilities it develops, which reflect the choices of the early team and its culture. Due to imprinting, these choices have an outsized impact on the overall evolution of the venture.

- The resources of a start-up include the tangible assets (e.g., machinery, financing) and intangible assets (e.g., intellectual property and know-how) controlled by the organization. The capabilities are what the organization can do with those resources to deliver value to customers. Unique and hard-to-imitate systems of resources and capabilities can achieve sustained competitive advantage for a firm.

- When a venture is formed, the resources and capabilities of the venture will be equivalent to those of the founding team. To leverage these scarce resources and knowledge, the team must form a clear hypothesis as to what additional resources and capabilities are necessary for value creation and successfully gain access to those resources and capabilities.

- The firm survival curve documents the association between the age of a new organization and likelihood of continued survival. Empirically, firms face a high likelihood of failure following founding, which declines with time.

- Sociologist Arthur Stinchcombe theorized that the high rate of failure of new organizations reflected the challenge of the liability of newness. Liability of newness captures the challenges new organizations face in defining their particular structure, routines, personal relationships, and culture.

- One of an entrepreneur's most significant organizational choices is with whom to cofound. Cofounders may bring many advantages to the venture, including their complementary skills and network access. However, disagreements among the founding team is an often-cited source of venture failure.

- A venture cannot build a high-performing organization along all dimensions—the founding team must prioritize. With a functional focus, a venture commits to prioritize investments in capabilities within a specific domain (or function).

CHOOSING YOUR ORGANIZATION

There are many ways you can choose to organize a venture. But start-up founding teams cannot do everything: they must choose which resources and capabilities to prioritize and the early team and organizational culture required to support those choices.

IDENTIFY THE MOST NEEDED RESOURCES AND CAPABILITIES FOR THE VENTURE

Create a Shortlist of the Resources and Capabilities Required to Deliver Value

- Generate a list of the resources and capabilities you will need for the venture to create and capture value from your idea. At a basic level, describe how each resource or capability contributes to value creation.

- Using this list, specify which resources and capabilities are most essential to value creation and capture.

STRATEGICALLY ANALYZE AND ASSESS YOUR RESOURCES AND CAPABILITIES SHORTLIST

Consider Developing Essential Resources and Capabilities for the Venture Internally vs. Acquiring Them Externally

- Founders and early team: Evaluate the skills and capabilities of the founding team to create and capture value from the idea. Determine which complementary skills and network access may be missing from the founding team.

- Functional or integrative focus: Consider which function the organization might emphasize to deliver value using a functional focus (e.g., engineering, design, or marketing). Then contrast that with the capabilities required to use a more integrative focus.

- Culture: Think about how a functional or integrative focus impacts the desired team culture.

- Make or buy: Evaluate the trade-offs of whether to quickly acquire the best products and capabilities available globally or whether to develop and then improve them internally. Estimate the commitments required and the viability of alternative paths.

REFINE YOUR ORGANIZATIONAL ALTERNATIVES THROUGH EXPERIMENTATION AND LEARNING

Conduct Low-Commitment Learning

- Identify steps to acquire or develop essential resources and capabilities internally versus externally.

- Pinpoint players within your business ecosystem who could help develop or access essential resources and capabilities.

- Generate a test to evaluate the ability of organizational alternatives to create and capture value.

By contrast, with an integrative focus, an organization commits to not prioritizing any particular function but instead to making investments that allow the functions to work together in a coordinated and effective manner.

- A choice of where to prioritize also reflects a choice about which activities to operate internally, or "make," and which to source externally, or "buy."

- Culture is how a start-up communicates the internal capabilities it wants to prioritize as it builds and grows its team.

- Choosing an organization is choosing how the start-up will work to create and capture value from the idea. It is choosing not only how the start-up will navigate the liability of newness and survive, but also the resources and capabilities that will provide it with an ongoing competitive advantage.

KEY TERMS

organization (p. 191)   capabilities (p. 194)
constrained (p. 191)   the liability of newness (p. 200)
imprinting (p. 192)   functional focus (p. 205)
resources (p. 194)   integrative focus (p. 206)

REVIEW QUESTIONS

1. What can be accomplished by establishing an organization that cannot be accomplished by a lone entrepreneur?

2. How does the establishment and growth of the organization of a firm allow an entrepreneur to create and capture value?

3. Relative to an established firm with existing resources and capabilities, why might organizational choice be even more critical for a start-up?

4. Define the terms "resources" and "capabilities" as they relate to an entrepreneurial venture. How do these two terms differ from one another?

5. According to Howard Stevenson, entrepreneurship is the "pursuit of opportunity beyond resources currently controlled." What does this definition mean in terms of a venture's organizational choices?

6. What is the firm survival curve? What are three distinctive empirical findings related to firm survival that might inform entrepreneurial strategy?

7. What is the liability of newness? What are the implications of the liability of newness for the early organizational choices of an entrepreneur?

8. Why are the experiences and backgrounds of cofounders so important for a new venture? How can the choice of cofounders enhance the likelihood that a venture is able to survive and grow?

9. What are the key consequences of choosing a more functional vs. integrative focus?

10. What are the key factors shaping whether to "make" or "buy" a given resource or capability?

11. Why does an entrepreneur need to choose their organization? How do initial organizational choices impact the survival and evolution of an entrepreneurial venture?

DISCUSSION QUESTIONS

Answer the following series of questions and scenarios either in class discussions or by writing a short response.

1. Tony Hsieh and his cofounders made very distinctive choices regarding their organization in the founding and scaling of Zappos. What were some of the key choices that enabled the unique resources and capabilities that Zappos was able to build? How would you compare those choices to the "average" firm in e-commerce? How did the development of those unique resources and capabilities impact the value of Zappos when it was acquired by Amazon in the late 2000s?

2. Kevin, an economics student, is considering how to pursue an opportunity that involves building interactive robots that can help the elderly with simple tasks around the house. He has watched videos on YouTube and other social media that show prototype robots developed in university labs accomplishing tasks such as folding laundry, cooking simple meals, and moving heavy boxes upstairs. Moreover, he has undertaken detailed primary market research that suggests that many retirees would pay a significant amount (more than $1,000) for a robot assistant that could perform these tasks. What are the obstacles Kevin faces to translate his idea into a reality? Even if Kevin's underlying idea is valuable, why might it be difficult for him to succeed in building an organization that realizes this opportunity? What can he do to overcome these challenges?

3. The liability of newness—the high rate of failure for ventures in the first few years after their founding—is one of the most distinctive and robust empirical patterns relating to entrepreneurship. What are the underlying factors that give rise to the liability of newness? What might an entrepreneur do as they develop their venture to guard against the liability of newness and so enhance their potential success over time?

4. Kate is a software engineer considering entrepreneurship based on her passion for sustainable local agriculture. She is thinking about developing an app-based platform whereby local farmers and restaurants could be matched depending on the availability of particular produce and the needs of local chefs. Her roommate, Angelica, is a chef and has lots of contacts in the local restaurant community. Kate and Angelica are debating whether to cofound the firm together. What factors should they think about as they consider whether to become cofounders? If they were to choose three topics to talk about and agree upon before founding the firm, what topics should they choose and why?

5. Eric and Maria's newly founded start-up plans to leverage recent advances in artificial intelligence to create more effective customer service voice assistance. They have limited funds and are debating whether to purchase cutting-edge computers they can customize and adapt to implement their technology or "rent" computing resources from cloud providers (such as Amazon Web Services or Google) that will allow them to get started immediately. The drawback is that these rentable resources are less tailored to their project. What factors might Eric and Maria consider as they contemplate this choice? If they do choose to rent at first, how might that affect the evolution of their technology and organization over time?

6. The organizational choices of start-ups reflect in many cases the resources and capabilities of their local environment. Can you identify a successful local start-up that has benefited from its founding in your area? Why was this start-up able to take advantage of the local environment, and how did the local environment influence the evolution and growth of the venture?

SUGGESTED READINGS

Baron, James N., Michael T. Hannan, and M. Diane Burton. "Building the Iron Cage: Determinants of Managerial Intensity in the Early Years of Organizations." *American Sociological Review* 64 (1999): 527–47.

Baron, James N., Michael T. Hannan, and M. Diane Burton. "Labor Pains: Change in Organizational Models and Employee Turnover in Young, High-Tech Firms." *American Journal of Sociology* 106 (2001): 960–1012

Burton, M. Diane, Jesper B. Sørensen, and Christine M. Beckman. "Coming from Good Stock: Career Histories and New Venture Formation." In *Research in the Sociology of Organizations*, edited by Michael Lounsbury and Marc Ventresca, 229–62. Greenwich, CT: JAI Press, 2002.

Bussgang, Jeffrey. *Entering StartUpLand: An Essential Guide to Finding the Right Job*. Boston: Harvard Business Review Press, 2017.

Eisenhardt, Kathleen M., and Claudia Bird Schoonhoven. "Organizational Growth: Linking Founding Team, Strategy, Environment, and Growth among U.S. Semiconductor Ventures, 1978–1988." *Administrative Science Quarterly* 35, no. 3 (1990): 504–29.

Eisenmann, Tom. *Why Startups Fail: A New Roadmap for Entrepreneurial Success*. New York: Currency, 2021.

Hsieh, Tony. *Delivering Happiness: A Path to Profits, Passion, and Purpose*. New York: Business Plus, 2010.

Ruef, Martin, Howard E. Aldrich, and Nancy M. Carter. "The Structure of Founding Teams: Homophily, Strong Ties, and Isolation among U.S. Entrepreneurs." *American Sociological Review* 68 (2003): 195–222

Stinchcombe, Arthur L. "Social Structure and Organizations." In *Handbook of Organizations,* edited by James G. March, 142–93. Chicago: Rand McNally, 1965.

Turco, Catherine J. *The Conversational Firm: Rethinking Bureaucracy in the Age of Social Media*. New York: Columbia University Press, 2016.

Wasserman, Noam. *The Founder's Dilemmas: Anticipating and Avoiding the Pitfalls That Can Sink a Startup*. Princeton, NJ: Princeton University Press, 2012.

Ayr Muir

Ayr Muir was working in consulting but had entrepreneurial ambitions to one day found his own clean energy consulting firm. While his underlying passion for creating an environmental impact remained steady, a project with a large soft-drink company shifted his entrepreneurial direction. In studying the food industry, Muir came to believe that the fast food industry was the primary contributor to skyrocketing levels of obesity, heart disease, high cholesterol, and diabetes. Soon after, he reviewed a UN report documenting that nearly 50% of all human-generated greenhouse gas emissions were from meat and livestock. Muir felt that for the sake of people's health and the planet the food industry needed to do better. This became the motivation for Clover, a fast-casual, locally sourced vegetarian restaurant. Muir set out to build a convenient, affordable, and, most importantly, tasty alternative to traditional fast food that would convince even the most ardent burger lover to go meat-free at least a few times a week.

Doing so would be no easy task. The fast food industry is notoriously complex, and that's before you try to build a delicious vegetarian menu relying only on fresh (no freezers!), local, seasonal ingredients. Muir knew he had a lot to learn. First, he set out to understand the established leaders. He toured local McDonald's restaurants and worked part-time at Burger King and Panera Bread. Hours behind the counter as well as the grill convinced him he could build something better.

During a leave from his consulting job, Muir wanted to quickly test his idea before he needed to return to his job or commit full-time to Clover. He designed a low-cost, low-commitment experiment to learn more about his idea, grounded in assumptions that there would be broad

To test out his idea, Ayr Muir used a simple organizational structure—a food truck.

interest and demand for a meatless fast-food menu and that he could consistently deliver those menu options for roughly the same price as a Big Mac. As a laboratory for his culinary and entrepreneurial experiments, Muir opened a food truck near a campus.

Questions

1. Which hypotheses would the food truck allow Muir to test? What capabilities and resources would he be required to develop or leverage in order to conduct his tests? Where should Muir look to obtain these resources and capabilities, and how might he attract them to his food truck?

2. If the food truck experiments prove successful and Muir decides to open a restaurant, what additional resources and capabilities will Clover need to acquire or develop?

Katrina Lake, founder and CEO of Stitch Fix

ENTREPRENEUR'S DILEMMA Finding a way to create value for customers usually means doing so in the face of competition. Though simply avoiding competition entirely might sound ideal, creating value for customers attracts competitors. While entrepreneurs can't avoid competition, they can choose the nature of the competition they are likely to encounter. Entrepreneurs must make careful choices because these will greatly impact the growth and evolution of the firm.

CHAPTER OBJECTIVES

- Explain why start-ups need to choose their competition
- Identify key complementary assets established firms possess that either must be accessed or replicated to compete
- Explain why the disclosure problem presents challenges to entrepreneurs
- Evaluate the trade-off between cooperating and competing with established firms
- Consider how orienting toward execution can give a venture a long-term competitive advantage, and how investing in control creates entry barriers against competition in the future

8

CHOOSING YOUR COMPETITION

While clothes shopping is often sold as fun and exciting, for many people it is frustrating, time-consuming, and inconvenient. This was the problem that Katrina Lake set out to tackle in 2011 when she started her company, Stitch Fix.

The core idea of Stitch Fix was simple: use artificial intelligence to take the fashion likes of individual users on social media (e.g., on Instagram and Pinterest) and get detailed information about a subscriber's body type and fit preferences to help Stitch Fix stylists curate looks for customers to consider and predict a set of clothing they would want to buy. Stitch Fix customers are then sent, without doing any shopping, a selection of clothing at regular intervals. If the customers do not like any of the selected pieces, they can return them. However, Stitch Fix believed its algorithms and AI would be good enough that returns would be relatively rare. Apparently, they were: in 2017, the company went public with a value of $1.6 billion. Though Stitch Fix's stock price has had its ups and downs, the company has grown substantially since; at one point, it employed several thousand people, from stylists to data scientists.

When starting out, the Stitch Fix team could have chosen to partner and use their methods and technology with an existing retailer—especially retailers trying to compete online. In this scenario, Stitch Fix might have used the retailer's existing distribution and logistics networks as well as its customer base to help build and grow the start-up. Doing so would follow classic business strategy, since among other reasons, it minimized challenges in building and managing inventory.

Consider, for a moment, how such a relationship might have evolved if, say, Stitch Fix had pursued a partnership with J.Crew. Stitch Fix would have access to many of the resources and capabilities of J.Crew, including its inventory management systems and existing loyal customers. J.Crew would enhance its

| CHOOSE YOUR CUSTOMERS | CHOOSE YOUR TECHNOLOGY |
| CHOOSE YOUR COMPETITION | CHOOSE YOUR ORGANIZATION |

In this chapter we focus on Choices around Competition, including key ideas like whether to cooperate or compete.

Like Stich Fix, Warby Parker chose to take on a large player by competing against Luxottica, a company with an almost monopoly position in the eyeware market.

competitor A firm that provides a similar product or service (or otherwise solves the same or similar customer need) to a start-up's chosen customer

online presence by providing its customers individualized curated clothing selections, hoping that this would increase J.Crew online sales while decreasing returns.

However, to best match customers' individual tastes and fit Stitch Fix's curation algorithms require a breadth of products from multiple designers and suppliers. If Stitch Fix's algorithm suggests items from direct J.Crew competitors, like Banana Republic or Club Monaco, or an independent line, its J.Crew partner will lose potential sales, possibly from its own website. More concerning, Stitch Fix might introduce existing J.Crew customers to brands they find they like even more, not only costing J.Crew the immediate sale but also a long-term customer. The Stitch Fix team felt that partnerships with existing retail brands would yield conflicts and, potentially, restrictions that would keep either party from realizing their desired outcome.

Instead, Stitch Fix took a different approach, partnering with many new and relatively unknown brands. These small and young brands benefited from exposure to new customers, particularly those whose style and fit matched closely to the brands, and Stitch Fix benefited from the range of clothing lines to draw upon when curating selections. Though in later years Stitch Fix would add more well-established brands, such as Theory and Kate Spade, no single brand would hold a dominant position. Stitch Fix competed by offering something unique compared with the brick-and-mortar retail giants it might have partnered with.

With Stitch Fix, we see the importance of strategically choosing your competition. Entrepreneurs need to carefully consider the competition they will face in formulating their strategy. Stitch Fix decided to challenge the larger retailers directly as a core aspect of its strategy. To quote Katrina Lake: "I'm fascinated by retail experiences and how untouched they were by modern technology in the 21st century. . . . I recognized that other retailers might suffer Blockbuster's fate if they didn't rethink their strategy."[1] Lake is not alone. Many start-ups have similarly shunned partnerships with traditional, established firms to bring forward their own expanded services. For instance, Warby Parker took on Luxottica, the world's largest eyewear company, behind brands such as LensCrafters, Pearle Vision, Ray-Ban, and Sunglass Hut. Uber and Lyft built platforms on the premise that people would ride in other people's cars, rather than building out an improved reservation and tracking system for taxis and car services in the mobile phone age. Of course, plenty of other start-ups think differently. In its early days, Microsoft developed a partnership as an exclusive supplier to IBM when it could have chosen to deal with more computer and electronics manufacturers. As we will see in this chapter, choosing your competition is both a fundamental choice for the business and sometimes an organizing principle for future strategic choices a start-up makes.

8.1 Why Do Start-Ups Have to Choose Their Competition?

All businesses must compete. A **competitor** is a firm that provides a similar product or service, or solves the same or similar customer need to a start-up's chosen customer. Of course, some competitors overlap more closely than others. However, to capture value, an entrepreneur must choose and implement an approach that creates value for customers above what competitors can provide now and in the future. This is why entrepreneurs are often asked about their start-up's competitive advantage, what investor Warren Buffet calls their **moat**. This advantage lets them capture more value than their competitors, and then protect and maintain their advantage.

moat A start-up's competitive advantage that allows it to capture value at a rate higher than its competitors, and then protect and maintain the advantage

Yet for any entrepreneur with a promising idea to create meaningful customer value, they do not really have an option that avoids competition, except in rare circumstances (e.g., when a government establishes a broad legal monopoly over a broad area of the economy). This is because either you are creating value in a way that is competitive with an already existing offering or company, or you have identified a new way to create value that encourages others to also serve those customers with similar (perhaps even identical!) products and services.

To understand the power of competition, let's step back to another era. In 1978, Dan Bricklin was an MBA student at Harvard Business School. Sitting in class, he watched the repetitive process his professor used to slowly derive financial analyses and forecasts by hand. Each revision to an assumption (or mistake!) required redoing a portion of the analysis, and sometimes the entire analysis, again by hand. Then the same process, albeit a longer one, would repeat in Bricklin's own project group each night as they tackled the week's assignments. Envisioning a faster method that allowed for quick modifications of inputs and assumptions, Bricklin came up with the idea for an electronic spreadsheet. His first product, called VisiCalc, was revolutionary: an electronic spreadsheet that distilled 20 hours of tedious number crunching by hand into just 15 minutes on a computer. In 1979, Bricklin and MIT grad student Bob Frankston founded Software Arts to launch a commercial version of the software.

In many ways, the VisiCalc spreadsheet was the first killer app of the PC industry (**Figure 8.1**). Neither Bricklin nor Frankston was prepared for VisiCalc's instant popularity. It quickly garnered the highest sales of any software program. The Apple II computer—initially the only computer VisiCalc operated on—benefited dramatically, as many users (including businesspeople at then Apple competitor Tandy) purchased Apple II computers simply to gain access to VisiCalc.

Yet by 1985, Software Arts was defunct, having lost the spreadsheet wars. After VisiCalc's launch, copycats flourished, and it was ultimately another competitor, Lotus 1-2-3, that won the market. Lotus was itself a start-up, founded by Mitch Kapor, a former employee of Software Arts. Though Kapor deserves significant credit for scaling up the electronic spreadsheet business during the earliest phases of the PC industry, the unfortunate fate of Software Arts teaches important lessons. Software Arts had all the elements of a promising start-up, including a great idea, a visionary founder, a solid grasp of customer needs based on experimentation, and a feasible plan of implementation. However, it failed to build a profitable business. Why did this happen?

There are a few key things to observe about this story. First, competition is a powerful force! If a business creates value, then you can expect that others will try to compete. While the idea behind VisiCalc—the electronic spreadsheet—proved to be among the most influential innovations of the personal computer revolution, most of the value of this idea was captured by others, including Lotus and, later, Microsoft.

Second, imitating VisiCalc was rather easy. It and Software Arts lacked a strong competitive advantage. Unfortunately, despite being a groundbreaking idea, there were few things that later entrants and established companies

FIGURE 8.1 VisiCalc: The First Electronic Spreadsheet

Dan Bricklin's first electronic spreadsheet product, VisiCalc, though simple by today's standards, was a game changer for the industry.

Philo T. Farnsworth vs. RCA. Popular consensus has it that it was Philo T. Farnsworth, a farm boy from Utah, who was the original inventor of the television. But Radio Corporation of America (RCA), wanting to get in on the TV race, attempted in the 1930s to claim that one of its own employees had in fact invented the television years earlier. It did this to avoid having to pay royalties to Farnsworth for the rights to produce and sell TVs. RCA's claim was challenged through the U.S. Patent Office and ultimately rejected, awarding the original patent to Farnsworth. But this challenge process was slow. By the time the process concluded and RCA finally agreed to pay royalties to Farnsworth, World War II had begun. This prevented companies from producing and selling consumer electronics in the United States for the duration of the war. Once the war finally ended, there were only a few years left on Farnsworth's patent. Once this patent expired, he was no longer owed royalties. RCA was able to mass-produce TVs without paying or crediting Farnsworth at all. Because he was not able to translate his value creation into value capture, he largely missed out on the financial benefit of his invention for the rest of his life.[a]

could not quickly copy and improve upon. Normally, start-ups will include formal intellectual property protection for their brands or concepts, or have other competitive advantages with unique equipment, resources, or personnel that help sustain profits even if competitive entry is possible. While Software Arts had taken steps to protect the copyright, it had prioritized getting VisiCalc out into the hands of customers at the expense of developing capabilities to stay ahead of competitors.[2]

VisiCalc is not alone. History is littered with innovators and entrepreneurs who did not capture the value they created with their innovative idea (see the sidebar on **Philo T. Farnsworth vs. RCA**). The overwhelming conclusion of research on innovation-based entrepreneurship is that entrepreneurs translating value creation into value capture is the exception rather than the rule.

BUILDING YOUR MOAT

The moral of this story for Software Arts would seem to be that the cofounders should have taken more steps to protect their work, to build their moat. Indeed, whether entrepreneurs are aware of it or not, they often invite competition when they validate their value creation hypothesis. Because of this, entrepreneurs must also construct a hypothesis on how they will compete. As crystallized by Michael E. Porter, the founder of the field of competitive strategy, "the job of the strategist is to understand and cope with competition."

Specifically, while an entrepreneur must compete in some domain, relative to existing firms, entrepreneurs have far more latitude in the tools they use to cope with competition. Interestingly, building a moat is but one tool. And the choice to build a moat comes with key trade-offs for the start-up since doing so requires significant resources—of time and investment, and, moreover, imposing strategic constraints on the ongoing venture.

As we will see in the rest of this chapter, competition is something all ventures face. But there is considerable scope to change where the venture competes (its position among other products in the market), whom the venture competes against (established firms or other start-ups), and when that competition arises (now or in the future). All of these choices must align also with other strategic choices—customer, technology, and organization. We can use those relationships to help sort through coherent strategies for entrepreneurs.

8.2 The Forces That Shape Competition

What choices can a start-up make to cope with competition? It starts with understanding how aspects of a chosen industry and competitive forces within it already affect how a firm can be profitable. Both the choice of industry *and* the choice of market position within that industry will impact the type of value and profitability a start-up should pursue. While average industry profitability on investment in the United States has been measured at around 9%, industries vary substantially in their average profitability: from the shoe industry, which has average profitability of over 33%, to the airline industry, with an average profitability of roughly 3% (see **Figure 8.2**).

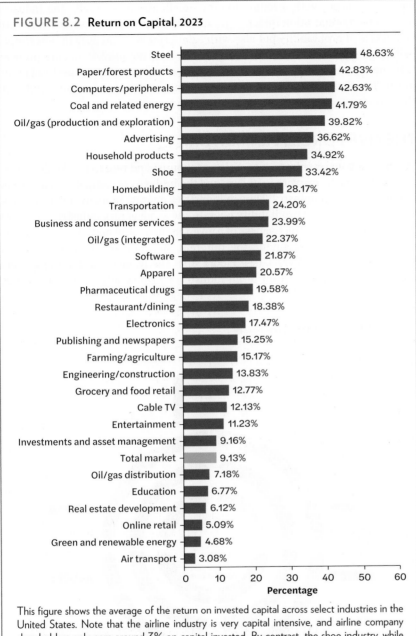

FIGURE 8.2 Return on Capital, 2023

Industry	Percentage
Steel	48.63%
Paper/forest products	42.83%
Computers/peripherals	42.63%
Coal and related energy	41.79%
Oil/gas (production and exploration)	39.82%
Advertising	36.62%
Household products	34.92%
Shoe	33.42%
Homebuilding	28.17%
Transportation	24.20%
Business and consumer services	23.99%
Oil/gas (integrated)	22.37%
Software	21.87%
Apparel	20.57%
Pharmaceutical drugs	19.58%
Restaurant/dining	18.38%
Electronics	17.47%
Publishing and newspapers	15.25%
Farming/agriculture	15.17%
Engineering/construction	13.83%
Grocery and food retail	12.77%
Cable TV	12.13%
Entertainment	11.23%
Investments and asset management	9.16%
Total market	9.13%
Oil/gas distribution	7.18%
Education	6.77%
Real estate development	6.12%
Online retail	5.09%
Green and renewable energy	4.68%
Air transport	3.08%

This figure shows the average of the return on invested capital across select industries in the United States. Note that the airline industry is very capital intensive, and airline company shareholders only earn around 3% on capital invested. By contrast, the shoe industry, while involving substantial capital, earned over 30%, largely because brand and style advantages distinguished them from their competitors in the eyes of consumers.

SOURCE: Aswath Damodaran, "Margin/ ROIC by Sector (US)," updated January 2023, https://pages.stern.nyu.edu/~adamodar/New_Home_Page/datafile/mgnroc.html.

But there is substantial variation in the profitability among the players within an industry. For instance, Southwest has consistently outperformed the profitability of its peers in the airline industry. That said, as Warren Buffet famously quipped, "When an industry with a reputation for difficult economics meets a manager with a reputation for excellence, it is usually the industry that keeps its reputation intact." Attractive industries are those not only with high levels of profitability but also with significant size and growth. But simply looking at an industry's historical profitability does not provide an entrepreneur with the information needed to understand how the industry will perform in the future. For that, an entrepreneur needs to understand how current trends will shape the competitive pressures within the industry.

THE FIVE FORCES FRAMEWORK

Synthesizing insights from economics, economist and researcher Michael Porter developed a framework to understand the intensity of competition and profitability within an industry. Though industries operate in many different ways, the forces that shape profitability operate the same across industries. Porter's work evaluates the attractiveness of a given industry and how any value within it was likely captured among the different stakeholders by assessing what he described as Five Forces (see **Figure 8.3**). His framework describes forces that govern the competition in an industry, and how attractive it is overall.

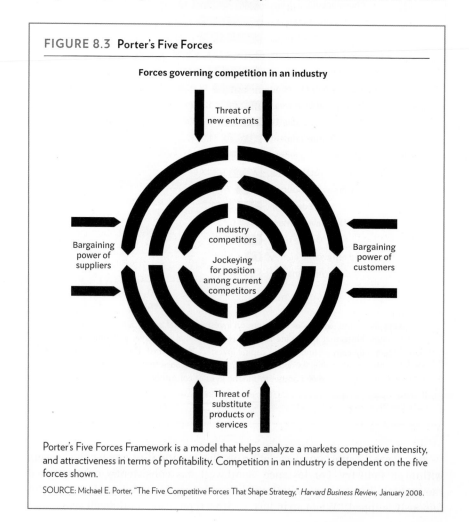

FIGURE 8.3 **Porter's Five Forces**

Forces governing competition in an industry

Threat of new entrants

Bargaining power of suppliers

Industry competitors

Jockeying for position among current competitors

Bargaining power of customers

Threat of substitute products or services

Porter's Five Forces Framework is a model that helps analyze a markets competitive intensity, and attractiveness in terms of profitability. Competition in an industry is dependent on the five forces shown.

SOURCE: Michael E. Porter, "The Five Competitive Forces That Shape Strategy," *Harvard Business Review*, January 2008.

Chapter 8: Choosing Your Competition

No matter the industry, Porter named certain threats to account for, including the degree of rivalry among existing competitors, the threat of substitute products or services, and the threat of new entrants. If there are a number of substitute goods with low switching costs for consumers or the barriers to entry into the industry are low, these factors can increase the competitive pressures within an industry. Similarly, if suppliers or buyers have a high degree of bargaining power, this can increase industry pressure, as they are able to capture a higher degree of the value created. By using the Five Forces framework, entrepreneurs can assess the attractiveness of an industry before they choose to enter it.

In some cases, this analysis might lead an entrepreneur to choose another industry to serve. For instance, consider how industry information might shape an entrepreneur's choices in introducing a new product, as in the case of Sarah Kauss. Conscious of the impact of plastic waste on the planet, Kauss had consistently carried a reusable water bottle since her days as an accounting student at the University of Colorado. However, according to Kauss, these bottles were "more appropriate for camping than the conference room." She set out to bring reusable water bottles into the boardroom. Instead of entering the crowded water bottle space in the camping or athletic market, she chose the professional accessories market. Kauss positioned her S'well water bottle product as an eco-friendly, stylish "hydration accessory" (**Figure 8.4**). The quality, design, and price point (well above existing reusable bottles) were aligned with her choice to target executives and compete in a market space of professionals otherwise not using reusable water bottles. In line with her decisions, Kauss selected potential partners who reinforced this market position, spending a fair amount of early effort convincing high-end retailers to try out the unusual accessory. Then, a feature in *O, The Oprah Magazine*, as well as a partnership with Starbucks, opened the doors to further partnerships and retailers, though Kauss still declined opportunities with big-box retailers (mass market S'ip by S'well products would follow later). By 2016, revenues exceeded $100 million.[3] By focusing on the high-end accessory market, Kauss chose not only a better industry but also one where she was better positioned to achieve advantage.

Significantly, as captured in the above example, the Five Forces framework guides strategic choice of market position *within* an industry. Instead of placing a product as a clear substitute to what incumbent firms are offering, do you try to find a different entry point to address customer needs that are either not met or are underserved by existing players? In Kauss's case, these were high-end customers and retailers. By understanding the key players within a competitive environment, entrepreneurs might foresee shifts in competition as well as how the industry will evolve and grow. They then can position themselves to take advantage of those trends in the market. For instance, if your rivals are making products at a high cost, you should think about whether you can produce a low-cost alternative. Alternatively, if your rivals make a product that targets one set of customers, you should produce one that targets a different set.

POSITIONING AND PATHS TO PROFITABILITY

One path toward sustained profitability can come from achieving a low-cost position in the market. If a start-up can come to market with a product or service whose cost is significantly below that of potential rivals, then that firm can gain market share by targeting price-sensitive customers with low prices and invest in resources and capabilities to operate in the long term at a lower-cost position than competitors. For example, in the airline industry, Herb Kelleher (with a now less well-known partner Rollin King) founded Southwest Airlines in 1971 using a "no-frills" approach to airline travel that revolutionized the industry. In the early days, rather than feature travel to glamorous international locations, Southwest Airlines focused on travel within the state of Texas, where at the time prices were not controlled by government regulations. More importantly, Kelleher implemented practices designed to transport individuals between cities on a lower-cost basis than established airlines. Southwest did not assign seats, which created much quicker boarding processes. It only used one type of aircraft, which saved on maintenance and repair costs, and famously only served peanuts! These choices made sense for Southwest's price-sensitive customers, and established players like American, United, and Delta could not match Southwest's offering for many decades. These airlines' processes and business models were generally built premised on providing a higher level of service for their customers, which also came at a higher cost.

However, a low-cost position is not the only way to achieve a degree of insulation from competitors. A second alternative is to compete with a unique offering that provides higher value for at least some customer segment that is poorly served by existing offerings. In many industries, it is not the lowest-cost firms that are the most profitable but those firms that can provide the most *differentiated* value for their customers (while also recognizing that other customers in the market may be indifferent to that unique offering). For example, Barry Nalebuff, a best-selling author and professor who teaches strategy, negotiation, innovation, and game theory, had challenged his MBA classes at Yale for many years to identify opportunities for customers that are not served or possibly underserved by the current offerings. During a class focused on the beverage industry, a student, Seth Goldman, wondered why prepackaged drinks such as soda and iced tea came only in a sugar-free, zero-calorie offering or with an extremely high level of sweetness (and calories!). A refreshing iced tea that was just a "tad sweet" with only a few calories was simply not in the marketplace. Several years later, Goldman and Nalebuff developed this product, experimenting with new types of tea flavors and ingredients, ultimately bringing to market a drink named Honest Tea. As it turned out, their hypothesis about the potential for a tea with an intermediate level of sweetness was validated; loyal customers (including President Barack Obama) were regular and price-insensitive consumers for this offering, and ultimately Honest Tea was acquired by Coca-Cola in 2012.[4] But it is not simply strategy professors who succeed with a differentiated strategy. In a recent study, researchers have shown that entrepreneurs who position their initial offering with more differentiation relative to products or services offered by established firms raise more initial funds and have improved long-term success.[5]

The first competitive challenge facing an entrepreneur is choosing an economic environment in which it is possible to not only create but also

For a time, Honest Tea established a differentiation that made it a favorite drink of many people, including then-president Barack Obama.

Chapter 8: Choosing Your Competition

capture economic value. But even in a favorable strategic environment, a start-up needs to establish a position for its product, service, or platform that provides it with some form of isolation from the competitive pressures in that strategic environment. The firm needs to strive to reach the "strategy frontier": a model for value delivery that achieves a given level of value creation at the lowest possible cost. But achieving competitive advantage depends not simply on creating value but also on doing so in a way that is somehow isolated or immune to the actions of potential competitors. In short, the goal for an entrepreneur in choosing their competition is to achieve a "lonely" place on the strategic frontier.

8.3 The Logic of Value Capture

The problem with the advice to choose a lonely place on the strategic frontier is that this may be more easily said than done. Firms such as Southwest Airlines, Honest Tea, or even Enterprise Rent-A-Car (discussed in Chapter 7) ultimately achieved a durable position in the marketplace by somehow establishing the resources and capabilities, as well as a market position, that provided some degree of protection from direct competition. But this raises a new question: *What factors shape a firm's ability to establish a competitive advantage?*

For an established enterprise, this is a complicated question. For these firms, competitive advantage may be driven by sources as disparate as long-standing customer relationships, particular capabilities developed within the firm over time, or even synergies among business units across the globe. However, for an entrepreneur, the logic of competitive advantage—not simply creating but also capturing value—is more straightforward. Specifically, it is not simply enough to have an idea; an entrepreneur has to make choices about how to bring that idea to life and commercialize it. **Commercialization** is the process by which a new product, service, or platform is brought to market, and so is how an entrepreneur turns their idea into a specific reality.

But the process of commercialization comes with two challenges. As articulated by renowned business professor and entrepreneur David Teece, *two broad factors fundamentally shape the ability of an entrepreneur to capture value from their idea:*

1. *Ease of imitation of the innovation*
2. *Ownership of complementary assets*

Entrepreneurs are often concerned that others will copy their idea. Though risk of idea theft is sometimes overstated, it may lead entrepreneurs to delay engagement with customers, experimentation, or other critical activities to prevent others from copying their innovation. This risk may be more or less pronounced in certain ecosystems or classes of innovation. For example, a key factor is the strength of intellectual property rights and the degree to which those rights protect the entrepreneur's idea in a particular region of the world. As we discussed in Choosing Your Technology (Chapter 6), intellectual property rights can take a number of different forms, from patents to trade secrets. Yet even in regions with strong enforcement of intellectual property rights, there are some types of innovations where either intellectual property protections are limited

commercialization The process by which a new product, service, or platform is brought to market

Complementary Assets

Simply put, for any venture, it's hard to go it alone. In his research, University of California professor David Teece highlighted the need for complementary capabilities or assets to commercialize an innovation, writing: "In almost all cases, the successful commercialization of an innovation requires that the know-how in question be utilized in conjunction with other capabilities or assets."[a] These may include manufacturing, distribution, and sales. They may also include more specialized components, such as key information channels (e.g., pharma drug approval), other components of the system (e.g., specialized software for hardware innovations), or complementary capabilities or components. Teece noted that "computer hardware typically requires specialized software, both for the operating system, as well as for applications." And further, even when an item like a computer is designed with "plug compatible components . . . certain complementary capabilities or assets will be needed for successful commercialization." For example, Netflix was initially successful with customers having ready access to DVD players and now relies on customers' easy access to fast streaming on smart televisions.[b]

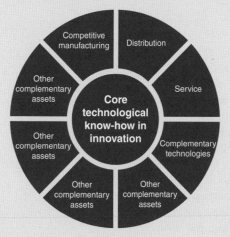

Complementary assets needed to commercialize an innovation

---

or offer limited protection from clever workarounds. In these environments, Teece noted, the profits from the innovation would not go to the entrepreneur but rather to the producer, manufacturer, or other owner of the resources, capabilities, and infrastructure required to bring the innovation (or copies of it) to market.

Unfortunately for start-ups, established firms—in many cases, potential competitors of the entrepreneur—often already have the existing processes, resources, and capabilities required to commercialize the idea, deliver value from it, and move it to market. They already have what are referred to as **complementary assets**, which include distribution, marketing, and legal services, to name a few (see **Using the Research: Complementary Assets**). In many cases, an entrepreneur must instead create these from scratch, which can be especially challenging when the assets are highly specialized or difficult to acquire or build. Fortunately, entrepreneurs can avoid duplication, delay, and risk in building them by cooperating with established businesses where they are in place. For instance, even in the digital age, it is very risky for authors simply to write a book and hope for success. There are already many books competing for the attention of readers. To boost a book's chances, an author partners with a publisher to certify and improve their book's quality before it is marketed and advertised and distributed to retailers. For other businesses, the activities may be much more formidable. For instance, a biotech venture developing a new

complementary assets Existing processes, resources, and capabilities that are required to commercialize an idea, deliver value from it, and move it to market

Chapter 8: Choosing Your Competition

drug cannot simply launch it. The drug needs to undergo a long process of testing and application to obtain regulatory approval before it is marketed to sophisticated practitioners. Because of this lengthy testing and approval process, biotech ventures often partner with established pharmaceutical companies to commercialize their discoveries. But while partnership can be especially lucrative and allow an entrepreneur to create a broad impact by leveraging the complementary assets of their partner, it does present a problem. Can your partner be trusted?

THE DISCLOSURE PROBLEM

Bob Kearns had a dream. He wanted to innovate for Ford. Kearns was an engineer who, growing up in Michigan after World War II, developed a long-standing admiration for the car company and what it had achieved. But it wasn't until he was driving in a punishing rainstorm that he had his big idea: What if he could make windshield wipers work better?

At the time, windshield wipers on vehicles had two settings: fast and slow. What is more, they just moved back and forth continuously. You may not realize it, but today's windshield wipers operate more like a blinking eye. They swipe, then pause, and then swipe again. The wiper is not continually moving and distracting but more unobtrusive, like a blink. While the notion of a variable speed wiper was not new, Kearns's big insight was to build it based on the burgeoning field of electronics.

It took years, but Kearns cracked the problem and fitted his wiper to his Ford Galaxie. He drove it down to the Ford plant, where Ford engineers pored over the mechanism. They didn't see it all, though, because the main electronics were housed in a black box. What is more, Kearns had applied for patents on his design. Nonetheless, he tried to be helpful. Kearns went away with instructions as to how to become a supplier to Ford. He subjected his design to tests in his own basement and eventually passed muster. But to his surprise, Ford did not want to be supplied by Kearns. Instead, they employed him for a time, but it didn't work out.

Seven years later, Kearns was at the Detroit Auto Show where Ford presented a new car with an intermittent windshield wiper. To his dismay, it was identical to the design he had driven down to the Ford plant years earlier. Over the next few years, other carmakers in the United States and around the world released cars with the same feature. In no case was Kearns being paid or even acknowledged.

The story of the intermittent windshield wiper highlights a risk that many entrepreneurs face when pursuing a cooperative commercialization strategy: to get a deal requires disclosing many elements of the core idea and technology of the business. However, an idea is not something that is tangible. Instead, it is just information that can be easily appropriated without paying the person who came up with the innovation in the first place. This **disclosure problem** was highlighted by Nobel Prize–winning economist Kenneth Arrow when describing why it is harder to create markets for information than physical products. Put simply, to sell an idea, the buyer needs to see it. But when that has been done, they no longer need to pay for it. Thus, an entrepreneur either risks expropriation like Kearns experienced (see the sidebar on **Greg Kinnear**) or instead has to sell an idea, sight unseen, normally at a far lower payment. Disclosure threatens the value that can be captured through cooperation and can make it preferable to try and compete instead.

disclosure problem The risk the entrepreneur faces that to sell an idea, a buyer needs to see it; but after disclosing the idea, the buyer no longer needs to pay for it

Greg Kinnear. The story of Bob Kearns got the Hollywood treatment in 2008 with the movie *Flash of Genius*, with Kearns played by Greg Kinnear.[a] Ironically, Kinnear's own ties to the disclosure problem ran quite deep. Back in 1990, he came up with an idea for a reality show that he pitched to ABC; later, that network released *America's Funniest Home Videos*. Kinnear sued ABC for idea theft and eventually won on appeal. Bob Kearns's son Dennis posted on a blog after hearing of this link that he was "amazed at how seamlessly he stepped into the role of Bob Kearns."[b]

But competing was not an option for Kearns. He might have been shrewder and threatened to hand the design over to Ford's competitors, having Ford pay him to avoid such competitive sabotage. Instead, Kearns fell back on his patents. Back in the 1960s, patent protection was not as strong as it is today; patents did not receive a big boost in effectiveness until 1984. It took two decades and a lost marriage, but Kearns (and eventually his children) won the day against Ford and others in a multimillion-dollar settlement. But the cost to Kearns was higher than that. Over the years, Kearns—a brilliant engineer—had been turned into a lawyer rather than an innovator.[6]

The disclosure problem is something that faces many entrepreneurs. To be sure, patents and other intellectual property protection can assist entrepreneurs in negotiating arrangements with less risk of expropriation. But such protections are not always ironclad or certain. While an extreme case, Bob Kearns's experience speaks to a more general challenge facing entrepreneurs: simply coming up with a "good idea" is not enough to capture value from that idea. Instead, even for successful entrepreneurs, the value from successful commercialization is, in the vast majority of cases, much higher than the value the entrepreneur can capture from their idea.

How can entrepreneurs navigating this challenging environment make sure that their innovations both create value *and* capture value? *Part of the answer is realizing that competition is a choice. Not only can entrepreneurs choose their industry and position within that industry, but also they can choose and shape the environment they face. In particular, entrepreneurs are able to choose with whom and how to compete.*

8.4 Cooperation vs. Competition

Not all competitors are alike. For most entrepreneurs, there is no "blue sky" opportunity where they produce a product so new that it does not displace other products. As entrepreneurs bring new ideas to the world (i.e., creation), they invariably displace the products based on older ideas (i.e., destruction). The automobile displaced the horse and buggy. Smartphones displaced cell phones, which displaced pagers. And ridesharing companies like Uber and Lyft are displacing older taxi and limo services. As we read in an earlier chapter, economist Joseph Schumpeter famously called this process "the gale of creative destruction."

For businesses that established themselves and found market leadership with older ideas, the rise of new technologies that may destroy their competitive advantages is not something they will necessarily stand by and watch happen. To preserve their market leadership, they may aggressively pursue these new technologies and leave their past businesses behind. These businesses may also need to play a role in accelerating the destruction of their legacy businesses. That is not an easy task. Their reluctance to do so may present opportunities for entrepreneurs who, unencumbered by such legacies, can take advantage of sluggish response from established firms.

But entrepreneurs may also prefer not to take on established firms competitively, worried that they may wake a sleeping bear. Another approach is to find opportunities to cooperate with established businesses and align their otherwise conflicting interests (see **Mini Case: Replacement Effect**).

Replacement Effect: Who Has the Incentive to Resist Innovation?

When entrepreneurs introduce an innovation that quickly transforms a market, some shame the large, established businesses for missing an obvious opportunity and tout the risk appetite of the entrepreneurs. However, this underplays the distinct concerns about and incentives against innovating that established firms have but entrepreneurs do not have to contend with. Identifying and understanding these differences—what economist Ken Arrow deemed "the replacement effect"—can yield strategic opportunities for entrepreneurs.

Established firms face a clear trade-off when introducing a new technology or innovation. While the new product may garner new customers, it will likely shift existing customers away from the business's existing products (cannibalizing those products' sales). In this case, the value the firm derives from the innovation is the difference between the sales of the new product and the likely sales of the existing product in the absence of the new product. An entrepreneur, unconstrained by existing products, faces no such trade-off. While large, established firms weigh their concerns and resist innovation, it may offer entrepreneurs the opportunity to enter the market successfully.

In practice, the replacement effect only applies to a subset of the innovations and product introductions a large, established business may consider. Before basing their strategy on incumbent firms' inability to respond, entrepreneurs should articulate a clear hypothesis about why the established competitor has incentives to resist innovation.

For instance, complementary products and services as well as product enhancements and upgrades may grow a firm's market. Established firms have incentives to adopt these innovations. Consider the case of Eastman Kodak, the once-ubiquitous supplier of cheaper cameras and film. The release of the digital camera was a threat to all aspects of Kodak's business. Kodak recognized this and was, in fact, one of the first to introduce a successful digital camera, the Kodak EasyShare. The company had hoped that people taking pictures using the camera would use Kodak services to print out physical copies. This made sense until it turned out that people were happier sharing (and taking) pictures with their phones.

Eventually the EasyShare camera fizzled out. But in other cases, established camera makers were successful (e.g., Zeiss found ways of selling its camera lenses and other technology to smartphone makers).

Kodak's EasyShare was an attempt to benefit from the innovations of digital cameras.

Thus, a fundamental strategic choice for any entrepreneur is whether their ideal route to commercialization is to cooperate with established businesses or construct an independent value chain, which usually will compete with established businesses. In a sense, competing with established businesses can be an easier path for the simple reason that you do not have to talk to or negotiate with them. There is no need for permission. You can start your business and compete.

The flip side is that the established businesses have no reason to care about the success of your business or the idea it is based on, and so competition, when it comes, might be fierce. For this reason, many new businesses find cooperation attractive. Cooperation requires searching for and finding established businesses to partner with, and then negotiating the terms of that cooperation. A good negotiation will focus first on what mutual benefits a partnership can create before turning to who gets what. There are two broad classes of benefits that can arise from negotiating a cooperative agreement with established businesses: accessing complementary assets and avoiding head-to-head competition.

ACCESSING COMPLEMENTARY ASSETS

During the 2000s, no company dominated the mobile device industry like BlackBerry (then called Research in Motion, or RIM). Its mobile device, with its small hardware keyboard, was an engineering marvel revered by its consumers, primarily business customers, who wanted to be able to email anywhere (**Figure 8.5**). However, making email work effectively on mobile networks optimized for voice communications was no easy task. BlackBerry initially had to develop hardware infrastructure for that purpose, which it also had to run. As one history of the company's founding describes:

FIGURE 8.5 **The Blackberry Craze**

The BlackBerry was a consumer favorite among business customers and celebrities alike. They prized it for its ability to handle a far greater array of personal and professional tasks than a typical mobile phone was capable of. Here, Kim Kardashian can be seen using hers while on the go.

In the early days, the BlackBerry service was unique in that RIM provided everything needed to make it work: the device itself, the software that made it run, the servers that routed email from the wired network, and the airtime that RIM leased from mobile-phone carriers. In other words, RIM adopted a highly integrated organizational model, which enabled the company to retain control over and coordinate all aspects of its service.[7]

But maintaining what was, in effect, a separate global communications network was not a way to scale that business. This led BlackBerry to seek out licensing partnerships with other mobile infrastructure providers such as Nokia and the mobile carriers themselves. BlackBerry went from acquiring, managing, and charging customers itself to having its product sold through mobile networks that maintained the relationship with those very same customers. As one of BlackBerry's founders, Jim Balsillie, stated, "By offering to license, RIM was able to access the innovative resources of the entire industry . . . leaving [it] able to focus on what it did best: wireless e-mail. We are a middleware. And that is a really useful place to be."[8] In other words, BlackBerry eventually leveraged the complementary infrastructure and then sales and marketing channel assets of others.

That said, it is possible to overstate the importance of such assets. There is a difference between the specialized regulatory management skills needed by a biotech start-up vs. other needs an entrepreneur may have. For example, at the most basic level, all entrepreneurs need office supplies to run their business and "cooperate" by purchasing these from existing businesses. By contrast, there are very few businesses with the drug approval skills required to certify the particular therapeutic categories a biotech venture may pursue. Needing these specialized and somewhat unique complementary assets drives a choice of cooperation.

CHOOSING TO COMPETE

Using the existing complementary assets held by established firms may play less of a role in value creation for a start-up. Constructing its own, distinct value chain offers a higher degree of operational freedom, and also enhances a start-up's ability to capture value once that value chain is in place. By constructing its value chain, a start-up avoids possibly giving incumbent players some control over how the idea is commercialized. These players might have incentives to thwart or slow down the entry of a start-up's innovation if it threatens current offerings. Additionally, the value chain of potential partners may not work well for the segment of consumers a start-up intends to serve. In those cases, despite the costs of constructing its own value chain, it could be even more costly to try to work with established partners and traditional channels.

Consider Dropbox, a service that allows people to easily store and synchronize files in the cloud. Launched in 2008, Dropbox had over 1 million users only a year later and 50 million just three years later. This growth quickly grabbed the attention of established firms. Apple, which had long struggled to launch cloud services for its Macintosh users, approached Dropbox's founders, Drew Houston and Arash Ferdowsi. Apple praised their remarkable growth as well as the underlying technology; notably, the green check mark (**Figure 8.6**) that appeared upon successful sync revealed a fair amount of knowledge and capabilities on the founders' part. In 2011, Houston and Ferdowsi met with then Apple CEO Steve Jobs, who tried to persuade them to sell Dropbox to Apple for a (rumored) nine-digit amount.

Though Apple could have provided Dropbox with immediate resources to continue its rapid scaling and expand to other services, the founders quickly declined Apple's offer. As Houston recalls, "[Jobs] started trolling us a little bit, saying we're a feature, not a product, and telling us a bunch of things like that we don't control an operating system so we're going to be disadvantaged, we're going to have to figure out distribution deals, which are risky, and sort of a bunch of business-plan critiques. But then he was like, 'Alright, well I guess we're gonna have to go kill you, basically.' Maybe not in those words, but pretty close."[9] Six months later, iCloud was announced.

For Apple, Dropbox was a potential solution to difficulties it had in the space. For Dropbox, if Jobs was right and the innovation was simply a feature, teaming with Apple was an opportunity to integrate it into the existing Apple platform serving hundreds of millions of users while realizing a strong financial exit for the team. However, if Jobs was wrong, as Houston believed, it was giving up an opportunity to build a more valuable, independent company focused on different things than Apple. In 2021, Dropbox had a stock market value of $11 billion, adding two whole digits beyond Apple's offer (more on Dropbox's story appears in Chapter 12).

FIGURE 8.6 **Dropbox's Green Check Mark**

The technology behind Dropbox's green check mark was something its founders felt would help it compete with a huge company like Apple.

AVOIDING HEAD-TO-HEAD COMPETITION

The second class of benefits that comes from cooperation is avoiding **head-to-head competition**. Although it has other effects, competition reduces the total profits firms can earn, and so firms have incentives to minimize it. As Adam Smith pointed out almost 250 years ago, this is something that potentially benefits both established firms and the start-up.

Ultimately, the choice between competition and cooperation is fundamental and drastically shapes the direction of the venture: though entrepreneurs do not have the luxury of choosing *not* to compete, the decision to collaborate with established firms means they face a more limited and significantly different competitive landscape than if they choose to compete with them (see **Mini Case: The Race for Synthetic Insulin**).

STRIKING A DEAL

Both accessing and not re-creating complementary assets and avoiding head-to-head competition are reasons why cooperative deals can be desirable for start-ups and established businesses. While antitrust laws can mitigate the potential for cooperation, these usually involve moves such as mergers and acquisitions, entrepreneurial exits that are a potential milestone of venture success. Instead, *the cooperation we are considering here is the earlier choice of whether the entrepreneur orients themselves toward the interests of established firms rather than against them*. For example, if an entrepreneur takes a more cooperative approach, they should focus on how their idea reinforces an established firm's value proposition with their customers (e.g., these are more likely to be more mainstream customers, and so they may need to standardize the product more quickly). Further, the entrepreneur should orient their technology choices in a way that integrates with the systems and offerings of the established player. For example, they can emphasize their compatibility and their role as a value-added service.

The company they build will also be different. A company that seeks to compete with established firms must build out—quickly—the full value chain. And it often benefits from a more open and fluid structure as the founding team and early employees each become a "jack-of-all-trades." More cooperative approaches likely will have a team that can work in an effective way with larger organizations (more suits, fewer jeans), and will invest in developing a comparative advantage in only those specific capabilities and problem areas that they plan to offer as their specialty.

However, in choosing a path, an entrepreneur will be interested in what their share in a cooperation will be. While some of this depends on relative skill in negotiating, it also is driven by how each would fare under competition. Working against a start-up would be the cost of duplicating complementary assets in order to enter. As mentioned earlier, these costs vary from industry to industry and change depending on the product. However, these costs may also relate to whether entrepreneurs have multiple options for partners. If a particular partner's complementary assets are not truly unique, an entrepreneur can investigate multiple ways to enter the market without building out their own value chain.

Also impacting the entrepreneur's bargaining position will be the nature of competition that might arise. If an incumbent firm feels comfortable in fending

The Race for Synthetic Insulin

Perhaps no case of choosing your competition has been more intensively studied than the patent race for human insulin that occurred in the late 1970s.[a] The development of a human insulin product represented the first commercially oriented product in the novel field of biotechnology and was closely watched at the time by industry observers and public policymakers. In the 45 years since the successful development of insulin by the start-up firm Genentech, the case of human insulin has been used again and again as an example to motivate different models of technological competition.

Most analysts date the commencement of this case of competition to a research conference hosted by Eli Lilly in May 1976. As the world's leading producer of insulin for diabetics, Lilly arranged the conference to assess whether novel recombinant DNA (rDNA) tools could produce human insulin, providing a higher-quality substitute to the pork and beef insulin then used in the treatment of diabetes. While molecular biologists were extremely excited by the possibilities of rDNA from a scientific perspective, few analysts or scientists believed that there would be important commercial applications in the near future; moreover, most of the main researchers were employed by universities, limiting their incentives and opportunity to explore commercial applications.

The research meeting, along with Lilly's continued research funding and commitments to license commercializable technology, helped researchers see that rDNA research could generate financial returns. As a result, three separate research teams pursued programs aimed at the "expression" of the human insulin gene (a necessary condition for commercial exploitation of rDNA techniques). Two of the teams, based at the biology/biochemistry departments of Harvard and the University of California, San Francisco, were essentially university research labs diverting attention and resources away from purely scientific projects and toward the commercially relevant human insulin project. The third team was initiated by Genentech, a start-up biotechnology firm founded by an entrepreneur (Bob Swanson) and a scientist (Herbert Boyer), which operated outside of the confines of a university.

In contrast to the university-based competitors, Genentech chose to pursue an alternative research strategy—gene synthesis—which was more amenable to commercialization prospects because it was not subject to burdensome NIH regulations governing the use of genetic materials.

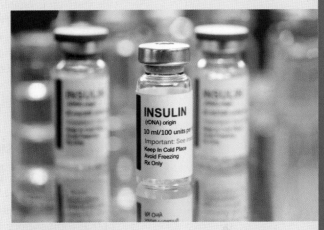

A vial of synthetic insulin

Each research team separately pursued human insulin synthesis, under the threat of being beaten by another team. In August 1978, Genentech researchers successfully synthesized the human insulin gene in bacteria, opening the door to the first commercial application of biotechnology. Then, one day after their experiment was validated, Genentech signed an exclusive license agreement with Eli Lilly. This agreement granted Lilly the manufacturing rights to Genentech's intellectual property; Lilly also contracted with Genentech to collaborate on certain scale-up activities where Genentech would have greater expertise. One of the distinctive features of the negotiations around this license was that Lilly maintained an aggressive position through negotiations, always de-emphasizing Lilly's need for the technology (it could continue to use animal insulin) and discounting claims by Swanson of the viability of the product.

What is perhaps most interesting about this case is that it is, by all accounts, not unique for the biotechnology industry. With a few exceptions, biotechnology firms either license their technology to a large established firm (which retains responsibility for FDA approval procedures, marketing, and so on) or are purchased outright by such a firm through an acquisition.

SOURCE: Scott Stern, "Incentives and Focus in University and Industrial Research: The Case of Synthetic Insulin," ch. 7 in *Sources of Medical Technology: Universities and Industry* (Washington, DC: National Academies Press, 1995).

off that competition, the entrepreneur's bargaining position will be weaker. By contrast, if the entrepreneur's idea generates a competitive threat, then even if competition would drive the profits of both parties to zero, it may do much more harm to the established firm than to the start-up. This could give the start-up considerable leverage. That said, if the intensity of competition is so strong that the start-up is unable to cover the costs of entry, then the entrepreneur's bargaining position will be weaker. Moreover, as we will discuss in more detail later in this chapter, if the established firm can easily imitate the entrepreneur's idea and product, then the entrepreneur's competitive options may be nonexistent. The tougher a competitor the start-up is anticipated to be, the better its bargaining position will be too. Put simply, in any cooperation, value capture depends on the alternative competitive path.

8.5 Choosing How to Compete: Control vs. Execution

Competition is not just about whom you compete with; it is also about the terms of that competition. There are, in fact, a number of choices that entrepreneurs make that shape how they compete (based on investments they have preemptively made to protect their market position or on capabilities they develop to ensure their products are valuable to customers in a sustained way). Broadly speaking, two distinct modes—control and execution—summarize these choices. Control involves trying to capture as much of the market as possible, reducing the amount of future competition. In contrast, execution involves trying to create the best possible product at the lowest price and adapting quickly to competitors rather than trying to eliminate them. We will illustrate how each represents orientations entrepreneurs can choose.

CONTROL

A common approach for choosing how to compete is to make a concerted, up-front effort to alter the prospects of future would-be competitors and, ideally, discourage them from competing with the venture as it grows. That is, control the market so that competition does not emerge.

Control is often a choice preferred by entrepreneurs because continual competition is not for everyone. PayPal cofounder and venture capitalist Peter Thiel is certainly not a fan:

> Creative monopoly means new products that benefit everybody and sustainable profits for the creator. Competition means no profits for anybody, no meaningful differentiation and a struggle for survival.[10]

He is not alone. Economics professors have long noted that perhaps the greatest benefit from a monopoly is a quiet life. And it is this push that is behind the oft-cited claim that entrepreneurs should build a company with a moat to protect against future competition. The idea of a moat is that a barrier to entry is erected that prevents would-be competitors from taking a venture's customers. To be sure, while the path of execution does not necessarily imply that profits will be low, it does require competition in an ongoing sense within the market. Wouldn't it be better to take over a market and just keep it?

If an entrepreneur could just be handed a monopoly and protection from competition for free, then perhaps this would be an obvious choice. However, this is very rarely the case. To protect your business from future competitors, you must make early and costly investments. A famous, quite literal example of this comes from the mid-1910s, when the Stark Brothers Nursery of Missouri acquired the rights to distribute the Golden Delicious apple tree developed by A. H. Mullins of West Virginia. However, lacking intellectual property rights, the brothers protected this innovation by building a cage (complete with alarm) around the apple tree to prevent would-be competitors from taking cuttings from the tree, which would allow them to replicate and sell the fruit tree and its delicious apples (**Figure 8.7**).[11] These steps were not only costly but also slowed the brothers' ability to quickly market their new (and delicious!) apples.

Let's consider a more modern example. For a technology-driven start-up, investments in formal intellectual property protection, though expensive, allow it to create a technology that is **proprietary**. Doing so excludes direct competition while also significantly enhancing bargaining power in

proprietary The legal right of a company to be the sole owner of a given type of technology

---

FIGURE 8.7 Golden Delicious Apple Tree

The Stark Brothers were intent on protecting their new apple tree, the Golden Delicious, from those who might steal it. A simple apple seed would not allow another would-be entrepreneur to plant a Golden Delicious apple tree, but a cutting from a tree would be all one would need to grow a sapling. Wary of thieves, the brothers developed an early form of intellectual property protection: they built wooden cages with bells around each of their trees. To ward off "delicious" competition, the brothers needed to make up-front investments to protect and control their innovation before the world discovered the value of the new variety and its potential demand among consumers.

network effects When value for a product depends on other people's use of the product, and vice versa

economies of scale When a firm can achieve a lower average cost through an increase in the overall quantity produced

branding A company image and reputation that customers associate with its products

This chapter's video shows how Microsoft used network effects and control to build a global company.

negotiations with potential supply chain partners. However, formal intellectual property protection such as patents is not the only way that the founding team can maintain control over their idea. Trade secrecy, proprietary methods or algorithms, and even employment practices such as non-competes can serve a similar purpose, helping to control who has access to the technology, even as they share the basic "idea," early prototypes, or even commercial products with others. Much like the Stark Brothers' apple tree cage, an early focus on control involves not only significant investments but also a real trade-off in moving quickly into the market.

Proprietary technology is one way that an entrepreneur can potentially protect themselves from future competition. Others can be even more lucrative. One that has received greater notice in the digital age is **network effects**. As we discussed in "Choosing Your Customer" (Chapter 5), network effects arise when the adoption decisions by one consumer are impacted positively by those of others. Microsoft initially introduced its Office suite of products, including Word, Excel, and PowerPoint, for the Apple computers that had initial traction in the personal computer market. However, through its role in the operating system software for personal computers supported by IBM, it expanded its products across different systems. As the use of desktop computers grew throughout the workplace, having a set of products that worked with hardware easily and allowed collaboration and document sharing among multiple people gave rise to a network effect. Cultivating this standard has allowed Microsoft to maintain its place as one of the world's most valuable companies for over three decades.

Microsoft had other advantages too. Computer software is a business with **economies of scale**; the more units that are sold, the lower the average cost of each one. Therefore, Microsoft invested heavily to ensure its software operated efficiently on or between almost all IBM-compatible computers. The payoff was creating a very large market and an extremely low possible average cost. This first allowed Microsoft to do enterprise deals and volume discounts that undercut potential competitors' pricing. It then protected the company from others looking to get into the market, as it would require scale to compete with Microsoft. In addition, by having many customers who understood its product, how it worked, and its reliability, Microsoft developed a reputation and a brand that helped it acquire new customers. Such **branding** requires long-term investments in marketing and sales—and having products that deliver on their promise. But critically, any new entrant hoping to compete for Microsoft's existing customers faces a hurdle from being unknown. This is perhaps why, when competitors to Microsoft's Office products did emerge, they came from companies like Apple and Google, who had brand names of their own.

Thus, while an execution path might allow a start-up to quickly enter and compete in the market, control requires investment and can delay market entry. Protecting technology, developing systems with network effects, establishing scale economies, and building a brand takes time. It may be some years before revenue outweighs even operational costs, and it is far from certain that the future payoff in terms of a valuable market with barriers to entry will arise. Moreover, while the start-up's future may not have ongoing competitive pressure, it is highly likely that, at the onset, the start-up will have to compete aggressively for the market position it needs to start building its protective moat. *In effect, rather than compete within the market, businesses investing in control are competing for the market itself.*

EXECUTION

There is an alternative to seeking control, and that is to focus on execution. This involves choosing not to try and build barriers against future competition but instead choosing to face that competition head-to-head when it arises and being prepared for it.

In the 1990s, when Marc Benioff first saw a web browser, he wondered why it was typically being positioned as a means for consumers or end users to access the Internet. If consumers could use the web to interact with Amazon, why couldn't salespeople use it to interact with their own customers? Prior to the establishment of his company, Salesforce.com, salespeople, if they used information technology at all, would be constrained to enterprise software solutions for customer relationship management (CRM) that were housed on internal networks and walled off from the outside world. What is more, these systems were static and would not evolve with user needs. In founding Salesforce, Benioff sought to bring sales into the digital age with a suite of services designed to empower salespeople in their jobs. As part of this, he introduced the notion of "software as a service." The applications would evolve and change as the needs of salespeople themselves changed. Benioff's applications would be housed on what we now call cloud computing. They would update automatically. They would be born on the Internet.

There was an important strategic element to this plan. Cloud computing was not uniquely available to Salesforce. What was to stop competitors from providing their own services should Salesforce prove successful? The answer, really, was nothing, and Benioff knew it. That meant that there was no possibility of really building a moat around this business. To be sure, Benioff could have made it difficult for users to switch, but to do so would require making it hard for them to start using his applications in the first place. But that involved its own costs. Benioff's vision was to produce a service that was customer-focused and responsive. But if there was limited take-up, that feedback would not be provided, and hence, his product development strategy would be at risk. Thus, it made more sense to focus on execution as a path that was consistent with the type of position Salesforce wanted to establish in the market, even if that left it vulnerable to future competition.[12]

When entrepreneurs say that they are "focusing on execution," one could be forgiven for thinking that this should be an obvious thing for all businesses to do. After all, doesn't "execution" mean "doing things well and efficiently"? However, all decisions face trade-offs. As entrepreneurs have limited resources and time, when they focus on one thing, they must choose not to do something else. When Marc Benioff decided to focus on ensuring his customers could gain immediate value from his CRM services, that meant he had to invest in capabilities—software developers, cloud infrastructure, and the like—to start developing customer-facing features. It also meant he could not afford to invest in ways that might cause customers to be locked in for a longer term. These investments in the longer term might diminish the quality of the immediate-term value Benioff wanted to deliver.

What, then, is the plan for profitability and value capture when an entrepreneur invests in execution? After all, they will face competition and, as we saw before, competition can threaten value capture even if competition is great for consumers. The answer is that *the execution entrepreneur intends to profit by having a competitive advantage as a competitor within a market*. To be sure, if you produce the same thing as everyone else at the same cost, you should not expect to earn profits. But if you produce a better product (for at least some market segments) at a lower cost, you can earn profits. And if the capabilities that allow you to differentiate your product or deliver it more efficiently require investment and experience that cannot be quickly replicated by competitors, then so long as you continue to invest in those capabilities, you can be profitable even in the face of competition and for a long period of time. The Salesforce team knew that they didn't have a lock on the market. Future innovations would come and compete with them, certainly for specific sales applications. Thus, they understood that they had to continue to execute well to maintain their market position over time.

EXECUTION VS. CONTROL

Similar to the choice between competition and collaboration, the choice between execution and control is crucial. Of course, not all ideas can be patented or receive effective intellectual property protection, and innovations vary with how "leaky" they are. Potential competitors may have the ability to imitate the idea or potential partners might be able to exploit it without you. For any given idea, however, entrepreneurs need to consider how their venture might evolve if they focus on execution—competing on the basis of speed and agility—vs. control—competing on the basis of strong bargaining power and a reputation for enforcing control over their idea. From a customer choice perspective, entrepreneurs focusing on execution are more likely to start by choosing a narrower customer segment, prioritizing learning from early adopters. In contrast, a control-oriented start-up, though slower, may be able to position itself to broader markets when it does enter. At the same time, execution-oriented start-ups are more likely to iterate on its technology (ride the S curve) rather than focus on transferable and generalizable technologies that are subject to standardization. Finally, the choice between execution and control is likely to have a significant impact on the company you build. For example, where execution-oriented start-ups are more likely to encourage iterative experimentation and learning, control-oriented start-ups will still undertake experimentation but in a more deliberate and decisive fashion.

8.6 Concluding Thoughts

When Katrina Lake had the idea to use artificial intelligence to augment and enhance the ability of stylists to curate clothing recommendations (and to do so at scale), she could have taken her start-up along many different paths. Yet no path would have isolated Stitch Fix entirely from competition. For any start-up whose underlying idea creates meaningful value, an entrepreneur does not have a choice that involves an absence of competition. Even in those cases where the product or service does not create value in a way that directly competes with existing firms, the discovery of a new way to create value often invites competition from existing firms as well as other entrepreneurs. By evaluating the structure of an industry, entrepreneurs can better understand how value is likely to be captured among industry stakeholders and better position their firm. Moreover, by actively choosing with whom and how to compete, entrepreneurs can shape the competition they will ultimately face (see **Putting It Together: Choosing Your Competition**).

CHOOSING YOUR COMPETITION

For a given idea, you have the freedom to choose with whom and how to compete.

CONSIDER COLLABORATION VS. COMPETITION

Collaborate: Identify Potential Partners

- Gauge the availability of key complementary assets or resources (human, intellectual, or physical) your start-up will need.
- Determine if you can contract for key complementary assets rather than build out yourself.
- Identify potential partners to help you build or acquire key complementary assets or resources. Can collaboration create value for both firms?

Compete: Identify Likely Competitors

- Evaluate the market conditions. Create a shortlist of current market players with products that will likely be impacted by your idea when it is brought to market.
- Consider the potential competitive responses by evaluating their strengths and weaknesses, strategic commitments, and past competitive actions. Identify strategies they might use like defensive pricing and imitation, and how to their slow responses.

EVALUATE INVESTMENTS IN EXECUTION VS. CONTROL

Consider How to Use Control of an Idea to Compete

- Assess which parts of your core idea are most susceptible to replication or work-around by others, and how this might impact the venture.
- Assess which parts are difficult to replicate and how they will create and capture value.
- Evaluate approaches and costs to exert control over your idea, including network effects, scale economies, branding, and using IP rights.

Consider How to Use Execution to Compete

- Consider your start-up's ability to stay ahead of the competition. How will customer feedback and rapid iteration help the venture stay ahead?
- Identify the resources and capabilities your start-up will need to execute quickly.

NARROW THE COMPETITIVE ALTERNATIVES

Conduct Low-Commitment Learning

- Contrast how different competitive choices will affect what you and your team learn, the capabilities you build, and your competitive advantage.
- Evaluate the success and failures of previous partnerships and collaborations in your industry. Identify partners who have a track record of successful collaborations with start-ups.
- Identify a critical, low-cost experiment to test these core competitive hypotheses.

Chapter 8 Review: Choosing Your Competition

CHAPTER TAKEAWAYS

- In order to capture value, an entrepreneur must choose and implement an approach that allows them to create value for customers in the face of both existing and potential competition. Simply put, if a start-up is profitable, it can expect that others will enter to compete with it.

- Porter's Five Forces framework allows one to evaluate the attractiveness of a given industry and recognize how value is likely to be captured among the different stakeholders.

- Given the industry structure, firms can choose their market position within an industry to achieve sustained profitability. Two common approaches are a low-cost strategy and a differentiation strategy.

- Commercialization is the process by which a new product, service, or platform is brought to market.

- Ease of imitation of the innovation and ownership of complementary assets shape the ability of an entrepreneur to capture value from their idea.

- Disclosing information about an idea to figure out the "price" for the idea, evaluating the potential of a collaboration, or otherwise seeking resources often reduces the potential for value capture.

- Cooperating with established players allows the entrepreneur to leverage the established player's complementary assets to commercialize the idea and avoid head-to-head competition.

- Competing with established players requires constructing a distinct value chain. Still, it allows the entrepreneur to have a higher degree of control over how the idea is commercialized and enhances the start-up's ability to capture value.

- Entrepreneurs choose not only with whom to compete but also how. A focus on execution centers on developing and continually building capabilities, whereas a focus on control involves preemptively making investments to protect a market position.

KEY TERMS

competitor (p. 220)
moat (p. 221)
commercialization (p. 227)
complementary assets (p. 228)
disclosure problem (p. 229)

head-to-head competition (p. 234)
proprietary (p. 237)
network effects (p. 238)
economies of scale (p. 238)
branding (p. 238)

REVIEW QUESTIONS

1. Why is it difficult for an entrepreneur to capture value from their idea even if it creates value?

2. Why are complementary assets important for commercialization? What are examples of complementary assets that are difficult for entrepreneurs to build or acquire?

3. Outline Porter's Five Forces framework. Why is this an important tool for understanding an industry, and what are the key implications for entrepreneurs?

4. What is a low-cost strategy, and what firm choices are involved in establishing this market position? Conversely, what is a differentiated strategy, and what firm choices are involved in establishing this market position?

5. Summarize the challenges the disclosure problem presents to entrepreneurs.

6. What are the benefits and risks of competing with established players? What early choices must an entrepreneur make?

7. What are the benefits and risks of collaborating with established players? What early choices must an entrepreneur make?

8. Why is there a trade-off between control vs. execution?

9. Why must an entrepreneur choose its competition? What are the trade-offs if the entrepreneur simply gets started without making a choice?

DISCUSSION QUESTIONS

Answer the following series of questions and scenarios either in class discussions or by writing a short response.

1. Miguel is working on a new smartphone game where users solve simple puzzles based on information about local retail stores. While his friends love playing the game (and many local retailers are interested in experimenting with the game as a new advertising channel), Miguel is unsure about whether this idea will serve as the foundation for a profitable business. Plus, he has yet to protect the idea in any way. His friend Joyce is encouraging him to just launch the app to see if it gains traction, emphasizing that he does not need to worry about competition as he is the first to pioneer this game. If the game is indeed attractive to both users and local retailers, will Miguel be able to avoid competition simply by being the first to commercialize this idea?

2. Famed investor Warren Buffett once quipped, "When a manager with a reputation for brilliance tackles a business with a reputation for bad economics, the reputation of the business remains intact." Why do entrepreneurs face challenges in establishing profitable businesses in industries with "bad economics"? What is an example of an entrepreneur who has overcome the challenge laid out by Buffett?

3. Nadira and her family plan to open a motel on the outskirts of their town, just off the exit from the interstate highway. Nadira's father has visited existing nearby motels and intends to simply imitate those motels in terms of amenities and design. Nadira argues to her father that their motel might be far more profitable if they were able to offer a unique approach, even if that would cost more money upfront. For example, no lodging within 25 miles offers a fully equipped fitness center. Why might Nadira's proposal to feature a fitness center allow her family to potentially operate a

more profitable motel? What are some potential arguments against her proposal? Beyond simply installing a gym, what would her family need to do to implement this proposal? How might the guests for this motel end up being distinctive relative to travelers staying at nearby motels?[13]

4. Some innovative start-ups such as biotechnology firms Genentech and Moderna have been able to capture significant value from their innovation, while others—such as the one founded by Dan Bricklin, the creator of the first spreadsheet, VisiCalc—developed valuable innovations but failed to capitalize on their idea. Why might entrepreneurs face challenges in their ability to capture value from their innovation? What factors do you think are most important in shaping the degree to which an entrepreneur is able to capture value from their idea?

5. Some of the most successful start-ups since 2000 have ultimately been acquired by the largest established firms in their industry. For example, YouTube was bought by Google, and Instagram was bought by Facebook. What are the advantages of "cooperating" with incumbents as an entrepreneur? What are the challenges of cooperation? For those entrepreneurs pursuing cooperation, who is their competition?

6. Miguel (from Discussion Question 1) is thinking about how to take a systematic approach toward commercializing his mobile retail puzzle game. One of his advisers, Edward, is adamant that the first step Miguel should take is to establish a patent or other intellectual property rights over his novel game idea. Miguel's friend Joyce, however, insists that patents are usually not used to protect mobile games. She says that all Miguel will be doing will be wasting time and money that could be more effectively spent on learning from customers. What are the potential advantages of Edward's approach? What are the potential advantages of Joyce's approach? Why might Miguel find it challenging to follow both pieces of advice?

FOR FURTHER READING

Gans, Joshua, Erin L. Scott, and Scott Stern. "Strategy for Start-Ups." *Harvard Business Review*, May–June 2018.

Gans, Joshua, and Scott Stern, "The Product Market and the Market for "Ideas": Commercialization Strategies for Technology Entrepreneurs." *Research Policy* 32, no. 2 (2003): 333–50.

Porter, Michael E. "The Five Competitive Forces That Shape Strategy." *Harvard Business Review*, January 2008.

Teece, David. "Profiting from Technological Innovation: Implications for Integration, Collaboration, Licensing, and Public Policy." *Research Policy* 15, no. 6 (1986): 285–305.

Katherine Homuth

"A woman's education consists of two lessons: never leave the house without stockings, never go out without a hat," claimed Coco Chanel. The hat was for wearing. The extra pair of stockings were for backup. Why? There was a good chance that the pair you were wearing wouldn't last the outing. They would run, which was a signal they would soon fall apart and you'd have to replace them while out. After a century, the problem had never been solved, and it was still top of mind. As comedian Phyllis Diller once said, "Women want men, careers, money, children, friends, luxury, comfort, independence, freedom, respect, love, and a three-dollar pantyhose that won't run."

Katherine Homuth, from Mississauga, outside of Toronto, recalled her grandmother appealing for a reinvention of pantyhose. Homuth, who had already sold her first venture, ShopLocket (an e-commerce start-up platform), at age 23, had the same thought as many others: "It seemed like such a bizarre thing; how do we have self-driving cars and space travel, but something as simple as a pair of pantyhose that doesn't rip when you put it on doesn't exist?" She also knew that if the problem of robust pantyhose could be cracked, they wouldn't sell for three dollars but 30 to 40 times more. Three dollars was something you paid for an item if it wouldn't last the day. One hundred dollars is what you pay for something you can use over and over again.

In 2017, Homuth decided to tackle the problem. Without textile experience, she explored and worked with suppliers to find a material that wouldn't rip, would be comfortable, lightweight, and water resistant, and would look good. A tall order, but Homuth's timing was just right. New advances in material science brought forth new polymers that would serve her purposes, and she seized on them, creating a virtually indestructible pair of tights she called Sheertex. Homuth brought Sheertex to Toronto's Creative Destruction Lab in 2018, the same time she launched a Kickstarter campaign. Having cracked the pantyhose problem, a big question loomed: *How should it be taken to market?*

There were lots of options. Having no manufacturing experience, let alone for textiles, perhaps the sensible option was to partner with an existing, established brand. But the pantyhose industry was built around disposability,

Sheertex founder Katherine Homuth pictured wearing a pair of rip-resistant Sheertex tights

and there was concern that brands would not be open to changing the entire model. Sheertex's material advances were being patented, and so Homuth could license that technology and allow others to use the material to make better products. This might go beyond pantyhose. Or perhaps she could brand the material like Gore-Tex had done decades ago for its waterproof and breathable fabric.

Questions

1. Consider the options available to Homuth. What value might collaboration with an established firm provide both the start-up and the potential partner?

2. What concerns might each have regarding the collaboration?

3. Should she stick to pantyhose or explore licensing the technology for broader applications?

4. Alternatively, what complementary assets would Homuth need to acquire to launch Sheertex as a standalone competitor to established hosiery firms?

SOURCE: Sean Silcoff, "'Unbreakable' Pantyhose Startup Sheertex Overcomes Disruptions in Quest to Make Over Industry," *Globe and Mail*, April 5, 2021, https://www.theglobeandmail.com/business/article-unbreakable-pantyhose-startup-sheertex-overcomes-disruptions-in-quest.

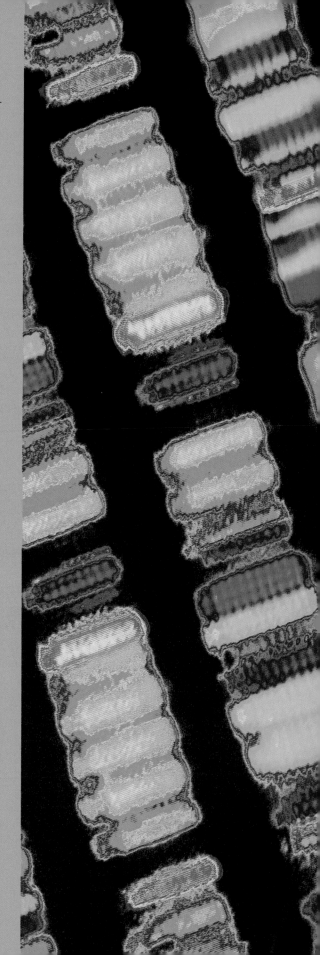

PART 3

FOUR STRATEGIES: HOW CHOICES WORK TOGETHER

W e have now covered four domains of choice—customer, technology, organization, and competition—that together form the strategy of an entrepreneurial venture. But these choices cannot be made independently of one another. They have to work together. In the next four chapters, we will illustrate four broad strategies—Intellectual Property Strategy, Disruption Strategy, Value Chain Strategy, and Architectural Strategy—and the core choices entrepreneurs make with each, devoting one chapter per strategy.

Where to next? Opportunities in genetics or healthcare in general have been pursued and are being pursued by many entrepreneurs. But how this is done depends on the strategy chosen.

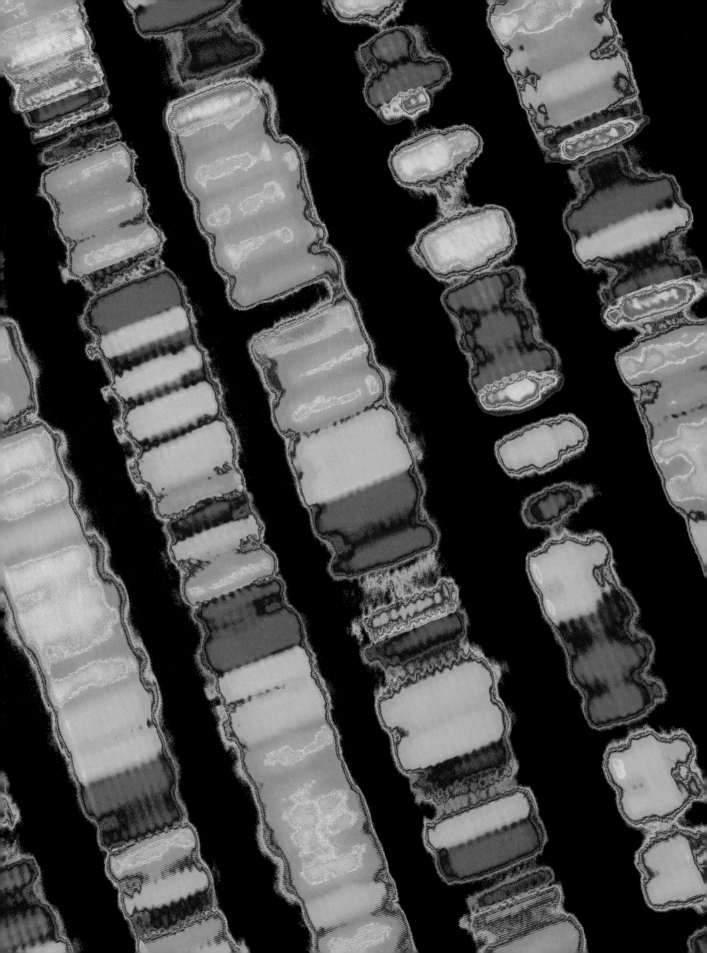

The Entrepreneurial Strategy Compass

There are two dimensions of competition choice that are particularly important in all four strategies: with whom to compete and how to compete. These give rise to the four types of strategy that can, in turn, guide the other choice domains. To start to understand this, we introduce the **Entrepreneurial Strategy Compass** below. The compass guides entrepreneurs by showing the best strategy to use depending on the initial directions chosen by the entrepreneur for a given idea.

To start, consider the entrepreneur with their idea at the center of the compass. For any given idea and entrepreneur, there will be choices that orient the venture more toward competition than collaboration, and other choices that require the company to invest more in execution than control. These decisions form the axes and directions of the compass. The degree of competition/collaboration and execution/control that the entrepreneur chooses for their venture will direct them toward the most effective strategy and thus shape both their venture and the complementary choices they will make in terms of customer, technology, and organization.

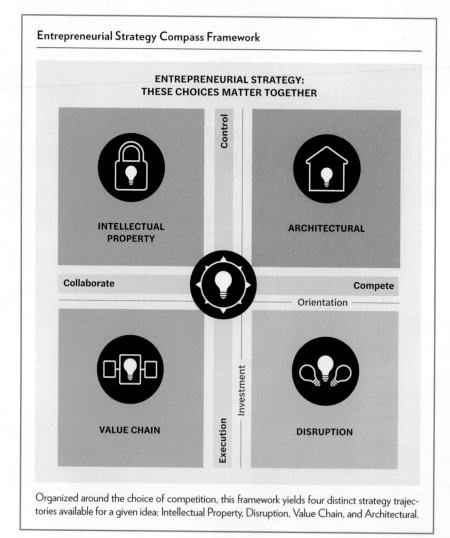

Entrepreneurial Strategy Compass Framework

ENTREPRENEURIAL STRATEGY:
THESE CHOICES MATTER TOGETHER

Control

INTELLECTUAL
PROPERTY

ARCHITECTURAL

Collaborate

Compete

Orientation

Investment

VALUE CHAIN

Execution

DISRUPTION

Organized around the choice of competition, this framework yields four distinct strategy trajectories available for a given idea: Intellectual Property, Disruption, Value Chain, and Architectural.

Professors Want a Quiet Life Compared to Their Students

In academic environments, most new ideas and discoveries are typically first disclosed through an academic paper. At this point, the potential entrepreneur behind the idea faces a lot of latitude in how to bring the idea to market. In a recent study, we evaluated the difference between professors and students in their approach to this process.

Faculty members (at least in the United States) are often encouraged to commercialize innovation through their institution's technology licensing office. First, faculty may owe their universities a duty of disclosure that can be enforced given their ongoing employment. These offices may also have experience in managing some of the complexities of controlling intellectual property. This is important to faculty who often have limited time to really invest in the type of learning that would be associated with execution. In contrast, student inventors are exactly the opposite: they have limited institutional support to obtain formal intellectual property but are free to simply walk off campus and "get stuff done" (e.g., Mark Zuckerberg was able to simply drop out of Harvard to pursue the development of Facebook [then called TheFacebook]), and they often embrace the iterative interaction with customers that is essential to learning and experimentation.

To investigate this more carefully, we examined a systematic sample of "paper-start-up pairs"—ventures whose origins are in an academic paper (think Google and the Google algorithm developed while Sergey Brin and Larry Page were students at Stanford), focusing on whether the founding team included a student, professor, or both. After accounting for differences across different "ideas" (e.g., some ideas are simply more "patentable" than others or may be associated with a more rapid process of market introduction), we evaluated how the choices of professor founders differed from that of student founders.

The results are dramatic: professors are more than twice as likely to commercialize their idea with a patent application within a year of the publication of the paper, while students are able to reach early-stage milestones more quickly, including incorporation, their first round of financing, and even the timing of their initial product introduction. What this illustrates is that time to market, for example, is not simply a function of the "idea."[a] Instead, you see how founders face a choice of how to manage that idea through execution (at the expense of control) or vice versa, and the impacts that choice has on the idea's performance.

Entrepreneurs can use this compass to help explore and search for strategies around their idea. This involves considering the potential of an idea or the capabilities of the entrepreneur; it also takes into account the preferences and aspirations of the entrepreneur.

For example, some entrepreneurs have a strong commitment to "openness." Even if it looks more profitable for their idea to use a control strategy, they may prefer to choose an execution strategy in line with their internal values, possibly around collaboration too. (see **Using the Research: Professors Want a Quiet Life Compared to Their Students**). In fact, this framework offers meaningful guidance for any entrepreneurial idea placed in the middle of the compass. For instance, though a biotechnology start-up usually pursues a patent given the nature of the industry, biotechnology start-ups will face choices about how intensively to file and enforce intellectual property (over just their core ideas or the core ideas plus all the associated tools and data), and how open they might choose to be with the scientific community. The Entrepreneurial Strategy Compass is a guide to help you resolve these trade-offs and point you toward strategies and choices that work with other aspects of your growing firm. By understanding alternative ways that your idea can create and capture value, entrepreneurs can make decisive choices that reinforce each other, enhancing the potential for venture success over time.

Dolby technology has become a standard in sound technology, particularly in theaters. It succeeded by using a novel IP strategy as it was getting started.

ENTREPRENEUR'S DILEMMA Entrepreneurs pursuing an intellectual property (IP) strategy must find partners (e.g., individuals and other businesses) who will create the most value when they bring this IP to customers. However, the best partners often have significant bargaining power that limits how much value an IP entrepreneur can capture. Entrepreneurs selling IP must ensure that their partners can create value while, at the same time, not accumulate excessive bargaining power.

CHAPTER OBJECTIVES

- Describe the tools of IP strategy, including patents, trademarks, and copyright
- Identify the customer, technology, organization, and competition choices an entrepreneur makes that comprise an IP strategy
- Detail how to envision deals to sell ideas and learn who to sell them to
- Explain the value creation hypothesis for an IP strategy
- Explain the value capture hypothesis for an IP strategy
- Understand why ventures pursuing an IP strategy end up becoming ideas factories

9

INTELLECTUAL PROPERTY STRATEGY

I n recent decades, anyone in the market for a stereo system or watching a film in theaters would be guaranteed to come across the Dolby name. Invented by its eponymous founder Ray Dolby in 1965, Dolby Laboratories' patented technologies greatly improved the sound quality in recordings and grew to become a global standard, gaining and retaining a position of market leadership for 50 years. Dolby technology was first used in Stanley Kubrick's *A Clockwork Orange* in 1970 and then, notably, in George Lucas's *Star Wars* and Steven Spielberg's *Close Encounters of the Third Kind*. The technology changed how people experience films, elevating the level of emotional intensity films c ould convey.[1]

However, Dolby Laboratories achieved its multibillion-dollar valuation with limited direct interaction with film directors, music producers, or audiophiles. Instead, it decided to license its proprietary technology to audio product developers and manufacturers, including Sony, Bose, Apple, and Yamaha, among many others. But how did Dolby become a brand itself, one that some of the biggest brands in the world decided to feature along with their own?

It started back in the 1960s, when Dolby was far from being a household name. Ray Dolby, a PhD physicist, had invented a technology that could reduce background noise in audio recordings without quality reduction. In doing so, Dolby had created a unique piece of **intellectual property** (IP), which are creations of the mind, such as inventions; literary and artistic works; designs; and symbols, names, and images used in commerce. Dolby's first move was to license the Dolby-technology IP to KLH, a high-end audio equipment manufacturer. While he also flirted with manufacturing Dolby products himself, Dolby eventually made the conscious decision to stick to pure licensing to avoid competing with licensees.

intellectual property (IP) Creations of the mind, such as inventions; literary and artistic works; designs; and symbols, names, and images used in commerce

Intellectual Property strategies require entrepreneurs to collaborate while at the same time maintaining control of their idea.

intellectual property strategy (IP strategy) A start-up strategy invested in controlling its technology while collaborating with established firms to create value for these firms' final consumers, IP strategy must create value for the end customers of existing firms while also maintaining control and bargaining power for the start-up after disclosing its idea

Dolby's decision to serve end customers from an arm's length may seem odd relative to familiar start-up models built on the ideas of rapid and continual customer response. But many ventures, including Dolby, have secured extraordinary returns creating businesses and exploring opportunities using **intellectual property strategy** (IP strategy). These include familiar brand names like Google, Apple, and Coke; a host of technology companies like Qualcomm, lens maker Leica, and microchip designer Arm; and people who license their brand name to use with a product (such as George Foreman for a grilling machine and Michael Jordan for Nike's Air Jordans). By definition, an IP strategy involves a start-up that is invested in *control* over its technology while also being oriented toward *collaboration* with established firms to create value for these firms' final consumers. *IP strategy must create value for the end customers of existing firms, while at the same time maintaining control and bargaining power for the start-up after disclosing its idea.*

Turning back to Dolby, his approach is instructive because of the clever, three-pronged strategy he used to maximize his IP. First, he protected his technology with multiple patents (described later) so he could stake and defend his core technological advance. His second strategy was less obvious. While licensing would be the key revenue component for Dolby, he decided to incentivize development of uses and products with Dolby technology by not charging high fees for these types of licenses. For example, because Dolby's technology would work best reducing noise in cassette tapes if the cassettes themselves were recorded with Dolby processes in mind, he did not charge fees for using the technology to create prerecorded cassettes; instead, he chose to earn fees on the cassette players that incorporated the Dolby technology (**Figure 9.1**). Doing so made Dolby technology in cassettes ubiquitous and created a widespread demand for cassette players with Dolby noise reduction features (usually a distinctive Dolby button). The button itself became synonymous with effective noise reduction to consumers. This pricing model continues today; Dolby does not charge fees for media like games and movies produced in Dolby Digital Surround Sound but charges for the equipment that plays them.

Further, Dolby wanted stringent control on the quality of those uses. To ensure that playback would be of high quality, Dolby technology could not be

FIGURE 9.1 **Dolby's Strategy in Action**

This 1980s era cassette tape (left) player utilizes Dolby Noise Reduction (Dolby NR) and has Dolby branding (right). Dolby's strategy created great demand for cassette tape players that utilized his technology.

incorporated into a device without Dolby's preapproval. This reinforced Dolby's corporate identity of quality technology and matched it with customers with similar priorities. Building this reputation helped Dolby earn and grow license fees even *after* his initial patent had expired.

Ultimately, Dolby pursued a classic intellectual property strategy to focus his creative energies on a core area of innovation. It places an entrepreneur's idea into an established market to achieve two related purposes:

This chapter's video explores how Dolby used an IP strategy to bring gold-standard audio technology to a variety of industries.

1. It enhances the value of products that established firms develop and sell, matching an entrepreneur's idea with firms that own key complementary assets needed to commercialize that idea.
2. It provides the entrepreneur (and their idea) with the power to receive committed payments prior to the sale of those downstream products.

But while selling ideas in the marketplace is increasing,[2] it is a bit of a puzzle as to why IP strategies are not more commonplace.[3] The answer, in part, is that the nature of ideas makes it difficult for entrepreneurs as well as buyers to successfully navigate the marketplace for ideas.[4] An IP entrepreneur must demonstrate that their IP provides opportunity for downstream firms and, in so doing, entails considerable risks. Navigating these challenges begins by understanding what constitutes an intellectual property strategy for a start-up. Entrepreneurs must also recognize the choices that give the strategy the best chance of realizing value from the idea.

9.1 Creating and Capturing Value with an IP Strategy

An IP strategy is premised on distinct value creation and value capture hypotheses. Let's start with value creation.

An IP strategy's value creation hypothesis is that the start-up's idea can generate value for the customers of established firms. It creates this value by integrating this idea or innovation into existing products, services, or the value chain of established players. To do so, these established firms must have the capabilities to meaningfully understand and absorb the start-up's *technology* into their existing systems. So rather than focusing exclusively on bleeding-edge research without regard to compatibility or integration, IP start-ups must focus on developing general and transferable innovations. Entrepreneurs must build a team with high inventive capacity and the necessary capabilities to facilitate technology transfer. In other words, the start-up will have an identity that emulates Dolby's culture of making "the inventors the heroes of the company."[5] They will become an "ideas factory" for firms, emphasizing their role as innovators and "thinkers" within the industry.

IP start-ups must also confront a value capture hypothesis: Will the IP entrepreneur be able to control their idea and associated intellectual property assets (e.g., patents, trademarks, copyrights, trade secrets) to capture value by extracting significant and sustainable revenues from established firms?

This first requires a start-up to create value for those established firms (and their downstream customers). But success hinges on whether it can establish significant bargaining power and develop a reputation for effective and tough enforcement of its IP.

If you sell something to someone, and they don't like how it works, often you can arrange to have them return it, and you can offer it again. This is not the case with IP; once a seller has revealed an idea to a buyer, the seller can't take it back. Buyers, however, can have a hard time establishing even a basic understanding of the value of the IP they are buying.

At a fundamental level, IP entrepreneurs are in the business of selling ideas. Ideas differ from other products in some fundamental ways. First, a buyer of an idea is not able to assess how good the idea is—that is, its quality—without actually seeing (and as a result, knowing!) the idea. This type of information asymmetry between buyers and sellers does happen in other markets; however, those settings offer remedies not available for ideas. For example, consider buying a used phone from a friend or acquaintance. It is hard to know if the phone works properly without using it for a while. To buy a used phone without trying it, you would really have to trust what the seller is telling you about the phone or have a way of returning it if it does not work as promised. Unlike phones, trust can work to sell ideas, but returns cannot happen. Once you have disclosed an idea to a buyer, they know it. There are no take backs. As a result, buyers are often unwilling to pay the full value for an undisclosed idea; they simply have no way of verifying the true value of the idea or returning it if the value was overstated.

The second difference between ideas and other products that makes selling them even more challenging is that ideas are what economists call a non-rival good. That means that my consumption of an idea does not physically prevent your consumption of it. We both can use and build on the idea. Taken with the inability of buyers to assess an undisclosed idea's quality, this presents a difficult situation for idea sellers. If you are an idea seller, you may want to disclose a good idea to show that it is, in fact, good. But for this to work you must give the buyer the option to choose whether to buy it or not once you have disclosed the idea. However, what is stopping an unscrupulous buyer from simply claiming the idea is not good while continuing to use the idea themselves (with no intention of paying you)? This disclosure problem means that in selling IP, you either (1) disclose the idea and risk someone taking or otherwise expropriating the idea and not paying you for it or (2) do not disclose the idea before you sell it. In the latter case, the buyer will scale down their willingness to pay for it, because they are unsure of the idea's quality.

9.2 The Tools of IP Strategy

The fundamental challenge in implementing an IP strategy is managing the disclosure problem. Fortunately, governments realized these issues long ago and have developed some important legal protections during the past two centuries that help entrepreneurs protect their ideas.

PATENTS, COPYRIGHTS, AND TRADE SECRETS

The first set of tools are *formal laws of intellectual property protection* (see **Table 9.1**) designed to prevent use of ideas commercially without the permission of the original inventor or creator. In particular:

- **Patents** give inventors the right to exclude the use of ideas by others.
- **Copyrights** give creators the right to exclude others from making copies of the original idea.
- **Trade secrets** are designed to allow inventors to disclose ideas to partners and employees and prevent them from disclosing them to others.

TABLE 9.1 Overview of Formal Intellectual Property Protections

	REQUIREMENTS	RIGHTS	EXAMPLES
Patents *Inventions*	In order to obtain a patent, an inventor must submit an application with the government patent office demonstrating that the proposed invention is *novel*, *non-obvious*, and *useful*. The application must disclose the necessary details to put the invention into practice and not simply outline the broad idea. There are three patent types: • ***Utility patent***: This is by far the most common type of patent. It is used for a new and useful process, machine, article of manufacture, or composition of matter, or any new and useful improvement thereof. • ***Design patent***: Used for a new, original, and ornamental design for an article of manufacture. • ***Plant patent***: Used for a newly identified or discovered and asexually reproduced distinct variety of plant. If the patent is granted, the details of the invention are disclosed and become public record. Patent protection must be applied for in each country, though treaties exist to ease the filing burden.	A patent grants the right to *exclude* others from making, using, offering for sale, or selling the invention within the country or importing into the country. Others seeking to do so must obtain a license from the patent holder. Patent protection is for a finite period of time, which is 20 years in the United States. Importantly, patent protection does not grant the right to make, use, offer for sale, or sell the invention. *Freedom to Operate (FTO)* analysis is necessary to ensure that the final product or service can be made and sold without infringing on the patents of others. In such cases, a license is needed.	Patent 3,789,409 "Navigation system using satellites and passive ranging techniques" (GPS navigation)
Copyrights *Original works*	Unlike patent protection, copyright protection is automatically granted upon the creation of a fixed (permanent), original work of authorship stored in a tangible medium (e.g., new painting on a canvas, new song recorded). Copyright includes both published or unpublished materials, including literary, dramatic, musical, artistic, and certain other intellectual works. Although registration with the government copyright office is voluntary, registration offers authors enhanced protections should they seek to enforce their rights in a court of law. Once registered, the work becomes part of the public record. Most countries recognize copyright protections granted in other countries.	A copyright provides the holder exclusive right to reproduce the copyrighted work as well as prepare derivative works, distribute copies, perform publicly, or display publicly. Those seeking to do so must seek permission from the copyright holder. Copyright protection is for a finite period of time, generally the author's lifetime plus 70 years in the United States. Expired works enter the public domain and may be used freely. The *Fair Use* doctrine allows for unlicensed use of copyrighted-protected works in a set of specific, non-commercial use cases, including for criticism, news reporting, teaching, and research.	*Harry Potter* series (books and films)
Trade secrets *Techniques*	Trade secrecy protection allows businesses to protect valuable proprietary information from being disclosed. The information may include a formula, pattern, device, method, technique, or process. For a business to claim trade secret protection, the information must be: • not generally known or readily derived; • commercially valuable because of its secrecy; and • protected by reasonable efforts on the part of the firm to maintain its secrecy. In contrast to both patent and copyright protection, trade secrecy (as the name implies) favors secrecy over public disclosure.	A trade secret is protected against unauthorized commercial disclosure. Lawyers may assist a venture in protecting the secret and preventing disclosure (e.g., when an employee leaves the firm). Unlike patent and copyright protections, trade secrecy protection does not expire. However, if the information is independently derived or accidently or otherwise disclosed, the protection is lost.	Coca-Cola's formula Google's search algorithm

SOURCES: "Learning and Resources," U.S. Patent and Trademark Office, accessed June 13, 2013, https://www.uspto.gov/patents-getting-started/general-information-concerning-patents; and Copyright, U.S. Government Copyright Office, accessed June 13, 2013, https://www.copyright.gov.

Each of these is designed to prevent people from taking or expropriating an idea being disclosed to them. Trade secrets allow ideas to be disclosed to employees and partners while also restraining them from taking those ideas elsewhere. Patents and copyrights allow entrepreneurs to disclose ideas to would-be buyers so that the buyers can evaluate their quality and the entrepreneurs have at least some legal recourse if no payment is received (see **Using the Research: Rolling the Dice** on p. 258). In other words, the goal of such protection is to make transactions involving ideas work more like transactions on other goods.

TRUST: TRADEMARKS AND BRANDS

The second set of tools to protect IP is designed to promote trust. A good example of this is a **trademark**—a word, phrase, symbol, and/or design that identifies and distinguishes the source of the goods of one party from those of others.[6] Trademark protection can be granted by the government, but it also comes automatically with first and continual use of the mark. It includes protection for identifying aspects of your product, like its *brand,* that establish important parts of your company's identity to the market (see the sidebar on **Most Valuable Brand Names** and **Table 9.2**).

Trademark protection allows inventors and sellers to protect their name from being used by others. Building a reputation for selling high-quality goods involves many consumers having experience with a seller and communicating their trust in some manner. However, once that is done, other sellers may want to disguise themselves as the trusted seller to profit from the established brand's good name (for instance, selling low-quality, fake Nike sneakers). If this is possible, it erodes sellers' incentives to develop that reputation in the first place. Trademarks allow sellers to protect their name and prevent its use by others. In the process, it helps protect their reputation and investments in trust. For idea sellers, like Dolby, this reputation means they can sell ideas prior to disclosing them to buyers. Similarly, in the early days of personal computing, Intel developed its brand by building trust not only with electronic manufacturers but also with end users. Their "Intel Inside" campaign and logo (**Figure 9.2**) contributed to ongoing demand for their products and has been called "one of the most successful branding campaigns in history."[7]

However, just like a patent or copyright, the strength of the tool comes from the ability of the owner to credibly claim they will sue. PayPal, owner of the popular Venmo payment app, was quick to sue start-up loan app Lenmo for trademark infringement, citing "obvious imitation" and an attempt to deceive customers.[8] PayPal's action was likely not only intended to prevent this attempt to leverage its name and reputation for gain (and potentially hurt customers) but also to send a signal to other would-be infringers.

As such, founding teams should take care that their name and trademark are not infringing on others' rights before beginning to sell and build their own reputation. Beyond a simple test of considering other brands in similar product spaces and the likelihood of confusion for customers, entrepreneurs should also conduct a search of the records of the Patent and Trademark Office. In many countries, this is available online. It is at uspto.gov in the United States and the Intellectual Property Office website at Canada.ca. By preemptively warding off

Most Valuable Brand Names. The reputation and trust a brand builds over time can generate considerable value to an organization. The brand name signals the quality and experience customers *and* potential partners expect from the organization. A strong brand can facilitate purchasing decisions, pricing power, and partnership agreements. According to a ranking by *Forbes,* the following firms had some of the most valuable brands in the world in 2022, with Apple's brand leading the list.

TABLE 9.2 **Top 20 Most Valuable Brands in 2022**

RANK	BRAND	BRAND VALUE (IN BILLIONS)
1	Apple	$241.2
2	Google	207.5
3	Microsoft	162.9
4	Amazon	135.4
5	Facebook	70.3
6	Coca-Cola	64.4
7	Disney	61.3
8	Samsung	50.4
9	Louis Vuitton	47.2
10	McDonald's	46.1
11	Toyota	41.5
12	Intel	39.5
13	Nike	39.1
14	AT&T	37.3
15	Cisco	36.0
16	Oracle	35.7
17	Verizon	32.3
18	Visa	31.8
19	Walmart	29.5
20	GE	29.5

SOURCE: Marty Swant, "The World's 20 Most Valuable Brands," *Forbes*, accessed June 13, 2023, https://www.forbes.com/powerful-brands/list.

potential confusion and infringement, entrepreneurs can avoid headaches once their venture has successfully built its own name and reputation.

LICENSING AGREEMENTS AND BEYOND

By selling ideas it owns, an IP start-up creates value by finding firms with complementary assets that, when paired with the idea, will solve a customer need. Ultimately, ideas do not create value on their own and need to be embodied in products, distributed in often well-established networks, and then marketed to reach a wide audience. IP start-ups often look for appropriate existing firms with those assets that could create new products with the start-up's IP. By licensing an idea to established firms, entrepreneurs can find a path to market that does

FIGURE 9.2 **Intel Inside**

For several decades, the slogan "Intel Inside" (shown here on a 2020 Lenovo laptop) became synonymous with the quality and performance of the computer a customer was buying.

Rolling the Dice: The Probabilistic Nature of Patents

It is not uncommon for entrepreneurs, particularly first-time entrepreneurs, to view intellectual property rights as either granted or not. And, if granted, for those rights to possess near-mythical levels of power in securing a monopoly or, at the very least, a significant competitive advantage for their invention. However, this view overlooks the details of the intellectual property system and may leave the entrepreneur at a significant disadvantage when they attempt to use their patent's protections against competitors or others infringing on their invention.

Recent research in economics and law views patents not as discrete and well-defined but as *probabilistic*

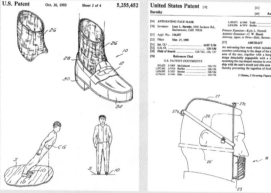

Each year hundreds of thousands of patents are filed, from the off-beat to the gravity defying. However, the strength of any patent is not known until it is tested.

property rights. The research shows that for the hundreds of thousands of patent applications filed each year, there is uncertainty over whether the patent will be granted, and, if granted, uncertainty about the patent scope (i.e., how much of the invention will be covered by the patent), the time to patent grant, and, finally, the enforceability of the issued patent itself. This means that even for an issued patent, the strength (and scope) of patent protections are not entirely known until tested. Though inventors may have some sense of the degree, or probability, that the patent will hold, they are unlikely to know the true strength of their protections until they attempt to deploy those protections.

While most committed applicants eventually receive a patent (upward of 90%), only a small percent of those are ultimately commercially valuable—few patents are ever included in any infringement lawsuits (less than 2%) and only a tiny fraction ever reach trial judgment (only 0.1%). However, of those patents litigated (likely the most economically important), a sizable proportion are found to be fully or partially invalid (up to 50% at the appeals court level) and, as a result, the value of the patent disappears entirely or is markedly reduced. It is a catch-22: to enforce the rights of the patent, one must be prepared to roll the dice that the patent rights might be taken back or considerably diminished.

What does this mean for entrepreneurs? It means the value of a patent depends on whether the entrepreneur can credibly claim that they will sue (if licensing negotiations break down) *and* that their patent will be upheld at trial or even on appeal. This requires making early investments to develop a strong IP strategy and build IP assets and capabilities. For instance, entrepreneurs should select their IP lawyers carefully and proactively work with them to diligently draft their patent(s) and build a portfolio of patents around key technologies and inventions. If one patent is invalidated, the others may continue to protect the invention.

SOURCE: Mark A. Lemley and Carl Shapiro, "Probabilistic Patents," *Journal of Economic Perspectives* 19, no. 2 (2005): 75-98, https://pubs.aeaweb.org/doi/pdf/10.1257/0895330054048650.

not require building up those complementary assets while also choosing not to compete with those established firms.

Licensing agreements tend to come in two forms, **fixed fee** and **price plus percent**. The optimal licensing contract for an invention depends on a number of criteria, in particular (1) the clarity of the market value of the invention (specifically, how it relates to the final product), (2) whether the license is exclusive, and (3) the financial constraints and relative bargaining power of both the patent holder (the licensor) and firm seeking to license the technology (the licensee).

In a *fixed fee* licensing arrangement, the contract specifies a set amount the licensee will pay the patent holder, either as an up-front payment or in a predetermined payment schedule, to license the patent. This contract type has the benefit of providing a reliable cash stream; however, it may limit the entrepreneur's ability to capture additional returns if the patent application is particularly successful. For instance, the potential value of a patent related to a prospective pharmaceutical treatment has a wide variance. If the science pays off, it may be worth hundreds of millions; however, if the treatment fails in clinical trials, the patent may have limited to no value. Licensing the invention at an early stage may allow a small biotech to focus on further research while a larger pharmaceutical company (with experience) takes the drug through clinical trials. A fixed fee licensing arrangement would provide up-front cash to the biotech but provide no additional upside should the treatment prove medically and commercially successful. However, by separating the contract from the outcome, the biotech's cash flow is not tied to the decisions of others or delayed for years as the treatment moves through clinical trials.

By contrast, in a *price-plus-percent* licensing arrangement, the biotech company would share in the ultimate market success of the commercial application of its licensed invention. In a price-plus-percent contract, the licensee pays both an up-front fee (the price) plus a percentage of future sales. This approach can be risky; perhaps the pharmaceutical company cannot bring the drug to market. It also requires a far more detailed set of contract terms (e.g., how sales will be measured, when payments will be made) and an ongoing relationship between the parties. However, for those products or services where the licensed invention is a significant proportion of the value of the final good or service, this approach can generate substantial rewards for the venture if entrepreneurs are patient.

Licensing isn't just about pricing terms. Licenses can lead to alliances that greatly improve a start-up's ability to develop its innovations. This was shown to be the case in economist Gary Pisano's seminal studies of the biotechnology industry.[9] An instructive case was his analysis of the initial strategy of Millennium Pharmaceuticals. Millennium was founded in 1993 by Mark Levin, a chemical engineer. Levin had previously worked for the legendary biotechnology firm Genentech and had a brief stint in biotechnology venture capital. The Human Genome Project had just begun, and Levin, along with geneticist Raju Kucherlapati, believed that it would eventually open up significant commercial potential. Namely, the two believed they could revolutionize the process of drug discovery that was, until that point, largely random. They felt that if obtaining a genetic road map could be made systematic, this would greatly improve the predictability and speed of identifying genes that would be suitable drug targets. In the long run, using genomics in this way could lead to personalized drugs

fixed fee A licensing agreement that specifies a set amount the licensee will pay the patent holder, either as an up-front payment or in a predetermined payment schedule

price plus percent A licensing agreement in which the licensee pays both an up-front fee (the price) plus a percentage of future sales

FIGURE 9.3 Mapping the Human Genome

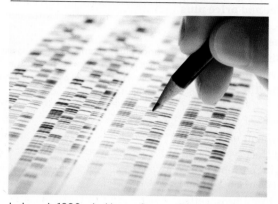

In the early 1990s, the Human Genome Project started to create maps of genetic sequences. The Millennium team believed they could apply their experience and research to help companies find the best targets for new and more personalized pharmaceuticals.

tailored to maximize a treatment's outcome while minimizing symptoms for individuals (**Figure 9.3**).

To get started, Millennium assembled a star team of researchers in this emerging field and began looking for potential pharmaceutical partners for funding. Exploiting their knowledge from the Human Genome Project, the team planned to identify new drug targets—disease-causing genes—that aligned with the portfolios of these pharmaceutical companies. These drug targets, the information assets, would be Millennium's initial product. Soon after, Millennium found its first partner, Roche, a company interested in finding targets in two disease categories: obesity and Type II diabetes. These were areas where the potential demand for a treatment was known to be large and where Millennium's team already had considerable expertise. Roche funded Millennium's research with $70 million over five years, contracting with it to focus on identifying small molecules for those disease categories.[10] A key term to this plan was Millennium only selling the knowledge for those categories to Roche while retaining the rights to explore targets in other areas. That agreement was one of the biggest, most significant biotech alliance deals at the time, and Millennium took up-front cash rather than the promise of a future stream of revenues common to other biotech alliances.[11]

9.3 The Four Choices That Shape an Intellectual Property Strategy

In most cases, a successful scenario for an intellectual property strategy is what occurred between Millennium and Roche: an established firm makes a significant payment for access to the idea (exclusive or otherwise). This leaves the entrepreneur free to reinvest and produce IP they can market to other established firms. Simply put, an IP strategy rests on the premise that the start-up can specialize and focus on innovation while leveraging the resources and capabilities of partners to fully commercialize their ideas.[12] For an IP strategy, how should an entrepreneur set the four key choices—customer, technology, competition, and organization—to maximize their probability of success?

CHOOSING YOUR CUSTOMER

An important starting point for an intellectual property strategy is the entrepreneur's choice of **customer**. IP strategy is unique in that, to implement it, an entrepreneur needs to know who their customer is on two levels: (1) Who are the final, end customers who will gain value from their idea? and (2) Who are the established firms serving those end customers that are willing to pay in order to provide that defined value?

This process of identifying these two customers is in some sense the primary criteria. For Dolby, it was obvious that its technology needed to be embedded

customer (IP strategy) Customer considerations for the IP strategy include determining who the final end customers are who will gain value from the idea and who the established firms are that are willing to pay to provide that defined value

260   Chapter 9: Intellectual Property Strategy

in devices to succeed, so it needed to target the companies that built them. For Millennium, like many biotechnology ventures, its licensees would be established pharmaceutical companies that possessed the resources to transform the idea into marketable products. However, even there, Millennium made a key strategic choice to target specific therapeutic categories *within* pharmaceutical companies rather than making deals with the entire company. Its customers were thus divisions within companies and the separate budgets controlled by their division heads. This left Millennium free to negotiate deals to use its technology with divisions within other pharmaceutical companies.

In many respects, finding that first customer is the experiment being undertaken by an intellectual property strategy (see **Mini Case: Bluefin Labs**).

Failure to find that first licensee would indicate that the technology is not easily transferable or perhaps the value created for end consumers is not of significant enough value. Thus, this would imply the idea might have to be developed further or perhaps deployed using a different strategy.

CHOOSING YOUR TECHNOLOGY

Given that an IP strategy is predicated on finding a customer with the ability and incentive to integrate your idea into its own products, the choice of **technology** must permit a seamless integration. That is, the technologies should be general components that fit in easily with technologies used in existing value chains. An ideal technology would be a modular innovation that could be slotted right into an established firm's operations with little to no integration costs. This is essentially what Dolby was able to produce, allowing its noise reduction technology to be added as a component to existing stereo and audio systems.

If the technology is not modular, then to become a salable piece of intellectual property requires the start-up to invest in further development, often to the point where the IP is seen as truly proven. This is the precise challenge Atomwise, a biotech start-up founded by Abraham Heifets, is facing. Like Millennium, Atomwise's business plan uses know-how, this time from supercomputers and a proprietary algorithm, to try to expedite the drug discovery process by narrowing down the field of possible drug candidates. However, Atomwise requires potential licensees to provide large quantities of data to first train its algorithm. So far, it has had to train and prove out its software using only data obtained through non-financial partnerships with local hospitals, hoping this will lead to deals with pharmaceutical companies.

A similar pattern can be seen in the choices made by screenwriters in developing movie ideas. While not considered high tech, movie idea development is

Bluefin Labs: Product Focus and Its First Customer

Social TV analytics start-up Bluefin Labs was founded in 2008 by MIT professor Deb Roy and PhD student Michael Fleischman. The company was created as Twitter and other social media companies took off and rapidly gained popularity, which drove the complementary rise of a host of social media analytics companies. Bluefin Labs was one of these, though it was distinctive in focusing its advanced technology for measuring "sentiment" expressed specifically by television viewers within Twitter and other social media platforms. In a nutshell, it measured discussions about TV that were taking place on these platforms, in a way that was particularly useful for improving the purchasing behavior of TV advertising buyers (the customers of TV networks). Therefore, it was a powerful tool in the arsenal of TV network media placement sellers too.

Roy and Fleischman's choice to focus on this single problem was crucial for establishing licensing contracts with TV networks. It also attracted the attention of Twitter itself, which acquired Bluefin in early 2013 for approximately $90 million and appointed Deb Roy as the chief media scientist of Twitter.

Bluefin created value by focusing on the sentiment of a particular market segment, television viewers.

technology (IP strategy) The choice of general components that fit in easily with technologies used in existing value chains

FIGURE 9.4 Movie Spec or Movie Pitch

Ideas for movies can be sold as specs or pitches. *The Hangover* was sold as a pitch.

entrepreneurial in that it is a key input into the development of movies, each one a separate innovation. In this industry, writers have a choice. They can sell an idea to a studio either as a "pitch" involving just the storyline, or a "spec" that provides a complete script. For instance, sold pitches include *Barbie*, *The Wedding Crashers*, and *Mr. and Mrs. Smith*, while sold specs have included *Basic Instinct*, *The Hangover*, and *Don't Worry, Darling* (**Figure 9.4**).[13] From a studio's perspective, it is easier to observe the quality of a spec relative to a pitch, while from the writers' perspective, there is value in locking down a deal as a pitch prior to investing in developing a complete script for a spec.

As it turns out, when writers are of an unknown quantity, they are more likely to sell specs rather than pitches. A known writer is more likely to sell pitches than specs. Research by Professor Hong Luo found that moving from zero writing credits to one or more writing credits increases the chance of a writer selling a spec by 100%.[14] This illustrates another general principle of technology with IP start-ups: those who are new to the industry should look to technologies that are developed (like specs) and whose performance is more proven to be successful (like a writer with at least some track record of success).

CHOOSING YOUR COMPETITION

For an IP start-up, the choice of how to use competition depends on the nature of its intellectual property assets and the dynamics of its potential licensees' industry.

At a basic level, if a start-up has secured a patent or trademark, it controls a tangible product or asset that can be described, licensed, and transferred to others. Founding teams should license this asset exclusively if there are only a few dominant firms in the industry, as these firms will have a high ability and willingness to pay in order to exclude access to competitors[15] and subsequently grow their own market share.[16] In contrast, founders should license more widely if there are a number of firms in the industry, as the ability to pay for exclusivity may be lower than the sum of all the firms' willingness to pay for access.[17] As an example, when Genentech first pioneered synthetic insulin in the 1978 insulin race (see Chapter 8), it licensed the product exclusively to Eli Lilly. Lilly had been intensely investing in bringing commercial insulin to market before its main competitor Novo Industri did.[18]

More recently, another race has been underway to develop and apply the revolutionary CRISPR technology for editing genes, which was invented by Jennifer Doudna and Emmanuelle Charpentier and won them the 2020 Nobel Prize in chemistry. Doudna and another leading CRISPR researcher, Feng Zhang, along with their teams and collaborators, have competed aggressively to advance the science underlying CRISPR technology. Both Doudna and Zhang have also founded start-ups to further develop the innovative technology. Doudna's Caribou Biosciences has been developing a broad range of applications for the tool and has given exclusive licenses to start-up Intellia Therapeutics, global pharmaceutical company Novartis, and international biosciences company DuPont to commercialize applications in distinct markets.[19] In this way, this company is following a similar road map to Genentech's deal with Eli Lilly, focusing its start-up efforts on developing the tool and pairing it with exclusive licenses. In Caribou Biosciences' case, it is trying to accelerate the development, application, and commercialization of the CRISPR gene editing technology across human and animal therapeutics, genomics, agriculture, biological research, and industrial biotechnology.[20] By choosing to cooperate with established market leaders to commercialize its efforts, Caribou Biosciences can focus on developing its revolutionary technology while leveraging the advantages of its partners.

However, if a start-up does not have formal intellectual property protection, is located in a country with relatively weak institutions for enforcement, or operates in an industry with a poor track record of upholding IP, the founding team must take a different approach. First, they should work with established firms known for their focus on the long term and a track record of success in developing new ideas. Firms like these are generally also known for protecting IP. If they do not, IP founders quickly start bringing ideas to competitors.[21] For example, toy companies purchasing new toy ideas could easily take concepts from pitches given by potential inventors (**Figure 9.5**). However, to do so would damage their reputation and reduce the flow of potential toy ideas coming their way. A similar risk appears for movie pitches. If a studio became known for appropriating a pitch, this would deter writers and others pitching to that studio and hurt it in the long run.

Another strategy is trying to develop an innovation that allows an entrepreneur or creator to play licensees off one another. For example, Garth Risk Hallberg's 900-page novel, *City on Fire*, set off a bidding war between 10 publishers for publishing rights. Hallberg, who was an unknown author pitching his debut novel, certainly had a riveting book, but he had also been clever with his strategy. Before even approaching publishers, Hallberg sent his manuscript to award-winning movie producer Scott Rudin, whose known literary tastes aligned with his novel. Rudin ended up optioning the movie rights, which paved the way for Hallberg to pit publishers against each other in a bidding war that gave him a $2 million payout.

Though choosing long-term-oriented licensees and creating a product that multiple firms could want exclusively are strategies that can work, it is safe to say that the absence of IP protection does limit the competitive choices that are part of IP strategy.

FIGURE 9.5 The Annual Toy Fair in New York City

Toy designs can be easy to copy. However, if a toy manufacturer develops a reputation for copying or taking designs, it's unlikely that successful designers will bring their ideas to that company in the future. Pictured here is the annual toy fair held in New York City.

CHOOSING YOUR ORGANIZATION

At its essence, a successful start-up pursuing an IP strategy will become an **ideas factory**: a place where new ideas are conceived and developed to become complementary innovations for established firms. This focus drives the final

ideas factory A place where new ideas are conceived and developed to become complementary innovations for established firms

choice for an intellectual property entrepreneur: how to establish their organization. Building a successful ideas factory means having:

1. people with high capacities for innovation and invention, often achieved by hiring leading researchers and innovators, and
2. people with high negotiating strength, often achieved by hiring IP lawyers and business development personnel.

The returns from an IP strategy critically hinge on how well the entrepreneur exploits established firms to pay for these ideas, firms which could already be either current or potential competitors. To do so, the entrepreneur needs an external presence with a reputation for tough dealmaking. Early on, Millennium Pharmaceuticals made investments in its business development personnel so it could negotiate effectively with larger pharmaceutical companies. It is also a potential reason why venture capitalists with strong reputations for successful dealmaking are sought after by IP firms and why venture capital funding is frequently connected with IP strategies.[22] With an IP strategy, it is simply better in the marketplace to be feared rather than loved.

Moreover, because the focus of an IP strategy is on finding the right established firm partners, the venture is, in a sense, born global. It must choose a location that makes it available to the largest number of potential partners possible. This was reflected in Millennium Pharmaceuticals' choice of location—Cambridge (MA)—to be near a large number of potential pharmaceutical companies that the founders could regularly interact with and try to partner with.

Furthermore, by closely integrating innovative and negotiating capabilities, an IP start-up can maximize its "invention-to-license" cycle. An example of this type of organization is Getty Images, a B2B provider of high-quality images, founded in 1995 by Jonathan Klein and Mark Getty. Getty Images is the leading provider of top-notch images and videos to businesses, specifically for use by advertisers, graphic designers, corporations, publishers, and media companies. It originally housed 30,000 images but now boasts a collection of 80 million, selling to a million customers worldwide. Getty Images' approach has been to grow its collection by acquisition and via a platform that rewards photographers and videographers.

Since its founding, Getty has relied on copyright laws to protect its image assets and has built an active legal team tightly integrated into innovation and strategic decisions. This stops the purchasers of one image from selling or giving away copies to others. Ensuring that this business model actually works requires a deep understanding of existing legal systems and options—not just in the United States but also globally. License terms must be constructed, violations noted and, where appropriate, legal action undertaken. Thus, Getty acquired Israeli company PicScout in 2011 to help it identify the digital fingerprint of its images that appear online, even ones that had been edited, to help protect its IP. In addition, Getty Images' very active legal department often becomes publicly involved in claims against smaller businesses. This is hardly the identity of a socially friendly company, which is precisely the point. The identity chosen with an intellectual property strategy is rarely a friend-making one.

It should be noted that, more so than in other strategies, IP start-up founding teams must be able to handle the potential media and industry scrutiny that comes with enforcing ownership of intellectual property. They need to be comfortable with the fact that sometimes the path to implementing an effective IP strategy is not a particularly friendly one. Nate Myhrvold, for example, is the founder and CEO of Intellectual Ventures (**Figure 9.6**), a firm devoted to acquiring a large portfolio of patents with the goal of licensing them at the same time as aggressively litigating against infringers. Myhrvold and his firm have both come under attack (Peter Thiel labeled the firm a "parasitic tax on the tech industry"[23] and CNET dubbed it the "most hated company in tech"[24]). Despite the heat, being a tough enforcer of its IP has been a core driver of Intellectual Ventures' revenues and growth.

FIGURE 9.6 Nate Myhrvold

Myhrvold's firm Intellectual Ventures is built on aggressive IP acquisition and enforcement.

HOW THE FOUR CHOICES FIT TOGETHER

Let's use **Figure 9.7** (p. 266), which highlights and illustrates a framework of how the choices of an IP strategy work together. Let's go through each choice, using the elements of the Dolby case in the chapter-opening story to provide a real world example.

COMPETITION CHOICE An IP strategy involves both collaboration with established firms and heavy investment in control. In starting his venture, Dolby made an important early decision to license his technology to existing companies and not try to create his own product to compete with them. Of course, he had patented these technologies early on to protect his control of the core ideas.

CUSTOMER CHOICE That collaboration means that value is created when established firms create more value for their existing users. Hence, the IP entrepreneur will want to choose partners (i.e., the venture's customers) whose own customers will benefit the most from the innovations being licensed. In light of this, Dolby first chose end users and listeners of Dolby-recorded products as his end customers. He gave away his technology to people creating recordings so those recordings would benefit from it. When consumers knew this was available, they looked for cassette players that had this technology; Dolby made his money licensing the technology to makers of cassette players having to respond to this demand. But Dolby also required these makers to let him pre-approve how they used his technology, to make sure his partners had similar priorities as he did.

TECHNOLOGY CHOICE Typically, this favors technological choices that appeal to a wide variety of potential partners and so are both general (useful to many established firms) and can slot into the value chain at the component level. This combination of multiple partner options and lower costs for incorporating the technology in existing products assists in putting the IP entrepreneur in a position to capture more value. In Dolby's case, his solution could enhance any established partners' technology in this market. Eventually, the component aspect of this product expanded out of cassette tapes and to many other forms of media.

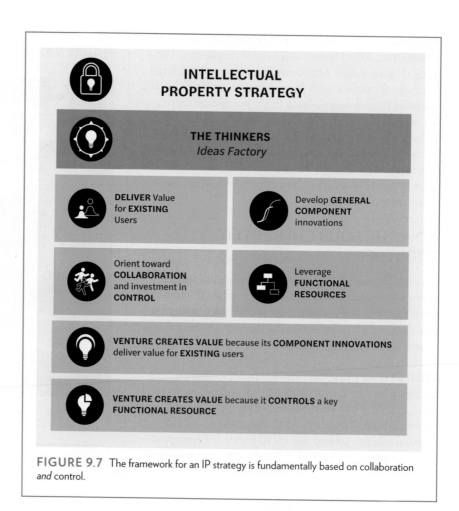

FIGURE 9.7 The framework for an IP strategy is fundamentally based on collaboration *and* control.

ORGANIZATION CHOICE By being part of a value chain rather than operating the whole chain, particular functions are more important than others. This drives an IP entrepreneur to choose an organization that prioritizes those particular functions over having more general, integrated capabilities. Dolby of course focused only on developing his technology and licensing it, and not every other aspect required for consumers to use it. He built an organization based around his IP, rather than trying, for example, to build audio components and sell them through retailers. He left many other parts of this value chain to established players.

9.4 One-Off Opportunities

Thus far, we have mainly highlighted examples of sustained IP start-ups, or ideas factories that continually reinvest in generating new inventions and products for licensing. There is, however, another flavor of IP strategy worth highlighting, one in which an inventor holds a more diminished role in the continued development of the idea. In this case, once the entrepreneur has established their IP, they make the choice to partner or sell, and then the partner or buyer makes the other choices necessary to create a viable product. We saw Lonnie Johnson doing this when he sold his Super Soaker in Chapter 1. Another example is the case of the George Foreman Lean Mean Fat-Reducing Grilling Machine. Despite its namesake, this grill was originally invented by Michael Boehm, who patented the grill's angular design. In the early days, Boehm faced significant challenges in communicating the unique value of the angled grill—a faster cooking time with less fat and grease—to potential manufacturers and customers. After more than a year of failed efforts, Boehm decided the key was to target an individual who was particularly likely to find significant value in the product and would serve as the ultimate reference to mainstream customers. In particular, he recalled that George Foreman, the two-time heavyweight boxing champion and Olympic gold medalist, "ate two burgers before every fight and that he and his sons were all burger freaks" who emphasized a healthy diet as part of their training.[25] After sending an early prototype of the grill to Foreman and his team, Boehm convinced Foreman to serve as spokesperson[26] and combined the two IP assets—the grill patent and George Foreman's trademark—into one overall license. Salton Inc. eventually bought the license and brought the product to market, manufacturing and selling over 150 million units worldwide.[27] Foreman would ultimately earn hundreds of millions of dollars from his successful endorsement and marketing of the grill—many times more than he had earned from his boxing career.[28] After striking the original deal, Boehm had almost zero involvement with his Lean Mean Fat-Reducing Grilling Machine and returned to his career as a serial inventor.

Inventor Michael Boehm partnered with George Foreman to create an IP asset that was incredibly valuable, the George Foreman Grill.

Boehm's case, juxtaposed with that of our earlier examples of Dolby, Millennium, and Getty Images, among others, illustrates how IP strategy in action can actually take on two distinct forms. On the one hand, it can take on an ideas factory model of continually developing new innovations through the reinvestment of licensing revenues in growing internal inventive capacity. On the other hand, it can be a simpler plan like that of Boehm's—taking an idea, developing it to some transferable stage, and then ceding control of the idea entirely by selling it to downstream firms that take the venture from there. As entrepreneurs think about IP, they should consider the type of company and career they aspire to build. In both situations, the path toward implementing an IP strategy involves careful planning and a clear understanding of how they intend to create and capture value, their four choices, and how they will test their underlying hypotheses.

9.5 Putting IP Strategy to the Test

After you have made and clearly articulated your choices, it's time to test them. For IP strategy start-ups, the ultimate test of your hypotheses is whether (a) you can find a downstream firm to be a potential partner or licensee (i.e., your innovation creates sufficient value for them) and (b) you can find a contractual arrangement with that firm that pays you a sufficient return (i.e., you can capture sufficient value).

FIGURE 9.8 LiquiGlide

With limited resources, Liqui-Glide chose to test its chances of success by focusing on food processing and packaging only. LiquiGlide is now used in Colgate Elixir toothpaste, making the product more sustainable because consumers can use "the last drop."

AN IP STRATEGY'S VALUE CREATION HYPOTHESIS

For an IP strategy, the value creation hypothesis is that value will be created because the start-up's component innovations will deliver value for existing users. More broadly, start-up teams must grasp how the existing value chain functions and develop a plan for how their innovation might fit in and enhance its overall value. IP start-up teams must develop, at a relatively early stage of their venture, a clear sense of how they will create meaningful value for a well-defined group of final customers. Then, they need to make their choices and commitments with that customer group in mind.

Consider Dave Smith, who during his PhD research developed an algorithm that generated hundreds of liquid-solid combinations for new self-lubricating coatings. When he launched his start-up, LiquiGlide, Smith had limited resources and needed to identify which element of his idea he should patent first. Forced to carefully consider how LiquiGlide would create value, he hypothesized that end consumers of "sticky" foods such as peanut butter, ketchup, and honey would value a non-stick-packaging experience. Furthermore, his hypothesis was that LiquiGlide's coating technology could be relatively easily incorporated into existing food-packaging processes (**Figure 9.8**).[29] Thus, Smith invested in securing a patent over "self-lubricating surfaces for food packaging and food processing equipment."[30] In doing so, he decided not to invest time and resources as intensively toward other substances where the application seemed less clear, or where entry was more complex.

TESTING VALUE CREATION: WHO WILL PARTNER WITH YOU?

The first step in testing value creation is to identify potential licensees/partners and their requirements. This information-gathering process is not precise but starts with creating a list of potential partners. You can build this list using sources such as industry connections, insider knowledge, surveys, conference participation, and general marketing research.

For each potential partner, you should be able to articulate how your idea (and with what level of further development by you) would create value for that potential licensee or partner specifically. You should also look for public or connected network knowledge of comparable licensing deals and information about litigation involving these potential partners. The best partners will show signs of allowing flexible growth rather than of sticking more to the letter of contracts.

Further, you will likely need to gather more information on potential partners' customers and industry as well as details regarding their current business and long-term strategy. Interviewing customers, attending trade shows, and otherwise engaging their stakeholders can provide further insight into how you might best create value for them and how to frame the way your technologies will fit in with their existing systems.

Finally, you need to gather information on the likelihood of potential partners reaching a commercially attractive arrangement with you. To do so, continue to pursue public knowledge about the partner, especially around any comparable licensing or other IP deals. Look for evidence of litigation and examine it. Ask contacts in the industry, including other customers or partners in that space. You want to use all information available to determine whether they will be good partners. In some cases, companies will have developed a reputation for being a fair partner—this is something that Cisco Systems is known for.

ONE CAUTIONARY TALE, AND TWO SUCCESSES

The value of carefully considering the prospects you might work with can be illustrated by the case of deCODE Genetics, founded by Icelandic scientist Kári Stefánsson in the 1990s. Stefánsson had the idea to use Iceland's limited gene pool as a genomics resource to identify genes that were associated with certain diseases (**Figure 9.9**). However, rather than identifying and prioritizing potential licensees and exploring their disease interests, deCODE focused initial resources on sorting out the regulatory issues around unlocking Icelanders' genetic information.[31] After spending much time navigating Iceland's constitution and political dynamics, deCODE was able to create a genetic database of Icelandic people. But identifying these genes did not in itself reveal treatments or blockbuster drugs. deCODE was unable to find a customer interested in licensing its intellectual property. In 2010, having burned through $600 million of capital, deCODE declared bankruptcy and later was quietly brought into Amgen.

deCODE demonstrates the importance of clearly identifying what value existing firms may gain from access to your intellectual property and to marshal resources to that end. The activities of deCODE, while scientifically successful, were not focused sufficiently on value creation to find a sustainable model for long-term success.

When entrepreneurs do undertake appropriate due diligence, the result can be markedly different. Millennium did this when carefully selecting an initial partner. It put together a star team of researchers and found an initial partner in Roche, an established pharmaceutical firm, which provided funding and was an early customer for Millennium. This approach allowed Millennium to test the value creation hypothesis for its IP strategy, which was to discover whether other targeted firms also saw the potential in taking an idea and using it to build out new products. To do so, Millennium would have to build a brand and expertise, and then see if other partners were interested in taking on the subsequent risks.

In the case of Millennium, the timing was right. Genomics was receiving significant public investment and was in the beginning of its technological development. Pharmaceutical firms wanted to be at the forefront of that development to reinvigorate their processes of drug discovery. Failure to do so might leave these firms far behind in any races to find treatments and secure valuable patents on drugs themselves. Ultimately, Millennium succeeded in

FIGURE 9.9 deCODE and Iceland

The company deCODE tried to harness the unique opportunity of studying the genes of the population of Iceland, a community tightly connected genetically because of its geography. Unfortunately, while deCODE created a useful resource, it could not harness its commercial potential.

building 20 of these alliances in its first few years and gathering more than $2 billion of funding.[32]

In another famous example, when Microsoft's founder, Bill Gates, was negotiating a contract with IBM for the development of MS-DOS for its new PC products, he was only offered lump-sum payments from IBM. But Gates learned that IBM was not interested in ownership of the software, and rather than asking IBM for an additional royalty on each copy sold, he asked to be able to license MS-DOS to other manufacturers. This turned out to be critical for Microsoft. It was able to broadly license its software to other manufacturers, becoming the de facto operating system standard for all personal computers.[33]

AN IP STRATEGY'S VALUE CAPTURE HYPOTHESIS

But a solid value creation hypothesis, while necessary, is not sufficient. IP strategy founders also need to articulate a theory of how they intend to capture part of the value that they are creating. *For an IP strategy, a venture will capture value because it controls a key function resource*—that is, an intellectual property asset including patents, trademarks, or copyrights. That control is the means by which founding teams intend to secure enough bargaining power to extract rents even after disclosing their idea during licensing negotiations. More specifically, it is that control that they intend to use to prevent well-resourced existing firms from taking their idea without payment.

In many cases, an idea will be able to create value but not secure revenues from the perspective of an IP entrepreneur. At one extreme, merely disclosing an idea to a well-resourced downstream firm may permit the firm to threaten or actually take the idea without payment. Moreover, by construction, non-disclosure is not an option in an intellectual property strategy, as any would-be purchaser must have a strong signal as to the idea's quality. Consequently, an IP entrepreneur must have a notion of the set of instruments and tactics it can employ to prevent such outcomes.

For Millennium Pharmaceuticals, as already noted, it secured a star team in an emerging area and constructed a model whereby that team could be used across many areas, limiting the incentives of any one pharmaceutical company to replicate that team. In addition, it hired key business development personnel and legal advisers to ensure a smooth but strong process of dealmaking. This strategy turned out to be successful, with the Roche deal followed by deals with three more major pharmaceutical companies over the next two years. Each deal earned a higher up-front licensing fee and greater ongoing payments for milestones and even royalty payments for subsequent marketed drugs (see **Figure 9.10**). When it was acquired by a pharmaceutical firm two decades later, Millennium was one of the most successful biotech firms of its generation, worth $8.8 billion.

Millennium Pharmaceuticals illustrates the important emphasis IP strategy founders must place not only on controlling its key intellectual property assets but also on building the capabilities to earn and grow revenues from those assets. This means establishing bargaining power with downstream firms through conscientious investments that build both a strong negotiating team and a reputation for enforcement (e.g., a willingness to defend patents in the face of competitors who may look to infringe or invalidate them).

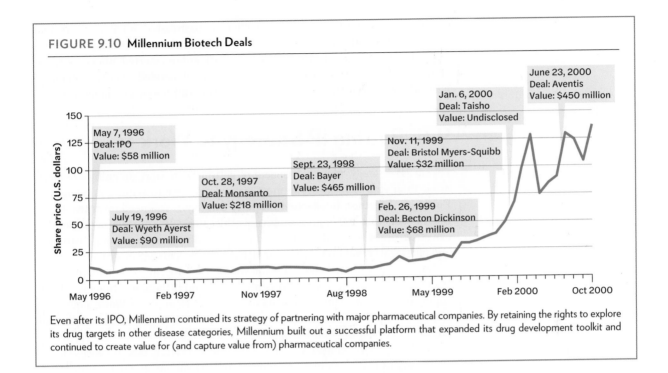

FIGURE 9.10 **Millennium Biotech Deals**

May 7, 1996
Deal: IPO
Value: $58 million

July 19, 1996
Deal: Wyeth Ayerst
Value: $90 million

Oct. 28, 1997
Deal: Monsanto
Value: $218 million

Sept. 23, 1998
Deal: Bayer
Value: $465 million

Feb. 26, 1999
Deal: Becton Dickinson
Value: $68 million

Nov. 11, 1999
Deal: Bristol Myers-Squibb
Value: $32 million

Jan. 6, 2000
Deal: Taisho
Value: Undisclosed

June 23, 2000
Deal: Aventis
Value: $450 million

Even after its IPO, Millennium continued its strategy of partnering with major pharmaceutical companies. By retaining the rights to explore its drug targets in other disease categories, Millennium built out a successful platform that expanded its drug development toolkit and continued to create value for (and capture value from) pharmaceutical companies.

TESTING VALUE CAPTURE: CAN YOU DEFEND YOUR IP?

Testing value capture requires determining what form of intellectual property protection can be obtained for your idea and whether it can be defended in any court proceedings. This includes assessing whether any disclosures you might make in negotiations with potential partners could be subject to effective reverse engineering. Many university technology licensing offices (e.g., the MIT Technology Licensing Office and the University of Toronto Innovation and Partnerships Office at the authors' institutions) provide support for navigating this process. Outside of universities, many law firms specialize in intellectual property, and related commercialization activities within your field may also be a useful resource.

Consider the case of Bob Kearns, whom we encountered in Choosing Your Competition (Chapter 8). Recall that Kearns invented the intermittent windshield wiper in 1962 after being inspired by a rainy-day drive. Kearns, a physics professor with no prior business expertise, developed a working prototype and pitched the concept to Ford Motors. Though he had a patent, Ford ended up reverse-engineering his design and adding the wipers to its latest line of automobiles without paying Kearns.[34] What ensued was over two decades of litigation in court as Kearns tried to capture the value he had created with his invention. It was not until 1995, after $10 million in legal fees and many years of lost time, that Kearns saw a payout of $30 million.[35]

Kearns's case is a clear warning that if you are considering an IP strategy, you must do the research and due diligence on how much control and protection you can receive over your idea, and learn how effective that protection has been in court against violators. For example, Qualcomm invested in patent protection for various key components of cell phones at a time when others believed patents would be of limited protection. Its legal investigations asserted otherwise. Qualcomm built a significant patent portfolio that has generated profits, in an otherwise fiercely competitive hardware market, from cell-phone manufacturers.

9.6 Putting IP Strategy to Work

For an IP strategy, the core aspects of getting your start-up going are clear; other than your core idea, the most critical resource to acquire is talent (see **Putting It Together: Intellectual Property Strategy**). You need inventive talent that can generate and improve upon novel ideas as well as negotiating talent that can structure strategic deals, understand the evolving needs of your customers, and take legal action to enforce your IP if necessary. This will often translate into an important locational choice for the start-up, identifying where talent may be readily available, where labor costs are lower, and if these locations will likely supply potential new hires for years to come. For example, D-Wave, a quantum computing start-up founded by Geordie Rose, needed to build a team of quantum physicists, computer scientists, and mechanical engineers. Rose ended up basing the company in Vancouver, Canada, where he had strong ties and access to the University of British Columbia's physics and astronomy graduate students. As this venture was located in Canada, Rose also qualified for lucrative tax incentives to hire Canadian researchers and engineers,[36] and he faced limited competition for this top talent.[37] By locating near pools of appropriate personnel, Rose could build an initial team and then have access to a long-term pool of scientific and engineering talent on an ongoing basis.

Another related consideration for IP start-ups is where the existing, potential partner firms and their end customers are concentrated. Millennium, for example, chose a strategic location right in the heart of Cambridge's Kendall Square, where numerous pharmaceutical companies—its potential licensees—were headquartered. This helped Millennium command a superior bargaining position rather than be tied to only one or two potential customers close by. Easy access to more potential customers also improved the Millennium team's bargaining position in the long run by giving them options and alternatives when negotiating.

INFORMATION GATHERING

Ongoing data collection can help inform whether your hypotheses are or continue to hold true. The central challenge for IP start-up founding teams, however, is that they often will not have a direct channel or relationship with end consumers. Often, your idea is more likely to be integrated into an existing product rather than operating as an independent physical product. Thus, the ability to gather information and evaluate your progress, particularly in validating your value creation hypotheses, will be an ongoing challenge.

For example, we recently advised a start-up that developed a software algorithm that could learn and "predict" consumer preferences, thus allowing online retailers to customize the products they marketed to each consumer. The founders wanted to gather information about how effective their algorithm was in driving conversions, but their customers, the retailers, wanted to control

INTELLECTUAL PROPERTY STRATEGY

A start-up gains control of an idea through intellectual property rights and trades in the "market for ideas."

EVALUATE YOUR FOUNDING TEAM AND PROPOSED BUSINESS MODEL

What Will You Control and Trade in the Market for Ideas?

- Briefly outline the founding team's "unfair" advantage, skills, and passion as they relate to the idea and how these align with the proposed strategy.
- Articulate how your business model will leverage the innovation.

DESCRIBE CUSTOMER, TECHNOLOGY, ORGANIZATION, AND COMPETITION CHOICES

Customer: Deliver Value for Existing Users

- Describe how your idea will enhance value for a range of existing companies and their end users.
- Specify a subset of "final" end users and the established firms serving those customers and describe why the established firms will pay for your product or service.

Competition: Orient toward Collaboration and Invest in Control

- Identify key competitors and how to approach established firms.
- Specify your intellectual property assets and how your venture can establish control of the invention through patents, trademarks, copyrights, or trade secrets.

Technology: Develop General Component Innovations

- Describe how the IP can—or eventually could—be readily integrated into a number of potential partners' existing value chains.
- Evaluate the technology's performance and outline key performance metrics.

Organization: Leverage Functional Resources

- Evaluate your venture's ability to build on the IP. Highlight key hires. Describe the desired culture.

SHARPEN YOUR VALUE CREATION HYPOTHESIS AND VALUE CAPTURE HYPOTHESIS

Create Value with Component Innovations That Deliver Value to Existing Users

- Articulate how your idea would create value for potential licensees or partners.
- Gather information on potential partners' customers and industry, their current business and long-term strategy, and comparable licensing or IP deals.

Capture Value by Controlling Key Functional Resources

- Assess whether necessary disclosures made in negotiations could result in reverse engineering of the idea.
- Research how much control and protection you can have over your idea.

that data and run the backend of the software themselves. In this situation, the founders were faced with a trade-off between the long-term benefits of gathering information to improve their algorithm and the short-term benefits of ceding that control to have satisfied paying customers.

Presented with this potential constraint, IP start-ups need to think carefully about ways they can gather this information, whether by including it in deal terms, investing in testing with end consumers, building a relationship with licensees, designing their product to have a built-in feedback component, or other tactics. The point is that as an IP strategy founder, since you do not have a direct relationship with end consumers, it is especially important for you to think through how you will continue to gather information and test your hypotheses as you grow.

9.7 Concluding Thoughts

In the era of the "lean start-up" where firms pivot to move to what seem to be viable opportunities, start-ups formed around plans to identify, protect, and develop IP have been, in a sense, sidelined. However, for entrepreneurs considering how to turn their idea into a tangible business opportunity, an IP strategy is a viable path—perhaps even more so for those entering developed industries. For example, a study of hundreds of start-ups found that start-up teams entering industries where there were established firms with key complementary assets were 86% more likely to use formal intellectual property protection in their idea.[38]

Chapter 9 Review: Intellectual Property Strategy

CHAPTER TAKEAWAYS

- An intellectual property strategy start-up is focused on control but is oriented toward cooperation with established firms in the industry.

- The value creation hypothesis for an IP strategy is that integrating the start-up's idea or innovation into an established firm's existing products, services, or the value chain will generate value for them.

- The value capture hypothesis for an IP strategy is to have a clear theory about why and how the start-up team can use control over their idea and associated intellectual property assets to extract significant and sustainable revenues from established firms.

- It can be challenging for a start-up to sell its ideas. Ideas differ from other products in a few fundamental ways: First, buyers are unable to carefully assess the quality of the idea without actually learning the idea, and yet, once the buyers know the idea, the seller is neither able to take back the idea nor is the buyer able to return the idea. Second, ideas are non-rival goods, which means that an individual's use of an idea does not prevent others from using the idea themselves. These two features of ideas create the disclosure problem.

- Managing the disclosure problem in an IP strategy requires that inventors must understand and leverage the formal laws of intellectual property protection. Patents, copyrights, and trade secrets prevent employees, partners, and others from expropriating or taking the idea disclosed to them.

- To successfully collaborate with an established firm, an IP start-up should seek licensing agreements with firms that have complementary assets and that can create new products for their existing customers with the start-up's IP.

- The customer choice in an IP strategy is to choose (1) end consumers who will gain value from the idea, and (2) the established firms that serve those end customers and will pay to provide the IP's value to them. Innovators must understand both of these customers.

- The technology choice in an IP strategy should work toward a seamless integration with the system and technologies used on existing value chains. An ideal technology, therefore, should be a modular innovation that could be slotted right into an established firm's operations with limited integration costs.

- The competition choice in an IP strategy is to first control an idea itself by investing in intellectual property assets and then cooperating with incumbent firms. If the start-up can't obtain formal IP protection, it needs to pursue long-term licensees with established partners that have an established reputation for protecting IP.

- The organization choice in an IP strategy is to build capabilities in conceiving and developing ideas that will be complementary innovations for established firms and capabilities for tough dealmaking and intellectual property protection.

KEY TERMS

intellectual property (IP) (p. 251)
intellectual property strategies
   (IP strategies) (p. 252)
patents (p. 255)
copyrights (p. 255)
trade secrets (p. 255)

trademark (p. 256)
fixed fee (p. 259)
price plus percent (p. 259)
customer (IP strategy) (p. 260)
technology (IP strategy) (p. 261)
ideas factory (p. 263)

REVIEW QUESTIONS

1. How does a start-up create and capture value from an intellectual property strategy?

2. What are the main factors that make it difficult to "sell" ideas that have not yet been incorporated into a specific product, service, or platform? Why might buyers be skeptical about purchasing an "idea"? What risks might sellers face if they provide information about their idea to potential buyers?

3. The choice of how to use competition for a start-up pursuing an IP strategy depends on the nature of its intellectual property assets. What is the purpose of intellectual property protection? Define the three types of intellectual property protection and provide an example of when each is used.

4. Patents are a critical tool within an IP strategy. What rights do patents establish for their owners? Does the grant of a patent to a start-up guarantee that the start-up is able to protect its idea? Why or why not?

5. What is the potential value that a start-up may be able to gain from trade secrecy? Why might it be difficult to establish a licensing agreement based on an idea that is protected only through trade secrecy? How might a start-up overcome these challenges?

6. A cooperative licensing agreement between a start-up and established firm can include (among other provisions) a fixed fee plus some form of royalty payments. What is the difference between a fixed fee and royalty payment? Describe each of these types of payments and the differences between them.

7. Start-ups pursuing an intellectual property strategy are encouraged to choose a "final" customer (i.e., the final user of the product or service that leverages the start-up's idea) in order to deliver value to existing users of the partners they work with. What is the logic behind this recommendation?

8. What role does modularity in design or innovation play in facilitating an IP strategy? How does modularity facilitate arm's-length collaborations with established firms?

9. One advantage of an IP strategy is the ability to leverage the resources and capabilities of established firms. What is an example of a resource a start-up might be able to access through a partnership? What is an example of a capability a start-up might be able to leverage through a partnership? Explain why each of these might be important for a start-up, and how they differ from each other.

10. What are the key risks for a start-up in establishing an open-ended alliance with a more established player? Why might a start-up nonetheless initiate such an approach in the earliest stages of its venture?

11. Describe one way to test whether a potential idea can create value through an IP strategy. What are the potential risks and challenges in implementing this entrepreneurial experiment?

12. Some of the most successful IP entrepreneurs are located in the heart of geographic clusters closely related to their innovations (e.g., Silicon Valley for information technology or Cambridge (MA) for biotechnology). Why does location within a cluster facilitate an IP strategy? Are there any risks to locating within a leading cluster?

DISCUSSION QUESTIONS

Answer the following series of questions and scenarios either in class discussions or by writing a short response.

1. Elaine, a graduate student in chemical engineering, has developed a chemical catalyst that might have important applications for semiconductor manufacturing. Along with her faculty adviser, she has been working with staff at the technology licensing office at her university, who are going through the early steps of drafting and filing patent applications to protect her technology. However, Elaine is uncertain about what *else* she should be doing to

implement an IP-oriented strategy to commercialize her innovation. What are three concrete steps you would recommend to Elaine that she could do before leaving graduate school that would allow her to decide whether to launch a venture leveraging her technology? Which one of these three steps would you recommend she do first?

2. While the patent applications that might protect her innovation are still pending (an uncertain process that could take 3–4 years), Elaine is approached at a conference by Babak, a leading researcher in a large semiconductor firm. Babak invites Elaine to give a brown bag seminar at the company to talk about her research and the potential for collaboration. What factors might Elaine consider when choosing whether to accept the invitation? What are the potential benefits of talking with this group, and what are the potential risks? What steps might Elaine take to make it more likely that she can establish a successful partnership that allows her to both create and capture value?

3. Still waiting on the status of her patents and in the early stages of negotiation with Babak's firm for a research alliance, Elaine enters a university "pitch" competition and wins $100,000. Now that it seems like her research may result in a real start-up, she is considering using her prize money to hire her first non-technical employee. What are the key skill sets or capabilities that you would recommend Elaine prioritize in hiring her first employee? What responsibilities or functional activities might she entrust to this employee?

4. Raoul is an undergrad computer science student passionate about soccer and his favorite team, Manchester United. In his free time, he has developed a unique database and analytics that allow for understanding the specific value that players bring in terms of defense (a notoriously difficult area for sports analytics). Raoul has been posting some of the insights from his data and algorithm on social media and has attracted about 10,000 new followers. The media team at the English Premier League (which includes Manchester United) reaches out to see if Raoul would like to develop a collaboration with the league for use by teams, players, and perhaps even fans. As a first step, Raoul would like to conduct primary market research (PMR) so that he can better articulate the type of value he and his algorithm might create (and for whom). What steps might Raoul take to undertake PMR? Which groups should he talk with? What questions should he ask? What hypotheses should he try to validate? Do you believe that it is important for Raoul to undertake detailed PMR before he negotiates an agreement with the Premier League? Why or why not?

5. President Abraham Lincoln once quipped that the patent system "added the fuel of interest to the fire of genius" (and Lincoln was himself the inventor on a patent!). Why do formal intellectual property rights such as patents provide "the fuel of interest" for potential innovators? What are the costs of the patent system in terms of promoting innovation and competition?

6. You are considering whether to apply for a patent on an invention but would like some insight into the patent system. Your friend suggests a challenge: Look at recently issued patents to see the process by which patents are granted, the protections that are obtained, and how that patent fits into the broader intellectual property of the grantee. Specifically, she recommends going to the Official Gazette for Patents of the United States Patent and Trademark Office and looking over recently issued patents from the last

few weeks. To dig in further, she suggests you consider the following three questions for one patent (be sure to review the full text of the patent):

- *Process.* Who invented this technology, and who received the patent? How long did it take to receive the patent? How many examples of "prior art" are cited references in the patent record? Is any "non-patent" prior art cited?

- *Substance.* How much of the invention was disclosed? Do you believe that someone trained in the field (i.e., "the art") of this broad technological area could reverse-engineer based on the patent disclosure? What IP rights were actually received? Can you think of an example where this inventor might be able to sue for patent infringement?

- *IP strategy.* How does this patent fit into the overall patent portfolio of the company? Is this the first patent the company has been issued, or is it part of a portfolio? Do you think this patent would be a credible bargaining chip in the context of negotiations with a potential commercialization partner?

FOR FURTHER READING

Arora, Ashish. "Licensing Tacit Knowledge: Intellectual Property Rights and the Market for Know-How." *Economics of Innovation and New Technology* 4, no. 1 (1995): 41–49.

Arora, Ashish, Andrea Fosfuri, and Alfonso Gambardella. *Markets for Technology: The Economics of Innovation and Corporate Strategy.* Cambridge, MA: MIT Press, 2004.

Arora, Ashish, and Alfonso Gambardella. "The Changing Technology of Technological Change: General and Abstract Knowledge and the Division of Innovative Labour." *Research Policy* 23, no. 5 (1994): 523–32.

Gans, Joshua S., David H. Hsu, and Scott Stern. "The Impact of Uncertain Intellectual Property Rights on the Market for Ideas: Evidence from Patent Grant Delays." *Management Science* 54, no. 5 (2008): 982–97.

Gans, Joshua, and Scott Stern. "Incumbency and R&D Incentives: Licensing the Gale of Creative Destruction." *Journal of Economics and Management Strategy* 9, no. 4 (2000): 485–511.

Gans, Joshua, and Scott Stern. "The Product Market and the 'Market for Ideas': Commercialization Strategies for Technology Entrepreneurs." *Research Policy* 32, no. 2 (2003): 333–50.

Hegde, Deepak, and Hong Luo. "Patent Publication and the Market for Ideas." *Management Science* 64, no. 2 (2018): 652–72.

Hellmann, Thomas. "The Role of Patents for Bridging the Science to Market Gap." *Journal of Economic Behavior and Organization* 63, no. 4 (2007): 624–57.

Luo, Hong. "When to Sell Your Idea: Theory and Evidence from the Movie Industry." *Management Science* 60, no. 12 (2014): 3067–86.

Lonnie Johnson

As introduced at the end of Chapter 1, as a child Lonnie Johnson was a tinkerer growing up in Mobile, Alabama. His mother recalled that he "tore up his sister's baby doll to see what made the eyes close."[a] A scholarship brought him to Tuskegee University in 1969 where he earned mechanical and nuclear engineering degrees. That led to a path that took him to NASA to work on the Galileo mission to Jupiter and then the Mars Observer at the Jet Propulsion Laboratory.

Johnson continued to tinker in his spare time. One of those inventions was an environmentally friendly heat pump that used water rather than Freon, a refrigerant. He used that insight to make a gun—specifically, a water gun. It was the invention that would change the toy industry: the Super Soaker.

About 200 million Super Soakers have been sold throughout the world. But Johnson didn't make them. Instead, he sold the invention to the Larami Corporation. An article in the *New York Times* described that moment as Johnson tried to sell his invention:

> He waited nervously for a meeting with toy executives at Larami, a pink Samsonite suitcase on his lap. Inside the suitcase was a new kind of water gun. Instead of a pistol that piddled out a thin stream, this toy was engineered to spray water dozens of feet. "I had bought a milling machine and made all of the parts myself out of PVC pipe and Plexiglas," Johnson says. . . . Johnson knew that the toy industry could be fickle. "It's like the entertainment industry. You can't predict whether a song is going to be a hit and how everyone will react to it." When he finally stepped into the conference room, Johnson didn't say much. Instead, he opened up his suitcase and pulled out a water gun, with a cartoonish plastic bulb mounted on top, that looked like a prop from "Plan 9 from Outer Space."
>
> "Does it work?" Myung Song, the company president, wanted to know. Johnson pumped the gun and pulled the trigger. Water blasted across the room and splatted against the far wall. There was a stunned silence. "Wow," Song said.[b]

A deal was soon struck in 1989 and the toy itself is now legendary.[c]

The Super Soaker 100 was released in 1990.

Johnson's Super Soakers have generated over $1 billion in sales worldwide. His story is an example of how, despite the salient need for IP start-ups to form well-grounded value creation hypotheses and invest in building value capture capabilities, an IP strategy can be the most scalable strategy for turning an idea into significant, global impact.

Use this scenario and the case above to answer questions 1–3. As part of a college class, a student team developed a smartphone app that integrates with modified water guns to provide an augmented reality gaming experience. Among the different game modes the team created, one that allows participants to "paint" virtual canvases on their phones using their physical water guns and sidewalks has gone viral on campus. Excited about this early success, the team has decided to launch a start-up to commercialize their idea and is seeking your advice.

Questions

1. Drawing on your knowledge of IP strategy and entrepreneur Lonnie Johnson's experience inventing and commercializing popular toys. What choices would you recommend their start-up take to commercialize the innovation?

2. What are the advantages in working with an established firm, such as Johnson did with Larami Corporation?

3. What are the potential hurdles in reaching a collaboration deal?

SOURCE: "Company Profile," Johnson Research and Development, accessed June 13, 2023, http://www.johnsonrd.com/ie/co/coprofile.html.

Reed Hastings, founder of Netflix is shown in 2006 with shelves of DVDs to mail to customers. Hastings wanted to break the cycle of trips to stores to rent and return videos.

ENTREPRENEUR'S DILEMMA Disruptive start-ups face a formidable dilemma. They must enter a market dominated by long-established, incumbent firms with proven capabilities to resist overt competition. A disruptive start-up's path to success requires taking on these incumbents and triggering their defensive actions to defeat competitors, moves that typically worked in the past to squash challengers. Overcoming this opposition means start-ups must have a plan to displace the incumbent with an entry strategy that does not trigger the competitive capabilities that made incumbents successful.

CHAPTER OBJECTIVES

- Describe the tools needed to pursue a disruption strategy
- Characterize how large firms are slow to respond to disruption
- Explain how the four choices (customer, technology, competition, organization) need to work together to take on an incumbent
- Describe the first steps some companies have taken to execute their disruption strategy

10

DISRUPTION STRATEGY

As Reed Hastings tells it, Netflix was born when he was charged a $60 late fee after renting *Apollo 13*. Back in the 1990s, if you wanted to watch a movie at home, on your own schedule, you would go to a store with a lending library of videos and rent a physical copy of a videotape or DVD. Of course, like all libraries, borrowing meant two trips, one there and one back. Hastings wanted to break that cycle, though his initial experiments at doing so were not that different. He first decided to create a new venture with a video lending library that instead used the mail for deliveries and returns. When Netflix started in 1997, you paid a fee for each Netflix rental and late fees applied. But starting with this simple model allowed him to learn about the demand and cost of offering this service through the mail and question ways to improve it. For example, Hastings wondered why Netflix should not have a subscription model that allowed you to have a few DVDs out at the same time. And if that was the case, why should Netflix care if you kept them for a week, two weeks, or months? Instead, why not give the customer the choice of when to send one back to get a different DVD? And if all of those proposals were good ideas, instead of concentrating on blockbuster titles, why not offer a selection of DVDs that was much larger than would fit into a physical store? Could Netflix target the "long tail" of movie watchers, a new and underserved customer segment of movie buffs and cinephiles with a much wider range of tastes than could be satisfied in a typical video store? By targeting this customer, the big video chains would, for that same reason, not see Netflix as an immediate threat.

Hastings decided to try out all these ideas. At an operational level, these strategies were reinforced by the choices of key hires. Netflix made early hires that helped gain access and support from independent movie studios and then built a deep online catalog with their offerings. Netflix also took advantage of

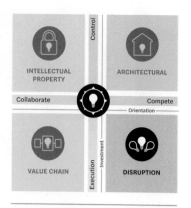

As you will see in section 10.2, Disruption strategies require execution and competition.

disrupter A venture or company that causes fundamental change through innovation, moving into poorly served areas and reinforcing their value to customers through iterative learning

innovation Where new ideas or change are brought to an existing product, idea, or firm; a new product or way of doing something that improves on what was previously available

technological trajectory A technological trajectory is the path of innovation in a specific field; can also be defined as a branch in the evolution of a product or service's technological design

the relatively low bargaining power of independent studios. Other hires helped Netflix develop a collaborative relationship with the United States Postal Service to fulfill customer orders, usually on an overnight basis.

In isolation, any one of these decisions and resource commitments might be questionable. However, taken together, Netflix created a new value delivery system that was very popular with customers and worked exceptionally well as an integrated strategy. This led first to its domination of the DVD rental market and later powered its proactive transition to the new opportunity of online streaming. By making a series of choices reinforcing its disruptive strategy, Netflix did not simply identify a new technology curve ahead of incumbents; it also overcame traditional entry barriers to realize market leadership.

The Netflix story is familiar to many ambitious start-ups: move into areas poorly served by existing players and focus on reinforcing the customer value proposition using iterative experimentation and learning. Simply put, Netflix chose to be a **disrupter**, a venture or company that causes fundamental change through innovation, moving into poorly served areas and reinforcing their value to customers through iterative learning. As we will read in the next section, the consequences of disruptive **innovation**, where new ideas or change is brought to an existing product, idea, or firm, can often be fatal for established firms. Yet, surprisingly, little attention has been paid to what constitutes a disruption *strategy* for a start-up. We will do so in this chapter, including the choices that give the strategy the best chance of realizing value from an idea itself.

10.1 The Origins of Disruption

In Chapter 6, we learned about the S-curve pattern of development with technology and how slow starts often lead to rapid advancements before improvements level off. This S-curve relationship has direct and broad implications for technology strategy and is the basis of studies of the disruption of successful market leaders.

Going back to Joseph Schumpeter (introduced in Chapter 2), economists and other scholars have emphasized the potential role of entrepreneurship in the process of "creative destruction" and how start-ups can leverage new **technological trajectories** to overcome established sources of market power. Recall that these trajectories are single paths or branches in the evolution of a product or service. The technology S curve (**Figure 10.1**) provides a way to visualize that process and better understand the interplay between technological innovation and competitive dynamics. Influential studies of the coevolution of technology and markets across industries by William Abernathy and Jim Utterback emphasize that established firms' power often comes from their leadership and ability to achieve rapid S-curve-shaped advancements with their core technology.[1] But the leadership positions that established firms maintain with a current technology path, or S curve, often come at

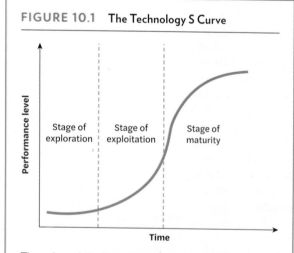

FIGURE 10.1   The Technology S Curve

This relationship shows how technology performance can increase rapidly after initial slow development. Disruptive firms can try to recognize and capitalize on these new opportunities.

the expense of being able to move to a different technology. To take one of many examples, Kodak was founded by in 1888 by George Eastman to commercialize advances in the then-emerging technology of chemical photographic processing. Kodak became the leading company in commercial film and dominated that industry for more than 100 years. However, its strength in this area, in a way, acted as a deterrent to jumping to digital photography. Kodak ceded its leadership as digital technology became the norm and eventually went into bankruptcy.

During the 1990s, scholars Rebecca Henderson and Kim Clark and then Clay Christensen, crystallized this dynamic through several important industry studies. These studies documented both the ability of established firms to innovate *within* a certain technological trajectory and their challenges (and even failure) to transition *across* trajectories. For example, Christensen coined the term "disruptive innovation" in his famous study of the disk drive industry in the 1970s and 1980s (this study led to his even more famous book, *The Innovator's Dilemma*). In this exhaustive study, Christensen documented that, over the course of nearly 20 years, it was start-ups rather than incumbents that were able to pioneer each meaningful format change in disk drives. In particular, this occurred as disk drives became smaller and smaller, shrinking through 14-inch, 8-inch, 5.25-inch, 3.25-inch, and then 2.5-inch drives (**Figure 10.2**). In most of these moves, established firms were not the first to transition, ignoring the next market change because those people were not their customers. Christensen documented how the incumbent firms seemed to be paralyzed by the interplay between organizational resistance and customer dynamics, which slowed them down relative to start-ups able to exercise strategic freedom. Others have noted that because new technologies often had lower performance than existing ones, incumbent firms felt they were making a rational decision by staying with the current technology. With some technologies, incumbents simply did not have the capability to respond to the disruption. Blockbuster, for example, was built on a model around people coming

The Netflix we know today has converted to a completely streaming model, moving on from a key part of its original, disruptive innovation.

This chapter's video showcases how Netflix used a disruption strategy to target underserved customers in the movie rental business.

FIGURE 10.2 Disk Drives

In Clay Christensen's groundbreaking study, disk drive companies in the 1970s, 80s, and 90s could not adapt to product improvements by new competitors. Early free-standing disk drives (left) were replaced by smaller and more integrated disk drives (right), which were later replaced by even smaller versions, and so on.

FIGURE 10.3
Thermostat Innovation

A recent technological disruption has been the move from classic home thermostats (top), a market dominated by Honeywell, to smartphone-enabled ones. Honeywell's slow movement in this market created an opportunity for start-ups like Nest (bottom).

into its stores and renting videos. It simply did not have the systems and capabilities in place to switch to Netflix's subscription modes.[2]

However, the key insight for start-ups is that an emerging technological trajectory may pose a challenge for established firms—and this opens a window of opportunity for a new player. For example, very recently, Honeywell, the established leader in home thermostats with their iconic circular design, was slow to leverage the potential of smart thermostats that could communicate with smartphones. This delay gave Nest an opening to gain a foothold in the market, allowing it to become not only an attractive acquisition target for Google but also a significant competitive player in the smart home industry (**Figure 10.3**).

Of course, a start-up does not have the luxury of looking back from the future to trace out an already existing technological path. Instead, entrepreneurs must choose to engage with an emerging path in advance of key technical breakthroughs or market success. Nest founder Tony Fadell pursued the link between cloud computing and thermostat design well before others placed significant weight on this as a priority area. *Entrepreneurs face real uncertainty about what is technologically feasible, and any number of experts will offer different assessments about what is likely. It is by breaking down this uncertainty in a systematic way that entrepreneurs can take a proactive approach toward choosing their disruptive technology.*

10.2 Creating and Capturing Value with a Disruption Strategy

By definition, a disruption strategy involves a start-up that is focused on *execution* but oriented toward *competition* with established firms in the industry (see Chapter 8 for a review of these concepts).

Some of the most famous examples of disruptive start-ups were low-cost airlines such as Southwest, Ryanair, and Virgin Airlines (see sidebar on **Ryanair**). These airlines offered no-frills but very cheap airline services that loaded on higher fees for checked baggage and seat choice. Some even charged for in-flight toilet access! They also emphasized fast airport turnaround of standardized jets with limited routes to keep costs down. Their targets were incumbent major airlines that had previously thrived behind regulatory barriers to entry that kept prices high. Those incumbents faced challenges as the disruptive entrants targeted their most profitable routes.

The central challenge of a disruption strategy is figuring out how the start-up's idea can deliver value to consumers that are underserved by established firms. At the same time, the strategy must ensure that those established firms do not respond aggressively before the start-up has traction in the market. Further, the value creation hypothesis underlying a disruption strategy is that the start-up's idea leads to the development of system innovations and the discovery of value for new users. Entrepreneurs must clearly articulate why their intended customer is unhappy or unserved by offerings from existing firms and why their idea can be implemented in a way that provides compelling value to one or more groups currently unserved (or poorly served) by those existing firms.

A CONUNDRUM

However, a disruptive start-up must confront a unique conundrum in its value capture hypothesis. Simply put, if the start-up's idea is so good, and its market potential is so large, why won't the established firms respond in a timely fashion? Entrepreneurs must develop a theory for why the established firms will be slow to respond and how they intend to stay ahead when there is a competitive threat.

Importantly, entrepreneurs should avoid a glib analysis that simply assumes that all incumbents cannot respond—the history of potentially disruptive innovations is filled with as many companies that survived disruptive attacks (see **Mini Case: Browser Wars** on p. 286) as incumbents that succumbed to the threat of disruptive innovation (Blockbuster, Bed Bath & Beyond, Kodak, Cisco Webex, Radio Shack, Brookstone, and chains such as Toys "R" Us, JCPenney, and Lord & Taylor). Instead, entrepreneurs should ground their disruptive strategy in an understanding of the particular ways in which the incumbents they face may be disadvantaged in response to their idea. These could include:

- *The potential of cannibalizing existing businesses:* Directly confronting the start-up would jeopardize current revenues from their core customers
- *Organizational inertia:* Incumbents often have significant challenges managing and implementing change across different divisions
- *The incumbent may be skeptical or misperceive the value offered by the disruptive start-up:* Incumbents often have a strong commitment to performance measures that are valued by existing customers but are *not* valued by the emerging customer segment

Ideally, disruptive start-ups base their strategy on attracting niche customers and employing a nascent **technology**. This rising technology is radical enough for established firms to have a hard time reacting to it and is also on a trajectory that could lead to broader market success by integrating with other available products or systems. Nest, for example, ticked all these boxes by using early but developing digital Internet technology, competing against Honeywell's then-analog thermostat system, and linking to smartphone technology that was becoming commonplace.

TWO STEPS

Choosing a disruption strategy involves two steps:

1. *Putting the strategy to the test*
2. *Putting the strategy to work*

In the first step, the start-up team must evaluate the likelihood that their value creation and value capture hypotheses can be satisfied. In other words, how likely is it that directly entering the market, executing and experimenting with their disruptive idea, and exposing this idea to others (particularly incumbents)

Ryanair. Ryanair was one of the original disruptive airlines. Launched in 1985, it first failed when trying to compete directly with incumbent British Airways. It offered low prices but also amenities like business class and a frequent flyer program. In 1990, it changed strategies—slashing its lowest fares to £59 (around $100 at the time) and getting rid of all frills to be a low cost/no frills airline. Two years later it made its first profit.[a]

technology The application of scientific innovation to a product or venture

Browser Wars: How Microsoft Reacted to Netscape

As an undergraduate at the University of Illinois Urbana-Champaign, Marc Andreessen had been part of the team at the National Center for Supercomputing Applications that developed Mosaic, one of the first—and certainly most influential—graphic web browsers. Though hard to imagine now, in the mid-1990s few tech leaders, including Microsoft's Bill Gates, understood the speed and magnitude with which the Internet would transform their industry. However, for others, including Andreessen, Mosaic provided a first clear picture of the commercial potential of the Internet.

Now defunct, Netscape's original web browser was a runaway hit, but Microsoft was able to defend against it with deep pockets and a user base it could leverage to use its response: Internet Explorer.

Heading to California after graduation, 24-year-old Andreessen met James Clark, cofounder of Silicon Graphics, and together they decided to found Netscape to build on Andreessen's earlier work. Recruiting much of the team from Mosaic, Netscape's rise was swift, and its browser, Netscape Navigator, quickly dominated as both a technological and market leader. Growing at a breakneck pace, within the first 16 months the venture would expand to 500 employees, take 70% of the browser market, conduct an IPO at a valuation of $2.7 billion, and fall square in the sights of Microsoft's targets. After an unproductive meeting between the future competitors, which Andreessen famously compared to "a visit by Don Corleone" of *The Godfather* ("I expected to find a bloody computer monitor in my bed the next day"), the full power of Microsoft came for Netscape.[a]

Microsoft used the excitement around the release of its Windows 95 operating system to promote its new competing browser, Internet Explorer. Though technologically inferior to Navigator, Microsoft made Internet Explorer widely available, easily accessible, and free online. By year's end, the two browsers were technologically on par, but only Internet Explorer sat preinstalled on the majority of Windows 95 machines. Microsoft then leveraged its market power (and deep pockets) to persuade online service providers to replace Navigator with Internet Explorer as their preferred browser. For the average web user, the performance and ubiquity of Internet Explorer left little need to search for a different web browser. This marked the end for Netscape. By 1998, only three years after Netscape's IPO, Microsoft controlled the majority of the browser market and America Online (AOL) announced its intention to acquire Netscape. Interestingly, having felled Netscape, Microsoft's Internet Explorer itself was outcompeted by Mozilla's Firefox and Apple's Safari, both of which eventually lost their market share to Google's Chrome, the browser that is dominant today.

will provide sufficient customer feedback and learning? And will the start-up also have time to scale without eliciting a timely or effective responsive from established players?

In the second step, putting a disruptive strategy to work means making and implementing choices to improve the start-up's chances for creating and capturing value. This includes choosing customer groups poorly served by existing firms that will particularly value the innovation and serve as engaged and useful sources for experimentation. It also means leveraging and iterating technology to stay ahead, even as other start-ups and established firms respond. This is the world of the "lean start-up" (introduced in Chapter 4 and expanded upon in Chapter 13), a company built around prioritizing customer feedback and experimentation at the expense of short-term profitability.

To clarify the power of disruptive strategies and identify some of the critical challenges in their scope and implementation, we first take a deeper dive into the nature of their value creation and value capture hypotheses, outline the four choices that underlie a disruption strategy, and then define the methods for putting a disruption strategy to the test and to work.

10.3 The Tools of Disruption Strategy

A key part of a disruption strategy requires identifying and understanding the strengths and weaknesses of incumbents. Ideally, entrepreneurs want to formulate a strategy that initially targets the weaknesses of incumbents and avoids their strengths. Let's spend a moment understanding these.

WHAT TO AVOID: INCUMBENTS' STRENGTHS

An incumbent's strength falls into three categories:

1. ***Incumbents have already invested in and control complementary assets and resources that make it less costly to bring products to market and add value to downstream customers.*** For instance, most successful incumbents have a strong brand name and understand how to market to their customers. A new venture must start from scratch and thus will face difficulties in attracting customers who are already loyal to an incumbent's brand and reputation (see **Mini Case: T.I's Enduring Legacy** on p. 288).
2. ***Incumbents can deploy resources quickly to meet competitive threats.*** An incumbent facing disruptive competition can create new divisions that can compete head-to-head with start-ups that are gaining traction. Incumbents, already operating at scale in the market, can sometimes create viable competitive offerings at just the time a start-up is hoping to quickly and easily capture market share. This can undermine confidence in the start-up's ability to capture, build, and maintain that market share and then obtain outside funding for ongoing scaling activities.
3. ***Incumbents have secured advantages in the past that have given them a favorable position in the industry.*** In some cases, incumbents have a monopoly or near-monopoly position with all of the profits and benefits that flow from that. If entry by a disrupter succeeds, however, they will end up in a situation that is far less attractive. Once an incumbent comes to believe that competitive entry is possible, it has a strong incentive to take preemptive actions that will make that entry difficult, repel the disrupter, and defensively maintain its current position. For entrenched incumbents, their incentives to play defense may be stronger than the incentives for disruptors to try to gain a foothold in the market.

TI's Enduring Legacy

The sustaining market power of Texas Instruments' graphing calculators is baffling to many a student. In an era where the standard smartphone offers much the same functionality and beyond with the addition of countless $0.99 apps, how is the $100+ graphing calculator still a staple of most high school and college math classrooms?

Beaten to the market by nearly five years by Casio and Hewlett-Packard, Texas Instruments introduced their first graphing

The classic TI-83 Plus graphing calculator.

calculator, the TI-81, in 1990 and quickly dominated. Though the TI-81 offered some technological advantages (particularly its software functionality), its emphasis on the needs of educational users allowed it to take and hold the market for over 20 years. Texas Instruments understood that high school and college students wanted portability, robust handling, and ease of use. Moreover, it knew that students typically used what educators used and that educators sought standardization in design (of keyboards and function menus) and companion teaching materials that allowed the technology to enhance, not distract from, learning.

The firm engaged leading high school instructors, including members of the National Council of Teachers of Mathematics, in the design process (leading to clear improvements in the later TI-83 model) and in facilitating the diffusion of the new technology into more classrooms. These early adopters served as both sources of learning and references for the firm, promoting Texas Instruments' teaching materials and newsletters. Texas Instruments would subsequently partner with many of these instructors to develop its own teaching program, T³, which provided training and resources for educators seeking to incorporate graphing calculators into their classroom. It also continued to develop companion products, such as educator versions of their calculators that could be connected to an overhead projector for teaching. Soon, so ubiquitous were Texas Instruments calculators that textbooks defaulted to providing problem solutions with instructions for TI devices (leaving Casio and HP users in search of a manual). Later approval by the College Board for AP and SAT exams hindered entry by new devices, such as smartphones, as students wanted to practice with the device they would use on the "big day."

Though Casio, HP, and later smartphone apps would sometimes supersede the technological capabilities of Texas Instruments' graphing calculators, the relationships, capabilities, and brand Texas Instruments built while engaging and serving the educational community were key complementary assets. They prevented others from dislodging Texas Instruments from the classroom and from its position as market leader.

All three of these advantages can make head-to-head competition against incumbents difficult, costly, and very risky. Thus, the disruptive entrepreneur will want to develop tools that avoid such competition—at least until they are strong enough to match or beat incumbents. In formulating their strategy, disrupters will want to target incumbents' weak points.

WHAT TO TARGET: INCUMBENTS' WEAK POINTS

As with strengths, incumbents have three weak points:

1. ***Not all of the incumbent's customers value the incumbent's products equally.*** There will always be some customers whose willingness to pay for an incumbent's product is close to the price they pay now, but others will be open to new options with different value propositions. For example, those customers may be dissatisfied with some of the choices incumbents make in product design. Going back to the original computer hard drive market, this was the case with incumbent hard drive makers' primary customers, who used them with mainframe computers. The incumbent companies produced hard drives that had a large amount of storage but were then necessarily larger and more power-hungry. To emerging personal computer users, this was a poor trade-off. Consequently, there was an opportunity for new entrants to supply smaller and lower-powered drives that targeted those customers. In the words of Clay Christensen, they tried to be "cheaper, simpler, smaller, and frequently, more convenient to use." With this trade-off, new entrants could match an incumbent's price while providing more value to some customers and capturing share. And because these customers were not the incumbent's best customers, losing them would be less likely to provoke a response. More recently, we see a similar case playing out with computer chips. While these had once emphasized central processing power, many now focus on narrower tasks like graphic processing to create videos and generative artificial intelligence.

2. ***A new technology opens an opportunity for entrants.*** Though this technology might underperform the old technology used by incumbents, it has the potential for a faster trajectory of improvement and superior performance in the long run. For Christensen's hard drive case, we saw that though hard drives supplied by new entrants for smaller computers may have had poorer performance because of their smaller size and power specifications, there was potential for improvement. While a small drive might never have as much storage as a larger drive, the trade-off of size for storage would become lower and lower, causing even the highest-end customers to prefer the new technology in the long run (see **Deep Dive: Differing S Curves** on p. 290). We have seen this continue with all types of hardware as they moved from mainstream to mobile computing, such as smartphones and tablets. New chip designs that reduced power consumption dramatically required dramatic shifts in mindset for development and innovation that new entrants could take advantage of.

3. ***Incumbents can be slow to change, hampering their ability to respond to entrants.*** While an incumbent may face long-term incentives to defend its domain, those incentives are much weaker in the short term. This is especially so when you consider that it may not be sure whether an entrant represents a true competitive threat or not, and that meeting that competitive threat is costly. It often requires giving price discounts to all of an incumbent's customers. If the new entrant is not as strong, this means a large loss in profits to protect against an entrant that may only appeal to a small portion of the market. Precisely because an incumbent

Differing S Curves

Comparing only the present forms of competing technologies can be deceiving. They may not reflect dramatic differences in the rate of performance improvements. Consider the classic case of the disk drive industry. In the early 1990s, 14-inch-diameter drives were clearly superior in storage capacity to the smaller 3.5-inch and 2.5-inch drives. However, the drives were on distinct S curves with differing rates of improvement, and the potential for improvement was greater for the smaller drives. While early on smaller sizes offered advantages only for niche customer applications such as mobile computing, as the storage capacity of these smaller drives dramatically increased, the size-for-storage trade-off disappeared for most mainstream customer needs.[a]

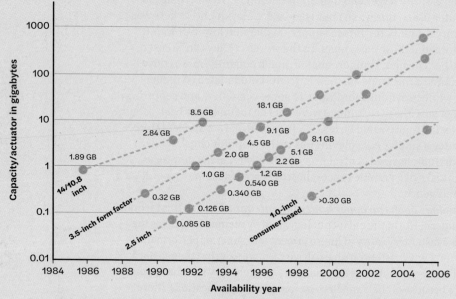

In the disk drive wars of the 1980s and 1990s, the largest-format disks started out with substantial advantages in capacity over smaller formats. However, this advantage disappeared quite rapidly.

SOURCE: Edward Grochowski, "Emerging Trends in Data Storage on Magnetic Hard Disk Drives," 1999, https://pdfs.semanticscholar.org/ad6e/3bc8598c5cf7eee4f715e3ebdbe1825d4080.pdf.

cannibalization A market dynamic where a company's new product competes with an older product, resulting in a loss of sales and profits; can also happen when a competitor's product replaces a company's product or service

has a large number of customers who are likely to stay with it, using new tactics to deal with an entry involves **cannibalization** of profits an incumbent would have expected to earn. No one wants to give up profits unnecessarily, and so an incumbent may choose not to respond until it is sure a competitive threat is real. However, in some circumstances, the response may come too late. This has perhaps been most apparent for brick-and-mortar retailers who were slow to move to online selling, allowing newcomers such as Amazon to gain traction (see **Using the Research: The Replacement Effect**).

The Replacement Effect: Why Blockbuster Couldn't Respond to Disruption

Many a postmortem of Blockbuster's abrupt demise features Netflix cofounder Reed Hastings's trip to Blockbuster's headquarters in Dallas. There, he proposed Blockbuster acquire the small start-up for $50 million and also let Netflix run Blockbuster's online presence. Hastings would make the trip to Dallas a few more times, each with the same response from Blockbuster executives: Are you kidding us? These critiques, benefiting generously from hindsight, often criticize Blockbuster CEO John Antioco for lack of vision in not seizing the Netflix opportunity and note that at the time of Blockbuster's bankruptcy, only 10 years later, Netflix was valued at $13 billion.[a]

The reality, of course, was a bit more complex. Blockbuster was well aware that innovation would alter the industry landscape. In fact, it was exploring a number of approaches and partnerships (including with Enron) to provide video on demand (VOD). At the time of Hastings's first trip to Dallas in early 2000, however, there was little rush to introduce VOD or online DVD rentals. Blockbuster's nearly 9,000 retail stores were doing well, and they were continuing to grow. Netflix's relatively small and unprofitable operation seemed to offer little to the large incumbent.

Blockbuster faced an all-too-common dilemma: in considering adopting an innovation, incumbent firms face a trade-off between potential profits from the new product or services and the real losses to the existing, profitable business as some current customers switch to the new product. Coined "the replacement effect" and studied by Nobel Prize winner Kenneth Arrow, this explains why an innovation often creates (at least in the short term) more value for a new entrant than for incumbent firms. For Blockbuster, VOD or online DVD rental was unlikely to yield many new customers. Instead, it was more likely to shift some existing customers online and out of their existing retail stores, taking their add-on popcorn and candy sales at checkout and their late fees with them. As such, the value to Blockbuster of adopting the online DVD rental service Netflix proposed was the profits from the new online service minus the profits from the existing retail business. Blockbuster had little incentive to hasten the demise of its retail operation. By contrast, new entrants, such as Netflix, face no trade-off (there are no existing services!) and, as a result, have a stronger incentive to adopt innovations. By the time Blockbuster felt the threat of Netflix and other innovators (such as Redbox), it was too late to respond.

One of Blockbuster's challenges was imagining how to replace a very profitable in-store renter who might make add-on purchases at the store. This photo from a Blockbuster shows candy, games, and used DVDs that customers could buy at checkout.

Thus, *while head-to-head competition plays to an incumbent's strengths, strategies that target niche markets or underserved customers are less likely to provoke an incumbent reaction. This is where incumbents are weakest in both their ability and incentives to respond.* Disruption requires a plan that targets these attributes initially while avoiding "waking the beast."

10.4 The Four Choices That Shape a Disruption Strategy

In choosing to pursue a disruption strategy, a start-up needs to set the four key choices—customer, technology, competition, and organization—for a particular strategic outcome. The success scenario for start-ups pursuing a disruption strategy is one where they become one of a few larger players in the market. Let's review these choices along with some successful examples.

CHOOSING YOUR CUSTOMER

In a disruption strategy, entrepreneurs should find those customer segments that are

a. underserved by existing firms; and
b. can be served better by the new technological opportunity accompanying the new idea.

These underserved customer segments exist typically because established firms have not found it worthwhile to develop solutions for their needs, either because they are too small or their preferences are at odds with the incumbents' current customers.

Consider, for example, Rent the Runway (RTR), the online apparel and accessory rental company we learned about in Chapter 1. RTR was inspired by a dilemma faced by the sister of founder Jennifer Hyman: she did not want to wear a dress she already owned to an upcoming event, as it had already been seen in photos on social media, but she could not afford the dresses she wanted to wear.[3] Hyman and her cofounder, Jennifer Fleiss, saw an opportunity to serve this target market segment of (a) young, fashion-oriented women (b) with limited disposable incomes who (c) wanted to wear high-end clothing but (d) could not afford to do so and (e) might not live in places where they could easily buy these fashions in the first place. Existing retailers of high-end brands catered solely to those who could afford to purchase these expensive (and very profitable) dresses. Even if the existing retailers might have considered offering rentals, it is likely that this would be at odds with their messaging to current customers on the value of new items. Furthermore, RTR felt it could use an online approach to rent out each item of clothing through its website to women across the United States and maintain this approach for many years. Through this focused choice of targeting an unserved market segment and creating value for them by leveraging a new technological opportunity, Rent the Runway was able to reach revenues of $100 million in 2014.[4]

CHOOSING YOUR TECHNOLOGY

As discussed earlier in this chapter, with a disruption strategy, the choice of technology should focus on an emerging technology S curve. Those nascent technologies tend to be unexploited by established firms in the industry. Hence, there are opportunities to provide new services using these technologies and opportunities for ongoing investment that significantly improve their performance.

A classic example of this is Amazon, which was founded by Jeff Bezos not because he was a book lover but because he saw that the Internet would change the way people shopped for goods in many categories. At the time, physical retail was still the predominant strategy. Even early e-commerce computer companies trying to disrupt the desktop industry dominated then by IBM still might have on-the-ground tech support (like Dell), or actual stores where customers could see computers before ordering them online (like a Dell competitor named Gateway).[5] Amazon's decision to focus purely online was thus a key technological decision. Incumbent book retailers believed browsing bookstore shelves was a critical part of the sales process and, therefore, mostly had not adopted e-commerce. By being completely online, Amazon was also able to serve an untapped market for "long tail" (e.g., niche topics) books that did not command sufficient sales to be carried on shelves but taken together amounted to significant sales. More recent examples are seen with products like mattresses (Casper) and eyeglasses (Warby Parker), items that at one time most consumers would have mainly felt comfortable buying in person (**Figure 10.4**).[6] Interestingly, as both companies have expanded, they have added product showrooms to attract more traditional customers.

FIGURE 10.4 **Casper**

In 2014, Casper thought it could find a market segment of customers willing to buy a mattress by mail order. As with a lot of disruptive ideas, many were skeptical. In the words of Neil Parikh, then Casper's chief strategy officer, "At the beginning, we met with dozens of investors who all said, 'No one is ever going to buy a mattress online. This is a dumb idea, don't do it.'"

Taken together, disruption entrepreneurs making their choice of technology should focus on new technological opportunities that have been underexploited and with a trajectory for improvement. At the same time, these new opportunities should be more costly for established firms to adopt, at least in the short run. In some cases, as Clay Christensen has emphasized, this involves adopting technologies that may be noticeably less focused on characteristics the industry holds as important. In the case of Amazon, Casper, and Warby Parker, these characteristics included physical browsing and shopping. Working with a frontier technology also gives companies the opportunity to iterate and continuously improve. Amazon developed a recommendation algorithm that helped drive repeat sales with customers, and Warby Parker made ongoing improvements in smartphone technology to let people see how glasses would look superimposed on their faces.

CHOOSING YOUR COMPETITION

A disruption start-up is, by definition, one that has chosen to take a competitive stance against established firms in the industry and to compete through execution. By choosing not to invest in control over their idea, disruption strategy entrepreneurs will inevitably face the threat of imitative competition from incumbents and new entrants alike. They must try to delay this response as long as possible, which means not calling out the established firms by publicly declaring disruption (what has been called "mooning the giant"). Disruption start-ups should position the start-up in a way that takes advantage of the

FIGURE 10.5 Disrupting the Market for Currency Exchange

The business of currency exchange was industry-driven by large players and storefront locations of banks and services like Western Union, as seen here. TransferWise (now known as Wise) sought to disrupt it.

market embeddedness of established firms to prolong the period before they respond.

In other words, it is important for these entrepreneurs to employ a "judo strategy," a concept in which a company uses speed and flexibility to outmaneuver a competitor. Consider, as a basic example, an industry where an incumbent sells a money transfer service with a $10 fee to 100 customers. If a disruptive start-up enters and offers to serve all 100 customers at a $5 fee, then the incumbent is forced to respond by matching or undercutting the start-up and driving it out of the market. If, instead, the disruptive start-up entered with a $5 fee positioned to only target and serve five of these customers, especially if these customers were costly for the incumbent to serve (e.g., higher marketing costs to convert or higher transaction costs), then the incumbent will find it more profitable to accommodate entry and continue serving its 95 other customers at the original fee.

This example[7] illustrates the actual case of TransferWise, launched in 2011 by Kristo Käärmann and Taavet Hinrikus (and now known as Wise). The inspiration came when Käärmann moved to the UK from Estonia and discovered he had to pay 12% in bank fees to move money from his Estonian bank to his UK account; at the same time, Hinrikus, who worked in the UK but owned a home in Estonia, was facing the same fees to convert pounds to kroons to pay his mortgage. Realizing they could avoid fees by having Käärmann pay for Hinrikus's mortgage in kroons and Hinrikus transferring the pounds equivalent to Käärmann, their idea for a peer-to-peer, low-cost money transfer service was born. Up against large incumbent competitors such as banks and existing money transfer services (e.g., Western Union, MoneyGram) (**Figure 10.5**), TransferWise employed a judo strategy by initially concentrating on European expats transferring pounds and euros. Furthermore, it was a completely online service and only accepted bank account transfers from individuals and not enterprises. In other words, TransferWise would still be inaccessible to the three core revenue streams for banks and money transfer services: the unbanked, the largest markets for remittances (e.g., India, China, Mexico), and enterprises. Over the past four years, despite raising significant venture capital, it has continued its judo strategy to evade a strong incumbent response by adding only 14 currencies (USD, CAD, and European currencies like the krona, lari, and franc) and focusing exclusively on Western consumers.

CHOOSING YOUR ORGANIZATION

The self-described motives of disruption entrepreneurs tend to embrace Schumpeter's notion of "creative destruction" in that the process of innovation requires "incessantly destroying the old [and] creating [the] new."[8] At heart, disruption strategy entrepreneurs are building on their ideas, with a theory and a belief that they can take advantage of hidden weaknesses in established firms and gain a stronghold before these firms can react. Time is of the essence for disruption start-up entrepreneurs, and they must move fast, developing products that can be quickly put into the market for customer feedback and improvement, all with limited resources. Erik Ries coined the idea and the movement of the "lean startup," focusing on how disruption strategy start-ups must operate leanly and hustle in order to afford continuous experimentation. In addition, this focus on speed in the face of limited resources requires disruption entrepreneurs to locate nearby talent pools that can support rapid experimentation and execution.

To illustrate this more clearly, consider the case of razor start-up Harry's. Harry's was founded in 2011 by Jeffrey Raider and Andy Katz-Mayfield on the hypothesis that they could develop higher-quality razors at a more affordable price than market behemoths Gillette and Schick and sell them with an online, direct-to-consumer approach. Raider and Katz-Mayfield launched their web store and began selling razors immediately, working with their suppliers to incorporate customer feedback in their product development. But they soon realized that what they needed was the talent and capabilities to both iterate and build the best razor for their brand more rapidly. To really succeed, they needed to own the supply process for their product and not outsource to the cheapest existing manufacturer. At only nine months old, the start-up took steps to integrate and then purchase a 93-year-old German blades manufacturer named Feintechnik[9] (**Figure 10.6**). A German magazine dubbed this move "a curious combination of U.S. entrepreneurial spirit and German engineering." Though time will tell if Harry's will succeed in achieving creative destruction, this case illustrates the willingness to make a rapid move to bring the needed talent and skills into a company. It also reflects an identity built around lean experimentation and being "hustlers" who bring innovation into an "old" market.

Ultimately, disruption entrepreneurs need to ensure that the capabilities they intend to be the source of long-term competitive advantage are integrated and prioritized in their organization design. They need to focus on developing their most important and disruptive capabilities by continual experimentation and market learning. Everything else, initially at least, can be outsourced so as to access the best practices in a timely manner.

FIGURE 10.6 **A Key Organizational Choice for Harry's**

Harry's had a coherent-enough strategy to convince investors that it should purchase German razor manufacturer Feintechnik, located in Eisfeld, Germany (shown here), for its disruptive venture.

HOW THE FOUR CHOICES FIT TOGETHER

As with an IP strategy, what constitutes a disruption strategy is how each of the four choices—customer, technology, competition, and organization—fit together. **Figure 10.7** updates the framework we saw in the IP chapters for the four key choices made with a disruption strategy, a strategy focused on creative destruction and being "hustlers." Let's go through each, using the elements of the Netflix story to provide a concrete example.

CUSTOMER CHOICE This involves disruption focused on finding and launching with new customers, potentially those in underserved segments ignored by the major players. For Netflix, the general idea was to use the Internet to let the customer order movies from home. By having DVDs come by mail, Netflix

FIGURE 10.7 This figure shows the core choices and value capture and creation elements of a disruption strategy, a strategy of creative destruction and "hustlers."

provided value to customers who did not want to travel to video stores and select items. But who were those customers? They were those patient enough to wait for the mail to come and who were able to plan what they might watch a few days in advance. In other words, they were not the customers who had to see this week's hit movie, or at least some movie, right now. They were effectively new users. They were the ones looking to see movies that were more niche, personalized, and less mass market. That meant ensuring that those customers had even more choices of titles than would be available in a local video store.

TECHNOLOGY CHOICE For Netflix, satisfying new customers meant choosing to pursue a new technological trajectory. Customers ordering DVDs on the Internet, managing the inventory, and mailing them efficiently required ordering and logistics advances and a new process or **specialized system** for the venture. The Netflix team needed to focus their core time and effort to develop a specialized technology system that would follow, and gain advantage from, their new technological trajectory.

specialized system An interface or process that is created uniquely for a particular venture

ORGANIZATION CHOICE Given the speed needed for a disruption strategy and innovations required to develop a specialized system, disruption strategies work to integrate "leanly" with complementary and available resources. Start-ups make choices that build these **integrative capabilities** with existing resources. In the case of razor start-up Harry's, it meant working to buy a specialized blades manufacturing plant in Germany. For Netflix, it meant closely partnering with the U.S. Postal Service as a complementary aid with distribution and, of course, mailing and handling returns of DVDs. Netflix's decision to build an organization with integrated capabilities allowed it to easily interface with and account for deliveries.

integrative capabilities A company's ability to work and fit with complementary and available resources

COMPETITION CHOICE Finally, in all of this, did traditional video stores have any complementary assets that might be important and create a reason for a Netflix partnership? As it turned out, they did not. Moreover, every mailed DVD was potentially a lost rental for those physical stores. So, Netflix, having made these other choices, ended up as the incumbents' direct competition, which is the core competition choice of a disruption strategy. Though there may have been another way to execute this idea and avoid competition, other disruption choices make it inevitable. Moreover, there was little to stop others from imitating Netflix with a similar approach—including incumbents, which is what they eventually tried to do. Therefore, Netflix like other disrupters, needed to be better and cheaper than its rivals by focusing on execution. The end result was a set of choices that made sense together and was coherent. You could see why one choice complemented—that is, reinforced—another.

COHERENCE

While making choices that cohere is important in any strategy, harnessing complementary opportunities across choices is particularly important for high-growth entrepreneurs. When each investment or choice reinforces prior decisions and so reinforces how the start-up creates and captures value, a venture can establish a distinctive approach and identity that can resist competitive imitation, even by more well-resourced firms. At the other extreme, uncoordinated decision-making can lead to costly (even fatal) mismatches: in particular, not taking advantage of key opportunities because of the lack of resources. Consider where Harry's might be if its entrepreneurs had not had the resources and joint commitment to buy a specialized razor manufacturer. Or where Netflix would have been if its team had also decided to build a network of shops to serve people who did not want to wait for the mail to deliver a DVD.

Another advantage of coherence is that it can assist in managing the strategy, which is particularly important when pursuing a disruption strategy. Because an entrepreneur's time is an especially scarce resource, a coherent strategy means parts that coordinate. Consider that a natural instinct in a start-up is to micromanage. However, with the right team, the people working with you can understand the plan and so remove the need to micromanage. The idea is simple: if you can articulate the plan and vision, which choices are being committed to and which actions will not be done, others on your team will have a coherent framework to guide their path.

We saw a version of this when Jeff Bezos announced that Amazon would have low prices and that it would figure out how to deliver on that. That commitment sent the organization a message about how each employee's choices should be made. Specifically, if a choice requires a high price to make sense, then it should not be done.[10]

10.5 Putting Disruption Strategy to the Test

As an entrepreneur evaluating how a disruption strategy can be used to translate your idea into a growing venture, you must begin by putting your key hypotheses to the test. As with other strategies, this means clearly articulating the four choices you will make, and how each, when combined with the others, is theorized to create and capture value. Then you must design strategic experiments to test the validity of your hypotheses. For a disruption strategy start-up, the ultimate tests of your hypotheses are

a. whether you can find customers who are unhappy with the current offerings available from existing firms;
b. if you can find evidence of market inertia, organizational inertia, or numerous potentially disruptive technologies facing incumbents; and
c. whether you can take advantage of this by executing your idea quickly.

A DISRUPTION STRATEGY'S VALUE CREATION HYPOTHESIS

Disruption strategy entrepreneurs need to accept that choosing a path of customer feedback–oriented execution requires disclosing their core idea. In most cases, this is an irreversible decision. Thus, *entrepreneurs must have a well-grounded hypothesis as to why their venture will provide novel value to consumers who have been traditionally ignored (or poorly served) by existing firms. They need to assess if they can feasibly develop a new value chain with a rate of improvement likely to outperform existing value chains.*

Consider the case of Uber, founded in 2009 by Garrett Camp and Travis Kalanick on the idea that mobile and other IT technology could make taxi and limo service more reliable for consumers.[11] Uber first launched in San Francisco with a focus on bringing together limo drivers with idle capacity and busy professionals with high (but not super-extravagant) disposable income. Though their idea originally stemmed from frustration with taxis, Camp and Kalanick recognized an opportunity to bring together two groups underserved by traditional incumbents. On the one hand, limos and black cars were often underutilized in major cities, serving a handful of clients, often through a reservation system where lengthy delays were common. On the other hand, busy working professionals were frustrated with using taxis, especially the processes of street-hailing or ordering by phone but did not have the habitual routines or the same personal budget to become traditional clients of black cars and limos. Camp and Kalanick's initial idea was to create a limo timeshare powered by mobile technology, which eventually evolved into a spot market for chauffeured trips that would unite supply—the idle bandwidth of limo drivers—with demand—professionals underserved by taxis. Mobile technology then offered the opportunity to track car and passenger locations in real time using GPS, and the potential for a seamless interface of ordering a taxi and cashless transactions, emphasizing a ratings system rather than tipping. Uber's combination of interacting features—leveraging the idle capacity of the black car drivers, exploiting the emerging functionality of GPS-enabled smartphones, and adopting standards and approaches that made it easy to pay and eliminate tipping—realized a novel value proposition for customers in a way that overturned several different assumptions of established players in the industry. Uber's model was so popular with customers in most markets that it was able to challenge an existing and heavily regulated taxi/transportation industry. It broke into markets where taxi companies sometimes had an almost cartel-like hold on these transportation services.

In short, any disruption start-up must be able to state clearly how it hopes to create value for consumers. For example, Uber hoped to create value for customers with a simplified and reliable process for obtaining a car that was affordable. For drivers, Uber hoped to create more income for them by generating more rides during idle periods. With a value creation hypothesis in hand, the start-up can test, sharpen, and iterate that hypothesis until it can make a decisive value proposition for at least one customer group. Let's see how this is done.

TESTING VALUE CREATION

The first step in testing a value creation hypothesis is to identify potential customer segments and their requirements; more specifically, the founding team must find customers who are unserved by existing businesses. One approach is first to evaluate where and how key incumbents have positioned their products and then identify the "missing" poorly served segments. Entrepreneurs can analyze incumbents' marketing materials, sales messaging, and their "reference" customers, for example, analyzing what types of customers are featured on their website or what customers appear in use cases or on incumbents' social media channels. When serial entrepreneur Jeff Lawson was looking for a way to send SMS texts at scale to users of his software products, he first approached existing telecom infrastructure and communications system providers. Through these meetings, he realized that these incumbents were geared toward large Fortune 500 companies.[12] This helped Lawson uncover an insight upon which he founded his start-up Twilio: small and medium-size enterprises (SMEs) and start-up entrepreneurs like himself were poorly served, as they could not afford the physical telecom infrastructure these providers delivered.

After identifying an unserved customer, the disruption strategy entrepreneur should evaluate if, in fact, their idea can meet the customer's needs and create value for them. This information can come from interviews with potential customers and running experiments to test if they value the solution. For example, consider fashion start-up Ministry of Supply (**Figure 10.8**), which in its earliest stages gave away a small batch of its novel T-shirts (made with temperature-regulating

FIGURE 10.8 **Ministry of Supply Boutique in New York**

Ministry of Supply used a small batch of its new T-shirts to find out if customers valued its clothing made of high-tech materials. Its high-end boutique in New York highlights the company's use of NASA materials by displaying a space suit in the front window.

materials developed by NASA) to colleagues and friends to get their feedback. The start-up then followed up on that experiment by selling its shirts to test if there was willingness to pay. With fewer than 50 shirts and in a matter of weeks,[13] the founding team gathered important insight into what these underserved customers really valued.

A DISRUPTION STRATEGY'S VALUE CAPTURE HYPOTHESIS

Next, entrepreneurs need to articulate their theory of how they intend to capture part of the value that they create. *As a first step, they must think through how to achieve customer growth without provoking a response from established firms, which requires forming a theory as to why these firms will be slow to respond.*

Strategy research has identified two core reasons why established firms can be slow to respond:[14]

- **Market inertia**: Incumbents are focused on serving their core customers. At the earliest stages of a disruptive technology, they have to consider the impact it has on the revenue streams from existing customers. Because they have to balance between their current business and the uncertain but potentially disruptive new business model, they can't move as quickly as start-ups not faced with this trade-off.

- **Organizational inertia**: Incumbents often have multiple divisions with competing interests. Even if some executives recognize the potential of a disruptive technology, they must convince others that the opportunity is worth pursuing even if it risks jeopardizing the overall company brand or making an existing division obsolete.

To make this concrete, let's look again at Salesforce, founded by Marc Benioff in 1999. Benioff, a longtime senior employee at Oracle, recognized an opportunity in the customer relationship management (CRM) space against his current employer. Oracle had strong market leadership in CRM, primarily serving large Fortune 500 companies through hands-on sales and customer service experience (e.g., Oracle clients often had their own dedicated Oracle employee). Benioff hypothesized that he could instead leverage cloud computing to develop a lower-cost, software-as-a-service-based CRM product that even SMEs and start-ups could afford. Given Benioff's deep insight into the organizational structure and customer service model at Oracle, he hypothesized that Oracle would not respond immediately because doing so would require the company to make many changes. Oracle would need to adopt cloud computing, a different pricing model (low monthly SaaS fees rather than large multiyear licenses), a different customer strategy (SMEs and start-ups in addition to Fortune 500s), and a different organizational structure (building up the software team and reducing the traditional emphasis on outside sales). Benioff's value capture hypothesis helped clarify both to entrepreneurs and early investors how they could exploit and capitalize on the then-new cloud computing technology S curve before Oracle would respond. The case of Salesforce, now an 80,000-employee company with a $200 billion market cap,[15] illustrates the importance of entrepreneurs analyzing established firms and gathering enough information to convince themselves that these firms will be slow to respond.

The second step is to determine if the start-up can execute quickly while evading incumbent detection and reaction. Though intuitively this may not seem possible to test, disruption strategy entrepreneurs should spend time exploring why these customers have been underserved by incumbents and why this nascent technology has not yet been exploited. A good starting point is to consider if incumbents are simply unaware that these customers and technology opportunities exist or if they have chosen not to address them now. Entrepreneurs can search the media, customer forums, and industry publications to see if either their customer choice, technology choice, or both have been discussed before. In doing this exercise, entrepreneurs should also observe how and if new ideas and trends get coverage in the press and in trade publications.

Another exercise is estimating how long entrepreneurs think it will take for an established firm to replicate the start-up's activities once the firm perceives it as a significant threat. How long will it take it to organize a meaningful response? Will it need to hire new personnel or develop new supply chains to respond to the disruptive threat? Where will the start-up be by that time, assuming that the incumbent moves a little faster than anticipated? In practice, this can include researching LinkedIn or elsewhere to find out what kinds of skills employees of the established firm already have. Or perhaps more effectively, engaging a former incumbent employee as a consultant or adviser may turn up more concrete answers to these questions. This way, disruption strategy entrepreneurs can, like Marc Benioff, identify what investments incumbents must make to launch a response and estimate how much time they have before needing to hold off a response from established firms.

10.6 Putting Disruption Strategy to Work

With the strategy in place, the precise steps to take next are of course dependent on the opportunity itself. However, almost all disruptive start-ups will take three major actions as part of their game plan.

1. ***Build relationships and a dialogue with your underserved customer base.*** This can entail hiring a customer engagement employee who comes from that specific segment and who can help a start-up find and cultivate a group of its customers to provide feedback. In the case of Uber, an early hire was a specialized salesperson who would enter individual cities and hold recruitment events for potential drivers.

2. ***Build a minimum viable product (MVP) to test and iterate quickly.*** Start-ups should design a minimal version of their technology so that it can be iterated fast. Even though a final version of the product may require significant investment to bring it fully into the market, developing an MVP that addresses basic pain points gets it into customers' hands as soon as possible. Entrepreneurs can then measure how customers react. For example, how many people will sign up and meaningfully use the MVP? What percentage are willing to put down their credit card information?

Is Disruption Overhyped?

Ever since Clay Christensen introduced the term "disruptive technologies," "disruption" has become a catchword for entrepreneurship, especially in Silicon Valley. There has been a tendency to see everything as "disruptive" and to see all start-ups as "disrupters." Even established firms like the *New York Times* have been trying to disrupt themselves. This gives the impression that the only path for entrepreneurs to be successful is to disrupt some market or industry. While not the only approach, research has shown that in recent times, ventures looking to disrupt have attracted more funding than others.[a]

It is true that much innovation requires creating new products that displace or destroy those that stand in markets before them. But as this book has emphasized, entrepreneurs have a choice as to whether they pursue disruption or not. While this chapter has explored

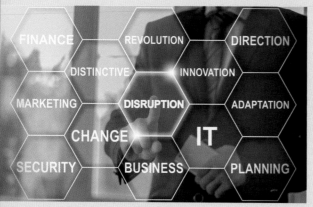

Are people classifying every type of new business venture as "disruption"?

strategies closely related to the popular image of a disrupter—those who opt to compete as well as focus on execution—there are other options available in choosing your competition; in particular, choosing to cooperate with existing businesses. In other words, disruption is not the only path.[b]

Moreover, researchers have explored precisely when it is more possible that a disruptive strategy is likely to be successful. Business strategist and Dartmouth professor Rod Adner has shown that the characteristics of a product and how they combine to satisfy the wants of niche customers is critical in the success of disruption.[c]

In the end, however, the theory of disruption as it was originally cast has, according to Harvard historian Jill Lepore, a narrow application:

> Disruptive innovation is a theory about why businesses fail. It's not more than that. It doesn't explain change. It's not a law of nature. It's an artifact of history, an idea, forged in time; it's the manufacture of a moment of upsetting and edgy uncertainty. Transfixed by change, it's blind to continuity. It makes a very poor prophet.[d]

Indeed, Yale economist Mitsuru Igami measured the effect of disruption in the disk drive industry and found that 57% of the gap between incumbent and start-up innovation arose because incumbent firms feared disrupting their existing businesses.[e] In that regard, it stands alongside other theories that also look at business failure and its relationship to the myriad constraints on established firms in their innovation choices, constraints that aren't faced by new ventures.

The MVP does not need to be perfect; in fact, it should not consume too many resources to deploy. Part of the disruption development process is engaging with customers in a repeated, iterative "build-measure-learn" loop to shape the product and start-up. For instance, in 2022 the start-up artificial intelligence firm OpenAI launched a very simple MVP called ChatGPT to allow a large number of users to interact with its new large language models. The purpose of this was to explore use cases and evaluate the safety of the product. Somewhat surprisingly for such a simple product, it became the most adopted new product in history, gaining over 100 million users in less than two months.

An MVP is often the first step in getting a disruptive start-up moving. As Erik Ries explains, the start-up should be "developing a minimum viable product (MVP) to begin the process of learning as quickly as possible. Once the MVP is established, a startup can work on tuning the engine."[16]

3. ***Accordingly, entrepreneurs need to build an organization that engages their customers, prioritizes customer feedback, and is capable of acting quickly on that feedback.*** This may require the start-up to locate near a supply of less expensive, competitive talent, helping grow the start-up's capacity to experiment in a lean and rapid manner. At one extreme, we saw Harry's actually buy an entire company to get the capabilities that it needed. More commonly, a start-up will locate in an area where key resources are nearby or actively recruit people with the specialized skills needed to execute more effectively.

10.7 Concluding Thoughts

A start-up entrepreneur pursuing a disruptive strategy tries to create value by exploiting a novel technological trajectory (a new *technology* S curve). In the process, they are developing a new value chain differentiated and isolated from established players (see **Putting It Together: Disruption Strategy** on p. 304). Disruptive entrepreneurs must focus on new *customers* that are poorly served by existing firms and products. Because the value chain is novel and the resources may be limited, a disruptive strategy must have significant iteration and experimentation with initial customers. Often, this experimentation takes place in local markets before going global, as companies like Uber debuted in one city before expanding.

Ultimately, the essence of a disruptive strategy is to take advantage of weaknesses in the ability of incumbent firms to react and turn this into a "window of opportunity" as an entrant. Discussions of the idea of disruption can make it seem like disrupters are everywhere, and some have said that entrepreneurs are trying to "disrupt" everything (see **Using the Research: Is Disruption Overhyped?**). "Disruption" is used so much that some entrepreneurs focus on it as the only way to go forward. But this book makes it clear that this is not the case. We have seen this already with IP strategy and will look at two others—value chain strategy and architectural strategy—in the coming chapters.

DISRUPTION STRATEGY

Undertaking "creative destruction," a disruptive strategy initially creates value for customers poorly served by existing firms and uses rapid iteration to ultimately disrupt established firms.

EVALUATE YOUR FOUNDING TEAM AND PROPOSED BUSINESS MODEL

How Will You Be Able to Disrupt?

- Outline the team's "unfair" advantage, skills, and passion as they relate to the idea.
- Articulate how your business model will rapidly innovate to deliver value to poorly served users and beyond.

DESCRIBE CUSTOMER, TECHNOLOGY, ORGANIZATION, AND COMPETITION CHOICES

Customer: Deliver Value for New Users

- Explain why niche customer segments are dissatisfied or underserved by existing firms. Describe how your idea creates value for them.
- Evaluate how these customers provide a pathway to the mainstream market.

Technology: Develop Specialized Innovations

- Describe how emerging technology can create new offerings and why it is underexploited by established firms in the industry.
- Evaluate the technology's performance, outline key performance metrics, and specify requirements to iterate and continuously improve along those performance metrics.

Organization: Build Integrated Capabilities

- Identify capabilities that will be long-term competitive advantages and how to continually improve them.
- Decide how to quickly scale up other capabilities with the limited resources available.

Competition: Orient toward Competition and Invest in Execution

- Identify established firms that make head-to-head competition difficult and weaknesses that may limit their ability and incentives to respond.
- Specify steps your start-up can take to delay competitive response while also prioritizing lean experimentation and iteration.

SHARPEN YOUR VALUE CREATION HYPOTHESIS AND VALUE CAPTURE HYPOTHESIS

Create Value for New Users with Innovations

- For the proposed niche customer group, articulate how your idea would create novel value and provide a pathway to a mainstream market.
- Conduct interviews and low-commitment experiments to test if they value your idea.

Capture Value by Focusing on Execution

- Articulate how your venture will sustain early market growth without provoking a competitive response.
- Gather information on constraints of the established firms; estimate the time it will take them to replicate your activities when perceived as a threat.

Chapter 10 Review: Disruption Strategy

CHAPTER TAKEAWAYS

- The value creation hypothesis for a disruption strategy uses a start-up's idea to develop a system innovation and discover value for new users, typically groups that are unserved (or poorly served) by the incumbents' offerings.

- A value capture hypothesis for a disruption strategy requires an entrepreneur to have a clear theory why incumbent firms will be slow to respond, and how the start-up will stay ahead when there is a competitive threat.

- Head-to-head competition with incumbent firms is challenging because incumbents possess built-in advantages like control over complementary assets and resources, being able to deploy those resources quickly in response to new threats, and having an established and favorable position in the industry.

- To successfully compete with an incumbent firm, the disrupter must understand the incumbent's weak points. There are three common weak points: (1) some of an incumbent's existing customers do not feel they are being served well by its offerings, (2) an emerging technology trajectory with the potential to overtake the one incumbents use becomes available to entrants, and (3) incumbents usually resist responding until certain the competitive threat is real because of the risk of cannibalization of current sales.

- The customer choice in a disruption strategy should be a segment that is poorly served by existing firms and will benefit from the value that an emerging technology could deliver.

- The technology choice in a disruption strategy should be an emerging technology S curve unexploited by established firms in the industry. It will have the potential to overtake the existing trajectory and will be costly for the established firms to adopt, at least in the short term.

- The competition choice in a disruption strategy is to compete against incumbent firms by focusing on idea execution versus idea control. While this comes with the threat of imitative competition, the disrupter should position their start-up in a way that will delay this response.

- The organization choice in a disruption strategy prioritizes integrated capabilities that leverage existing market resources. Doing so helps the team conduct ongoing experimentation and learning.

KEY TERMS

disrupter (p. 282)
innovation (p. 282)
technological trajectory (p. 282)
technology (p. 285)

cannibalization (p. 290)
specialized system (p. 296)
integrative capabilities (p. 297)

REVIEW QUESTIONS

1. How does a start-up create and capture value in a disruption strategy?

2. What are the primary challenges a start-up faces if it competes directly with an incumbent firm? What advantages does an incumbent hold in response to a direct competitive threat?

3. What are the three most critical weaknesses of an incumbent that a disruptive entrant might be able to leverage?

4. Define *cannibalization*. Why might the potential for cannibalization limit an incumbent's response to the entry of a new product or service from a start-up?

5. Why might a start-up have an advantage relative to an incumbent firm in exploring the earliest stages of a new technological trajectory (i.e., a new technology S curve)?

6. What types of customer groups are particularly attractive from the perspective of a disruptive entrant? How can customer choice by a start-up limit the timing and nature of competitive response?

7. What are the most critical organizational challenges a disruptive start-up must overcome? How can a disruptive start-up establish a new organization that overcomes some of the "liability of newness" (as discussed in Chapter 7)?

8. Describe one way to test whether a potential idea can create value through a disruption strategy. What are the potential risks and challenges in implementing this entrepreneurial experiment?

9. Why are opportunities for learning and experimentation often riskiest in a disruption strategy?

10. What are the main risks and drawbacks of implementing a disruption strategy? What choices can a start-up make to mitigate these potential challenges?

DISCUSSION QUESTIONS

Answer the following series of questions and scenarios either in class discussions or by writing a short response.

1. Antonio and Julia both are both obsessed with sneakers. They love wearing stylish sneakers but also care about the fit and comfort of those sneakers, particularly at the gym. While the styles offered by major brands such as Nike and Adidas have expanded over time, Antonio and Julia are frustrated by the inability to truly personalize sneaker styling (i.e., the outer design) and functionality (i.e., fit and support) at the same time. They are exploring how to leverage advances in 3D printing to create "on-demand" sneakers that would allow for a personal style in a sneaker that is just right for each individual. Using a disruption strategy approach, they are planning to focus the next summer on developing this idea into a potentially viable business. What are three concrete steps you would recommend that Antonio and Julia take over the course of a summer to decide whether they should pursue this opportunity? What are the most critical hypotheses that the duo should attempt to validate? Can you suggest a way that they might be able to do so?

2. Rent the Runway entrepreneurs Jennifer Fleiss and Jennifer Hyman planned from an early stage to use an online platform to scale their idea of renting designer dresses for formal events. However, their initial tests of their idea were in-person activities such as organizing gatherings at local colleges where women would be able to try on and then rent dresses from the fledging start-up (see p. 292). What hypotheses about their plan could they validate through an in-person test? What is one hypothesis that they would *not* be able to test until they built a working online platform? Do you agree with their choice to first focus on in-person experiments? Explain why or why not.

3. One element of a disruption strategy is a so-called judo approach. In this method, a start-up turns what seems to be strengths of existing firms into disadvantages. Doing so helps the start-up avoid a direct competitive response from these firms. For example, in its earliest days, Netflix took advantage of the fact that since Blockbuster maintained a large retail footprint that made its stores accessible to nearly all Americans, it was reluctant to embrace an online model for movie rentals. Any Blockbuster sales through that channel likely cannibalized their sales from existing retail locations. Using examples in this text or that you research in outside sources, identify another start-up that has implemented this type of judo approach, describing what it did. In particular, what choices did the start-up make that induced a trade-off for the established firm? Why did the established firm find it so difficult to respond? What happened to the start-up and established firm over time?

4. Aileen is a venture capitalist considering how to invest in sustainable food. She has been very impressed by advances in plant-based meat substitutes such as the Impossible Burger and Beyond Meat. But she also believes that this is a broad opportunity and that plant-based protein alternatives are at the cusp of a long period of growth and improvement (in terms of taste, texture, cookability, etc.). Aileen is hearing a pitch from Chetana, whose start-up has created a lab-based vegan substitute for traditional eggs. This new egg-like offering has already received positive feedback and too many orders to handle from Chetana's beachhead market of committed vegans. In this pitch, Aileen asks Chetana how she plans to bring this product to a broader market. What might Chetana do to enable her innovation to grow beyond her initial segment? Why might Aileen wonder if the success in the beachhead market may not lead to a broader set of market segments? Do you think this start-up might succeed even if it never is able to move beyond the initial beachhead customer segment?

5. One of the critical elements of a disruption strategy is rapid experimentation and learning to allow for multiple iterations of a novel product or service. While learning and iteration can uncover new ways to create customer value, a rapid process of experimentation might inadvertently lead to potential harm (for customers, the venture, or other stakeholders). For example, in a study, Dana Kanze and her collaborators have documented that start-ups that utilize the term "disruption" or variants in their firm description have much higher rates of workplace injuries and other safety violations.[17] Given this information, what is a setting where you would recommend against the rapid experimentation method emphasized in a

disruption strategy? What would be the potential harms of rapid experimentation in that setting, and how might you overcome those challenges in the context of an alternative approach?

6. Over the past two decades, the potential for disruption has led many incumbent firms to be more willing to disrupt themselves. For example, after successfully overtaking Blockbuster in the video rental industry, Netflix disrupted itself by embracing streaming services and investing in its own production company. If you were advising a large established firm facing potential competition from a disruptive entrant, what are some general strategies and approaches you might suggest for it to maintain and extend its leadership? What strategic options does an established firm have to mitigate the threat coming from a disruptive entrant?

FOR FURTHER READING

Adner, Ron. "When Are Technologies Disruptive? A Demand-Based View of the Emergence of Competition." *Strategic Management Journal* 23, (2002): 667–88.

Christensen, Clayton M. *The Innovator's Dilemma: When New Technologies Cause Great Firms to Fail*. Cambridge, MA: Harvard Business Review Press, 2016.

Christensen, Clayton M. "The Rigid Disk Drive Industry: A History of Commercial and Technological Turbulence." *Business History Review* 67, no. 4 (1993): 531–88.

Gans, Joshua. *The Disruption Dilemma*. Cambridge, MA: MIT Press, 2016.

Gans, Joshua. "Keep Calm and Manage Disruption." *Sloan Management Review* 57, no. 3 (2016): 83–90.

Gans, Joshua. "To Disrupt or Not to Disrupt." *Sloan Management Review* 61, no. 3 (2020): 40–45.

Kanze, Dana, and Sheena S. Iyengar. "Startups That Seek to 'Disrupt' Get More Funding Than Those That Seek to 'Build.'" *Harvard Business Review*, November 2017.

Lepore, Jill. "The Disruption Machine." *New Yorker*, June 2014.

Dave Gilboa and Neil Blumenthal

When Dave Gilboa lost his glasses—a $700 setback—he spent weeks saving for a replacement pair and complaining about the cost to his friend and MBA classmate Neil Blumenthal. The price of glasses exceeded that of an iPhone.[a] Blumenthal had come to business school after working at VisionSpring, a nonprofit providing low-cost glasses to low-income communities in India and El Salvador. At VisionSpring, he learned that the eyeglass industry was centered on high prices and high margins and largely controlled by the $20-billion-dollar Italian giant Luxottica. The conglomerate controlled over 80% of the industry through its various subsidiaries, including key brands (e.g., Ray-Ban, Oakley) and physical retail locations (e.g., Sunglass Hut, LensCrafters).[b] Luxottica focused primarily on high-margin brands sold through physical retail locations, with over 73,000 employees operating in multiple divisions across 130 countries.[c] Gilboa and Blumenthal, along with two other MBA compatriots who ultimately left the company, founded Warby Parker in 2010 with the objective of disrupting the eyeglass industry. Their strategy focused on offering designer-style glasses at a low price (less than $100 versus $400 for traditional frames), leveraging the ability to access low-cost Chinese manufacturing and focus exclusively on an online retail channel. Warby Parker targeted hip, socially conscious yet budget-constrained students and young professionals (in other words, themselves), emphasizing their cool eyeglass frame designs and their commitment to donate a pair of glasses to VisionSpring for each pair of glasses sold. Warby Parker has executed quickly and consistently, scaling to more than $100 million in annual revenues and over 500 employees in less than five years. As of late 2023, there has been no direct competitive response from Luxottica.[d]

The entrepreneurs of Warby Parker reasoned that young students and professionals found stylish Luxottica-branded glasses prohibitively expensive, and that much of the costs and stylings of traditional retail infrastructure held little appeal for these demographics. Warby Parker thus focused on those eyeglass purchasers who had a taste for stylish frames but who were willing, in exchange for a much lower price, to take the time to receive a prescription from an optometrist and identify their precise sizing through an in-home trial (involving multiple eyeglass

While providing a broad market product, Warby Parker founders Neil Blumenthal (left) and David Gilboa targeted a market of younger, stylish customers willing to work with technology to get a better deal on eyeglasses.

frames sent through the mail). Of course, that gave the Warby Parker team incentive to identify how to ensure a smooth process for distributing glasses through the mail and to limit their selection of styles to establish a distinctive Warby Parker "look and feel."[e] Importantly, Warby Parker's early customers have been an effective reference for follow-on customer segments and have allowed its diffusion into broader market success and to reach channels (such as traditional physical retail locations) that it avoided in its earliest stages.

Questions

1. Describe Warby Parker's value creation hypothesis. What early choices did the founding team make that were consistent with a disruption strategy?

2. Warby Parker's value capture hypothesis was premised on the fact that Luxottica would be delayed in effectively responding to its entry into the market. Explain the logic of why Luxottica was slow to respond to Warby Parker's entry.

Founders of the IT firm Infosys Technology (from left to right), Nandan Nilekani, N. S. Raghavan, Kris Gopalakrishnan, Narayana Murthy, S. D. Shibulal, and K. Dinesh are pictured in 2014. Along with a seventh founder, Ashok Arora, they felt they could bring access to Indian engineering talent to foreign multinationals.

ENTREPRENEUR'S DILEMMA Positioning a new venture within an existing value chain means selling to established businesses. The dilemma entrepreneurs face is how to provide value for the customers of those businesses without having a direct relationship with those customers themselves. Also, how does a venture encourage other players in the value chain to make investments that support its capabilities and role and not others that would encourage stronger competition?

CHAPTER OBJECTIVES

- Describe the tools of value chain strategy, including teams, firm boundaries, strategic alliances, and trust relationships
- Explain how to sell to incumbents and build bargaining power
- Understand how the customer, technology, organization, and competition choices need to work together to sell to incumbents
- Understand why ventures pursuing a value chain strategy end up focusing on developing their core competencies

11

VALUE CHAIN STRATEGY

In the early 1980s, Narayana Murthy and six of his colleagues from Patni Computer Systems in Pune, India, borrowed $250 USD from his wife, Sudha, to cofound a new venture, Infosys. Trained as electrical engineers and computer programmers at one of the prestigious Indian Institutes of Technology (IIT), the team believed in a simple yet novel vision: to become a globally successful Indian software corporation providing solutions for the world's biggest corporations. This vision was quite contrarian at the time: India during the 1980s had only a limited market economy (most economic activity was highly regulated by the government), poor infrastructure (it took Infosys more than a year to get a telephone connection), and a low level of globalization. Further, private companies were severely limited in how they could attract foreign capital or work with multinational companies.

The Infosys team recognized that the growing number of highly trained English-speaking computer scientists and engineers graduating from India's best technical universities (including the IITs) might provide an unfair advantage. At the time, global corporations were rapidly increasing the scale and complexity of their information technology (IT) systems. These new IT systems normally came with their own complicated implementation challenges. Though many of these new Indian engineers possessed the technical skills to solve these problems, and at a wage much lower than that of engineers in the United States or Europe, there were few, if any, ways for corporations to access this talent in a systematic or scalable way. Infosys wanted to solve this problem.

Infosys was built on what Murthy described as three interrelated principles: (1) the criticality of customized software in creating a competitive advantage for a corporation, (2) globalization, and (3) professionalization of the entrepreneurial venture.[1] While many companies were aware of the potential for customized

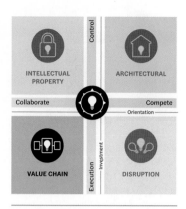

In Value Chain strategies, companies need to work with incumbent firms while maintaining their bargaining power.

software and globalization to enhance their performance, relatively few had the internal capabilities to take advantage of this potential. Infosys saw that these large corporations could benefit from partners that specialized in customized software for global corporations, and especially those using lower-cost Indian engineering talent.

Realizing this possibility required that those companies could trust these new partners in India. To build trust in Infosys, Murthy and his team chose to adopt practices big and small that showed a high level of professionalism and corporate governance.[2] For example, relative to other Indian software engineering firms at the time, Infosys worked closely and collaboratively with its global clients. Doing so required a more iterative approach and that all employees maintained a high level of English proficiency. Infosys committed itself to a high level of transparency through audited financial statements and adopted a formal dress code. Over time, these choices slowly helped Infosys build an unparalleled reputation for professional integrity, especially on the part of its management team.

With these principles in practice, Infosys was able to establish long-term partnerships with global corporations like Reebok, Rockport, and Jockey. While this success invited imitation and competition (the concept of outsourcing is something anyone can do), the capabilities and reputation that Infosys established during its early years built an advantage relative to other firms. Infosys maintained this advantage over an extended period in which demand for custom software was growing rapidly. By being the "father of the Indian software industry," Murthy and his team simultaneously became the preferred employer for the most talented graduates of the IITs and the preferred partner in India of multinational companies.

With this powerful **value chain** strategy, Infosys established itself as a leading global software company. Broadly, this strategy focuses on a particular stage (i.e., a link in a chain) that adds value to a product and combines with stages provided by others to create and add value across all stages. Infosys became the go-to company to knit a company's IT processes together. Between 1990 and 2014, Infosys registered dramatic and sustained growth led, in succession, by four of its cofounders (its first non-founder CEO took over in 2014). By 2020 Infosys earned revenues of more than $13 billion and employed more than 250,000 individuals across more than 50 countries. Moreover, beyond its financial performance, Infosys established a viable and much-imitated model for the Indian software industry.

11.1 Creating and Capturing Value with a Value Chain Strategy

The central challenge of a value chain strategy has two parts: how to implement the start-up's idea in a way that reinforces and enhances the value chain of an existing incumbent, and how do to this while still also establishing and maintaining bargaining power within that value chain. We saw that Infosys is a value chain venture focused on superior and/or unique execution while collaborating or partnering with established firms. Value chain entrepreneurs must clearly articulate what is missing from the value proposition and value chain of existing firms and why integrating the entrepreneur's

value chain A process or activity where value is added to a product across sequence of stages

idea will benefit the existing firms' end customers. For Infosys, this meant developing customized software solutions in partnership with established firms in industries like software, apparel, and retail. Infosys's work gave these firms new insights to create and deliver more valuable products at lower costs.

Thus, the value creation hypothesis underlying a value chain strategy is that the start-up's idea can create compelling value for the end customers of existing firms. This includes customers the firm has now and those the firm would like to attract.

Of course, an entrepreneur must also determine how they will capture this value, forming a value capture hypothesis for their venture. They need to articulate how they will establish and maintain bargaining power with firms while simultaneously creating value for their final customers. Simply put, if the idea creates value for end customers, why won't established firms imitate and bypass the start-up? Unlike intellectual property strategy, maintaining bargaining power in a value chain strategy does not come through direct control over its idea, but by developing unique capabilities and resources that provide leverage with its value chain partners.

Effective value chain entrepreneurs often focus on a single "horizontal" layer of the value chain where their expertise and capabilities are unrivaled (**Figure 11.1**). For example, a company might try to completely run a horizontal such as sales, product development, or planning and sell this specialized service to other businesses. Establishing this position largely depends on the team that the founder can build. In fact, there is probably no entrepreneurial strategy where the initial team plays a more important role. The team must integrate innovators, business development leaders, and supply chain partners so the value of its team is more than the value of the individual players. These organizational capabilities must translate into enhanced differentiation or cost advantage for the established firms. Even if the venture's innovation enhances the competitive advantage of the overall value chain, a value chain entrepreneur will only capture value if other players in the value chain cannot replicate the value the venture provides.

A top choice of its global customers, Infosys also became the top employment choice of students from technical universities, including branches of the Indian Institute of Technology.

FIGURE 11.1 Horizontal Layers of a Value Chain

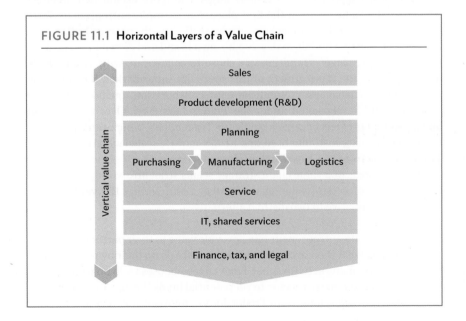

Satisfying the Need for Outsourced Personnel Services. In 1976, Janice Bryant Howroyd left her North Carolina hometown for Los Angeles with $900 and used it to build a company that put the "humanity" in human resources. After a stint as a temporary worker, Howroyd founded The ActOne Group out of a small office in Beverly Hills. She started by making full-time job placements for companies and then switched to temporary placements.[a] Today, The ActOne Group, which includes other brands such as Agile-1, contracts with more than 17,000 businesses in 34 countries.[b]

TWO STEPS

As with other strategies, choosing a value chain strategy involves two steps:

1. *Putting the strategy to the test*
2. *Putting the strategy to work*

In the first step, the value chain entrepreneur must evaluate the likelihood that their value creation and value capture hypotheses can be met. How likely is it that they can enter a market with their idea and create novel value for existing end customers, demonstrating enough value that existing firms will pay for and build sufficient, unique capabilities to maintain bargaining power with these firms?

In the second step, putting a value chain strategy to work requires making and implementing strategic choices that improve their chances of creating and capturing value. For example, a venture might identify customers who are valuable to existing firms but might become even more valuable if these incumbents embrace a new technology. It means building a company around "helping" existing firms rather than "disrupting" them and becoming an irreplaceable part of the value chain (see the sidebar on **Satisfying the Need for Outsourced Personnel Services**).

Next, we take a deeper dive into the tools of the value chain strategy, the four choices underlying a value chain strategy, and the value creation and value capture hypotheses that must be validated.

11.2 The Tools of a Value Chain Strategy

Value chain entrepreneurs want to establish a position *within* a larger value chain, proactively choosing which layers of the value chain to participate in. This lets an entrepreneur working with constraints potentially leverage the resources and capabilities of a usually larger and more established architect who created a value chain in the first place. For example, entrepreneur Terry Kroll developed a tasty snack—pretzels stuffed with peanut butter—and faced the choice of whether to develop his own brand and distribution or work with an existing player. He ultimately chose to collaborate with Trader Joe's, benefiting from the rapid growth of this speciality supermarket. But Kroll had to accept the supermarket's conditions for collaboration, including that the product would be marketed under the Trader Joe's label. Over time, peanut butter–stuffed pretzels became a staple for Trader Joe's, which caters to a very loyal, even cultlike, customer base, and Kroll's venture scaled with the growth of Trader Joe's across the United States (**Figure 11.2**).[3]

While the logic of a value chain strategy seems straightforward, the strategy is complex. A successful value chain strategy requires that the venture offer superior value relative to two distinct alternatives.

1. The value chain entrepreneur must provide value to their partners above and beyond what their architect could choose to do on their own. For example, there are many activities that Trader Joe's chooses to do on its own, including an extensive process to vet potential items through an internal tasting panel led by long-term Trader Joe's employees. It is very difficult

FIGURE 11.2 Peanut Butter Pretzel

The peanut butter pretzel was a unique product Terry Kroll brought to Trader Joe's right as that company was growing. In 2014, Kroll noted he was selling $9 million annually of the product to the grocery chain.

for an entrepreneur to provide meaningful value for activities that are the core focus of the value chain architect; an entrepreneur could try to replace Trader Joe's choice process but would probably be rebuffed, as Trader Joe's sees this process as part of its success.

2. At the same time, the venture must offer value to its partners that is superior relative to *other* potential suppliers (including other start-ups). This is harder than it may seem. For example, in 2014 Terry Kroll sued Trader Joe's when the supermarket chain cut Kroll's firm out of the supply chain by directly contracting with the firms that manufactured Kroll's tasty pretzel snacks.

A value chain entrepreneur's aim is to become the preferred provider for chosen partners, who then offer a comprehensive value proposition to their final customers. Next, we will explore the tools a value chain entrepreneur uses.

TEAM

The first critical tool is the team: the design and interdependence of the team play a unique role in a value chain strategy.

Consider the case of PayPal, formed in 2000 through the merger of two exploratory start-ups—Confinity and x.com. The founders of PayPal were a group of young technologists and entrepreneurs, including Elon Musk, Max Levchin, and Peter Thiel. They built their initial team carefully, hiring people they already knew and trusted: Thiel recruited former colleagues from the student publication the *Stanford Review* for business roles; Levchin hired engineering friends from his alma mater, the University of Illinois Urbana-Champaign. With these combined technical and business capabilities, PayPal built an innovative email payments product and identified a large and growing beachhead market for that product—eBay auctions. PayPal's platform let auction sellers accept credit cards even if they did not qualify for a traditional credit card merchant account. It also let auction buyers choose from different payment options without the risk of divulging a credit card number to a stranger. By offering a secure, low-cost solution for online transactions that benefited both auction sellers and buyers, PayPal enhanced the value of the eBay platform and quickly established itself as the most popular transaction solution for eBay auction participants.

In this example, we see that PayPal was not built on a single technological breakthrough, but through mutually reinforcing components that reflected the distinct capabilities of the founding team. Though at the time there were a number of alternatives to PayPal and numerous start-ups considering how to navigate the regulatory maze around online payments, PayPal combined its founding team's insights to create a unique service that reinforced and extended the eBay platform. This drove PayPal's own IPO and subsequent acquisition by eBay in 2002 at a valuation of $1.2 billion. Reflecting on PayPal's journey in 2006, Peter Thiel explained, "We had an incredible team at PayPal. Four years after the fact, I think it is far more incredible than we realized at the time."

The first element of a team is, of course, the individuals who make up the team. Attracting talent is critical for the value chain entrepreneur. As emphasized in Chapter 7, founders must offer cofounders and early employees a reason

In this chapter's video, learn how PayPal used a value chain strategy to provide the secure payment platforms underlying companies such as eBay.

to forego other opportunities, and recruiting these early team members depends on developing a shared understanding and shared incentives.

However, the value of a team is more than simply the ability to attract exceptional talent. If a start-up discovers and creates value through the insights and creativity of a single individual, an established firm might simply hire that individual outright or consult with them alone. But when the skills and insights of multiple team members are integral to the start-up, potential partners will collaborate with the firm as a whole rather than try to cherry-pick the most talented individuals.

FIRM BOUNDARIES

The second tool is how an entrepreneur designs their **firm boundaries**. These boundaries delineate the set of activities under the purview of the start-up. By extension, they also define those activities that are the responsibility of other players within the value chain (including the value chain architect). Firm boundaries structure the relationship between the start-up and the broader value chain.

The choice of firm boundaries (including how fluid a boundary should be) is both critical and challenging since different choices lead to different trade-offs for the firm. Boundaries shape the ways a firm will collaborate with others by defining the distinct role played by the start-up and the unique value it might create. On the one hand, a more fluid approach (at least at the outset of the relationship) might help a value chain entrepreneur *discover* novel value for current (or adjacent) customers. This might mean exploring the commercialization of a technological innovation, experimenting with alternative business models, redesigning specific products or features according to customer feedback, or streamlining processes to reduce cost or improve operations. Exploring these alternatives requires a high level of collaborative learning between the start-up team and their partners, and the structure of firm boundaries shapes the effectiveness of these collaborations. A start-up might need to interact with current customers (e.g., to conduct interviews and observe behavior) and collaborate with the value chain architect to help create new products or services for its customers. Choosing to work with a more ambiguous and cooperative boundary at the outset may help the venture and the firm iterate and learn.

In contrast, a well-defined firm boundary divides responsibilities for different activities within the value chain between the start-up and the established firm. Both organizations focus on activities they are particularly well-suited for and avoid duplicative investment. For instance, most large consumer goods companies, such as Kellogg's, Coca-Cola, or even Apple, rank branding and marketing as among their most critical assets, and one might assume that these companies rely on their own internal capabilities to develop and build their brand identity. However, the vast majority of national or global brand advertising is handled by independent advertising agencies. Working collaboratively with a small number of select clients (usually no more than one in any given industry or market), these agencies are responsible for creating and implementing the brand strategy, marketing materials, and advertising campaigns for their client's core products and services. Thus, advertising agencies develop capabilities and approaches that create value for their clients, so client firms can focus on developing and delivering the actual products and services.

firm boundaries Limits that set the responsibilities and activities of a firm in a value chain

FIGURE 11.3 Advertising and Marketing Value Chain Entrepreneurs

(a)   (b)

One of Kellogg's most beloved brand characters, Tony the Tiger (a) originated not in the halls of the large multinational food manufacturing company, but from value chain entrepreneur Leo Burnett and his legendary advertising company, Leo Burnett Company. Another entrepreneur, David Williams, centered his data processing firm, Merkle (b), on having the best talent and using the power of data streams in marketing and advertising for its clients.

This structure provides an opportunity for an advertising agency entrepreneur with a novel approach toward branding and marketing that could apply across different industries. For example, while most advertising traditionally had focused on product descriptions or price, Leo Burnett believed that a more durable brand could be built through a "soft sell" approach in which an advertisement featured a memorable, realistic experience where the product is being used. This unique perspective became the cornerstone of the Leo Burnett Company, which developed some of the most iconic brands and messages of the twentieth century, including Tony the Tiger and United Airlines' "Fly the Friendly Skies" slogan (**Figure 11.3a**). Even the design of the Glad sandwich bag was the brainchild of Burnett and his team. More recently, many advertising and marketing start-up firms have been focusing on maximizing and utilizing data for their clients. For example, at the age of 25, David Williams acquired and became the 24th employee of a small firm focused on data processing, Merkle.[4] Over the years, concentrating on organic growth and talent acquisition led it to a mission to "empower the world's leading brands to transform their data, technology, and organizational capabilities."[5] Merkle was fully acquired by the advertising firm Dentsu for approximately $1.5 billion in 2020 (**Figure 11.3b**).

MAKE VS. BUY

The most obvious approach to structuring firm boundaries is to be a supplier of an intermediate product or service as part of a value chain of a larger firm. For a larger firm, each stage of a value chain is associated with a "make vs. buy" decision, where the firm compares the overall value created from maintaining a particular set of functions or capabilities in-house (i.e., "make") to the value

Nobel Prize Winners on Outsourcing

The make vs. buy decision defines what will be done inside the business instead of outsourced. Nobel laureate Ronald Coase famously postulated that the costs of transacting in the market were a key reason for making rather than buying business functions. Procuring external functions is sometimes easy, especially when you can buy services in a competitive market. But at other times, doing so requires key specifications of quality standards and delivery timing. This

The make vs. buy decision of whether to outsource has been considered by several Nobel Prize economists.

often occurs for start-ups developing products that require physical manufacturing. In the latter case, outsourcing requires careful attention to contracting so that terms are not changed after an agreement, as another Nobel laureate, Oliver Williamson, warned about. Doing so requires experience, deal-making skills, networks to assess the reputation of suppliers and, of course, lawyers. Those costs can add up. But this doesn't imply that outsourcing has costs and internal sourcing is "free." As Nobel laureate Oliver Hart and economics professor John Moore pointed out, if getting needed quality is an issue from an external supplier, it can be just as difficult internally. The difference between the two is that you may be in a superior bargaining position when you control key assets required to complement the efforts of talent.

The challenge of implementing this approach is that the well-defined boundaries needed to capture value from the relationship may come at the expense of the insight needed to identify how to create value for a specific partner in the first place. The choice to buy rather than to make is ultimately a choice of the larger firm, which will also hold most of the bargaining power. Though a highly structured supply relationship may be the *goal* of a value chain entrepreneur, obtaining the information needed to get started can make this difficult to establish at the start.

---

outsource Obtaining a good or service through an outside supplier, in place of obtaining one from this in-house

created if it partners or **outsources** with an external entity to obtain these goods or services (i.e., "buy") (see **Using the Research: Nobel Prize Winners on Outsourcing**). A value chain entrepreneur can induce a firm to "buy" if the entrepreneur can offer a well-defined set of component parts or services that (1) significantly reduces cost or (2) offers more quality than what is available internally or externally. For example, a start-up might develop a new process that creates incremental value for a partner firm's current customers or that expands the partner firm's customer base to an adjacent or complementary sector.

STRATEGIC ALLIANCES

Specifying firm boundaries at the start of a partnership can be challenging. An alternative is to establish a strategic alliance. A strategic alliance creates a formal but fluid relationship between the two firms. It delineates a domain of collaborative activity with the possibility of establishing a more structured relationship after achieving certain milestones. The value of a strategic alliance comes from combining the collaborative and iterative nature of this more fluid approach with the longer-term potential to divide responsibilities, and payments, between the firms if it becomes more structured.

To see the value of alliances, consider the case of the network hardware company Cisco, which has pursued strategic alliances with start-up firms as a central tool in maintaining its leadership. Cisco is the dominant firm and value chain architect of networking hardware, including products such as routers and services such as server management. While most companies in this industry maintain collaborative agreements with start-ups, most are managed on a case-by-case basis. In contrast, starting in the mid-1990s under the leadership of John Chambers, Cisco developed and implemented a comprehensive approach to work with start-up innovators. First, Cisco identified start-ups working in an area that could be valuable to them. Then, Cisco would establish a strategic alliance to understand the ways in which the firms might work together to create new value for Cisco's customers, establish trust, and identify the motivation and career goals of the start-up team. These alliances let Cisco and the start-up identify how to structure a more long-lasting relationship. In some cases, this meant shifting toward an ongoing supply relationship. Importantly, in other cases, this would lead to Cisco acquiring the start-up outright and purposefully on favorable terms for the start-up. Cisco championed the use of strategic alliances as a way to find technology and new teams and ultimately became the preferred acquirer of promising start-ups in the hardware networking industry (**Figure 11.4**).[6]

FIGURE 11.4 Cisco Acquisitions

Cisco notes on its website: "Our acquisition strategy brings new technologies and business models to Cisco" and then goes on to list them over 23 alphabetized pages.

The Cisco experience is far from unique. Strategic alliances have become a standard way for a start-up firm and a larger firm that is its industry's value chain architect to explore potential ways to work together on an ongoing basis.[7] These start-ups normally achieve higher valuations too. However, while this collaboration is beneficial to the partner firm, the lack of clear boundaries can be a disadvantage to a start-up; the partner firm may be able to absorb the unique knowledge or insights of the start-up, placing the start-up in an even weaker bargaining position. For this reason, start-ups pursuing a strategic alliance must choose a partner with a strong reputation (or incentive) for working effectively with new ventures.

TRUST

Many value chain entrepreneurs rely at least at first on simply trusting potential partners until an agreement is reached. A value chain strategy means a commitment to execution at the expense of control, and these entrepreneurs may decide to work informally at first with a medium or large player within their industry. Though the start-up might not capture any value from the relationship, an informal engagement with a larger player helps a start-up when it can provide value for a potential partner without having to commit to that partner too early in the process.

Consider the early history of Sun Microsystems, a general-purpose workstation company founded by Andy Bechtolsheim, Vinod Khosla, Bill Joy, and Scott

McNealy in 1982 around the principle that the "network is the computer." While their first product gained success within universities, penetrating the larger and more sustainable OEM market proved to be a much tougher sell. (OEM stands for original equipment manufacturer; an OEM makes products from other manufacturers' components). About one year after its founding, Sun was locked in a battle to serve as the supplier for Computervision, the leading OEM computer reseller of the early 1980s. The customers of Computervision were demanding advanced workstation technology, and Khosla and his team believed that the solutions promoted by Sun would be a game changer for these customers. However, the viability of Sun as a venture was at stake when the CEO of Computervision informed Khosla that they had selected Apollo, Sun's leading competitor, as Computervision's supplier. Khosla countered with an extraordinary offer: in exchange for becoming the exclusive supplier to Computervision, Sun promised to allocate half of its workforce to the Computervision contract, give Computervision the right to use the Sun technology on its own production lines, and, moreover, agree to this deal at a price of zero! Khosla believed that, even though Sun would not be paid for its initial work, Sun could prove the value of its team and technology to Computervision over time. However, that belief also depended on *trusting* Computervision to give Sun a chance to prove itself and make itself indispensable to Computervision. To this end, Khosla leveraged access to his team, carefully rationing contact with Sun's technology gurus Bechtolsheim and Joy. This enhanced Sun's bargaining power over time, ultimately creating and capturing value by providing a valuable service that Computervision could no longer live without (**Figure 11.5**).

FIGURE 11.5 **Sun Microsystems**

The Sun Microsystems team proved crucial to providing unique value to Computervision's end customers. Vinod Khosla (pictured here in 2022) made a bold deal to work with Computervision that helped Sun develop its capabilities, earn broader credibility within the emerging workstation industry, and flourish as one of the superstar computer companies of the 1980s and 1990s.

While Khosla's choice to simply trust Computervision worked out for Sun, a trust-based relationship with a larger firm is challenging for most start-ups. Trust-based economic relationships can work when two parties or members of a network have a long-standing existing relationship so that each party is able to demonstrate their reliability to the others. Futher, this relationship must be likely to persist into the future so that each party does not have an incentive to take short-term advantage of their partners. Almost by definition, neither of these conditions holds for a start-up trying to work within the value chain of larger, more established enterprises. The start-up does not have a long-standing track record and is not guaranteed to survive in the future. The resulting imbalance in power between the start-up and the established firm is amplified when the start-up needs the opportunity to demonstrate its value to its potential partners.

In some cases, the founder's reputation in the industry helps overcome this challenge. For example, the start-up's founders may be trusted former employees of the larger firm. And some value chain architects (such as Cisco discussed earlier) proactively nurture a reputation as a reliable start-up partner. However, in many circumstances, when a value chain entrepreneur relies on trust-based relationships without a path toward either an alliance or a contractual supply relationship, they end up yielding the bargaining power in the relationship to the incumbent firm, to the long-term disadvantage of the start-up.

11.3 The Four Choices That Shape a Value Chain Strategy

Simply put, in most cases, a successful scenario for a value chain strategy is one where other firms contract with the entrepreneurs for a significant payment for their execution capabilities. This provides entrepreneurs with resources to reinvest and further develop their core competencies, becoming even more of an asset. With this in mind, for a value chain strategy, how should an entrepreneur set the four key choices—customer, technology, competition, and organization—to maximize their probability of success?

CHOOSING YOUR CUSTOMER

Recall that to be successful, a value chain strategy must create value for a group of customers served by the partner firm. Value chain entrepreneurs reinforce the value proposition of an existing firm, either by enhancing or improving what it does or by reducing its costs. Value chain entrepreneurs must articulate a value proposition that will be meaningful for a partner firm's existing customers, or those that are a priority for them to obtain. Notably, this differs from the "fringe" customers that are the first targets for a disruptive strategy.

Consider Schoology, founded in 2009 by Jeremy Friedman, Ryan Hwang, and Timothy Trinidad, who started collaborating in an entrepreneurship class at Washington University in St. Louis. The three founders of Schoology focused from the outset on integrating cloud-based educational support tools into traditional classrooms, an approach that differed from other start-ups at the time that sought to disrupt traditional education. Rather than trying to immediately sell a particular product or service, their early focus was gaining feedback from educators about how an interactive system could enhance the learning experience. In doing so, the team found that many of their early assumptions were incorrect: "When we pitched the first version of Schoology, high schools hated it. [Doing so] brought our act together and got us to where we are today."[8] Specifically, teachers highlighted the importance of controlling student cyberbullying or flirting, prompting the team to give educators higher control over how the platform was used. With this iterative process, they rapidly gained insight into developing a more "social" learning management system, which they successfully deployed across tens of millions of users across all 50 states and more than 130 countries by 2016.

It is useful to highlight how customer choice in a value chain strategy differs (in a subtle way) from customer choice in an intellectual property strategy. In an intellectual property strategy, the start-up and the firms it collaborates with have a good idea about whether and how value will be created with some IP. In a value chain strategy, the start-up firm and established players engage, experiment, and learn together to *discover* exactly how (and for exactly whom) they should target their offering. For example, in the early history of online grocery shopping, 1990s start-up Peapod did not try to compete with established grocery chains but served as a value-added complement to the traditional industry. Through this collaboration, it identified professional women as a specific type of target customer. It gained an understanding of important features that they valued, like automating repeat orders and scheduling delivery for specific times.[9] These targeted experiments during its formative stage let it build a base of knowledge and develop specialized capabilities. Since then, Peapod has led the online grocery business for nearly 20 years. After a 2020 acquisition, it is now called Peapod Digital Labs and, according to its website, it tries to make the entire "grocery experience better every day."[10]

CHOOSING YOUR TECHNOLOGY

Frequently, value chain entrepreneurs are in business to integrate emerging technology into the operations of existing players. But fusing new technology into an older value chain can present a distinct and difficult challenge for an entrepreneur. Often, both the start-up and their partners want to take advantage of emerging technologies that incumbent firms have yet to exploit. By assimilating this emerging technology (and the promise of its new S curve) into its value chain, an incumbent will enhance how it creates value and avoid potential disruption by a competitive start-up. But because the incumbent firm usually does not want to abandon its prior technology and infrastructure, a value chain entrepreneur cannot simply develop a whole new system. Instead, the challenge (and the opportunity) of technology choice in a value chain approach is identifying how the emerging technology can extend rather than replace the current technology S curve.

Consider how Mick Mountz harnessed the value that robotics could bring to warehouse automation through his start-up Kiva Systems (**Figure 11.6**). Mountz got the

FIGURE 11.6 **Kiva Systems**

Kiva Systems robots are each positioned under and ready to move a shelf of goods at an Amazon warehouse in Tracy, California.

idea for Kiva Systems working in Silicon Valley for Webvan, a late 1990s start-up that, unlike Peapod, attempted to disrupt the traditional grocery store industry with online grocery shopping. After Webvan went bankrupt during the dot-com crash of the early 2000s, Mountz moved back to the East Coast. He realized that, though Webvan had pursued a failed strategy, integrating robotics into warehouse operations was a meaningful and underdeveloped opportunity. Along with Peter Wurman and Raffaello D'Andrea, Mountz founded Kiva Systems not to compete with established companies but to explore how to integrate emerging advances in robotics systems in their operations. Specifically, warehouse logistics involve two key steps—"picking" (i.e., finding an item on a warehouse shelf) and "packing" (i.e., sorting the item into an appropriate box for delivery). While humans traditionally completed both of these tasks, Mountz and his team believed that they could develop a robot that could completely automate "picking" while leaving humans to do the "packing" step. Early investor Bain Capital introduced them to the leadership of Staples Office Supplies, which was moving toward online ordering rather than in-store sales. Mountz and his team worked with Staples to develop a standardized robotic trolley and software to control it. The robotic trolleys dramatically reduced the role of humans in the picking stage and enhanced their productivity in the packing stage. Over the next several years, Kiva Systems iteratively improved the performance of the trolleys and determined how to best use them as a *specialized component* they could apply across different warehouse configurations and product categories. With this approach, the team established a small but meaningful set of partnerships with leading retailers, including the Gap, Walgreens, and Crate & Barrel, and then Amazon. In 2012, Amazon acquired Kiva Systems outright, integrating more than 200,000 robots across its warehouse operations over the next decade.

Ultimately, Kiva Systems succeeded in integrating an emerging technology for those retailers, producing significant value. It succeeded because, rather than simply investing in the power of the new technology, the team prioritized creating a bridge between the new technology (robots picking) and old technology (humans packing). More generally, entrepreneurs can explore using technology to improve existing firms' interfaces and how firms collaborate in product development, but in a way that is compatible with a firm's primary use case. A value chain strategy depends less on the intrinsic value of the technology (as might be the case in a disruptive strategy) than on making sure it meaningfully integrates with the technology an incumbent firm uses.

CHOOSING YOUR COMPETITION

Successfully capturing value with a value chain strategy requires establishing a meaningful bargaining position with partners. The price that a value chain entrepreneur can charge depends on the strength of their position relative to their partner. This is shaped by two distinct forms of competition.

1. Can a start-up establish itself as the "preferred" partner in a particular domain? If the value created can be produced by many other firms, then the incumbent firm will play different value chain firms off one another, bargaining over price.
2. Can the partner duplicate the activities of the partnership? If the partner can do most of what is needed itself, the threat of that substitution will hang

FIGURE 11.7 McDonald's Clamshell

This clamshell container solved a problem that McDonald's did not want to deal with or try to replicate, and in the process clamshell creator Jon Huntsman Sr. became a key part of its value chain.

over the relationship and undermine the bargaining power of the start-up. However, if incumbent firms cede responsibility for a set of activities to the start-up, the start-up will accumulate bargaining power over time, as it gradually improves and adds to its specialized capabilities and resources.

To see both of these competitive effects in action, consider the introduction of the clamshell container by Jon Huntsman Sr. During the early 1970s, Huntsman perceived an opportunity to leverage his background in the petrochemical products industry to provide more effective containers for the rapidly growing fast-food industry. Specifically, McDonald's had introduced its iconic Big Mac sandwich just a few years earlier but faced the problem that the packaging would often leak. Huntsman recognized that using Styrofoam shells would address the leakage problem and maintain heat and taste (**Figure 11.7**). Though McDonald's initially expressed no interest in partnering with Huntsman, Huntsman demonstrated the potential value of the clamshell in the form of a limited experiment with Burger King. With its success, Huntsman could begin negotiating with McDonald's in a more systematic way. Importantly, Huntsman rapidly expanded the capacity and the capabilities (especially the precision) of Styrofoam production for the food industry. Given its internal priorities on developing new food products rather than containers and given that it did not have alternative options to do what Huntsman did, McDonald's simply established a long-term partnership. Huntsman ultimately produced hundreds of millions, if not billions, of clamshell containers for McDonald's, becoming a billionaire in the process. Indeed, the economic sustainability of this product line was not undermined by competition but by growing awareness and appreciation for the negative environmental consequences of petrochemicals, prompting a shift in the 2000s back to wrapped paper packaging.

CHOOSING YOUR ORGANIZATION

One of the most challenging aspects of choosing a value chain strategy is establishing an organization to partner with other firms at segments of their value chain. While control-oriented strategies organize a team's identity around a specific IP or technology, and disruptive entrepreneurs can leverage an unfettered entrepreneurial spirit, value chain entrepreneurs must establish a distinctive role and identity not centered on an idea they control or by pitting themselves against the world. Instead, the organization of a value chain start-up is centered on developing and growing its core competency. Value chain start-ups form an organization that fulfills an irreplaceable function in the value chain with a functionally specialized team and unique capabilities. They can't be just good but must be the very best at something, such that value chain partners cannot or do not want to imitate and expropriate from the start-up.

This is something that Judith Faulkner understood. In the late 1970s, Faulkner, without outside funding, saw an opportunity to computerize and track patient information and founded a company called Epic. She wasn't the only one. A well-funded competitor, Cerner, founded by three Arthur Andersen consultants, moved quickly and gained market leadership before going public just three years after its founding. Epic took a slower route, with just 69 customers by 2000. As it turned out, that timing was just right, as one of the United States' biggest HMOs, Kaiser Permanente, was looking to replace its old IBM system with up-to-date technology. Cerner and Epic competed for the deal, but whereas Cerner had a key presence of salespeople, Epic chose to let Kaiser's team see what they wanted within the company, treating them "like a colleague, not a customer." Epic won the deal and, with that prize, expanded rapidly. The records of 40% of the U.S. population now are on Epic through its integrated MyChart interface, where each version retains the brand of the partner healthcare systems (see the sidebar on **Judith Faulkner and Epic**).[11]

This victory reflected a critical part of Epic's culture. It focused on execution, which meant developing a system that met its customer needs. That meant selling itself without a hard sale. Despite having billions of dollars in revenues, only 1% of its 9,000-plus employees are in sales and marketing, with only five senior salespeople and no commissions to anyone. Epic does not try to grab as many customers as possible but instead seeks only those who are fit to work with Epic. In fact, Faulkner wants customers to come to her company. Epic's system is based on a half-century-old programming language that plays into the hospital's desire for reliability. In other words, Faulkner has built a company culture based on transparency to customers, no special treatment or deals, and, hence, no need for sales pressure or expertise.

HOW THE FOUR CHOICES FIT TOGETHER

To review, a value chain strategy is built on the idea that it is a partner that enhances the market power of a partner firm. However, it does so in a way that establishes and sustains bargaining power for the start-up. A value chain strategy's key element is carefully positioning the venture to serve a particular "layer" of the value chain in a unique and distinctive way. Doing this can be difficult and will leave start-ups with a low level of bargaining power within their relationships if the integration is not handled strategically.

Understanding how the four key choices in a value chain strategy work together helps a venture establish a stronger position. Let's review these using **Figure 11.8** on page 326, which shows the key choices in a value chain strategy, and see how these were applied by Infosys.

ORGANIZATION CHOICE Value chain strategies are built on having resources that excel in a specific function. Rationing access to key members of an integrated team helps establish the value that a firm can offer within a relationship, highlighting the role of organization choice in shaping the success of a value chain strategy. Infosys did this by harnessing the growing resource of English-speaking engineering graduates from India's prestigious IITs. The founding team saw that they could build an organization with this talent to improve the processes at large global firms at a lower price.

CUSTOMER CHOICE Value chain strategies help a partner firm find more value for that firm's high priority-customers. But a value chain firm must understand

Judith Faulkner and Epic. Computer programmer Judith Faulkner started Epic in her basement. Decades later, Epic has grown to become one of the largest healthcare technology firms in the United States, headquartered on a sprawling thousand-acre campus in Verona, Wisconsin, and Faulkner is one of the country's wealthiest self-made billionaires, according to *Forbes*. In leading the over 9,000-person company today, Faulkner still focuses on the same principles that first made Epic a valuable partner for health systems—a relentless commitment to recruiting top talent, protecting its customer-service-centric culture, and avoiding distractions. Showing this specialty, Epic develops all its software itself.[a]

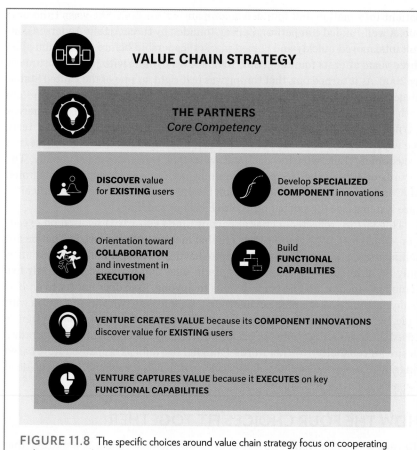

FIGURE 11.8 The specific choices around value chain strategy focus on cooperating and executing with an incumbent firm, but in a way that maintains control for the start-up.

and choose both customers: the end customer as well as the firm trying to serve them. In this sense, Infosys understood that the products and services provided by the large companies it partnered with, like Reebok, would have more value because of how it would improve and better integrate the IT processes of these large companies.

TECHNOLOGY CHOICE A value chain entrepreneur helps partners integrate an emerging technology into a firm's existing operations and business processes. The entrepreneur does so by providing a specialized component that extends the firm's current technology and embeds the value chain entrepreneur directly into the processes of the partner firm. For Infosys, a core principle was the "criticality of customized software [created by Infosys] in creating a competitive advantage for a corporation."[12]

COMPETITION CHOICE Value chain strategy ventures join forces with partners, working to be seen as trusted collaborators. However, the founding team must always exert control over their resources; what they offer must be seen as unique and not something the established firm can easily imitate. In its early days, Infosys worked hard to establish trust with new partners, from its transparency in business relations to its standards of professionalism. Over time, it became a premier employer for ITT grads, which burnished its reputation and cachet in the market.

11.4 Putting a Value Chain Strategy to the Test

The ultimate tests for a value chain start-up and its hypotheses are

a. whether it can attract talent with scarce and unique capabilities;
b. whether it can find customers that can be better served by the start-up's expertise, technology, process improvement, or unique offerings; and
c. whether it can integrate its idea without disclosing key knowledge that may be used for reverse engineering.

Let's see how real-world entrepreneurs have performed these tests to find out whether their idea or hypothesis can create and capture value.

A VALUE CHAIN STRATEGY'S VALUE CREATION HYPOTHESIS

We have seen that value chain entrepreneurs must have a *well-grounded hypothesis of why their team will be able to provide additional unique value either through enhanced consumer benefit or lower costs to those customers who are already being served by established firms* (for another example, see **Mini Case: How Sensassure Aligned Its Product with Customer Needs** on p. 328). And to prove this, they must run experiments and tests that show credible evidence of why their team and its value creation hypothesis will provide unique value to an established firm's customers. Consider Shahid Khan, a Pakistani emigrant to the United States who began working in the automobile parts industry while studying at the University of Illinois in the late 1960s. Khan became an early employee of auto parts manufacturer Flex-N-Gate, attempting to improve the company's car bumper production and installation processes. At that time, a typical bumper had 15 separate components, which then had to be fastened together in manufacturing. As part of the early engineering team at Flex-N-Gate, Khan believed that a bumper could be "stamped" from a single piece of steel, essentially eliminating the costly and time-consuming processes of putting the individual pieces of a bumper together. However, the only real way to demonstrate this value was to test the idea on an existing automobile assembly line. To do so, Flex-N-Gate collaborated with Jeep, which then had only a small market share (mostly government sales). Tests with Jeep and later ones with emerging Japanese companies for pick-up trucks let Flex-N-Gate prove that its product was more reliable for end customers and reduced the costs of complex assemblies.[13]

However, though Flex-N-Gate was able to test the potential for value creation, the path toward value capture became more challenging. Specifically, when General Motors (then the leading automobile manufacturer in the world) decided

How Sensassure Aligned Its Product with Customer Needs

Constructing their value creation hypothesis within a value chain strategy was a key challenge for the Sensassure founding team. Started by a 20-year-old business student from the University of Alberta, Canada, Sameer Dhar (along with Tim Ahong and Jeremy Dabor), Sensassure sought to create "smart" diapers for elder care. Dhar had seen that continence management was a large pain point in nursing homes. Typically, residents wearing diapers were awoken every two hours to be checked, disturbing their sleep and adding an extra burden on staff. By placing Sensassure's sensors on the diapers, staff could be alerted if there was a real need to change someone rather than just sticking to a schedule. It seemed like a no-brainer idea in value creation for residents and a new product category—underwearables—to boot.

The natural customers for Sensassure's product were nursing homes. However, it quickly became apparent that, in Canada, there was little reason for those homes to pay for the product. Being primarily government funded, the value Sensassure created

Sameer Dhar

in continence management was not aligned with how those homes were funded. So Dhar and his team left for the United States, where competitive pressures in nursing homes were more apparent and good continence management was not just a pain point but also a potential source of competitive advantage in attracting residents and their families. While providing a sensor to manage continence was a clear technical proposition, its founders quickly realized that detection was not enough. The new device had to be integrated into the workflow of nursing homes. How to do that, however, was not at all clear.

The first problem the team faced was that it was hard to get residents to agree to participate with prototype devices that looked like a scary set of wires attached to their undergarments. However, upon describing this quandary to one of their professors (and an author of this textbook), he suggested they should each "take one for the team" and test the device on themselves. Uncomfortable though that was, they and their new employees (as part of an initiation ritual) wore and used the device. This greatly accelerated the testing process as well bringing a new appreciation of comfort requirements.

Fresh off that undertaking, when it came to learning how to integrate the device into workflows, the twenty-something founders took their entire operation to Maryland, where they were allowed to spend six months living in an aged-care facility owned by a chain, Lorien. That experience enabled them to understand both technical and organizational challenges and ultimately develop a system that created value for nursing homes as well as their residents. They also learned the ins and outs of elder care and developed close relationships with staff and residents.

After spending months piloting and refining their solution and integrating it with nursing home partners, Sensassure was acquired just two years later by the Swedish global hygiene company, SCA, in what was a very successful exit for both its founders and investors.

to adopt the Flex-N-Gate design across all its vehicles, it chose to work with a larger and more established supplier to scale the innovation developed by Flex-N-Gate. By this time, Khan was the owner of Flex-N-Gate; after briefly leaving to start his own company, Bumper Works, in 1978, he was able to exploit its success to purchase Flex-N-Gate several years later.[14] While many entrepreneurs

Shahid Khan's belief that a bumper could be stamped from a single piece of steel led to deals with Japanese automakers, his company eventually becoming the leading bumper manufacturer in the world, and Kahn fulfilling his dream of owning professional sports franchises.

might be bitter, Khan noted, "It really was the right thing for them [GM]. We had no business going from making 200 bumpers a day to 40,000."[15] Instead, Khan focused on working with the rapidly expanding Japanese manufacturers, most notably Toyota, which allowed Flex-N-Gate to eventually establish itself as the leading producer of bumpers in the world; for example, its bumpers were included on more than two-thirds of vehicles sold in 2011. By 2020 Flex-N-Gate registered more than $8 billion in annual sales, and Shahid Khan had already been able to parlay his successful leadership in the bumper industry to achieve his childhood dream of owning a sports franchise, purchasing the NFL's Jacksonville Jaguars in 2012 (**Figure 11.9**) and the Premier League's Fulham Football Club just one year later.

A VALUE CHAIN STRATEGY'S VALUE CAPTURE HYPOTHESIS

As illustrated in the case of Flex-N-Gate, without clear control over its technology, a start-up's value chain partners can learn from the start-up at the very early stages of the relationship and then bypass it once the partners are able to extract the knowledge and know-how they need. Flex-N-Gate could not initially serve GM, which could implement Flex-N-Gate's advances itself. To overcome this challenge, *a value chain entrepreneur must go beyond and have a hypothesis of why they will serve a crucial, irreplaceable role in the value chain for existing firms.*

Both of the core tools of a value chain strategy are critical for enabling this process of value capture.

1. Team: A value chain entrepreneur can establish bargaining power through the cohesion and interdependence of their team. The team is the source of the tacit knowledge and knows how to realize the promise of the innovation; they can efficiently and creatively solve implementation problems or develop a continuous stream of innovation.
2. Firm boundaries: Through the proactive choice of firm boundaries, the value chain entrepreneur provides unique value by developing specific, tailored capabilities. Often, this is accomplished by establishing excellence at a specific "layer" of the value chain where the value chain architect has either less capability or strategic focus.

A prime example of this is the Taiwanese technology firm Foxconn, which has long focused on developing capabilities in precision electronics manufacturing. It found early success in this field in the 1980s as the lowest "total cost" manufacturer for early electronics products like the massively popular gaming system Atari 2600 (**Figure 11.10a**). This experience tested Foxconn's ability to serve as a critical layer in this electronics value chain. It also established the team and firm boundaries that have been crucial for the company's success over time. Foxconn is now responsible for nearly 40% of electronics manufacturing globally and is the largest single private employer in China (with nearly 1.5 million employees as of 2013). While Foxconn has been involved in controversies regarding its labor force (including concerns over working conditions, wages, and the incidence of employee depression and suicide), it has become one of the largest single companies in the world without engaging directly with final customers (i.e., the ultimate buyers of devices it manufactures, such as the iPhone or Nintendo Switch: **Figure 11.10b**) or with the process of initial product design and innovation that is the hallmark of many of its clients. Indeed, this division of labor between Foxconn and its value chain partners reinforces the competitive advantage of each: design- and customer-oriented firms focus on innovation and customers, and Foxconn focuses on the manufacturing supply chain and the manufacturing process.

FIGURE 11.10 **Video Games: Then vs. Now**

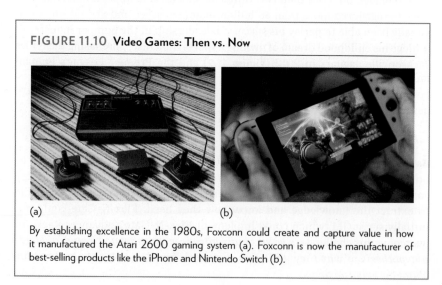

(a)　　　　　　　　　　　　　　　　(b)

By establishing excellence in the 1980s, Foxconn could create and capture value in how it manufactured the Atari 2600 gaming system (a). Foxconn is now the manufacturer of best-selling products like the iPhone and Nintendo Switch (b).

11.5 Putting a Value Chain Strategy to Work

With a strategy chosen, entrepreneurs need to start putting it to work by following three essential steps:

1. Carefully plan for and build a team based around the unique capabilities of the start-up. Value chain entrepreneurs should be "slow to hire, fast to fire" and prioritize finding people who can be integrated into the team and corporate culture.
2. Consider their proximity to the sources of talent they need to attract and access when locating their start-up. Another key consideration is identifying where existing firms are currently based; co-location could be a valuable way to foster trust and collaboration throughout the early product-development process.
3. Invest in business development, building strong relationships with their customers. Customers must be willing to support the development of the product and think of the start-up as their preferred partner. Value chain start-ups must also invest in acquiring people with strong negotiating abilities; their business success is driven by how well they arrange their contract terms with partners.

Perhaps there is no better example of the ability to put a value chain strategy to work over the past decade than Stripe. Founded in 2010 by Irish brothers Patrick and John Collison, Stripe worked on what many considered a pedestrian problem: online payment processing. Services such as PayPal and traditional credit card companies such as Mastercard and Visa had established reasonably secure and reliable payment processing in the early 2000s. However, the Collison brothers recognized the emerging payment problems that cloud-based start-ups such as Instacart and DoorDash would face. These start-ups maintained relationships with a wide variety of vendors, each with their own system, and had relatively small customer transactions that made the fees of most traditional solutions burdensome. To address these challenges, the Stripe team developed a simple yet elegant solution in which a single payment processing protocol could be used across a wide range of payment systems at a low per-transaction cost. The use of Stripe helped other platforms to rapidly onboard their customers at a much lower level of complexity and cost. For example, Airbnb could bring new hosts into its network by providing a simple Stripe solution for payments. By focusing on other start-ups as its initial customers, Stripe built the capabilities and infrastructure to serve as a critical—and nearly invisible—transaction layer where both start-ups and established firms rapidly process and account for their online business revenue. In 2023, Stripe was valued at $50 billion.

11.6 Concluding Thoughts

In many respects, a value chain strategy is a natural and often feasible path to commercializing an entrepreneur's idea. The existing value chain itself defines a functional role for the venture as a partner that will be successful if the entrepreneur can build an organization that focuses on a core competency, allowing it to execute on building functional capabilities (see **Putting It Together: Value Chain Strategy** on p. 332). The challenge is that other actors along the value chain will,

VALUE CHAIN STRATEGY

Discover new value for existing users by providing a best-in-class solution in collaboration with an established partner.

INTRODUCE THE FOUNDING TEAM AND PROPOSED BUSINESS MODEL

What Is Your Core Competency?

- Outline the team's "unfair" advantage, skills, and passion as they relate to the idea.
- Articulate how your business will discover new value with your partner organization.

DESCRIBE CUSTOMER, TECHNOLOGY, ORGANIZATION, AND COMPETITION CHOICES

Customer: Discover Value for Existing Users

- Describe how your idea will reinforce the value proposition of an existing firm by enhancing or improving current offerings or reducing costs; specify how this will discover new value for the established firm's customers.

Technology: Develop Specialized Component Innovations

- Describe how emerging technology extends rather than replaces the established firm's current technology.
- Evaluate the technology's performance and outline key performance metrics; specify how the technology must meaningfully integrate into existing systems.

Organization: Build Functional Capabilities

- Identify the unique capabilities needed for an irreplaceable, best-in-class function.
- Prioritizing these in your organizational design, briefly describe how the firm will recruit and retain that team.
- Describe the culture that facilitates continued innovation, business development, and trust with a partner organization.

Competition: Orient toward Collaboration and Invest in Execution

- Identify key competitors.
- Determine whether a potential partner has a track record of working with start-ups and if it has the capabilities or incentives to imitate or expropriate from the start-up.
- Specify the steps your start-up can take to be and stay the "preferred partner."

SHARPEN YOUR VALUE CREATION HYPOTHESIS AND VALUE CAPTURE HYPOTHESIS

Create Value with Component Innovations That Discover Value

- Articulate how your idea integrated with an established firm creates a continuous stream of innovation for customers.
- Generate experiments that demonstrate this value.

Capture Value by Executing on Key Capabilities

- Assess how the team's cohesion, interdependence, and choice of firm boundaries will establish and shape the start-up's bargaining position.
- Conduct due diligence on the potential partner's failure with prior collaborations.

while appreciating and encouraging value creation by the venture as a partner, try to suppress the unique role of the venture and their reliance on the capabilities the venture builds.

This tension places a considerable challenge on continuing management. The established partner firm has to permit the venture, itself a potential competitive threat, to exist. At the same time they expect a level of execution from the venture that is high enough for that partner to refrain from considering other options or doing it on their own. As we will discuss in a later chapter, when this tension is difficult to resolve, the value chain start-up becomes a natural candidate for acquisition and control by one of its partners as an exit option.

Chapter 11 Review: Value Chain Strategy

CHAPTER TAKEAWAYS

- A value chain strategy focuses on execution but is oriented toward cooperation with established firms in the industry.

- The value creation hypothesis for a value chain strategy leverages the start-up's core competency to create new value for the customers of an existing firm as well as those they want to attract.

- The value capture hypothesis for a value chain strategy should describe why the start-up will serve a crucial, irreplaceable role in the value chain for existing firms.

- Being able to attract and assemble talent is critical to the success of a value chain entrepreneur. A value chain start-up must leverage the team's learning, insights, and capabilities to create new value in a value chain.

- Firm boundaries define the set of activities that is the start-up's responsibility and those done by other players within the value chain (including the value chain architect). Choosing this boundary shapes how the start-up will collaborate with the value chain architect and other players in the market and the unique value it creates.

- At each stage in the value chain, the value chain architect makes a "make vs. buy" decision, comparing the value from "making" functions or capabilities internally to "buying" them by using an external partner. The value chain architect might "buy" from a start-up if it offers component parts or services that either (a) significantly reduce cost or (b) enhance quality relative to other options.

- A strategic alliance is a formal but fluid relationship between two firms. It describes an area of collaborative and iterative activity with the possibility of establishing a more structured relationship after certain milestones are achieved.

- In some cases, a value chain entrepreneur may find it worthwhile at first to work informally with a medium or large player within their industry, relying on trust until an agreement is reached.

- The customer choice in a value chain strategy is to select both the consumers who will ultimately gain value from the idea and the incumbent firm serving them.

- The technology choice integrates an emerging technology as a specialized component within the operations of an older value chain. Innovations will help extend the firm's technology but not replace it.

- The competition choice is to collaborate with incumbent firms. This is done by investing in the unique, specialized execution capabilities of the start-up team to shape the bargaining position of the start-up.

- The organization choice is to build a functionally specialized team with unique capabilities. The team then fulfills an irreplaceable function in the value chain.

KEY TERMS

value chain (p. 312)

firm boundaries (p. 316)

outsource (p. 318)

REVIEW QUESTIONS

1. How does a start-up create and capture value in a value chain strategy?

2. What are the primary challenges a start-up team faces if they choose to collaborate with incumbent firms but have no control over their idea? Why might incumbents have the upper hand when it comes to early-stage collaborations with execution-oriented start-ups?

3. What are the two most critical "tools" available to a value chain entrepreneur? For each tool, briefly describe how it allows a start-up to enhance its ability to create and capture value through a value chain strategy.

4. What are the key challenges a start-up team faces in building and retaining an effective team? What can a founding team do to build their team as part of a value chain strategy?

5. Define *make vs. buy*. Why might a start-up choose to "make" rather than "buy" a particular capability? Why might a start-up choose to "buy" rather than "make"?

6. What are the advantages of a strategic alliance approach to a value chain strategy? Why might strategic alliances allow a start-up to overcome some of the key challenges of a value chain strategy?

7. Start-up teams pursuing a value chain strategy are encouraged to choose a final customer (i.e., the final user of the product or service that leverages their idea) to discover value for their partners' existing users. What is the logic behind this recommendation?

8. What role does the development of a core competence play in a value chain strategy? Why might a start-up that develops a core competence succeed as one element of a larger value chain?

9. What is the core hypothesis that an entrepreneur should test in a value chain strategy? What other players might that entrepreneur need to get on board to perform a meaningful test?

10. What are some key implementation factors that allow a value chain entrepreneur to succeed over the longer term? Why are each of these important, and what challenges does a start-up face in putting a value chain strategy to work?

11. Many successful value chain start-ups choose to locate close to their partner. Why might locating near larger value chain partners be particularly important?

DISCUSSION QUESTIONS

Answer the following series of questions and scenarios either in class discussions or by writing a short response.

1. Minjun and Soomi are colleagues in the medical device industry. Minjun has considerable expertise in the regulatory process, while Soomi is an expert in user-centered design. Over dinner at an industry conference, they agree that, too often, patients' perspective is undervalued in the product development process to reduce potential regulatory hurdles. They believe that a firm that combines a user-centric design approach and incorporates regulatory concerns from the outset might offer a powerful new opportunity for traditional medical device firms. They plan to meet one day a week to work on this potential idea. Given their time constrains, what are three concrete steps you recommend that Minjun and Soomi accomplish over the course of six months to decide whether they should pursue this opportunity? What are the most critical hypotheses in their idea to validate? Can you suggest a way to do so (or not)?

2. Earlier in the chapter, we discussed how the Schoology founders Jeremy Friedman, Ryan Hwang, and Timothy Trinidad integrated feedback from educators to improve their product. For example, rather than allow a "free-for-all" environment on the platform, educators placed a high premium on moderated discussions. Because the founders valued opinions like these, teachers were given a high degree of control over how the platform was used. Using the information you have, describe why listening and learning from educators was so important for Schoology (i.e., how did they turn feedback into action?). Do you agree with the Schoology founders' choice to focus first on educators, perhaps at the expense of students? Or do you think there may have been better paths to take? Support your answer with information from the chapter about the best way to execute a value chain strategy.

3. One element of a value chain strategy is developing a trust-based relationship between the value chain start-up and more established firms. For example, Infosys cofounder Narayana Murthy maintained a high level of professionalism within Infosys, adopting corporate governance practices such as audited financial statements that were above and beyond what was required of Indian firms at that time. What role did these trust-oriented commitments by Infosys play in shaping its relationships with global companies? Why is it hard for a start-up to establish a reputation as a trusted partner? What might a value chain start-up do to help nurture such a reputation in its earliest days?

4. Oliver's goal is to bring actionable metrics and strategy to established companies who are seeking to create more diverse, equitable, and inclusive (DEI) workplaces. He has developed a unique metrics-based approach that allows potential partners to assess their historical DEI performance and develop

and implement actionable strategies to reach DEI objectives. While Oliver initially believed he could simply license his methodology to firms using a hands-off approach, he has found that successful collaboration with a partner requires significant and sustained effort and time by him and his team. However, once the system is finally working within a firm, many clients can incorporate the metrics directly into their day-to-day operations. Given this information, what do you think might help Oliver establish partnerships with established companies (i.e., how does his start-up create value with its partners)? Briefly, why might the start-up face challenges in capturing value over the longer term? What are some alternatives to an open-ended consulting arrangement that might help Oliver and his team to capture more value over time?

5. One critical element of a value chain strategy is creating a "bridge" between the technology and designs of established firms and emergent technology that might pose a disruptive threat. For example, Kiva Systems integrated warehouse robotics into the existing processes and operations of logistics-intensive firms (such as Staples and, ultimately, Amazon), allowing these established players to leverage the value created by advanced robotics while maintaining much of their preexisting organizational structure. Using examples you have seen in the chapters or from outside research, identify an established firm that formed a partnership with a start-up to integrate a technology that might otherwise have been disruptive. Did the established firm successfully integrate the new technology into its established value chain? What happened to the start-up that helped to facilitate the transition?

6. Many value chain entrepreneurs find their ability to grow limited by the relatively narrow scope of their position within the value chain. A number would like to implement a strategic pivot toward a more control-oriented approach (such as an intellectual property strategy or even an architectural strategy where they compete with their former partners). Why might a value chain entrepreneur be interested in this type of strategic pivot? Describe challenges they are likely to face. Are there specific steps they might undertake to navigate such a transition successfully?

FOR FURTHER READING

Alvarez, Sharon A., and Jay B. Barney. "How Entrepreneurial Firms Can Benefit from Alliances with Large Partners." *Academy of Management Perspectives* 15, no. 1 (2001): 139–48.

Hamel, Gary, Yves Doz, and C. K. Prahalad. "Collaborate with Your Competitors—and Win." *Harvard Business Review*, February 1989, https://hbr.org/1989/01/collaborate-with-your-competitors-and-win.

Hart, Oliver, and John Moore. "Property Rights and the Nature of the Firm." *Journal of Political Economy* 98, no. 6 (1990): 1119–58.

Prahalad, C. K., and Gary Hamel. "The Core Competence of the Corporation." In *Knowledge and Strategy,* edited by Michael H. Zack, 41–59. New York: Routledge, 2009.

Tripsas, Mary. "Unraveling the Process of Creative Destruction: Complementary Assets and Incumbent Survival in the Typesetter Industry." *Strategic Management Journal* 18 (1997): 119–42.

Nick Rellas

When recent college graduate Nick Rellas found himself at home craving a beer, he found it odd that he could order almost everything—taxis, pizza, even a handyperson—through his mobile phone, yet he could not get a six-pack. Collaborating with his former classmate Justin Robinson, Rellas found that many independent liquor stores did, in fact, offer delivery services, but as these stores had little online presence, online delivery was not an integral aspect of their business. Rellas and Robinson founded Drizly to serve as the "21st century middleman"[a] for beer, wine, and liquor. They developed a streamlined mobile app and website that allows users to input their location; browse and purchase from an inventory of beers, wines, and spirits; and redirect that sale to a local liquor store partner that then fulfills their order in a timely way (including charging the customer, verifying customer ID for age purposes, and making the delivery). As one of Drizly's earliest partners, David Gordon, owner of Gordon Fine Wines, a small chain of stores in the Boston area, explains, "I thought [teaming up with them] was a good fit for the things we wanted to do with the business . . . a lot of retailers in the state are not innovative . . . [Drizly] brings a lot more relevance to the market."[b]

Drizly had great success during the COVID-19 pandemic, seeing a its revenue increase by four times and successfully obtaining $50 million in additional funding. Eventually it was acquired by Uber for $1.1 billion in 2021; although it was later folded into Uber's Uber Eats business in 2024.[c] While several elements of Drizly's story are familiar within the world of growth start-ups (a pair of twenty-somethings spot a weakness in current industry practices, develop a mobile app, and raise millions in financing), Drizly consciously stayed away from the word "disruptive." As Rellas explained, "We're not trying to rip down an industry and build it back up. . . . All we're doing is trying to give small businesses tools to be more profitable at the end of the day."[d] Drizly followed

Nick Rellas in 2015 in the Drizly office in Boston

a *value chain strategy*—playing a vital role in extending an existing value chain by helping local liquor stores (many of which are localized monopolists) boost retail sales through a value-added offering to their traditional end customers.

Questions

1. What was Drizly's value creation hypothesis? How did Drizly create value for local liquor stores? How did it create value for the customers of local liquor stores (i.e., local liquor buyers)? What early choices did the founding team make that were consistent with a value chain strategy?

2. Take the perspective of Drizly founders Nick Rellas and Justin Robinson in the early days of their start-up. How would you build your team to enhance the ability of Drizly to become the preferred partner for liquor stores? What functions and capabilities would you prioritize? How would you recruit experienced talent to your still-nascent start-up to fill these roles?

Today, Bloomberg technology is everywhere in the world of finance. However, this was an entirely new business architecture when it launched.

ENTREPRENEUR'S DILEMMA Ventures trying to build a new business architecture must create a new value chain while ensuring they have elements in place to control their future competition. Their dilemma is guaranteeing that customers will invest in and add value to their new business architecture, while ensuring that these investments do not also enhance the competitive position of existing value chains.

CHAPTER OBJECTIVES

- Understand that an architectural strategy is oriented toward competition and focuses on control
- Describe the tools of architectural strategy, including economies of scale and scope, sustainable differentiation, and platform design
- Identify the customer, technology, organization, and competition choices made as part of an architectural strategy
- Understand why ventures pursuing an architectural strategy end up focusing on going from "zero to one"

12

ARCHITECTURAL STRATEGY

I n 1981, Michael Bloomberg, a tech-savvy star stock trader, was fired from his Wall Street job. This unexpected career shock offered him a chance to explore an opportunity he had spotted in the industry: bringing computers into the trading room to "make a difference in the world of money and investing."[1] Bloomberg observed that, contrary to the traditional approach to trading, the information technology revolution was providing traders with large amounts of new information. As traders were starting to use this technology, it was changing trading to, as he says, "rely more on mathematical skills, and less on guts."[2] Bloomberg realized he was in a unique position to combine his engineering background and securities experience to bring the full and often untapped value of this new information technology across the financial services industry.

Recruiting three former trading colleagues,[3] the founding team focused on how to combine real-time financial data and networked computers to create meaningful value for financial professionals. Their exploration pushed them to construct the core of their new platform for this industry: a physical terminal that could not only display financial data as it came in but also let users run sophisticated financial analyses.

Bloomberg L.P.[4] then chose a business model where customers could use this platform on a proprietary basis. Financial services firms would lease the Bloomberg Terminal for their employees on a per-terminal, per-month basis so that Bloomberg L.P. would earn a recurring revenue from each trader who used the terminal. Leasing these terminals also let Bloomberg L.P. maintain tight control over how traders used the devices. The firm could manage how it delivered and supported product features while also limiting the potential for the lessees to share these resources with each other. Believing that these terminals offered differentiated value relative to existing products in the financial news industry,

An Architectural Strategy works to with a new value chain or platform that it builds and then controls.

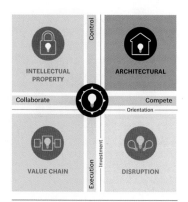

In Michael Bloomberg's words, "We went against giants, and giants are usually easy to beat."

Bloomberg focused his early efforts at winning customers among the most demanding and influential Wall Street firms. Merrill Lynch, one of the largest Wall Street brokerages, became Bloomberg's first customer.

Over the next 15 years, the Bloomberg Terminal became a ubiquitous standard for Wall Street traders. While the core interface of the platform remained the same, Bloomberg introduced tightly coupled complementary services, including a rapid and secure messaging system that let traders interact with others on the platform and a tailored real-time financial news feed that kept them aware of broader events that might impinge on financial markets. Bloomberg also had an organization built around serving customers using the terminal. Anytime, anywhere around the globe, customers with questions about using the terminal could contact the New York office for help and the answers they needed.

In effect, Bloomberg used what we term an *architectural strategy* in his venture. This strategy sees an entrepreneur work to build, control, and compete in an industry with an entirely new value chain, which can be driven by a new business platform. When successful, it is a very powerful strategy where control of the needed resources gives the entrepreneur real longevity even in a very competitive marketplace. We see that Bloomberg's terminal and platform created an entirely new value chain based on accessing and using financial information, one that the firm tightly controlled as it engaged its competitors. In the words of one Bloomberg executive, "All we ever talked about was the terminal . . . the terminal is front and center. It's all about the terminal. Everything is built for and is on the terminal."[5] Through this focus, Bloomberg has established and retained market leadership in the financial information services industry for multiple decades. In 2001, Michael Bloomberg actually took a leave of absence from his company to run for mayor of New York City, a position that he won and then was reelected to twice. One indication of the longevity of the competitive advantage of the Bloomberg platform is that, despite taking a leave of absence for more than a decade from the company, Michael Bloomberg's fortune as founder of Bloomberg L.P. actually doubled during his time in public office. As of 2023, Bloomberg has leased about 365,000 terminals for about $2,500 per month (with essentially no discounting), and the platform is the de facto standard interface for most financial services professionals.[6]

12.1 Creating and Capturing Value with an Architectural Strategy

Using an architectural strategy means conceiving and creating an entirely new value chain in the marketplace, rather than boosting the performance of an existing one. The central challenge of an architectural strategy for a start-up team is figuring out how their idea can deliver value to customers while, at the same time, maintaining control over their concept as they compete directly against incumbents for their core customers. Even so, an architectural strategy is distinct from a disruption strategy because the start-up must commit up front to specific product features, interfaces, or relationships to compete against established firms *and* maintain control over its underlying idea. Recall that in a disruption strategy, the start-up tries at first to compete against incumbents, but in a way that does not seem like a threat, at least at the beginning. In contrast, an architectural strategy is the entrepreneurial strategy closest to traditional ideas of **competitive strategy** that also applies to more established firms. As we saw with Bloomberg, far from operating at the fringes, it focused at an early stage on the most demanding and influential customer base and competed directly against the incumbents of the time.

Further, compared with other strategies we have seen in the last three chapters, architectural strategy is inherently more confrontational (relative to existing players) than one premised on cooperation (i.e., intellectual property or value chain) and more immediately commitment-oriented relative to the ongoing learning and experimentation associated with disruption. This makes architectural strategy both risky, since there is a higher level of up-front commitment, and more complex, since the venture needs to design and control a new value chain from the outset. Its core advantage comes from the value in attracting and then controlling resources essential to a successful new value chain. As described by PayPal cofounder Peter Thiel, starting a completely new business from "zero to one" allows a start-up to not only pioneer an idea in the marketplace but also establish the foundations for an enduring advantage (see sidebar on **Going from Zero to One**).

In this strategy, the central challenge and *value creation hypothesis* is how to make the up-front commitments to translate an idea into a novel value chain that creates demonstrable value for consumers. More specifically, how will the entrepreneur build out the value chain to provide a product or service at a lower cost, a greater value, or a combination of lower cost and greater value, by connecting stakeholders through their new platform? As an example, Bloomberg L.P. was built on the hypothesis that offering large quantities of real-time financial data would provide differentiated value from traditional financial media providers. Bloomberg hypothesized the firm could "alter the balance of power between the buy and sell sides"[7] of stock trading by increasing transparency and facilitating a more efficient market.

The *value capture hypothesis* is that the start-up can control the core idea by making strategic commitments to protect itself from inevitable competition from incumbents and entrants. This strategy can be like architecting a house, or as Warren Buffet describes it, building an "economic moat" around the idea to protect it.[8] Control can include investing in formal intellectual property protection (e.g., patents, copyrights, trademarks) or acquiring physical assets that competitors would need to purchase or develop to compete. It can also mean commitments the entrepreneurs make to thwart imitation, often a "secret sauce" in the product or process design that is hard to replicate, increasing consumer lock-in. For example, early on, Bloomberg invested in developing a system-wide secure messaging feature across all its terminals. As former Bloomberg director Matt Turck explains, "In its relevant target market, everyone is on [the messaging service] and uses it all day to communicate with colleagues, clients, and partners."[9] The messaging service created strong demand-side economies of scale, or network effects, such that as the number of traders on Bloomberg Terminals increased, the more valuable the Bloomberg Terminal became, making it increasingly harder for imitators to enter and start from square one (**Figure 12.1** on p. 342).

To clarify the architectural strategy and its costs and benefits further, we next take a deeper dive into the value creation and value capture hypotheses, outline

Going from Zero to One. The advantages (control, novelty) and challenges (direct competition, uncertainty) of an architectural strategy stem from building an entirely new value chain from scratch—going from "zero to one." In his 2014 book with the same name, Peter Thiel wrote, "The act of creation is singular, as is the moment of creation, and the result is something fresh and strange."[a]

FIGURE 12.1 The Bloomberg Keyboard

The Bloomberg terminal's keyboard contains easy access to its messaging service and the IB (Instant Bloomberg) chat system, which it advertises as "the center of the Bloomberg Terminal experience."

the four choices that underlie an architectural chain strategy, and then provide methods to put this strategy to the test and to work.

12.2 The Tools of Architectural Strategy

Architectural strategy is premised on the idea that designing and then controlling the key resources for a *new* value chain can deliver value superior to that which is currently provided in the marketplace. The key challenge of an architectural strategy is to choose and implement a precise design or approach that creates value while also maintaining sufficient control over the design to capture that value. For a start-up to do so successfully usually means using three strategic tools:

1. Achieving a low-cost position through economies of scale and scope
2. Realizing higher willingness to pay with core customers through a unique and differentiated product offering that cannot be easily imitated
3. Developing and managing a core platform that leverages direct and indirect network effects to achieve market lock-in

In short, the success of an architectural strategy centers on not simply coming up with a good idea but implementing it in a way that establishes and sustains advantage in the face of potential competition. Consider the business strategy pursued by King Gillette in the early 1900s that we first saw in Chapter 6. Razor blades in the nineteenth century were not only expensive but also required significant care and maintenance. While the concept and potential value of a "disposable" razor blade had been recognized since at least the 1850s,

FIGURE 12.2 Gillette

An army-issued Gillette safety razor kit, complete with a razor head, handle, pack of disposable blades, and a carrying case

Gillette was the first to develop a better product and a strategy to succeed in the marketplace. First, he took nearly a decade to refine the design and manufacture of a blade that was of high enough quality to give a clean shave and could be produced at a low enough cost so individuals could replace the blades regularly. Gillette then invested significantly in protecting his innovation through patents, trademarks, and secrecy in the manufacturing process and by working with influential potential adopters in the marketplace. While maintaining control is very important, creating incentives for people to take actions that reinforce your chosen architecture is critical. In Gillette's case, the U.S. Army was a key buyer during World War I, providing a whole generation of young American men with their first exposure to Gillette products (**Figure 12.2**). Interestingly, at the outset, Gillette sold each razor at a significant price premium ($5 for the handle and first set of blades); however, as the patents on his initial product expired, he shifted the pricing strategy, selling the razors for a nominal charge but charging more for replacement blades. Gillette would earn a high return on each purchase of a new set of blades, which had a low unit cost.

When pursuing an architectural strategy, think of yourself as not selling a product but instead developing a platform. King Gillette's success encapsulates how an entrepreneur can use the three key tools of an architectural strategy. Let's now look at each in more detail.

ECONOMIES OF SCALE AND SCOPE

The first critical tool is the ability to achieve a lower-cost position through **economies of scale and scope**. Economies of scale and scope arise when a firm can achieve a lower average cost through increasing the quantity produced of a single good, or by producing two or more things together at cheaper cost.

This chapter's video discusses how Gillette used an architectural strategy to revolutionize the way we shave.

economies of scale and scope
When a firm can achieve a lower average cost through an increase in the overall quantity produced of a single good, or by producing two or more things together at a cheaper cost than separately

Developing a Taste for CHEP's Pallet

In World War II, the Australian government set up an entity to handle defense supplies, largely shipped on wooden pallets. The end of the war left millions of these pallets unused in Australia, all painted a distinctive blue. When a new government came to power in 1949, it decided to privatize what was then called the Commonwealth Handling Equipment Pool (CHEP), which eventually became part of a transportation and logistics business, the Brambles corporation. While not a start-up in the strictest sense, it was an independent, innovative business. Since 2000, CHEP has enacted an architectural strategy for global expansion for pallets that has given it a virtual monopoly in many countries.

How did this happen? One reason is that in the United States, for example, the standard unit pallet was manufactured by a highly competitive set of small, local producers and often sold to recyclers who would break down and resell the wood. The technology had not changed much in half a century.

A stack of blue CHEP pallets, ready to be used for shipping.

Another reason: the dispersed nature of pallet production had made innovation difficult. To build a better, more durable pallet required more expense. However, as most pallets would be purchased and then stored or discarded, there was no demand for a more expensive pallet even if it was of higher quality.

CHEP changed the business model of the pallet industry. First, it developed a higher-quality pallet that was an inch taller, cleaner, and more uniform than a standard pallet. The pallet's design was also changed to make it more forklift friendly and liftable from four rather than two directions. Second, to justify this new design, CHEP went for scale. There are now a quarter of a billion pallets in the world with the distinctive blue paint and "Property of CHEP" emblazoned on the sides. Third, to overcome the usage issue associated with higher quality, CHEP chose not to sell pallets but to rent them. CHEP would control the pallets over their lifetime. Fourth, CHEP needed a way to keep track of all its pallets and ensure they were re-rented rather than, say, recycled. CHEP decided to invest in an army of "asset retrieval specialists" (think former cops) who visited shipyards and identified the blue pallets. It took considerable expense initially—both legal and otherwise—to retrieve the pallets, but adhering to its motto to "never leave a pallet behind," the firm established a reputation that caused recyclers to stay away from CHEP pallets. Today, CHEP has an uneasy relationship with recyclers; it pays a nominal fee to these companies to return pallets.

In the end, CHEP's pallets were a cheaper proposition for logistics. In 2010, Costco moved to only accept shipments on CHEP pallets. Thus, CHEP started to achieve some benefits of controlling a standard resource, alongside the scale efficiencies that can accompany management of a shared asset—in this case, a humble wooden pallet.

SOURCE: Tom Vanderbilt, "How Pallets Move the World," *Sydney Morning Herald*, August 16, 2012, https://www.smh.com.au/business/how-pallets-move-the-world-20120815-248mc.html.

Though conceptually straightforward, leveraging economies of scale and scope is difficult for a start-up. A new firm lacks the existing physical capital, infrastructure, knowledge, and demand to achieve an immediate low-cost position. One of the principal ways that companies achieve economies of scale is through "learning by doing." This happens when a firm builds up knowledge over time as it produces and distributes its products and learns how to systematically lower costs as it does (and also improve other factors like its reliability, operations, etc.). (See **Mini Case: Developing a Taste for CHEP's Pallet**.)

But many start-ups seek to leverage the potential for economies of scale and scope as part of their overall architectural strategy. For example, as discussed in Chapter 6, Elon Musk explicitly stated in his "Secret Tesla Motors Master Plan": "The strategy of Tesla is to enter at the high end of the market, where customers are prepared to pay a premium, and then drive down market as fast as possible to higher unit volume and lower prices with each successive model."[10] In so doing, Musk echoed perhaps the most important historical case of realizing an architectural strategy through economies of scale: Ford Motor Company. Henry Ford founded the Ford Motor Company in 1903 on the conviction that he could build a better automobile manufacturing company. Ford's hypothesis was that by using modular design and an assembly line production system, he could engineer a more efficient and affordable car. Over the course of five years, Ford experimented with multiple different prototypes and production models of his car, from the Model A onward. In 1908, he and his team realized his hypothesis with the launch of the Model T, a car that was not only functional but also affordable for middle-class incomes. Achieving this for the mass market depended critically on the experimentation and learning that came from models A though S, where Ford learned how to dramatically reduce the costs of automobile production and assembly. In fact, Ford's value creation hypothesis resonated so strongly that the Ford Model T was considered the most influential car of the twentieth century, selling over 15 million vehicles.[11]

SUSTAINABLE DIFFERENTIATION

The second tool for an architectural strategy is creating a unique and differentiated offering to the marketplace. As emphasized in Chapter 5, for any product, service, or platform to succeed it needs to create value for consumers relative to the costs of delivering that value. One of the most important ways that entrepreneurs create value is to introduce a new good, service, or platform that creates more value for some meaningful group of customers (though not necessarily all potential customers).

But being the first to offer a new product, service, or platform that provides value to customers inevitably (and somewhat ironically) attracts the attention and interest of potential competitors and imitators. A start-up must maintain enough control of its position to withstand the impact of follow-on competition, often through formal intellectual property protection (such as patents and trademarks), the development of a brand to distinguish itself from competitors, and particular design elements that are difficult to imitate. Consider, for example, the founding of the doll company American Girl by Pleasant Rowland in 1986 (see Chapter 15). Initially motivated by a desire to stimulate young girls' interest in history,[12] Rowland developed a unique line of dolls complete with period costumes and historic backstories. Relative to other dolls and toys of the time, Rowland invested a higher amount up front in each doll's design and degree of uniqueness (each one came with an individual story), along with a premium price (**Figure 12.3** on p. 346). By connecting doll collecting with unique storytelling (two traditionally separate domains), Rowland created a "system" and brand for value creation that were simultaneously protected by formal intellectual property rights and hard for would-be competitors to imitate. Specifically, whereas the bulk of the toy and doll industry was evolving toward a more cost-conscious

FIGURE 12.3 American Girl Dolls

American Girl dolls on display at the company's flagship store in New York City.

approach based on imitative competition, the American Doll franchise continued to invest in creating premium experiences for its customers. This ultimately led to the opening of unique retail experiences in the form of American Girl Place, exclusive outlets offering tea parties and haircuts for both children and dolls. American Girl is now owned by Mattel, which purchased the company from Rowland for $700 million in 1998.

PLATFORM DESIGN

The third tool is **platform design**. A platform design is simply how a firm organizes groups of users so they can interact with each other through the platform and realize value from their interactions. For example, the value created by a social media platform such as Instagram for any given user depends not only on the intrinsic properties of the platform itself (e.g., its user interface) but also on who else is using the app and how they are engaging with it. Are popular celebrities joining the platform, and if so, which ones? How are they posting, and what types of posts do they make? Entrepreneurs can choose how to design the functionality and governance of a platform to first attract users in ways that will increase the value within the platform. Then they can capture value by identifying which types of users will pay to enable premium functions.

While potentially very powerful, there are key challenges of platform design for a start-up. To understand these, we can contrast how platform design differs from the more traditional tools of architectural strategy, economies of scale and scope, and sustainable differentiation. Relative to platform design, these classical approaches are essentially under the control of the firm. Achieving

platform design How a firm organizes groups of users so they can interact with each other through the platform and realize value from their interactions

lower cost or making design and branding choices involve choices that are directly under the firm's control, as long as it can attract or acquire the resources and capabilities necessary to do so. In contrast, a significant and necessary source of value is produced when others adopt and use the platform, and when other companies develop ancillary and complementary products and services around it.

While the role of networks and interfaces in shaping value has long been appreciated (at least since the development of networks such as the telegraph and telephone in the nineteenth century), recognizing the centrality of platform design in shaping value creation and capture is more recent. Starting in the 1980s, both academic researchers as well as entrepreneurs began to recognize explicitly the potential role of network effects in an overall entrepreneurial strategy.[13] Perhaps the key insight was that when the value of a platform to a user increases because of the number of other users on the platform (a "network effect"), then the platform's value creation depends on the intrinsic value of its design *and* whether it has attracted users that others find valuable to interact with through the platform.

To see the power of this insight, consider the early entrepreneurial strategy of one of the most valuable companies in the world, Microsoft.[14] When a young Bill Gates dropped out of Harvard in the mid-1970s to take advantage of advances in microcomputing, he formed the then-contrarian hypothesis that it was possible to design and distribute software that was independent of any individual computer system. First with his cofounder Paul Allen, and then quickly joined by his college friend Steve Ballmer, Gates worked to develop a simple programming language that could take advantage of the new computing technology. The choices that established Microsoft's dominance were made in 1980 when Gates and the Microsoft team simultaneously established a relationship with IBM, by far the largest computer company of the time, while also retaining control over the underlying software they developed for IBM—MS-DOS.[15] Gates wanted to control these rights because he believed that he would be able to sell MS-DOS to multiple potential vendors of computing systems. This would stimulate software development by Microsoft and others built on the MS-DOS system, creating increasing amounts of value for potential computer buyers. At that time, purchasers were mostly companies introducing their first personal computers into the workplace. To be clear, the role of how network effects could shape and drive an effective entrepreneurial strategy was uncertain. For example, Steve Jobs at Apple focused far more on the intrinsic value of his product's design, supported by a small number of in-house applications, for early users of the Mac. However, Gates's choice to design software whose success was premised on the importance of network effects propelled Microsoft to establish its long-term dominance of the software industry.

Despite the promise of platform design, succeeding poses considerable challenges. A start-up has neither an existing set of customers that can be encouraged to adopt the platform at relatively low cost nor the bargaining power over other potential contributors to the value chain. To clarify, introducing a successful platform design is also difficult for very established firms. A "platform wannabe" must (1) choose and commit to a platform design that encourages a significant level of use while (2) maintaining control over the core factors that create and capture value.

Five Coring Questions

Coring is a process that creates a framework for describing the central idea and interactions of a platform.[a] As part of the process, there are five questions start-up teams must answer.

1. **What sides of the platform should be brought together?** Sometimes this answer is a simple one; for example, Airbnb's founders knew they were trying to bring hosts and guests together, replicating the experiences of a host looking to find a short-term renter (or "couch surfer" at the platform's start) but eliminating the challenges. In other situations, there may be more than two groups. For instance, media platforms bring together content providers and consumers, and then advertisers to those consumers. This often involves two linked platforms that evolve in concert.

2. **What is the unit of value on a platform?** This describes what the platform is trying to maximize. Sometimes it means just counting the number of people on either side of a platform, but in other situations it is their interaction (or matching) that matters. These interactions involve trade-offs. At times it is easier to increase matches per person by restricting users on one side of a market (as occurs when you want to vet one side for quality/safety). Other times, that information is not readily available, so the platform prioritizes having a thick market with tools given to users to surface quality information they might need.

3. **What is the pricing structure?** A platform has *referral users* who bring others to the platform, and *monetization users* who pay the platform provider for services. These can be the same people, or they can be distinct—and notably, distinct by design. For instance, in social media platforms, advertisers pay to place ads and so are monetization users. Consumers are referral users who bring their and others' attention, providing "eyeballs" for advertisers.

4. **How will the platform be governed?** Rules and regulations will need to be set so that interactions on the platform are safe for various users. This may mean rules of behavior but also ratings of that behavior. This may also require monitoring, either by people or algorithms. There are many choices for regulations, and getting it right can be the difference between having an effective platform or not.

5. **What is your plan to control interactions on the platform?** This is a difficult question. Many who build platforms aspire to have theirs operate autonomously and will not intervene to regulate actions. However, many platforms have encountered privacy issues, bad actors, and other activities that have necessitated interventions. Having a plan to deal with ongoing user management issues can be the difference between maintaining a platform and having virtuous cycles turn into vicious ones.

coring A process that creates the framework describing the central idea and interactions of the platform

Let's examine both factors more closely, starting with the design. The first element of platform design that a start-up must choose is its **coring**, the framework that describes the the central idea and interactions of the platform (see **Deep Dive: Five Coring Questions**). At the center of any platform is a key technology or interface that is the foundation for how all others can create value by working with the platform. For instance, Google's initial idea was to improve Internet searches through its novel PageRank algorithm, so named because of its inventor Larry Page and its unique way of scoring influence among web pages. PageRank was Google's coring. At a critical junction, Google then faced the decision of whether to be a product or a platform. If the Google founders had opted for their idea to be a product, users could have been charged a fee to use its Internet search algorithm, or some other Internet company might have licensed Google's search engine. The founders instead chose Google to be a platform, to

Chapter 12: Architectural Strategy

give its search algorithm away for free and to make money from users indirectly by selling advertising. Critically, Google's core advertising technology was not simply "eyeballs" but the quality of the consumers it brought to advertisers. Realizing that a user's search behavior signaled intent, Google placed keyword auctions at the core of its business. These instantaneous auctions made advertisers bid for priority for sponsored spots ahead of unpaid (or organic) search results. While Google engages with multiple partners—from smartphone makers to online publishers—all of this promotes the use and value of the advertising products that Google tightly controls.

The second factor to consider in implementing an architectural strategy is **tipping**, or what actions or features will push, or "tip," a customer's decision to use a platform in your favor and away from a competitor. When there are network effects involved, if there are competing platforms, they will often have aggressive competition for the market. This competition for the market through aggressive tipping tactics is a hallmark of competition among alternative platform designs.

To see how tipping works, let's first consider how YouTube started. In 2005, three former PayPal employees, Chad Hurley, Steve Chen, and Jawed Karim, saw a new opportunity in online video after they had failed to launch an online dating site using uploaded videos. They realized that when news events involved a video element—such as the infamous Super Bowl halftime show incident with Janet Jackson and Justin Timberlake—it was difficult to find videos about the event online. They wanted ordinary people to be able to upload and distribute videos. With this decision, YouTube was born. One key choice the cofounders made was to have the service be free to all users, whether uploading videos or viewing them. In just a year, the plan had worked: 25 million videos had been uploaded and 2 million people were visiting their site each day. The site was so impactful that in 2006 it was *Time* magazine's person of the year. (Well, technically, the person of the year was "you," but the inspiration was YouTube.) The service was acquired by Google that year and remains the dominant video hosting site to this day.

YouTube's success came from tipping. When people look for videos, most tend to use one service. As a result, if you also want your video to be found, it makes sense to use the same service you use for search. These network effects pushed, or tipped, the market toward one single, dominant video hosting service. Achieving that tipping point required a combination of choices to make video uploading and viewing easy and cheap, and importantly, making it easy to find these videos too (**Figure 12.4**). Prior to YouTube, video watching required your computer and a separate app like RealPlayer or Windows Media Player, which took up valuable storage space on your hard drive. There were video streaming services, such as Broadcast.com founded by Chris Jaeb, Mark Cuban, and Todd Wagner in 1995, but these were devoted to livestreaming events and did not allow user uploads. Prior to acquiring YouTube, Google had attempted to compete with it using Google Video. However, YouTube's initial decisions had already tipped the market in its favor.

tipping The actions or features that will push, or "tip," a customer's decision to use a platform in your favor and away from a competitor

FIGURE 12.4 YouTube

The key to YouTube's success was the founding team setting conditions to be the place where people looked for, watched, and uploaded videos.

The combination of a platform's coring and its tipping potential is integral to how it can create a new value chain. Because platform design requires a significant level of up-front investment and commitment, early mistakes can be costly and undermine the overall potential of a start-up's underlying idea. As such, platform design requires detailed planning and potentially aggressive competitive moves at earlier stages than other strategies. This makes both the initial hypothesis and how the four key choices of customer, technology, competition, and organization are first made together even more paramount.

12.3 The Four Choices That Shape an Architectural Strategy

In most cases, a successful scenario for an architectural strategy sees an entrepreneur building and controlling a distinct value chain that takes a market from zero to one. How should an entrepreneur set the four key choices—customer, technology, competition, and organization—to maximize their probability of success?

CHOOSING YOUR CUSTOMER

In an architectural strategy, the choice of customer should be those who are the most desirable in the industry, not only for the start-up but also incumbents. Ideal customer characteristics include having high influencer value and serving as a reference case for other customer segments. These types of customers make the start-up well positioned to "cross the chasm" (discussed in Chapter 5). This is in stark contrast to a disruption strategy where the initial customer choice targets oddball, poorly served customers undesirable to traditional incumbents.

Consider the case of Facebook, founded by Mark Zuckerberg in 2004. Despite its now global ubiquity, Facebook did not start out as a global platform; instead, it initially served an elite, influential group of college students: the Harvard undergraduate population. This meant that, as a new social network that relied on authentication of friendship links, Facebook was tapping into a crowd that already had existing links. Thus, Facebook was building off the top of existing networks as an exclusive "club." This was in contrast to, say, MySpace, which from its start emerged as a public space. After learning from Harvard students, Facebook opened access to other Ivy League colleges and then national ones, relying on friendship links across users to generate a new layer of social interaction. It then opened up to students from other educational institutions such as high schools, and to certain companies including Apple and Microsoft. It took two full years before Facebook was open to all, although it still required that new users be connected and authenticated by friends already on the platform.

Facebook's strategy shows how customer choice can facilitate control over the platform. First, by limiting the initial set of customers, Facebook could engage in more experimentation without damaging its ability to grow beyond that group. Second, experiments within this limited set of customers could teach Facebook about what might interest the broader set. By targeting the college-age segment, the Facebook team learned a lot from early adopters about social interactions using digital technologies. This data shaped how Facebook developed as it moved to the early majority and laggard markets. Third, exclusivity can simply raise the desirability of being part of the network. Finally, when network effects will come from the sum of local connections, an efficient means of garnering adoption is to start with a critical mass in tightly connected local groups and build out from there.[16] Facebook did all of these things, leading to spectacular growth in just a decade.

CHOOSING YOUR TECHNOLOGY

In an architectural strategy, the start-up should focus on a new technology S curve that it can control as it progresses in performance. This will maintain its leadership over potential rivals. In the case of Dropbox (whose 2007 founding was introduced in Chapter 8), the idea was to leverage the burgeoning cloud computing build-out to provide computer users with remote file hosting. Founder Drew Houston realized that existing services suffered from issues of reliability due to the technical challenges in continually uploading rapidly changing files—such as documents and spreadsheets. He decided to make technological choices that built Dropbox based on "delta updates"—not uploading whole files but just the changes in those files. This dramatically increased the reliability of the service and naturally dovetailed into an efficient means of recovering previous file versions.

Later, Apple, Microsoft, and Google all released their own cloud storage platforms. However, Dropbox was able to withstand that potential competition because its technology delivered a new and clearly difficult-to-replicate architecture for cloud storage that no other firm could match in reliability.[17] Thus, Dropbox's growth was rapid and, moreover, it was able to establish its leadership position while established firms created competitive responses. Today, though operating in a highly competitive market, Dropbox still maintains almost 18 million paying customers and $2.3 billion in annual sales.[18] In this respect, it is a textbook case of how controlling an architectural innovation (and its corresponding secret sauce) is a mechanism by which an entrepreneur can profit from investing in control. Notably, Dropbox has also signaled it is moving into AI in its platform, as it seeks to be first to market or a "first mover" in how customers use this technology with their files (see the sidebar on **Dropbox's Focus on Trust in Its AI**).[19]

CHOOSING YOUR COMPETITION

In considering how to choose competition, it is important to return to the idea of building an economic moat. Rather than trying to fly under the radar of incumbents as in a disruption strategy, architectural entrepreneurs must forecast what the incumbent response will be and prepare to safeguard their start-up against the inevitable competition. To erect a moat, the architectural founder needs to understand what part of their idea is the linchpin that they must invest in protecting. Consider, for example, the iconic Coca-Cola Company, worth more than $240 billion USD as of 2023[20] and accounting for over 41.9% of the soft drink market.[21] Throughout its nearly 130-year history, the company has

Dropbox's Focus on Trust in Its AI. In a recent blog post, founder Drew Houston noted that trust would be a key part of how Dropbox used AI in its platform, and that AI would clearly be part of its coring and tipping strategies for the future. Houston wrote: "To 'be worthy of trust' has long been at the center of everything we do at Dropbox . . . Our AI principles have been developed with this standard in mind."[a]

experimented with many aspects of its supply chain, from bottling (e.g., licensing to third-party bottlers vs. in-house ownership of bottling), to stocking, to sales and marketing, but at its core, it has carefully protected "Merchandise 7x," the secret formula for Coca-Cola, ever since it was invented by Coca-Cola founder John Pemberton in 1886.

In a similar way, architectural entrepreneurs must identify on how many fronts they will choose to face competition. In other words, with any idea, there are numerous complementary tasks, functions, and assets that can support the creation of customer value. Architectural entrepreneurs must determine which functions and tasks they plan to fulfill and which they plan to partner with complementary providers to achieve. Entrepreneurs must understand the interplay between their choices of customer and technology with their own capabilities and ambitions, and also how their choice of competition will inspire would-be competitors to either compete with or become complementary providers for the start-up. For example, Slack (introduced in Chapter 4) was designed to help facilitate communication between team members in a work setting, especially as an alternative to email or clunky enterprise communication platforms. Slack's founder knew it needed to offer multiple functions—from customer management to document storage to video conferencing—to become the standard communication platform. Rather than building all those services in-house, however, Slack focused on controlling the front end of the experience with a seamlessly designed user chat interface while building third-party partnerships and integrations with incumbent solutions (e.g., Zendesk, Dropbox). By turning these incumbents into partners rather than competitors, Slack substantially narrowed its pool of competitors.

CHOOSING YOUR ORGANIZATION

Organizational commitment is implicit in any architectural strategy. To be successful, ventures must commit to certain paths, pricing, and quality, and its organization must reflect and support what will remain an unchanged set of integrated resources. Though customers or even investors may not initially understand or like the idea before its release, entrepreneurs must make investments in building a new value chain around it.

Consider, for example, AngelList, a platform for start-up fundraising founded in 2010 by Naval Ravikant and Babak Nivi. Initially it only bridged introductions between high-potential start-ups and prospective angel investors. Then Ravikant and Nivi had the vision to also facilitate actual equity-based financial transactions through their platform. At the time, however, it was unclear if angel investors would be willing to put capital behind entrepreneurs without offline due diligence and meetings, nor was it clear that regulators would even be willing to permit that type of financial investment activity. Ravikant, however, was extremely convinced of the importance of his idea, explaining that "we had to force transparency into the system" (**Figure 12.5**). He rallied a group of industry leaders and lobbied Washington to change regulations to allow for equity crowdfunding, and at one point secured over 5,000 entrepreneur signatures on a petition.[22] Eventually, in 2013, new legislation known as Title II of the JOBS Act went live, which made it easier for start-ups

FIGURE 12.5 **AngelList**

To make his platform successful, Naval Ravikant was willing to do whatever was necessary, including lobbying for new legislation to allow for equity crowdfunding.

and small businesses to secure new funding. Soon after, AngelList launched its online equity crowdfunding product. Just one year later, despite initial reservations, angel investors and start-up entrepreneurs alike embraced the platform, with over $104 million USD invested in 243 start-ups.[23] Lobbying policymakers may be on an extreme end of the spectrum, but the underlying point is that architectural entrepreneurs must possess not only a clear vision but also a strong belief that helps drive them toward making significant commitments, even in the face of doubt from others.

Peter Thiel offered useful advice for architectural entrepreneurs going from "zero to one": they should ask themselves the essential question, "What valuable company is nobody building?"[24] As Thiel explains, the challenge architectural entrepreneurs face is that "it's always hard to come up with new truths that people have not yet understood . . . it also requires a bit of courage because you often have to go against social convention in pursuing certain lines of business. People discourage you from doing things that are strange and new."[25] Perhaps the concept of "zero to one" is best illustrated when considering Thiel's venture Palantir, cofounded with Joe Lonsdale, Alex Karp, and Stephen Cohen. Palantir arose at a time in which it did not fit the mold of a software start-up, as it did "not help you share, message, pin, post or chat."[26] In contrast, the company's core product, the Palantir Gotham, is big data mining software for search, discovery, and analysis of both structured and unstructured data. In fact, when it launched, the company was such a novel concept that, according to Karp, most "American venture capitalists seemed allergic to the company . . . A Kleiner Perkins exec lectured the Palantir entrepreneurs on the inevitable failure of their company for an hour and a half."[27] Eventually, it secured financing from venture capital firm In-Q-Tel and proceeded to onboard the CIA, NSA, and FBI as early customers for the Palantir Gotham. Though some early-stage venture capitalists could not see it at the time, Palantir successfully built what former CIA chief David Petraeus described as "a better mousetrap when a better mousetrap was needed."[28] Palantir not only targeted a void in the industry left by incumbents such as Booz Allen and Lockheed Martin, but it also built an organization around being boldly different in the face of discouragement from the start-up industry.

HOW THE FOUR CHOICES FIT TOGETHER

An architectural strategy is an extremely ambitious strategy (**Figure 12.6**). Let's use Figure 12.6 and the chapter's original example about Bloomberg L.P. to see how the four choices are made together.

TECHNOLOGY CHOICE At its heart, an architectural strategy exploits a new technology curve to architect an entirely new value chain ecosystem, which

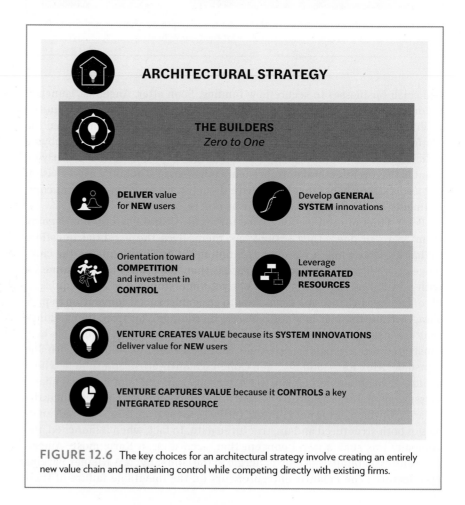

FIGURE 12.6 The key choices for an architectural strategy involve creating an entirely new value chain and maintaining control while competing directly with existing firms.

might involve integrating a venture downstream in the final part of a value chain or building a platform or multi-sided market of novel *customer* combinations. We saw Bloomberg L.P. do this by creating an entirely new technology through its terminals and the services on them and showing how this would benefit existing financial firms.

Further, an architectural strategy requires carefully choosing which stages of the value chain to participate in (or not) and, most importantly, taking active leadership of the entire value ecosystem. Challenges arise in part because of the very high level of coordination and execution that is required in delivering your product: for example, even though your enterprise is just a start-up, an architectural strategy requires that you consider how your actions as the platform leader shape the value and investments made by other members of the ecosystem too. For Bloomberg, this meant getting big customers to invest in his terminals.

ORGANIZATION CHOICE The *organizational* requirements of an architectural strategy are formidable, often with a sophisticated inward-looking organization that can reinforce a platform's core, and external-facing divisions to manage and maintain the business ecosystem it gradually creates. At Bloomberg L.P., Michael Bloomberg's original partners included a great technologist and a great salesperson. Throughout its history, Bloomberg L.P. has worked to build a culture of service to customers and loyalty to the firm. This reflects a more general idea that platform architects serve as platform "hubs" with interactions between multiple stakeholders through control over an interface or access point.

COMPETITION CHOICE In terms of *competition*, these companies are often competing "for" the market rather than "in" the market. Architectural strategy entrepreneurs immediately go head to head with established players, and Bloomberg L.P. chose to go after all the major financial information players with its terminals.

CUSTOMER CHOICE Instead of trying to compete with underserved customers, architectural strategy entrepreneurs want to change the market and be noticed. Michael Bloomberg started out by trying to recruit one of the best and most profitable firms, Merrill Lynch, as his first customer. This immediately established his business as a viable option for any customer.

Taken together, architectural strategies are both the most ambitious yet most risky of the strategies within the entrepreneurial strategy compass.

12.4 Putting Architectural Strategy to the Test

For architectural start-ups, the ultimate test of their value creation and capture hypotheses is (a) whether they can create defined value by architecting a new value chain in the marketplace and (b) whether they can secure sufficient, durable control to protect their idea against competition.

AN ARCHITECTURAL STRATEGY'S VALUE CREATION HYPOTHESIS

An architectural founder must have a *well-grounded hypothesis as to why their idea of a new, integrated value chain or platform will be of clear value to customers.* This is easiest to do if the hypotheses are using traditional strategic tools like economies of scale and scope to create a low-cost position or successfully differentiating a unique product offering in a way that others will find difficult or too costly to imitate. The essential hypothesis is to create new value for customers either by lowering the underlying cost structure or by offering a product or service that is currently "missing" from the marketplace.

The nature of the value creation hypothesis for platform design is a bit more subtle. It is fundamentally about how to bring together multiple actors ("sides") of a platform in a way that increases the value end consumers receive, while also potentially lowering transaction costs. The process of identifying how different sides of the platform fit together and the rules that govern their interaction are the building blocks of a field known as market design.

Consider the case of eHarmony, founded in 1998 by Dr. Neil Clark Warren and Greg Forgatch as an online couple-matching platform. Though existing dating platforms existed (e.g., Match.com), eHarmony's entrepreneurs hypothesized they could develop a new kind of dating market aimed exclusively at those seeking a serious relationship. Rather than following the industry standard of offering low-cost, easy sign-ups, eHarmony opted to set a high monthly price, require prospective customers to answer over 400 questions, and approve only 80% of applicants for the platform. The rationale was that by having a stringent selection filter, eHarmony would develop a novel platform that created differentiated value in the industry, emphasizing its dating market's quality over quantity. Only allowing those serious about relationships to join the platform also increased the odds that its customers would be able to find someone ready for a similar type of commitment. eHarmony's carefully developed value creation hypothesis led it to become a multimillion-dollar business with over 20 million registered users[29] and numerous successful marriages.

Having a strong conviction in their idea is particularly salient for architectural entrepreneurs, as is whether they have the needed resources and compatible profile for their idea. This is because, unlike a disruption or value chain strategy where customer feedback is a necessary input in the idea's iterative development, architectural entrepreneurs face the issue of customers (and sometimes also investors, reporters, or mentors) having a hard time conceptualizing what a new value chain will look like and how it will offer better value than existing options. In other words, as Y Combinator founder Paul Graham observes, it is easy to "unconsciously judge larval startups by the standards of established ones. [It's] like someone looking at a newborn baby and concluding 'there's no way this tiny creature could ever accomplish anything.'. . . It's harmless if know-it-alls dismiss your startup. They always get things wrong . . . The big danger is that you'll dismiss your startup yourself."[30]

To avoid this, an architectural entrepreneur should "do things that don't scale,"[31] creating and testing on a small scale the totality of the experience and value creation possibility that could ultimately be part of a larger platform experience. For example, in its early days, Airbnb was premised on its entrepreneurs' hypothesis that they could drive customer willingness to rent through a peer-to-peer platform by serving as a professional, trusted intermediary. To test this theory, they traveled to New York City, rented professional cameras, and physically went to their handful of early renters' homes to take well-lit, professional photos to upload to Airbnb's website. Though they had not yet built the capabilities to onboard renters in such a professional manner, the positive results from this experiment made them confident their value creation hypothesis was on the mark and that they should continue architecting this new value chain.

AN ARCHITECTURAL STRATEGY'S VALUE CAPTURE HYPOTHESIS

Architectural entrepreneurs also need to be able to articulate *what will prevent others from imitating the core idea of the venture and providing immediate or long-term competition.* In many cases, an idea will have clear value but will not be secure from competitive forces. While this issue is a traditional strategic challenge, for a start-up using an architectural strategy, demonstrating this new value to consumers of incumbents with only limited resources puts it at risk of imitative competition. Thus, architectural strategy entrepreneurs must carefully plan and think through how they will build a house or an economic moat around the idea.

Careful planning is necessary because it forces entrepreneurs to outline the commitments they will invest in, how to avoid commoditization of the "foundation" of their house (i.e., their core idea), and how they will secure the capital to enforce control. As we read earlier, controlling the idea usually means creating economies of scale; increasing customer switching costs; controlling access to key assets like raw materials, distribution channels, locations, or brand identities; and protecting and safeguarding trade secrets.

And where disruption entrepreneurs may be able to start executing with little planning and worry about monetization later, architectural entrepreneurs cannot simply run small tests. Architectural entrepreneurs must show their plan has sufficient evidence of an upside to raise the required financing to thwart competition.

Of course, many modern architectural entrepreneurs plan to create value through a platform that can connect different stakeholders together. The value capture question for these entrepreneurs is a bit more nuanced—can they control access to the value created by combining these different stakeholders? These entrepreneurs must articulate the distinct sources of platform value they are creating, how they will "core" the market (i.e., how they will make their underlying idea essential to the market), and how they will "tip" the market toward their platform (i.e., how they will shape market dynamics such that they become the platform of choice).[32] When the restaurant reservation platform OpenTable got started (see Chapter 4), its founder Chuck Templeton decided a vital element for success would be securing the most difficult side of the market first: the restaurants. As he dug in further, he realized that most restaurants had limited or no computers or Internet-based technologies in their operations. OpenTable decided to not only offer a reservation platform but also provide support for restaurants to establish their own in-house computer terminals. As Templeton recalls, in the earliest days of the business, "[OpenTable was] the one running wire through the rafters to get power and connectivity" (**Figure 12.7**). To tip the market toward OpenTable, Templeton targeted the most influential, powerful restaurants first. "We were able to get the top 20 restaurants and the next 50 would all want to be where those top 20 were—there began to be a critical mass on the website," he says.[33] OpenTable also charged very competitive prices, offering consumers bookings free of charge and billing restaurants a very low SaaS (software as a service) price in return for both a reservation system and information on customer demand and preferences. The early planning Templeton did in thinking through how to create novel value, core the market, and tip it toward OpenTable allowed the start-up to build a strong base of top restaurants in the United States and withstand competition from incumbents and new entrants alike, retaining market leadership nearly two decades later. OpenTable was acquired by Priceline for $2.6 billion in 2014.

Architectural entrepreneurs must decide early on to build a product- or platform-centered business. Though it is possible to move from one to the other, having strategic clarity is important in shaping how they design the start-up to capture value. For example, even though demand-side economies of scale or network effects could be used to enforce control around both product- and platform-based ideas, product-based ideas will likely emphasize indirect network effects and becoming the standard. To illustrate: Suzy's ownership of an iPad will not affect the value of an iPad to Jelani, but the more iPads that are purchased, the more iPad apps will be developed.[34] On the other hand, platform-based ideas will likely emphasize direct network effects and achieving

FIGURE 12.7 **OpenTable**

Around 2001, OpenTable's strategy was to do everything it could to establish strong and continuing connections with restaurants, including providing IT services to independent local restaurants..

enough critical mass to tip the market and establish a monopoly. As an example, if Parvati or Dae is the first to join a social network like Facebook, it has no value. As each additional new member joins the platform, the value for everyone increases. Ideally, the platform will reach a certain tipping point in size such that the market momentum drives the platform to become the market leader.[35]

Finally, to test the value capture hypothesis, it is important to consider how to protect and control the core secret sauce of the idea, planning what resources (financial, human, and infrastructure) are needed to ensure that the core product, service, or platform design is maintained on a proprietary basis. Architectural entrepreneurs need to think through how they will protect their idea and how they will secure the resources to build and sustain that protection. This is particularly salient since many of the most successful application platforms with active developer communities are bankrolled by well-endowed large corporations (e.g., Apple App Store, Android App Market) or launched after significant financing (e.g., Facebook launched its Facebook platform in 2007 after it already had 20 million active users and over $240 million in funding).[36] Simply saying that you intend to build a platform where others will build applications is not enough.

12.5 Putting Architectural Strategy to Work

After gathering enough information to convince yourself that your underlying hypotheses are correct and correspond best to an architectural strategy, you can put your hypotheses to work (for a summary, see **Putting It Together: Architectural Strategy** on p. 360).

In an architectural strategy, it is critical to ensure that you can secure the necessary capital to build and enforce control over your idea. Architectural entrepreneurs must be prepared to defend their idea against competition earlier, as they will be targeting existing customers of incumbent firms. Therefore, an architectural founding team should carefully think through how much outside financing is required and the types of characteristics (e.g., their ethos and expectations) that make up the ideal funding partner. Implementing an architectural strategy often requires large amounts of up-front investment (especially relative to disruption) in planning and making strategic commitments to build an entirely new value chain. Thus, architectural entrepreneurs must be diligent in assessing fit and buy-in with potential investors and ensure that they will not be pressured to execute quickly before they have had a chance to establish control.

As a final story, in October 2002, a mere four months after he sold his last start-up to eBay, a young Elon Musk explained to a group of students at Stanford that U.S. space exploration risked becoming uncompetitive, especially in the face of developments in Russia and China. He believed it was necessary for private enterprises to enter the arena, bringing in an injection of entrepreneurial spirit.[37] It may have seemed incredible at the time for a fledgling start-up to manufacture rockets, but just four years later, Musk's new company, SpaceX, funded by some of his own fortune as well as private equity, won a contract from NASA.[38] With an ultimate goal of enabling people to travel commercially to space and back, SpaceX has been focused for now on building advanced spacecraft, putting

ARCHITECTURAL STRATEGY

A venture creates a new value chain across multiple stakeholders, controlling, and integrating resources.

EVALUATE YOUR FOUNDING TEAM AND PROPOSED BUSINESS MODEL

How Will You Craft a New Value Chain?	• Outline the founding team's "unfair" advantage for this idea. Articulate how the new value chain's business model coordinates and delivers new value to multiple stakeholders.

DESCRIBE CUSTOMER, TECHNOLOGY, ORGANIZATION, AND COMPETITION CHOICES

Customer: Deliver Value for New Users	• Describe how your idea creates value for highly desirable customers who might serve as a reference for the mainstream market.
	• Specify a subset who of customers who will promote your control of the platform.
Technology: Develop General Systems Innovations	• Describe how emerging technology reinforces the new value chain.
	• Evaluate technology performance and create key performance metrics; specify activities to control and maintain technology leadership and performance improvement over time.
Organization: Leverage Integrated Resources	• Describe the inward-looking organization required to strengthen your platform and the external-facing requirements needed to manage and maintain the business ecosystem.
	• Briefly describe key hires and your desired organizational culture.
Competition: Orient toward competition and invest in control	• Identify competitors including established firms and start-ups and forecast their likely response to your entry. Identify vital components of your idea and how to protect them.
	• Consider competitive functions and tasks you will do, and where you will partner.

SHARPEN YOUR VALUE CREATION HYPOTHESIS AND VALUE CAPTURE HYPOTHESIS

Create Value with Systematic Innovations that Deliver Value for New Users	• Describe how the platform creates value through traditional schools like economics of scale or scope or through differentiation or market design.
	• Test the total experience on a small scale.
Capture Value by Controlling Key Integrated Resources	• Determine the economic moat around your idea, and outline commitments needed to create economies of scale, increase switching costs, control assets, and protect trade secrets.
	• Explain the financial, human, and infrastructure resources required and how to acquire these resources.

FIGURE 12.8 SpaceX

SpaceX has remained notoriously secretive about its manufacturing and design process since its inception in the early 2000s, choosing not to file for patents and instead relying solely on trade secrets as a means to protect its core ideas. This approach has allowed the team to stay ahead of incumbent competitors like Lockheed and Boeing, ultimately helping them secure manufacturing contracts with NASA.

it in competition with incumbents like Lockheed Martin and Boeing.[39] Over the past years, despite its relative openness about its failed rocket launches, SpaceX has been secretive about its manufacturing and design. It has not even filed for patents, out of the belief that "the best way to ensure that our investment in ground-breaking research and development stays safe is to keep it confidential. Therefore, [SpaceX] relies heavily on trade secrets to prevent [its] innovations from being taken outside the U.S."[40] (**Figure 12.8**).

12.6 Concluding Thoughts

An architectural strategy is in some ways an interpretation of traditional strategy for the modern entrepreneur. It emphasizes taking on a competitive positioning, carefully developing a plan, and balancing the ability to deliver clear customer value while also retaining control over the core idea. The challenge is that it is difficult to compete against existing firms on a head-to-head basis as a start-up. Almost by definition, a resource-constrained start-up subject to the "liability of newness" finds it difficult to assemble and manage the resources and capabilities to compete from the outset for the most demanding customer groups within the marketplace.

This tension is intensified when considering platform design, one of the leading tools by which start-ups realize an architectural strategy. To attract users to a new platform, it is important to offer a compelling value, which itself depends on the participation and engagement of other actors on the platforms (other users, complementary services, or applications). Because of the higher level of risk and failure with this strategy, making design and governance choices and expending the up-front financial resources to enable tipping require a high initial level of commitment by the start-up. Yet, this commitment can ultimately allow the venture to create significant and lasting value.

Chapter 12 Review: Architectural Strategy

CHAPTER TAKEAWAYS

- An architectural strategy involves a start-up focused on control but oriented toward competition with established firms in the industry.

- The value creation hypothesis for an architectural strategy is premised on translating the start-up's idea into a novel, integrated value chain that creates demonstrable value for consumers.

- The value capture hypothesis for an architectural strategy involves a clear theory as to why control of key resources will allow the start-up to prevent others from imitating the core idea of the venture.

- In order to establish and then sustain competitive advantage with an architectural strategy, an entrepreneur can utilize three tools: (1) achieve a low-cost position through economies of scale and scope, (2) realize higher willingness to pay with core customers through a unique and differentiated product offering, and (3) develop and manage a platform core that leverages direct and indirect network effects to achieve market lock-in.

- A platform design is how a firm organizes groups of users so that they can interact with each other through the platform and realize value from their interactions. A start-up team must choose both a coring and tipping strategy for their platform design that ensures the potential for significant value capture over an extended period from their new value chain.

- The customer choice in an architectural strategy should be the segment most desirable in the industry not only for the start-up but also for incumbents. The customers chosen should also have the ability to serve as a reference for other customer segments.

- The technology choice in an architectural strategy should be centered on a new technology S curve that allows the start-up to control and maintain leadership over the technology as it improves rapidly in performance.

- The competition choice in an architectural strategy are incumbent firms that the start-up faces head-on by focusing on control over the venture's core idea, through investment in key resources. It requires building an economic moat to safeguard against inevitable competition.

- The organization choice in an architectural strategy involves integrating resources to reinforce the platform core while also investing in external-facing divisions to manage the ecosystem over time.

KEY TERMS

competitive strategy (p. 341)
economies of scale and scope (p. 343)
platform design (p. 346)

coring (p. 348)
tipping (p. 349)

REVIEW QUESTIONS

1. How does a start-up create and capture value from an architectural strategy?

2. What are the primary challenges a start-up faces in choosing an architectural strategy from the outset? Why might start-ups find it difficult to specify at the earliest stages of their venture how they can create and capture value through an architectural strategy?

3. What are the three critical tools available to a value chain entrepreneur? What are the key differences between each of these tools? Briefly describe how the use of each tool might allow a start-up to create and capture value through an architectural strategy.

4. Define *economies of scale or scope*. How might a start-up use economies of scale or scope to establish and sustain competitive advantage? What are the key challenges for a start-up to achieve economies of scale or scope?

5. Define *sustainable differentiation*. How might a start-up leverage differentiation to establish and sustain competitive advantage? What are key challenges for a start-up to achieve sustainable differentiation?

6. Define *platform design*. How might a start-up use platform design to establish and sustain competitive advantage? What are the key challenges for a start-up to achieve a successful platform design?

7. What are the two key elements of a platform strategy? What are three platform design choices that contribute to defining a platform "core"? What are three tactics that might allow a start-up to "tip" the market toward its platform?

8. Start-ups pursuing an architectural strategy through the establishment of a new platform bring together multiple "sides" of a market to facilitate economic and social transactions that might not otherwise occur. Why is it hard to learn about whether a particular platform design creates value before implementing it at some level of scale?

9. A defining feature of an architectural strategy is a high level of commitment. What role do early strategic commitments play in an architectural strategy? How does a commitment-oriented approach potentially help an architectural strategy start-up get from "zero to one"?

10. What are the core hypotheses an entrepreneur should seek to test as part of an architectural strategy? What are the challenges of implementing tests of these hypotheses in the absence of significant investment and commitment?

11. What are some of the key implementation factors that allow an architectural strategy entrepreneur to succeed over the longer term?

12. Many successful architectural strategy start-ups design and scale novel platform ecosystems that bring together users and stakeholders that might not otherwise interact. Why does the establishment of a platform that allows different "sides" of a platform to interact in a new way potentially create value in the context of an architectural strategy?

DISCUSSION QUESTIONS

Answer the following series of questions and scenarios either in class discussions or by writing a short response.

1. Anton and Francesca are both in the early planning stages for their (separate) weddings. They are frustrated by the sheer amount of time and effort it takes to find venues that are just right for the type of wedding they want. As well, a mutual friend, Hugo, owns a beautiful rustic property he would like to rent out occasionally for events, but he finds it difficult to market it. Anton and Francesca believe there might be a potential for an "Airbnb for wedding venues," which would allow couples to search through unique venues that might offer a more distinctive wedding experience than traditional hotels or catering halls. Spurred by early enthusiasm from friends, including some also in the process of wedding planning, as well as from Hugo on the venue side, they agree to spend the upcoming summer exploring whether such a venture might be worth pursuing. What are three concrete steps you would recommend to Anton and Francesca that they could accomplish over the course of three months to help them decide whether to pursue this opportunity? What are the most critical hypotheses the team should attempt to validate, and can you suggest a way that they might be able to do so (or not)?

2. Motivated by a trip to Colonial Williamsburg and her frustration with what was available on the market, American Girl founder Pleasant Rowland wrote a postcard to a good friend: "What do you think of this idea? A series of books about 9-year-old girls growing up in different times in history, with a doll for each of the characters and historically accurate clothes and accessories with which girls could play out the stories?" To implement this idea, Rowland created three high-quality, emotionally resonant dolls that combined backstories rich in historical detail with the opportunity for young girls to play with dolls in an interactive way. Why was it important that Rowland develop full-fledged characters and stories to test her value creation hypothesis? Why do you think her initial dolls proved a success when there were other dolls such as Barbie already in the marketplace? Why do you think that American Girl has been able to sustain itself as a distinctive brand for more than 30 years?

3. One element of a platform-based architectural strategy is the development of a platform core that structures the relationship between the different sides of the market that the platform is organizing. For example, from the

outset, Michael Bloomberg offered a proprietary terminal (the "Bloomberg machine") that connected busy (and price-insensitive) traders and market analysts with financial news and information sources, creating a synthesized stream of financial market information. How would you describe how Bloomberg created value for the different sides of the financial news and trading marketplace? What role did the development of a proprietary system play in facilitating his ability to capture value from this platform? What factors do you believe have allowed Bloomberg to sustain leadership in this area for more than four decades?

4. Javier is an avid collector and occasionally a seller of antiques, and he is continually frustrated by the challenges of both buying and selling in this market. Historically, most transactions in the antiques market depend on negotiations with mom-and-pop local dealers or through individual sales in social networks. Also in this specialized market, there are antiques shows and auctions for buyers and sellers as well as trusted intermediaries such as individuals who can certify the authenticity and potential auction value of items (as seen on, for example, *Antiques Roadshow*). Motivated by the success of start-up platforms like Airbnb and Care.com (see **Case: Care.com**), Javier is designing a platform that would simultaneously allow for real-time buying and selling but would also include the ability to authenticate and provide a fair price estimate for pieces listed on the platform. What sides of the platform should be brought together? What is the unit of value on the platform? What is the pricing structure (i.e., how would Javier get paid)? How will the platform be governed? How might Javier control interactions on the platform to create a real-time market for antiques?

5. One critical element of an architectural strategy is the ability to create an economic moat through which a start-up can establish and sustain competitive advantage. For example, by integrating itself deeply into operations of restaurants, OpenTable was not only able to revolutionize online reservations but maintain a strong relationship with restaurants on the platform over time. Can you identify a successful start-up platform that created a meaningful economic moat, one that not only created value but has allowed the platform designer to capture value over time? What were the key commitments or choices the start-up team made early in the platform's history that enabled them to establish and sustain market leadership? Why was this start-up platform able to deter direct competitors?

6. Architectural strategy is usually the most risky entrepreneurial strategy a founding team considers. An architectural strategy combines a high level of up-front commitment (often requiring significant fundraising) with an offering that competes within a broader market context. Given these challenges, why might start-up entrepreneurs be interested in pursuing an architectural strategy? What advantages does a successful architectural strategy offer over alternative strategic paths?

FOR FURTHER READING

Bresnahan, Timothy F., Shane Greenstein, and Rebecca M. Henderson. *Schumpeterian Competition and Diseconomies of Scope: Illustrations from the Histories of Microsoft and IBM*. Chicago: University of Chicago Press, 2011.

Chen, Andrew. *The Cold Start Problem: How to Start and Scale Network Effects*. New York: Harper, 2021.

Cusumano, Michael A., Annabelle Gawer, and David B. Yoffie. *The Business of Platforms: Strategy in the Age of Digital Competition, Innovation, and Power*. New York: Harper Business, 2019.

Gawer, Annabelle, and Michael A. Cusumano. "How Companies Become Platform Leaders." *Sloan Management Review*, January 1, 2008.

Parker, Geoffrey G., Marshall W. Van Alstyne, and Sangeet Paul Choudary. *Platform Revolution: How Networked Markets Are Transforming the Economy—and How to Make Them Work for You*. New York: Norton, 2016.

Thiel, Peter, with Blake Masters. *Zero to One*. New York: Crown, 2014.

Sheila Lirio Marcelo

As introduced in Chapter 3, Sheila Lirio Marcelo was already a successful businessperson when she encountered a difficult year. She was establishing herself as a business leader while caring for two young children when her father suffered a heart attack. Marcelo needed to hire nannies, tutors, and babysitters for her children and a caregiver for her parents. She was an immigrant to the United States from the Philippines and had graduated from Harvard Business School. Both experiences gave her entrepreneurial energy and a desire to build a business. When faced with the struggles of procuring basic household care, she swung into action and, in 2006, Care.com was formed.

Care.com is a freemium model—anyone can search the site and be matched with caregivers without paying a fee. The company earns money from users who pay extra for a premium membership that offers a full range of search results. It also offers businesses services to help their employees find care. It does not earn revenue from matches or caregivers.

To build a platform of caregivers who could be confidently matched with those in need, reliability was critical. Marcelo could not simply open the door to anyone wanting to be a caregiver. They had to be qualified, pass (preliminary) background checks, and keep obtaining favorable reviews from those who hired them. However, ensuring that these checks worked well has been an issue for the business; several problems arose early on from hiring candidates with criminal histories. Vetting procedures were strengthened over time as a result.

Still, Care.com offered no guarantees. Ultimately, whether a caregiver was trustworthy was something only a customer with contact with them could establish. Marcelo called this "shared responsibility."[a] Even full background checks were the responsibility of the customer. But there were incidents where caregivers were unsuitable or worse, engaging in criminal actions. Care.com has struggled to find the right balance but has aimed to be safer than word-of-mouth references. The issue is striking a balance between being able to attract a large number of caregivers to the site while ensuring a safe transaction process.

Sheila Lirio Marcelo

Over time, this balance appears to have been maintained, with the site growing steadily. Care.com has expanded to Canada and Europe, and today it offers babysitting, tutoring, pet sitting, senior care, and housekeeping. It was briefly listed on the New York Stock Exchange before becoming private again at a valuation of $500 million in 2020.

Questions

1. How would you articulate Care.com's value creation hypothesis? How did the company create value for caregivers (e.g., nannies)? How did it create value for the those in need of caregiving services (e.g., parents)?

2. Given the information in this case, what early choices did Sheila Lirio Marcelo make that were consistent with an architectural strategy? How did she architect a new value chain?

3. If you were advising Marcelo on designing the early Care.com platform, what recommendations would you have made about how the platform should be governed? What key features or functions would you have recommended? Would you have prioritized caregiver safety more stringently?

PART 4

PUTTING IT TO WORK

In Parts 1–3 of this text, we studied how entrepreneurs form ideas, the choices that entrepreneurs will make around them, and how these choices will lead to different strategic approaches for their business. Now we will discuss how to put this all together—the tools to aid with planning and decision-making, the ways you might decide to try to fund this idea, and whether to include (or not include) plans to scale the idea. It is time to put all your plans to work.

As you will see in Chapter 13, to make that strategic choice, you must ensure you have all the information you can get without making a commitment. That means experimentation and learning. You want to explore or test at least two strategic plans before committing to implementing one. That requires formulating clear value creation and capture hypotheses to tell when things are working and, perhaps as important, when things are not working and you need to pivot.

With a plan in hand, entrepreneurs will need to consider financial resources, the subject of Chapter 14. These will fund your ability to attract talent and make other investments to implement your strategic choice. But those financial resources are not free. You will need to persuade potential funders with both information and a share of future returns. Having done that, you'll find that many opportunities require a plan to scale your ideas, the subject of Chapter 15. Growth itself is not a given but a choice, and the ways in which you seed the ground for future growth are part of your strategic plan, including how you will find financing and talent for your venture.

The founders of Spotify thought the idea of streaming music services was a good one but the strategy was wrong. With another strategy for this idea, they were able to scale and succeed with an IPO.

Eric Ries's idea behind the "lean startup" was to bring a much more disciplined approach to entrepreneurship.

ENTREPRENEUR'S DILEMMA In the first three parts of this book, we have explored ideas behind entrepreneurship, choice, and types of strategy. In particular, we have seen that for a given idea, there are typically many strategies to pursue around it. But how many do you have to consider before you can choose? Where do you start? When do you stop? In this chapter, you will learn how to conduct a process to choose an entrepreneurial strategy and begin to put it into action. This process shows you how to Test Two and Choose One.

CHAPTER OBJECTIVES

- Understand the elements of the Entrepreneurial Strategy Canvas
- Construct an informative Entrepreneurial Strategy Canvas and its supplemental Strategic Coherence and Linkages Canvas and Learning and Experimentation Canvas
- Ensure the four choices in any entrepreneurial strategy come together, are consistent, and make sense
- Use value creation and capture hypotheses to outline a Plan A and Plan B for your venture
- Describe how iterative experimentation can lead to finding product-market fit or to changing strategies
- Explain how the Test Two, Choose One tool helps entrepreneurs deal with uncertainty and choose a path forward

13

FROM STRATEGY TO ACTION

The bursting of the 2000 dot-com bubble ended then-22-year-old Eric Ries's dream of growing his start-up into the "next big thing." Along with two of his undergraduate classmates, Ries had cofounded Catalyst Recruiting, which created a platform where college students could share their professional portfolios with potential employers, similar to the fledgling LinkedIn. Their approach to use financing to "get big fast" had come at a tremendous cost. Without a clear sense of direction, in his words, "hard work and perseverance don't lead to success."[1]

Ries put these insights to work a few years later in his second venture, a virtual world he called IMVU (see the sidebar on IMVU in Chapter 4 for more information). Instead of simply committing to an up-front plan, Ries premised IMVU almost from its start on the potential insights to be gained by customer experimentation and learning. Rather than focusing on the profitability to be harvested from early customers, Ries thought of customers as "lab rats" testing the rapid cycles of product introductions and offerings he produced. These tests generated enormous information about customer wants and needs. For example, Ries and his team undertook an A/B test where 50% of customers were simply provided with a display offering "3D instant messaging" and the other 50% were offered "avatar chat." The ultimate product they would design would be determined by the empirical results of this test (e.g., the customers' likelihood of sign-up and long-term adoption of an idea) instead of the less-informed opinion of the internal team.

Ries was influenced by his mentor, the start-up guru Steve Blank, who has championed the idea of developing start-ups through first developing an idea of who their customers are. Ries's core insight was that start-up success was not a completely predictive science, nor was it complete luck. The success of new

Steve Blank mentored Eric Ries and championed the concept of developing an idea of the customer first, urging founders to get out and talk to people.

ventures depended on adopting an engineering approach, using a mindset of building, measuring, learning, and iterative product development and positioning. He explored these ideas further, delving into how to apply powerful ideas developed by the Japanese lean manufacturing movement to the process of experimentation and learning in start-up firms. This essential insight formed the nucleus of the "lean startup" movement founded by Ries, ushering in a powerful shift away from a luck-driven "rags to riches" vision of entrepreneurship toward a more disciplined approach based on iterative learning through continual feedback.

To explore why Ries's methodical approach is so powerful, this chapter will discuss the value of first designing and choosing an entrepreneurial strategy, building on steps and ideas discussed in previous chapters. Next we will introduce and expand on the Entrepreneurial Strategy Canvas and provide a practical yet rigorous approach for how to use testing as a key process in choosing your entrepreneurial strategy. Our framework focuses on the sometimes elusive nature of entrepreneurial experimentation and learning, highlighting the need to reduce the uncertainty surrounding a proposed strategic path. However, rather than simply using that process to shine light on "one true path," the framework suggests that founders with a good idea will ultimately face a choice among promising strategic alternatives. The process of testing toward a moment of choice, Test Two, Choose One, offers a practical approach that embraces learning and experimentation while also resolving the paradox of entrepreneurship.

13.1 Why You Need to Choose an Entrepreneurial Strategy: A Review

Throughout this book, we have discussed many key ideas for finding and pursuing opportunities. Let's take a moment to review them together in this section.

- *For a given idea or opportunity, entrepreneurs usually can craft alternative routes to translate the idea into reality. Being able to do so should be seen as a sign of a promising idea.*

Alternative routes may come from different customer groups or alternative technological trajectories, using distinct resources and capabilities, or targeting different partners, competitors, and competitive tactics. However, to give an idea the best chance of success, an entrepreneur must eventually focus their attention and their resources. They must make choices! Moreover, these choices cannot be made in isolation—the respective choices must cohere, reinforce the value each provides, and form an entrepreneurial strategy.

- *As an entrepreneur, often working alone or with a small team, it can seem overwhelming to construct and evaluate alternative strategies and determine the best path forward.*

At the outset, there is fundamental uncertainty about the value of the core idea and if options to pursue it will be feasible or successful. This uncertainty presents several challenges. To make a choice, the entrepreneur must explore alternative paths for commercializing the idea and doing so can be costly. Further, it is difficult for an entrepreneur to learn and keep all their options open; trying to get clear signals about an idea can lead to committing to a specific path.

- *Reducing uncertainty requires experiments on the most critical assumptions. But the most critical assumptions may be difficult if not impossible to test without a significant level of commitment.*

Consider the case of Napster. When Shawn Fanning and his uncle John Fanning founded the peer-to-peer music sharing service Napster in 1999, the two Fannings and their cofounders (including serial entrepreneur and Facebook's first president, Sean Parker) were generally aware that the design of their service— which used the unauthorized peer-to-peer distribution of copyrighted music— was likely, but not necessarily, illegal (**Figure 13.1**). One relatively low-cost test the team undertook to assess the legal risks facing Napster was to hire an attorney to provide a nonbinding legal opinion about the lawfulness of the service. The lawyer argued that since Napster was a peer-to-peer network and did not actually host the underlying files, the service did not violate copyright law. In a separate, concurrent test, they launched the service for free to see what would happen. Though the early-stage founders and investors believed that they could overcome any legal difficulties through trial-and-error iteration of their model, the free service grew rapidly. This growth eventually led to legal action and a $26 million liability being imposed on the young company. While their initial legal opinion was relatively inexpensive, fast, and low commitment, its fidelity was also low. Napster

FIGURE 13.1 **Napster**

In this photo, Shawn Fanning reacts to a ruling that Napster was an illegal service. His early test of hiring a lawyer to investigate this idea had suggested that it might not be illegal.

eventually learned about its true legal position through a test that ultimately bankrupted the company.

Napster's second test of launching its free service committed it to choices without understanding the validity of key critical assumptions. By not limiting the growth of its user base during an experimental stage, the founders did not limit their liability. However, in this case, a limited test might not have been valuable; without a lot of people willing to share a very wide variety of music files, the service might never have caught on.

- *Trade-offs around a test's criticality, its fidelity, and its opportunity cost raise questions of how to best design and sequence experiments while limiting early commitment.*

On the one hand, exploring the most critical assumptions early on can mean making unintended commitments before this learning process is finished. It is tempting to first explore aspects of an idea and strategy that involve the lowest cost and commitment, even if that means focusing effort on less critical assumptions. On the other hand, experiments on less critical assumptions might not reduce uncertainty in a meaningful way. It is easy for some entrepreneurs to use the potential for unintended commitment to avoid confronting their most critical assumptions.

- *It is best to use a strategic process of learning and experimentation that truly helps assess whether the idea is worth pursuing.*

At the outset, an entrepreneur may first need to test the technical feasibility of the core idea and whether it is viable. This may involve prototyping and other forms of experimentation. Once the idea has been deemed technically feasible, the entrepreneur can move on to low-commitment testing to investigate potential strategies around an idea and assess their feasibility. Next, an entrepreneur might test different combinations of technology, customers, and competitors to see how they might interact and whether the idea is likely to succeed.

Once a potential strategy has been identified, high-commitment testing may be necessary to determine whether it is viable and whether it is worth pursuing. For example, an entrepreneur might implement the strategy on a small scale to see how it performs and to gather feedback from customers and other stakeholders. Once a strategy has been chosen, within-strategy testing can help the entrepreneur refine and improve their strategy over time. They may continue to test different approaches to technology, organization, and competition and use the results to adjust and improve the venture's overall performance.

- *Finally, you cannot test what you cannot state. At the earliest stages of exploring an entrepreneurial strategy, the focus should be on formulating rather than simply conducting tests.*

Stating a hypothesis clearly is often the most important and necessary step toward developing a test for it. Trying to determine the most critical assumptions underlying a strategy can sometimes surface a way to test even these assumptions in a low-cost, high-fidelity way (see **Using the Research: Rapid Entrepreneurial Experimentation and Learning in the Cloud**). As we will emphasize

Rapid Entrepreneurial Experimentation and Learning in the Cloud

The advent of inexpensive cloud computing in the early 2010s illustrates how having a platform for low-cost experimentation dramatically accelerates the process of entrepreneurial learning. Researchers have shown that the introduction in 2006 of Amazon Web Services (AWS), where users "rented" space on the cloud on an affordable fractional basis, enabled start-ups to host online experiences at very low cost and grow with demand.[a] AWS did not materially change the cost of running an established business (running your own cloud versus renting were roughly comparable in price once you achieved large scale). But this change in the cost of experimentation helped new ventures actively learn about the viability of their idea and strategy and do so before making large fixed investments that might commit them to a specific path (or doomed idea). A wide range of then-new ventures, such as Airbnb, Dropbox, and Uber, used AWS for small-scale customer experiments.

The AWS cloud helped entrepreneurs run tests at a very low level of cost and commitment.

The move toward cloud computing was a key factor driving the rise of early-stage angel financing. Financiers now placed a much larger set of smaller bets on start-up ventures in the hope that a "spray and pray" strategy would find winners. That is, instead of investing in only a few start-ups, financiers provided more ventures with enough financing to test their basic ideas in the cloud. Using these tests, the backers then invested in further rounds of financing for those ventures that had de-risked their idea and strategy. Not surprisingly, decreasing the cost of experiments broadened the scope of ideas and the number of founders receiving initial and follow-on investment.

later in this chapter, a particularly effective means for clarifying the key assumptions is the Test Two, Choose One method.

13.2 The Elements of an Entrepreneurial Strategy

In past chapters, we have learned about the four critical choices facing early-stage ventures and how they relate to each other in the Entrepreneurial Strategy Compass. Now, let's see how to use these four choices and the compass to articulate alternative entrepreneurial strategies, and then choose one. To start, we will see that this choice process requires some initial formal business planning. But as we have emphasized, formulating an entrepreneurial strategy requires embracing that a start-up faces considerable uncertainty and must engage in significant learning and feedback. With this in mind, let's see how we can use business planning to make concrete choices even though outcomes from entrepreneurial strategies are fundamentally uncertain.

ENTREPRENEURIAL STRATEGY CANVAS

To focus this process, let's use a tool we call the Entrepreneurial Strategy Canvas (**Figure 13.2**). The canvas has 12 elements corresponding to core ideas in previous chapters. It is designed to provide a structured way to describe and state the important choices in an entrepreneurial strategy. By preparing a canvas for each strategy, it also becomes easy to compare one against the other. Let's see how this works.

PRE-STRATEGY ELEMENTS: IDEA, PASSION, AND UNFAIR ADVANTAGE

At the top of the canvas (in orange) are things that cannot, or cannot easily, be changed. The first element is the statement of your **core idea**. As we discussed in Chapter 3, this is your fundamental insight about the entrepreneurial opportunity you face. It describes what your venture intends to do without referencing any particular strategic element. Shortly, we will show you a process to work through and clearly state your core idea. *Your core idea is something that will not change as you develop and consider alternative strategies on other canvases.*

The second and third elements in the yellow section are where you describe your **unfair advantage** and **passion** (Chapter 2), respectively, the characteristics you have that will shape or constrain how you value the commercialization routes you take with your business. For instance, you might want to develop a venture in a particular location, or you might feel strongly that your venture should be environmentally friendly. Similarly, you might feel you have a specific knowledge base, skill, or unfair advantage to harness. Articulating these here will help you, potential team members, and others supporting you (like mentors) choose between different strategies. These parts of the canvas will let you and others know what might drive your choice and what competitive advantages you might have in realizing the opportunity and any given strategies.

CORE STRATEGIC HYPOTHESES: VALUE CREATION AND VALUE CAPTURE

The next two elements are at the bottom of the canvas in blue and are where you make clear statements of your **value creation and capture hypotheses**. We locate these at the bottom of the canvas because, along with the decisions in yellow, they frame the entire emphasis of the venture. In many ways, they are the most important elements in building your entrepreneurial strategy. These hypotheses draw a clear, logical line describing what must be true for your venture to succeed. Because success isn't guaranteed, in creating these, it can also help to consider what must *not* happen—the things that would make your hypothesis false.

Further, to find out if these hypotheses are correct, you will need to make choices about both, while understanding you do not know if either hypothesis is correct in the first place. As we will see in a later chapter, it is only by doing this that you can make a subsequent decision to continue the venture, to switch to an alternative strategy, or to abandon the venture entirely.

core idea The fundamental entrepreneurial opportunity and insight that a venture will be built on

value creation and capture hypotheses Hypotheses that frame the entire emphasis of your venture, drawing a clear, logical line describing what must be true for your venture to succeed

Chapter 13: From Strategy to Action

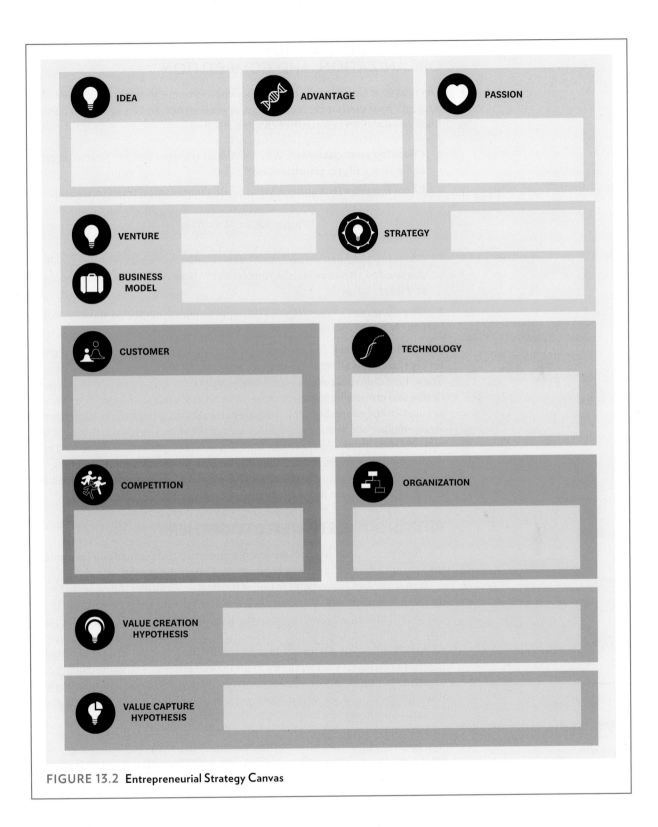

FIGURE 13.2 Entrepreneurial Strategy Canvas

CORE STRATEGIC CHOICES: CUSTOMER, TECHNOLOGY, ORGANIZATION, AND COMPETITION

The next four elements are the four key choices underlying your entrepreneurial strategy: your *customer*, *technology*, *organization*, and *competition* choices. Each was a subject of an earlier chapter. In brief:

- *Choosing your customer:* What customer segments do you plan to target, and which will you prioritize first?

- *Choosing your technology:* What broad technological trajectories and innovations will you exploit in your venture? Will you work with an established technology and its development S curve, or try to look for another one that may emerge?

- *Choosing your organization:* What resources and what capabilities will you need to attract to launch your venture? How will you organize people and their skill sets?

- *Choosing your competition:* Who will be your competitors, and how will you choose to compete (or possibly cooperate) with them?

While addressing specific choices beyond those highlighted here will be critical for every start-up, all ventures need to confront, at a minimum, these four choices. These four domains cover a significant swath of the critical choices for venture design and growth, highlighting those most central and consistent, though not an exhaustive encyclopedia for all contingencies a start-up might face. Each strategy you formulate will include a choice for each of these. As you resolve those choices, you will state them clearly in the four boxes on the canvas. In describing each choice, you want to make sure that it is clear to your cofounders, mentors, and advisers which customer segment you have chosen, for instance, and which sets of customers you have not selected (at least temporarily).

PUTTING THE STRATEGY TOGETHER

The final three elements in light green summarize the venture and its strategy: the venture's *name*, the overall **strategy**, and **business model**.

If your choices correspond to one of the four descriptive strategies that make up the Entrepreneurial Compass, you can state this in the strategy box. In the last four chapters, we have outlined the four most common strategies for start-ups. Though each has distinct trade-offs, each also includes a coherent set of choices that provide a pathway that gives your idea the best chance of translating into a reality. Of course, the entrepreneurial strategy you choose may not fit exactly into one of the four strategies from the Entrepreneurial Compass. This is acceptable, but it will mean more work in identifying the value creation and capture hypotheses and may increase the trade-offs your venture faces.

Finally, the business model box should build on the chosen strategy, describing succinctly how the venture will make money in an ongoing way. For instance, what product or service will you specifically sell? How will you sell it? With your entrepreneurial canvas in place, you now have a vision of the type of venture you might be growing as a result of your strategic choices, and you can begin sharpening those choices. The canvas also provides a ready-made set of hypotheses with assumptions that, if true, should create and capture value from the strategy.

strategy The combination of elements that make up the four key choices underlying an entrepreneurial opportunity: customer, technology, organization, and competition

business model Builds upon a venture's strategy to describe how it will make money in an ongoing way

13.3 Entrepreneurial Strategy Coherence

linkages The underlying connections formed between each of the four elements of your entrepreneurial strategy

Thus far, we have considered the process for making each of the four key choices separately. In reality, the choices cannot be made in this manner but instead have to fit together with **linkages** that reinforce one another. In this sense, we say they have *strategic coherence*.

Understanding how different choices reinforce others simplifies your process of arriving at a full strategy. The Strategic Coherence and Linkages Canvas shown in **Figure 13.3** will help you explore and understand these. When you make one choice of, say, customer, you should be considering your choices of technology, competition, and organization in terms of how they reinforce your choice of customer. Notably, we started with customer in this example because it is the choice that, in our experience, drives the process for many entrepreneurial ventures. Another popular starting point is the choice

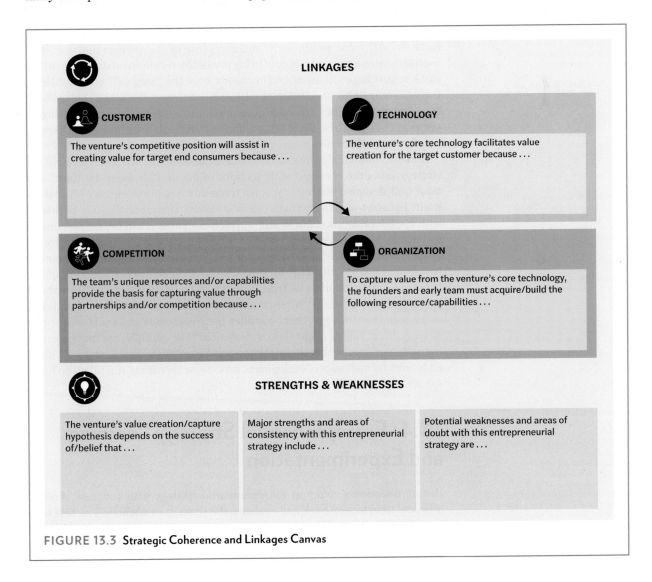

LINKAGES

CUSTOMER
The venture's competitive position will assist in creating value for target end consumers because . . .

TECHNOLOGY
The venture's core technology facilitates value creation for the target customer because . . .

COMPETITION
The team's unique resources and/or capabilities provide the basis for capturing value through partnerships and/or competition because . . .

ORGANIZATION
To capture value from the venture's core technology, the founders and early team must acquire/build the following resource/capabilities . . .

STRENGTHS & WEAKNESSES

The venture's value creation/capture hypothesis depends on the success of/belief that . . .

Major strengths and areas of consistency with this entrepreneurial strategy include . . .

Potential weaknesses and areas of doubt with this entrepreneurial strategy are . . .

FIGURE 13.3 **Strategic Coherence and Linkages Canvas**

of technology, perhaps leveraging research from a lab or a new innovation. If you start with either of these, or possibly even organization or competition, the key is making sure the follow-on choices reinforce each other and form a coherent strategy.

If there are choices that do not fit or make sense together, you will not achieve strategic coherence. While some customer groupings will reinforce other strategic choices, different customer groups—though perhaps attractive or on par with each other in terms of their viability—may be inconsistent with those other choices. For example, if a start-up is planning to stay at the forefront of technology over time and so continually be on the bleeding edge of innovation, then ideal customer groupings are those willing to tolerate failure and encourage experimentation. Alternatively, if the start-up is instead attempting to establish its technology as a broad standard (perhaps at the expense of incorporating every potential follow-on bell and whistle), then the founding team might prioritize more mainstream customer groupings at an earlier stage. They will do so to ensure that they are building a standards-setting process and broader organizational capabilities beyond technological expertise. As discussed in Chapter 10, Netflix's early focus on film buffs at the expense of mainstream movie renters complemented its core strategy of using predictive recommendation algorithms and low-cost acquisitions of DVD versions from the "long tail" of movie titles. Understanding how the choice of customer reinforces the other choices (e.g., from first employee hires to mode of competition) is among the most challenging yet most clarifying insights as a start-up tries to translate its idea into a foundation for competitive advantage.

Finally, a founding team should evaluate the strengths and weaknesses of the strategy using the corresponding sections of Figure 13.3. Even the "best" and most well-designed strategies involve trade-offs. That is the nature of strategy itself! For start-ups, those trade-offs may involve commercialization pathways with considerable uncertainty still unresolved. These could be, for instance, a technology not quite ready for proof of concept or a particularly novel customer value proposition that is yet to be borne out. Founders should sharpen their key hypotheses and identify what must be true for their value creation and capture hypotheses to turn out to be true. Next, they should consider the strengths of the strategy. For instance, where are the strongest areas of coherence and consistency in the strategy? Then, consider the weaknesses and trade-offs of this strategy. What routes might this strategy close? For example, are there promising customer groups that this strategy would ignore? Or does it require a more ambitious technological development process or recruiting top talent to build specific capabilities?

13.4 Entrepreneurial Strategy Learning and Experimentation

Having designed a coherent entrepreneurial strategy with concrete choices, it is now time to step back and evaluate the strategy as a whole. The first step is to focus again on the value creation and capture hypotheses. The critical assumptions underlying those hypotheses are opportunities for experimentation and learning.

For any given idea and strategy, there is a set of hypotheses that must turn out to be true for the strategy to succeed. Among many factors, some of these include the presence of a paying customer, feasible technology and organization, and a commercialization path that creates and captures value on a sustainable basis. Similarly, the founding team should identify assumptions in their strategy that if proven false would make it difficult for the venture to succeed along this commercialization path. Having identified these assumptions, entrepreneurs need to identify opportunities for experimentation and learning to explore and hopefully validate these hypotheses. In our Learning and Experimentation Canvas (**Figure 13.4**), you should complete the Experimentation section with this information.

Being clear and sharp on the most critical hypotheses facing the venture is important; it helps the team identify the underlying opportunity and risks facing a venture, test their entrepreneurial strategy, and focus their time and attention on ensuring that critical hypotheses turn out to be true. For example, when Netflix cofounders Reed Hastings and Marc Randolph were exploring the potential for a mail-order movie rental service, they realized that a

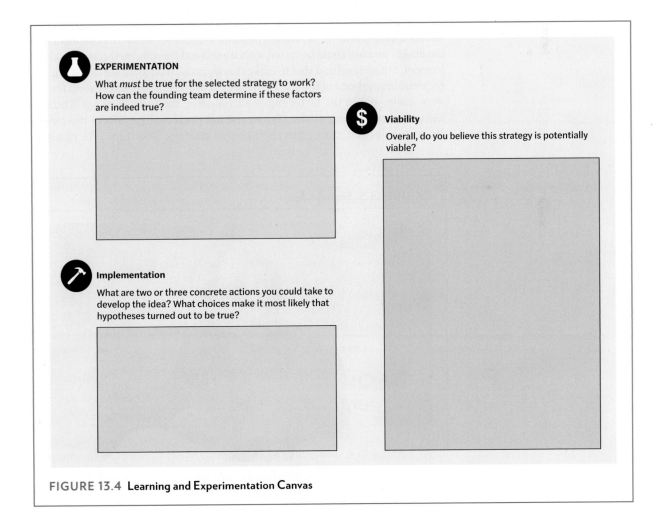

EXPERIMENTATION

What *must* be true for the selected strategy to work? How can the founding team determine if these factors are indeed true?

Viability

Overall, do you believe this strategy is potentially viable?

Implementation

What are two or three concrete actions you could take to develop the idea? What choices make it most likely that hypotheses turned out to be true?

FIGURE 13.4 **Learning and Experimentation Canvas**

critical assumption was that they could send DVDs by mail smoothly and efficiently. Rather than debate the point in the abstract or assume its validity, they mailed CDs to themselves in a regular envelope.[2] While Hastings and Randolph could not test every element of their model, this simple test gave them a high level of confidence to further develop and learn about other aspects of their strategy before committing to it.

Like Hastings and Randolph, entrepreneurs should look for concrete actions they can implement that test their strategy. In our canvas in Figure 13.4, there is an Implementation section specifically for this purpose. Unlike scientists, entrepreneurs can shape the world to give their hypotheses and tests (and venture) the best chance of success. Consider the case of a custom framing start-up, Framebridge. Founder and CEO Susan Tynan (**Figure 13.5**) founded Framebridge with an explicit focus on the customer. Indeed, it had been a challenge she faced as a consumer that led her to entrepreneurship: after collecting four National Parks posters during a trip with her sister, she set out to frame the posters. But she found this led to both a lengthy process at a design studio and an expensive (over $1,600!) set of standard metal frames that she hated.[3] Tynan founded Framebridge on the hypotheses that customers would purchase custom frames and framing services online, sending their mementos and photos to the company for framing, if the process was reliable, simple, affordable and included custom-design services. The basic hypotheses about the customer and the design process could be tested with traditional framing methods and skilled framers. But she realized that to make this work as an ongoing service at scale, it required innovations in the standard framing process, in the way custom frames were made, and in the technologies surrounding the logistics space. Through thoughtful technology choice, Tynan and her team could reinforce their value for customers and strengthen their overall strategy. The team prioritized an

---

FIGURE 13.5 **Framebridge**

Susan Tynan realized that to make her strategy work, she would have to dramatically change how the entire framing process works.

early focus on logistics and making commitments like raising venture capital to develop best-in-class logistics and design capabilities. Innovation in logistics continues to be a hallmark of the company.

As a final step, entrepreneurs must evaluate the hypotheses' key risks and areas of uncertainty. Stepping back and evaluating everything you know, how viable is this plan? This is the red final section in Figure 13.4. Of course, after doing all this work, it may solidify your feelings about the opportunity, or you may come to a different conclusion. But in Tynan's case, she felt a multibillion-dollar market was ripe for innovation, and an increasing focus on home design, customization, and Internet-based services meant customers were eager for such a company. She felt certain of the market potential. However, to do it properly, she knew that the risks would include needing significant resources and uncertainty about building out the logistics and meeting demand. Ultimately, she identified investors who saw the promise of the opportunity as well as her strategy for realizing that opportunity. Only three years after founding, Tynan had secured a partnership with Target, and Framebridge was on its way to reshaping the framing industry.

13.5 The Strategy for Start-Ups' Performance Bump

Founders only learn the true value of their ideas when they take action. Many entrepreneurs find that identifying value creation and value capture hypotheses and the associated strategic choices to be a challenging and sometimes time-intensive process. Confronting the uncertainty and the very real trade-offs of alternatives can be difficult, as is leaving behind potential alternatives and confronting risks head on. As such, let's review why taking a systematic strategic approach to entrepreneurship is valuable.

First, one of the chief benefits is clarifying an entrepreneur's or a team's understanding of the essence of their idea and the potential value it can create. By debating alternative strategies' strengths and weaknesses, founding teams sharpen their understanding of what is unique or distinctive about their idea and the core resources or capabilities they possess and will leverage.

Second, research has shown that formal planning processes pay off. In a critical study, researchers Francis Greene and Christian Hopp analyzed data on 1,088 founders. They compared the viability of start-ups that undertook a process of formal (or informal) planning versus those that did not.[4] The researchers found that the start-ups founded by teams that undertook a planning process were more likely to launch and continue an operation, achieve sales for their product or service, and sustain profitability. They then questioned whether these two sets of founding teams and start-ups were similar. Perhaps the planners were more skilled, or perhaps they planned because they had better information about whether their ideas had greater potential or otherwise were distinct. However, controlling for effects of the founder's skill and the idea's quality, Greene and Hopp found that planning significantly increased the likelihood of the viability and performance of the business. In their words: "We find that it pays to plan."

In another study, researchers focused on whether forming concrete hypotheses about the start-up idea and using a scientific approach as the venture was implemented would yield benefits.[5] This team with three members from

Bocconi University in Italy designed a randomized control trial of 116 Italian start-ups, where they divided a set of founders with similar quality, nascent venture ideas into two groups. In the first group, founders received advice about how to build and scale their business. In the second group, the founders also received advice about how to form hypotheses on assumptions underlying their venture and follow a scientific approach to testing and validating (or disproving!) these hypotheses. After these courses, the researchers followed the ventures for over a year. Ultimately, those in the second group, who had received advice on how to pursue their entrepreneurship activities with a scientific approach, were more likely to have generated more precise information to guide their decision-making. Above all, this group earned greater revenue than those ventures that did not receive advice on hypothesis testing.

However, planning can become a mechanism or an excuse to never get started. A strategic approach to entrepreneurship is not an excuse for over-analysis or decision paralysis. Sitting on the sidelines does not move the idea to reality, no matter how well-crafted the strategy. Entrepreneurship requires that entrepreneurs and founding teams commit to action.

13.6 Experimenting to an Epiphany

Moving from commitment-free exploration to action means embracing iterative experimentation, the process central to formulating an entrepreneurial strategy and at the heart of entrepreneurship. Doing so requires both paying attention to the information experiments provide and being willing to adjust your choices as new information comes in. Like other aspects of entrepreneurship, which experiments you pursue are a choice. With limited resources and the distinct possibility that some experiments will close off options, entrepreneurs must understand what they are trying to learn.

Steve Blank, introduced earlier in the chapter as Eric Ries's mentor, wrote an influential manifesto, *The Four Steps to the Epiphany*, in which he described how the process of iterative experimentation results in clarity about the path forward. In a nutshell, the "steps to the epiphany" prioritize performing experiments with customers to identify a clear way for the venture to create and capture value from an underlying idea. Noted venture capitalists Andy Rachleff and Marc Andreessen have echoed this idea, emphasizing that the path to the epiphany is to undertake experimentation until the venture achieves what Rachleff calls "product-market fit."[6]

FIGURE 13.6 **Product-Market Fit**

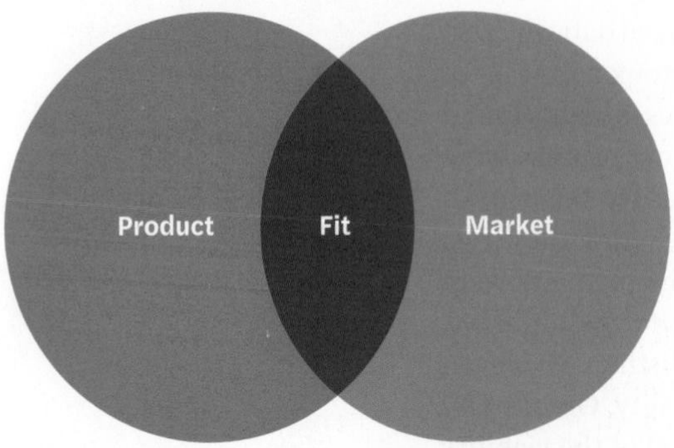

In the words of Marc Andreessen, "Product-market fit means being in a good market with a product that can satisfy that market."

PRODUCT-MARKET FIT

What is product-market fit? It is a process of refining your choice of customer to find the best market segment (**Figure 13.6**).[7] Consider the music streaming service Spotify, which faced some distinct choices about which customers to target. Prior to recent ventures like Spotify, the first inroads into music streaming were by platforms that did not, initially, license music rights from music copyright holders. One of the earliest was Napster, founded by Shawn Fanning, John Fanning, and Sean Parker. A court order shut Napster down, and it was never able to revive itself as a lawful service. While many analysts saw the bankruptcy of Napster as proof that peer-to-peer unlimited streaming music distribution could never be profitable, Swedish entrepreneur Daniel Ek hypothesized that services such as Napster, LimeWire, and Pirate Bay had pursued a good idea with a fundamentally flawed strategy. In his words, "you can never legislate away from piracy." Along with cofounder Martin Lorentzon, Ek launched Spotify as a legal streaming site that compensated artists based on the popularity of their music on the site. Ek and Lorentzon initially limited Spotify to the Swedish market, experimenting over several years to figure out how to collaborate effectively with the music industry, work out the operation of the technology platform, and develop potential sources of revenue (e.g., advertising versus subscription). By achieving product-market fit within the Swedish market, the founders (and investors) of Spotify gained confidence that a profitable streaming music service could be launched on a global basis, resulting in a 2017 IPO valuing Spotify at $26 billion.[8]

To recognize possible product-market fit, founding teams should already have validated multiple critical assumptions with high-fidelity tests. Ideally, only one or two critical assumptions remain untested. When there are many untested assumptions, the probability of success is lower. First recognizing product-market fit and implementing a specific entrepreneurial strategy are key to the success of any venture.

In this chapter's video, learn how Spotify achieved product-market fit in the streaming industry.

COSTS OF COMMITMENT

Once a venture achieves product-market fit and commits to an entrepreneurial strategy, it will continue to experiment, focusing on how to reach its potential. It will serve chosen customers, evolve its technology, and work to establish and sustain a competitive position. It will hire key personnel, leverage resources, and build capabilities. Essentially, implementing the strategy matures the start-up into a functional organization.

But it is important to emphasize the costs of commitment. Before committing to a particular path, a venture can still assess multiple alternatives and choose. Once the core choices within a particular entrepreneurial strategy are implemented, the costs of pivoting rise significantly. As we discussed in Chapter 5, online grocer Webvan, founded at the peak of the dot-com boom, implemented a strategy that turned out to be based on faulty assumptions. The founding team overestimated the level of demand and underestimated the technological complexities of warehouse logistics and the costs of a competitive online delivery service. Their commitment left them unable to alter their strategy (i.e., pivot) toward an alternative. They could not, for example, imitate Peapod's successful and less capital-intensive business that provides ordering and delivery for existing grocery stores. Webvan's inability to switch was due to the team's commitments to competition with traditional supermarkets, costly leases on warehouses, and heavy investments in technology, as well as a mismatch between the expectations raised during their IPO and the smaller, more gradual market growth that a profitable alternative would have.

But changes are possible. There are three common scenarios where strategies change *after* an initial choice of one strategic path.

1. ***Gradual change.*** Elements of implementing a given strategy will likely change based on direct experience. For example, the details of pricing, product characteristics, or precise positioning against competitors are all likely to change over time.

2. ***Changes in response to favorable news.*** Strategies can change to take advantage of favorable circumstances. For example, a company that is founded within a value chain strategy may realize it can architect a new value chain, necessitating a transition to an architectural strategy. While Microsoft was essentially founded as a value chain company, Bill Gates leveraged its contract with IBM as the cornerstone of an architectural strategy where first DOS and then Windows became the dominant platform of the new personal computing ecosystem. Alternatively, a venture that pursued a disruptive strategy may pivot toward a more collaborative approach once it is established, partnering with the incumbent players the founding team formerly competed against.[9]

3. ***Changes in response to failure.*** When early feedback indicates that a strategy is not succeeding, the venture can try to pivot away from it. Pinterest was launched as a mobile-first fashion commerce platform, but its founders quickly realized that users were not interested in purchasing items through their phones but instead storing photo collections of items they might explore later. CEO Ben Silbermann and his cofounders shifted Pinterest toward exclusively curating and sharing collections of online content (**Figure 13.7**), building a base of more than 465 million monthly users as of 2023 (though capturing value from these users remains somewhat elusive).[10]

FIGURE 13.7 **Pinterest**

Pinterest shifted to a strategy of having users create and share collections.

Chapter 13: From Strategy to Action

"Testing to the epiphany" provides the start-up with confidence but not certainty about the value of a particular strategic path (although it reduces the uncertainty). Choosing a path means implementing that strategy. Identifying a clear "best path forward" through testing focuses the venture on the pursuit of that path.

13.7 Test Two, Choose One

At this point, you have been introduced to a process and strategic canvases to help develop an entrepreneurial strategy and consider how to find product-market fit through testing. But now, we want to describe the power of doing the process twice. This idea lies in what we saw in Chapter 4, that an idea worth pursuing almost always has multiple viable paths to follow. It is likely that there will be multiple potential customers to be served (even as initial markets), multiple technological solutions, multiple ways to organize, and multiple ways to compete. By developing two strategies about an idea at the outset, you are helping to confirm its potential. Further, you are not locking yourself into the results of one set of product tests. When entrepreneurs explore multiple potential paths, and identify only a single viable path to success, they may be tempted to identify that path as the achievement of product-market fit. Instead, this should be weighed against the possibility that there is a hidden or implicit assumption that might undermine it. Specifically, if all but one commercialization route is likely to fail, how robust can this single route to success be?

Developing two strategies rather than just one is more than doubly useful for entrepreneurs. Developing two options around an idea, including business plans for each, is literally the least one can do in order to ensure that there is an opportunity to make a considered choice. If an entrepreneur's core idea is really that transformative, they owe it to that idea to create a choice between different strategic options to commercialize that idea. That being said, while we advocate testing two strategies, there may well be returns to considering even more strategies. But aiming for two gives entrepreneurs an achievable goal in strategy formulation.

TEST TWO

This brings us back to our earlier best practice: the Test Two, Choose One process. It starts by designing a strategy using the canvases and questions described earlier in the chapter. Entrepreneurs and teams should iterate on it until they have a strategy they believe is viable. *However, having identified a viable strategy, the founders should start again and develop a second strategy, using the same process.* Then, both of these strategies should be tested—this is the "Test Two" part of the process—so that the most promising path to success can be chosen.

Critically, the founders should seek to design and then test a second strategy whose value creation and capture hypotheses are fundamentally distinct from those in their first strategy. An effective way to do so is to consider a dramatically different choice for one of the key domains. For instance:

- What would it mean if the venture served an entirely different customer?
- Instead of collaborating with a potential incumbent, can the venture choose to compete with them?

- Is there a different technological trajectory to use, or can their current technology be used in a different way?
- Is there a different specialized set of capabilities the firm can advertise as their expertise?

The key is to explore other viable choices that craft an entirely different, viable strategy. The entrepreneur or founding team should then iterate the process they followed to craft the initial strategy.

With at least two viable entrepreneurial strategies, the team should test and evaluate the differences across those two strategies. Besides the differences in the key domains of choice, they should consider the differences with questions like:

- How is the uncertainty in realizing this opportunity different along these two paths?
- What will you learn about the idea and strategy along one path but not along the other path (and vice versa)?
- Does one involve earlier commitment (and closed doors earlier) or involve sharper trade-offs?
- What are the day-to-day activities of these respective companies?
- What would success look like for the venture with each of these strategies?
- Will the founding team be unable to do both strategies at the same time?
- Does pursuing one route foreclose permanently the potential for the venture to pursue the other route?

In considering the differences, the founding team will confront uncertainty. One pathway may be full of promise but have more uncertainty than the alternative pathway. In evaluating and testing the two, consider if there are sources of uncertainty that, if resolved, would alter your choice of strategy to pursue. Assess whether there are tests you could run that would provide greater clarity and allow you to choose between these alternatives.

CHOOSE ONE

Finally, the founding team must make a choice, commit to an entrepreneurial strategy, and begin the steps to implement it. As we have seen, *a strategic approach to entrepreneurship moves beyond trying to figure out which one of these paths is "right" or "wrong" and instead focuses entrepreneurs on proactive experimentation and learning to understand the key trade-offs between options. Then the entrepreneur or team can choose the path that best aligns with their objectives and resources.* The overall viability of these alternatives becomes less important, since each comes with its own profile of costs and benefits. The fit between the founders, their particular circumstances and motives, and the strategy becomes paramount.

Two related considerations help guide the moment of choice. First, some strategies might simply be more feasible in the near term due to the availability of local resources or near-term opportunities. For example, if one strategy focuses on a local market where the founders already live, the value of being able to take advantage of resources and connections that are close at hand can be a deciding factor. Many entrepreneurs report relying on near-term factors in early decisions. Rather than reflecting an absence of using strategy, this pragmatic focus is consistent with taking advantage of near-term opportunities to implement their broader idea.

Second, beyond the pragmatism of local opportunities, choice is ultimately guided by which strategy achieves broader objectives and missions important to the entrepreneur. Some strategies might more closely align with customer groups that the founders aim to serve, while others might involve a lower level of risk and be more consistent with the risk tolerance of the founding team. *Once the founders have undertaken a rigorous process to identify viable alternatives, that process can be resolved; the founders can decide how their internal motivations should take precedence over potential external rewards.* They may have their own passions, values, and capabilities that drive them to favor one strategy over another.

13.8 Concluding Thoughts

By their very nature, start-ups face a wide range of choices. Founding teams cannot implement all of the options that are available to them and so face uncertainty at the moment of founding about the relative value creation and capture associated with at least some of those options. As such, the most crucial task for a start-up team at the founding is not simply to "just do it" but instead to learn what "it" to "do" (see **Putting It Together: From Strategy to Action** on p. 390).

As Eric Ries's work brought to the forefront, a key component of entrepreneurship is the process of entrepreneurial experimentation and learning. However, the value of such experiments is higher when guided by an entrepreneurial strategy process. A strategic approach to experimentation emphasizes that commitment-free learning and analyses (e.g., cost-benefit calculations) is an important step for eliminating clearly suboptimal paths but is insufficient for entrepreneurs aiming to create an ambitious growth business. Until entrepreneurs face the conundrum of having to leave behind an equally attractive potential business path, they have not yet reached the entrepreneurial edge of their idea.

Chapter 13 Review: From Strategy to Action

CHAPTER TAKEAWAYS

- For most ideas (especially good ideas!), entrepreneurs can readily craft alternative strategic routes to take advantage of it.

- To give an idea the best chance of success, an entrepreneur must focus their attention and their resources. They must design and choose an entrepreneurial strategy.

- The Entrepreneurial Strategy Canvas is a tool that helps define the key elements of an entrepreneurial strategy. It includes the pre-strategy elements (idea, passion, and unfair advantage) as well as the core strategic hypotheses (value creation and value capture) and the core strategic choices (customer, technology, organization, and competition) of the entrepreneurial strategy being developed.

FROM STRATEGY TO ACTION

How do you explore, learn, and decide what to do? Use these three tools to help you.

ENTREPRENEURIAL STRATEGY CANVAS

Construct a Plan to Translate Your Idea into a Venture

- State the core idea and your "unfair" advantage and passion.
- Specify your hypotheses as to how your venture will create and capture value.
- Identify the core choices: which customers will you serve, how will you innovate, how will you build your team, and with whom and how will you compete?
- Summarize the venture and its strategy, including the venture's name, overall strategy, and business model.

ENTREPRENEURIAL STRATEGY COHERENCE

Evaluate the Plan as a Whole

- Determine how the core elements of the strategy fit together.
- Consider the strengths and weaknesses of the strategy: what must be true for the strategy to work?
- Identify opportunities for experimentation to strengthen your hypotheses. Specify two to three concrete actions you could take to implement the strategy.

TEST TWO, CHOOSE ONE

Learn about Two Alternative Strategies and Choose One

- Construct and evaluate at least two viable strategic paths for the venture. Make sure they involve distinct core choices by changing at least the value creation hypothesis or value capture hypothesis.
- Evaluate the differences between the two strategies. Beyond the core domains of choice, consider the uncertainty, opportunities for learning, and commitments involved with each strategy.
- Generate a test you could conduct to choose between these alternatives. Consider whether choosing one imposes costs on transitioning or pivoting to the other.
- Choose the strategy that best aligns with your objectives for becoming an entrepreneur and leverages your skills and resources.

- The choices comprising an entrepreneurial strategy are not made independently, as each choice should link to other strategic choices and reinforce the value they provide.

- At the earliest stages of exploring an entrepreneurial strategy, entrepreneurs must focus on formulating rather than simply conducting tests. The act of stating a hypothesis clearly is often the most important step toward developing a test for that hypothesis. You cannot test what you cannot state!

- Clearly stating the most critical hypotheses facing the venture allows the founding team to effectively test their entrepreneurial strategy and determine if they are true.

- The process of designing and evaluating an entrepreneurial strategy clarifies key choices, disciplines entrepreneurial experimentation and learning, and provides a concrete road map for the commercializing of an idea.

- The Test Two, Choose One process tests two possible strategies, but does not try to resolve all uncertainty with each idea or the alternative strategic paths. Instead, it works to gather enough information to make an informed choice.

- By engaging in this iterative process of testing and learning, entrepreneurs can make a more informed decision about which strategic path to pursue.

- In the long run, choosing an entrepreneurial strategy is guided not simply by the relative economic and financial returns but also by an entrepreneur's wish to achieve their broader objectives and missions.

- Ultimately, choosing your entrepreneurial strategy means making an active choice to leave alternative strategies behind, at least temporarily.

KEY TERMS

core idea (p. 376)
value creation and capture
   hypothesis (p. 376)

strategy (p. 378)
business model (p. 378)
linkages (p. 379)

REVIEW QUESTIONS

1. Why do you need to choose an entrepreneurial strategy?

2. Outline and explain the elements of the Entrepreneurial Strategy Canvas. Which elements change and which stay the same as an entrepreneur formulates alternative strategic routes for their idea? Explain.

3. How do the four core strategic choices—customer, technology, organization, and with whom and how to compete—relate to the value creation and value capture hypotheses?

4. Why must the choices within the Entrepreneurial Strategy Canvas have linkages with each other? What challenges will entrepreneurs face if their choices are not coherent?

5. What steps should an entrepreneur undertake to learn more about a given strategic route before choosing and committing to the path?

6. In what ways is a systematic strategic approach to planning valuable for entrepreneurs? Do such benefits require a lengthy process?

7. How does an entrepreneur's approach to learning and experimentation evolve as they develop alternative entrepreneurial strategies, choose one, and then implement, and achieve product-market fit for, a given entrepreneurial strategy?

8. What types of changes are likely to occur after an entrepreneur has chosen and committed to a particular entrepreneurial strategy? Explain.

9. Describe the Test Two, Choose One process. Explain how this process allows an entrepreneur to follow their passion.

DISCUSSION QUESTIONS

Answer the following series of questions and scenarios either in class discussions or by writing a short response.

1. Pick one of your favorite start-ups—this could be a well-known venture, an enterprise found from research online, or one from your university ecosystem, local community, or region—and use it to complete the Entrepreneurial Strategy Canvas. In doing so, try to re-create the founding team's early idea and strategic choices. Then, in a few paragraphs, briefly evaluate their early entrepreneurial strategy. For example, what do you consider their dimensions of early uncertainty? What trade-offs did they face in moving their idea and strategy forward?

2. After completing Question 1, use its early idea and the canvas to develop your own idea based on it. To do so, create new value creation and value capture hypotheses for the idea (Tip: Start with different core strategic choices!). Then, evaluate this entrepreneurial strategy. How does this strategic path differ from the one the actual entrepreneurs chose? Why do you think they chose the route they ultimately selected instead of the one you have just created?

3. Consider the following scenario before you answer the questions. Following the Test Two, Choose One approach, Gregory, a barbecue enthusiast, has developed multiple alternative viable strategies for his idea, a compact oven design, using the Entrepreneurial Strategy Compass as his guide. He is now weighing two strategies. Following an intellectual property strategy, his first approach involves seeking licensing agreements with players across a range of industries as he continues to push forward oven design and research. Alternatively, following a disruption strategy, Gregory is considering launching a compact grill based on his technology for apartment residents, who lack the space and approval for traditional outdoor grills and may provide the pathway to disrupt the traditional grilling market with his designs.

   Briefly describe steps can Gregory take to learn about these alternative paths before choosing one. In doing so, what early commitments are required for each of these strategies? Does one strategy allow for more learning and experimentation over time? How does that shape the early choices Gregory faces?

4. Consider the following scenario before you answer the questions. After a summer internship at a gaming company, Meera has an idea for a new offering missing from the market. Using a value chain strategy, she has developed a promising entrepreneurial strategy that could effectively realize her idea by working in collaboration with the gaming company where she interned.

Meera has set up a meeting with her team from the company to discuss the opportunity. She is seeking your advice on deal terms and next steps to implement the strategy. You think it may be wise for Meera to consider a few alternative ("Test Two"!) entrepreneurial strategies before choosing one. However, Meera contends there is no need for alternatives; she knows she will choose this strategy because she wants to work with her old company.

Why might it be valuable for Meera to consider alternative strategies even if she still chooses the value chain strategy she has developed? How might she be better prepared for her upcoming meeting by having considered alternative strategic routes for her idea? Are there any other steps you would recommend that Meera do in advance of the meeting?

5. Use your own entrepreneurial idea and the Test Two, Choose One process to complete the Entrepreneurial Strategy Canvas. First, use the canvas to design an entrepreneurial strategy. This will require you to iterate a few times until you feel you have identified a potentially viable strategy that could serve as the foundation for further learning and experimentation. Next, start again and design another entrepreneurial strategy. Importantly, for this iteration, design an entrepreneurial strategy whose value creation and capture hypotheses are fundamentally different from the first strategy (for instance, choose a different customer). With both strategies in hand, step back and evaluate them.

Beyond the disparities in the domains of choice, what are the key differences across these strategies? What learning and experiments could you conduct to better understand these strategies? What initial steps would be required to implement them? Finally, which would you choose?

SUGGESTED READINGS

Bingham, Christopher B., and Kathleen M. Eisenhardt. "Rational Heuristics: The 'simple rules' That Strategists Learn from Process Experience." *Strategic Management Journal* 32, no. 13 (2011): 1437–64.

Gans, Joshua, Erin L. Scott, and Scott Stern. "Strategy for Start-Ups: First Answer Two Questions; Then Explore Four Paths." *Harvard Business Review*, May–June 2018, https://hbr.org/2018/05/strategy-for-start-ups.

Murray, Fiona, and Mary Tripsas. "The Exploratory Processes of Entrepreneurial Firms: The Role of Purposeful Experimentation." In *Business Strategy over the Industry Life Cycle*. Vol. 21, edited by Joel Baum and Anita McGahan, 45–75. *Advances in Strategic Management*. Elsevier JAI, 2004. (Earlier version distributed as Harvard Business School Working Paper No. 04-031.)

Osterwalder, Alexander, and Yves Pigneur. *Business Model Generation: A Handbook for Visionaries, Game Changers, and Challenger.* New York: Wiley, 2010.

Scott, Erin, and Scott Stern. "The Best Startup Ideas Have Multiple Paths to Success." *Quartz at Work*, August 3, 2021, https://qz.com/work/2041928/the-best-startup-ideas-have-multiple-paths-to-success.

Zott, Christophe, and Raphael Amit. "The Fit between Product Market Strategy and Business Model: Implications for Firm Performance." *Strategic Management Journal* 29, no. 1 (2008): 1–26.

Michael Martin

Upon graduating in 2012, Michael Martin landed his first job at an investment firm in New York City. After a late night at the office, he was walking down a deserted street when a man followed him. As Martin recalled, "I couldn't make a phone call, since this individual was following me." Instead he pulled out his phone, opened his Uber app, and called a car. When the impromptu rescue vehicle pulled up, he jumped in, relieved, and thought, Why can I push a button for food, a car service . . . but I still have to dial a number for 911? He couldn't even text 911 in that emergency situation. It was then that the idea for RapidSOS was born.

In particular, Martin thought about how response time all too often determines whether an emergency victim survives and that a "911 brought into the smartphone age" could be transformative. He realized that to move forward, he had to understand and engage directly with the emergency response system community. Traveling the country in a borrowed car, Martin visited over 350 dispatch centers, talking with various players in the emergency response ecosystem. While some expressed interest, the more common response was a resistance to rapid change. Martin realized how deeply beholden the industry was to twentieth-century technology. To gain traction in the medium term, he would need to somehow integrate a technological solution into the existing 911 infrastructure rather than attempt to replace it entirely.

To develop this technology, he joined forces with Nick Horelik, a nuclear engineering PhD student similarly drawn to the challenges in emergency response (as an undergraduate, he had answered a suicide prevention hotline and recalled the challenges of locating individual students in emergencies). Martin and Horelik undertook a process to develop and test a technology with the power to substantially reduce emergency response time. In concrete terms, a user interacted with an app called Haven, which provided a simple way to reach emergency responders. RapidSOS then created a back end that supplied a seamless connection between Haven and the local emergency response system, which would simply receive an emergency call with appropriate location information.

In founding RapidSOS, Martin and Horelik were frank as to the mission of their start-up: they were in the business

In founding his venture, Michael Martin first identified multiple business options to pursue.

of saving lives. The key question was how to translate this potential into a concrete go-to-market strategy. "We were all over the map in terms of what was interesting to us," Martin recalled, because "we saw value in a number of segments." The team sat down to consider what they considered to be a set of viable options:

1. RapidSOS had received significant interest from the insurance industry about potential partnerships. These organizations would provide and promote the Haven app to their customers, perhaps through cobranding or an insurance application with RapidSOS inside. The RapidSOS team articulated two distinct sources of value for these potential partners: First, the Haven app offered an opportunity for insurance companies to provide a new source of value to their customers, enhancing customer engagement and brand appeal. Second, the app had the potential to reduce the costs of emergency incidents and also possibly save lives. Actuarial studies based on the enhanced speed of response that would be enabled by the RapidSOS app indicated a potential value of $18 per member per year in terms of reduced insurance claims. From a product-development standpoint, a partnership with an insurance company would not require any significant innovations; it would instead involve close integration and enhancement with the

app developers at the partner company. It would be important to align the look and feel of the app with the priorities and branding of the partner.

2. The alternative would have RapidSOS focus first on delivering its OneTouch 911 technology to "burning platform" users—that is, a few specific populations more likely to require emergency care and for whom a timely and accurate response was critical, such as those at risk of heart attack, those who suffered from epilepsy, and seniors. These groups, already well aware of the limitations of the current 911 system, also closely aligned with the mission orientation of RapidSOS, since adoption by them would most likely have a transformative impact on all users of the emergency response system. To implement this approach, the key would be to establish partnerships with organizations like the American Heart Association (AHA), the Epilepsy Foundation of America (EFA), or AARP. While these groups were unlikely to provide a direct revenue stream to RapidSOS, this approach would allow the start-up to gain traction with critical user communities. At the same time, it was unclear whether gaining traction with these early users would translate into a more general transformation of emergency response.

Questions

1. Compare and contrast how these strategies would differ in terms of the four choices (customer, technology, organization, and competition). Provide at least one concrete example of why the RapidSOS team has to choose among the alternatives, rather than being able to "do it all."

2. Can you propose an experiment or test that would allow Martin to choose between the alternative strategies you have described? How would the experiment yield data or information that would allow Martin and his team to choose between alternatives?

3. Given the information you have right now, which strategy would you recommend, and why? What concrete steps would you take to implement your proposed strategy?

In obtaining financing for their start-up WhatsApp, Jan Koum (right) and Brian Acton (left) prioritized options that would let them retain control of their venture and shared their vision for how it would grow.

ENTREPRENEUR'S DILEMMA Most new ventures must acquire financial resources to explore an opportunity and then implement their chosen strategy. Yet normal channels to obtain financing can lead to the founding team ceding control of the venture, including choices about its direction and impact. Ultimately, entrepreneurs must make careful and measured choices about how they will finance their venture.

CHAPTER OBJECTIVES

- Understand why start-ups have to choose their financing
- Compare and contrast the trade-offs of financing alternatives
- Describe staged financing and how it complements early-stage experimentation and learning processes

FINANCING

14

As a teenager, Jan Koum immigrated to Mountain View, California, from a small rural town outside Kyiv, Ukraine, and quickly developed an interest in computing. In 1997, while still a student at San Jose State University, he joined Yahoo!, the most popular search engine of the time, which had recently undergone an IPO. Through the dot-com boom and bust of the early 2000s as well as the expansion of the Yahoo! platform, including the launch of its enhanced advertising system, Koum's almost decade-long stint at the company gave him a strong perspective on the evolving industry. Perhaps most critically, he built a strong relationship with his coworker, friend, and subsequent start-up cofounder Brian Acton.

In late 2007, after working together for nine years, Koum and Acton left Yahoo! to travel the world. Upon returning to California, the pair applied for jobs at Facebook, and both were rejected. Koum, however, became fascinated by the emerging Apple App Store and the potential of a wide array of iPhone apps. In particular, Koum envisioned an app that allowed your contacts to post status updates, and he quickly set about incorporating a company and building the code for an app he dubbed "WhatsApp" (which sounded like "what's up?"). With Apple's introduction of push notifications, the app and Koum's nascent venture quickly transformed. He discovered that his early adopters were using the status messages as an instant messaging service to communicate at no cost with friends and family across the globe. Koum quickly launched WhatsApp 2.0, introducing the now-familiar messaging interface. As his user base grew, Koum recruited his friend Acton to help design the evolving platform; Acton would ultimately join as cofounder months later.

Acton proved instrumental not only in expanding the design of WhatsApp, but also in attracting early resources to the venture, collecting a $250,000 angel

Acton and Koum felt strongly about the business model of their creation. Koum kept a handwritten note by Acton near his desk that said, simply: "No Ads. No Games. No Gimmicks."

This chapter's video highlights how WhatsApp founders made strategic financing choices to maintain control over the direction of their venture.

investment from a group of former Yahoo! colleagues.[1] Using these resources, the pair expanded the team, built out WhatsApp beyond the iPhone platform, and expanded the features within the app, including photo sharing. Within a few years, WhatsApp was a dominant app across the globe, with users more than willing to pay the $1 fee to download it. With this revenue stream in hand, Koum resisted the idea of accepting venture capital investment to further grow and scale the company. In particular, he was concerned venture capitalists (VCs) might push the company to prioritize advertising, which he and Acton were against after their experiences at Yahoo![2]

However, Jim Goetz, a partner at Sequoia Capital, ultimately proved to be an instrumental strategic adviser for the venture. In 2011, Koum and Acton chose to accept $8 million from Sequoia with the promise that the VC would not push them into the advertising business.[3] As the user base continued to grow to hundreds of millions with a staff of fewer than a hundred, the pair decided to seek more funding. They turned down a range of eager venture capital firms and again accepted investment from Sequoia, which had previously demonstrated a commitment to the cofounders' vision and provided valuable strategic advice. Sequoia's subsequent $50 million investment allowed WhatsApp to move into a larger building, double its staff, and continue to expand features within the app.[4] In 2014, WhatsApp was acquired by Facebook for over $19 billion, with Koum and Acton continuing to lead their team. Later, the two left Facebook over a disagreement with the company related to monetizing WhatsApp through advertisement.[5]

Koum and Acton used financing to implement and scale their entrepreneurial strategy and realize their vision for WhatsApp. In selecting Jim Goetz and Sequoia as their investors, the founders sought not only financial resources but key knowledge and advice, as well as partners equally committed to their vision. It takes patience for founders to choose the financing and investors that will best enable and scale their entrepreneurial strategy. In this chapter, we will examine why an entrepreneur must choose among alternative sources of financing and investors. Choosing strategically means considering the value each financing option provides the venture, and how each option affects control and ownership of the venture.

14.1 Why Does a Start-Up Need to Choose Its Investors?

Finance is among the most important and challenging domains of choice for a new venture. While selecting your investor is a key choice, it is not a core part of a venture's strategy. Instead, it is a choice that should support early experimentation and the strategy the entrepreneur chooses.

Most new businesses have to invest financial capital to establish themselves before generating enough revenue to cover their underlying operating costs. For some ventures, the up-front expenditure required may be modest, or the founding team may already have access to financial resources; if sufficient capital is available, the team can focus on choosing their customer, technology, organization, and competition without having to make separate choices about how to attract external financial investors. But for many start-ups, attracting investors emerges quickly as a crucial early step in the venture's development. Financing is a necessary input for key activities—from technology development to manufacturing to fielding a sales force—that are required to test and implement an entrepreneurial strategy. Because of this, attracting investment to the venture becomes the first key tests of the team and its underlying idea. In too many cases, raising capital becomes almost an end in itself. Ventures can become too focused on raising money with an idea and not on how the money they raise will help put their idea and strategy to work.

Financing serves two related but distinct functions for a start-up. First, financial resources let a start-up team explore their underlying idea and how to commercialize it. Primary market research to assess alternative customer groups, experiments to compare technologies, and building prototypes to gain early customer feedback all require real resources, and financing at the earliest stages should facilitate it. As we saw in Chapter 7, Tony Hsieh, the founder of the online shoe store Zappos, fundamentally created a new "bet the company" plan as his venture struggled during the 2000 recession. His plan was to enhance the online shoe purchasing experience through significant investment in inventory. Hsieh recounted in his memoir that he was willing to invest the remainder of his own personal financial resources in order to "either save Zappos or ensure our speedy demise" by testing his value creation hypothesis. Simply put, this example illustrates how risking capital in an early-stage venture can facilitate the resolution of uncertainty.

Secondly, financial capital lets start-ups make commitments to implement their chosen strategy. Once a strategy has been selected, obtaining investment capital may be required to establish a supply chain, marketing and distribution channels, or particular features or services. In contrast to investments made to inform choices, this second role is about implementing choices that have already been made. Once Ray Kroc had identified the core elements of the system that he believed would allow new McDonald's outlets to succeed, the McDonald's corporation reorganized itself to focus on implementation (**Figure 14.1** on p. 400). It effectively became the source of start-up funding for purchasing new locations that would then be leased to new franchisees. In this case, the financing provided by McDonald's to franchisees was the means by which McDonald's constrained franchisees, ensuring consistent quality and standards across all outlets.

RISK AND INVESTMENT CAPITAL

Broadly speaking, investments in start-ups break down into investments seen as **risk capital** or **investment capital**. Risk capital investments are made with the intention of being speculative and forward thinking, but also with the expectation of high reward. These types of investments are made early on to finance experimentation and learning. Investment capital investments are made to fund business activities to build products or offer services and come when ventures are turning their choices into reality. While separate ideas, the reality is that most investments and financing are made with goals that contain a mix of risk capital and investment capital. For example, an early-stage angel investor might still invest with an emphasis on activities that ensure that the company begins to earn revenues sooner rather than later. Or traditional business loans from banks often allow for some degree of design and planning. However, capital—most notably **venture capital** (introduced in Chapter 2)—is explicitly structured for the purposes of resolving uncertainty. Venture capital is equity raised to finance

risk capital Investments made with the intention of being speculative and forward thinking, but also with the expectation of high reward

investment capital Investments made to fund business activities to build products or offer services; these come when ventures are turning their choices into reality

venture capital Equity raised to provide financing to start-ups and small businesses that investors believe have long-term growth potential

FIGURE 14.1 Ray Kroc and McDonald's

In building out his franchise model, Ray Kroc (at right) believed that regardless of location, McDonald's restaurants would consistently and efficiently deliver value to customers in line with the system he had designed. The financing provided by McDonald's to franchisees both assists the opening of locations and includes elements to ensure consistent quality and standards across all of them. Pictured with Kroc is Fred Turner, who rose from grill operator to eventually become CEO and chairman of McDonald's.

start-ups and small businesses that investors believe have long-term growth potential. Other forms of capital such as collateralized bank loans are primarily structured for the purposes of investment; the bank lends you money to purchase or finance something that you will pay off over time.

More subtly, different potential investors—even within a given "class" such as venture capital—vary significantly in terms of their orientation between risk and investment capital. While these investors are choosing whether or not to invest in a particular start-up, it is equally true that founders need to choose investors that align with their underlying strategy, orientation, and stage of business. For example, if the venture is still at an exploratory stage, one investor may encourage a high level of early commitment to an initial plan or idea, perhaps dooming the venture by heading down a poor direction without enough investigation. Understanding both the types of investment, and when and how they will be pursued and used, is a central challenge for a venture. Doing so proactively helps entrepreneurs make sure their fund-raising goals and their venture's strategic goals align.

14.2 Start-Up Financing Alternatives

Choosing investors starts with first identifying the type and scale of financing entrepreneurs need to test and implement their entrepreneurial strategy. All forms of financing come with a different set of benefits and costs. Understanding the alternative sources of financing helps founders match their financing to the overall goal and requirements of the venture. Let's start by reviewing each one.

BOOTSTRAPPING The most straightforward way to gain financing for a venture is not through an external investor but directly from customers' purchases. Since profitable and sustainable ventures must create customer value, **bootstrap financing**—investing the revenues that are in excess of direct costs of serving early customers—is a powerful way of testing whether value is being created, conducting experiments to learn more about potential customers, and ultimately investing in scaling a business. For example, Sara Blakely founded Spanx with just $5,000 of her own savings, and thereafter used only revenue generated directly from the business to finance its expansion. This customer-led growth enabled Spanx to grow to sales of over $300 million per year while allowing Blakely to maintain 100% of the equity in her company. Blakely finally took outside investment when she sold control of Spanx to Blackstone Investments for $1.2 billion.[6] In recent years, bootstrapping has been made easier with the emergence of crowdsourcing funding programs like Kickstarter. Over the past decade, an increasing number of start-ups have turned to these platforms to help them directly access and raise revenue from potential customers for a given product (see the sidebar on **Raising Money on Kickstarter**). Bootstrap financing also has the benefit that the "investors," the first buyers of the product, are not making an assessment of the overall business but, instead, are making a purchase decision. All that matters is whether the product provides direct value to them and is not a forecast of demand for the entire marketplace.

The downside of bootstrapping is that for many start-ups, choosing and implementing their strategy requires significant up-front capital. They need money either to do the type of experiments that will inform their strategy's success or build out aspects of their business.

SELF-FINANCING For founders with the available funds or assets, one possibility is to self-finance the early stages of a venture. Self-financing is simple

bootstrap financing Investing the revenues that are in excess of direct costs of serving early customers

Raising Money on Kickstarter. The popular crowdfunding platform Kickstarter launched in 2009. As of fall 2023, its website notes that "22 million people have backed a project, $7,561,408,162 has been pledged, and 245,883 projects have been funded." An important rule for the platform: "Everything on Kickstarter must be a project. A project has a clear goal, like making an album, a book, or a work of art. A project will eventually be completed, and something will be produced by it."[a]

to implement (you need not negotiate over the equity split with yourself) and helps members of a founding team clarify their level of personal commitment. When Mark Getty, an heir to the Getty fortune, cofounded Getty Images in 1995 with Jonathan Klein, his personal investment caused early skepticism about the potential for the venture. However, Getty simply had the funds to invest in assembling an unparalleled collection of images and become the leading creator and curator of still imagery. At the same time, self-financing magnifies the level of risk borne by an entrepreneur and isolates the founder from the feedback gained from external funding. When former World Series champion Curt Schilling launched a new multiplayer online game, *Kingdoms of Amalur: Reckoning*, he initially made a significant personal investment, with a focus on retaining a maximal equity share. Despite receiving significant negative feedback from a variety of venture capitalists (who were excited to meet with a baseball legend but turned off by the prospects for the overall venture), Schilling spent the vast bulk of his Major League wealth as well as more than $75 million in taxpayer-subsidized loans from Rhode Island when the game would not scale. Ultimately, while self-financing allows a founder to retain control, because external financing depends on the positive judgment of a third party, it can provide the founder with useful information about their idea.

FRIENDS AND FAMILY FINANCING Not surprisingly, the most common source of early-stage external financing is not through institutional sources but through founders' own networks, including their friends and family. Grounded in the founders' personal relationships, friends and family financing simultaneously provides access to finance and feedback while reducing some of the risks associated with attracting early-stage finance. Most notably, a central challenge of early-stage finance—particularly for risk capital where the entrepreneur is learning about options to choose a strategy—is the potential for conflicts with early-stage investors to distract from identifying an effective path for the venture. In the extreme, a potential investor can require the entrepreneur to disclose significant information about the underlying idea and their insights and then simply "steal" it for their own venture. More commonly, the uncertainty and lack of clarity about an idea at its earliest stages puts entrepreneurs at a disadvantage in their initial attempts at seeking capital from professional investors.

Friends and family financing can help to mitigate these challenges, due to the higher level of trust and the established and ongoing personal relationship between the entrepreneur and their investors. Family financing comes with its own challenges, including conditions that arise when intermingling personal and professional objectives for the venture. For example, when Jimmy John Liautaud graduated high school (second to last in his class), his father wanted him to go into the army while Jimmy wanted to start a business. His father agreed to provide $25,000 in exchange for a promise that Jimmy would enlist in the army if the business was not profitable within a year.[7] Faced with this deadline and limited budget, the younger Liautaud researched the idea of opening a hot dog stand first but discarded this idea when he found that the necessary equipment cost too much. He decided to focus on developing and selling sandwiches and offered only four types of sandwiches at his first store, which, in fact, turned a profit in year one. Growing from a single shop in Charleston, Illinois, there are almost 3,000 locations of Jimmy John's Gourmet Sandwiches as of 2023 (**Figure 14.2**).[8]

FIGURE 14.2 Jimmy John's

Jimmy John Liautaud financed his first store with the support of his father, though with his father's conditions too. He decided to open a sandwich shop because that is what he could afford.

NON-DILUTIVE GRANTS Beyond individual financing or friends and family, start-ups can gain access to up-front funding through institutional sources such as grants, loans, and equity financing (e.g., venture capital). Though limited to a small number of use cases and often involving a demanding and competitive application process, early-stage grants provide start-up capital without requiring collateral, debt repayment, or equity dilution. For example, in the United States, the Small Business Innovation Research (SBIR) program (**Figure 14.3**)

FIGURE 14.3 America's Seed Fund

America's Seed Fund for technology and scientific solutions, administered by Small Business Innovation Research (SBIR), grants funds to applicants to develop their proof of concept and technology prototype before commercialization.

SOURCE: America's Seed Fund, accessed September 12, 2023, https://beta.www.sbir.gov.

provides more than $2.5 billion annually for R&D projects for small (and young) businesses, including up to $300,000 for a Phase I grant, which less than 15% of applicants successfully earn, as well as larger grants of up to $2 million for Phase II.[9] Not limited to innovation funding, other grant programs target entrepreneurship by particular groups, affiliations (e.g., students, alumni, or projects coming out of a university), or new business formation in particular locations (e.g., enterprise zones).

LOANS The most common form of institutional capital for start-ups are loans. Primarily arranged through traditional banks, a bank loan for a new business provides up-front capital, often with some limitations on how the funds are to be used, in exchange for a promise of repayment with interest over the life of the loan. For many businesses, loans are the primary form of investment capital. Loans are useful for businesses seeking to purchase or improve equipment or structures to implement a particular strategy. The tangible capital goods purchased with the loan are collateral that retains some value even when the start-up itself is unsuccessful. For example, in the immediate aftermath of the 1906 San Francisco earthquake, A. P. Giannini traversed the devastation to offer loans to individuals to rebuild their businesses. These proactive loans by Giannini's Bank of Italy, at that time a fledgling start-up providing financing for immigrants and the middle class, were a key impetus for San Francisco's rapid bounce back from the earthquake. While some of the businesses that received loans were ultimately unable to recover from the earthquake, the investments they made in the community helped the city as a whole. (For more on A. P. Giannini, see the sidebar on **A. P. Giannini's Choices.**)

Loans offer entrepreneurs up-front capital while not diluting equity. As long as the start-up can repay the loan plus whatever interest accrues, it need not share the gains from success with the lender. This benefit comes with a corresponding cost: repayment imposes higher operating costs on the venture, and the lender can take control of the assets of the business if the loan is not repaid on a timely and regular schedule. This type of debt therefore has an ironic consequence; with it, the start-up might be able to capture more of the upside, but it encourages entrepreneurs to make choices that ensure that they can meet their debt repayments, perhaps at the expense of the overall value creation potential of the venture. For example, in an experiment conducted in Kolkata, India, micro entrepreneurs who had to begin repaying a loan immediately upon receipt of their loan had lower rates of investment and long-run profits than those who were provided with a "grace period" to experiment, and perhaps experience some failures, before having to begin repayment (see **Using the Research: Reducing Stress and Rewarding Risk in Microfinance**).

This experiment highlights an important (and often overlooked) aspect of loan financing for start-ups: the precise terms and conditions governing the loan can significantly influence the incentives and choices of the start-up. The precise loan rate and repayment period, the degree of discretion afforded the entrepreneur, and the conditions under which the lender gets control are all terms to be negotiated. In other words, loan financing involves a complex up-front negotiation that requires entrepreneurs to specify their entrepreneurial strategy. As a result, while loan financing can be an extremely effective form of investment capital, it is less suitable as a source of risk capital to explore and choose the firm's strategy in the first place.

A. P. Giannini's Choices. A. P. Giannini's father immigrated to the United States from Italy during the California Gold Rush. Having started his career in the produce industry, Giannini founded the Bank of Italy in San Francisco in 1904 to provide support to immigrants and middle-class workers. Committed to serving these customers instead of the wealthier clients on whom other banks focused, Giannini made a number of choices to align his bank with his customers. These choices included making loans based on the potential opportunity, rather than the current collateral, and staying open until 9 pm (well past the traditional banking hours of 3 pm) for workers.[a] Within 20 years, Bank of Italy in San Francisco had grown to become the third largest bank in the United States, and it remained committed to the needs of immigrants and workers. In 1930, it would become Bank of America, the largest bank of the time.

Reducing Stress and Rewarding Risk in Microfinance

Microfinance operations, like the one pioneered by the Grameen Bank (see Chapter 2), loan money out in small amounts, typically with weekly repayment contracts to impose discipline on the borrower. This repayment schedule is also seen as building relationships of trust with the lender, as the loan officer meets with the client regularly. However, researchers Erica Field, Rohini Pande, Jeanette Park, Natalia Rigol, and John Papp wanted to see if changing these terms affected repayment.

They studied a microfinance operation named Village Financial Services (VFS) in Kolkata, India, that provides loans exclusively to women who typically have a household income of less than $2 per day. They experimented with different repayment contracts for borrowers working with VFS to study how repayment was affected and how much financial stress borrowers experienced. In the initial study, 1026 borrowers were randomly assigned to either weekly or monthly repayment schedules. Replicating this study with another 740 borrowers, the researchers also conducted interviews on financial stress. In a subsequent experiment with 845 more borrowers, clients were given either the standard two weeks before their initial payment or a two-month grace period.

The researchers found that switching to monthly payments did not impact loan repayment, and clients reported being less worried about their ability to repay their loans,

Kolkata, India

reducing their financial stress. More importantly, having the two-month initial grace period made clients twice as likely to invest in a new business. In three years, those with grace periods had 57.1% higher profits, 19.5% higher household incomes, and 80% more business capital. Although grace-period clients were three times more likely to default on their loan, reflective of the increased time granted to start riskier businesses, they had a higher return rate if successful.

SOURCE: Erica Field et al., "Microfinance Repayment Schedules in West Bengal, India," *Innovations for Poverty Action*, May 14, 2014, https://poverty-action.org/microfinance-repayment-schedules-west-bengal-india.

EQUITY FINANCING With equity financing, founders attract risk capital specifically to do the experimentation and learning required to choose and implement the venture's entrepreneurial strategy. Whereas loan financing comes in exchange for repayment and the right to control the firm's underlying assets when the venture performs poorly, equity financing does not involve any guarantee of repayment of the initial investment. Instead, it offers investors a share of the profits of the firm when the venture succeeds. Sharing the upside of success has a significant impact on how entrepreneurs choose their investors and the role of those investors in a venture. On the one hand, founders can choose investors that are optimistic (relative to other potential investors) about the potential of the venture. When an investor believes that the venture has the potential to be very valuable, they will be willing to invest on relatively favorable terms for the founding team. At the same time, investors with an equity stake in the firm have strong incentives relative to debt holders to help the firm reach its growth potential, either through active involvement in the business (e.g., advice)

The Birth of Venture Capital

In the wake of World War II, Brigadier General and Harvard Business School professor Georges Doriot recognized that, while the growth of the economy depended on the availability of risk capital for new ventures, financial regulation and institutions established during the Great Depression would direct capital toward established enterprises operating on public markets. Doriot had been involved in the New Products Committee, a group of leading New England civic and business leaders that was attempting to chart a new path for the New England economy based on early-stage industries leveraging new technology and innovation. Not content to play a passive role, Doriot

Georges Doriot spearheaded the use of venture capital.

and his collaborators established a new type of enterprise, American Research and Development Corporation (ARD), which would attract institutional capital but then use an active process of screening and hands-on involvement to invest in new enterprises.

With ARD, Doriot was not only establishing a new investment fund but also building a new type of firm: a venture capital firm. Doriot was explicit that venture capital firms could uniquely accelerate technology development and scaling and provide the risk capital required to establish and grow new industries. But to do so, Doriot insisted the firm would not just be speculating by "choosing winners" but would shape ventures and the people who ran them. Doriot famously (though not inclusively) quipped: "I am building men and companies."

To achieve his vision, Doriot did not focus his own fundraising efforts on large institutional investors such as MIT and Investors Mutual, or on the funds controlled by wealthy families that were the prevailing vehicle for risk capital. In addition, and perhaps less strategically, ARD issued tradable shares to the public. Doing so raised additional capital but likely placed pressure on the fledgling firm to realize near-term earnings on its investments at the expense of long-term capital gains.

Though early returns were modest, ARD's eventual spectacular success with Digital Equipment Corporation (DEC) legitimized and popularized venture capital as an organizational form. "The General" not only provided the financing for a new generation of start-ups but, perhaps more importantly, served as the founder of the new venture capital industry.

or through providing access to resources (e.g., networking). For example, when supermarket executives Leo Kahn and Thomas Stemberg developed the concept for Staples, the first office supply superstore, the principal financing came from the private equity firm Bain Capital; perhaps more importantly, the then-CEO of Bain Capital, Mitt Romney, joined the board and became heavily involved in setting and enabling the strategic direction of Staples. Staples benefited from Romney's more than a decade of consulting experience at Bain & Company and an associated rich network in related industries.

VENTURE CAPITAL For growth-oriented start-ups, there are a number of specialized forms of equity financing. The most common is venture capital. As originally conceived by World War II general Georges Doriot (see **Mini Case: The Birth of Venture Capital**), venture capital firms are designed to attract external financing from large institutional investors and focus that capital on a much smaller number of firms than a traditional investment company. VC firms do not simply provide financing; they also provide direct input into the development and implementation of the start-up's entrepreneurial strategy. This model was refined over time to provide high-powered financial incentives to the individual venture capitalists themselves, who would receive a significant fraction of the upside of the returns achieved through their investments.

The venture capital model has proven influential for entrepreneurial financing because of how it aligns the interests of investors and founding teams. It is also influential because venture capitalists, at their best, can help realize the potential of young firms. For example, when Jim Clark and Marc Andreessen sought financing in 1994 for Mosaic Communications (the company behind Netscape, the first commercially oriented web browser), John Doerr of the VC firm Kleiner Perkins Caufield & Byers shared their vision about the inherent value of the Internet, a minority view at the time. But Doerr then actively worked to drive Netscape's early success. He helped develop the initial Internet business ecosystem and, thus, the value of Netscape's web browser, by making complementary investments and broadly evangelizing the transformative power of the Internet. Even more critically, Doerr and partners Kevin Compton and Doug Mackenzie assisted Netscape's Clark and Andreessen in recruiting experienced and skilled executives, including CEO Jim Barksdale. These experienced hands led the venture as it rapidly iterated its product, went public at a valuation of $2.2 billion, and moved into Microsoft's targets, all in less than 16 months. Kleiner Perkins Caufield & Byers's $5 million investment ultimately yielded a $400 million return.

As in the example of Netscape, venture capital has been the early source of capital for many of the most successful ventures. For example, even though the venture capital industry invests in only 15,000 firms per year, more than one-third of all firms that eventually achieve an IPO receive early-stage venture capital financing. And for the first several decades of its existence, the venture capital industry itself secured high returns for those lucky enough to invest in it: during the 1990s its returns were well above any other asset class in the United States.

CONVERTIBLE NOTES While venture capital is typically conceived as an equity investment, most early-stage venture capital financing is actually in the form of convertible debt. This is a form of investment where venture investors can recover any remaining assets from the firm if the firm goes bankrupt but also share in the upside of investments that prosper by "converting" their debt into equity. This conversion is done based on an agreed-upon formula connected to predetermined milestones. As an example, a start-up's founding team might receive $1 million from a venture capitalist in exchange for 25% of the equity in their company. A key implication of this investment is that it has now assigned a $3 million "pre-money" valuation to the venture. The $1 million of additional capital results in a $4 million "post-money" valuation. The contract might also include terms where the venture capital investors earn back their investment, often with a built-in return, in case the firm shuts down prior to another round of financing. While this type of contract might seem unfair to founders, convertible debt contracts are designed to provide maximum incentives for entrepreneurs to focus their efforts on achieving an upside outcome.

ANGEL FINANCING Venture capitalists are, of course, not the only type of equity financing available for a new venture. Angel financing combines some of the informality associated with friends and family financing with the networks and experiences of traditional venture capitalists. Where venture capitalists invest on behalf of their limited partners, angel investors put their own personal wealth at risk. By and large, an initial round of angel financing will come at an earlier stage and in a smaller amount than the first round of venture capital. But there is a strong interconnection between angel financing and venture capital. Often, angel financing provides risk capital to entrepreneurs to develop an entrepreneurial strategy that will be implemented with follow-on venture capital investment.

Individual angel investors frequently focus their investments in their local environment, and entrepreneurs will often be introduced to them through their social networks. Angel investors commonly attempt to combine resources by establishing a local angel group or investment club that leverages the social networks and search activity of each angel while also diversifying across a larger angel portfolio.

EQUITY CROWDFUNDING Most recently, we have seen experiments with equity crowdfunding. Equity crowdfunding platforms such as AngelList give entrepreneurs an opportunity to attract investment from a wide group of investors who assess investment opportunities online. The venture receives funding only when a critical mass of funding is raised through the platform. While equity crowdfunding reaches a larger, more diverse group of potential investors, the large number is a double-edged sword. Entrepreneurs will need to manage the crowd and will not benefit from the expertise or networks of key investors. Equity crowdfunding requires far more disclosure and transparency than traditional crowdfunding. The only information that a founding team needs to provide backers of a non-equity project are details about the product or service that people are preordering, while equity crowdfunding requires far more transparency around the venture's entrepreneurial strategy. Despite these challenges, equity crowdfunding is attractive to entrepreneurs who may not have ready access or networks connected to alternative forms of equity financing. There is some evidence that equity crowdfunding is a particularly effective approach for women entrepreneurs or those operating outside of traditional hubs of entrepreneurial activity.

Choosing among these alternatives is both challenging and consequential for founding teams. The trade-offs between options depends first on the availability of specific alternatives (i.e., how costly would it be in terms of time and effort to attract financing of a given type), and then on the precise terms and conditions of each alternative. In the extreme, founding teams can be caught in a catch-22, where risk capital is required to explore and choose a strategy, yet the absence of a clear entrepreneurial strategy limits the venture's ability to attract capital on favorable terms. In the next sections, we explore how to confront and solve these challenges.

14.3 The Founder's Dilemma

With early-stage investments, entrepreneurs will typically face a choice about how much control over their venture they are willing to give up to obtain an investment, including the size of the investment and the network of the investors.

The Founder's Dilemma. Now the dean of the School of Business at Yeshiva University, Noam Wasserman described the founder's dilemma while a business school professor at Harvard. Broadly, his research found that entrepreneurs who ceded control of their business by giving up equity built a more valuable business. However, this usually meant that the founder was replaced by an experienced CEO. Wasserman felt that founders needed to choose to be "rich" by giving up company control or be "king" by working to maintain control at the expense of some wealth.

SOURCE: Noam Wasserman, "The Founder's Dilemma," *Harvard Business Review*, February 2008, https://hbr.org/2008/02/the-founders-dilemma.

As emphasized by Noam Wasserman, an entrepreneur's choice to either cede equity at an early stage to gain access to better venture partners, vs. maintain a higher level of control over their venture, is the "founder's dilemma." Is it better to have a smaller fraction of a larger pie or a larger fraction of a smaller pie? (See the sidebar on **The Founder's Dilemma**.)

At first glance, the obvious choice might be to simply choose a smaller fraction of a very large pie. This minimizes the entrepreneur's risk and overall effort, while still allowing for a large potential return. For example, Bob Langer, one of the most prolific scientists and inventors at MIT, has been involved in more than 30 start-ups (and more than 1,300 patents). In nearly all cases, Langer cedes the bulk of equity and control rights to the investors and managers at an early stage, serving only in an advisory capacity to the start-up. Simultaneously, Boston-based venture capital firm Polaris Ventures has a significant portion of its portfolio directed toward start-ups from Langer's lab, with over $200 million invested across more than 20 companies. By focusing exclusively on idea production while having the independent ventures control strategy and implementation (resulting in a history of both hits and misses), Langer-affiliated start-ups have achieved more than $23 billion in market value in 2017.[10]

But ceding control comes at the expense of retaining authority. Many people become entrepreneurs at least in part to be their own boss. Since most new ventures are founded with only modest growth ambitions (e.g., running one or a small number of local restaurants rather than creating a national restaurant chain), entrepreneurs whose financing needs are modest may choose financing that helps them achieve this goal.

More subtly, a second potential cost of ceding control is relinquishing rights to determine the role, if any, that an entrepreneur or team will play in the venture. While an entrepreneur may end up with more wealth from ceding control, they also may be concerned with how their experience within their venture impacts their career and professional development. Consider the case of Martin Eberhard, who, along with Marc Tarpenning, was a cofounder of the earliest version of Tesla Motors.

The two initially welcomed the 2004 Series A investment led by Elon Musk, who then became chair of the young company. Early enthusiasm about this partnership turned to frustration as Eberhard was sidelined over time and Musk took greater managerial control. Though Eberhard benefited financially from his involvement in Tesla, the initial investment from Musk limited his career trajectory within Tesla and exposed him to criticism from Musk. Eberhard left Tesla in 2007.

Ceding control is not simply a matter of career ambitions; it also implies loss of authority. Key entrepreneurial strategy choices are resolved not only by analyzing what is best for the financial viability of a venture but also which alternative best fits the decision-makers' broader objectives for the venture. Ceding control in advance of choosing an entrepreneurial strategy may have a large influence on the identity and culture of the eventual firm that is built. Turning back to an example in Chapter 1, if Walt Disney had allowed himself to be bought out by Charles Mintz, the company might still have gone on to become a leader in animation. But it is exceedingly unlikely that the firm would have realized Disney's distinctive vision for what animation could be.

THE ROLE OF CHOICE

The entrepreneurial choice process plays a central role in resolving the founder's dilemma. It surfaces multiple strategic directions for a venture and then helps an entrepreneur choose a direction based on its financial potential and alignment with the objectives and missions of the founding team. Ceding control of a venture prior to selecting an entrepreneurial strategy puts that core set of choices in the hands of investors rather than in the hands of the founding team. To be clear, obtaining risk capital might be necessary for an entrepreneur to fund the experimentation and learning needed to choose a strategy. Raising this capital is not an end in itself but is done to fund the choice process and implementation of the choice. In other words, founding teams should be wary of surrendering control simply to raise funds. Once a strategy has been chosen, entrepreneurs may be able to attract investors aligned with that strategic direction. Doing so should lessen the strategic costs of ceding control.

Of course, managing this trade-off in practice is difficult. Even the most proactive entrepreneurs with a strong underlying idea will find themselves trading off between control and commercialization.

With that said, founding teams can ease the founder's dilemma in two ways:

1. Take a proactive approach to the timing, stages, and sequencing of investment alternatives.
2. Seek investors who not only support the underlying idea but also are in alignment their choice of entrepreneurial strategy.

14.4 Staged Financing

Even when a venture will require a very significant level of investment, founding teams can still make two important choices:

1. When to seek investment
2. What type of investment to seek

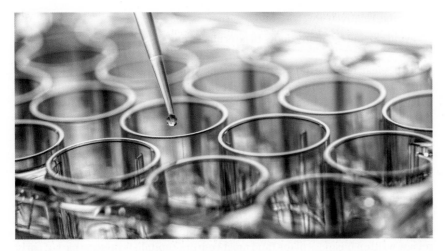

Funding Stages in Pharmaceutical Trials. The stages in government pharmaceutical trials offer clear markers for staging rounds of funding. The four major steps listed by the FDA in the drug development process, with intermediate steps in between, are:

- Step 1: Discovery and development
- Step 2: Preclinical research
- Step 3: Clinical research
- Step 4: FDA drug review

SOURCE: "The Drug Development Process," U.S. Food and Drug Administration, accessed September 12, 2023, https://www.fda.gov /patients/learn-about-drug-and-device-approvals /drug-development-process.

The sequencing and timing of outside investments is a powerful way for entrepreneurs to align their funding with their chosen strategy.

In a strategic approach to entrepreneurship, formulating and implementing strategic experiments creates a practical guide for how to sequence early-stage entrepreneurial financing. *Each financing stage should correspond to a critical set of entrepreneurial experiments. This lets both founders and investors assess the overall viability of the venture and the relative value of strategic directions.* In the biotechnology industry, for example, it is routine for the size and expected duration of each financing round to accord closely to the requirements of clinical trials in the drug development process (see the sidebar on **Funding Stages in Pharmaceutical Trials**). Teams can deploy capital to maximize the possibility of a successful drug trial while allowing investors an opportunity to step away from an investment if the results are poor.

This principle can be an equally powerful tool for structuring customer experiments. Jennifer Fleiss and Jennifer Hyman, founders of the online fashion start-up Rent the Runway (Chapter 1), used a small seed round of financing and an invitation-only customer list to test the core of their "reserve-and-rent" approach to fashion during the 2009 holiday season. Their key finding was that customer interest was so high that their main challenge was managing the disappointment of those who could not be accommodated due to limited inventory. They concluded that they had achieved product-market fit and established the central tenets of their entrepreneurial strategy. Doing so prompted them (and their initial investors) to pursue an aggressive round of additional financing to scale their venture.

GOALS OF STAGING

The question, then, is not whether to sequence experiments with stages of financing but how to do so. Both entrepreneurs and investors will want to sequence investments that are highly informative without committing the firm too heavily toward any particular strategy. In general, early experiments should

- clarify the overall value of the idea;
- clearly test key assumptions about any particular entrepreneurial strategy;

- involve relatively low cost; and

- avoid closing too many doors to alternative paths.

To be clear, because most experiments have multiple objectives, like maximizing learning while minimizing cost and commitment, the design and sequencing of experiments will require hard trade-offs. Often the most important assumption to test may not be the cheapest experiment to conduct.

Further, investors have a somewhat different additional goal when considering the value of an entrepreneurial experiment. Where entrepreneurs are primarily interested in testing the value of a given idea and strategy, investors also use the process of experimentation to assess and learn about the quality and strength of the founding team.

Consider, for example, the pervasive role of the pitch presentation as a means for evaluating early-stage ventures. In principle, it would be possible to simply review written business plans (and most venture capitalists do so as part of early screening processes) or engage in an open-ended discussion. However, one of the rituals associated with raising early-stage funds from angels or venture capitalists is having entrepreneurs perform a polished pitch presentation, followed by fielding tough questions about the venture in real time (often in a relatively combative back-and-forth). Though preparing for a pitch presentation arguably diverts entrepreneurs' time and shifts ventures away from describing complex strategies, it lets investors assess whether founding teams have the personal capabilities to recruit early-stage employees, persuade customers, and lead a growing organization. Of course, these processes do not come without biases: learning from pitches prioritizes some types of leadership styles over others. And pitch presentations may hold implicit biases against entrepreneurs from certain demographics, such as women and underrepresented minorities. But potential investors simply use pitches as part of the process of entrepreneurial experimentation to choose whether to invest in the founding team.

HOW MUCH RISK CAPITAL IS NEEDED?

The amount of financing raised should be enough to meaningfully test the most critical experiments that need to be conducted. The runway provided to founding teams should be long enough to conduct a meaningful set of experiments but short enough to inform simply whether and how to proceed. As described in the last chapter, in the "lean startup" approach pioneered by Eric Ries, a start-up's runway is measured by the number of pivots it has left before running out of funding.[11]

Of course, the amount of financing required to implement an experiment is itself uncertain; **bridge financing**, often in the form of a loan between two formal rounds of equity financing, can fund experiments that inform the next step of strategic choice. Over the past two decades, third-party lenders have come to play an increasingly significant role, particularly in providing loans collateralized by patents, offering additional resources to finalize an experiment before a new financing round.[12]

However, a crucial consideration for entrepreneurs is that a large fraction of all venture-backed firms replace key members of the early management team at a relatively early stage. In early risk financing, investors assess that while the

bridge financing Often comes in the form of a loan between two formal rounds of equity financing and can fund experiments that inform the next step of strategic choice

idea and associated strategy have the potential to succeed, the addition of a more professional management approach or particular expertise is required too (see the sidebar on **Aileen Lee and Cowboy Ventures**). This should further highlight that attracting risk capital is qualitatively different from raising investment capital. Investment capital is aimed at implementing a strategy, while risk capital is aimed at the learning needed to choose and implement this strategy. While both entrepreneurs and investors share an interest in choosing and implementing a successful strategy, this alignment is not perfect. Frequently, investors want to help to enhance the value of the firm but also weaken the power and centrality of the founding team.

14.5 Choosing Your Investor

The founder's dilemma seems to crystallize the central challenge of entrepreneurial finance: how should founding teams raise capital when doing so cedes ownership and control to investors who may not have the founders' best interests in mind? Overcoming this dilemma is not simply a matter of having the good luck to land beneficent investors. Instead, it requires transforming the decision of *whether* to work with an investor to the choice of investor to work *with*.

Consider Honest Tea, founded in the late 1990s by Seth Goldman and his former strategy professor Barry Nalebuff. Within two years of its launch, the founders were convinced that their core idea—lightly sweetened organic iced teas (with calories only 10% that of traditional sweetened teas)—was viable and that their next stage of growth would require several million dollars before the venture would earn positive cash flows. When they received an offer from venture capitalists, that offer came with a significant loss of control over the future direction of Honest Tea. Rather than simply accept or reject that offer, the founders instead pursued separate offers from angel investors that offered immediate financial resources, were more closely aligned with their goals, and required far less loss of control. Goldman and Nalebuff purposefully altered the calculus of their decision from the harsh trade-offs of the founder's dilemma to a choice between alternative visions for their venture. As Goldman noted later in an address to Congress concerning entrepreneurship and job growth, "Because we were careful, in Honest Tea's first ten years we 1) managed to stay in business, and equally important, 2) we managed to keep control of the business."[13]

As we see with Honest Tea, surfacing multiple sources of funding enhances the bargaining power of the founding team, which is especially important for unproven entrepreneurs. However, this enhanced bargaining position may be best used not by pushing the valuation or ownership upward, but to access the complementary, non-financial resources each potential investor possesses that may assist the founding team. Access to these non-financial resources may come as part of a negotiation with a certain investor team as well as from choices between different investors. The value of these resources can be significant. Wharton professor David Hsu found that entrepreneurs were not only three times more likely to accept offers from high-reputation venture capitalists; they were also prepared to accept a lower valuation to do so.[14] But the founding team should also believe that the investors have a shared vision, at least for the short term.

So what happens when investor and founder goals no longer align? When Cisco cofounders Sandy Lerner and Leonard Bosack accepted $2.6 million from venture capitalist Don Valentine for 30% of their revenue-generating company, all parties shared a common goal of dramatically growing the young, highly promising venture. However, the founders were soon startled by Valentine's abrupt appointment of a new CEO who viewed the founders as a key limitation to the organization's growth; the CEO quickly shifted the company's focus to new customer segments and removed Lerner from her company (Bosack followed shortly thereafter). Though Cisco would go on to perform exceptionally well, and Lerner and Bosack were financially rewarded through their minority ownership, the founders regretted accepting Valentine's investment.

14.6 Concluding Thoughts

Financing is a critical tool of start-up growth and development. However, despite the range of financing alternatives and growing investment in early-stage startups, the choice of financing is among the most challenging domains of choice for a new venture. When made effectively, this choice supports early experimentation and learning and subsequent implementation and scaling of the chosen strategy (see **Putting It Together: Financing**). The WhatsApp founders' choice to accept financing reflected their clarity about the value they sought to create for customers, as well as the trade-offs they were willing to make in the early days to remain committed to their chosen path. This transformed their decision from whether to accept financing to which investor to work with and when to bring them onboard. They chose an investor who significantly shared their vision for the venture and could provide critical advice and resources. This highlights the importance of considering not just financing options, but also the non-financial resources and specific terms and conditions with each option. Doing so helps an entrepreneur choose the one that best aligns with the goals and objectives of the founding team.

FINANCING

Obtaining financing is a challenge as well as an important opportunity and choice for a new venture.

IDENTIFY START-UP FINANCING ALTERNATIVES

Explore the Available Funding Opportunities for Your Strategy

- Indicate the requirements for the venture to effectively bootstrap its initial launch and growth. Outline the trade-offs for your chosen strategy.
- List sources of non-dilutive grants in your region and industry. Describe the application and evaluation process for any relevant programs.
- Consider what you would be able to commit to the venture. Determine if any opportunities exist through early-stage external financing from your own networks, including your school, friends, and family.
- Identify several equity financing sources for early-stage ventures in your sector, including any relevant angel investor groups, crowdfunding platforms, or venture capitalists.

STAGE YOUR FINANCING

Align the Timing of Investment with Experimentation

- Outline and sequence the critical set of entrepreneurial experiments, prioritizing at the earliest stages relatively low-cost tests that clarify the overall value of the idea and validate key assumptions associated with your chosen strategy.
- Estimate the resources and commitments involved in achieving each milestone.
- Specify financing alternatives for each stage and its associated trade-offs.

CHOOSE YOUR INVESTOR

Weigh Control vs. Resources

- Consider the "founder's dilemma." Determine your preferences regarding control of the ongoing venture vs. access to resources to experiment, establish, and scale your venture.
- Evaluate the financing alternatives, prioritizing those that align with your preferences for control and for realizing your choice of entrepreneurial strategy.

Chapter 14 Review: Financing

CHAPTER TAKEAWAYS

- Finance is among the most important and challenging domains of choice for a start-up. The choice of financing should support early learning and experimentation and, ultimately, the entrepreneurial strategy chosen by the founding team.

- Start-up financing serves two related but distinct functions. Risk capital lets the founding team explore their underlying idea, resolve associated uncertainty, and choose how they will commercialize the opportunity. Once an entrepreneurial strategy has been chosen, investment capital lets the venture establish capabilities or implement features to deliver value to the customer.

- Some of the most common finance options are bootstrapping, self-financing, friends and family, non-dilutive grants and loans, and equity financing. Entrepreneurs should consider both the availability of given options and the specific terms and conditions associated with each alternative.

- The founder's dilemma posits that while retaining ownership (and avoiding equity investment) allows founding teams to capture a higher fraction of the value they create and exercise a greater degree of choice over the evolution of the start-up, accepting outside investment brings a higher level of capital and non-financial resources to de-risk and grow their start-up.

- Ceding control of a venture prior to selecting an entrepreneurial strategy puts that core set of choices in the hands of investors rather than in the hands of the founding team. It is important to remember that raising capital is not an end in itself but, instead, is serving the process of choosing and then implementing the overall entrepreneurial strategy.

- Choosing the sequencing and timing of investment is a powerful way for founding teams to align the funding of their venture and their learning and experimentation, choice of an entrepreneurial strategy, and implementation of that strategy.

- Surfacing multiple sources of external financing enhances a venture's bargaining power in those negotiations. Entrepreneurs may best utilize this advantage to access investors or financing with non-financial resources that will best assist the founding team.

KEY TERMS

risk capital (p. 399)
investment capital (p. 399)
venture capital (p. 399)

bootstrap financing (p. 402)
bridge financing (p. 412)

REVIEW QUESTIONS

1. What is the difference between *risk capital* and *investment capital*? Define each of these terms and explain how they are different from each other.

2. For each of the following terms, provide a definition that distinguishes that form of financing from others, and provide one example of how that form has been used by an entrepreneurial venture:

   a. Bootstrapping

   b. Non-dilutive grants

   c. Crowdfunding

   d. Bank loans

   e. Venture capital

3. Emilio is planning to launch a food delivery service that will cater to businesses in the local office park. He has already developed a prototype website and also has established relationships with local restaurants interested in partnering with him. Based on his research, he is fairly confident that if he can raise $100,000 in up-front capital to purchase delivery vehicles and undertake staff training, he will be able to establish a profitable business within six months with annual profits of at least $200,000. Is a bank loan or venture capital a more appropriate form of financing for this venture? Why?

4. Karen is seeking financing for a new social media platform that will use proactive content moderation to reduce negative interactions on the platform and prioritize mental health. Her uncle, Phil, a retired dentist, has at family gatherings expressed interest in providing funding for her entrepreneurial ventures. What are the advantages and potential drawbacks that Karen might consider before approaching Uncle Phil for start-up capital?

5. What are the main advantages and disadvantages of using online crowdfunding platforms as an initial source of capital for a start-up company? How does reward-based crowdfunding differ from equity crowdfunding?

6. What is the founder's dilemma? Why do founders face a trade-off between attracting financing at an early stage and maintaining control over their venture?

7. Rajiv is thinking of building a start-up focused on leveraging advanced machine learning to produce on-demand personalized stories and activities for children.

   a. Consider the earliest stages of this venture, where Rajiv has an idea but has not yet learned enough to figure out whether the idea is worthwhile to pursue, and, if so, what choices he would like to make as part of his entrepreneurial strategy. What types of financing might be appropriate for Rajiv to explore as he undertakes learning and experimentation? Would a bank loan be appropriate for this stage?

   b. Now consider a later stage where Rajiv has undertaken experiments that have validated the market opportunity and allowed him to identify a feasible and potentially profitable path toward large-scale commercialization. What types of financing might be appropriate for Rajiv to explore at this later stage? Would a bank loan be more appropriate now than in the earlier stage?

DISCUSSION QUESTIONS

Answer the following series of questions and scenarios either in class discussions or by writing a short response.

1. As we read early in this text, Howard Stevenson felt that "Entrepreneurship is the pursuit of opportunity in advance of resources currently under control." What are the most critical challenges that entrepreneurs face in raising financing at the earliest stages of a venture? Why might financing be a more substantial challenge for a start-up vs. an established firm?

2. Sara Blakely was able to launch Spanx, a line of footless body-shaping pantyhose, with only $5,000 from her own savings, and grew the firm for more than 20 years without external investors. What are the benefits and costs of bootstrap financing a start-up venture? What are some key ways a bootstrapping approach impacts the growth and evolution of a firm?

3. Musical theater actors traditionally have been taught to do separate warm-ups for their voice (for singing) and their body (for dancing). Based in New York City, Adebayo, a leading vocal coach, and Deidre, a leading dance coach, have developed an innovative integrated vocal and dance warm-up that is a big hit with their mostly professional students. The pair estimates that demonstrating their approach in a clear way in the form of a professional online video requires $50,000 for up-front costs in production, filming, and editing. To launch their "Broadway Warm-Up" in the broader market, Adebayo and Deirdre are considering a rewards-based crowdfunding campaign to gain initial funding for their venture. What are the strengths of this approach? What risks might they face? What are some challenges they are likely to encounter after they have raised money through crowdfunding?

4. Perin and Eric are at the earliest stages of launching a venture focused on enhancing infrastructure for on-the-go electric vehicle charging. Perin has a strong technical background and has done research on how to enhance the speed of the charging process, and Eric is conducting primary market research exploring what different users might value in such a service. To date, they have not yet settled on their precise customer target or technical approach. Perin estimates that conducting a prototype experiment to demonstrate technical feasibility of their approach would involve an up-front cost of $500,000, and Eric estimates they will incur another $100,000 in costs to develop a network of potential users before they realize a meaningful level of revenue. They are considering trying to take out a bank loan to open their business but have also been approached by an equity investor who would be willing to provide $750,000 in exchange for a 25% equity stake in the company. What are the strengths and weaknesses of these two alternative approaches to financing their venture? What challenges might they face in applying for a bank loan at this point? And what challenges might they face in the future if they move forward with an equity investor?

5. Cassie and Jeong are both passionate participants in cosplay ("costume play"). They wear elaborate, unique costumes, role-play particular

characters and stories, and attend events such as Comic-Con. The duo has launched an online platform, cosmosii, that will allow cosplay enthusiasts to be matched with specific costume makers to realize their individual vision. Cassie and Jeong have been successful at nurturing growth within this online community and have been approached by a venture capitalist, Eddie, who would like to help them scale their venture on an accelerated basis. Eddie believes that serving the existing cosplay community is only a first step. He would like to transform and enlarge the platform, primarily by serving the market for high-end children's Halloween costumes. In exchange for 51% of the company, Eddie is willing to invest $50 million to enable this scaling. Why might Cassie and Jeong accept or reject this offer? If Eddie owns 51% of the company, what concerns might they have about the evolution of the platform?

6. Della is building a company in personalized skincare that leverages cutting-edge machine learning technology to match specific skincare products to particular individuals. She has been accepted into a prestigious entrepreneurial accelerator where she will receive mentorship and then have an opportunity to participate in a Pitch Day for investors. In addition to these value-added opportunities, the accelerator provides $100,000 in seed capital in exchange for a 5% equity share in her company (Della currently has no other investors). She is deciding whether to participate in the accelerator and has an opportunity to meet with the accelerator leadership. What are three or four questions that she might ask the accelerator leadership to determine whether this potential investor is a good match for her venture?

7. The vast majority of financing for early-stage ventures is led by local investors. What is an example of an investor or financing approach used by a start-up in your region that you believe accelerated and enhanced the ultimate impact and growth of that venture? Are there examples where promising start-ups were unable to attract financial resources despite having a good idea and strategy?

8. If you were to seek out external investors within your own ecosystem, what would you look for when choosing your investor? Are there investors or channels that you would find particularly attractive? Why?

FURTHER READING

Da Rin, Marco, and Thomas Hellmann. *Fundamentals of Entrepreneurial Finance.* New York: Oxford University Press, 2020.

Feld, Brad, and Jason Mendelson. *Venture Deals: Be Smarter Than Your Lawyer and Venture Capitalist.* 4th ed. New York: Wiley, 2019.

Hallen, Benjamin L. "The Causes and Consequences of the Initial Network Positions of New Organizations: From Whom Do Entrepreneurs Receive Investments?" *Administrative Science Quarterly* 53, no. 4 (2008): 685–718.

Hellmann, Thomas, and Manju Puri. "The Interaction between Product Market and Financing Strategy: The Role of Venture Capital." *Review of Financial Studies* 13, no. 4 (2000): 959–84.

Hellmann, Thomas, and Manju Puri. "Venture Capital and the Professionalization of Start-Up Firms: Empirical Evidence." *Journal of Finance* 57, no. 1 (2002): 169–97.

Hsu, David H. "Venture Capitalists and Cooperative Start-Up Commercialization Strategy." *Management Science* 52, no. 2 (2006): 204–19.

Kerr, William R., Ramana Nanda, and Matthew Rhodes-Kropf. "Entrepreneurship as Experimentation." *Journal of Economic Perspectives* 28, no. 3 (2014): 25–48.

Kortum, Samuel, and Josh Lerner. "Assessing the Contribution of Venture Capital to Innovation." *RAND Journal of Economics* 31, no. 4 (2000): 674–92.

Lerner, Josh, Ann Leamon, and Felda Hardymon. *Venture Capital, Private Equity, and the Financing of Entrepreneurship.* New York: Wiley, 2012.

Alejandro Velez and Nikhil Arora

Alejandro Velez and Nikhil Arora's entrepreneurial journey started in an ethics course their senior year at the University of California, Berkeley. Both were intrigued when their professor noted that "gourmet mushrooms can grow on spent coffee grounds," and a friendship developed as the pair tried their hands at growing their own mushrooms in buckets in their small college kitchen. From that early experiment, the friends started to explore whether this idea could be the foundation of a business. After using a $5,000 initial grant from their university for additional experiments, the pair's mushrooms earned the seal of approval of renowned chef Alice Waters, who served the coffee-grounds-grown fungus at her restaurant Chez Panisse, a pioneer in the culinary farm-to-table movement.[a] On the strength of this evidence in hand, the pair decided to decline their corporate job offers and pursue organic, urban farming.

Back to the Roots was founded with a mission to help children and families better understand "where food comes from, by helping them experience the magic of growing it themselves."[b] In particular, Velez and Arora wanted to make gardening easy and accessible. Their early products were small, simple kits that allowed those in apartments or without large backyards to grow mushrooms and vegetables at home. As their venture has grown, they have expanded their range of products from seeds and soil to breakfast cereal.

The entrepreneurs have leveraged a range of financing for this experimentation and growth. Over the five years after their initial grant from UC Berkeley, the pair raised funds by selling their delicious mushrooms at local farmers markets and launching a Kickstarter campaign to develop their innovative Water Garden, a small, inexpensive aquaponics kit. They also obtained a loan to move operations and increase production.[c]

Back to the Roots then raised venture capital investment. In early 2016, it raised $5 million, including $3 million from equity-based crowdfunding source CircleUp, investors' start-up accelerator Agency of Trillions (founded by Tony Robbins and Peter Guber), TOMS founder Blake Mycoskie, Annie's cofounder John Foraker, Clif Bar CEO

Nikhil Arora (left) and Alejandro Velez (right) pictured with their organic grow kits

Kevin Cleary, and others.[d] Later that year it raised another $10 million, led by Acre Venture Partners, a fund formed by Campbell Soup.[e]

Questions

1. Using this case and the information in the chapter, describe some of the benefits and limitations to Velez and Arora when they initially raised funds by selling their mushrooms at local farmers markets.

2. Briefly describe what the advantages were of using a Kickstarter crowdsourcing campaign to fund Back to the Roots's Water Garden aquaponics kit. What were the risks of such a campaign (even if the campaign successfully raised the targeted funds)?

3. Use the Internet to learn more about the sources where this company received later stages of funding. What is your assessment of where Velez and Arora chose to seek and accept financing to grow their product line and distribution partnerships? Beyond financing, what resources might these funding sources have provided Back to the Roots that might have been useful in achieving their short-term objectives and long-term mission?

When Melanie Perkins created Canva, it was built on an idea to make design tools something anyone could succeed with, an idea with a blueprint for growth and scale built into it.

ENTREPRENEUR'S DILEMMA Scaling requires a large level of investment and commitment. Entrepreneurs face a dilemma, as that level of commitment can draw more attention and more competition from incumbent firms and often requires the entrepreneur to cede power to attract more resources. By not scaling, value creation is reduced, but the entrepreneur can keep a greater share of the value.

CHAPTER OBJECTIVES

- Understand why scaling is a choice that entrepreneurs face when they achieve initial success
- Recognize the implications of the Penrose effect on venture growth
- Consider the balance, imprinting, and power challenges facing entrepreneurs when scaling
- Understand the findings of the Greiner curve for the evolution of organizational structure and leadership
- Classify the different approaches businesses use to scale strategically

15

SCALING

Melanie Perkins became an entrepreneur at age 15. She sold hand-knitted scarves at boutiques around her hometown of Perth, Australia. Perkins created custom labels advertising that the scarves were handcrafted, hoping that customers would forgive any imperfections in her designs. While attending the University of Western Australia, she continued working in design by tutoring students on how to use Adobe Photoshop to promote their own products, projects, and activities. There she had an epiphany: her job should not exist. It should not take at least a semester of training for an individual to complete basic tasks in Photoshop. That might be fine for those who want to make a career of design. But what if they were just dipping in for smaller projects like, say, a high school yearbook?

In 2007, with her partner, Cliff Obrecht, Perkins pursued her vision of making design tools for the rest of us. They created a new venture, Fusion Books, to help students easily design yearbooks. They could simply drag and drop photos, adjust layouts, and collaborate throughout the design process. It turned out to be a perfect but intense niche market. Perkins and Obrecht chose to take a handcrafted approach for each customer. They would walk each school through the design and publication process. The undertaking was time-intensive, but it gave the founders immediate feedback on what worked and what did not. They learned, for instance, that customers didn't just want to drag and drop; they also wanted to click and edit. Over the course of five years, with intense iterative feedback and design, Fusion Books grew to be the largest yearbook company in Australia and expanded to New Zealand and France.

However, Perkins still had her original vision in mind. She had set out to improve all design tools and only scratched the surface in revamping the school

scale In entrepreneurship, when a business is adding revenue faster than it is adding costs

yearbook market. Indeed, her yearbook customers were asking for more tools for their other activities and projects. Thus, in 2013, having secured initial funding, Perkins launched Canva to bring design tools to the web in an intuitive way. By the end of its first year, Canva had 750,000 users. Today, it has over 130 million users and is worth A$25 billion (after reaching a high of A$40 billion in 2021), partnering with large U.S. firms such as FedEx Office and Office Depot.[1]

How did Canva grow this big so fast? The answer was embedded in its plan. To beat Adobe Photoshop and open up design to more users, Canva had to be everything Photoshop was not. It was not enough just to get a customer to Canva's website and let the customer take it from there. The customer had to experience the product and want to explore it within the first few minutes. However, what Perkins found is that customers were reluctant to start exploring Canva. Many had been told that design is hard and should be left to the experts. To overcome these hesitations, Canva experimented with a number of onboarding approaches designed to give customers "quick wins" and project designs that they would feel proud to share with others. These changes made the product more accessible and built customers' confidence in their ability to use the product. They also spurred a network of organically arising influencers touting the product as customers shared their finished work with others.

Canva became a company primed for growth. Perkins's vision was to bring design tools to the masses, creating Canva as a cheaper alternative to professional graphic design that gave users more power *without the learning cost*. In doing so, Canva jettisoned a central cost of customer acquisition, namely the start-up "costs" of time and effort customers incur when learning to use a new product or technology. It created simple tutorials that brought even complicated design tools within reach. By understanding and solving the problem of learning costs for consumers, the company had thus made investments and choices designed to create rapid growth. It was built for **scale**.

The seeming paradox of Canva's growth is that it started by doing things that were the opposite of scaling: onboarding customers with a very hands-on approach. However, this was part of the plan. Canva's goal was ultimately to automate and simplify a huge component of the design process. This meant the founders first had to understand not only what to automate, but also how to do so in a way that was intuitive for the mass consumer. The idea that building for scale starts with doing things that seemingly are not scalable is a theme that runs through many start-ups. But it also leads to an important insight: scaling is hard. It takes time to get from zero to a few customers. However, do that process correctly and the move to scale can then accelerate: a slow start followed by a flood of activity is typical of many start-ups.

In this chapter, we will examine what entrepreneurs need to be mindful of in choosing and strategically planning for this type of scale and growth. When a strategy finds success, an entrepreneur must make an active choice to scale. This chapter considers that choice plus other choices entrepreneurs face as they build on their success and take a business to scale. While many of those choices will be made as success is taking place, as we see with Canva, some of the trade-offs entrepreneurs face when scaling can be softened by choices made as part of their initial entrepreneurial strategy.

This chapter's video explores how lower customer acquisition costs let Canva scale rapidly.

Canva was built with the idea of making design easier for the masses, essentially eliminating a start-up "cost" for many customers. This led it to scale rapidly once the idea caught on.

15.1 Why Do Start-Ups Have to Choose to Scale?

The scaling of businesses can be characterized in a few different ways. Some entrepreneurs aim for sales growth, while others set targets for the number of employees to hire or the amount of capital to raise. There is the ubiquitous benchmark of market share that compares revenue and resource size to other businesses. Scale should mean generating high profits by the venture creating and capturing value. This is what leads businesses to receive a high and sustainable equity valuation.

But even for an initially successful firm, growing to scale is far from inevitable. Some firms achieve a high rate of growth, while others remain stable, contract, or eventually fail. From this perspective, differences among firms might seem to be attributable to differences in the quality of the opportunities being pursued, the quality of the people working in the venture, the overall execution, or even to luck. Given the circumstances that must come together for most businesses to succeed, successful entrepreneurship can seem akin to purchasing a winning lottery ticket!

However, *while growth may be difficult to predict, the pursuit of growth is a choice.* Growth only occurs when an entrepreneur makes a choice—perhaps carefully considered or perhaps off the cuff—to hire a new employee, seek a new investor, or build out an element of their supply chain. Attracting and acquiring new resources and capabilities draws on the scarce time and attention of the founding team, and the process of growth only occurs through engagement and initiative by the founders and other employees of the firm.

There is nothing that precludes an entrepreneur from establishing an organization using their personal resources (e.g., their time, capital, and skills) and then maintaining that organization as a small business. *The choice not to grow is far more common than the choice to pursue growth.* Among newly formed businesses in the United States in the early 2000s that survived more than four years, the majority did not increase their number of employees at all, and less than 4% grew to more than 10 employees.[2] Moreover, the fact that most businesses remain small does not reflect a failure to achieve positive growth but rather an entrepreneur's choice to not pursue growth in the first place. According

Many businesses are started with no intention of scaling but rather with the goal of providing meaningful opportunity for the entrepreneur and value for their community.

Konoa's Headphone Struggles

Konoa was founded in 2015 to provide wireless headphones that could modulate the level of external noise, which might let bikers listen to music but also hear oncoming cars. It received enough preorders to raise more than $7 million in capital. However, after more than 18 months of delays beyond the initial promised delivery date, the company began shipping a product that was quickly panned: online reviewers claimed that, though the $300 product came in a nice case and had a nicely designed T-shirt, the process of syncing the earphones to the app did not work, the promised audio augmentation functionality did not perform, and the audio was filled with feedback or cut out entirely.

Of course, Konoa pursued a promising opportunity; wireless headphones with essentially the same features were successfully commercialized shortly after Konoa's demise. Konoa also succeeded in attracting early-stage capital, employees, and suppliers. But ultimately, Konoa could not take advantage of those resources to build capabilities and deliver a product that would create meaningful customer value in a timely and effective way. While the founding team chose to pursue a growth path and had a good idea, their other choices led to their failure.

Konoa had the right idea—headphones that would work better for bikers—but the wrong execution.

to the Panel Study of Entrepreneurial Dynamics (PSED II), less than 25% of entrepreneurs have a desire to grow to be "big," and less than 10% of new entrepreneurs seek to grow their firm to be more than 10 employees over their first five years of operation. In the same survey, many entrepreneurs noted the value they placed on the ability to be their own boss, maintain flexible hours, and choose activities and opportunities that interest them.[3] Not surprisingly, the opportunities being pursued by these entrepreneurs neither require nor meaningfully benefit from growth. Small establishments—a restaurant, medical or legal practice, or even the corner dry cleaner—make up a significant majority of all new businesses, and most of these "Main Street" businesses are providing an existing service to a local market and creating value for those local consumers. Many require a modest but meaningful level of investment capital at the outset (or perhaps over the first few months) and then can achieve a stable level of business activity over an extended period of time.

But for those entrepreneurs who choose to pursue a growth path, there is no guarantee that it will occur or will be sustainable. An entrepreneur may be able to attract significant financial resources, engage in extensive hiring, and even bring a product to market, only to find that there is little to no demand for their product. For example, in Chapter 5 we learned about how Segway launched its product but failed to create value for customers from the start. The Pebble watch, which we discussed in Chapter 7, had a far better market reception, but it failed to capture value on an ongoing basis as it was out-executed by competitors. It is also possible to pursue growth but make choices and investments that do not deliver value for customers in any meaningful way (see **Mini Case: Konoa's Headphone Struggles**). The failure of Segway, Pebble, and Konoa and the legions of other start-ups that pursue aggressive growth and then do not deliver value for customers highlights the uncertainty fundamental to pursuing an opportunity built on the idea of eventual growth.

But just because growth is uncertain does not negate the fact that growth is a choice. At its heart, an entrepreneur's choice to pursue growth is the choice of how quickly—and in what ways—to expand the resources and capabilities of that organization over a specific amount of time.

15.2 A Useful Regularity: The Law of (Almost) Proportional Growth

The most common type of business organization is a *firm*, a for-profit business formed as a corporation, limited liability company, or partnership.[4] We consider a firm's growth to be the change over time in its quantity of human, physical, and financial resources, and its development of processes and structures (and even organizational culture) that enable capabilities.

Growth can be positive or negative: a firm can become bigger or smaller, its capabilities can expand or erode, and the overall resources and capabilities available at a moment in time reflects the growth that has occurred between the time of founding and that moment.

Growth is important because, as they found their businesses, most entrepreneurs do not have all the resources and capabilities they need to achieve their goals. As we stated in the last section, growth is required to create and capture value, and how and when to grow is a choice. Entrepreneurs must choose what resources and capabilities to acquire or access, in what sequence and time frame, and how to structure those resources and capabilities within their firms.

THE PENROSE EFFECT

However, growth is a costly and complex process. Economist Edith Penrose first captured this complexity in her book *The Theory of the Growth of the Firm*, where she used detailed case studies to identify both the importance of growth for organizations and the central challenge of achieving that growth. Her central insight—the **Penrose effect**—is premised on the observation that at any moment in time, firms are limited in the available resources and managerial capabilities needed for growth. To grow, a firm must attract, acquire, and then manage the introduction of new resources and capabilities. As such, adding *new* resources and capabilities to grow the firm inherently must utilize the *existing* resources and capabilities of that firm. Even when there is no ambiguity about what resources and capabilities a firm needs to develop, the scarcity of current resources limits the rate that a firm can introduce new resources and capabilities. Essentially, for any firm, there are limits on its growth rate at any point in time (**Figure 15.1**).

Penrose effect The fact that as businesses grow, managerial and resource constraints tend to be a limiting factor

---

FIGURE 15.1 The Penrose Effect

The Penrose Effect points out that firms have only so many resources and managerial capabilities they can use to grow. For example, attending and recruiting new people at this job fair uses resources that could be directed somewhere else, and training and managing these new employees will require additional resources.

the law of (almost) proportional growth Because firm growth is enabled by existing resources and capabilities, a firm's growth potential at a moment in time depends at least in part on the size and age of that firm at that moment in time

This relationship impacts all organizations, no matter their size or maturity. Even a long-standing organization with reasonable resources—say a midsized state university—faces significant challenges in introducing new programs or classes beyond those already in place. Hiring new staff or faculty takes time and effort, and this time and effort comes at the expense of teaching existing classes to current students.

With that said, the Penrose effect perhaps most significantly impacts start-ups. To test and implement an entrepreneurial strategy, a new firm almost always needs resources and capabilities beyond those under its control at the time of founding. But attracting and acquiring resources takes time and attention away from implementing the strategy itself. So even when a founding team is clear about the direction in which they would like to grow, the Penrose effect creates a challenging dilemma as they seek to make that growth a reality. In this way, the Penrose effect not only captures a central challenge facing founders but also provides a foundation for perhaps the single most important fact about the growth of organizations: **the law of (almost) proportional growth**. *Because firm growth is enabled by existing resources and capabilities, a firm's growth potential at a moment in time depends at least in part on the size and age of that firm at that moment in time.* For example, the process of attracting and hiring the first employee for an organization is much more challenging and costlier than hiring an additional employee once the firm has achieved a meaningful scale.

THE POTENTIAL FOR GROWTH

The simple observation in the preceding paragraph has an important consequence: the potential for firm growth tends to be on a percentage rather than an absolute basis. When a firm is young and small, a given percentage increase in the size of the firm, say a 50% growth rate, will be relatively small in absolute terms. For example, a firm growing from two cofounders working full-time by adding one full-time employee has grown by 50%. Achieving that same growth rate for a larger firm, say one that now has 50 employees, requires hiring not one but 25 new employees. Put another way, it would be extremely difficult and therefore highly unlikely for a firm with only two individuals to be able to add 25 new employees in its first year. It is similarly true that adding a single employee would represent a much more modest challenge for a firm that has already grown to 50 individuals. In short, because the Penrose effect implies that the "challenge" of growth is roughly proportional to the current size of the firm, it also implies that the potential for growth is roughly proportional to the size of the firm (see **Using the Research: Gibrat's Legacy**).

Of course, just because the potential for growth is proportional to the current size of the firm does not mean that all firms grow at the same rate. Exactly the opposite is true. While some firms achieve a high rate of growth relative to their current size in a given year, others either stagnate, decline in absolute size, or go out of business. This variation has a profound influence over time. While the vast majority of all new ventures either fail or attain only a limited size after a few years, a very small number of ventures sustain a high

Gibrat's Legacy

The idea that persistent differences in the percentage growth rates of firms result in large differences in the eventual size of firms was documented by French economist Robert Gibrat. He proposed that the growth rate of firms was independent of their size, and that the extreme variation in the eventual size of firms within a given industry (or even the entire economy) was because of a few "lucky" firms that were able to maintain a persistently high percentage growth rate increase over time.

There have been a few key modifications to Gibrat's law: most notably, across most industries, young firms have both a higher rate of exit but, if they survive, also achieve a higher average rate of growth. In other words, relative to established firms, start-ups are simultaneously more likely to fail but, if they avoid failure, grow at a proportionately faster rate during their first few years of operation. The law of (almost) proportional growth highlights the idea that while the potential for firm growth is constrained by the existing level of resources and capabilities, the growth process for firms that are ultimately successful tends to

Gibrat's research has led to the idea that if new firms can survive, their growth rates are much faster than those of established firms.

be more rapid at the earliest stages of the firm. The largest enterprises emerge by realizing a persistent and high growth rate over an extended period of time.

level of growth for an extended period of time (see **Deep Dive: Pioneers of Sustained Growth** on p. 430). Because of this, even if a group of firms are founded at the same time with roughly the same initial resources and capabilities, only one or a small fraction of those firms may over time come to dominate the industry or opportunity these firms are pursuing. For example, suppose Firms A and B both achieve positive growth each year, but Firm A achieves a 100% growth rate and Firm B achieves a 25% growth rate (which would still be impressive): after just 10 years, Firm A would be *more than 100 times* larger than Firm B! Interestingly, even though it would be small relative to Firm A, Firm B would nonetheless be nearly 10 times as large as a firm that did not grow at all.

Economists have a particular notion about how some businesses can achieve growth after initial success: replication. Manufacturers can build another plant and retailers can launch more outlets. In principle, there is no reason why the latest plant cannot be at least as productive as the first one. Businesses have constant returns to scale—meaning they can scale as far as demand will take them.

In practice, there are some common resources that might be shared across business units that can give rise to advantages, especially at lower levels of

Pioneers of Sustained Growth

Besides Penrose and Gibrat, there are some notable academics who have been very influential in pioneering scaling strategies and identifying key trade-offs in achieving that growth.

- **Alfred DuPont Chandler** was perhaps the first historian to examine the success of the world's largest companies. Chandler studied some of the foremost industries of the 1960s and asked how they came to be. For instance, he noted that at the turn of the twentieth century, there were many car companies, but within a few decades, three dominated: Ford, General Motors, and Chrysler. In each case, what separated these three from the competitive pack was that they made large investments in manufacturing and distribution to realize economies of scale and scope and push others out of the market. This same trend, with the eventual market leaders being few in number, was observed across many industries, from chemicals to computers.

- **John Sutton** examined a similar familiar set of patterns from the lens of the 1980s and 1990s. He noted that it was not simply the ability to reach scale that allowed a few firms to dominate industries but that the investments in scale were a strategic choice.

As markets for new products grew, Sutton noted, this should have allowed for more firm entry. Instead, incumbent firms escalated the scale of their investments and adopted technologies with scale advantages to beat out others in competition with them. Sutton argued that a primary fact of scaling was not that there were fixed costs but that firms were making the strategic choice to invest in the high fixed level of the costs.

- **Rebecca Henderson** focused on the most innovative businesses—in particular, those that relied on continual innovation to both improve their products and be ready to recognize and exploit radical new technological opportunities. She identified a fundamental trade-off when businesses scale: they could organize themselves to beat others in product quality in the current technological generation or they could make sure they were in a position to exploit changes in later technology generations. However, they could not do both. Thus, businesses had a strategic decision to either push for immediate market leadership or build in capabilities to create long-term sustained advantages even if they were never number 1 in the market.

output that increase returns to scale. However, for most businesses, those common resources have their limits and will be subject to decreasing returns at a point. The underlying logic in principle is that replication provides a way in which start-ups can scale, though it may present challenges in both the short term and the long term.

15.3 Choosing to Scale

Choosing to grow and scale is, in many cases, the most actionable choice facing entrepreneurs. However, that choice involves a critical trade-off for founders. On the one hand, rapid growth introduces new resources and capabilities to the firm that help create and deliver value. Particularly when entrepreneurs are pursuing an opportunity that might attract competitors, enabling rapid growth is critical for realizing value. For example, while the opportunity to pursue electric scooter rentals was not limited to any one individual or firm,

FIGURE 15.2 Bird Scooter Rentals

Bird chose to scale and grow so quickly that it caused many launch cities (including Los Angeles, pictured here) to wonder how to handle this new business.

early entrants such as Bird in 2017, founded by ex-Uber employee Travis VanderZanden, chose to raise capital rapidly. This let Bird preemptively launch a dense network of electric scooter rental franchise operations that scaled more quickly than other entrants. This choice to grow rapidly had its consequences, with many municipalities struggling to determine whether to allow electric scooter rentals and whether the service was safe or even desirable for their citizens (**Figure 15.2**). Despite these challenges, Bird grew over its first three years to more than 1,000 full-time employees and raised more than $700 million to support an army of scooters and "chargers" (gig workers maintaining and recharging scooters on a per-scooter basis) in more than 300 cities around the world.[5] Even after the Covid pandemic in 2020 led to a dramatic short-term reduction in scooter use (and potentially allowed other competitors to catch up), Bird leveraged its early growth to not only maintain but also extend its dominance in the emerging electric scooter rental market. In short, succeeding with an opportunity depends in many cases on the timeliness with which the organization takes advantage of that opportunity. Entrepreneurs may therefore choose to accelerate growth as quickly as possible, leveraging rapid growth into a position of extended leadership in an emerging market.

However, the Penrose effect highlights that rapid growth is a challenge on its own terms. Choosing a more rapid growth rate uses current resources and capabilities intensively. In many cases, this is the personal time, skills, and financial resources of the founding team, and it can exert immediate pressure

The Scaling Learning Curve

In the 1930s, engineers noticed that the cost of producing airframes (the body of airplanes without the engine) fell in proportion to the total labor hours needed to produce them in the past. This generated the notion of a "learning curve," the relationship between an activity and how more efficient those performing the activity became over time. For airframes, the relationship was given by the cube root of the size of the workforce at a plant.

Research on how aircraft frames are manufactured gave rise to the idea of the learning curve.

The idea that productivity can improve as people learn how to be better, faster workers with experience has endured. In management strategy, this is seen in the idea that firms with more experience tend to be able to build superior capabilities and productivity than younger firms. This may be seen not only in broad business skills, such as marketing and manufacturing, but also in ways that impact strategy choices. For instance, when a business competes, it can take advantage of how it will improve through learning by doing.

What this means is that when it comes to scaling, one of the great inputs an entrepreneur can bring is their own experience in scaling other ventures. Thus, we often see serial entrepreneurs who start one business but then go on to successfully build others (e.g., Steve Jobs, Reid Hoffman, Richard Branson, Oprah Winfrey). This also means that in scaling, ventures can benefit from bringing in mentors and even senior management with experiences that the venture lacks. For instance, Google famously appointed Eric Schmidt, the former CEO of Sun Microsystems and Novell, to be its CEO for a decade before handing the reins back to one of its founders, Larry Page. As it was scaling, Page simply had no similar experience.

on the firm and especially less experienced leaders (see **Using the Research: The Scaling Learning Curve**). Further, pursuing rapid growth may actually harm or destroy the firm in the process. To see these dynamics in action, contrast the growth of Bird (described above) with that of Tink Labs. Tink Labs was founded in 2012 by Terence Kwok to provide local smartphones for travelers through partnerships with leading hotel chains such as Hyatt Hotels and Shangri-La Hotels and Resorts. These phones would let travelers make local calls and avoid expensive roaming charges, and potentially offer hotels another way to provide services to their visitors.[6] After tailoring the handsets to the needs of hotels and their guests and establishing a successful beachhead in Hong Kong, Kwok focused on a similar plan of rapid international expansion. This expansion included raising more than $125 million in venture capital and expanding Tink Labs' geographic footprint to more than a dozen offices with more than 400 employees serving 80 countries and hundreds of thousands of hotel rooms.[7] However, this very rapid process of growth doomed Tink: the organization not only failed to succeed in the new markets it entered, but the focus on growth blinded Kwok and his team to changes in their core markets. The growth of services like Viber and WhatsApp and the decrease in international roaming charges for visitors to Hong Kong made their service less valuable. Less than 24 months after undertaking rapid global growth and being declared Hong Kong's first "unicorn," Tink Labs declared bankruptcy, and its concierge handset business was sold for a nominal sum. Kwok and his team could not simultaneously build a global organization and maintain a focus on their existing offerings in Hong Kong and Southeast Asia.

The difficulties of navigating the potential of growth with its costs and challenges are not unique. Ventures that choose to scale face three key challenges.

1. ***The balance challenge:*** Ensuring the organization can grow in a balanced manner
2. ***The imprinting challenge:*** Building on the foundation and commitments of their entrepreneurial strategy
3. ***The power challenge:*** Understanding the necessary changes in power that will accompany this transformation

We next examine all three in detail.

15.4 The Balance Challenge

Though it's easy to characterize the failure of Tink Labs as due to expanding too quickly, the challenge of growth is more complicated: growth itself changes the nature of the organization. At the moment a firm is founded, the organization is represented simply by the founding team and the resources and capabilities they bring to the organization. In most cases, this makes it highly fluid and flexible, leverages the strengths of individuals, and perhaps delays implementing activities where the team has less experience or skill. In many cases, founders maintain overlapping and vaguely defined roles, and the early team's frequent communication fosters learning and coordination across the team. At this early stage, each member of the founding team often operates more like a generalist than a specialist or functional manager.

Growing beyond this early team involves two challenges of **balance**.

1. The founding team must balance the ongoing activities of the venture with the activities required to grow the organization. As highlighted by the work of Penrose and Gibrat, the current size and resources of the venture constrain the firm's growth. To scale, the founding team must prioritize the recruiting, hiring, and onboarding of new team members over some of the activities that have driven their success. With competing demands on the founding team—acquiring and serving customers, developing the technology and product, and coordinating with partners—many start-ups choose to rush the hiring process so they can remain focused on achieving key, external milestones. However, a lack of attention and balance in developing the organization can lead to a haphazard hiring process. This might distract the founding team, further inhibit the growth of the venture, and

balance Favoring all aspects of the business equally; for example, maintaining the ongoing activities of the venture while also focusing on growing in the organization for the future and not pursuing one at the expense of the other

limit the organization's ability to achieve those very key milestones. This distraction can result in either bad hires who must be let go and the start of a new recruiting process or strong hires whose work is poorly coordinated.

2. While potentially advantageous at the moment of founding, the fluidity of the early founding team becomes both more difficult and less valuable to maintain as the firm grows. In most cases, new employees are hired to fulfill specific functional roles (e.g., sales, R&D), and even though early employees are often provided with some equity in the firm, a hierarchy is established between the members of the founding team and more traditional employees of the organization. The growth of the firm involves not only an increase in the size of the organization but also a change in its structure.

Growing organizations can find it challenging to establish new structures, hierarchies, and routines. Defining specific roles and structures takes time, and the effort of setting up the organization comes at the expense of engaging with customers or developing new or better products or services. Even pragmatic concerns are costly. Hiring the *first* full-time employee usually requires identifying and recruiting a potential employee, defining a job title and responsibilities for that individual, and overcoming complex administrative hurdles like payroll, taxation, and acquiring required employee benefits like workers' compensation insurance.

Taken together, at the outset, start-ups are unbalanced; they must favor one aspect of the business over another. In very simple terms, as they begin, start-ups either have to prioritize demand—ensuring that customers have a great experience and come back for more—or supply—ensuring that resources are in place that can scale naturally when demand comes in. This means that success brings about the costs of this imbalance. There is either a shortage—that is, more customers than you can reliably serve—or a surplus—more capacity to serve customers than you have. To scale, those elements need to be brought back into balance (see **Mini Case: Shopify and Scaling with Platforms**).

SurveyMonkey is an example of a start-up that confronted the balance challenge. SurveyMonkey is a ubiquitous web tool to survey customers or anyone else and analyze the results. Today it is a public company with 25 million users and hundreds of millions in revenue per year. But back when Selina Tobaccowala (see the sidebar), cofounder of Evite, joined SurveyMonkey as VP of engineering and product in 2009, there were just two developers and 10 customer service agents. In other words, the company had the marketing orientation bringing in demand, but the technical resources to supply the product at scale were lacking. The situation was not sustainable. Services like backing up the data so critical to customers were inadequate. Tobaccowala hired specialists for growth so that the business would be balanced and sustainable.

By contrast, Starbucks (which we first encountered in Chapter 4), found itself locally successful with just 11 stores and 100 employees. But it was still incurring losses when its founder Howard Schultz decided to solve a major potential imbalance: retaining good employees. Despite not being profitable, he made the decision to invest heavily in employees with some very (at least for the 1980s) unconventional moves. Specifically, he decided to give

Selina Tobaccowala. Selina Tobaccowala founded and scaled Evite, an event invitation platform, straight out of college. After a successful exit for the venture, Tobaccowala joined Ticketmaster Europe as a senior software executive. In 2009, she was recruited to join the small SurveyMonkey team; the enterprise was generating millions in revenue but needed to scale the platform and the team behind it. As she planned for rapid growth, Tobaccowala drew from her experience at Evite and Ticketmaster. She focused on improving one area of the platform at a time, made critical hires, including a UX designer and a head of engineering (stealing both from LinkedIn), and started to launch globally. Within five years, her team grew to over a hundred engineers, and SurveyMonkey would support 17 languages and 28 currencies, with 45% of its business based outside the United States.[a]

Shopify and Scaling with Platforms

One way in which start-ups can resolve imbalances is by creating a platform that helps others outside the firm invest in its value proposition. A good example of this was done by Shopify (whose founder, Tobi Lütke, we first encountered in Chapter 3). Shopify had successfully launched with tools to help online retailers set up and manage their shops. But by 2009, Lütke was still looking for the "real" growth opportunity. He decided he was not simply building a product, but that Shopify should aim to become a platform with additional innovations and support for his customers. Rather than assuming Shopify could do that itself, Lütke opened up the platform to allow app developers to market and sell apps operating within the Shopify experience directly to customers. This was a bold move. "What we did to get the platform off the ground is to basically leave all of the economics for Shopify on the table and give it to the third-party app developers," Lütke explains.[a] The Shopify app store quickly populated, attracting more users (demand) and more developers (supply). As a result, 10 years later in 2018, Lütke claimed that Shopify had crossed the "Gates line," which comes from a remark from Bill Gates: "You are not a platform until the people who are building on you make more money than you do."[b] In fact, Shopify businesses were making over $80 billion in sales while app developers made about $500 million.

To achieve the scale it wanted, Shopify had to become a platform for the success of outsiders who would improve its functionality.

all employees health insurance and stock options. And not just full-timers but part-time employees too, a first for the United States. With such inducements in place, Starbucks was in a position to grow rapidly. Four decades later it has over 36,000 stores in 84 countries.[8] Starbucks's investment in employees continued with a free college tuition program in 2014. In China, to raise the perceived status of working for Starbucks, health insurance benefits were expanded to an employee's parents. Today, of course, Starbucks is being challenged by a different imbalance as it confronts unionization efforts, with many workers questioning whether the company and Schultz himself are living up to its original ideals.

15.5 The Imprinting Challenge

The second scaling challenge is that the choices entrepreneurs have already made matter. Their chosen entrepreneurial strategy has imprinted on the start-up (see Chapter 7 for more on imprinting). When firms consider a growth strategy, the entrepreneurs have already established a beachhead with key customer groups, built their products with specific technologies, chosen whether to partner with established firms or not, and built organizations that prioritize certain resources and capabilities. These choices shape the behaviors, processes, and routines of the start-up, then persist and are difficult to change.

The persistence of different organizational structures and routines has long been of interest to sociologists. In a study of U.S. college fraternities and their respective structures and long-standing traditions, sociologist Arthur Stinchcombe identified how the external environment at the time of its founding shaped different waves of fraternities and how those differences in structure remained over a hundred years later.[9] Remarkably, sociologists have found that the early structures of organizations of all types, shaped by the environment at founding, persist well after such structures still benefit the organization and newer organizational models have emerged. In particular, the Stanford Project on Emerging Companies (SPEC) explored how prior experience and founding choices at a set of high-tech start-ups in Silicon Valley shaped their early organizational form, the persistence of that structure, and the implications for start-up performance.[10] SPEC found that the ventures' initial organizational model, or blueprints, affected the evolution of bureaucratic intensity and organizational structure, investment in specific resources and capabilities, timing of CEO succession, and likelihood of the venture going public. One of the most distinctive observations from the SPEC studies was that the particular configuration of the founding team seemed to have a long-term impact on a venture as it scales. For example, ventures founded by a strong individual leader developed a higher level of centralized control even as the firm expanded, while firms founded with more equality across roles among team members maintained a lower level of hierarchy as they scaled.

Consider the case of W. W. Norton & Company, the publisher of this book. Norton was founded in 1923 by William W. Norton and his wife Mary "Polly" Dows Norton with the idea that "leaders in their fields—not mere popularizers—should 'bring to the public the knowledge of our time.'"[11] Rather than simply competing for authors with a proven track record, the founders wanted to endow their editors with the freedom and independence to identify and support the emerging authors of their era, serving as partners in assisting these authors (and their ideas) to reach the masses. One way the founders chose to build an organizational culture focused on this independence occurred at William's death at the age of 54. Polly Norton at that time decided to make Norton an employee-owned company, on the condition that the employees pledged to keep the company independent. A hundred years later, the company remains employee owned (**Figure 15.3**), with a legacy that has supported transformational ideas and national bestsellers such as *The Feminine Mystique* by Betty Friedan, *A Clockwork Orange* by Anthony Burgess, and *Liar's Poker* by Michael Lewis, and hundreds of new authors and titles each year. With an emphasis still today on employee autonomy, Norton remains a leader in the challenging (and ever-changing) book publishing industry.

Of course, founders also have some degree of choice about whether and when imprinting will impact their scaling. If a particular organizational choice is appropriate at the earliest stages of a venture, this does not necessarily mean it will be appropriate as the organization matures. Proactive awareness of imprinting and its consequences can help teams build on those elements that

FIGURE 15.3 W. W. Norton, Independent and Employee Owned

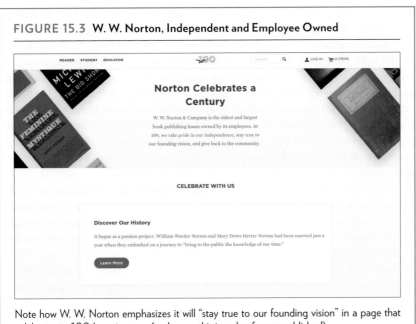

Note how W. W. Norton emphasizes it will "stay true to our founding vision" in a page that celebrates its 100th anniversary (and yes ... this is a plug for our publisher!).

have driven growth while pruning or reorganizing elements that have outlived their usefulness.

Nonetheless, the persistence of early start-up choices means that different approaches to scale may be more favorable to a given venture than others. Start-ups are building off different foundations for growth and will require different approaches to scale. Simply put, the blueprint for scale begins at founding.

15.6 The Power Challenge

Growth lets entrepreneurs move beyond the constraints of their own time and expertise by drawing upon the capabilities and resources of others. But this is not simply a choice to attract and acquire resources and capabilities. The choice to grow is either implicitly or explicitly a choice to navigate the challenge of establishing specific structures, routines, and a hierarchy where none exist. The choice to grow is a choice to be not simply an entrepreneur but also a leader.

Becoming a leader and manager requires an entrepreneur to confront how they will shape the **power structure** within their organization and their position in it. At founding, an entrepreneur chooses how to allocate their own time and resources. When they draw on external resources, the entrepreneur must choose how to allocate the time and resources of other people. For instance, they might closely direct activities or provide broad discretion. They might choose narrowly defined job activities or allow for fluidity between roles. But regardless of their organizational choice, their role is inherently changed by now leading and managing an organization.

power structure The hierarchy of power defined by how to best allocate the time and resources of other people throughout the organization

This transformation can itself impede growth; in each phase of growth, entrepreneurs must choose how to reconfigure both the organization and their own role. Each of these shifts will involve learning and adaptation, which take time and attention to implement and may need to be reconsidered or even reversed. Different members of the founding team, or even early employees or investors, might disagree about whether a particular organizational approach is effective or not, or what role they would like to play in the growing firm. There may be competing visions as to the importance and relative power of different stakeholders and functional areas (i.e., sales, R&D). As a consequence, the process of growth can often be chaotic and contentious.

One of the more counterintuitive experiences for first-time entrepreneurs is that their success may result in them being replaced by a more experienced executive. This "paradox of success" occurs because as an entrepreneur achieves venture milestones, investors may "professionalize" the start-up with leadership and executives for the next stage in the organization's growth.[12] Studies have shown that not only is founder replacement rather common,[13] but doing so increases the probability of a successful exit such as acquisition or IPO.[14] Some founders are surprised at the power investors may wield over the company. While external investors might bring resources to grow the company, they likely will come at the cost of the founder's control and leadership (see the sidebar on **Ben Horowitz**). Understandably, this transformation of power and organizational structure can be disorienting for the founder(s) and the team.

Ben Horowitz. Besides founding several start-ups, Ben Horowitz is known for starting the venture capital firm Andreessen Horowitz with Netscape founder Marc Andreessen. Horowitz also authored a book about start-ups called *The Hard Thing about Hard Things: Building a Business When There Are No Easy Answers.* In it, he notes that founders have difficulty as businesses scale. He argues that while founders are integral to the first stage of a venture, as the venture grows and becomes complex, they do not have the skills needed to lower costs, manage far greater numbers of employees, streamline operations, and many other core challenges that larger firms face.[a]

15.7 The Greiner Curve and Growth Playbooks

The consequences of the balance challenge, the imprinting challenge, and the power challenge come together to form the central insight behind the Greiner curve (**Figure 15.4**). It maps out the distinct phases of growth for a firm as it achieves meaningful scale. Developed by Professor Larry Greiner, the model identifies five phases of organizational evolution, each characterized by a unique set of challenges and opportunities that can ultimately result in an organizational crisis and organizational evolution.

1. **Creativity phase:** In the early creativity phase, the organization is fluid and focused on experimentation and learning. This phase comes to an end with a leadership crisis as the founders must choose a path forward, building on what they have learned.
2. **Direction phase:** In the direction phase, the team expands and is focused on achieving clear milestones, which requires establishing an organizational hierarchy. A crisis can occur as more autonomy is required by the individuals within the teams.
3. **Delegation phase:** As the organization grows, more responsibility is delegated to the teams, which become more specialized in skills and objectives and seek more control over their operations.

Chapter 15: Scaling

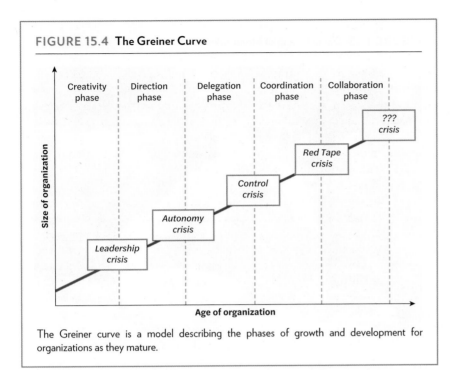

FIGURE 15.4 The Greiner Curve

Creativity phase | Direction phase | Delegation phase | Coordination phase | Collaboration phase

Size of organization

Age of organization

Leadership crisis

Autonomy crisis

Control crisis

Red Tape crisis

??? crisis

The Greiner curve is a model describing the phases of growth and development for organizations as they mature.

4. **Coordination phase:** In the next phase, the organization must focus on coordinating the increasingly specialized and distinct teams to maintain alignment and achieve key milestones. This process can become overly bureaucratic and filled with red tape.

5. **Collaboration phase:** In the collaboration stage, the final phase of the Greiner curve, the organization seeks to create more interdependencies between the teams to encourage continued innovation to drive continued growth.

Taking a step back, we see in this figure that while in each phase a firm achieves a higher level of scale, there also is a change in the nature of how the firm is managed. Where the earliest phase of a firm is characterized by creativity and fluidity, later phases show a higher level of structure and hierarchy. Critically, the transition between phases is a source of potential crisis. While entrepreneurs or eventually professional managers must make the choice to transition into the next phase, doing so means restructuring the organization, not only in size but in its design and management. This restructuring requires individuals to change their roles and even their relationship to the firm. For example, transitions between phases may result in the departure of early employees who wanted to be involved in a more fluid start-up environment. In the extreme case, the crisis during the transition can lead to the failure of the firm: founders who disagree on the direction for the next stage of the firm may find it difficult to maintain their commitment to that firm.

The Greiner curve also has an impact on the relationships among members of a growing team. When emerging chef David Chang (**Figure 15.5**) sought to scale his wildly popular Momofuku Noodle Bar in New York City by opening

FIGURE 15.5 David Chang of Momofuku

David Chang, chef and founder of the Momofuku restaurant group, received countless accolades from delighted guests and earned James Beard Foundation awards and Michelin stars. He rose to success by blending flavors and techniques from his Korean heritage with seasonal produce and other cuisines.

up new restaurants Momofuku Ssäm Bar and Momofuku Ko in the mid-2000s, he found that the time and attention to the new locations came at the expense of maintaining the quality at the Noodle Bar. Whether it was a new recipe design or how to structure the dining experience at the new restaurants, the choice to open additional venues meant Chang neglected efforts at improvement and training of new employees at the old restaurant. When he visited the Noodle Bar, Chang found that multiple elements of what made the Noodle Bar "special" had begun to erode during his absence; he found his frustration and often visible anger necessitated multiple meetings and interventions, which came at the expense of planning for the new restaurants! While Chang ultimately overcame these growing pains and the Momofuku group has since grown to more than 20 restaurants, the challenges of scaling are often at the heart of some of the most difficult interpersonal conflicts within any growing organization.[15]

THE GROWTH PLAYBOOK

To navigate the Greiner curve, entrepreneurs cannot follow a prespecified growth "recipe" because there are too many differences across start-ups. Instead, entrepreneurs can benefit from the concept of a **growth playbook**, a guide that identifies particular sequences or priority areas to focus on during the growth process. A playbook in principle helps entrepreneurs be systematic in pursuing growth and be more effective in implementing choices.

growth playbook A guide that identifies particular sequences or priority areas to focus on in the growth process

In general, achieving growth in the face of the Greiner curve involves at least three distinct steps.

1. Entrepreneurs must build an organization to test and validate their core value creation and value capture hypotheses. Regardless of how quickly the firm grows, the critical test for the survivability of the firm is its ability to identify a way of creating value for customers and capturing that value on an ongoing basis.

2. Entrepreneurs must start the process of growth in a way that also navigates the inevitable conflicts and challenges of growth. Achieving growth requires not simply replicating the structure of the early organization at a larger scale but fundamentally transforming that organization, including the roles played by the founding team. Not establishing an organization with the potential to scale fundamentally undermines its ability to ever do so.

3. Finally, the organization must have a plan for how to manage growth and how to acquire or build the resources and capabilities needed to grow. Entrepreneurs can only realize their ambitions for growth if they attract the employees, investors, suppliers, and other stakeholders that will help transform their idea into a meaningful reality. This means building the design and culture of the organization in a way that is sustainable.

Each of these steps is challenging, and achieving all three of them is even more so. Key choices in each step are made with relatively little information about the "right" decision and few opportunities to conduct informative experiments or tests. Finally, each step is consequential and involves a significant level of commitment—each choice shapes the direction and identity of the firm.

Perhaps an even bigger challenge is simply prioritizing and sequencing the choices required for growth. Having clarity about which choices are most important and guidance about how to implement them focuses an entrepreneur on those aspects of the organization that are most critical for the growth of the firm. Entrepreneurs who lack knowledge or are confused about how to grow often expend time and attention on choices that may not matter at the expense of choices that are more critical. Paralysis in decision-making, holding off on key choices due to prolonged uncertainty and doubt, and a chaotic environment discourage others from being willing to join, fund, or engage with the firm.

Failing to choose a path to grow can itself lead to the failure of the firm. In a seminal study of start-ups funded by venture capital that ultimately failed to grow, more than 60% of the respondents identified organizational factors as one of the most—if not *the* most—critical factors that led to the firm's failure.[16] A more recent study examined more than 450 venture-backed start-ups, including firms that have grown and those that have not. Those start-ups that lacked structure or were unable to develop a positive culture had a much lower rate of success. For example, companies that failed to develop a formal organizational structure succeeded at less than half the rate of those that implemented a structured organizational design.[17]

Essentially, achieving a structured path toward growth does not occur by accident. Entrepreneurs can take a proactive, strategic approach to growth by using a growth playbook. Playbooks draw on the experience and insights of those who have already attempted to pursue growth, whether they succeeded or failed. Many of the key choices facing founders are common across start-ups. For example, to attract early employees or investors, founders must choose how much equity to allocate to these early stakeholders. While that allocation may be different for different start-ups, entrepreneurs can benefit from understanding decisions that have been made before.

While no single growth playbook has proven effective for all start-up firms, there are nonetheless key insights from leading playbooks that have proven effective in shaping firm growth. Let's look at some particularly influential ones, which differ from each other in one key variable: speed of growth.

STEADY, SUSTAINED GROWTH This is a classic plan of attack built on the idea of establishing success and then growing it over time. An example that shows this approach is the growth of Walmart.

Walmart is currently the largest single private sector employer in the United States (with more than 2 million employees), with a Walmart now within 15 miles of more than 90% of all Americans. Walmart actually began as a single store in Rogers, Arkansas, founded by Sam Walton, who already had more than a decade's worth of experience in founding and managing retail stores in small towns. Walton perceived that, relative to the variety stores and department stores dominant at the time (such as J. C. Penney and Sears), there was an opportunity for discount stores to thrive by focusing less on the margin on any individual item and more on the volume of sales achieved across the widest variety of items. While the potential for a discounting strategy is likely highest once a retailer has achieved significant scale and can negotiate significant volume discounts, Walton nonetheless experimented with a discount-focused strategy with only a single, relatively small store. For example, he found that aggressive pricing on specific items (such as ladies' underwear at four for a dollar) might attract customers to the store, who would then be enticed to purchase a wider range of items as long as all items were of high quality but priced on a competitive basis. While other discount retailers were able to grow, and both Woolco and Kmart actually grew more quickly than Walmart in the early years, the persistent and long-term growth of Walmart ultimately overshadowed all its physical retail competitors (**Figure 15.6**).

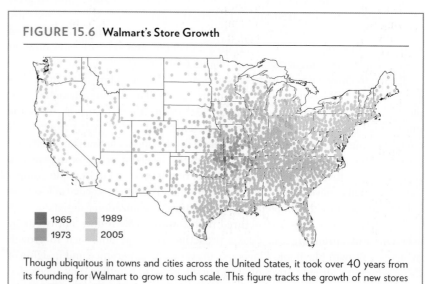

FIGURE 15.6 **Walmart's Store Growth**

■ 1965 ■ 1989
■ 1973 ■ 2005

Though ubiquitous in towns and cities across the United States, it took over 40 years from its founding for Walmart to grow to such scale. This figure tracks the growth of new stores across these four decades.

SOURCE: Emek Basker, "The Causes and Consequences of Wal-Mart's Growth," *Journal of Economic Perspectives* 21, no. 3 (2007): 177–98.

FIGURE 15.7 Amazon's Employee Growth

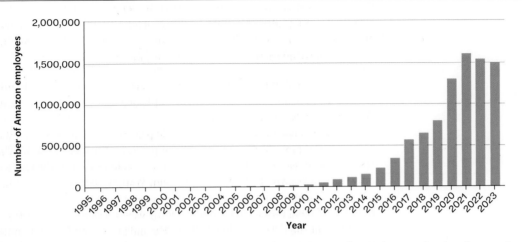

By 2020, Amazon had built an organization of over 1 million employees, reflective of more than two decades of sustained growth. During that time, Amazon expanded its team, built new capabilities (e.g., Lab126), and acquired established organizations (e.g., Zappos, Whole Foods).

SOURCE: Harry McCracken, "Amazon's Wild 24-Year Ride, from 11 Employees to 600,000-Plus," *Fast Company*, April 11, 2019, https://www.fastcompany.com/90331689/amazons-wild-24-year-ride-from-11-employees-to-600000-plus.

By the mid-2000s, Walmart earned annual revenues of more than $300 billion, nearly 10% of all retail workers in the United States worked at a Walmart, and Walmart alone accounted for nearly 15% of Chinese imports into the United States. Importantly, while Walmart has continued to grow and nearly double in size from the early 2000s to 2020, its relative dominance has ebbed. Amazon, founded in 1994, has followed a similar playbook and has been able to maintain a persistent growth rate in sales and employment, growing from fewer than 10,000 employees in the early 2000s to more than 1,200,000 employees in 2020. It challenges Walmart for retail leadership in the United States and abroad (**Figure 15.7**).

Both Walmart and Amazon chose steadier paths for growth. For Walmart, it was physical outlet by physical outlet. For Amazon, it was product vertical by product vertical. In each case, they used past experience to work out the kinks to have successful rollouts in the future. The trade-off, however, is that the pace of scaling was actually slower than the unbalanced model many start-ups choose for rapid growth.

NAIL IT THEN SCALE IT Developed by Nathan Furr and Paul Ahlstrom, this idea emphasizes the importance of first testing and validating the key hypotheses for value creation and value capture at a small scale before pursuing the resources and capabilities required to scale that solution more broadly. The "Nail It Then Scale It" playbook focuses founders on a single market or customer segment to test whether the underlying idea and solution are viable, and to experiment and develop an organization for value delivery. It is only when entrepreneurs have identified a repeatable business model—a reliable system for generating revenue and delivering value to customers—that they should devote time and attention to the process of scaling more broadly.

Consider OpenTable, first introduced in Chapter 4. While the basic concept behind OpenTable was straightforward (enabling diners to make online reservations with the restaurant of their choice in the local area), implementing this idea was more challenging. Founder Chuck Templeton and his team went through an extensive process of experimentation to find ways of delivering meaningful value for restaurants before they would adopt OpenTable for customer reservations. Focusing on just a handful of cities and restaurants at first, Templeton discovered that a practical online reservation system must also synchronize the seating and staffing plans for restaurants. With this insight in hand, and after developing software and a small team that could do so, OpenTable was then able to rapidly expand to most major cities in the United States, with adoption by leading restaurants and a critical mass of patrons. The idea of Nail It Then Scale It prioritizes meaningful exploration and experimentation at the earliest stages, only turning to growth after core challenges have been resolved.

BLITZSCALING LinkedIn founder Reid Hoffman (**Figure 15.8**) has long emphasized the importance of "blitzscaling," the idea of trying to scale more rapidly than competitors.

While there are many benefits of an approach that prioritizes steady, sustained growth, blitzscaling prioritizes speed over efficiency to move from a successful entrant to market maker. Undertaken with the intention to either win the market or fail trying, blitzscaling, as coined by Hoffman, involves developing an organizational capability for execution and evolution in the face of considerable uncertainty. Hoffman scaled PayPal as COO and its "firefighter-in-chief," cofounded and scaled LinkedIn as its CEO through its acquisition by Microsoft, and has advised companies such as Airbnb and Flickr as an investor. He tells

---

FIGURE 15.8 Reid Hoffman

Reid Hoffman, a successful entrepreneur and adviser, has long advocated that start-ups should scale with speed as a priority.

entrepreneurs that they need to "accept the risk of making the wrong decision and willingly pay the cost of significant operating inefficiencies in exchange for the ability to move faster" because the "cost of being too slow is greater."[18] While many a scaling playbook focuses exclusively on "hacks" for customer and revenue growth, blitzscaling also focuses on the organizational growth required to deliver those results. Similar in nature to the Greiner curve, blitzscaling views the organization as evolving through key stages that require distinct management styles and organizational forms that prioritize growth of different areas of the organizations. Simple processes guide decision-making such as hiring, and leaders ignore at least temporarily broken processes and routines that are not essential to achieving the next steps along the pathway to growth. As Hoffman describes it, "If classic start-up growth is about slowing your rate of descent as you try to assemble your plane, blitzscaling is about assembling that plane faster, then strapping on and igniting a set of jet engines (and possibly their afterburners) while you're still building the wings."

USING WHAT'S AVAILABLE

Growth playbooks provide founders with guidance about how to focus their scarce time and effort. But the most fundamental constraint on growth for most firms is that they have little access to the resources and capabilities required to grow. When a founding team lacks the wide set of resources and capabilities that they will need to scale, that founding team can simply focus first on what's available: the resources and capabilities that are the *most* accessible in terms of time, effort, and complexity. Rather than needing to articulate a complete growth strategy, a start-up team can instead focus on what is at hand to see if they can validate their core idea and hypotheses. This process of improvising based on what is available—known as bricolage—means focusing on the resources and capabilities abundant in the local environment and using what is available to overcome challenges that require costly or hard-to-obtain resources. Empirical researchers have evaluated the extent to which firms undertake bricolage and have found that running these types of local, exploratory experiments using what's available is connected to the degree to which a young firm is able to innovate and grow.

15.8 Concluding Thoughts

The choice to grow a venture is not an abstract choice but is instead grounded in choosing to expand specific resources and capabilities or adopt a particular organizational approach or culture (see **Putting It Together: Scaling**). The timing, nature, and extent of that growth are grounded in the choice by the founding team to pursue it to realize their vision and ambitions for their venture. Even when they agree about the need for growth, they might disagree about exactly how to pursue that opportunity (and which potential paths to leave behind). A more technical cofounder might be interested in prioritizing the development of technology, while a more marketing-oriented cofounder might be interested in directing the scarce resources of the firm to bring the current technology to market. Neither of these perspectives is right or wrong but instead reflects

SCALING

New ventures don't just grow on their own but do so because of proactive choices and actions.

GROWTH IS A CHOICE

Consider the Benefits of Scale

- Weigh the benefits and trade-offs of growth. Describe how scale will allow you to achieve your objectives for the venture and entrepreneurship.
- Identify the key learning required to prepare to scale. Generate opportunities to experiment, test, and learn along these dimensions from activities that do not scale.
- Specify key resources and capabilities required to scale, including hiring new employees, building new teams, adding new investors, or developing the supply chain.

CONFRONT THE CHALLENGES OF GROWTH

Map Out Key Constraints of Scaling Your Entrepreneurial Strategy

- Consider the consequences of balancing growth with the ongoing activities of your early-stage start-up. Identify which aspects of the business you'll need to focus on for growth, including identifying key hires, structures, or routines necessary to prioritize those aspects of the business. Briefly describe how these activities might constrain other key aspects of the business.
- Describe how the early choices you make in choosing your entrepreneurial strategy will imprint on the organization for long-term viability and growth. Identify any early-stage organizational choices that may be no longer appropriate for growth.
- Evaluate how the founding team's position and power within the organization will likely evolve as the venture draws on the resources and capabilities of others, builds scale, and establishes a successful ongoing venture.

MAKE A PROACTIVE CHOICE

Translate Your Idea to Impact

- Indicate how alternative growth playbooks align with your objectives as an entrepreneur and confront the challenges of scaling the entrepreneurial venture you have identified.
- List key steps to build and reshape the venture to achieve the next stage in its growth. Make a proactive choice to move your venture forward.

differences among the founding team in how they would like to grow the firm. In each case, the growth of the organization involves choosing what to commit to (for example, to focus on hiring R&D workers versus salespeople) and what organizational goals and associated structures to prioritize (such as providing rewards for long-term innovation or short-term revenue).

Ultimately, however, the choice to grow is choosing the route for commercialization along a given path. The balance, imprinting, and power challenges require the founding team to direct their attention away from current operations to iteratively build and reshape the organization to achieve the next stage in its growth. In so doing, they must confront the impact they want to create from the venture and their very role in creating that impact.

Chapter 15 Review: Scaling

CHAPTER TAKEAWAYS

- Building for scale often involves first doing activities that seemingly are not scalable. Learning from these activities can better enable the founding team to prepare for growth and scale these activities.

- After successfully implementing an entrepreneurial strategy, an entrepreneur must make an active choice to scale. Choosing to scale only occurs when the founding team makes choices to grow, such as hiring new employees, seeking new investors, or building out an element of their supply chain.

- The Penrose effect states that for business growth, managerial and resource constraints tend to be limiting factors. This implies that there are brakes on a business's growth rate.

- The law of (almost) proportional growth notes that the potential for firm growth at a moment in time tends to be on a percentage basis of the current size of the firm, as the growth of the firm is enabled (and as a result, constrained) by the existing resources and capabilities of the venture.

- In order to effectively grow, the organization must confront three challenges: the balance challenge, the imprinting challenge, and the power challenge.

- The balance challenge: The founding and early team must balance the ongoing activities of the venture with the activities required to grow. This is a profoundly unbalanced process, often temporarily requiring prioritizing one aspect of the business over another and thereby straining other aspects of the venture.

- The imprinting challenge: The early choices the founding team made in choosing and testing their entrepreneurial strategy establish a foundation for the organization to grow and often have a long-term impact on the evolution of the venture as it scales.

- The power challenge: As the venture grows and draws upon the capabilities and resources of others, the choices the founding team makes shape the power structure within their organization and their own position within that structure.

- A consequence of these challenges is mapped in the Greiner curve. Each distinct phase of growth involves a higher level of scale, accompanied by distinct leadership challenges and requiring a change in the nature of how the firm is organized and managed.

- Growth playbooks help firms understand ways that they can grow. They are a guide that identifies particular sequences or priority areas to focus on in the growth process. Three popular ones are Steady, Sustained Growth; Nail It Then Scale It; and Blitzscaling.

KEY TERMS

scale (p. 424)
Penrose effect (p. 427)
the law of (almost) proportional
   growth (p. 428)

balance (p. 433)
power structure (p. 437)
growth playbook (p. 440)

REVIEW QUESTIONS

1. In 2013, Melanie Perkins and her cofounders built on the niche market success of Fusion Books to build Canva as an online tool "empowering the world to design" (see chapter introduction). What are three concrete actions Perkins and her team took that enabled Canva to grow?

2. Less than 25% of all entrepreneurs report having a goal of scaling their venture. What are three motives an entrepreneur might prioritize that would lead them to choose *not* to scale?

3. In your own words, describe the law of (almost) proportional growth. Why does the Penrose effect imply that firm growth might be (on average) proportional to the current size of a firm?

4. Why is it difficult for ventures to grow in a balanced manner?

5. Consider the findings from the Stanford Project on Emerging Companies (SPEC; see "The Imprinting Challenge"). According to the SPEC data, when founders depart their start-up and are replaced by a new CEO, the new CEO is able to rapidly eliminate any "imprint" of the original founders on the organization. Briefly describe the underlying scaling challenges that result in the findings observed in the SPEC data.

6. Describe the "paradox of success" and its effect on the power structure and growth of a venture.

7. In your own words, describe the first three phases of the Greiner curve. How does the crisis at the transition of each of these phases reflect tensions described in the balance challenge, the imprinting challenge, and the power challenge?

8. What are the key recommendations of growth playbooks such as Nail It Then Scale It and Blitzscaling? What are the key differences in the advice these playbooks would offer?

DISCUSSION QUESTIONS

Answer the following series of questions and scenarios either in class discussions or by writing a short response.

1. Erik has launched an event management platform, automating processes for event planning so that they take minutes rather than hours. He has successfully implemented the first stages of his entrepreneurial strategy, creating a valuable offering that allows couples to efficiently coordinate their wedding venue and vendors. As he and a few early team members have grown their operation in Ontario, Canada, they have each filled many different roles in the organization: manually onboarding new venues, adding and automating new features, and providing real-time customer support to couples facing all types of wedding hiccups (and the occasional disasters!). Despite not marketing in neighboring Quebec, Erik and his team have received a number of inbound requests from couples and venues in the region to join the platform. Erik is excited to start scaling and has visions of serving all of North America. However, the team is overwhelmed by the current demand, and their nights and weekends are taxed providing customer support, leaving little time to build out the platform, feature-wise or geographically. Prepare two alternative recommendations as to how Erik should proceed. What are the trade-offs to these alternative paths to scale?

2. Anita, a software engineer, and Ishaan, a recent MBA, have successfully launched an online platform for personalized skin-care products. At the time of founding, the pair decide to separate engineering and marketing activities so that each can work most efficiently in building their business. As the company starts to grow, they increasingly find that there is poor communication across the two teams and, as a result, poor alignment between the needs of the market and the capabilities of the platform. The venture, which started as a pioneer in the space, is quickly being overtaken by competitors. Ishaan believes the two teams need to be integrated and restructured to recapture the innovative spark they achieved in the early days of the platform. Anita is concerned this will reduce the agility that has allowed them to experiment and iterate quickly. What might be some of the challenges in integrating the two teams? How might the founders' roles be affected by this transition? How can the founders counter inertia and resistance to these changes?

3. Uber, a pioneer in the rideshare industry, was founded in 2009 by Garrett Camp and Travis Kalanick; they first launched their service in San Francisco in 2010. By 2013, the company had expanded across the United States and begun an aggressive international expansion campaign. In each market, the start-up famously "sought forgiveness rather than permission" in navigating around local regulations and the existing taxi industry while the founding team worked to shape regulation in the emerging rideshare industry. Internally, they developed a "win at all costs" culture to achieve these results. What were the benefits and trade-offs of taking this approach to reach rapid international scale? How might this "win at all costs" culture manifest in other areas of the organization? In what ways might it be difficult to change this cultural imprint even after the early team departs?

4. Many start-ups often appear to be overnight success stories. However, as we saw in the chapter, even Walmart and Amazon took decades of sustained growth to achieve their impressive scale. Select a start-up from your university or region that has achieved scale and map their growth. What choices have been instrumental to achieving growth? What key resources and capabilities did they add as they grew? How has their top management team and organization transformed during these periods of growth?

5. Experimentation and learning are key to a strategic approach to entrepreneurship. How does the nature of the hypotheses tested, experiments conducted, and opportunity costs expended evolve from early opportunity exploration, entrepreneurial strategy choice and development, and scaling?

6. In his book *The Founder's Dilemmas*, Noam Wasserman says that founders must choose whether to be "rich" or be "king." What type of leader do you think each of these represents? Describe the implications of each choice on the potential for founder control and venture growth. Why might it be difficult to maintain control and achieve growth?

SUGGESTED READINGS

Brown, Shona L., and Kathleen M. Eisenhardt. "The Art of Continuous Change: Linking Complexity Theory and Time-Paced Evolution in Relentlessly Shifting Organizations." *Administrative Science Quarterly* 42, no. 1 (1997): 1–34.

DeSantola, Alicia, and Ranjay Gulati. "Scaling: Organizing and Growth in Entrepreneurial Ventures." *Academy of Management Annals* 11, no. 2 (2017): 640–68.

Eisenmann, Thomas R., and Alison Berkley Wagonfeld. "Scaling a Startup: People and Organizational Issues." Harvard Business School Entrepreneurial Management Case No. 812-100, February 23, 2012.

Furr, Nathan R., Fabrice Cavaretta, and Sam Garg. "Who Changes Course? The Role of Domain Knowledge and Novel Framing in Making Technology Changes." *Strategic Entrepreneurship Journal* 6, no. 3 (2012): 236–56.

Graham, Paul. "Things That Don't Scale." *Paul Graham* (personal website), July 2013. http://paulgraham.com/ds.html.

Greiner, Larry E. "Evolution and Revolution as Organizations Grow." *Harvard Business Review* 50 (1972): 37–46.

Hannan, Michael T., M. Diane Burton, and James N. Baron. "Inertia and Change in the Early Years: Employment Relations in Young, High Technology Firms." *Industrial and Corporate Change* 5 (1996): 503–36.

Hoffman, Reid, and Chris Yeh. *Blitzscaling: The Lightning-Fast Path to Building Massively Valuable Companies*. New York: Crown, 2018.

Marx, Matt, Joshua S. Gans, and David H. Hsu. "Dynamic Commercialization Strategies for Disruptive Technologies: Evidence from the Speech Recognition Industry." *Management Science* 60, no. 12 (2014): 3103–23.

McDonald, Rory, and Cheng Gao. "Pivoting Isn't Enough? Managing Strategic Reorientation in New Ventures." *Organization Science* 30, no. 6 (2019): 1289–318.

Pleasant Rowland

The American Girl line of dolls, introduced in Chapter 12, was the brainchild of Pleasant Rowland. Rowland had been a teacher, TV news anchor, and textbook writer for two decades before she founded the company that brought American Girl dolls to the market in 1986. It was on a visit to Colonial Williamsburg that she had the idea that girls might become more interested in history if they could identify with dolls who came from different times. Soon after, she wrote out her vision and became convinced that, as an idea, it was compelling—simply because she would have loved the dolls as a child and, as an adult, she would love to give them to children. Though perhaps an unlikely entrepreneur, Rowland's instincts were strong and pushed her forward despite skepticism (Rowland once summarized initial reactions as "Are you kidding? Historical dolls in the day and age of Barbie?"[a]).

More than a vision, Rowland had clarity on the product features required to create value for children and adults alike as well as the team and capabilities needed to consistently deliver that value. The dolls Rowland envisaged were expensive ($82 then) and too large for toy and department stores to stock them. She wanted them to be cherished items so children would really become invested in them. But in a toy industry used to selling cheaper products on a mass scale, implementing that vision would require a distinct retailing approach. So, in that pre-Internet era, Rowland chose to sell them herself through a catalog; this allowed her to structure the marketing of the dolls around her historical vision. "From its inception, it was a doll company, a toy company, a clothing company, a publishing company, and a direct mail company all at once," Rowland said at a 25th anniversary celebration.[b] "But in truth, from its beginning vision, it was a company that was bigger than the sum of all those parts. It was a girl company, and anything that was good for girls, was ours to give them."[c] The product was an immediate success, with $1 million in sales that year. But, something that is extremely rare in toy markets, it was an enduring success and a brand that would continue to grow over the next three decades.

Walk into an American Girl Place or visit its website and you know very quickly who its target customer is: kids. It is a vast retail space where a kid can find a doll that looks like them, clothes for the doll, matching clothes for the kid, accessories for both, a place to get their hair done (yes, both kid and doll), and also a place to take tea. There are also books that place each doll in some American historical context. And not just mild stories, but stories that involve poverty, hardship, racism, child abuse, and war.

Rowland built that foundation, and then in 1998 she opened her visionary stores and sold the company to Mattel for $700 million the same year.

Questions

1. As Pleasant Rowland was recruiting her early team, what capabilities would she need to build in the organization to design, develop, and sell these historical dolls and their stories through a catalog? What functional areas should she have prioritized first? Why?

2. In 1998, when Rowland chose to further grow American Girls and launch the American Girl stores, what additional resources and capabilities would she have needed to recruit and build? What were the advantages and disadvantages of partnering with Mattel to grow? What other routes were available to American Girl? How should Rowland have decided which route to pursue?

GLOSSARY

balance Favoring all aspects of the business equally; for example, maintaining the ongoing activities of the venture while also focusing on growing in the organization for the future and not pursuing one at the expense of the other

beachhead customers The very first potential customers for a new product or service

bootstrap financing Investing the revenues that are in excess of direct costs of serving early customers

branding A company image and reputation that customers associate with its products

bridge financing Often comes in the form of a loan between two formal rounds of equity financing and can fund experiments that inform the next step of strategic choice

business model Builds upon a venture's strategy to describe how it will make money in an ongoing way

business risk The probability of several business outcomes occurring, especially the risk of failure

cannibalization A market dynamic where a company's new product competes with an older product, resulting in a loss of sales and profits; can also happen when a competitor's product replaces a company's product or service

capabilities In business, what a firm is able to do

choice-based approach An approach to entrepreneurship focused on identifying choices and opportunities first, and then actively making choices about these potential entrepreneurial paths

choice challenge A problem that occurs when a venture has many options to consider, but also tight constraints on how many options can reasonably be explored

combinatorial innovation The arrangement of different technological elements in a novel way

commercialization The process by which a new product, service, or platform is brought to market

competitive strategy The series of choices a business makes in order to gain and sustain a competitive advantage, that is, conditions that allow it to control scarce resources or offer unique product offerings in a market

competitor A firm that provides a similar product or service (or otherwise solves the same or similar customer need) to a start-up's chosen customer

complementary assets Existing processes, resources, and capabilities that are required to commercialize an idea, deliver value from it, and move it to market

constrained In entrepreneurship, the idea that you have limited resources to draw on, especially financial, that limit what an entrepreneur can do

copyright An official protection that provides the holder exclusive right to reproduce a certain work as well as prepare derivative works, distribute copies, perform publicly, or display publicly

core idea The fundamental entrepreneurial opportunity and insight that a venture will be built on

coring A process that creates the framework describing the central idea and interactions of the platform

creative destruction The act of creating new innovations that upend established firms and markets

customer Any person, group, or organization who will pay a business money for any of its goods or services

customer (IP strategy) Customer considerations for the IP strategy include determining who the final end customers are who will gain value from the idea and who the established firms are that are willing to pay to provide that defined value

customer acquisition cost (CAC) The total amount of money a company spends to gain a new customer

Customer Adoption Lifecycle The breakdown of market adoption patterns into five customer types: innovators, early adopters, early majority, late majority, and laggards

disclosure problem The risk the entrepreneur faces that to sell an idea, a buyer needs to see it; but after disclosing the idea, the buyer no longer needs to pay for it

disrupter A venture or company that causes fundamental change through innovation, moving into poorly served areas and reinforcing their value to customers through iterative learning

domains of choice Areas in which entrepreneurs will be faced with the need to make decisions, including customers, technology, organization, and competition

early adopters The first customers to adopt a new technology or service who may be characterized as application enthusiasts; seeking a revolution; demanding but collaborative

economic choice A decision made to pursue one path of action over another after analyzing the relative benefits of each

economies of scale When a firm can achieve a lower average cost through an increase in the overall quantity produced

economies of scale and scope When a firm can achieve a lower average cost through an increase in the overall quantity produced of a single good, or by producing two or more things together at a cheaper cost than separately

effectual reasoning A set of five key principles by which entrepreneurs make early venture decisions, centered on the means that an entrepreneur can use to build opportunities

entrepreneur A person who forms, pursues, and turns their business idea or product into a reality

entrepreneurial experimentation A systematic process in which an entrepreneur "tests" a plan with potential ways to create and capture value from an idea

entrepreneurial hypothesis A *new* way to create and capture value that others have yet to implement successfully

entrepreneurial opportunity The set of circumstances that allows a potential founder to create and capture value by establishing a new business

entrepreneurial path A plan or way for an entrepreneur to execute and ideally succeed with their idea

entrepreneurial strategy A practical and systematic framework of the core choices that entrepreneurs make to translate ideas into a reality

exploitation The second stage of a technology S curve, a focus on what is available in the short term, making use of existing technological solutions

exploration The first stage of a technology S curve, a focus on the long term and emerging technological options

firm boundaries Limits that set the responsibilities and activities of a firm in a value chain

fixed fee A licensing agreement that specifies a set amount the licensee will pay the patent holder, either as an up-front payment or in a predetermined payment schedule

functional focus Where a venture decides it will make a clear investment in specific capabilities within a business area to create value

fundamental uncertainty A challenge around whether an entrepreneur is realistically conceptualizing business scenarios around their idea

growth playbook A guide that identifies particular sequences or priority areas to focus on in the growth process

head-to-head competition Two firms directly competing for the same customer base with similar products or services

hypothesis A testable assumption for solving or addressing a particular problem or opportunity

ideas factory A place where new ideas are conceived and developed to become complementary innovations for established firms

imprinting The idea that the identity, passion, and early decisions of founders have an outsized impact on the overall evolution of the venture

individual-opportunity nexus The closely connected relationship between a specific opportunity and an individual

inherent value A customer's worth to an organization, derived from their willingness to pay for a start-up's products and/or services

innovation Where new ideas or change are brought to an existing product, idea, or firm; a new product or way of doing something that improves on what was previously available

innovation diffusion The process of how new ideas and technologies spread among customers and markets

innovation-driven enterprises (IDEs) Businesses formed to leverage a specific innovation, such as a new business model or technology, but which often require specialized expertise and external funding

integrative capabilities A company's ability to work and fit with complementary and available resources

integrative focus Where a business does not make any particular function high performing but aims to make the functions themselves work together in a coordinated and effective manner

intellectual property (IP) Creations of the mind, such as inventions; literary and artistic works; designs; and symbols, names, and images used in commerce

intellectual property strategy (IP strategy) A start-up strategy invested in controlling its technology while collaborating with established firms to create value for these firms' final consumers, IP strategy must create value for the end customers of existing firms while also maintaining control and bargaining power for the start-up after disclosing its idea

investment capital Investments made to fund business activities to build products or offer services; these come when ventures are turning their choices into reality

the law of (almost) proportional growth Because firm growth is enabled by existing resources and capabilities, a firm's growth potential at a moment in time depends at least in part on the size and age of that firm at that moment in time

learning challenge The difficulty an entrepreneur faces in learning as much as possible about each potential path before moving forward

the liability of newness The theory that young firms are more likely to fail because entrepreneurs lack essential knowledge or financial acumen as well as the structure, routines, personal relationships, and culture required for their organizations to function effectively

lifetime value (LTV) Estimates the total net profit a company can expect to generate from a customer throughout their entire relationship with the business

linkages The underlying connections formed between each of the four elements of your entrepreneurial strategy

market S curve A graph that shows the slow initial traction gained by a new product or service that is followed by a period of quicker gains before a final tapering off

maturity The final stage of a technology S curve where there are diminishing returns due to the fundamental limits of the technology

moat A start-up's competitive advantage that allows it to capture value at a rate higher than its competitors, and then protect and maintain the advantage

network effects When value for a product depends on other people's use of the product, and vice versa

noneconomic goal A goal not related to the economic outcome of a given venture

organization A larger, more formal, and less personal group, such as a business or school, set up with specific objectives in mind

outsource Obtaining a good or service through an outside supplier, in place of obtaining one from this in-house

paradox of entrepreneurship The process of learning and experimentation at the early stage of a start-up to choose a path forward that inevitably results in some level of commitment that closes off other strategic options

patent An official grant of rights that excludes other from making, using, offering for sale, or selling an invention with a county or importing into the country

Penrose effect The fact that as businesses grow, managerial and resource constraints tend to be a limiting factor

platform design The means by which a firm organizes groups of users so they can interact with each other through the platform and realize value from their interactions

power structure The hierarchy of power defined by an entrepreneur in order to best allocate the time and resources of other people throughout their organization

price plus percent A licensing agreement in which the licensee pays both an up-front fee (the price) plus a percentage of future sales

proprietary The legal right of a company to be the sole owner of a given type of technology

real options approach An approach where an entrepreneur gives themselves choices or options to make or abandon an investment

resources Assets that your organization is able to control or potentially access when needed

risk capital Investments made with the intention of being speculative and forward thinking, but also with the expectation of high reward

scale In entrepreneurship, when a business is adding revenue faster than it is adding costs

self-employment A form of individual entrepreneurship, including (but not limited to) gig workers, freelancers, independent salespeople, and specialized consultants

small and medium enterprises (SMEs) Businesses focused on solving well-defined problems with well-established solutions in their local market, with less uncertainty and well-understood risks

social entrepreneurship A business venture that combines a sustainable business model with the creation of broader social value

specialized system An interface or process that is created uniquely for a particular venture

strategic value The added value of some particular customers who prove more useful than others because they can unlock broader market segments

strategy The combination of elements that make up the four key choices underlying an entrepreneurial opportunity: customer, technology, organization, and competition

subsistence entrepreneurship The most common form of entrepreneurship, pursued as an alternative to traditional employment opportunities

technological disruption Establishing leadership in a market using technological innovation

technological innovation Value created that comes from reducing costs or producing a product or service that has not yet been brought to the marketplace at scale

technological trajectory A technological trajectory is the path of innovation in a specific field; can also be defined as a branch in the evolution of a product or service's technological design

technology The application of scientific innovation to a product or venture

technology (IP strategy) The choice of general components that fit in easily with technologies used in existing value chains

Test Two, Choose One A process in which entrepreneurs commit to only one business plan after considering multiple strategic alternatives and identifying at least two that are commercially viable yet difficult to rank

tipping The actions or features that will push, or "tip," a customer's decision to use a platform in your favor and away from a competitor

total addressable market (TAM) The overall revenue potential or market size for a particular product or service

trademark A word, phrase, symbol, and/or design that identifies and distinguishes the source of the goods of one party from those of others

trade secret Valuable proprietary information that a business wants to protect from being disclosed, including things like formulas, patterns, devices, methods, techniques, and processes

uncertainty The belief that the outcome of business decisions cannot truly be predicted or modeled

unique value The value provided either by improving an existing level of performance or a new dimension of performance that is poorly served by existing offerings

value capture The ability to realize personal value (financial and otherwise) from establishing and operating a new enterprise

value chain A process or activity where value is added to a product across sequence of stages

value creation Making customers better off via the product, platform, or service that is offered

value creation and capture hypotheses Hypotheses that frame the entire emphasis of your venture, drawing a clear, logical line describing what must be true for your venture to succeed

venture capital Equity raised to provide financing to start-ups and small businesses that investors believe have long-term growth potential

window of opportunity A time when a venture can explore an emerging opportunity that established firms may dismiss or discount

NOTES

CHAPTER 1

1. Sebastian Bron, "Is Cactus the New Coconut? Hamilton Native Pitches Fledging Prickly-Pear Beverage on 'Shark Tank,'" *Hamilton Spectator*, June 13, 2022, https://www.thespec.com /business/is-cactus-the-new-coconut-hamilton-native-pitches -fledging-prickly-pear-beverage-on-shark-tank/article_cb2fc426 -7f3b-5407-8b9d-ea5b505bab48.html.
2. Sergey Brin and Lawrence Page, "The Anatomy of a Large-Scale Hypertextual Web Search Engine," *Computer Networks and ISDN System* 30, no. 1–7 (April 1998): 107–17, https://doi .org/10.1016/S0169-7552(98)00110-X.
3. Jenna Wortham, "A Netflix Model for Haute Couture," *New York Times*, November 9, 2009, https://www.nytimes .com/2009/11/09/technology/09runway.html.
4. David Kindy, "The Accidental Invention of the Super Soaker," *Smithsonian Magazine*, June 21, 2019, https://www .smithsonianmag.com/innovation/accidental-invention -super-soaker-180972428.
5. Brian VanHooker, "The Oral History of the Super Soaker," *MEL*, July 20, 2020, https://melmagazine.com/en-us/story /super-soaker-oral-history.
6. Jordan Zakarin, "How Lonnie Johnson Invented the Super Soaker," *Biography*, January 26, 2021, https://www.biography .com/news/lonnie-johnson-invent-super-soaker.
7. Lonnie Johnson, "Lonnie Johnson: The Father of the Super Soaker," interviewed by William Kremer, *BBC News*, August 15, 2016, https://www.bbc.com/news/magazine-37062579; and Justin Wm. Moyer and Fred Barbash, "How a Black Inventor Beat the Odds to Create the Super Soaker," *Washington Post*, November 6, 2015, https://www.washingtonpost.com/news /morning-mix/wp/2015/11/06/how-a-black-inventor-beat -the-odds-to-create-the-super-soaker-just-inducted-in-the -toy-hall-of-fame/.

Mini Case: Paradox of Entrepreneurship

a. Ken Zurski, "Charles Mintz: Walt Disney, the Early Shorts, and 'Oswald the Lucky Rabbit,'" *Unremembered*, updated May 19, 2017, https://unrememberedhistory.com/tag/charles-mintz.
b. Sotheby's, "'It All Started with a Mouse'—90 Years of Mickey the Icon," accessed January 26, 2023, https://www.sothebys .com/en/articles/it-all-started-with-a-mouse-disney.

Using the Research: The Benefits of Systematizing Mentorship

a. For a description of the Creative Destruction Lab process, see Karim R. Lakhani, Hong Luo, and Laura Katsnelson, "Market for Judgement: Creative Destruction Laboratory," Harvard Business School Case 719-479, revised June 2020, https:// www.hbs.edu/faculty/Pages/item.aspx?num=55676.

Sidebar: Supergoop!

a. EY, "Entrepreneur of the Year US National Overall Award Winners," accessed June 26, 2023, https://www.ey.com/en_us /entrepreneur-of-the-year/molly-thaggard-amanda-baldwin -supergoop.

Case: Doorbot

a. Eric Beato, "Jamie Siminoff '99 and the Power of Entrepreneurial Thinking," Babson Thought & Action, April 19, 2021, https:// entrepreneurship.babson.edu/jamie-siminoff-commencement.
b. Entrepreneur, "The Origin Story of Ring," April 9, 2020, You-Tube video (*How Brands Are Born with Kristen Aldridge*), 07:51, https://www.youtube.com/watch?v=7tIVhl0cetw.
c. Jamie Siminoff, "The History behind Ring," Ring, September 26, 2014, https://blog.ring.com/about-ring/scrappy-dedicated -humbled-proud-and-excited-the-history-behind-ring.
d. Shark Tank Global, "Sharks Struggle to Understand Doorbot's Value," April 15, 2022 (*Shark Tank*, season 5, episode 9, aired November 15, 2013), YouTube video, 09:42, https://www .youtube.com/watch?v=um-iVXiXedc.
e. Jamie Siminoff, "First, I Lost on 'Shark Tank.' Then, I Sold My Startup for Over $1 Billion," interviewed by Emily Canal, *Inc.*, July/August 2018, https://www.inc.com/magazine /201808/emily-canal/how-i-did-it-jamie-siminoff-ring .html.

f. Minda Zetlin, "Amazon Just Bought Video Doorbell Company Ring for $1 Billion—5 Years after It Failed on 'Shark Tank,'" *Inc.*, February 28, 2018, https://www.inc.com/minda-zetlin/amazon-just-bought-video-doorbell-company-ring-for-1-billion-5-years-after-it-failed-on-shark-tank.html.

CHAPTER 2

1. Grace Bluerock, "24 Quotes on Success from Oprah Winfrey," *Entrepreneur*, January 29, 2016, https://www.entrepreneur.com/article/269979.

2. Ed Pilkington, "The Secretive World of Oprah Winfrey," *Guardian*, April 16, 2010, https://www.theguardian.com/tv-and-radio/2010/apr/17/secretive-world-oprah-winfrey.

3. "Our Brand Story," The Body Shop, accessed February 13, 2023, https://www.thebodyshop.com/en-us/about-us/our-story/a/a00002.

4. "About Us," accessed February 13, 2023, https://www.misfitsmarket.com/about-us.

5. Tristan L. Botelho, Daniel Fehder, and Yael Hochberg, "Innovation-Driven Entrepreneurship," NBER Working Paper, July 2021, https://www.nber.org/papers/w28990.

6. William Aulet and Fiona Murray, "A Tale of Two Entrepreneurs: Understanding Differences in the Types of Entrepreneurship in the Economy," SSRN, updated October 8, 2013, https://ssrn.com/abstract=2259740 or http://dx.doi.org/10.2139/ssrn.2259740.

7. "The State of Small Businesses Now," U.S. Chamber of Commerce, April 10, 2023, https://www.uschamber.com/small-business/state-of-small-business-now.

8. Aulet and Murray, "Tale of Two Entrepreneurs."

9. Kyle Stock and Venessa Wong, "Chipotle: The Definitive Oral History," Bloomberg, February 2, 2015, https://www.bloomberg.com/graphics/2015-chipotle-oral-history/.

10. Tom Eisenmann, "Entrepreneurship: A Working Definition," *Harvard Business Review*, January 10, 2013, https://hbr.org/2013/01/what-is-entrepreneurship#:~:text=It%20was%20formulated%20by%20Professor,a%20short%20window%20of%20opportunity; and Peter Cohan, "Harvard's Lion of Entrepreneurship Packs Up His Office," *Forbes*, June 15, 2011, https://www.forbes.com/sites/petercohan/2011/06/15/harvards-lion-of-entrepreneurship-packs-up-his-office/?sh=440893554e89.

11. Daniel Roberts and Kacy Burdette, "The History of an Iconic Sports Beverage: Gatorade Turns 50," *Fortune*, October 1, 2015, https://fortune.com/2015/10/01/gatorade-turns-50.

12. Christine Lagorio-Chafkin, "ClassPass Was a Beautiful Website and a Cool Company—with No Users or Investors. Here's How the Founder Turned It Around," *Inc.*, July 5, 2019, https://www.inc.com/christine-lagorio/classpass-payal-kadakia-fitness-founders-project.html.

13. Rob LaFranco and Chase Peterson-Withorn, eds., "The 400 Richest People in America," *Forbes*, accessed February 13, 2023, https://www.forbes.com/forbes-400/.

14. Barton H. Hamilton, "Does Entrepreneurship Pay? An Empirical Analysis of the Returns to Self-Employment," *Journal of Political Economy* 108, no. 3 (2000): 604–31.

15. Claire Rafford, "Ben & Jerry's Founder Reflects on Company, Socially Conscious Business Mission," *Observer*, March 21, 2018, https://ndsmcobserver.com/2018/03/ben-jerrys-founder-reflects/.

16. David Gelles, "How Payal Kadakia Danced Her Way to a $600 Million Start-Up," *New York Times*, August 16, 2019, https://www.nytimes.com/2019/08/16/business/payal-kadakia-classpass-corner-office.html.

17. Jamie Johnson, "10 Inspirational Oprah Quotes for Business Owners," CO, January 21, 2020, https://www.uschamber.com/co/start/strategy/inspirational-oprah-winfrey-quotes.

18. Farhad Manjoo, "MailChimp and the Un-Silicon Valley Way to Make It as a Start-Up," *New York Times*, October 6, 2016, https://www.nytimes.com/2016/10/06/technology/mailchimp-and-the-un-silicon-valley-way-to-make-it-as-a-start-up.html.

19. Jeff Haden, "Shark Tank's Barbara Corcoran Says Every Exceptional Person Suffers from Self-Doubt: How to Use Imposter Syndrome to Your Advantage," *Inc.*, March 13, 2020, https://www.inc.com/jeff-haden/shark-tanks-barbara-corcoran-says-every-exceptional-person-suffers-from-self-doubt-how-you-can-use-imposter-syndrome-to-your-advantage.html.

20. Anna Waldman-Brown and Georgina Campbell Flatter, "Scaling Sanergy: Growing a Promising Sanitation Startup," Case Study, May 2018, https://legatum.mit.edu/wp-content/uploads/2018/07/Sanergy-Case-Study_6.29.2018.docx.pdf.

21. Jonathan Rothwell and Steve Crabtree, "Not Just a Job: New Evidence on the Quality of Work in the United States," Gallup, October 20, 2019, https://www.gallup.com/education/267590/great-jobs-lumina-gates-omidyar-gallup-quality-report-2019.aspx; Jonathan Rothwell, "Earning Income on the Side Is a Large and Growing Slice of American Life," *New York Times*, December 18, 2019, https://www.nytimes.com/2019/12/18/upshot/multiple-jobs-united-states.html.

22. Ingrid Lunden, "Confirmed: Walmart Buys Jet.com for $3B in Cash to Fight Amazon," *TechCrunch*, August 8, 2016, https://techcrunch.com/2016/08/08/confirmed-walmart-buys-jet-com-for-3b-in-cash/.

23. "The Most Creative People in Business: 52. For Incubating Walmart's Business: Kate Finnegan," Fast Company, accessed July 13, 2023, https://www.fastcompany.com/most-creative-people/2018.

24. Gustavo Manso, "Experimentation and the Returns to Entrepreneurship," *Review of Financial Studies* 29, no. 9 (2016): 2319–40.

25. Jackson G. Lu et al., "'Going Out' of the Box: Close Intercultural Friendships and Romantic Relationships Spark Creativity, Workplace Innovation, and Entrepreneurship," *Journal of Applied Psychology* 102, no. 7 (2017): 1091–1108; and Jackson G. Lu, "Cultural Diversity Stimulates Entrepreneurship: Evidence from Two Large-Scale Natural Experiments," Academy of Management Annual Meeting Proceedings, July 26, 2011, https://journals.aom.org/doi/abs/10.5465/AMBPP.2021.10533abstract.

26. Ola Svenson, "Are We All Less Risky and More Skillful Than Our Fellow Drivers?" *Acta Psychologica* 47 (1981): 143–48.

27. Wikipedia, s.v. "Illusory Superiority," last modified January 30, 2023, https://en.wikipedia.org/wiki/Illusory_superiority.

28. Malcolm Gladwell, "The Sure Thing: How Entrepreneurs Really Succeed," *New Yorker*, January 18, 2010, https://www.newyorker.com/magazine/2010/01/18/the-sure-thing.

29. B. Zorina Khan, "Married Women's Property Laws and Female Commercial Activity: Evidence from United States Patent Records, 1790–1895," *Journal of Economic History* 56, no. 2 (1996): 356–88.

30. Lisa D. Cook, "Violence and Economic Activity: Evidence from African American Patents, 1870–1940," *Journal of Economic Growth* 19 (2014): 221–57.

31. Alison Wood Brooks et al., "Investors Prefer Entrepreneurial Ventures Pitched by Attractive Men," *PNAS* 111, no. 12 (2014): 4427–31.

32. Dana Kanze et al., "Male and Female Entrepreneurs Get Asked Different Questions by VCs—and It Affects How Much Funding They Get," *Harvard Business Review*, June 27, 2017, https://hbr.org/2017/06/male-and-female-entrepreneurs -get-asked-different-questions-by-vcs-and-it-affects-how -much-funding-they-get.

33. United States Census Bureau, "Women-Owned Businesses," March 31, 2017, https://www.census.gov/library/visualizations /2017/comm/women_owned_businesses.html.

34. United States Census Bureau, "Los Angeles County a Micro-cosm of Nation's Diverse Collection of Business Owners, Census Bureau Reports," December 15, 2015, https://www .census.gov/newsroom/archives/2015-pr/cb15-209.html.

35. Pierre Azoulay et al., "Age and High-Growth Entrepreneurship," *American Economic Review: Insights* 2, no. 1 (2020): 65–82.

36. LaFranco and Peterson-Withorn, "400 Richest People."

37. Asian American Hotel Owners Association, "The Foremost Resource and Advocate for America's Hotel Owners," accessed July 13, 2023, https://www.aahoa.com/home; Sudhin Thanawala, "Indian Hoteliers Test Clout in Lawsuits against Big Chains," AP News, July 8, 2021, https://apnews.com/article /lifestyle-health-travel-india-lawsuits4b2e2c86817293d2065 fc4c16b06ba08; Yudhijit Bhattacharjee, "How Indian Americans Came to Run Half of All U.S. Motels," *National Geographic*, September 4, 2018, https://www.nationalg eographic.com/culture/2018/09/south-asia-america -motels-immigration/https://www.nationalgeographic.com /culture/2018/09/south-asia-america-motels-immigration/; and Tunku Varadarajan, "A Patel Motel Cartel?" *New York Times*, July 4, 1999, https://www.nytimes.com/1999/07/04 /magazine/a-patel-motel-cartel.html.

38. Pierre Azoulay et al., "Immigration and Entrepreneurship in the United States," NBER Working Paper, September 2020.

39. Sari Pekkala Kerr and William Kerr, "Immigrant Entrepre-neurship," in *Measuring Entrepreneurial Businesses: Current Knowledge and Challenges,* John Haltiwanger et al., eds. (Chicago: University of Chicago Press, 2017), 187–249.

40. Britannica, s.v., "Coco Chanel," last updated April 26, 2023, https://www.britannica.com/biography/Coco-Chanel.

Uber

a. Josh Barro, "Uber's Plan to Lose Money on Each Transaction and Make It Up in Volume, Annotated," *New York*, April 26, 2019, https://nymag.com/intelligencer/2019/04/ubers-plan -to-lose-money-on-each-ride-make-it-up-in-volume.html.

b. Kellen Browning, "Uber Posts Record Revenue but Loses More Money from Investments," *New York Times*, August 2, 2022, https://www.nytimes.com/2022/08/02/business/uber -quarterly-earnings.html.

Steve Jobs

a. Katie Canales, "Laurene Powell Jobs Says It Took Her and Detail-Obsessed Husband Steve Jobs 8 years to Buy a Couch because They Couldn't Agree on One," *Business Insider*, September 8, 2022, https://www.businessinsider.com /laurene-powell-jobs-steve-jobs-8-years-with-no-couch-2022-9.

Barbara Corcoran

a. Taylor Locke, "Why Barbara Corcoran 'Felt Like an Absolute Fraud' after Selling Her Business for $66 Million," CNBC, updated January 12, 2021, https://www.cnbc.com/2020/02/27 /why-barbara-corcoran-felt-like-a-fraud-after-selling-her -business.html.

Mini Case: When an Entrepreneur Chooses More Than the Bottom Line

a. Yvon Chouinard, *Let My People Go Surfing: The Education of a Reluctant Businessman* (New York: Penguin Books, 2016).

b. "About 1% for the Planet," 1% for the Planet, accessed July 25, 2023, https://www.onepercentfortheplanet.org/about/mission.

Mini Case: Do You Need to Be an Expert?

a. Daniel Chase, "Nike Doesn't Need Roads," *Stock Price*, January 18, 2019, https://stockprice.com/stock-price-featured-content /nike-doesnt-need-roads-2019-01-18/.

Using the Research: Do Universities Produce Successful Entrepreneurs?

a. Edward B. Roberts, *Entrepreneurs in High-Technology: Lessons from MIT and Beyond* (New York: Oxford University Press, 1991).

b. David Hsu, Edward B. Roberts, and Charles E. Eesley, "Entre-preneurs from Technology-Based Universities: Evidence from MIT," *Research Policy* 31, no. 1 (2007): 159–82; and Edward B. Roberts, Fiona Murray, and J. Daniel Kim, "Entrepreneur-ship and Innovation at MIT: Continuing Global Growth and Impact," Martin Trust Center for MIT Entrepreneurship, 2015.

c. Illinois Innovation Index, "2019 University Entrepreneurship Index: Universities Drive New Venture Creation," Illinois Science and Technology Coalition, accessed July 25, 2023, https://www .istcoalition.org/data/index/2019-university-entrepreneurship-index.

d. Charles E. Eesley and Yong Suk Lee, "Do University Entrepre-neurship Programs Promote Entrepreneurship?" *Strategic Management Journal* 42, no. 4 (2021): 833–61.

Case: ConBody

a. Adam Davidson, *The Passion Economy* (New York: Vintage Books, 2020), p. 138, Kindle.

b. Noah Remnick, "Getting Fit, Prison-Style," *New York Times*, April 9, 2016, https://www.nytimes.com/2016/04/10/nyregion /at-a-gym-in-manhattan-fitness-tips-from-ex-convicts.html.

c. A. J. Harrington, "Cannabis Shop Run by Formerly Incarcerated Licensed to Open in New York," *Forbes*, April 6, 2023, https:// www.forbes.com/sites/ajherrington/2023/04/06/cannabis -shop-run-by-formerly-incarcerated-licensed-to-open-in -new-york/?sh=4c27ee79632c.

CHAPTER 3

1. Tina Seelig, "The Little Risks You Take to Increase Your Luck," produced by TED, August 28, 2018, YouTube video, 11:39, https://www.youtube.com/watch?v=PX61e3sAj5k.

2. Sara Blakely, "How Spanx Got Started," *Inc.*, transcript and video, January 20, 2012, https://www.inc.com/sara-blakely /how-sara-blakley-started-spanx.html.

3. See Kevin A. Bryan, Michael D. Ryall, and Burkhard C. Schipper, "Value Capture in the Face of Known and Unknown Unknowns," *Strategy Science* 7, no. 3 (2021): 157–89.

4. Mary Hance, "13 Things to Know about Trader Joe's," *Tennessean*, September 30, 2020, https://www.tennessean .com/story/life/shopping/ms-cheap/2020/09/30/trader -joes-13-things-to-know-about-popular-grocer /5860532002.

5. Qiuning Yang, "The Development of Entrepreneurship in China" (PhD diss., Freien Universität Berlin, 2012), https:// refubium.fu-berlin.de/bitstream/handle/fub188/7253 /Qiuning_Yang-dissertation.pdf.

6. Rajah Rasiah, Xin-Xin Kong, and Jebamalai Vinanchiarachi, "Moving Up in the Global Value Chain in Button Manufac- turing in China," *Asia Pacific Business Review* 17, no. 2 (2011): 161–74; Rajah Rasiah, Thiruchelvam Kanagasundram, and Keun Lee, eds., *Innovation and Learning Experiences in Rapidly Developing East Asia* (New York: Routledge, 2012); and Louisa Lim, "Chinese 'Button Town' Struggles with Success," NPR, August 22, 2006, https://www.npr.org/2006/08/22/5686805 /chinese-button-town-struggles-with-success.

7. James Dyson, interview by Guy Raz, *How I Built This*, NPR, July 22, 2019, https://www.npr.org/2019/07/19/743512256 /dyson-james-dyson.

8. Blakely, "How Spanx Got Started," *Inc.*

9. Victoria DiPlacido, "A Comprehensive Guide to Fenty Beauty," *Elle Canada*, September 7, 2017, https://www .ellecanada.com/beauty/makeup-and-nails/a-comprehensive -guide-to-fenty-beauty; and Adrianne Pasquarelli, "Marketer A-List 2018: Fenty," *AdAge*, December 3, 2018, https://adage .com/article/special-report-marketer-alist/marketer-a-list -2018-fenty/315798.

10. Natalie Robehmed, "How Rihanna Created a $600 Million Fortune—and Became the World's Richest Female Musician," *Forbes*, June 4, 2019, https://www.forbes.com/sites /natalierobehmed/2019/06/04/rihanna-worth-fenty-beauty /amp.

11. Scott Shane, "Prior Knowledge and the Discovery of Entre- preneurial Opportunities," *Organization Science* 11, no. 4 (2000): 448–69.

12. Damon J. Phillips, "A Genealogical Approach to Organizational Life Chances: The Parent-Progeny Transfer among Silicon Valley Law Firms, 1946–1996," *Administrative Science Quarterly* 47, no. 3 (2002): 474–506.

13. Steven Klepper and Sally Sleeper, "Entry by Spinoffs," *Manage- ment Science* 51, no. 8 (2005): 1291–306; and Rajshree Agarwal et al., "Knowledge Transfer through Inheritance: Spin-Out Generation, Development, and Survival," *Academy of Manage- ment Journal* 47, no. 4 (2004): 501–22.

14. Alex Konrad, "How Super Angel Chris Sacca Made Billions, Burned Bridges and Crafted the Best Seed Portfolio Ever," *Forbes*, March 25, 2015, https://www.forbes.com/sites /alexkonrad/2015/03/25/how-venture-cowboy-chris-sacca -made-billions/?sh=15d13d476597.

15. Colin Camerer and Don Lovallo, "Overconfidence and Excess Entry: An Experimental Approach," *American Economic Review* 89, no. 1 (1999): 306–18.

16. Alex Konrad, "Zoom, Zoom, Zoom! The Exclusive Inside Story of the New Billionaire Behind Tech's Hottest IPO," *Forbes*, April 19, 2019, https://www.forbes.com/sites/alexkonrad /2019/04/19/zoom-zoom-zoom-the-exclusive-inside-story -of-the-new-billionaire-behind-techs-hottest-ipo/?sh =7399b7fe4af1.

17. "The Clif Bar & Company Story," Clif Bar & Company, accessed May 4, 2023, https://www.clifbar.com/stories/the-clif-bar -and-company-story.

18. Nadia Hosni, "Triple Bottom Line: Clif Bar & Company," *Tonic*, July 7, 2010, http:/www.tonic.com/article/triple -bottom-line-clif-bar-and-company.

19. Arnold C. Cooper, Carolyn Y. Woo, and William C. Dunkelberg, "Entrepreneurs Perceived Chances for Success," *Journal of Business Venturing* 3 (Spring 1988): 97–108.

20. Thomas Åstebro, "The Return to Independent Invention: Evidence of Unrealistic Optimism, Risk Seeking or Skewness Loving?" *Economic Journal* 113, no. 484 (January 2003): 226–39.

21. Gilbert King, "The Rise and Fall of Nikola Tesla and His Tower," *Smithsonian Magazine*, February 4, 2013, https://www .smithsonianmag.com/history/the-rise-and-fall-of -nikola-tesla-and-his-tower-11074324; and A. J. S. Rayl, "Nikola Tesla's Curious Contrivance," *Air and Space Magazine*, September 2006, https://www.airspacemag.com /history-of-flight/nikola-teslas-curious-contrivance -10187565.

22. Walt Disney Company, "The Walt Disney Company Acquires the Baby Einstein Company," press release, November 6, 2001, https://thewaltdisneycompany.com/the-walt-disney-company -acquires-the-baby-einstein-company.

Using the Research: Entrepreneurs and the Scientific Method

a. Arnaldo Camuffo, Alessandro Cordova, Alfonso Gambardella, and Chiara Spina, "A Scientific Approach to Entrepreneurial Decision-Making: Evidence from a Randomized Control Trial," *Management Science* 66, no. 2 (2020): 503–1004.

Deep Dive: Knightian Uncertainty

a. "The Anti-Portfolio," Bessemer Venture Partners, accessed October 30, 2023, https://www.bvp.com/anti-portfolio.

b. Econlib, s.v., "Frank Hyneman Knight (1885–1972)," by David R. Henderson, accessed February 22, 2023, https://www .econlib.org/library/Enc/bios/Knight.html.

Using the Research: Schumpeter's Creative Destruction vs. Kirzner's Discovery

a. Joseph A. Schumpeter, Capitalism, *Socialism and Democracy*, 2nd ed. (New York and London: Harper, 1947).

b. Israel M. Kirzner, *Competition and Entrepreneurship* (Chicago: University of Chicago Press, 2015).

Mini Case: User Innovators Turned Entrepreneurs

a. "What Is the History of Khan Academy?" Khan Academy, accessed February 22, 2023, https://support.khanacademy.org/hc/en-us/articles/202483180-What-is-the-history-of-Khan-Academy.

b. Sonali Shah and Mary Tripsas, "When Do User-Innovators Start Firms? A Theory of User Entrepreneurship," in *Revolutionizing Innovation: Users, Communities and Open Innovation*, ed. Dietmar Harhoff and Karim R. Lakhani, 285–307 (Cambridge: MIT Press, 2016).

Using the Research: Effectual Reasoning

a. Saras D. Sarasvathy, "What Makes Entrepreneurs Entrepreneurial?" Darden Case Number UVA-ENT-0065, October 21, 2008, https://papers.ssrn.com/sol3/papers.cfm?abstract_id=909038.

Mini Case: Why Hamilton?

a. Rebecca Mead, "All about the Hamiltons," *New Yorker*, February 9, 2015, https://www.newyorker.com/magazine/2015/02/09/hamiltons.

Case: Shopify

a. SnowDevil Shopify demo store, https://www.snowdevil.ca/.

b. Trevor Cole, "Our Canadian CEO of the Year You've Probably Never Heard Of," *Globe & Mail*, November 27, 2014, https://www.theglobeandmail.com/report-on-business/rob-magazine/meet-our-ceo-of-the-year/article21734931.

CHAPTER 4

1. Michael Grothaus, "A Rediscovered 1997 Video Reveals Why Jeff Bezos Chose Books and Not CDs to Be Amazon's First Product," *Fast Company*, November 13, 2019, https://www.fastcompany.com/90430303/a-rediscovered-1997-video-reveals-why-jeff-bezos-chose-books-and-not-cds-to-be-amazons-first-product; unsigned summary of *An Executive Summary of the Everything Store: Jeff Bezos and the Age of Amazon*, by Brad Stone, The Investor's Podcast Network, accessed March 2, 2023, https://www.theinvestorspodcast.com/billionaire-book-club-executive-summary/the-everything-store.

2. Mark Abadi, "MacKenzie Bezos Played a Big Role in the Founding of Amazon and Drove across the Country with Jeff to Start It," *Business Insider*, April 4, 2019, https://www.businessinsider.com/how-mackenzie-bezos-met-jeff-bezos-2019-1; Erik Sherman, "20 Years of Amazon's Expansive Evolution," CBS News, July 15, 2015, https://www.cbsnews.com/news/20-years-of-amazons-expansive-evolution.

3. Gina Keating, *Netflixed: The Epic Battle for America's Eyeballs* (New York: Penguin, 2012); and Victoria Barret, "Dropbox: The Inside Story of Tech's Hottest Startup," *Forbes*, October 18, 2011, https://www.forbes.com/sites/victoriabarret/2011/10/18/dropbox-the-inside-story-of-techs-hottest-startup.

4. Tristan Walker interview by Kevin Cool, Stanford Graduate School of Business, July 15, 2022, https://www.gsb.stanford.edu/programs/mba/life-community/alumni/voices/tristan-walker.

5. Tristan Walker, interview by GIC Americas, *ThinkSpace*, March 31, 2021, https://www.gic.com.sg/thinkspace/enterprise-excellence/tristan-walker-founder-and-ceo-of-walker-and-company.

6. Hannah Smelter, "5 Women Leaders in the Professional World," CodeHer, April 2, 2021, https://www.codehergirls.org/post/5-women-leaders-in-the-professional-world.

7. "Bumble Founder Whitney Wolfe Herd: New Yorkers, You Inspire Us," The Beehive, accessed March 2, 2023, https://thebeehive.bumble.com/whitneyftob.

8. Lilly Smith, "How Bumble's Clever Design Helped the App Go Public," *Fast Company*, February 21, 2021, https://www.fastcompany.com/90603980/how-bumbles-clever-design-helped-the-app-go-public.

9. Scott Stern and Daniel Fehder, "PillPack Entrepreneurial Strategy Case," case study.

10. Ingrid Lunden, "Amazon Buys PillPack, an Online Pharmacy, for Just under $1B," *TechCrunch*, June 28, 2018, https://techcrunch.com/2018/06/28/amazon-buys-pillpack-an-online-pharmacy-that-was-rumored-to-be-talking-to-walmart.

11. Ellen Huet and Olivia Zaleski, "Silicon Valley's $400 Juicer May Be Feeling the Squeeze," Bloomberg, April 19, 2017, https://www.bloomberg.com/news/features/2017-04-19/silicon-valley-s-400-juicer-may-be-feeling-the-squeeze.

12. Katie Roof, "RIP Juicero, the $400 Venture-Backed Juice Machine," *TechCrunch*, September 1, 2017, https://techcrunch.com/2017/09/01/rip-juicero-the-400-venture-backed-juice-machine.

13. Theo Coetzer, "Maine Line: The Story of L.L.Bean," Habilitate, January 22, 2022, https://habilitateblog.com/maine-line-the-story-of-l-l-bean.

14. Alexandra Schwartz, "Rent the Runway Wants to Lend You Your Look," *New Yorker*, October 22, 2018.

Mini Case: If You Change Your Idea, You Have a New Venture

a. Mat Honan, "The Most Fascinating Profile You'll Ever Read about a Guy and His Boring Startup," *Wired*, July 7, 2014, https://www.wired.com/2014/08/the-most-fascinating-profile-youll-ever-read-about-a-guy-and-his-boring-startup.

Sidebar: Design Choices

a. Lilly Smith, "How Bumble's Clever Design Helped the App Go Public," *Fast Company*, February 21, 2021, https://www.fastcompany.com/90603980/how-bumbles-clever-design-helped-the-app-go-public.

Using the Research: Uncertainty in Start-Up Ideas

a. Erin L. Scott, Pian Shu, and Roman M. Lubynsky, "Entrepreneurial Uncertainty and Expert Evaluation: An Empirical Analysis," *Management Science* 66, no. 3 (2020): 1278–99.

Sidebar: IMVU

a. Eric Ries, *The Lean Startup: How Today's Entrepreneurs Use Continuous Innovation to Create Radically Successful Businesses* (New York: Crown, 2011).

Case: Spyce

a. Julie Barr, "Alumni-Founded Robotic Kitchen Cooks Up Tasty Meals," *MIT Alumni News*, July 2, 2018, https://news.mit.edu/2018/mit-spinoff-spyce-robotic-kitchen-cooks-tastymeals-0702.

b. Tracy Jiang and Davin W. Shi, "Spyce Sizzles into Harvard Square, Complete with Automated Kitchen," *Harvard Crimson*, January 28, 2021, https://www.thecrimson.com/article/2021/1/28/spyce-restaurant-opening.

c. Anissa Gardizy, "How Much Did Sweetgreen Pay for Robot-Kitchen Startup Spyce? $50 Million," *Boston Globe*, updated October 27, 2021, https://www.bostonglobe.com/2021/10/27/business/how-much-did-sweetgreen-pay-robot-kitchen-startup-spyce-50-million.

CHAPTER 5

1. Nicholas Eriksson et al., "Web-Based, Participant-Driven Studies Yield Novel Genetic Associations for Common Traits," *PLoS Genetics* 6, no. 6 (2010): e1000993, https://doi.org/10.1371/journal.pgen.1000993.

2. Thomas Goetz, "23AndMe Will Decode Your DNA for $1,000. Welcome to the Age of Genomics," *Wired*, November 17, 2007, https://www.wired.com/2007/11/ff-genomics.

3. Andrew Pollack, "Is a DNA Test a Medical Test or Just Informational? Views Differ," *New York Times*, March 20, 2010, https://www.nytimes.com/2010/03/20/business/20consumergenebar.html.

4. Pollack, "Is a DNA Test?"

5. "Largest Toppling Dominoes," uploaded on August 8, 2009, YouTube video, 4:01, https://www.youtube.com/watch?v=APoL-Gw9jMQ.

6. Zvi Griliches, "Hybrid Corn: An Exploration in the Economics of Technological Change," *Econometrica* (1957): 501–22.

7. Dan Elitzer, Profile, LinkedIn, accessed June 8, 2023, https://www.linkedin.com/in/delitzer.

8. "Ambition and Uncertainty as Bitcoin Experiment Nears," MIT Sloan School of Management, July 7, 2014, https://web.archive.org/web/20150910144822/http://mitsloan.mit.edu/newsroom/articles/ambition-and-uncertainty-as-bitcoin-experiment-nears.

9. Rob Matheson, "Bitcoin Study: Period of Exclusivity Encourages Early Adopters," *MIT News*, July 13, 2017, http://news.mit.edu/2017/bitcoin-study-period-exclusivity-encourages-early-adopters-0713; and Christian Catalini and Catherine Tucker, "When Early Adopters Don't Adopt," *Science*, July 14, 2017, 135–36, http://science.sciencemag.org/content/357/6347/135.

10. Doug Aamoth, "First Smartphone Turns 20: Fun Facts about Simon," *Time*, August 18, 2014, http://time.com/3137005/first-smartphone-ibm-simon; and Adam Pothitos, "The History of the Smartphone," *Mobile Industry Review*, October 31, 2016, http://www.mobileindustryreview.com/2016/10/the-history-of-the-smartphone.html.

11. "The Diffusion of iPhones as a Learning Process," Asymco, November 6, 2013, http://www.asymco.com/2013/11/06/the-diffusion-of-iphones-as-a-learning-process.

12. Geoffrey A. Moore, *Crossing the Chasm*, 3rd ed. (New York: HarperCollins, 2014).

13. Wikipedia, s.v. "Documentum," last modified March 21, 2023, https://en.wikipedia.org/wiki/Documentum.

14. Moore, *Crossing*, ch. 3.

Deep Dive: S Curve across Innovative Products

a. Richard Alm and W. Michael Cox, "Time Well Spent: The Declining Real Cost of Living in America," *Federal Reserve Bank of Dallas Annual Report*, 1997, 22, https://www.minneapolisfed.org/~/media/files/research/prescott/quant_macro/arpt97.pdf?la=en.

Using the Research: The Hazards of Ignoring Early Adopters

a. Christian Catalini and Catherine Tucker, "When Early Adopters Don't Adopt," *Science*, July 14, 2017, 135–36, http://science.sciencemag.org/content/357/6347/135.

CHAPTER 6

1. While this seems a long time ago, we should recall that humans landed on the moon in 1969.

2. Giovanni Dosi, "Technological Paradigms and Technological Trajectories: A Suggested Interpretation of the Determinants and Directions of Technical Change," *Research Policy* 11, no. 3 (1982): 147–62; and Richard N. Foster, *Innovation: The Attacker's Advantage* (New York: Summit, 1986).

3. "Haitz's Law," *Nature Photon* 1, no. 23 (2007), https://doi.org/10.1038/nphoton.2006.78.

4. Joshua Gans, *The Disruption Dilemma* (Cambridge, MA: MIT Press, 2016).

5. Jennifer Korn, "Google to Stop Selling Google Glass Smart Glasses, Shifting Focus to AR," ABC7 Eyewitness News, March 16, 2023, https://abc7chicago.com/google-news-what-is-glass-glasses/12963728.

6. Lucas Matney, "Once Poised to Kill the Mouse and Keyboard, Leap Motion Plays Its Final Hand," TechCrunch, May 30, 2019, https://techcrunch.com/2019/05/30/once-poised-to-kill-the-mouse-and-keyboard-leap-motion-plays-its-final-hand.

7. Jared Canfield, "12 Ways Pixar Beats Disney at Their Own Game," *ScreenRant*, April 4, 2016, https://screenrant.com/pizar-better-than-disney.

8. While Jobs managed Pixar in a way that encouraged a high level of creativity and exploration, he also was demanding (and perhaps did not maintain a tolerance for failure at all times). In one infamous episode known as "the whiteboard incident," cofounder Alvy Ray Smith and Jobs nearly ended up in a physical altercation. This prompted Smith to actually leave the firm before it reached its success with *Toy Story* and beyond.

9. Florian Ederer and Gustavo Manso, "Is Pay for Performance Detrimental to Innovation?" *Management Science* 59, no. 7 (2013): 1496–513.

10. Marcus Yam, "The Hubless, Carbon-Fiber Cyclotron Bike Looks Straight Out of 'Tron,'" Digital Trends, April 1, 2019, https://www.digitaltrends.com/outdoors/cyclotron-hubless-smart-bike.

Using the Research: Crash-Test Dummies and Choosing Meaningful Metrics

a. Jane Wu, "Innovation for Dummies? Exploring the Role of Metrics in Automotive Safety," Working Paper, November 6, 2021, https://ucla.app.box.com/s/ygfoqtm2yxy3oh2gjfeizdx6884w55lc.

Mini Case: Technology S Curves in Action

a. Malcolm Gladwell, "Smaller," *New Yorker*, November 18, 2001, https://www.newyorker.com/magazine/2001/11/26/smaller.

Deep Dive: Organizational Learning

a. James G. March, "Exploration and Exploitation in Organizational Learning," *Organization Science* 2, no. 1 (1991): 71–87.

CHAPTER 7

1. The story of Zappos is memorably recounted in Tony Hsieh's memoir, *Delivering Happiness: A Path to Profits, Passion, and Purpose* (New York: Grand Central Publishing, 2010).
2. Robert D. Hershey, Jr., "Jack Taylor, Founder of Enterprise Rent-A-Car, Dies at 94," *New York Times*, July 3, 2016, https://www.nytimes.com/2016/07/03/business/jack-taylor-founder-of-enterprise-rent-a-car-dies-at-94.html.
3. Rebecca Mead, "Just Add Sugar," *New Yorker*, October 28, 2013, https://www.newyorker.com/magazine/2013/11/04/just-add-sugar.
4. Steve Kovach, "How the Hot Startup That Stole Apple's Thunder Wound Up in Silicon Valley's Graveyard," *Business Insider*, December 17, 2016, https://www.businessinsider.com/how-smartwatch-pioneer-pebble-lost-everything-2016-12.
5. Stewart Thornhill and Raphael Amit, "Learning about Failure: Bankruptcy, Firm Age, and the Resource-Based View," *Organization Science* 14, no. 5 (2003): 497–509.
6. https://restaurant.org/research-and-media/research/.
7. Rajshree Agarwal, MB Sarkar, and Raj Echambadi, "The Conditioning Effect of Time on Firm Survival: An Industry Life Cycle Approach," *Academy of Management Journal* 45, no. 5 (2002): 971–94.
8. Thomas Hellmann and Manju Puri, "Venture Capital and the Professionalization of Start-Up Firms: Empirical Evidence," *Journal of Finance* 57 (2002): 169–97, https://doi.org/10.1111/1540-6261.00419.
9. Kit Hickley and Erin L. Scott, "Gimlet Media," Martin Trust Center for MIT Entrepreneurship, 2019.
10. Arielle Duhaime-Ross, "Driven: How Zipcar's Founders Built and Lost a Car-Sharing Empire," *The Verge*, April 1, 2014, https://www.theverge.com/2014/4/1/5553910/driven-how-zipcars-founders-built-and-lost-a-car-sharing-empire.
11. Duhaime-Ross, "Driven."
12. Randall Stross, *The Launch Pad: Inside Y Combinator* (New York: Penguin, 2013).
13. Michael Gorman and William A. Sahlman, "What Do Venture Capitalists Do?" *Journal of Business Venturing* 4, no. 4 (1989): 231–48, https://doi.org/10.1016/0883-9026(89)90014-1; and Steven N. Kaplan and Per Strömberg, "Characteristics, Contracts, and Actions: Evidence from Venture Capitalist Analyses," *Journal of Finance* 59 (2004): 2177–210, https://doi.org/10.1111/j.1540-6261.2004.00696.x.

14. Isabella Simonetti, "Peloton, Seeking to Cut Costs, Will No Longer Make Its Own Bikes," *New York Times*, July 12, 2022, https://www.nytimes.com/2022/07/12/business/peloton-bikes.html; and Peloton, "Peloton Exits Owned-Manufacturing and Expands Partnership with Leading Taiwanese Manufacturer Rexon," press release, July 12, 2022, https://investor.onepeloton.com/news-releases/news-release-details/peloton-exits-owned-manufacturing-and-expands-partnership.
15. Tom Eisenmann, *Why Startups Fail* (New York: Currency, 2021), p. 223, Kindle.
16. Om Malik, "'No Mobile Phones. You Must Look Me in the Eye,'" *Medium*, April 29, 2015, https://medium.com/backchannel/no-mobile-phones-you-must-look-me-in-the-eye-1c743fa8b137.
17. Lauren Collins, "House Perfect: Is the IKEA Ethos Comfy or Creepy?" *New Yorker*, October 3, 2011, http://www.newyorker.com/magazine/2011/10/03/house-perfect.
18. Catherine J. Turco, *The Conversational Firm* (New York: Columbia University Press, 2016).
19. James N. Baron and Michael T. Hannan, "Organizational Blueprints for Success in High-Tech Start-Ups: Lessons from the Stanford Project on Emerging Companies," *California Management Review* 44, no. 3 (2006): 8–36, https://doi.org/10.2307/41166130.

Sidebar: Pebble Watch vs. Apple Watch

a. Brad Moon, "Apple Watch vs. Pebble Time Round: Hands-On Showdown," *Forbes*, June 22, 2016, https://www.forbes.com/sites/bradmoon/2016/06/22/apple-watch-vs-pebble-time-round-hands-on-showdown/?sh=7cff819c2de2.

Using the Research: The Firm Survival Curve

a. Tiantian Yang and Howard E. Aldrich, "'The Liability of Newness' Revisited: Theoretical Restatement and Empirical Testing in Emergent Organizations," *Social Science Research* 63 (2017): 36–53, https://doi.org/10.1016/j.ssresearch.2016.09.006.

Mini Case: The "Traitorous Eight" and the Birth of Silicon Valley

a. *American Experience*, season 25, episode 3, "Silicon Valley," aired February 5, 2013, on PBS, http://video.pbs.org/video/2332168287.
b. "The Traitorous Eight Traitorously Leave Shockley Semiconductor," PBS, accessed May 9, 2023, https://www.pbs.org/transistor/album1/eight/index.html.

Deep Dive: Three Nobel Laureates on Make vs. Buy

a. David Frydlinger, Oliver Hart, and Kate Vitasek, "A New Approach to Contracts," *Harvard Business Review*, September–October 2019, https://hbr.org/2019/09/a-new-approach-to-contracts.

Mini Case: Choosing a "Human-Centered" Culture to Create Value for Customers

a. "What Eventbrite Did Early to Create 'Sustainable' Success," Women Mean Business, accessed July 11, 2023, https://www.womenmeanbusiness.ca/inspiring-content/what-eventbrite-did-early-to-create-sustainable-success.

CHAPTER 8

1. Katrina Lake, "Stitch Fix's CEO on Selling Personal Style to the Mass Market," *Harvard Business Review*, May–June 2018, https://hbr.org/2018/05/stitch-fixs-ceo-on-selling-personal-style-to-the-mass-market.
2. Dan Bricklin, *Bricklin on Technology* (New York: Wiley, 2009).
3. Elana Lyn Gross, "How Sarah Kauss Turned S'well into a $100 Million-Dollar Company," *Forbes*, April 4, 2018, https://www.forbes.com/sites/elanagross/2018/04/04/how-sarah-kauss-turned-swell-into-a-100-million-dollar-company/#4e1bf4301974.
4. Seth Goldman and Barry Nalebuff, *Mission in a Bottle: The Honest Guide to Doing Business Differently—and Succeeding* (New York: Currency, 2013).
5. Jorge Guzman and Aishen Li, "Measuring Founding Strategy," *Management Science* 69, no. 1 (2022): 101–18, https://doi.org/10.1287/mnsc.2022.4369.
6. John Seabrook, *Flash of Genius: And Other True Stories of Invention* (New York: Macmillan, 2008).
7. Deepak Somaya, David Teece, and Simon Wakeman, "Innovation in Multi-Invention Contexts: Mapping Solutions to Technological and Intellectual Property Complexity," *California Management Review* 53, no. 4 (2011): 47–79, https://doi.org/10.1525/cmr.2011.53.4.47.
8. Alex Frankel, "The Willing Partner," *MIT Technology Review*, July 1, 2005, https://www.technologyreview.com/2005/07/01/230701/the-willing-partner-2.
9. Libby Kane and Alyson Shontell, " 'You Either Got Chill Steve or Very Mean Steve': Dropbox Founder Remembers Being Summoned to Apple by Steve Jobs—Then Told His Startup Would Be Killed," *Business Insider,* June 14, 2017, https://www.businessinsider.com/drew-houston-dropbox-steve-jobs-2017-6.
10. Peter Thiel with Blake Masters, *Zero to One* (New York: Currency, 2014).
11. Petra Moser and Paul W. Rhode, "Did Plant Patents Create the American Rose?" *SSRN*, January 6, 2011, doi.org/10.2139/ssrn.1735015.
12. Eugene Kim, "CEO of $50 Billion Salesforce Shared His Epic Founding Story to Inspire a Small Business Owner," *Business Insider*, September 19, 2015, https://www.businessinsider.com/salesforce-benioff-shares-founding-story-2015-9.
13. This example draws on research by Michael Mazzeo, including "Competitive Outcomes in Product-Differentiated Oligopoly," *Review of Economics and Statistics* 84, no. 4 (2002): 716–28.

Philo T. Farnsworth vs. RCA

a. Joel Brinkley, "The Crime behind Every TV," *New York Times*, June 9, 2002, https://www.nytimes.com/2002/06/09/books/the-crime-behind-every-tv.html; and Dorsey & Whitney LLP, "The Top Ten Patent Wars," August 14, 2018, *JD Supra*, https://www.jdsupra.com/legalnews/the-top-ten-patent-wars-television-10-73080/#:~:text=Farnsworth%20rejected%20RCA's%20offer%20in,his%20own%20filed%20in%201923.

Using the Research: Complementary Assets

a. David Teece, "Profiting from Technological Innovation: Implications for Integration, Collaboration, Licensing, and Public Policy," *Research Policy* 15, no. 6 (1986): 285–305.
b. Teece, "Profiting."

Greg Kinnear

a. Allison Hope Weiner, "Lawyer Is Upping the Ante in Claims of Idea Theft in Hollywood," *New York Times*, July 27, 2006, https://www.nytimes.com/2006/07/27/movies/27gadf.html.
b. Dennis Kearns, comment on Joshua Gans, "A Tangled Web of Reality," *Core Economics*, January 27, 2009, https://economics.com.au/2009/01/27/a-tangled-web-of-fiction-and-reality.

Mini Case: The Race for Synthetic Insulin

a. A popular account of this research is provided in *Invisible Frontiers: The Race to Synthesize a Human Gene* (1988), an entertaining book by Stephen S. Hall.

PART 3

Using the Research: Professors Want a Quiet Life Compared to Their Students

a. Kenny Ching, Joshua Gans, and Scott Stern, "Control versus Execution: Endogenous Appropriability and Entrepreneurial Strategy," *Industrial and Corporate Change* 28, no. 2 (2019): 389–408, https://doi.org/10.1093/icc/dty040.

CHAPTER 9

1. Natasha Singer, "Ray Dolby, Who Put Moviegoers in the Middle of It, Is Dead at 80," *New York Times*, September 12, 2013, http://www.nytimes.com/2013/09/13/business/ray-dolby-who-put-moviegoers-in-the-middle-is-dead-at-80.html.
2. Ashish Arora, Andrea Fosfuri, and Alfonso Gambardella, "Markets for Technology and Their Implications for Corporate Strategy," *Industrial and Corporate Change* 10, no. 2 (2001): 419–51.
3. Joshua S. Gans and Scott Stern, "Is There a Market for Ideas?" *Industrial and Corporate Change* 19, no. 3 (2010): 805–37.
4. For more, see a rich and extensive literature, including Naomi R. Lamoreaux and Kenneth L. Sokoloff, "Market Trade in Patents and the Rise of a Class of Specialized Inventors in the 19th Century United States," *American Economic Review* 91, no. 2 (2001): 39–44; Joshua S. Gans and Scott Stern, "The Product Market and the 'Market for Ideas': Commercialization Strategies for Technology Entrepreneurs," *Research Policy* 32, no. 2 (2003): 333–50; and Ashish Arora and Alfonso Gambardella, "The Changing Technology of Technological Change: General and Abstract Knowledge and the Division of Innovative Labor," *Research Policy* 23, no. 5 (1994): 523–32.
5. Singer, "Ray Dolby."
6. "Trademark Basics," US Patent and Trademark Office, accessed June 13, 2013, https://www.uspto.gov/trademarks-getting-started/trademark-basics.
7. Youngme E. Moon and Christina L. Darwall, "Inside Intel Inside," Harvard Business School Case 502-083, revised October 2005, https://www.hbs.edu/faculty/Pages/item.aspx?num=29096.

8. Bill Donahue, "Venmo Hits Startup Loan App 'Lenmo' with Trademark Suit," *Law360*, July 8, 2019, https://www.law360.com/articles/1175846/venmo-hits-startup-loan-app-lenmo-with-trademark-suit.

9. Among other work, see Gary P. Pisano, *Science Business: The Promise, the Reality, and the Future of Biotech* (Cambridge, MA: Harvard Business School Press, 2006).

10. Moon and Darwall, "Inside Intel Inside."

11. Michael D. Watkins and Sarah G. Matthews, "Strategic Deal-Making at Millennium Pharmaceuticals," Harvard Business School Case: 5-902-002, September 27, 1999, https://hbsp.harvard.edu/product/800032-PDF-ENG?Ntt=Strategic%20Deal-Making%20At%20Millennium%20Pharmaceuticals.

12. Arora and Gambardella, "Changing Technology."

13. Although what precisely *The Hangover 3* was is anyone's guess.

14. Hong Luo, "When to Sell Your Idea: Theory and Evidence from the Movie Industry," *Management Science* 60, no. 12 (2014): 3067–86.

15. James J. Anton and Dennis A. Yao, "Little Patents and Big Secrets: Managing Intellectual Property," *RAND Journal of Economics* 35, no. 1 (2004): 1–22; and Joshua S. Gans and Scott Stern, "Incumbency and R&D Incentives: Licensing the Gale of Creative Destruction," *Journal of Economics and Management Strategy* 9 no. 4 (2000): 485–511.

16. Richard J. Gilbert and David M. G. Newbery, "Preemptive Patenting and the Persistence of Monopoly," *American Economic Review* (1982): 514–26; and Stephen W. Salant, "Preemptive Patenting and the Persistence of Monopoly: Comment," *American Economic Review* 74, no. 1 (1984): 247–50.

17. Yongmin Chen, "Strategic Bidding by Potential Competitors: Will Monopoly Persist?" *Journal of Industrial Economics* 48.2 (2000): 161–75.

18. Adam Brandenburger, Vijay Krishna, and Paul Barese, "Race to Develop Human Insulin," *Harvard Business Review*, 1991, 191121-PDF-ENG.

19. Knut J. Egelie et al., "The Emerging Patent Landscape of CRISPR–Cas Gene Editing Technology," *Nature Biotechnology* 34 (2016): 1025–31, https://doi.org/10.1038/nbt.3692.

20. "About," Caribou Biosciences, accessed June 13, 2023, https://cariboubio.com/about-us.

21. Gans and Stern, "Product Market."

22. These are findings from research by Wharton professor David Hsu, who found that high-reputation VCs acquired equity at a 10%–14% discount compared with other financiers (David Hsu, "What Do Entrepreneurs Pay for Venture Capital Affiliation?" *Journal of Finance* 59 (2004): 1805–44) and that VC-backed firms were more likely to engage in cooperation with established firms (David Hsu, "Venture Capitalists and Cooperative Startup Commercialization Strategy," *Management Science* 52 (2006): 204–19).

23. Ashlee Vance, "Silicon Valley's Most Hated Patent Troll Stops Suing and Starts Making," Bloomberg, September 4, 2014, http://www.bloomberg.com/bw/articles/2014-09-04/intel-lectual-ventures-patent-troll-funds-startups-new-products.

24. Jim Kerstetter and Josh Lowensohn, "Inside Intellectual Ventures, the Most Hated Company in Tech," CNET, August 21, 2012, http://www.cnet.com/news/inside-intellectual-ventures-the-most-hated-company-in-tech.

25. David Port, "Boost Your Brand," *Entrepreneur*, April 2, 2009, http://www.entrepreneur.com/article/201036.

26. Port, "Boost Your Brand."

27. Daniel Roberts, "George Foreman's Best Business Advice," *Fortune*, March 16, 2015, http://fortune.com/2015/03/16/george-foreman-business-advice.

28. Darren Rovell, "Foreman's Grill Deal: Best in Sports Marketing History?" CNBC, August 11, 2010, https://www.cnbc.com/id/38657945.

29. LiquiGlide, "Colgate Expands Use of LiquiGlide's EveryDrop™ Technology with Colgate Elixir Launch in Canada," press release, March 15, 2022, https://www.prnewswire.com/news-releases/colgate-expands-use-of-liquiglides-everydrop-technology-with-colgate-elixir-launch-in-canada-301502945.html.

30. US Patent 8,535,779, granted 2014. Jenny Eagle, "LiquiGlide Expands IP Protection after Global Interest in Its Slippery Coating, Food Navigator," September 9, 2014, http://www.foodproductiondaily.com/Processing/LiquiGlide-US-IP-patent-slippery-coating; and Nidhi Subbaraman, "LiquiGlide Sliding Fast Out of MIT into Success," *Boston Globe*, October 12, 2014, http://www.bostonglobe.com/business/2014/10/12/liquiglide-story-innovation-through-ketchup-toothpaste-hair-gel-and-airplane-wings/5yvcEc8MIyLOSSTTuTkOfI/story.html.

31. Michael Specter, "Decoding Iceland," *New Yorker*, January 18, 1999, 40–51.

32. Wikipedia, s.v. "Takeda Oncology," last modified April 9, 2023, https://en.wikipedia.org/wiki/Takeda_Oncolog.

33. Michael J. Miller, "The Rise of DOS: How Microsoft Got the IBM PC OS Contract," *PC Magazine*, August 12, 2021, https://www.pcmag.com/news/the-rise-of-dos-how-microsoft-got-the-ibm-pc-os-contract.

34. John Seabrook, "Flash of Genius," *New Yorker*, January 3, 1993, http://www.newyorker.com/magazine/1993/01/11/the-flash-of-genius.

35. Alec Matthew Klein, "Millions of Dollars Can't Wipe Away Pain," *Baltimore Sun*, March 26, 1995, http://articles.baltimoresun.com/1995-03-26/news/1995085007_1_kearns-walked-wipers-inventor.

36. "Scientific Research and Experimental Development (SR&ED) Tax Incentives," Government of Canada, accessed July 26, 2023, https://www.canada.ca/en/revenue-agency/services/scientific-research-experimental-development-tax-incentive-program.html.

37. Gillian Shaw, "Burnaby Quantum Computer Maker D-Wave Pulls in $29 Million in Funding," *Vancouver Sun*, January 28, 2015, http://www.vancouversun.com/technology/Burnaby+quantum+computer+maker+Wave+pulls+million+funding/10770082/story.html

38. Joshua S. Gans, David H. Hsu, and Scott Stern, "When Does Startup Innovation Spur the Gale of Creative Destruction?" *RAND Journal of Economics* 33, no. 4 (2002): 571–86.

Case: The Super Soaker

a. Tuskegee University, "Inventor, Alumnus Lonnie Johnson '73 Returns to Tuskegee for Feb. 23 Public Lecture," press release, February 19, 2018, https://www.tuskegee.edu/news/inventor

-alumnus-lonnie-johnson-73-returns-to-tuskegee-for-feb-23
-public-lecture.

b. Pagan Kennedy, "Who Made That Super Soaker?" *New York Times*, August 2, 2013, https://www.nytimes.com/2013/08/04/magazine/who-made-that-super-soaker.html?searchResultPosition=1.

c. Hasbro eventually purchased Larami Corporation in 1995.

CHAPTER 10

1. James M. Utterback and William J. Abernathy, "A Dynamic Model of Process and Product Innovation," *Omega* 3, no. e6 (1975): 639–56.

2. For a synthesis of the problems of incumbents, see Joshua Gans, *The Disruption Dilemma* (Cambridge: MIT Press, 2016), https://joshgans.medium.com/the-disruption-dilemma-56b05cc866d1.

3. Tiffany Black, "30 under 30: Jennifer Hyman and Jenny Fleiss, Founders of Rent the Runway," *Inc.*, 2016, http://www.inc.com/30under30/2010/profile-jennifer-hyman-jenny-fleiss-rent-the-runway.html.

4. Steve Bertoni, "How Mixing Data and Fashion Can Make Rent the Runway Tech's Next Billion Dollar Star," *Forbes*, August 20, 2014, http://www.forbes.com/sites/stevenbertoni/2014/08/20/how-mixing-data-and-fashion-can-make-rent-the-runway-techs-next-billion-dollar-star.

5. Britannica, s.v., "Dell Inc.," last modified June 21, 2023, https://www.britannica.com/topic/Dell-Inc.

6. Tom Huddleston Jr., "How Casper's Founders Went from $100,000 in Debt to Building a Billion-Dollar Mattress Start-Up," CNBC, April 10, 2019, https://www.cnbc.com/2019/04/05/how-caspers-founders-built-a-billion-dollar-mattress-start-up.html.

7. Adapted from David B. Yoffie and Mary Kwak, *Judo Strategy: Turning Your Competitors' Strength to Your Advantage* (Boston: Harvard Business School Press, 2001).

8. Joseph A. Schumpeter, *Capitalism, Socialism and Democracy* (New York: Harper, 1942).

9. Bernhard Warner, "Why This Shaving Startup Made a $100 Million Gamble on a 100-Year-Old Factory," updated May 9, 2019, *Inc.*, https://www.inc.com/magazine/201605/bernhard-warner/harrys-razors-german-factory.html.

10. This insight is explored by Eric van den Steen in "A Formal Theory of Strategy," Harvard Business School, 2014.

11. Jenna Wortham, "With a Start-Up Company, a Ride Is Just a Tap of an App Away," *New York Times*, May 3, 2011, https://www.nytimes.com/2011/05/04/technology/04ride.html.

12. Bruce Rogers, "Jeff Lawson's Twilio Disrupts Telecom Industry," *Forbes*, August 12, 2013, http://www.forbes.com/sites/brucerogers/2013/08/12/jeff-lawsons-twilio-disrupts-telecom-industry.

13. From author interview with founder.

14. Including Clayton Christensen, Rebecca Henderson, Shane Greenstein, and Kim Clark, among many others. See Gans, *Disruption Dilemma*, for a full discussion.

15. "Salesforce, Inc. (CRM)," Yahoo! Finance, accessed August 20, 2023, http://finance.yahoo.com/q?s=CRM.

16. Eric Ries, "Methodology," The Lean Startup, accessed October 27, 2023, http://theleanstartup.com/principles.

17. Dana Kanze, Mark Alexander Conley, and E. Tory Higgins, "Kanze, Conley, & Higgins, 2019 Motivation of Mission Statements: How Regulatory Mode Influences Workplace Discrimination," *Organizational Behavior and Human Decision Processes* 166 (2021): 84–103, https://doi.org/10.1016/j.obhdp.2019.04.002?.

Sidebar: Ryanair

a. Tom Boone and Pranja Pande, "The Story of Ryanair: Ireland's LCC Used to Be Anything but Low Cost," *Simple Flying*, October 5, 2023, https://simpleflying.com/ryanair-history/.

Mini Case: Browser Wars

a. W. Joseph Campbell, "The '90s Startup That Terrified Microsoft and Got Americans to Go Online," *Wired*, January 27, 2015, https://www.wired.com/2015/01/90s-startup-terrified-microsoft-got-americans-go-online.

Deep Dive: Differing S Curves

a. Edward Grochowski, "Emerging Trends in Data Storage on Magnetic Hard Disk Drives," 1999, https://pdfs.semanticscholar.org/ad6e/3bc8598c5cf7eee4f715e3ebdbe1825d4080.pdf.

Using the Research: The Replacement Effect

a. Marc Graser, "Epic Fail: How Blockbuster Could Have Owned Netflix," *Variety*, November 12, 2013, https://variety.com/2013/biz/news/epic-fail-how-blockbuster-could-have-owned-netflix-1200823443.

Using the Research: Is Disruption Overhyped?

a. Dana Kanze and Sheena S. Iyengar, "Startups That Seek to 'Disrupt' Get More Funding Than Those That Seek to 'Build,'" *Harvard Business Review*, November 24, 2017, https://hbr.org/2017/11/startups-that-seek-to-disrupt-get-more-funding-than-those-that-seek-to-build.

b. See Joshua Gans, "To Disrupt or Not to Disrupt," *Sloan Management Review*, February 19, 2020, pp. 40–45, https://sloanreview.mit.edu/article/to-disrupt-or-not-to-disrupt.

c. Ron Adner, "When Are Technologies Disruptive? A Demand-Based View of the Emergence of Competition," *Strategic Management Journal* 23, no. 2 (2002): 667–88, https://doi.org/10.1002/smj.246.

d. Jill Lepore, "The Disruption Machine," *New Yorker*, June 16, 2014, pp. 30–36, https://www.newyorker.com/magazine/2014/06/23/the-disruption-machine.

e. Mitsuru Igami, "Estimating the Innovator's Dilemma: Structural Analysis of Creative Destruction in the Hard Disk Drive Industry, 1981–1998," *Journal of Political Economy* 125, no. 3 (2017): 798–847, https://www.journals.uchicago.edu/doi/10.1086/691524.

Case: Warby Parker

a. Catherine Clifford, "Warby Parker Co-Founder on the Next Generation of Social Entrepreneurship," *Entrepreneur*, March 13, 2015, http://www.entrepreneur.com/article/243915.

b. Jessica Pressler, "20/30 Vision," *New York*, August 9, 2013, http://nymag.com/news/features/warby-parker-2013-8/index2.html.

c. "Who We Are," EssilorLuttoxica, accessed October 27, 2023, https://www.essilorluxottica.com/en/group/.

d. Max Chafin, "Warby Parker Sees the Future of Retail," *Fast Company,* February 17, 2015, http://www.fastcompany.com/3041334/most-innovative-companies-2015/warby-parker-sees-the-future-of-retail. When the Luxottica CEO was asked directly about Warby Parker in 2013, he remarked, "It's not a model, it's a brand . . . Very honestly, the more they do . . . the more our industry is in the center of the village and the happier we all are," quoted in Kyle Stock, "Luxottica, Rich on Ray-Bans, Sees Nothing to Fear in Warby Parker," Bloomberg, October 7, 2013, http://www.bloomberg.com/bw/articles/2013-10-07/luxottica-rich-on-ray-bans-sees-nothing-to-fear-in-warby-parker.

e. Dhani Mau, "Some People Are Buying 20–30 Pairs of Warby Parker Glasses a Year," *Fashionista,* June 26, 2014, http://fashionista.com/2014/06/warby-parker-growth.

CHAPTER 11

1. N. R. Narayana Murthy, *A Better India, a Better World* (New Delhi, India: Penguin, 2009).

2. Tarun Khanna and Krishna G. Palepu, "Globalization and Convergence in Corporate Governance: Evidence from Infosys and the Indian Software Industry," *Journal of International Business Studies* 35, no. 6 (2004): 484–507, https://doi.org/10.1057/palgrave.jibs.8400103.

3. Alfred Lee, "Pretzel Supplier Alleges Twisted Tale," *Los Angeles Business Journal*, February 16, 2014, https://labusinessjournal.com/manufacturing/pretzel-supplier-alleges-twisted-tale.

4. David Williams, Profile, LinkedIn, accessed July 18, 2023, https://www.linkedin.com/in/davidwilliams17.

5. "About Us," Merkle, accessed July 18, 2023, https://www.merkle.com/who-we-are/history-performance-marketing-agency.

6. "Acquisitions," Cisco, accessed September 20, 2023, https://www.cisco.com/c/en/us/about/corporate-strategy-office/acquisitions.html.

7. Sharon A. Alvarez and Jay B. Barney, "How Entrepreneurial Firms Can Benefit from Alliances with Large Partners," *Academy of Management Perspectives* 15, no. 1 (2001): 139–48, https://www.jstor.org/stable/4165716.

8. "Innovation," Washington University in St. Louis, accessed July 18, 2023, https://fuse.wustl.edu/2298-2.

9. "Our Company: Information for Students," Peapod, accessed November 15, 2023, https://web.archive.org/web/20160818115752/https://www.peapod.com/site/companyPages/our-company-info-for-students.jsp.

10. In more recent years, the entry of Amazon Fresh, Google Direct, and Instacart, among others, has introduced new competitive pressures.

11. Marc Eisen, "The Future of Madison's 'Epiconomy,'" *Madison Magazine*, September 7, 2020, https://www.channel3000.com/the-future-of-madisons-epiconomy.

12. "Infosys' Murthy: Sharing a 'Simple Yet Powerful Vision,'" *Knowledge at Wharton*, May 23 2001, https://knowledge.wharton.upenn.edu/article/infosys-murthy-sharing-a-simple-yet-powerful-vision/.

13. Tania Ganguli, "Shahid Khan Has True Rags to Riches American Story," *Florida Times-Union*, December 3, 2011, https://www.jacksonville.com/story/sports/nfl/2011/12/04/shahid-khan-has-true-rags-riches-american-story/987238007.

14. "About," Flex-N-Gate, accessed July 18, 2023, https://jobs.flex-n-gate.com/about#:~:text=Who%20Is%20Flex%2DN%2DGate,while%20pursuing%20his%20engineering%20degree.

15. Brian Solomon, "Shahid Khan: The New Face of the NFL and the American Dream," *Forbes*, September 5, 2012, https://www.forbes.com/sites/briansolomon/2012/09/05/shahid-khan-the-new-face-of-the-nfl-and-the-american-dream/#28b58b8450d2.

Sidebar: Satisfying the Need for Outsourced Personnel Services

a. Ron White, "How I Made It: Meet Janice Bryant Howroyd, the First African American Woman to Run a $1-Billion Business," *Los Angeles Times*, February 11, 2018, https://www.latimes.com/business/la-fi-himi-howroyd-20180211-htmlstory.html.

b. *Harvard Business Review*, "ActOne Group Founder Janice Bryant Howroyd: Never Compromise Your Values in a Quest to Succeed," February 2, 2023, https://hbr.org/2023/02/actone-group-founder-janice-bryant-howroyd-never-compromise-your-values-in-a-quest-to-succeed.

Sidebar: Judith Faulkner and Epic

a. Marc Eisen, "The Future of Madison's 'Epiconomy,'" *Madison Magazine*, September 17, 2020, https://www.channel3000.com/the-future-of-madisons-epiconomy/.

Case: Drizly

a. Lauren Landry, "The Alcohol Delivery Service Pouring Innovation into an Antiquated Industry," *Business Journals*, January 29, 2014, https://www.bizjournals.com/boston/inno/stories/profiles/2014/01/29/the-alcohol-delivery-service-pouring-innovation.html.

b. Steve Annear, "Drizly App Lets You Get Alcohol Delivered Straight to Your Door," *Boston Magazine*, May 14, 2013, https://www.bostonmagazine.com/news/2013/05/14/drizly-app-alcohol-delivery-boston/.

c. Aaron Pressman, "Last Call for Drizly: Liquor Delivery Service Shutting Down," *Boston Globe*, January 16, 2024, https://www.bostonglobe.com/2024/01/16/business/last-call-drizly-liquor-delivery-service-shutting-down.

d. Landry, "Alcohol Delivery Service."

CHAPTER 12

1. Michael Bloomberg with Matthew Winkler, *Bloomberg by Bloomberg* (New York: Wiley, 1997), foreword, p. v.

2. Bloomberg, *Bloomberg*, p. 149.

3. A mathematician, salesman, and software developer.

4. Originally named Innovative Market Solutions and rebranded to Bloomberg L.P. Myles Meserve, "How Michael Bloomberg Went from Bond Trader to Billionaire Media Mogul with One Incredible Machine," *Business Insider*, July 20, 2012, http://www.businessinsider.com/michael-bloomberg-biography-2012-7#he-invested-4-million-of-his-own-money-into-the-development-of-a-computer-system-that-could-provide-information-about-the-bond-markets-11.

5. Robin Wigglesworth, "Bloomberg Is Contemplating Life without Its Founder," *Financial Times*, April 20, 2023, https://www.ft.com/content/b998300e-d5d9-4104-a0de-dbdf0686eb14.

6. Zachary M. Stewart, "This Is How Much a Bloomberg Terminal Costs," *Quartz*, May 15, 2013, http://qz.com/84961/this-is-how-much-a-bloomberg-terminal-costs.

7. Richard S. Goldberg, *The Battle for Wall Street* (Hoboken, NJ: Wiley, 2009).

8. An economic moat refers to a business's ability to maintain competitive advantages over its competitors to protect its profits and market share. Chris Gallant, "How an Economic Moat Provides a Competitive Advantage," Investopia, updated August 8, 2023, http://www.investopedia.com/ask /answers/05/economicmoat.asp.

9. Matt Turck, "Can the Bloomberg Terminal Be 'Toppled'?" March 19, 2014, http://mattturck.com/2014/03/19/can-the -bloomberg-terminal-be-toppled.

10. Elon Musk, "The Secret Tesla Motors Master Plan (just between you and me)," Tesla, August 2, 2006, https://www .tesla.com/en_CA/blog/secret-tesla-motors-master-plan -just-between-you-and-me.

11. James G. Cobb, "This Just In: Model T Gets an Award," *New York Times*, December 24, 1999, http://www.nytimes. com/1999/12/24/automobiles/this-just-in-model-t-gets -award.html.

12. Julia Rubin, "All Dolled Up: The Enduring Triumph of American Girl," Racked, June 29, 2015, http://www.racked .com/2015/6/29/8855683/american-girl-doll-store.

13. Carl Shapiro and Hal R. Varian, *Information Rules: A Strategic Guide to the Network Economy* (Boston: Harvard Business School Press, 1998).

14. Annabelle Gawer and Michael A. Cusumano, *Platform Leadership: How Intel, Microsoft, and Cisco Drive Industry Innovation* (Boston: Harvard Business School Press, 2002).

15. There is an ongoing dispute about the ownership and originality of MS-DOS; see Klint Finley, "Was Microsoft's Empire Built on Stolen Code? We May Never Know," *Wired*, August 7, 2012, https://www.wired.com/2012/08/ ms-dos-examined-for-thef.

16. See Glen Ellison, "Learning, Local Interaction, and Coordination," *Econometrica* 61, no. 5 (1993): 1047–71.

17. In addition, Dropbox used a network-based reward for consumers who referred other users to the Dropbox service with more free storage and an easy and trustworthy way of sharing files between users.

18. Bret Schafer, "When Will Investors Stop Doubting Dropbox?" *Motley Fool*, May 3, 2023, https://www.fool.com/investing /2023/05/03/when-will-investors-stop-doubting-dropbox.

19. Schafer, "When Will Investors Stop?"

20. "CocaCola Net Worth 2010–2023," Macrotrends, accessed October 2, 2023, https://www.macrotrends.net/stocks /charts/KO/cocacola/net-worth.

21. M. Ridder, "Coca-Cola Company's Market Share in the United States from 2004 to 2021," Statistica, October 25, 2022, http:// www.statista.com/statistics/225388/us-market-share-of -the-coca-cola-company-since-2004.

22. Ondi Timoner, "How Naval Ravikant Risked It All to Pull the Veil Back on Venture Capital," *HuffPost*, December 7, 2013, https://www.huffpost.com/entry/how-naval-ravikant-risked _b_4047044.

23. Quentin Hardy, "Angel Investors Lend Expertise as Well as Cash," *New York Times*, March 31, 2015, https://www.nytimes .com/2015/04/02/business/dealbook/angel-investors-lend -expertise-as-well-as-cash.html.

24. Peter Thiel with Blake Masters, *Zero to One* (New York: Crown, 2014).

25. Peter Thiel, " 'Zero To One': How to Develop the Developed World," interview by Wade Goodwyn, NPR, September 13, 2014, http://www.npr.org/2014/09/13/348181054/peter-thiel -in-zero-to-one-how-to-develop-the-developed-world.

26. Andy Greenberg and Ryan Mac, "How a 'Deviant' Philosopher Built Palantir, a CIA-Funded Data-Mining Juggernaut," *Forbes*, August 14, 2013, http://www.forbes.com/sites /andygreenberg/2013/08/14/agent-of-intelligence-how-a -deviant-philosopher-built-palantir-a-cia-funded-data -mining-juggernaut/.

27. Greenberg and Mac, "How a 'Deviant' Philosopher."

28. Greenberg and Mac, "How a 'Deviant' Philosopher."

29. Tomio Geron, "The $100M Revenue Club: EHarmony Captures Hearts of VCs," *Wall Street Journal*, July 12, 2010, http://blogs.wsj.com/venturecapital/2010/07/12/the-100m -revenue-club-eharmony-captures-hearts-of-vcs.

30. Paul Graham, "Do Things That Don't Scale," July 2013, http:// paulgraham.com/ds.html.

31. Graham, "Do Things."

32. Annabelle Gawer and Michael A. Cusumano, "How Companies Become Platform Leaders," *MIT Sloan Management Review*, January 1, 2008, http://sloanreview.mit.edu/article /how-companies-become-platform-leaders.

33. "Founder Stories at 1871: OpenTable's Chuck Templeton," Doejo, June 13, 2012, http://doejo.com/blog/founder-stories -at-1871-opentables-chuck-templeton/#.VVItsdMzZ-U.

34. Hal R. Varian, "Economics of Information Technology," revised March 23, 2003, http://people.ischool.berkeley .edu/~hal/Papers/mattioli/mattioli.html#tth_sEc8

35. Gawer and Cusumano, "How Companies."

36. Brad Stone, "Microsoft to Pay $240 Million for Stake in Facebook," *New York Times*, October 25, 2007, https://www .nytimes.com/2007/10/25/technology/24cnd-facebook .html.

37. shazmosushi, "Elon Musk's 2003 Stanford University Entrepreneurial Thought Leaders Lecture," July 12, 2013, YouTube video, 47:58, https://www.youtube.com/watch?v=afZTrfvB2AQ.

38. The contract was to demonstrate cargo delivery to the International Space Station. A more recent (2015) contract allows SpaceX to compete for most NASA-funded missions. Jon Fingas, "SpaceX Gets the All-Clear to Launch Most NASA Science Missions," *Engadget*, May 17, 2015, http://www.engadget .com/2015/05/17/spacex-approval-for-most-nasa-missions.

39. http://www.spacex.com/mission/index.html.

40. James F. Kurkowski, "America Invents Act," U.S. Patent Office, November 8, 2011, http://www.uspto.gov/sites/default/files /aia_implementation/pur-2011nov08-space_exploration _tech_corp.pdf.

Sidebar: Going from Zero to One

a. Peter Thiel with Blake Masters, *Zero to One* (New York: Crown, 2014), p. 1.

Deep Dive: Five Coring Questions

a. Annabelle Gawer and Michael A. Cusumano, "How Companies Become Platform Leaders," *MIT Sloan Management Review*, January 1, 2008, https://sloanreview.mit.edu/article /how-companies-become-platform-leaders.

Sidebar: Dropbox's Focus on Trust in Its AI

a. Charlotte Trueman, "Dropbox Unveils Two AI-Based Products, Launches $50M AI Venture Fund," *Computerworld*, June 21, 2023, https://www.computerworld.com/article/3700078 /dropbox-unveils-two-ai-based-products-launches-50m-ai -venture-fund.html.

Case: Care.com

a. Kirsten Grind, Gregory Zuckerman, and Shane Shifflett, "Care.com Puts Onus on Families to Check Caregivers' Backgrounds—with Sometimes Tragic Outcomes," *Wall Street Journal*, March 8, 2019, https://www.wsj.com/articles /care-com-puts-onus-on-families-to-check-caregivers -backgroundswith-sometimes-tragic-outcomes-11552088138.

CHAPTER 13

1. Eric Ries, "The Lean Startup," Knowledge at Wharton, November 22, 2011, https://knowledge.wharton.upenn.edu/article /eric-ries-on-the-lean-startup.
2. Ashley Rodriguez, "Netflix Was Founded 20 Years Ago Today because Reed Hastings Was Late Returning a Video," *Quartz*, August 29, 2017, https://qz.com/1062888/netflix-was-founded-20 -years-ago-today-because-reed-hastings-was-late-a-returning-video.
3. Susan Tynan, "Our Story," Framebridge, accessed August 25, 2023, https://www.framebridge.com/about/our-story.
4. Francis J. Greene and Christian Hopp, "Are Formal Planners More Likely to Achieve New Venture Viability? A Counterfactual Model and Analysis," *Strategic Entrepreneurship Journal* 11, no. 1 (2017): 36–60, https://doi.org/10.1002/sej.1245.
5. Arnaldo Camuffo et al., "A Scientific Approach to Entrepreneurial Decision-Making: Evidence from a Randomized Control Trial," *Management Science* 66, no. 2 (2020): 503–1004.
6. Marc Andreessen, "Part 4: The Only Thing That Matters," Pmarchives, June 25, 2007, https://pmarchive.com/guide_to _startups_part4.html.
7. Tren Griffith, "12 Things about Product-Market Fit," Andreessen Horowitz, accessed August 25, 2023, https:// a16z.com/2017/02/18/12-things-about-product-market-fit-2.
8. Hamza Shaban and Renae Merle, "After Wall Street Debut, Spotify Valued at $26.5 Billion," *Washington Post*, April 3, 2018, https://www.washingtonpost.com/news/the-switch /wp/2018/04/02/spotify-ipo/.
9. Matt Marx, Joshua S. Gans, and David H. Hsu, "Dynamic Commercialization Strategies for Disruptive Technologies: Evidence from the Speech Recognition Industry," *Management Science*, 60, no. 12 (2014): 3103–23.
10. Erin Griffith, "Pinterest Prices I.P.O. at $19 a Share, for a $12.7 Billion Valuation," *New York Times*, April 17, 2019, https://www .nytimes.com/2019/04/17/technology/pinterest-ipo-stock. html; and "Your Audience Is Here," Pinterest Business, accessed August 25, 2023, https://business.pinterest.com/audience.

Using the Research: Rapid Entrepreneurial Experimentation and Learning in the Cloud

a. Michael Ewens, Ramana Nanda, and Matthew Rhodes-Kropf, "Cost of Experimentation and the Evolution of Venture Capital," *Journal of Financial Economics* 128, no. 3 (2018): 422–42, https://doi.org/10.1016/j.jfineco.2018.03.001.

CHAPTER 14

1. Parmy Olsen, "The Rags-to-Riches Tale of How Jan Koum Built WhatsApp into Facebook's New $19 Billion Baby," *Forbes*, February 19, 2014, https://www.forbes.com/sites /parmyolson/2014/02/19/exclusive-inside-story-how-jan -koum-built-whatsapp-into-facebooks-new-19-billion-baby.
2. Parmy Olson, "WhatsApp Cofounder Brian Acton Gives the Inside Story on #DeleteFacebook and Why He Left $850 Million Behind," *Forbes*, September 26, 2018, https://www .forbes.com/sites/parmyolson/2018/09/26/exclusive -whatsapp-cofounder-brian-acton-gives-the-inside-story -on-deletefacebook-and-why-he-left-850-million-behind.
3. Olson, "Rags-to-Riches Tale."
4. Olson, "Rags-to-Riches Tale."
5. Olson, "WhatsApp Cofounder."
6. Eliza Haverstock, "Sara Blakely Is a Billionaire (Again) after Selling a Majority of Spanx to Blackstone," *Forbes*, October 20, 2021, https://www.forbes.com/sites/elizahaverstock/2021/10/20 /sara-blakely-is-a-billionaire-again-after-selling-a-majority -of-spanx-to-blackstone/?sh=31783ed57d5c.
7. "About," Jimmy John Liautaud, accessed September 12, 2023, https://jimmyjohnliautaud.com/about-jimmy-john-liautaud.
8. "Jimmy John's History," Jimmy John's, accessed September 12, 2023, https://www.jimmyjohns.com/about-us/history.
9. "About," America's Seed Fund, accessed January 22, 2024, https:// www.sbir.gov/about#:~:text=As%20of%20October%202023%2C %20agencies,levels%20will%20require%20a%20waiver.
10. Steven Prokesch, "The Edison of Medicine," *Harvard Business Review*, March–April 2017, https://hbr.org/2017/03 /the-edison-of-medicine.
11. Eric Ries, *The Lean Startup* (New York: Random House, 2011), p. 160.
12. Yael Hochberg, Carlos Serrano, and Rosemarie Ziedonis, "Patent Collateral, Investor Commitment, and the Market for Venture Learning" *Journal of Financial Economics* (forthcoming). http://yael-hochberg.com/assets/portfolio/HSZ.pdf.
13. Seth Goldman, "Honest Tea's Seth Goldman Addresses Congress," *Inc.*, March 27, 2012, https://www.inc.com /seth-goldman/honest-teas-seth-goldman-addresses -congress.html.
14. David H. Hsu, "What Do Entrepreneurs Pay for Venture Capital Affiliation?" *Journal of Finance* 59, no. 4 (2004): 1805–44.

Sidebar: Raising Money on Kickstarter

a. "Pressroom," Kickstarter, accessed September 19, 2023, https://www.kickstarter.com/press?ref=global-footer.

Sidebar: A. P. Giannini's Choices

a. "A. P. Giannini," Who Made America, accessed October 16, 2023, https://www.pbs.org/wgbh/theymadeamerica/whomade /giannini_hi.html.

Aileen Lee and Cowboy Ventures

a. "Founder-First," Cowboy Ventures, accessed December 12, 2023, https://www.cowboy.vc.

Case: Back to the Roots

a. Esha Chhabra, "Two Founders Go from Growing Mushrooms in College to Building Out a National Brand," *Forbes*, January 30,

2020, https://www.forbes.com/sites/eshachhabra/2020/01/31/two-founders-go-from-growing-mushrooms-in-college-to-building-out-a-national-brand/?sh=168af0bc67ff.

b. "About," Back to the Roots, accessed December 12, 2023, https://backtotheroots.com/pages/our-story.

c. "Water Garden: Self-Cleaning Fish Tank That Grows Food," Kickstarter, accessed December 20, 2023, https://www.kickstarter.com/projects/2142509221/home-aquaponics-kit-self-cleaning-fish-tank-that-g; and "Back to the Roots," Main Street Launch, accessed December 20, 2023, https://mainstreetlaunch.org/project/back-to-the-roots/ https://backtotheroots.com/pages/our-story.

d. "Back to the Roots Ready to Grow Thanks to $5M Seed Round," Sustainable Brands, January 28, 2016, https://sustainablebrands.com/read/product-service-design-innovation/back-to-the-roots-ready-to-grow-thanks-to-5m-seed-round.

e. Samantha Hurst, "California Food Startup Back to the Roots Secures $10M During Series A Funding Round," Crowdfund Insider, June 6, 2016, https://www.crowdfundinsider.com/2016/06/86521-circleup-success-back-to-the-roots-secures-10m-during-series-a-funding-round.

CHAPTER 15

1. Connie Loizos, "T. Rowe Price Has Marked Down Its Stake in Canva by 67.6%," TechCrunch, June 2, 2023, https://techcrunch.com/2023/06/02/t-rowe-price-has-marked-down-its-stake-in-canva-by-67-6.

2. Erik Hurst and Ben Pugsley, "What Do Small Businesses Do?" Brookings Papers on Economic Activity 43, no. 2 (2011): 73–142.

3. Panel Study of Entrepreneurial Dynamics (PSED) background information, documentation, and data are available at http://www.psed.isr.umich.edu/psed/.

4. Will Kenton, "Firms: Definition in Business, How They Work, and Types," Investopedia, updated July 24, 2023, https://www.investopedia.com/terms/f/firm.asp.

5. Biz Carson, "Scooter Startup Bird Raises $275 Million in New Funding Round," Forbes, October 3, 2019, https://www.forbes.com/sites/bizcarson/2019/10/03/bird-raises-275-million-series-d-funding.

6. "Tink Labs," Failory, accessed September 18, 2023, https://www.failory.com/cemetery/tink-labs.

7. Mercedes Ruehl, "Inside the Unravelling of Tink Labs," Financial Times, August 16, 2019, https://www.ft.com/content/22ed37c0-b9b7-11e9-96bd-8e884d3ea203.

8. "Company Profile," Starbucks Stories and News, 2023, https://stories.starbucks.com/uploads/2023/02/AboutUs-Company-Profile-2.6.23.pdf.

9. Christopher Marquis and András Tilcsik, "Imprinting: Toward a Multilevel Theory," Academy of Management Annals 7, no. 1 (2013), https://doi.org/10.5465/19416520.2013.766076.

10. James N. Baron and Michael T. Hannan, "Organizational Blueprints for Success in High-Tech Start-Ups: Lessons from the Stanford Project on Emerging Companies," California Management Review 44, no. 3 (2006): 8–36, https://doi.org/10.2307/41166130.

11. "History of W. W. Norton," W. W. Norton, accessed September 18, 2023, https://wwnorton.com/who-we-are/history-of-w.-w.-norton.

12. Noam Wasserman, "Founder-CEO Succession and the Paradox of Entrepreneurial Success," Organization Science 14, no. 2 (2003): 149–72, http://www.jstor.org/stable/4135157.

13. Jing Chen and Peter Thompson, "New Firm Performance and the Replacement of Founder-CEOs," Strategic Entrepreneurship Journal, 9 (2015): 243-62, https://doi.org/10.1002/sej.1203; and Thomas Hellmann and Manju Puri, "Venture Capital and the Professionalization of Start-up Firms: Empirical Evidence," Journal of Finance, 57, no 1. (2002): 169–97, http://www.jstor.org/stable/2697837.

14. Michael Ewens and Matt Marx, "Founder Replacement and Startup Performance," Review of Financial Studies 31, no. 4 (2018): 1532–65, https://www.jstor.org/stable/48616686.

15. David Chang, Eat a Peach: A Memoir (New York: Clarkson Potter, 2020).

16. Michael Gorman and William Sahlman, "What Do Venture Capitalists Do?" Journal of Business Venturing 4, no. 4 (1989): 231–48.

17. Tom Eisenmann, Why Startups Fail: A New Roadmap for Entrepreneurial Success (New York: Random House, 2021).

18. Reid Hoffman and Chris Yeh, "The Blitzscaling Basics," Strategy and Business, October 1, 2018, https://www.strategy-business.com/article/The-Blitzscaling-Basics.

Sidebar: Selina Tobaccowala

a. "The Inside Story on How SurveyMonkey Cracked the International Market," Review, accessed September 18, 2023, https://review.firstround.com/the-inside-story-on-how-surveymonkey-cracked-the-international-market.

Mini Case: Shopify and Scaling with Platforms

a. "Be a Platform: Shopify's Tobi Lütke," podcast, February 13, 2020, Masters of Scale, audio, 32:10, https://mastersofscale.com/tobi-lutke-be-a-platform.

b. Semil Shah, "Transcript: @Chamath At StrictlyVC's Insider Series," Haystack, September 17, 2015, https://semilshah.com/2015/09/17/transcript-chamath-at-strictlyvcs-insider-series.

Sidebar: Ben Horowitz

a. Bradley Hendricks, Travis Howell, and Christopher Bingham, "Research: How Long Should a Founder Remain CEO?" Harvard Business Review, December 17, 2021, https://hbr.org/2021/12/research-how-long-should-a-founder-remain-ceo.

Case: American Girl

a. Laura Larrimore, "A Girl's Window into History," United States Patent and Trademark Office, accessed November 9, 2023, https://www.uspto.gov/learning-and-resources/journeys-innovation/field-stories/girls-window-history.

b. American Girl, "Pleasant Rowland Speaks at American Girl 25th Anniversary Tribute," November 29, 2011, YouTube video, 07:17, https://www.youtube.com/watch?v=_ltX5W6eZYw.

c. Julia Rubin, "All Dolled Up: The Enduring Triumph of American Girl," Racked, June 29, 2015, http://www.racked.com/2015/6/29/8855683/american-girl-doll-store.

CREDITS

PHOTOGRAPHS

Frontmatter

Icons: Shutterstock; **title page:** Sakchai Vongsasiripat/Getty Images; **Contents: Part 1:** Kathy deWitt/Alamy Stock Photo; **Part 2:** Liz Hafalia/The San Francisco Chronicle via Getty Images; **Part 3:** Gio.tto/Shutterstock; **Part 4:** Richard Levine/Alamy Stock Photo; **author photos: Gans:** Photo by Annika Gans; **Scott:** Photo by Darren Pellegrino; **Stern:** Photo by Scott Stern.

Part 1

Opener: pp. 2–3: Kathy deWitt/Alamy Stock Photo; **Chapter 1: p. 4:** Michael Desmond/© Disney General Entertainment Content/Getty Images; **p. 6:** Christopher Willard/© Disney General Entertainment Content/Getty Images; **p. 8 (left):** D. Hurst/Alamy Stock Photo; **p. 9:** JOKER/Martin Magunia/Ullstein Bild via Getty Images; **p. 10:** Creative Destruction Lab; **p. 12 (left):** Brian Friedman/Shutterstock; **p. 12 (right):** Bill Rowntree/Mirrorpix/Getty Images; **p. 13 (top):** Timon Schneider/Alamy Stock Photo; **p. 13 (bottom):** Kyle Ericksen/WWD/Penske Media via Getty Images; **p. 14:** SpeedKingz/Shutterstock; **p. 15:** Thomas S. England/Getty Images; **p. 19:** Supergoop!; **p. 22:** Adam Taylor/© ABC/Getty Images; **Chapter 2: p. 24:** Steve Jennings/Getty Images; **p. 26 (top):** © King World Productions/Courtesy: Everett Collection; **p. 26 (bottom):** PictureLux/The Hollywood Archive/Alamy Stock Photo; **p. 27 (left):** Tribune Content Agency LLC/Alamy Stock Photo; **p. 27 (center left):** PA Images/Alamy Stock Photo; **p. 27 (center right):** Colin Lenton; **p. 27 (right):** Rolf Adlercreutz/Alamy Stock Photo; **p. 30:** Rblfmr/Shutterstock; **p. 31:** Harvard Business School; **p. 32:** REUTERS/Alamy Stock Photo; **p. 33:** Ted Dully/The Boston Globe via Getty Images; **p. 34:** Noam Galai/Stringer/Getty Images; **p. 36:** Pictorial Press Ltd/Alamy Stock Photo; **p. 37:** David Howells/Corbis via Getty Images; **p. 38:** The Sanergy Collaborative; **p. 39:** ZUMA Press, Inc./Alamy Stock Photo; **p. 40 (top):** Thomas Concordia/Getty Images; **p. 40 (bottom):** Carlos Delgado/AP Images; **p. 41:** Jim Alcorn/Splash News/Newscom; **p. 42:** Libby March/Bloomberg via Getty Images; **p. 45:** AP Photo/Gerald Herbert; **p. 51:** Brad Barket/Stringer/Getty Images; **Chapter 3: p. 52:** DB Apple/picture-alliance/Dpa/Newscom; **p. 54:** REUTERS/Alamy Stock Photo; **p. 55:** Courtesy of STVP, the Stanford Engineering Entrepreneurship Center. Video still from: "From Inspiration to Implementation." Season 10, Episode 3 *of Entrepreneurial Thought Leaders*, recorded October 15, 2014. URL: https://ecorner.stanford.edu/videos/from-inspiration-to-implementation-entire-talk/; **p. 57:** Brian To/Variety/Penske Media via Getty Images; **p. 58:** MediaNews Group/Orange County Register via Getty Images; **p. 60:** Monticello/Shutterstock; **p. 61:** AP Photo/Chris Pizzello; **p. 62:** Pat Greenhouse/The Boston Globe via Getty Images; **p. 64 (top):** Boumen Japet/Alamy Stock Photo; **p. 64 (bottom):** Medicimage Education/Alamy Stock Photo; **p. 65:** Adrian Sherratt/Alamy Stock Photo; **p. 66:** Ryan DeBerardinis/Shutterstock; **p. 67:** The Chosunilbo JNS/Imazins via Getty Images; **p. 70:** Dpa Picture Alliance/Alamy Live News; **p. 71:** Patti McConville/Alamy Stock Photo; **p. 72:** David Paul Morris/Bloomberg via Getty Images; **p. 73:** Saras Sarasvathy; **p. 74:** Walter McBride/WireImage/Getty Images; **p. 75:** REUTERS/Alamy Stock Photo; **p. 76:** ZUMA Press, Inc./Alamy Stock Photo; **p. 78:** Kristoffer Tripplaar/Alamy Stock Photo; **p. 85:** NetPhotos/Alamy Stock Photo; **Chapter 4: p. 86:** Abaca Press/Alamy Stock Photo; **p. 89:** Andrew Yates/AFP via Getty Images; **p. 90 (left):** Patrick Fraser/Corbis via Getty Images; **p. 90 (right):** AP Photo/Richard Drew; **p. 91:** Farlap/Alamy Stock Photo; **p. 95 (right):** Davidd/Alamy Stock Photo; **p. 95 (left):** Jeff Haynes/AFP via Getty Images; **p. 97:** David Paul Morris/Bloomberg via Getty Images; **p. 98:** F11photo/Shutterstock; **p. 99:** ZUMA Press, Inc./Alamy Stock Photo; **p. 100 (left):** Boumen Japet/Shutterstock; **p. 100 (right):** Nikkimeel/Shutterstock; **p. 101:** Sean Locke/Stocksy; **p. 103:** Pat Greenhouse/The Boston Globe via Getty Images; **p. 105:** Franco Origlia/Getty Images; **p. 107:** Micharl Kovac/Getty Images; **p. 108:** William N. Finley IV/ZUMA Press/Newscom; **p. 109:** Doug Jones/Portland Press Herald via Getty Images; **p. 110:** Dennis Gilbert-VIEW/Alamy Stock Photo; **p. 110:** Littleny/Alamy Stock Photo Images; **p. 112:** Sharaf Maksumov/Shutterstock; **p. 113:** Indypendenz/Shutterstock; **p. 121:** AP Photo/Charles Krupa.

Part 2

Opener: pp. 122–23: Liz Hafalia/The San Francisco Chronicle via Getty Images; **Chapter 5: p. 126:** Peter Dasilva/The New York

Times/Redux; **p. 129:** David Bro/ZUMA Press/Newscom; **p. 132:** New Africa/Shutterstock; **p. 135:** Copyright © University of Nebraska, 2004. Accessed via: https://passel2.unl.edu/view/lesson/c3ded390efbf/9; **p. 136:** Andrew Harrer/Bloomberg via Getty Images; **p. 140:** Chris Willson/Alamy Stock Photo; **p. 141:** Maskot/Alamy Stock Photo; **p. 142 (top left):** AP Photo/Mark Lennihan, File; **p. 142 (top right):** ZUMA Press, Inc./Alamy Stock Photo; **p. 142 (center):** George Frey/Stringer/Getty Images; **p. 142 (bottom):** Charles Sykes/Shutterstock; **p. 144:** Julee Ashmead/Shutterstock; **p. 145:** Richard Levine/Alamy Stock Photo; **p. 146:** Stock-Asso/Shutterstock; **p. 147:** Liz Hafalia/The San Francisco Chronicle via Getty Images; **p. 149 (top):** Robyn Beck/AFP via Getty Images; **p. 149 (bottom):** Liz Hafalia/The San Francisco Chronicle via Getty Images; **p. 155:** Nouman Ahmad and Ian Burgess; **Chapter 6: p. 156:** SIPA USA/SIPA/Newscom; **p. 158:** Patrick Pleul/picture-alliance/dpa/AP Images; **p. 159 (both):** U.S. Department of Labor, https://www.dol.gov; **p. 162:** Rod Rolle/Stringer/Getty Images; **p. 164:** ImageBROKER/Alamy Stock Photo; **p. 167 (top left):** Bill Truran/Alamy Stock Photo; **p. 167 (top right):** Courtesy of the Rockefeller Archive Center; **p. 167 (bottom):** Courtesy of the Rockefeller Archive Center; **p. 168:** Lea Suzuki/The San Francisco Chronicle/Associated Press; **p. 171:** Laurence Dutton/E+/Getty Images; **p. 173:** Heather Kennedy/Getty Images; **pp. 176–77:** Plot courtesy of the National Renewable Energy Laboratory, Golden, CO; **p. 178:** © Buena Vista Pictures/Courtesy Everett Collection; **p. 179:** Cliff Hide News/Alamy Stock Photo; **p. 179:** Entertainment Pictures / Alamy Stock Photo; **p. 182:** J. Dorfman/MIT/Splash/Newscom; **p. 187:** Cole Burston/Bloomberg via Getty Images; **Chapter 7: p. 188:** William Widmer/Redux; **p. 190:** Ronda Churchill/Bloomberg via Getty Images; **p. 193:** Jack Garofalo/Paris Match via Getty Images; **p. 194:** Jonathan Weiss/Shutterstock; **p. 195:** Idealphotographer/Shutterstock; **p. 196:** Kent Raney/Alamy Stock Photo; **p. 197:** Ramin Talaie/Corbis via Getty Images; **p. 198 (top):** Dpa Picture Alliance/Alamy Stock Photo; **p. 198 (bottom):** Peppinuzzo/Shutterstock; **p. 201 (left):** Richard Levine/Alamy Stock Photo; **p. 201 (center):** Cultura Creative RF/Alamy Stock Photo; **p. 201 (right):** Anel Alijagic/Shutterstock; **p. 203:** Yana Paskova/The Washington Post via Getty Images; **p. 205:** © Wayne Miller/Magnum Photos; **p. 207:** PhotoStock-Israel/Alamy Stock Photo; **p. 209:** TT News Agency/Alamy Stock Photo; **p. 210:** AP Photo/Richard Drew; **p. 217:** Ted Fitzgerald/MediaNews Group/Boston Herald via Getty Images; **Chapter 8: p. 218:** Tribune Content Agency LLC/Alamy Stock Photo; **p. 220:** Robert K. Chin—Storefronts/Alamy Stock Photo; **p. 221:** Wikimedia Commons; **p. 222:** Science History Images/Alamy Stock Photo; **p. 225:** Randy Duchaine/Alamy Stock Photo; **p. 226 (top):** Shutterstock; **p. 226 (bottom):** EQRoy/Shutterstock; **p. 229:** © Universal/Courtesy Everett Collection; **p. 231:** Setiawan Anang/Shutterstock; **p. 232:** Everett Collection Inc/Alamy Stock Photo; **p. 235:** MedStockPhotos/Alamy Stock Photo; **p. 237:** Stark Bro's Nurseries & Orchards Co.; **p. 238:** Vulk/Shutterstock; **p. 245:** Copyright Sheertex Inc.

Part 3

Opener: pp. 246–47: Gio.tto/Shutterstock; **Chapter 9: p. 250:** Cfoto/ZUMAPRESS/Newscom; **p. 252 (both):** Konrad Zelazowski/Alamy Stock Photo; **p. 253:** Konrad Zelazowski/Alamy Stock

Photo; **p. 254:** ColleenMichaels/Depositphotos; **p. 256 (top):** Boggy22/Depositphotos; **p. 256 (center top):** Nyvlt_art/Depositphotos; **p. 256 (center bottom):** Kornienkoalex/Depositphotos; **p. 256 (bottom):** Rozelt/Depositphotos; **p. 257:** Tada Images/Shutterstock; **p. 258 (all):** United States Patent and Trade Office; **p. 260:** Klaus Ohlenschlaeger/Alamy Stock Photo; **p. 261:** Ryzhoz/Depositphotos; **p. 262:** © Warner Bros/Courtesy Everett Collection; **p. 263:** Richard Levine/Alamy Stock Photo; **p. 265:** Dan Lamont/Alamy Stock Photo; **p. 267:** Johnny Green—PA Images/Getty Images; **p. 268:** Pixelot/Alamy Stock Photo; **p. 269:** ImageBROKER.com GmbH & Co. KG/Alamy Stock Photo; **p. 279:** Fabian Posselt/Ullstein bild via Getty Images; **Chapter 10: p. 280:** ZUMA Press, Inc./Alamy Stock Photo; **p. 283 (top):** Phil Barker/Future Publishing via Getty Images; **p. 283 (bottom left):** Chris Pearsall/Alamy Stock Photo; **p. 283 (bottom right):** INTERFOTO/Alamy Stock Photo; **p. 283:** Kaspars Grinvalds/Shutterstock; **p. 284 (top):** Bruce Bisping/Star Tribune via Getty Images; **p. 284 (bottom):** Alexander Oganezov/Alamy Stock Photo; **p. 285:** Pio3/Shutterstock; **p. 286:** Megan Williams/ZUMA Press/Newscom; **p. 288:** Ken Howard/Alamy Stock Photo; **p. 291:** Andrew Barker/Alamy Stock Photo; **p. 293:** David Tran Photo/Shutterstock; **p. 294:** Matthew Ashmore/Alamy Stock Photo; **p. 295:** Bildagentur-online/Sunny Celeste/Alamy Stock Photo; **p. 299:** Robert K. Chin—Storefronts/Alamy Stock Photo; **p. 302:** Panchenko Vladimir/Shutterstock; **p. 309:** Fairchild Archive/Penske Media via Getty Images; **Chapter 11: p. 310:** Manjunath Kiran/AFP/Getty Images; **p. 313:** PradeepGaurs/Shutterstock; **p. 314 (top):** Phelan M. Ebenhack/AP Images for International Leadership Summit; **p. 314 (bottom):** Brent Hofacker/Alamy Stock Photo; **p. 315:** GK Images/Alamy Stock Photo; **p. 317 (left):** Sheila Fitzgerald/Shutterstock; **p. 317 (right):** Kristoffer Tripplaar/Alamy Stock Photo; **p. 318:** Feng Yu/Alamy Stock Photo; **p. 319:** Pavel Kapish/Alamy Stock Photo; **p. 320:** David Paul Morris/Bloomberg via Getty Images; **p. 322:** David Paul Morris/Bloomberg/Getty Images; **p. 324:** B Christopher/Alamy Stock Photo; **p. 325:** Steven Ferdman/Getty Images; **p. 328:** Courtesy Sameer Dahl/Photo by Jeff Cheong; **p. 329:** Action Plus Sports Images/Alamy Stock Photo; **p. 330 (left):** Retro Ark/Alamy Stock Photo; **p. 330 (right):** Wachiwit/Shutterstock; **p. 337:** Sean Proctor/The Boston Globe/Getty Images; **Chapter 12: p. 338:** Dpa Picture Alliance/Alamy Stock Photo; **p. 340:** Karjean Levine/Getty Images; **p. 341:** Dragon Images/Shutterstock; **p. 342:** Leo R Martins/Shutterstock; **p. 343:** Maurice Savage/Alamy Stock Photo; **p. 343:** Kristoffer Tripplaar/Alamy Stock Photo; **p. 344:** Redbrickstock.com/Alamy Stock Photo; **p. 346:** Patti McConville/Alamy Stock Photo; **p. 349:** Pixinoo/Shutterstock; **p. 351:** AP Photo/Richard Drew; **p. 353:** Noam Galai/Stringer/Getty Images; **p. 358:** Kumar Sriskandan/Alamy Stock Photo; **p. 361:** Trekandshoot/Alamy Stock Photo; **p. 367:** Alberto E. Rodriguez/Getty Images.

Part 4

Opener: pp. 368–69: Richard Levine/Alamy Stock Photo; **Chapter 13: p. 370:** Larry Busacca/Wire Image/Getty Images; **p. 372:** AB Forces News Collection/Alamy Stock Photo; **p. 373:** Abaca Press/Alamy Stock Photo; **p. 375:** GK Images/Alamy Stock Photo; **p. 382:** Kimberley White/Stringer/Getty Images; **p. 385:** Richard Levine/Alamy Stock Photo; **p. 386:** Blaize Pascall/Alamy

Stock Photo; **p. 394:** Courtesy of RapidSOS; **Chapter 14: p. 396:** Peter DaSilva/Polaris/Newscom; **p. 398:** Piotr Swat/Alamy Stock Photo; **p. 398:** Sebolla74/Shutterstock; **p. 400:** Everett Collection Historical/Alamy Stock Photo; **p. 401:** SeanShot/Getty Images; **p. 403 (top):** Tribune Content Agency LLC/Alamy Stock Photo; **p. 403 (bottom):** America's Seed Fund/Small Business Innovation Research (SBIR) and Small Business Technology Transfer (STTR); **p. 404:** Bettmann/Getty Images; **p. 405:** Radiokafka/Shutterstock; **p. 406:** Bettmann/Getty Images; **p. 409:** Abhijit Bhatlekar/Mint via Getty Images; **p. 411:** Cavan-Images/Shutterstock; **p. 413:** Steve Jennings/Getty Images for TechCrunch; **p. 421:** MediaNews Group/Bay Area News via Getty Images; **Chapter 15: p. 422:** Pedro Fiúza/NurPhoto/Getty Images; **p. 424:** Timon Schneider/Alamy Stock Photo; **p. 424:** Timon Schneider/Alamy Stock Photo; **p. 425 (left):** Ken Howard/Alamy Stock Photo; **p. 425 (center):** David Grossman/Alamy Stock Photo; **p. 425 (right):** The Photo Works/Alamy Stock Photo; **p. 426:** Prathankarnpap/Shutterstock; **p. 427:** B Christopher/Alamy Stock Photo; **p. 429:** Lionel Derimais/Alamy Stock Photo; **p. 431:** Mark Ralston/AFP/Getty Images; **p. 432:** Sina Salehian/Shutterstock; **p. 434:** David Paul Morris/Bloomberg via Getty Images; **p. 435:** DC Studio/Shutterstock; **p. 437:** W.W. Norton & Company, Inc.; **p. 438:** Martina Albertazzi/Bloomberg/Getty Images; **p. 440:** AP Photo/Diane Bondareff;

p. 444: Dpa Picture Alliance/Alamy Stock Photo; **p. 451:** Juana Arias/The Washington Post via Getty Images.

TEXT

Figure 2.2, p. 29: Figure reprinted from Global Entrepreneurship Monitor, 2020/2121 Global Report. © 2021 Niels Bosma, Stephen Hill, Aileen Ionescu-Somers, Donna Kelley, Maribel Guerrero, Thomas Schott, and the Global Entrepreneurship Research Association (GERA). Reprinted with permission. **Figure 2.8, p. 44:** Fig. 1 from "Investors Prefer Entrepreneurial Ventures Pitched by Attractive Men," *Proceedings of the National Academy of Sciences* 111, no. 12 (2014) 4427–31. Reprinted by permission of PNAS. **Chapter 5: Deep Dive (graph), p. 138:** Figure reprinted from *Time Well Spent: The Declining Real Cost of Living in America, 1997 Annual Report,* Federal Reserve Bank of Dallas. Reprinted with permission. **Figure 8.3, p. 224:** Reprinted by permission of Harvard Business Review. Exhibit: Forces Governing Competition in an Industry from "Five Competitive Forces that Shape Strategy" by Michael E. Porter, January 2008. Copyright ©2008 by Harvard Business Publishing; all rights reserved. **Chapter 9, p. 279:** "Who Made That Super Soaker?" by Pagan Kennedy, 02 August 2013. From *The New York Times*. © 2013 The New York Times Company. All rights reserved. Used under license.

COMPANY, BRAND, AND ORGANIZATION INDEX

NAME INDEX

SUBJECT INDEX